Lecture Notes in Computer Science 10704

Commenced Publication in 1973
Founding and Former Series Editors:
Gerhard Goos, Juris Hartmanis, and Jan van Leeuwen

More information about this series at http://www.springer.com/series/7409

Klaus Schoeffmann · Thanarat H. Chalidabhongse
Chong Wah Ngo · Supavadee Aramvith
Noel E. O'Connor · Yo-Sung Ho
Moncef Gabbouj · Ahmed Elgammal (Eds.)

MultiMedia Modeling

24th International Conference, MMM 2018
Bangkok, Thailand, February 5–7, 2018
Proceedings, Part I

 Springer

Editors
Klaus Schoeffmann
Alpen-Adria-Universität Klagenfurt
Klagenfurt
Austria

Thanarat H. Chalidabhongse
Chulalongkorn University
Bangkok
Thailand

Chong Wah Ngo
City University of Hong Kong
Hong Kong
China

Supavadee Aramvith
Chulalongkorn University
Bangkok
Thailand

Noel E. O'Connor
Dublin City University
Dublin
Ireland

Yo-Sung Ho
Gwangju Institute of Science
 and Technology
Gwangju
Korea (Republic of)

Moncef Gabbouj
Tampere University of Technology
Tampere
Finland

Ahmed Elgammal ⒾⒹ
Rutgers University
Piscataway, NJ
USA

ISSN 0302-9743   ISSN 1611-3349   (electronic)
Lecture Notes in Computer Science
ISBN 978-3-319-73602-0   ISBN 978-3-319-73603-7   (eBook)
https://doi.org/10.1007/978-3-319-73603-7

Library of Congress Control Number: 2017963755

LNCS Sublibrary: SL3 – Information Systems and Applications, incl. Internet/Web, and HCI

Printed on acid-free paper

This Springer imprint is published by Springer Nature
The registered company is Springer International Publishing AG
The registered company address is: Gewerbestrasse 11, 6330 Cham, Switzerland

Preface

These proceedings contain the papers presented at MMM 2018, the 24th International Conference on MultiMedia Modeling, held in Bangkok, Thailand, during February 5–7, 2018. MMM is a leading international conference for researchers and industry practitioners to share new ideas, original research results, and practical development experiences from all MMM-related areas, broadly falling into three categories: multimedia content analysis; multimedia signal processing and communications; and multimedia applications and services.

MMM 2018 received 185 submissions across four categories; 158 full research paper submissions, six special session paper submissions, 12 demonstration submissions, and nine submissions to the Video Browser Showdown (VBS 2018). Of the submissions, 75% were from Asia, 17% from Europe, 5% from North America, 2% from South America, and 1% each from Oceania and Africa.

Of the 158 full papers submitted, 46 were selected for oral presentation and 28 for poster presentation, which equates to a 47% acceptance rate overall. Of the six special session papers submitted, five were selected for oral presentation, which equates to a 83% acceptance rate overall. In addition, all 12 demonstrations and nine VBS submissions were accepted. The overall acceptance percentage across the conference was thus 54%, but 40% for full papers and 25% of full papers for oral presentation.

The submission and review process was coordinated using the EasyChair conference management system. All full-paper submissions were assigned for review to at least three members of the Program Committee. We owe a debt of gratitude to all these reviewers for providing their valuable time to MMM 2018.

We also wish to thank our organizational team: Special Session Chairs Suree Pumrin and Benoit Huet; Demonstration Chairs Wolfgang Huerst, Joemon Jose, and Suvit Nakpeerayuth; Video Browser Showdown Chairs Klaus Schoeffmann, Werner Bailer, Cathal Gurrin, Jakub Lokoč, and Kunwadee Sripanidkulchai; Publicity Chairs Kiyoharu Aizawa, Norliza Binti Mohd Noor, Celia Shahnaz, Karlsten Mueller, and Alexander Loui; Finance Chair Nisachon Tangsangiumvisai; Sponsorship Chairs Natawut Nupairoj and Widhayakorn Asdornwised; Registration Chairs Sukree Sinthupinyo and Charnchai Pluempitiwiriyawej; Publication Chairs Twittie Senivongse and Peerapon Vateekul; Local Arrangements Chairs Nakornthip Prompoon and Kultida Rojviboonchai; Web Chair Krerk Piromsopa; Webmaster Apinun Intarachaiya; Conference Secretariat Thittaporn Ganokratanaa, Tasaporn Intarachaiya, Itsara Wichakam, Kankawin Kowsrihawat, and Araya Pudtal.

We would like to thank Chulalongkorn University for hosting MMM 2018. Finally, special thanks go to our supporting team at Chulalongkorn University (Watchara Ruengsang, Sirinthra Chantharaj, Pitchayut Chitsinpchayakun, Ammarin Jetthakun, Kawin Liaowongphuthorn, Kissada Pornratthanapong, Chanatip Saetia, and Chavisa Thamjarat), as well as to student volunteers, for all their contributions and valuable support.

The accepted research contributions represent the state of the art in multimedia modeling research and cover a very diverse range of topics. We wish to thank all authors who spent their valuable time and effort to submit their work to MMM 2018. And, finally, we thank all those who made the trip to Bangkok to attend MMM 2018 and VBS 2018.

February 2018

Supavadee Aramvith
Yo-Sung Ho
Noel E. O'Connor
Thanarat Chalidabhongse
Klaus Schoeffmann
Chong Wah Ngo
Moncef Gabbouj
Ahmed Elgammal

Organization

MMM 2018 was organized by the Faculty of Engineering, Chulalongkorn University, Thailand.

Steering Committee

Phoebe Chen (Chair)	La Trobe University, Australia
Tat-Seng Chua	National University of Singapore, Singapore
Kiyoharu Aizawa	University of Tokyo, Japan
Cathal Gurrin	Dublin City University, Ireland
Benoit Huet	Eurecom, France
R. Manmatha	University of Massachusetts, USA
Noel E. O'Connor	Dublin City University, Ireland
Klaus Schoeffmann	Alpen-Adria-Universität Klagenfurt, Austria
Yang Shiqiang	Tsinghua University, China
Cees G. M. Snoek	University of Amsterdam, The Netherlands
Meng Wang	Hefei University of Technology, China

Organizing Committee

Honorary Chairs

Supot Teachavorasinskun	Chulalongkorn University, Thailand
Ming-Ting Sun	University of Washington, USA
Tat-Seng Chua	National University of Singapore, Singapore

General Chairs

Supavadee Aramvith	Chulalongkorn University, Thailand
Yo-Sung Ho	Gwangju Institute of Science and Technology, South Korea
Noel E. O'Connor	Dublin City University, Ireland

Program Chairs

Thanarat Chalidabhongse	Chulalongkorn University, Thailand
Klaus Schoeffmann	Alpen-Adria-Universität Klagenfurt, Austria
Chong Wah Ngo	City University of Hong Kong, SAR China
Moncef Gabbouj	Tempere University of Technology, Finland
Ahmed Elgammal	Rutgers University, USA

Special Session Chairs

Suree Pumrin	Chulalongkorn University, Thailand
Benoit Huet	Eurecom, France

Demonstration Chairs

Suvit Nakpeerayuth	Chulalongkorn University, Thailand
Wolfgang Huerst	Utrecht University, The Netherlands
Joemon Jose	University of Glasglow, UK

Video Browser Showdown Chairs

Kunwadee Sripanidkulchai	Chulalongkorn University, Thailand
Cathal Gurrin	Dublin City University, Ireland
Werner Bailer	Joanneum University, Austria
Klaus Schoeffmann	Alpen-Adria-Universität Klagenfurt, Austria
Jakub Lokoč	Charles University in Prague, Czech Republic

Publicity Chairs

Kiyoharu Aizawa	University of Tokyo, Japan
Norliza Binti Mohd Noor	Universiti Teknologi Malaysia, Malaysia
Celia Shahnaz	BUET, Bangladesh
Karlsten Mueller	Franhofer Heinrich Hertz Institute, Germany
Alexander Loui	Kodak Alaris, USA

Finance Chair

Nisachon Tangsangiumvisai	Chulalongkorn University, Thailand

Sponsorship Chairs

Natawut Nupairoj	Chulalongkorn University, Thailand
Widhayakorn Asdornwised	Chulalongkorn University, Thailand

Registration Chairs

Charnchai Pluempitiwiriyawej	Chulalongkorn University, Thailand
Sukree Sinthupinyo	Chulalongkorn University, Thailand

Publication Chairs

Peerapon Vateekul	Chulalongkorn University, Thailand
Twittie Senivongse	Chulalongkorn University, Thailand

Local Arrangements Chairs

Nakornthip Prompoon	Chulalongkorn University, Thailand
Kultida Rojviboonchai	Chulalongkorn University, Thailand

Web Chair

Krerk Piromsopa   Chulalongkorn University, Thailand

Webmaster

Apinun Intarachaiya   Chulalongkorn University, Thailand

Conference Secretariat

Thittaporn Ganokratanaa   Chulalongkorn University, Thailand
Tasaporn Intarachaiya   Chulalongkorn University, Thailand
Itsara Wichakam   Chulalongkorn University, Thailand
Kankawin Kowsrihawat   Chulalongkorn University, Thailand
Araya Pudtal   Chulalongkorn University, Thailand

Special Session Organizers

SS: Multimedia Analytics: Perspectives, Techniques, and Applications

Laurent Amsaleg   IRISA Lab, France
Cathal Gurrin   Dublin City University, Ireland
Björn Þór Jónsson   IT University of Copenhagen, Denmark
Stevan Rudinac   University of Amsterdam, The Netherlands

Program Committee

Thumrongrat Amornraksa   KMUTT, Thailand
Laurent Amsaleg   IRISA Lab, France
Le An   University of North Carolina at Chapel Hill, USA
Ognjen Arandjelovic   University of St. Andrews, UK
Sansanee Auephanwiriyakul   Chiang Mai University, Thailand
Esra Açar   Middle East Technical University, Germany
Werner Bailer   Joanneum Research, Austria
Amr M. Bakry   Alexandria University, USA
Ilaria Bartolini   University of Bologna, Italy
Jenny Benois-Pineau   LaBRI, University of Bordeaux, France
Benjamin Bustos   University of Chile, Chile
K. Selcuk Candan   Arizona State University, USA
Premysl Cech   Charles University, Czech Republic
Thanarat Chalidabhongse   Chulalongkorn University, Thailand
Savvas Chatzichristofis   Neapolis University Pafos, Cyprus
Edgar Chavez   CICESE, Mexico
Zhineng Chen   Chinese Academy of Sciences, China
Wen-Huang Cheng   Academia Sinica, Taiwan
Wei-Ta Chu   National Chung Cheng University, Taiwan
Tat-Seng Chua   National University of Singapore, Singapore
Vincent Claveau   IRISA – CNRS, France
Kathy Clawson   University of Sunderland, UK

Wei Zhang	Chinese Academy of Sciences, China
Wan-Lei Zhao	Xiamen University, China
Marissa Zhou	Dublin City University, Ireland
Xiaofeng Zhu	Guangxi Normal University, China
Arthur Zimek	University of Southern Denmark, Denmark
Roger Zimmermann	National University of Singapore, Singapore

External Reviewers

Konstantinos Avgerinakis	Information Technologies Institute, Greece
Long Chen	Northwest University of China, China
Klitos Christodoulou	Neapolis University of Pafos, Cyprus
Hannes Fassold	Joanneum Research, Austria
Frank Hopfgartner	The University of Glasgow, UK
Andreas Leibetseder	Alpen-Adria Universität Klagenfurt, Austria
Xinhui Li	Tianjin University, China
Meng Liu	Shandong University China
Eva Mohedano	Insight Centre for Data Analytics, Ireland
Eleftherios Spyromitros-Xioufis	Information Technologies Institute, Greece
Filareti Tsalakanidou	Information Technologies Institute, Greece
Stefanie Wechtitsch	Joanneum Research, Austria
Wolfgang Weiss	Joanneum Research, Austria
Jun Zhang	University of North Carolina at Chapel Hill, USA
Yihong Zhang	Kyoto University, Japan
Wanqing Zhao	Northwest University, China

Sponsors

Chulalongkorn University

Faculty of Engineering, Chulalongkorn University

CHULA ΣNGINEERING
Foundation toward Innovation

Thailand Convention & Exhibition Bureau

Springer Publishing

Contents – Part I

Full Papers Accepted for Oral Presentation

SS: Multimedia Analytics: Perspectives, Techniques and Applications

Contents – Part II

Demonstrations

Video Browser Showdown

Full Papers Accepted for Oral Presentation

A Markov Network Based Passage Retrieval Method for Multimodal Question Answering in the Cultural Heritage Domain

Shurong Sheng[1]([✉]), Aparna Nurani Venkitasubramanian[2],
and Marie-Francine Moens[1]

[1] Department of Computer Science, KU Leuven, 3001 Leuven, Belgium
{shurong.sheng,sien.moens}@cs.kuleuven.be
[2] Department of Electrical Engineering (ESAT), KU Leuven, 3001 Leuven, Belgium
aparna.nuranivenkitasubramanian@esat.kuleuven.be

Abstract. In this paper, we propose a Markov network based graphical framework to perform passage retrieval for multimodal question answering (MQA) with weak supervision in the cultural heritage domain. This framework encodes the dependencies between a question's feature information and the passage containing its answer, with the assumption that there is a latent alignment between a question and its candidate answer. Experiments on a challenging multi-modal dataset show that this framework achieves an improvement of 5% in terms of mean average precision (mAP) compared with a state-of-the-art method employing the same features namely (i) image match and (ii) word co-occurrence information of a passage and a question. We additionally construct two extended graphical frameworks integrating one more feature, namely (question type)-(named entity) match, into this framework in order to further boost the performance. The performance has been further improved by 2% in terms of mAP in one of the extended models.

Keywords: Multimodal question answering · Passage retrieval
Markov network · Graphical framework

1 Introduction

Multimodal question answering (MQA) refers to answering a textual query on an image. In the cultural heritage domain, MQA enables asking questions on images of cultural artifacts for visitors in museums, landmarks and other sites. This allows a personalized, engaged and natural way for people to interact with cultural relics which, to our best knowledge, doesn't exist yet.

A crucial component of an MQA system is the *passage retrieval* task that involves the identification of top-ranked passages that may contain the answer for a given question, thereby reducing the search space from a massive collection of documents to a fixed number of passages. Although passage retrieval in open-domain question answering (QA) is widely studied over the last decades, there

© Springer International Publishing AG 2018
K. Schoeffmann et al. (Eds.): MMM 2018, Part I, LNCS 10704, pp. 3–15, 2018.
https://doi.org/10.1007/978-3-319-73603-7_1

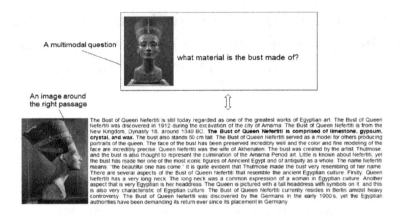

A multimodal question

what material is the bust made of?

An image around the right passage

The Bust of Queen Nefertiti is still today regarded as one of the greatest works of Egyptian art. The Bust of Queen Nefertiti was discovered in 1912 during the excavation of the city of Amarna. The Bust of Queen Nefertiti is from the New Kingdom, Dynasty 18, around 1340 BC. **The Bust of Queen Nefertiti is comprised of limestone, gypsum, crystal, and wax.** The bust also stands 50 cm tall. The Bust of Queen Nefertiti served as a model for others producing portraits of the queen. The face of the bust has been preserved incredibly well and the color and fine modeling of the face are incredibly precise. Queen Nefertiti was the wife of Akhenaten. The bust was created by the artist Thutmose and the bust is also thought to represent the culmination of the Amarna Period art. Little is known about Thutmose, yet the bust has made her one of the most iconic figures of Anncient Egypt and of antiquity as a whole. The name Nefertiti means "the beautiful one has come." It is quite evident that Thutmose made the bust very resembling of her name. There are several aspects of the Bust of Queen Nefertiti that resemble the ancient Egyptian culture. Firstly, Queen Nefertiti has a very long neck. The long neck was a common expression of a woman in Egyptian culture. Another aspect that is very Egyptian is her headdress. The Queen is pictured with a tall headdress with symbols on it, and this is also very characteristic of Egyptian culture. The Bust of Queen Nefertiti currently resides in Berlin amidst heavy controversy. The Bust of Queen Nefertiti was discovered by the Germans in the early 1900's, yet the Egyptian authorities have been demanding its return ever since its placement in Germany.

Fig. 1. An exemplary question-passage pair, the answer passage is retrieved by the model proposed in this paper

are few efforts on passage retrieval for MQA in the cultural heritage domain. In this paper, we address the task of retrieving passages (from a multimodal documentation) that contain the answers to a multimodal question. An exemplary question-passage pair is shown in Fig. 1. As in [13], we divide the multimodal questions into two categories: (i) the coarse *full-image* level questions on the entire image of an artwork, e.g., who is she?, and (ii) the finer *partial-image* level questions referring to the intricacies of an artwork, e.g., what happened to her left eye?

Compared with traditional passage retrieval in open-domain textual question answering, passage retrieval for MQA in the cultural heritage domain faces several key challenges. First, the multimodal setting injects some uncertainties into the passage retrieval problem, e.g., how to define the relevance of a passage and its associated images in the multimodal documents? How accurate is the definition of this relevance? Second, the text-based resources in the cultural heritage domain are often innately noisy, containing non-standard spelling, poor punctuation, obsolete grammar and word forms [7]. In addition, the information needs and tasks of cultural heritage users are often complex and diverse. For instance, the dataset we use in this paper covers 9 types of diverse questions with some of them being complex. Third, some questions inevitably have no answers due to historical reasons, in which case the questions should be classified as NIL questions, that is, having no answers. As we will see in Sect. 4.1, this may lead to propagated errors for the passage retrieval task in case the questions are wrongly classified. Moreover, *partial-image* level questions require deep reasoning of both the textual and visual parts of a question.

With the increasing interest in deep learning, huge efforts have been put into both the textual QA task and the MQA task [1,11] employing deep neural networks which need a large amount of question-answer pairs as training data and usually work on sentence-level answers (short answers). Due to the lack of large-scale training data and longer answers for MQA in the cultural heritage domain, current end-to-end deep neural networks cannot be directly applied in our task. In this paper, we propose a Markov network based graphical framework encoding the dependencies between a question's feature information and the passage containing its answer, with the assumption that there is a latent alignment between a question and its candidate answer. Experimental evaluation in terms of mAP shows that this framework achieves an improvement of 5% compared with the state-of-the-art proposed in [13] when using the same features namely (i) image match and (ii) word co-occurrence information of a passage and a question.

The main contributions of this paper are as follows: first, we propose and implement a weakly supervised Markov network based graphical framework to perform passage retrieval for MQA in the cultural heritage domain; second, we construct two extended forms of the framework integrating one more feature, namely (question type)-(named entity) match, to further boost the performance with 2% improvement in terms of mAP.

The remainder of this paper is organized as follows: Sect. 2 introduces related research, Sect. 3 describes the graphical frameworks, Sect. 4 discusses feature extraction experiments and gives an analysis of the final results, Sect. 5 concludes this paper and points out future research.

2   Related Work

Our work is mainly inspired by [17] that learns entity linking across animal objects of a video and textual mentions from corresponding subtitles. It achieves good results on their cross-modal (vision and language) entity alignment task in a video documentary about wildlife. In contrast to our work, the entity alignment in [17] is more straightforward, e.g., zebra as an object label in the video should be mapped to (ambiguous) mentions of zebra in the text side. While in our task, the alignment for a question and a passage is latent due to their corresponding semantic meaning, requiring a deeper reasoning.

Graphical frameworks are quite popular in performing information retrieval (IR) and question answering [10,15]. The difference between these frameworks is the way they encode dependencies in diverse graph structures. [10] focuses on dependencies between different terms while [15] emphasizes the evidence introduced by multiple passages by adding links between several passages sharing common words. In this paper, we encode the dependency of answer passages with feature-level evidence. Furthermore, we encode not only textual clues but also visual evidence i.e., the image match information of a question and a passage in a multimodal setting. [2] also performs passage retrieval in a feature based manner, while they represent features of a question-passage pair as a continuous feature vector, we perform this in a more compact and simple way by embedding them into a graphical framework as discrete variables.

3   Methodology

3.1   Task Definition

Given a multimodal question, we assume that there is a latent alignment in this question and its candidate answers due to some matching features among them. That is, the more closely a certain feature matches between a question and a passage, the more likely is the latent alignment between the question and the passage and vice versa. In this paper, we consider feature matches namely image match, word overlap and (question type)-(named entity) match. The first two features are the same as in [13] and the third feature is utilized to further improve the system performance.

This problem is formulated as follows: given a multimodal question q_i and a multimodal documentation D, a corresponding candidate passage set $P = \{pg_1, pg_2, ..., pg_j, ..., pg_n\}$ needs to be extracted from the documentation D, n is the number of candidate passages; the goal is to retrieve the passages containing the answers to question q_i; that is, to predict the probability that a passage pg_j contains the answer to question q_i based on the corresponding feature match information.

For the feature match information, we rely on three sources:

1. *Image match* between a passage and a question ($pg_j.image \leftrightarrow q_i.image$) where a passage image $pg_j.image$ refers to the image surrounding pg_j.
2. *Word co-occurrence* ($word\_overlap(q_i, pg_j)$) which refers to the word tokens occurring in both q_i and pg_j.
   The extended graphical models have an additional feature:
3. *Question type - named entity match* ($q_i.question\_type \leftrightarrow pg_j.entity$). As for certain types of questions in the dataset, i.e., 'Who' and 'Where' questions, e.g., who is this person? where are they from? the answers must contain named entities which are human names and location names respectively.

We address this task using a graphical model that encodes the dependencies between a question q_i's feature match and the candidate passage pg_j containing its answer, as described next.

3.2   Model

Pairwise Markov random fields (MRFs) forms a subclass of Markov networks which are associated with a set of node potentials and a set of edge potentials. The overall distribution is the normalized product of all the potentials (both node and edge) [4]. A pairwise MRF $G = <\{P^{answer}, PQ^{image}, PQ^{vec}\}, E>$ is constructed in this paper to judge whether passage pg_j is relevant to question q_i. This MRF G is called basic framework (BF) further in this paper, and it includes the following components:

- A set P^{answer} of nodes $p_j \in \{0, 1\}$ in the first row of Fig. 2(a) with $p_j = 1$ when pg_j contains an answer and otherwise 0. We define a node potential φ_{pj} for each p_j.

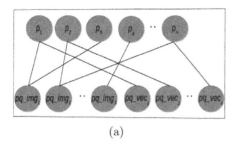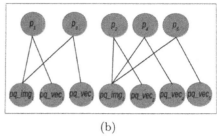

(a)   (b)

Fig. 2. (a): Basic framework structure. Each node in the first row refers to a binary variable denoting whether a certain passage contains an answer, and nodes in the second row denote image match and word co-occurrence features between a passage and question a question. The edges between the first and the second row encode corresponding dependencies. (b): Illustration of separated components in the basic framework

- A set PQ^{image} of nodes $pq\_img_j \in \{0,1\}$ in the left part of the second row in Fig. 2(a), denoting the match of passage image $pg_j.image$ and question image $q_i.image$. Here, $\varphi_{pq\_img_j}$ represents the node potential for pq_img_j.
- A set PQ^{vec} of nodes $pq\_vec_j \in \{0,1\}$ in the right part of the second row in Fig. 2(a), denoting the word co-occurrence of passage pg_j and question q_i. $\varphi_{pq\_vec_j}$ corresponds with the node potential for pq_vec_j.
- $\forall j$, two edges are built for p_j namely, $<p_j, pq\_img_j>$ and $<p_j, pq\_vec_j>$. Respective edge potential denoting the dependency weights between p_j and its connected node variables are referred to by φ_{edge_pj}.

The objective is to maximize the joint probability of all variables for the BF:

$$P = \frac{1}{Z} \prod_{\substack{p_j \in P^{answer} \\ pq\_img_j \in PQ^{image} \\ pq\_vec_j \in PQ^{vec} \\ edge\_pj \in E^{BF}}} \varphi_{p_j} * \varphi_{pq\_img_j} * \varphi_{pq\_vec_j} * \varphi_{edge\_pj} \qquad (1)$$

where Z is the normalization constant and E^{BF} is a set of the edges in the BF. The parameters in this equation are initialized as follows:

- As for φ_{p_j}, the potential value for p_j being 1 is a prior that allows to incorporate background knowledge (e.g., to indicate that certain passages are inherently related to certain questions). In our experiments, we use an uninformed prior, i.e., $\forall j$, we set $\varphi_{p_j} = 0.5$ with the assumption that all candidate passages have equal probability to be or not to be the answer to a question.
- $\forall j$, $\varphi_{pq\_img_j}$ are assigned in the same way as in [13]: for all candidate passages, the passages in a document right before or after a relevant image of a query image have node potential values of 1 for pq_img_j being 1, and this score is then discounted by a fixed number (0.2 in our case) which is the same for all documents for further away passages. Details on relevant image extraction are explained in Sect. 4.1.

- $\forall j$, $\varphi_{pq\_vec_j}$ is assigned as the cosine score between a question vector and a passage vector when pq_vec_j is 1. Details on cosine score computation are provided in Sect. 4.2. If a cosine score is 0, we assign the corresponding potential value to be a very small number near 0 to avoid side effects caused by 0 values.
- $\forall j$, φ_{edge_pj} is assigned empirically using a validation set.

Based on the assignments for $\varphi_{pq\_img_j}$, the number of its distinct values is fixed to M (6 in our case, i.e., 1, 0.8, 0.6, 0.4, 0.2, 0). Accordingly, we utilize M nodes to denote the image match information in the BF, i.e., the size of PQ^{image} is M. With this property, some passages share the same image match probability, i.e., different passages may be connected due to the shared image match feature. The size of P^{answer} and PQ^{vec} equals the number of candidate passages for q_i. Since each node p_j in the first row is only connected to its own feature match information regarding a question q_i, this framework is composed of several connected components as illustrated in Fig. 2(b).

3.3   Extended Models

One additional feature (question type)-(named entity) information has been integrated into the two extended frameworks shown in Fig. 3. We call the extended model with two rows in Fig. 3(a) as EF-1 and the other extended model with three rows in Fig. 3(b) as EF-2 further in this paper.

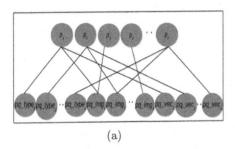 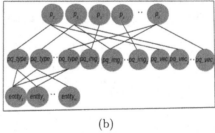

(a)   (b)

Fig. 3. (a): Extended framework 1 integrating (question type)-(named entity) match (pq_type_j) in the second row (left part). (b): Extended framework 2 integrating also named entity information in the third row

Compared with the BF, EF-1 and EF-2 have an additional set PQ^{type} of nodes $pq\_type_j \in \{0,1\}$ as shown in Fig. 3. These nodes denote the (question type)-(named entity) match of a question and a passage. Here, $\varphi_{pq\_type_j}$ represents the node potential of pq_type_j and is initialized empirically with pre-defined values according to corresponding match information extracted in Sect. 4.3. There is another set P^{entity} of nodes $entity_k \in \{0,1\}$ in EF-2 as shown in Fig. 3(b). Each $entity_k$ corresponds with an entity $entity\_k$ in the candidate passages where $entity_k$ is 1 when $entity\_k$ is the target entity to question q_i and 0 otherwise. Here, φ_{entity_k} refers to the node potential for $entity_k$. This potential is initialized as 0.5 when $entity_k$ is 1 with the hypothesis that an entity has equal probability to be or not to be the target answer for q_i. The size of P^{entity} equals the number of distinct named entities in the whole documentation. We construct an edge between the second and third row if and only if the question type and the named entities of the passage match. For example, if the given question q_i is a 'Who' question and passage pg_j has and $entity\_k$ referring to 'PERSON', then there is an edge $<pq\_type_j, entity_k>$. φ_{edge_entity} refers to corresponding edge potential denoting the dependency weights between the node variables in the second and third row in EF-2. Also, since several passages may share some named entities, there may exist loops between the second and the third row.

The extended models have similar objective functions as the one used in the BF expressed in Eq. (1). As for EF-1, the additional $\varphi_{pq\_type_j}$ should be added to the right side of Eq. (1) as an element for the product and both $\varphi_{pq\_type_j}$ and φ_{entity_k} should be added to Eq. (1) in the same way as for EF-2.

3.4   Inference and NIL Classification

If the graphical model has no cycles (e.g., basic framework and EF-1), belief propagation (BP) is employed as the inference method, otherwise when there are cycles (e.g., EF-2), loopy belief propagation (LBP) is applied. In either case, we use the implementation of [12]. Belief propagation works by passing real-valued messages along the edges between connected nodes and LBP starts from an initial set of node messages which are updated until convergence in an iterative manner. This way, the probability that passage pg_j contains an answer and the feature match information have mutual influence on each other. Using these inference algorithms, the aforementioned parameters for the three graphical frameworks (namely, edge potential φ_{edge_pj} in the BF, all edge potentials in the EF-1, all node and edge potentials in the EF-2) can be validated or updated respectively. The inference method yields a probability list $S_i = [s_1, s_2, ...s_j, ..., s_n]$ in which s_j refers to the probability passage pg_j containing the answer to question q_i. As in [13], a threshold s is used to ascertain that a question has NIL as its answer. i.e., q_i has NIL as its answer if $\forall j, s_j < s$.

4   Experiments and Results

There are two assumptions for the experiments introduced in this part: first, we benefit from the mature indoor positioning techniques for mobile devices e.g., Bluetooth, Wi-Fi positioning. Under these circumstances, the metadata (id, date, class, etc.) of the artwork regarding a multimodal question can be regarded as prior knowledge since the indoor position of visitors who ask these questions is known. Second, most digital archives of cultural heritage e.g., Europeana[1],

---

[1] http://www.europeana.eu/portal/en.

Google Arts & Culture[2] support searching by the metadata of an artwork and return its related documents accordingly. Hence, for each artwork in a museum room, its related documents can be regarded as prior knowledge with known metadata.

The feature extraction and model construction are preceded by two pre-processing steps: (i) all tokens in the questions and the documentation are converted to lowercase format; (ii) passages in the *related documents* concerning the artwork metadata of question q_i are extracted, to be added to the graphical model (instead of adding passages from all the documents).

4.1 Relevant Image Extraction

Full-image retrieval: Full-image retrieval is the process of extracting relevant images from the documents, in response to the coarse *full-image* level questions concerning the entire artifact. We employ manual annotation in this task as in [13], since the related documents for a multimodal question are prior knowledge, the relevant images can then be manually annotated for our small-scale dataset concerning a museum room.

Partial-image retrieval: Partial-image retrieval is the process of extracting relevant image parts from corresponding full images[3], in response to the finer *partial-image* level questions concerning only a part of an artwork. In this task, we need to further filter the relevant images for a partial multimodal question by excluding the parts of images that do not concern the partial question image. For example, full relevant images containing the upper body of Akhenaten are relevant for *full-image* level questions such as 'who is this man?' but not for *partial-image* question 'why is he barefoot?' whose question image is a photo of Akhenaten's feet. A convolutional neural network (CNN) based method is applied to perform this task wherein the question image is compared with the sub-images detected from the full relevant images using selective search [16]. CNN-based retrieval methods have constantly been proposed in recent years and are gradually replacing the hand-crafted local detectors and descriptors [19]. In this task, we extract the 4096-dimensional descriptor for an input image from the fully-connected (FC7) layer of AlexNet [6] pre-trained on ImageNet [3]. Cosine distance is then utilized to retrieve the relevant partial images for a certain query image. A threshold ($k = 0.3$) is set to filter out irrelevant sub-images. It yields a reasonable retrieval performance with an average accuracy of 0.60.

4.2 Word Co-occurrence Extraction

In this task, the questions and passages are represented as vectors in a common vector space, where each word represents an axis. A passage is represented as a bag-of-words (bow) as its vector is given by the number of word occurrences (or

---

[2] https://www.google.com/culturalinstitute/beta/.
[3] These full images are obtained by full-image retrieval described in the beginning of Sect. 4.

term frequency, tf), $pg_j = [\text{tf}_{1,j}, \text{tf}_{2,j}, \ldots, \text{tf}_{V,j}]$, where V is the vocabulary size, i.e., the number of distinct word types in the target collection. A textual query q_i is also represented as a V-dimensional vector in the same space. We compute the cosine similarity of a query vector and a passage vector to measure the word co-occurrence between them. Stop words are removed and stemming is applied in this procedure.

4.3   Question Classification and Named Entity Extraction

Question classification: We follow [14] for defining the question types. Question classification refers to classifying all questions into the pre-defined types. There are basically two different approaches for question classification: rule-based and machine learning based [5]. We implemented two simple cases of both methods. In the rule-based method, surface words 'who', 'identity', 'name' and 'whose' are applied to detect 'Who' type questions, while the word 'where' is used to detect 'Where' type questions. As for the machine learning based approach, we predict the category of the questions with logistic regression trained on the UIUC dataset[4]. The questions in the training and test set are represented as bag-of-words vectors which serve as the input for the logistic regression method. The question type classification in this study is a multi-class classification task. We employed a cross-entropy loss function for logistic regression, using the Scikit-learn library[5]. Since most of the recent learning-based and hybrid approaches use the taxonomy proposed by [8], and the category of the questions in the training set is different from this paper, we need to classify the predicted category to our pre-defined category according to their semantic meaning after the prediction phase.

Table 1. Evaluation results for question classification on 'Who' and 'Where' questions

		Precision	Recall	F1 score
Rule-based method	Who	0.97	0.95	0.96
	Where	1	0.9	0.94
Logistic regression	Who	0.425	0.9375	0.607
	Where	0.66	0.88	0.75

Table 1 shows the results of these two approaches. Notably, the rule-based method achieves better results in our task. The logistic regression has a relatively lower performance mainly due to the category difference between the training and the test set. Therefore, the rule-based method is utilized to obtain question types.

---

[4] http://cogcomp.cs.illinois.edu/Data/QA/QC/.

[5] http://scikit-learn.org/stable/modules/generated/sklearn.linear_model.LogisticRegression.html.

Table 2. Evaluation results for PERSON and LOCATION type named entities

	Precision	Recall	F1 score
PERSON	0.87	0.87	0.87
LOCATION	1	0.9	0.94

Named entity recognition: Stanford named entity recognizer (NER) [9] is employed to detect three types of named entities in the passages namely 'PERSON', 'LOCATION' and 'ORGANIZATION'. This NER may classify the same entity to different categories in different documents (based on the context). We employ a majority voting scheme to determine the category label. E.g., if 'Nefertiti' occurs as 'PERSON' 100 times and as 'ORGNIZATION' 50 times, we label it as 'PERSON' in the database. In this task, we assume that the named entity in the cultural heritage domain is not ambiguous, i.e., each named entity belongs to only one category.

The performance of the modified NER introduced in the previous paragraph is evaluated with 100 randomly sampled passages from the documentation as shown in Table 2. Evaluation for 'ORGANIZATION' entities was out of the scope of this paper.

4.4   Final Results of the MQA

A small validation dataset[6] is used to estimate the optimal values for parameters in the graphical frameworks and the threshold s for NIL classification introduced in Sect. 3. As for the dataset, there are 807 multimodal questions, 204 multimodal documents and 19587 corresponding paragraphs. Since some passages are filtered out by their constituted entity types in the extended models, the average number of potentially relavant passages per question in the extended models is less than that of the basic framework. This average number of potentially relevant passages per question is 1292 for the BF and 1109 for the extended models. Corresponding standard deviations of the potentially relevant passage numbers for the two model types are 1364 and 1301 respectively. Other details about the dataset can be found in [14].

There may be several answers to a question, we therefore apply the mean average precision method [13] to evaluate each model's performance. Mean reciprocal rank (MRR) [18] is also employed to evaluate the system's performance to find the top-ranked answer. NIL precision and recall [13] are computed to evaluate the system's ability to detect questions without ground-truth answers.

The evaluation results for the test set[7] are shown in Table 3. Notably, the BF achieves a mAP score of 0.13 for the *full-image* level questions. This is 5% higher than the best result (0.08) obtained in [13] which employs the same features namely image match and the word co-occurrence as in the BF but uses

---

[6] 20% of the data with 86 question-passage pairs.

[7] 344 *full-image* level questions and 385 *partial-image* level questions.

Table 3. Evaluation results for full-image and partial-image level questions

		mAP	MRR	NIL precision	NIL recall
Full	BF	0.13	0.17	0.31	0.77
	EF-1 (BF + additional feature)	0.14	0.18	0.34	0.77
	EF-2 (BF + additional feature)	0.15	0.19	0.35	0.76
Partial	BF	0.091	0.091	0.67	0.77
	BF + partial-image retrieval	0.092	0.092	0.67	0.77

Table 4. mAP scores for each type of questions. 'BF+' refers to 'BF + partial-image retrieval' as in Table 3 and '-' means there is no such type of questions

		What	When	Who	Why	Where	Which	How	Yes or no	Selective
Full	BF	0.13	0.06	0.13	0.09	0.04	0.02	0.5	0.19	0.06
	EF-1	0.13	0.06	0.13	0.09	0.07	0.02	0.5	0.19	0.06
	EF-2	0.13	0.06	0.12	0.09	0.19	0.01	0.5	0.18	0.10
Partial	BF	0.06	-	-	0.05	-	-	-	0.15	0.33
	BF +	0.06	-	-	0.05	-	-	-	0.16	0.33

them sequentially rather than complementarily. After integrating the additional feature namely (question type)-(named entity) match into the BF, the system performance is improved due to the excellent performance in detecting 'Where' questions as shown in Table 3. Here, EF-2 achieves better performance with a mAP score of 0.15 and a MRR score of 0.19. For *partial-image* level questions, the system works 1% better in mAP score when performing partial-image retrieval.

The mAP scores shown in Table 4 indicate the system's qualification in answering 'How' type questions in the *full-image* level question set. With the additional feature, better performance is achieved for 'Where' questions but not in the case of 'Who' questions mainly due to the propagated error of the NIL classification. On one hand some questions having ground-truth answers are wrongly classified as NIL questions with no answers, thus do not contribute to the final mAP score. On the other hand, some NIL questions are classified as questions with ground-truth answers, resulting in an average precision of 0[8].

5   Conclusion and Future Work

In this paper, we have proposed an MRF to perform passage retrieval for MQA in the cultural heritage domain. This framework encodes the dependencies between a question's feature match and the passage containing its answer. We built a basic framework incorporating two features: one textual (word co-occurrence)

---

[8] This reason is figured out by manually checking the mAP score for each 'Who' question in different models.

and one visual (image match) feature. We have also explored extended forms of this framework, by integrating one more feature, i.e., (question type)-(named entity) match. Experiments show that the basic framework improves over the state-of-the-art by 5% in terms of mAP computed over 344 multimodal questions, and the extended models obtain further improvement with an additional feature.

The graphical models are applied on a challenging small-scale dataset on which it is difficult to train a supervised model. In future work, we will investigate domain adaption methods which can leverage large-scale/external datasets and overcome the limits of the scale of our dataset.

Acknowledgments. This work is funded by the KU Leuven BOF/IF/RUN/2015. We additionally thank our anonymous reviewers for the helpful comments.

References

1. Andreas, J., Rohrbach, M., Darrell, T., Klein, D.: Neural module networks. In: Proceedings of the IEEE Conference on Computer Vision and Pattern Recognition, pp. 39–48 (2016)
2. Chen, T., Van Durme, B.: Discriminative information retrieval for question answering sentence selection. In: Proceedings of the 15th Conference of the European Chapter of the Association for Computational Linguistics, pp. 719–725 (2017)
3. Deng, J., Dong, W., Socher, R., Li, L.J., Li, K., Fei-Fei, L.: ImageNet: a large-scale hierarchical image database. In: Proceedings of the IEEE Conference on Computer Vision and Pattern Recognition, pp. 248–255 (2009)
4. James, G., Witten, D., Hastie, T., Tibshirani, R.: An Introduction to Statistical Learning, vol. 112. Springer, Berlin (2013). https://doi.org/10.1007/978-1-4614-7138-7
5. Jayalakshmi, S., Sheshasaayee, A.: Question classification: a review of state-of-the-art algorithms and approaches. Indian J. Sci. Technol. 8(29) (2015)
6. Krizhevsky, A., Sutskever, I., Hinton, G.E.: ImageNet classification with deep convolutional neural networks. In: Proceedings of the 25th International Conference on Neural Information Processing Systems, pp. 1097–1105 (2012)
7. Lawless, S., Agosti, M., Clough, P., Conlan, O.: Exploration, navigation and retrieval of information in cultural heritage: ENRICH 2013. In: Proceedings of the 36th International ACM SIGIR Conference on Research and Development in Information Retrieval, p. 1136 (2013)
8. Li, X., Roth, D.: Learning question classifiers. In: Proceedings of the 19th International Conference on Computational Linguistics, pp. 1–7 (2002)
9. Manning, C.D., Surdeanu, M., Bauer, J., Finkel, J.R., Bethard, S., McClosky, D.: The stanford coreNLP natural language processing toolkit. In: Proceedings of the Association for Computational Linguistics (System Demonstrations), pp. 55–60 (2014)
10. Metzler, D., Croft, W.B.: A Markov random field model for term dependencies. In: Proceedings of the 28th Annual International ACM SIGIR Conference on Research and Development in Information Retrieval, pp. 472–479. ACM (2005)
11. Oh, J.H., Torisawa, K., Kruengkrai, C., Iida, R., Kloetzer, J.: Multi-column convolutional neural networks with causality-attention for why-question answering. In: Proceedings of the 10th ACM International Conference on Web Search and Data Mining, pp. 415–424 (2017)

12. Schmidt, M.: UGM: a Matlab toolbox for probabilistic undirected graphical models (2007). https://www.cs.ubc.ca/~schmidtm/Software/UGM.html
13. Sheng, S., Moens, M.F.: Simple baseline models for multimodal question answering in the cultural heritage domain. In: Busch, C., Sieck, J. (eds.) Kultur und Informatik: Mixed Reality, pp. 119–132. Verlag Werner Hülsbusch, Boizenburg (2017)
14. Sheng, S., Van Gool, L., Moens, M.F.: A dataset for multimodal question answering in the cultural heritage domain. In: Proceedings of the COLING 2016 Workshop on Language Technology Resources and Tools for Digital Humanities (LT4DH). ACL (2016)
15. Sun, H., Duan, N., Duan, Y., Zhou, M.: Answer extraction from passage graph for question answering. In: Proceedings of the International Joint Conference on Artificial Intelligence, pp. 2169–2175 (2013)
16. Uijlings, J.R., Van De Sande, K.E., Gevers, T., Smeulders, A.W.: Selective search for object recognition. Int. J. Comput. Vis. **104**, 154–171 (2013)
17. Venkitasubramanian, A.N., Tuytelaars, T., Moens, M.F.: Entity linking across vision and language. Multimed. Tools Appl. **76**, 22599–22622 (2017)
18. Voorhees, E.M., et al.: The TREC-8 question answering track report. In: Text REtrieval Conference, pp. 77–82 (1999)
19. Zheng, L., Yang, Y., Tian, Q.: SIFT meets CNN: a decade survey of instance retrieval. arXiv preprint arXiv:1608.01807 (2016)

A Method of Weather Radar Echo Extrapolation Based on Convolutional Neural Networks

En Shi, Qian Li[✉], Daquan Gu, and Zhangming Zhao

National University of Defense Technology, Nanjing, China
public_liqian@163.com

Abstract. Weather radar echo extrapolation techniques possess wide application prospects in short-term forecasting (i.e., nowcasting). Traditional methods of radar echo extrapolation have difficulty obtaining long limitation period data and lack the utilization rate of radar. To solve this problem, this paper proposes a method of weather radar echo extrapolation based on convolutional neural networks (CNNs). To create a strong correlation among contiguous weather radar echo images from traditional CNNs, this method present a new CNN model: Recurrent Dynamic CNNs (RDCNN). RDCNN consists of a recurrent dynamic sub-network and a probability prediction layer, which constructs a cyclic structure in the convolution layer, improving the ability of RDCNN to process time-related images. Nanjing, Hangzhuo and Xiamen experimented with radar data, and compared with traditional methods, our method achieved higher accuracy of extrapolation and extended the limitation period effectively, meeting the requirements for application.

Keywords: Weather radar echo extrapolation · Deep learning
Convolutional neural networks · Image prediction

1 Introduction

Nowcasting convective precipitation has long been an important problem in the field of weather forecasting, especially for predicting disastrous weather [1]. The goal of precipitation nowcast is to precisely predict rainfall intensity in a timely manner in a local region over a relatively short period. Because precipitation nowcast requires more accurate forecasting resolution and time than other traditional rainfall or temperature predictions, this challenging operation has emerged as a popular research topic in the meteorological field [2]. At present, extrapolation forecasts based on radar echoes is the mainstay of precipitation nowcasting [3, 4]. More accurate and efficient prediction by radar echoes are crucial for improving the accuracy of short-term precipitation nowcast. The purpose of radar echo extrapolation is to predict the future position and intensity of radar echo based on current radar observations. The key to radar echo extrapolation is to obtain a reliable extrapolated echo image. The essence of radar echo extrapolation is based on the current and historical moments of radar echo images to predict the next unseen image. Existing methods for radar echo extrapolation can roughly be

© Springer International Publishing AG 2018
K. Schoeffmann et al. (Eds.): MMM 2018, Part I, LNCS 10704, pp. 16–28, 2018.
https://doi.org/10.1007/978-3-319-73603-7_2

categorized into two classes: centroid tracking methods and tracking radar echoes by correlation (TREC) methods [5].

The centroid tracking method relies on the reflectivity factor threshold to identify storms. It is mainly applied to the tracking of storms and difficult to predict large-scale precipitation echoes. The TREC methods predicts future echoes by calculating the correlation of radar echoes at several previous moments. Based on the TREC methods, researchers further developed continuity of TREC vectors (COTREC) [6] and difference image-based TREC (DITREC) [7] along with other methods, which are all widely used in precipitation forecasting. However, these TREC methods are only based on several past radar echo images, which are used to predict the next radar echo image. This results in defective data utilization. Effective forecast time usually cannot exceed one hour.

To solve this problem, we examine the challenging of weather forecasting via machine learning and propose a method of weather radar echo extrapolation based on CNNs. In recent years, there have been few studies on CNN-applied weather forecasting. Shi et al. proposed the convolutional long-short term memory network (LSTM) (i.e., ConvLSTM) by adding convolutional structures to fully connected LSTM (FC-LSTM) [8], which preserves previous training information, and then extended the forecasting period effectively. Singh et al. used convolutions within cyclic structures of recurrent neural networks (RNNs), exploiting both spatial and temporal dependencies in the data [9], which achieved state-of-the-art performance while reducing the model size four times compared to the conventional model. Inspired by these works, this paper presents a new CNN model, namely a recurrent dynamic CNN (RDCNN). Observing that a radar image in sequence can usually be approximated as a translation of the previous image, CNNs can be trained by a variety of weather radar images sorted chronologically to learn how echoes translate, thus predicting the next radar image in sequence. To accommodate the strong correlation between radar echo images at adjacent times, we modify the network structure based on traditional CNNs so that the convolution kernels can save the history information of the training process. The convolution kernels vary from input to input during testing. RDCNN is a more suitable model for radar echo extrapolation, which processes a series of time-related image sequences. In our experiment, we compare the RDCNN prediction to other baselines, including a strong COTREC method. We show that by using RDCNN, we gain accuracy of prediction improvements compared to the other baselines.

2 Preliminaries

2.1 CNNs

In recent years, CNNs have become increasingly popular in solving various computer vision applications, such as object recognition, objection localization, cancer detection, face recognition, and scene labelling [10–15]. What sets CNNs apart from other neural networks is the use of convolutional and sampling layers [10]. The convolutional layer computes the output feature maps by convolving the feature maps of the previous layer with a set of convolution kernels. The sampling layer reduces the resolution of its input

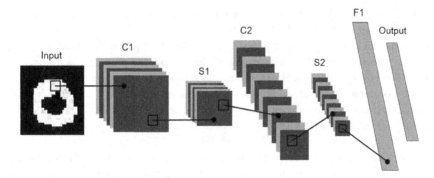

Fig. 1. A basic CNNs model with two convolutional layers (C1, C2), two sampling layers (S1, S2), and one classifier (F1).

feature maps. Therefore, compared with other neural networks such as back propagation (BP) neural network, CNNs can accelerate the training process greatly by processing images with less network weight parameters [16, 17], which is far more efficient. Figure 1 shows a basic CNNs structure. The convolutional layer computes the output feature via the following equation,

$$y_j = f\left(\sum_{i\in M} k_{ij} * x_i + b_j\right) \tag{1}$$

where $f(\bullet)$ is an element-wise non-linearity, such as a sigmoid or hyperbolic tangent; M is the set of input feature maps; x_i is the ith input feature map; y_j is the jth output feature map; b_j is the jth bias; the convolution kernels are denoted by k_{ij}; and the $*$ symbol is the convolution operator. The sampling layer computes the output feature via the following equation,

$$y_j = g(x_i) \tag{2}$$

where $g(\bullet)$ is a sampling function. We apply mean-pooling as sampling function, which takes the average gray-scale value of the pixels in the sampling area as the output of the function.

2.2   RNNs

In the conventional neural network model, we assume that all inputs (and outputs) are independent of each other. Thus there is no connection between the neurons of the same hidden layer. This results in the inability to deliver information and is the reason why traditional neural networks have difficulty dealing with time-related data. RNNs are a class of artificial neural network where connections between units form a directed cycle [18]. This allows them to exhibit dynamic temporal behavior. Unlike feed-forward neural networks, RNNs can use their internal memory to process arbitrary sequences of inputs. This makes them applicable to tasks such as speech recognition [19] or text recognition [20].

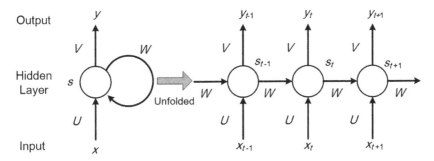

Fig. 2. Basic RNN model with one hidden layer, and its structure after unfolding.

RNNs perform the same task for every element of a sequence, with the output depending upon the previous computations. Figure 2 shows a typical RNN with a hidden layer being unfolded into a full network. The hidden state is calculated via the following recurrence equation,

$$s_t = f(Ux_t + Ws_{t-1}) \tag{3}$$

where x_t is the input at time step t and s_t is the hidden state at time step t. The function $f(\bullet)$ usually is a nonlinearity such as *tanh* or ReLU. The output is calculated as follows,

$$y_t = g(Vs_t) \tag{4}$$

where y_t is the output at time step t. The function $g(\bullet)$ usually uses softmax. We can set the hidden state s_t as the memory of the network. s_t captures information from all the previous time steps, and the output at time step t is calculated solely based on s_t.

RNNs store historical training information through its cyclic structure. Since radar echo extrapolation is a process based on time-dependent image sequences, a CNN model with cyclic structure is able to preserves the features of the former input images, and predict more reliable future radar echo images.

3   RDCNN Model

This paper proposes an RDCNN model, which combines a deep CNNs with a cyclic structure learned from RNNs. RDCNNs consist of a recurrent dynamic sub-network (RDSN) and a probability prediction layer (PPL), it obtains the characteristics of the radar echo image sequence, then predicts the next radar echo image. Figure 3 shows the overall structure of the model. When we use RDCNN to forecast future radar echo images. First, the RDSN processes four radar echo images to obtain two probability vectors, then the resulting probability vector and the last image in the input sequence are input to the PPL. Finally, the last image is convoluted with the probability vectors in the PPL to calculate the next radar echo image.

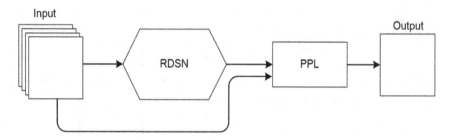

Fig. 3. Architecture of RDCNN. RDSN is a sub-network which computes probability vectors. The last image in the sequence and the probability vectors then input into the probability prediction layer to predict the next radar echo image.

3.1 RDSN

RDSN is the main part of RDCNN, which is a separate CNN model. The radar image sequence is input into the RDSN, and two one-dimensional vectors are calculated by the convolution layers, the sampling layer and the classifier. Traditional CNNs extract the image features alternately with the convolution layers and the subsampling layers. In contrast, the RDSN adds the hidden layer and constructs the cyclic structure with the convolution layer. Figure 4 shows the cyclic structure of RDSN. In the cyclic structure, the convolution layer is connected to the hidden layer, and the output feature maps of the convolution layer is processed by the hidden layer. Afterwards, the information is re-entered into the convolution layer at the next time step.

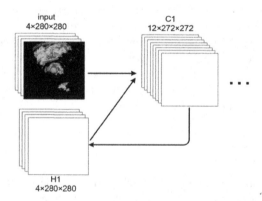

Fig. 4. The cyclic structure in RDSN consists of convolution layers and hidden layers.

The hidden layer processes the input feature map at the current moment and passes the result to the convolution layer at the next time step. with the cyclic structure, RDCNN is able to establish contact between input radar echo images at different times.

The overall structure of RDSN is shown in Fig. 5. The four radar images of size 280×280 are given as inputs to a convolutional layer (C1) with 12 convolution kernels of size 9×9. The resulting 12 feature maps are then passed to a sampling layer (S1) and a hidden layer (H1). S1 takes the max over 2×2 spatial blocks with a stride of 2, and H1 with four convolution kernels of size 9×9 compute four feature maps that input into C1 at next time step. The next three convolutional layers (C2, C3, C4) contain 32 filters of size 9×9. The resulting 32 feature maps are then passed to the next sampling and hidden layers. The sampling layers (S2, S2, S4) take the max over 2×2 spatial blocks with a stride of 2, and the hidden layers (H2, H3, H4) with eight convolution kernels of size 9×9 compute eight feature maps that input into corresponding convolutional layers at next time step. This is followed by another conventional convolutional layer (C5) with 32 filters of size 7×7. The resulting 32 feature maps are then passed to a classifier (F1) and a hidden layer (H5). H5, with eight parameters, computes eight feature maps that input into C5 at next time step, and F1 expands the feature maps into a column vector of size 521×1 and applies a softmax function to the column vector to calculate two probability vectors: VPV and HPV. These two vectors are calculated as follow,

$$\begin{aligned} \text{VPV} &= [\text{softmax}(WV \times a^{C5} + BV)]^{\text{T}} \\ \text{HPV} &= \text{softmax}(WH \times a^{C5} + BH) \end{aligned} \tag{5}$$

where a^{C5} is the column vector of size 521×1, WV and WH are two weight matrix of size 41×512, BV and BH are two bias matrix of size 41×1, $(\bullet)^{\text{T}}$ represents the matrix transpose, and symbol $\times$ represents the matrix's outer product operator.

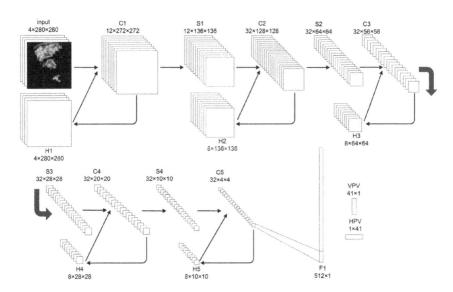

Fig. 5. The overall structure of RDSN with five convolutional layers (C1, C2, C3, C4, C5), four sampling layers (S1, S2, S3, S4), five hidden layers (H1, H2, H3, H4, H5), and one classifier.

According to the characteristics of the softmax function, VPV and HPV are positive and sum to 1, which could be considered as vectors of probabilities. It should be noted that when calculating the output feature maps at the hidden layer, we need zero padding to ensure that the resolution of output maps match with the input maps of the convolution layer.

3.2   Probability Prediction Layer (PPL)

The input of the PPL includes the last image in the sequence and the probability vectors calculated by RDSN. PPL computes the final predicted image through two convolution operations. Figure 6 shows how PPL works. It contains two network layers of DC1 and DC2. The VPV is taken as the convolution kernel of DC1 and convoluted with the last image in the sequence to get the feature map of size 240 × 280. The HPV is the convolution kernel of DC2 and is convoluted with the obtained feature map from DC1 to predict the next radar echo image.

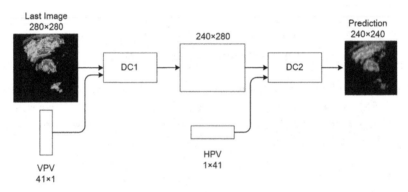

Fig. 6. The structure of PPL. DC1 takes the last image in the sequence and convolves it with VPV, DC2 takes the output of DC1 and convolves it with HPV to compute the next radar echo image.

Since the probability vectors VPH and HPV carry the characteristic of the input radar echo images, the calculations in the DC1 and DC2 can be regarded as the predictions in the vertical direction and horizontal direction.

4   Experiments

The RDCNN was developed, tested, and compared to alternatives using its own designed radar echo dataset for radar echo prediction. The experiment was carried out on a computer with 2.40 GHz CPU and 4 GB memory. In our experiments, the convolution kernels and weight matrix (include *WV* and *WH*) are initialized per the Xavier method [21]. All the bias parameters are initialized as zero vectors. The back-propagation algorithm is adopted in the training process, and the network parameters are updated by the gradient descent method with a momentum of 0.9. The learning rate is 0.0001, and the number of iterations is 40.

In the comparative experiment, the RDCNN and the mature COTREC algorithm are used to predict the three large-scale precipitation processes of 2016, which occurred at Nanjing on July 11, Hangzhou on August 20, and Xiamen on July 9. The future radar echo images are obtained by RDCNN and other baselines. Then we analyze the advantages and disadvantages of different radar echo extrapolation methods from both the prediction images and the precipitation nowcasting metrics.

4.1 Radar Echo Dataset

We create three radar echo datasets from CINRAD-SA-type Doppler weather radar data, and all the three are independent. The first dataset contains radar images taken in Nanjing, Jiangsu; the second dataset contains radar images taken in Hangzhou, Zhejiang; and the third dataset contains radar images taken in Xiamen, Fujian. Each dataset is split into a training set and a testing set. The three training sets contain 12,000 samples each, and the testing sets contain 1,000 samples each. There are five images for each sample, marked as $\{x_1, x_2, x_3, x_4, y\}$. Among them, $\{x_1, x_2, x_3, x_4\}$ is the input image sequence with size of 280×280, and $\{y\}$ is the ground truth for calculating error with size of 240×240. The time interval between images is 6 min. Figure 7 shows one sample from the dataset.

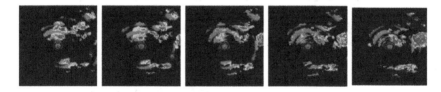

Fig. 7. A sample from Nanjing dataset taken in August 5, 2016.

4.2 Prediction Images Analysis

We apply the RDCNN and COTREC algorithms to predict the above three precipitation processes, and results are shown in Fig. 8. We can find that RDCNN can obtain more accurate prediction and can better estimate the generation and demise of precipitation echo. Although COTREC can provide sharper predictions than RDCNN, the accuracy of the predictions is generally not as precise as RDCNN, especially at the boundary. Additionally, the results of RDCNN suffer fuzzy effect. We believe that the fuzzy effect may be due to the inherent uncertainty of the task. That is, in long-term prediction, it is almost impossible to make accurate predictions for the entire radar map, especially when RDCNN has learned various transformation modes of precipitation during training.

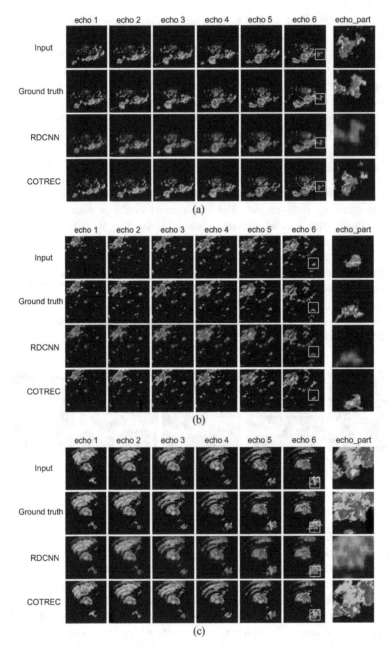

Fig. 8. Three prediction examples. All the predictions and ground truths are sampled with an interval of 6 min. From top to bottom: input frames; ground truth frames; prediction by RDCNN; prediction by COTREC. The echo_parts are the result of enlarging radar echo images in the red frames (a) Nanjing on July 11, 2016; (b) Hangzhou on August 20, 2016; (c) Xiamen on July 9, 2016. (Color figure online)

4.3 Precipitation Nowcasting Metrics Analysis

In Sect. 4.2 we evaluated RDCNN with other radar echo extrapolation methods from prediction images. Additionally, we evaluated these methods using several commonly used precipitation nowcasting metrics, including rainfall mean squared error (RMSE), critical success index (CSI), false alarm rate (FAR), and probability of detection (POD) [8]. The RMSE metric is defined as the average squared error between the predicted rainfall and the ground truth. Because our predictions are done at the pixel level, we need to convert the grayscale image into radar echo intensities and calculate the precipitation intensity through the Z-R relationship [22]. Then we calculate RMSE as follows,

$$\text{RMSE} = \frac{1}{N} \sum_{\Omega} \left[F(t_0 + \tau, x) - \widehat{F}(t_0 + \tau, x) \right]^2 \tag{6}$$

where Ω is the observation area; N is the total number of pixels; and precipitation intensity of the predicted rainfall and the ground truth on pixel x at time step τ is denoted by $\widehat{F}(t_0 + \tau, x)$ and $F(t_0 + \tau, x)$.

We then need to compare the prediction with the ground truth, pixel-by-pixel, when calculating CSI, FAR and POD. Every pixel in prediction and ground truth is marked as a 1 or 0 using a threshold of a 0.5 mm/h rainfall rate (indicating raining or not). Then, we count the numbers of 'hits' pixels (prediction = 1, truth = 1), 'misses' pixels (prediction = 0, truth = 1), and 'false' pixels (prediction = 1, truth = 0), and mark them as n_h, n_m and n_f. CSI, FAR and POD are defined as follows.

$$
\begin{aligned}
\text{CSI} &= \frac{n_h}{n_h + n_m + n_f} \\
\text{FAR} &= \frac{n_f}{n_h + n_f} \\
\text{POD} &= \frac{n_h}{n_h + n_m}
\end{aligned}
\tag{7}
$$

We apply the RDCNN and COTREC to predict the precipitation processes in Xiamen on July 9, 2016, and to calculate four precipitation nowcasting metrics over 15 prediction steps. Additionally, we use the last image in the sequence as a reference. Results are shown in Fig. 9 and Table 1. The predicted radar echo image gradually deviates from the last image as the forecast time grows. When the forecast time is short, both RDCNN and COTREC perform well. Over five extrapolated steps, RDCNN outperforms the COTREC algorithm, especially on RMSE and FAR. We infer that the reason RDCNN performs better because it has seen similar patterns during training, it can discover this type of sudden changes and give reasonable predictions in the forecasting.

In this paper, the limitation period of radar echo extrapolation is described by de-correlation time $L \cdot L$ is the time corresponding to the correlation between the predicted echo image and the ground truth falling from 1 to $1/e$. The correlation factor c is defined as follows,

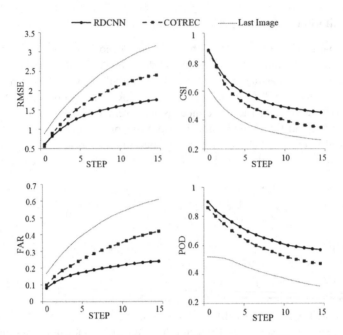

Fig. 9. Comparison of four precipitation nowcasting metrics on different models over 15 prediction steps.

Table 1. Comparison of average scores of different models over 15 prediction steps.

Model	RMSE	CSI	FAR	POD
RDCNN	1.376	0.573	0.187	0.682
COTREC	1.753	0.499	0.292	0.610
Last image	2.264	0.366	0.444	0.419

$$c(\tau) = \frac{\sum_{\Omega} \widehat{G}(t_0 + \tau, x) G(t_0 + \tau, x)}{\sqrt{\sum_{\Omega} \widehat{G}(t_0 + \tau, x)^2 \cdot \sum_{\Omega} G(t_0 + \tau, x)^2}} \tag{8}$$

where the grayscale of the pixel x in the prediction and the ground truth at time step τ is denoted by $\widehat{G}(t_0 + \tau, x)$ and $G(t_0 + \tau, x)$, respectively. The correlation factor ranges from 0 to 1; the higher the correlation factor is, the more similar two images are. This implies a more precise prediction. When c is less than $1/e$, it can be concluded that the predicted radar echo image is no longer valid, and the time is defined as the de-correlation time L, and L is used as the limitation period of radar echo extrapolation. Figure 10 shows that correlation factor c changes over forecast time during the three precipitation processes. We can find that the value of c decreases exponentially with the forecast time, compared with COTREC. The correlation factor c of RDCNN decreases

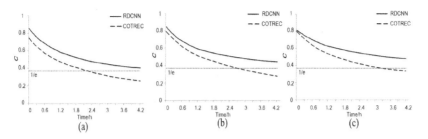

Fig. 10. Correlation changes over forecast time during the three precipitation processes. (a) Nanjing on July 11, 2016; (b) Hangzhou on August 20, 2016; (c) Xiamen on July 9, 2016.

more slowly. Finally, the de-correlation time of the COTREC method is approximately 2.4–3 h, and L of RDCNN is greater than 4 h, which indicates that using RDCNN can effectively extend the limitation period.

5 Conclusion and Future Work

CNNs have a far-reaching application prospect in the recognition and prediction of 2D images. At present, there is little research about CNN applications in the field of weather forecasting. In this paper, we have successfully applied the machine learning approach, especially with CNNs, to the challenging precipitation nowcasting problem. We regard radar echo extrapolation as a spatial-temporal sequence forecasting problem and propose a new CNN model, namely RDCNN, to solve the problem. RDCNN consists of RDSN and PPL, and constructs a cyclic structure between convolution layers and hidden layers, which improve the ability of RDCNN to process time-related image sequences. Through experimentation, we proved the effectiveness of RDCNN in radar echo extrapolation, especially in the boundary. RDCNN can predict the generation and demise of precipitation echo more accurately.

For future work, we will investigate how to optimize RDCNN to reduce the fuzzy effects of prediction, and to apply RDCNN to video-based action recognition.

References

1. Doviak, R.J.: Doppler Radar and Weather Observations. Courier Corporation, Chelmsford (1993)
2. Sun, J., Xue, M., Wilson, J.W., Zawadzki, I., et al.: Use of NWP for nowcasting convective precipitation: recent progress and challenges. Bull. Am. Meteorol. Soc. **95**(3), 409–426 (2014)
3. Reyniers, M.: Quantitative Precipitation Forecasts Based on Radar Observations: Principles, Algorithms and Operational Systems. Institut Royal Météorologique de Belgique, Uccle (2008)
4. Cheung, P., Yeung, H. Y.: Application of optical-flow technique to significant convection nowcast for terminal areas in Hong Kong. In: The 3rd WMO International Symposium on Nowcasting and Very Short-Range Forecasting, pp. 6–10 (2012)

5. Otsuka, S., Tuerhong, G., Kikuchi, R., et al.: Precipitation nowcasting with threedimensional space–time extrapolation of dense and frequent phased-array weather radar observations. Weather Forecast. **31**(1), 329–340 (2016)
6. Li, L., Schmid, W., Joss, J.: Nowcasting of motion and growth of precipitation with radar over a complex orography. J. Appl. Meteorol. **34**(6), 1286–1300 (1995)
7. Zhang, Y., Cheng, M., Xia, W., et al.: Estimation of weather radar echo motion field and its application to precipitation nowcasting. Acta Meteorol. Sin. **64**(5), 631–646 (2006)
8. Xingjian, S.H.I., Chen, Z., Wang, H., et al.: Convolutional LSTM network: a machine learning approach for precipitation nowcasting. In: Advances in Neural Information Processing Systems, pp. 802–810 (2015)
9. Singh, S., Sarkar, S., Mitra, P.: Leveraging convolutions in recurrent neural networks for doppler weather radar echo prediction. In: Cong, F., Leung, A., Wei, Q. (eds.) ISNN 2017. LNCS, vol. 10262, pp. 310–317. Springer, Cham (2017). https://doi.org/10.1007/978-3-319-59081-3_37
10. LeCun, Y., Bottou, L., Bengio, Y., Haffner, P.: Gradient-based learning applied to document recognition. Proc. IEEE **86**(11), 2278–2324 (1998)
11. Krizhevsky, A., Sutskever, I., Hinton, G.E.: Imagenet classification with deep convolutional neural networks. In: Advances in Neural Information Processing Systems, pp. 1097–1105 (2012)
12. Cireşan, D.C., Giusti, A., Gambardella, L.M., Schmidhuber, J.: Mitosis detection in breast cancer histology images with deep neural networks. In: Mori, K., Sakuma, I., Sato, Y., Barillot, C., Navab, N. (eds.) MICCAI 2013. LNCS, vol. 8150, pp. 411–418. Springer, Heidelberg (2013). https://doi.org/10.1007/978-3-642-40763-5_51
13. Sermanet, P., Eigen, D., Zhang, X., et al.: OverFeat: integrated recognition, localization and detection using convolutional networks. arXiv:1312.6229, arXiv preprint (2013)
14. Szegedy, C., Liu, W., Jia, Y., et al.: Going deeper with convolutions. In: Proceedings of the IEEE Conference on Computer Vision and Pattern Recognition, pp. 1–9 (2015)
15. Taigman, Y., Yang, M., Ranzato, M. A., et al.: DeepFace: closing the gap to human-level performance in face verification. In: Proceedings of the IEEE Conference on Computer Vision and Pattern Recognition, pp. 1701–1708 (2014)
16. Yang, W., Jin, L., Tao, D., et al.: DropSample: a new training method to enhance deep convolutional neural networks for large-scale unconstrained handwritten Chinese character recognition. Pattern Recogn. **58**(1), 190–203 (2016)
17. Huang, F.J., LeCun, Y.: Large-scale learning with SVM and convolutional for generic object categorization. In: IEEE Computer Society Conference on Computer Vision and Pattern Recognition, pp. 284–291 (2006)
18. Mikolov, T., Karafiát, M., Burget, L., et al.: Recurrent neural network based language model. In: Interspeech, vol. 2, p. 3 (2010)
19. Vinyals, O., Ravuri, S.V., Povey, D.: Revisiting recurrent neural networks for robust ASR. In: IEEE International Conference on Acoustics Speech and Signal Processing (ICASSP), pp. 4085–4088 (2012)
20. Sutskever, I., Martens, J., Hinton, G. E.: Generating text with recurrent neural networks. In: Proceedings of the 28th International Conference on Machine Learning (ICML-2011), pp. 1017–1024 (2011)
21. Glorot, X., Bengio, Y.: Understanding the difficulty of training deep feedforward neural networks. In: Proceedings of the Thirteenth International Conference on Artificial Intelligence and Statistics, pp. 249–256 (2010)
22. Uijlenhoet, R.: Raindrop size distribution and radar reflectivity-rain rate relationships for radar hydrology. Hydrol. Earth Syst. Sci. **5**(4), 615–627 (2001)

A Motion-Driven Approach for Fine-Grained Temporal Segmentation of User-Generated Videos

Konstantinos Apostolidis, Evlampios Apostolidis, and Vasileios Mezaris[✉]

Information Technologies Institute/CERTH, 6th km Xarilaou - Thermi,
57001 Thessaloniki, Greece
{kapost,apostolid,bmezaris}@iti.gr

Abstract. This paper presents an algorithm for the temporal segmentation of user-generated videos into visually coherent parts that correspond to individual video capturing activities. The latter include camera pan and tilt, change in focal length and camera displacement. The proposed approach identifies the aforementioned activities by extracting and evaluating the region-level spatio-temporal distribution of the optical flow over sequences of neighbouring video frames. The performance of the algorithm was evaluated with the help of a newly constructed ground-truth dataset, against several state-of-the-art techniques and variations of them. Extensive evaluation indicates the competitiveness of the proposed approach in terms of detection accuracy, and highlight its suitability for analysing large collections of data in a time-efficient manner.

1 Introduction

The recent advances in video cameras, combined with the widespread use of social networks (e.g. Facebook) and video sharing platforms (e.g. YouTube), led to a tremendous increase in the number of videos captured and shared by amateur users. Such user-generated videos (UGVs) can nowadays be recorded at any time and place with the help of smartphones and a variety of video cameras (such as GoPro action cameras) that can be attached to sticks, body parts or even drones. The ubiquitous use of video capturing devices supported by the convenience of the user to share videos through social networks and video sharing platforms, leads to a wealth of on-line available UGVs.

Analysing such video content, for generating high-level metadata that can be used for indexing and retrieval of it (e.g. concept and event detection), as well as for allowing fine-grained access to it (e.g. finding just the specific parts of videos that show a red sports car) is a requirement in many multimedia applications. The first step of most of such analysis pipelines is the identification of the video's temporal structure. For edited (i.e. professional) videos this typically corresponds to the detection of the video shots (i.e. sequences of frames captured uninterruptedly by a single camera) using a shot segmentation method, e.g. [2]. However, when dealing with UGVs the shot-level fragmentation is too coarse

© Springer International Publishing AG 2018
K. Schoeffmann et al. (Eds.): MMM 2018, Part I, LNCS 10704, pp. 29–41, 2018.
https://doi.org/10.1007/978-3-319-73603-7_3

and often fails to reveal useful information about their structure, since UGVs are most commonly captured uninterruptedly, thus being single-shot videos. Motivated by this observation, we developed a motion-driven algorithm to identify visually coherent parts (called sub-shots in the sequel) of a single-shot video, that relate to different actions taking place during the video recording. The proposed approach extracts the optical flow between neighbouring frames and evaluates its spatial distribution over frame sequences, to detect sub-shots. The conducted experimental evaluations illustrate the time-efficiency and superiority of the algorithm against other state-of-the-art sub-shot segmentation techniques.

2   Related Work

Several methods dealing with the temporal segmentation of videos into sub-shots have been introduced, most of which can be grouped in two main classes of methodologies. The techniques of the first class consider a sub-shot as an uninterrupted sequence of frames within a shot that only have a small variation in visual content. Based on this assumption, they try to define sub-shots by assessing the visual similarity of consecutive or neighbouring video frames. A rather straightforward approach that evaluates frames' similarity using colour histograms and the x^2 test was described in [26], while a method that detects sub-shots of a video by assessing the visual dissimilarity of frames lying within a sliding temporal window using 16-bin HSV histograms (denoted as "Eurecom segmentation") was reported in [11]. A different approach [3] estimates the grid-level dissimilarity between pairs of frames and segments a video by observing that the cumulative difference in the visual content of subsequent frames indicates gradual change within a sub-shot; a similar approach was presented in [20]. The method of [25] estimates the brightness, contrast, camera and object motion of each video frame using YUV histograms and optical flow vectors, and defines sub-shot boundaries by analysing the extracted features through a coherence discontinuity detection mechanism on groups of frames within a sliding window.

The methods of the second class segment a video shot into sub-shots based on the rationale that each sub-shot corresponds to a different action of the camera during the video recording. Hence, these approaches aim to detect different types of camera activity over sequences of frames, and define these frame sequences as the different sub-shots of the video. An early, MPEG-2 compatible, algorithm that detects basic camera operations by fitting the motion vectors of the MPEG stream into a 2D affine model, was presented in [18]. Another approach that exploits the same motion vectors and estimates the camera motion via a multi-resolution scheme was proposed in [12]. More recently, the estimation of the affinity between pairs of frames for motion detection and categorization was a core idea for many other techniques. Some of them use the motion vectors of the MPEG-2 stream (e.g. [22]), while others compute the parameters of a 3×3 affine model by extracting and matching local descriptors [8] or feature points [24]. The dominant motion transformation between a pair of frames is then estimated by comparing the computed parameters against pre-defined models.

[9] studies several approaches for optical flow field calculation, that include the matching of local descriptors (i.e. SIFT [21], SURF [4]) based on a variety of block matching algorithms, and the use of the PLK algorithm [6]. Contrary to the use of experimentally-defined thresholds for categorizing the detected camera motion, [16] describes a generic approach for motion-based video parsing that estimates the affine motion parameters, either based on motion vectors of the MPEG-2 stream or by applying a frame-to-frame image registration process, factorizes their values via Singular Value Decomposition (SVD) and imports them into three multi-class Support Vector Machines (SVMs) to recognize the camera motion type and direction between successive video frames. A variation of this approach [1], identifies changes in the "camera view" by estimating a simplified three-parameter global camera motion model using the Integral Template Matching algorithm [19]. Then, trained SVMs classify the camera motion of each frame, and neighbouring frames with the same type of camera motion are grouped together forming a sub-shot. Another threshold-less approach [17] aims to identify specific activities in egocentric videos using hierarchical Hidden Markov Models (HMM), while the algorithm of [14] combines the concept of "camera views" and the use of HMM for performing camera motion-based segmentation of UGVs. Finally, a study on different approaches for motion estimation was presented in [5].

Further to the aforementioned two general classes of methodologies, other approaches have been also proposed. [7] extracts several descriptors from the video frames (e.g. colour histograms and motion features) and subdivides each shot into sub-shots by clustering its frames using k-means clustering. [10,29] utilize data from auxiliary camera sensors (e.g. GPS, gyroscope and accelerometers) to identify the camera motion type for every video sub-shot or a group of events in UGVs, while other approaches define sub-shots by extracting and processing 3D spatio-temporal slices [23] or through statistical analysis [15].

The proposed method is most closely related to [9], in the sense that motion information is described by computing the optical flow field using the PLK algorithm, while it is similar to [8,16,24] in that motion information is again represented using the optical flow field (computed using other techniques, though). However, these previous approaches try to distinguish the type of camera motion via computationally-expensive techniques that involve the estimation of homography and affinity between pairs of frames, or the use of trained classifiers. In contrast, our algorithm efficiently identifies several kinds of video recording activities based on a lightweight process that finds the dominant motion in the four quartiles of the video frame, and compares the frame-level motion distribution against pre-defined motion models.

3   Proposed Method

The proposed algorithm segments a single-shot video into self-contained parts (called sub-shots) which exhibit visual continuity and correspond to individual elementary low-level actions that take place during the recording of the video.

These actions include camera panning and tilting; camera movement in the 3D Euclidean space; camera zoom in/out and minor or no camera movement. The detection of sub-shot boundaries and the identification of the performed action is based on the extraction and spatio-temporal analysis of motion information. The latter is computed using the optical flow between pairs of video frames. In particular each processed pair of frames initially undergoes an image resizing process that maintains the original aspect ratio of the video frames and makes their width equal to w. Following, each frame is spatially segmented into four quartiles. The most prominent corners in each quartile are then detected based on the algorithm of [28], and used for estimating the optical flow at the region-level by utilizing the PLK technique. Based on the extracted optical flow, a mean displacement vector is computed for each quartile, and the four spatially distributed vectors are treated as a region-level representation of the motion activity between the pair of analysed frames (left part of Fig. 1a, b and c).

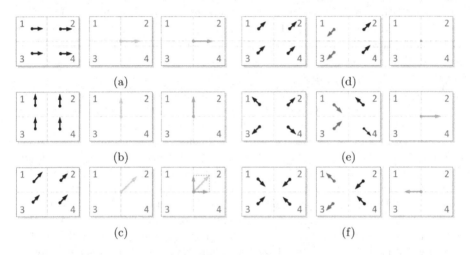

Fig. 1. Motion estimation process for (a) right displacement, (b) upward displacement, (c) diagonal displacement of the camera. Focal distance change estimation process in case of (d) displacement only at horizontal and vertical axes (similar to (c) - thus, no change in the z-axis), (e) forward displacement or zoom in, (f) backward displacement or zoom out.

For detecting and recognizing any displacement of the camera in the 2D space at the frame-level, the algorithm averages the four computed mean displacement vectors (middle part of Fig. 1a, b and c) and projects the resulting vector to the horizontal and vertical axis of the Euclidean space (right part of Fig. 1a, b and c). A horizontal-only camera displacement leads to a single x-axis vector (Fig. 1a), a vertical-only leads to a single y-axis vector (Fig. 1b), while a diagonal displacement results to a pair of x- and y-axis vectors (Fig. 1c). For identifying any camera activity at the depth level (i.e. the z-axis of the 3D space) the developed approach inverts the direction of the mean displacement vectors of the top- and bottom-left regions of the image (left and middle part of Fig. 1d, e and f), computes the vector sum of all four vectors and projects it on the x-axis (right part of Fig. 1d, e and f). As depicted in Fig. 1d, in case of camera movement at the horizontal and/or vertical axes only, the vector inversion process leads to a set of counterbalanced mean displacement vectors and thus, the magnitude of the projection is zero. However, in case of camera activity at the depth axis, the four mean displacement vectors do not maintain the same direction, but point either to the corners of the frame (Fig. 1e), forming a projection vector with positive magnitude, which indicates the existence of forward camera movement or camera zoom in operation; or to the centre of the frame (Fig. 1f), forming a projection vector with negative magnitude, that denotes the occurrence of backward camera movement or a camera zoom out operation.

Through the above mentioned process the proposed method computes for each pair of frames three values that represent the spatial displacement in x-, y- and z-axis. However, successive frames of a video, even with the standard frame-rate of 30 fps, usually exhibit high visual similarity, which is even more true for videos of greater frame-rates that can be captured using modern smartphones or action cameras (e.g. GoPro cameras, which support video recoding up to 240 fps). Guided by this fact, the aforementioned pair-wise motion estimation is not applied on every pair of consecutive video frames, but only on neighbouring frames selected through a sampling strategy with a fixed-step equal to 10% of the video frame-rate. Moreover, for facilitating the upcoming sub-shot segmentation analysis, the computed spatial displacement values, denoted as V_x, V_y and V_z in the sequel, are normalized in $[-1, +1]$ where: V_x (V_y) $= -1$ represents left (downward) displacement of frame pixels equal to 5% of the frame width (height), V_x (V_y) $= +1$ signifies right (upward) displacement of frame pixels equal to 5% of the frame width (height), V_x (V_y) $= 0$ denotes no displacement of frame pixels, $V_z = -1$ ($+1$) indicates increment (decrement) of the focal distance that causes inward (outward) spatial displacement of frame pixels equal to 5% of the frame's diagonal, and $V_z = 0$ indicates no change of the focal distance.

The normalized spatial displacement vectors V_x, V_y and V_z are then post-processed, as described in Algorithm 1, to detect the different sub-shots. Specifically, the values of each vector are initially subjected to low pass filtering in the frequency domain (sample rate equals video frame-rate; cut-off frequency empirically set as 1.0 Hz), which excludes sharp peaks related to wrong estimation of the PLK algorithm or quick changes in the light conditions (top row of Fig. 2). Each of the filtered vectors V_x', V_y' and V_z' is then processed for finding its intersection points with the corresponding axis, and the identified intersection points are stored in vectors I_x, I_y and I_z respectively (Fig. 2c). These intersection points are candidate sub-shot boundaries, since the video frames between a pair of consecutive intersection points exhibit a contiguous and single-directed camera movement, thus being a potential sub-shot according to the proposed approach. However, since most UGVs are captured by amateurs without the use of any professional equipment that ensures the stabilization of the camera, the developed algorithm filters-out fragments depicting minor motion by computing

---

Algorithm 1. Pseudo code of the proposed technique

Input: V_x, V_y, V_z: axes displacement vectors
Output: O': set of sub-shot boundaries

1: **function** PROCESSVECTOR(V)
2:     Low-pass filter V. Store in V'.
3:     Detect intersection points in V'. Store in I.
4:     Measure the total displacement between intersection points in I. Store in D.
5:     Select fragments with displacement $D > t$ as sub-shots. Store in B.
6: **end function**
7: $B_x \leftarrow$ PROCESSVECTOR(V_x)
8: $B_y \leftarrow$ PROCESSVECTOR(V_y)
9: $B_z \leftarrow$ PROCESSVECTOR(V_z)
10: Add in O the B_x and B_y fragments.
11: Extend O by adding B_z fragments that do not coincide with B_x and B_y fragments. Mark remaining parts of the video as fragments with no or minor movement.
12: Discard fragments less than 1 sec. Store in O'.

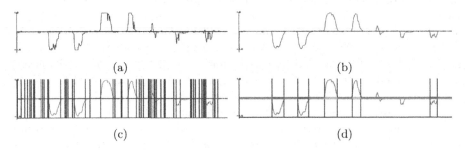

(a)   (b)

(c)   (d)

Fig. 2. Application of Algorithm 1 for a single normalized displacement vector: (a) initial values V_x, (b) low-pass filtered values V'_x, (c) detected candidate sub-shot boundaries in I_x, (d) selected sub-shot boundaries in B_x; red parts denote fragments with left displacement, orange parts denote fragments with right displacement and green parts denote fragments with no or minor movement. (Color figure online)

the total displacement over each fragment as the sum of the absolute values of the filtered displacement values V'_x, V'_y and V'_z of each pair of frames in the fragment. This process results in vectors D_x, D_y and D_z, which store the total displacement score of each defined fragment in the x-, y- and z-axis respectively. The video fragments with total displacement score less than an experimentally-selected threshold t, are discarded. In our evaluations (Sect. 4) $t = 12$, which leads to the best performance (expressed by F-score in Fig. 3). The determined fragments of each axis are stored in vectors B_x, B_y and B_z (Fig. 2d). A simple fusion process is then applied, that takes the union O of B_x and B_y fragments, extends it by adding B_z fragments that do not temporally coincide (either completely or partially) with B_x and B_y fragments, and marks the remaining parts of the video as fragments with no or minor movement. The final output of the algorithm (O') is formed by discarding fragments with duration <1 sec. through a process that equally dispenses their frames in the previous and the following sub-shot.

Fig. 3. The algorithm's segmentation effectiveness (expressed as F-score) for different values of threshold t. As shown in the graph, the best performance is achieved for $t = 12$, while any value in the range $[11, 14]$ leads to similar results.

4   Experiments and Results

Driven by the lack of publicly available datasets for evaluating the performance of the developed sub-shot segmentation algorithm[1], we built our own ground-truth dataset. This dataset is publicly available[2] and consists of:

- 15 single-shot videos of total duration 6 min, recorded in our facilities; these videos, denoted as "own videos" in the sequel, contain clearly defined fragments that correspond to several video recording activities.
- 5 single-shot amateur videos of total duration 17 min, found on YouTube; these videos are denoted as "amateur videos" in the sequel.
- 13 single-shot parts of known movies of total duration 46 min; these videos, denoted as "movie excerpts", represent professional video content.

Ground-truth segmentation of the employed dataset was created by human annotation of the sub-shot boundaries for each video, where each boundary indicates the end of a visually and temporally contiguous activity of the video recording device and the start of the next one (e.g. the end of a left camera panning, which is followed by a camera zooming). Overall, our dataset contains 674 sub-shot transitions. The performance of the developed algorithm was compared against other relevant state-of-the-art methods of the literature. Aiming to include in our evaluations several different categories of methods (presented in Sect. 2), we implemented:

- A straightforward approach (denoted S_HSV in the sequel) which assesses the similarity between subsequent video frames with the help of HSV histograms

---

[1] Some works reported in Sect. 2 use certain datasets (TRECVid 2007 rushes summarization, UT Ego, ADL and GTEA Gaze) which were designed for assessing the efficiency of methods targeting specific types of analysis, such as video rushes segmentation [3] and the identification of everyday activities [30] and thus, ground-truth sub-shot segmentation is not available for them.

[2] http://mklab.iti.gr/project/annotated-dataset-sub-shot-segmentation-evaluation.

and x^2 distance, and a variation of it (denoted S_DCT) that represents the visual content of the video frames using DCT features and estimates their visual resemblance based on the cosine similarity.

- A method (denoted B_HSV) similar to [26], that selects the first frame of the video F_a as the base frame and compares it sequentially with the following ones using HSV histograms and x^2 distance until some frame F_b is different enough, then frames between F_a and F_b form a sub-shot, and F_b is used as the next base frame in a process that is repeated until all frames of the video have been processed; a variation of this approach (denoted B_DCT) that represents the visual content of the video frames using DCT features and estimates their visual resemblance based on the cosine similarity was also implemented.

- The algorithm of [8] (denoted A_SIFT), which estimates the dominant motion between a pair of frames based on the computed parameters of a 3×3 affine model through the extraction and matching of SIFT descriptors; furthermore, variations of this approach that rely on the use of SURF (denoted A_SURF) and ORB [27] (denoted A_ORB) descriptors were also implemented for assessing the efficiency of faster alternatives to SIFT.

- An implementation of the best performing technique of [9] (denoted A_OF), which computes the optical flow using the PLK algorithm and identifies camera movement by fitting it to a 2×2 affine model containing parameters that represent the camera pan, tilt, zoom and rotation actions.

- Variations of the local-feature-based approaches documented in [9], that rely on the extraction and matching of SIFT, SURF and ORB descriptors (denoted H_SIFT, H_SURF and H_ORB, respectively) or the computation of the optical flow using PLK (denoted H_OF), for estimating the dominant motion based on specific parameters of the homography matrix computed by the RANSAC method [13].

For each one of the tested approaches we counted the number of correct detections (where the detected boundary can lie within a temporal window around the respective ground-truth boundary, equal to twice the video frame-rate), misdetections and false alarms and expressed them in terms of Precision (P), Recall (R) and F-Score (F), similarly to [1,2]. Time efficiency was evaluated by computing the ratio of processing time over the video's duration (a value below 1 indicates faster-than-real-time processing). All experiments were conducted on a PC with an i7-4770K CPU and 16 GB of RAM.

Table 1 reports the evaluation results of each compared approach, both separately on each of the three parts of the dataset, as described above, and on the overall dataset. According to these results, and regarding the different implemented methodologies, approaches that estimate the dominant motion based on a homography matrix seem to be more effective compared to the methods that rely on affine models or the assessment of visual similarity, with the latter one being slightly better compared to the affine-based methods in terms of recall. Among the examined similarity-based techniques, the use of HSV histograms results in better performance in terms of precision; however, the utilization of DCT features leads to remarkably higher recall scores, and thus a better overall

Table 1. Evaluation results for different sub-shot segmentation approaches (P: Precision, R: Recall, F: F-score).

Method	"Own videos"			"Amateur videos"			"Movie excerpts"			Overall dataset		
	P	R	F	P	R	F	P	R	F	P	R	F
S_HSV	0.31	0.28	0.30	0.23	0.09	0.13	0.28	0.44	0.34	0.28	0.36	0.32
S_DCT	0.54	0.88	0.67	0.14	**0.86**	0.25	0.25	**0.84**	0.38	0.22	**0.84**	0.36
B_HSV	0.30	0.09	0.14	**0.55**	0.09	0.16	0.43	0.12	0.18	0.44	0.11	0.18
B_DCT	0.50	0.23	0.32	0.36	0.40	0.38	0.43	0.24	0.31	0.41	0.27	0.32
A_OF	0.41	0.68	0.50	0.20	0.82	0.31	0.30	0.78	0.43	0.27	0.78	0.40
A_SIFT	0.55	0.62	0.59	0.20	0.09	0.12	0.30	0.14	0.19	0.33	0.17	0.23
A_SURF	0.54	0.64	0.58	0.29	0.30	0.29	0.36	0.25	0.30	0.36	0.29	0.33
A_ORB	0.40	0.25	0.30	0.09	0.02	0.03	0.46	0.02	0.05	0.38	0.05	0.08
H_OF	**0.98**	0.62	0.76	0.26	0.67	0.38	0.41	0.58	0.47	0.37	0.60	0.45
H_SIFT	0.90	0.74	0.82	0.27	0.78	0.39	0.35	0.63	0.45	0.34	0.66	0.45
H_SURF	0.88	0.73	0.80	0.26	0.70	0.38	0.36	0.64	0.47	0.36	0.66	0.46
H_ORB	0.85	0.67	0.75	0.18	0.76	0.30	0.30	0.73	0.43	0.28	0.72	0.40
Proposed	0.96	**0.90**	**0.93**	0.42	0.71	**0.53**	**0.48**	0.64	**0.55**	**0.52**	0.70	**0.59**

performance (F-score). Concerning the implemented affine-based techniques, the most efficient is the one that relies on the optical flow, showing the highest recall scores in all different video categories and comparable precision scores with the other related methods. Regarding the suitability of local descriptors for computing an affine model that helps with the identification of the performed movement, SURF are the most effective ones, SIFT perform slightly worse, and ORB exhibit the weakest performance. With respect to the evaluated homography-based approaches, the use of different local descriptors or optical flow resulted in similar efficiency, with ORB being the least competitive descriptor due to lower precision. The last row of Table 1 shows that the proposed algorithm is the best-performing one, achieving the highest F-score on all dataset parts and on the overall dataset. On the first collection of videos, the developed technique also exhibits the highest recall score, with the S_DCT being the second best, while its precision is slightly lower than the one achieved by the H_OF method. However, these two methods have lower precision and recall scores, respectively, resulting to a significantly lower overall performance. On "Amateur videos" the developed technique is again the best performing one, while the B_HSV and the S_DCT methods, that presented competitive precision and recall respectively, achieved significantly lower overall performance. Similar efficiency is observed when analysing single-shot parts of professional movies; the proposed approach is the best in terms of F-score and precision. All the above are reflected in the last three columns of Table 1, which show the superiority of the developed method over the other evaluated techniques in the overall dataset. An indicate example of how the algorithm segments a part of a UGV recorded by a camera that is moving right and then upwards, is presented in Fig. 4.

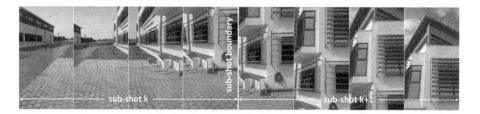

Fig. 4. A sequence of video frames (sampled for space and presentation efficiency) segmented by the proposed algorithm into two sub-shots; one related to a horizontal and one related to an upward camera movement.

With respect to the time-efficiency, as shown in Table 2, the more straight-forward approaches that segment a video based on the visual resemblance of video frames are faster that methods computing the parameters of affine models or homography matrices, as expected. Moreover, the use of DCT features outperforms the HSV histograms, while the extraction and matching of complex local descriptors (SIFT and SURF) is more computationally expensive compared to the matching of binary descriptors (ORB) or the extraction of optical flow for computing the affine or homography matrices. As shown, the proposed approach exhibits competitive time performance, being a bit slower than the straightforward similarity-based methods and faster than almost the entire set of the evaluated affine- and homography-based techniques. Its time efficiency permits sub-shot segmentation to be performed nine times faster than real-time analysis, while this performance can be further improved by introducing simple parallelization in the algorithm's execution. In fact, a multi-threaded software implementation of the proposed technique splits the group of analysed frames into four different and non-overlapping parts which are being processed (i.e. for extracting the optical flow among each pair of frames) in parallel on the CPU. The lightweight post processing of the computed displacement vectors for motion detection and recognition is still carried out using a single thread. Experiments on the same dataset showed 267% speed-up compared to the single-thread version, which means that the analysis of a single-shot video with the multi-thread implementation of the algorithm takes only 4.1% of the video's duration.

Table 2. Time-efficiency of the evaluated sub-shot segmentation approaches.

Method	S_HSV	S_DCT	B_HSV	B_DCT	A_OF	A_SIFT	A_SURF	A_ORB	H_OF	H_SIFT	H_SURF	H_ORB	Proposed
Proc. time % of video length	7.1	**2.9**	3.8	6.7	7.8	127.2	56.3	12.7	14.5	132.6	70.2	16.1	11.1

The above findings document that the proposed algorithm combines the time-efficiency of similarity-based approaches that rely on the extraction of lightweight visual descriptors (such as colour histograms and DCT features) with the detection effectiveness of more complex state-of-the-art techniques that estimate the dominant motion with the help of affine transformations and image homography. Moreover, the developed approach ensures the highest accuracy over different types of single-shots videos, while its time-efficiency makes it suitable for application in large collections of videos or real-time analysis of multiple video streams.

5 Conclusions

In this paper we proposed a framework for motion-driven sub-shot segmentation of UGVs and released a new dataset for evaluating sub-shot segmentation algorithms. The developed algorithm detects and recognizes several different types of video recording activities, such as camera pan, tilt, zoom and displacement, by computing the optical flow between neighbouring frames. Experimental evaluations showed that the developed segmentation algorithm outperforms other, more complex methods that rely on the extraction and matching of local descriptors, while it maintains the time-efficiency of more straightforward similarity-based approaches, being several times faster than real-time analysis.

Acknowledgements. This work was supported by the EU's Horizon 2020 research and innovation programme under grant agreement H2020-732665 EMMA.

References

1. Abdollahian, G., et al.: Camera motion-based analysis of user generated video. IEEE Trans. Multimed. **12**(1), 28–41 (2010)
2. Apostolidis, E., et al.: Fast shot segmentation combining global and local visual descriptors. In: Proceedings of the IEEE International Conference on Acoustics, Speech and Signal Processing, pp. 6583–6587 (2014). http://mklab.iti.gr/project/video-shot-segm
3. Bai, L., et al.: Automatic summarization of rushes video using bipartite graphs. Multimed. Tools Appl. **49**(1), 63–80 (2010)
4. Bay, H., et al.: Surf: speeded up robust features. In: Proceedings of the 9th European Conference on Computer Vision, pp. 404–417 (2006)
5. Benois-Pineau, J., Lovell, B.C., Andrews, R.J.: Motion estimation in colour image sequences. In: Fernandez-Maloigne, C. (ed.) Advanced Color Image Processing and Analysis, pp. 377–395. Springer, New York (2013). https://doi.org/10.1007/978-1-4419-6190-7_11
6. Bouguet, J.Y.: Pyramidal implementation of the affine lucas kanade feature tracker description of the algorithm. Intel Corp. **5**(1–10), 4 (2001)
7. Chu, W.T., et al.: Video copy detection based on bag of trajectory and two-level approximate sequence. In: Proceedings of the Computer Vision, Graphics, and Image Processing Conference (2010)

8. Cooray, S.H., et al.: An interactive and multi-level framework for summarising user generated videos. In: Proceedings of the 17th ACM International Conference on Multimedia, pp. 685–688 (2009)

9. Cooray, S.H., et al.: Identifying an efficient and robust sub-shot segmentation method for home movie summarisation. In: 10th International Conference on Intelligent Systems Design and Applications, pp. 1287–1292 (2010)

10. Cricri, F., et al.: Multimodal event detection in user generated videos. In: IEEE International Symposium on Multimedia, pp. 263–270 (2011)

11. Dumont, E., et al.: Rushes video summarization using a collaborative approach. In: Proceedings of the 2nd ACM TRECVID Video Summarization Workshop, pp. 90–94 (2008)

12. Durik, M., et al.: Robust motion characterisation for video indexing based on MPEG2 optical flow. In: International Workshop on Content-Based Multimedia Indexing, pp. 57–64 (2001)

13. Fischler, M.A., et al.: Random sample consensus: a paradigm for model fitting with applications to image analysis and automated cartography. ACM Commun. **24**(6), 381–395 (1981)

14. González-Díaz, I., et al.: Temporal segmentation and keyframe selection methods for user-generated video search-based annotation. Expert Syst. Appl. **42**(1), 488–502 (2015)

15. Guo, Y., et al.: Selecting video key frames based on relative entropy and the extreme studentized deviate test. Entropy **18**(3), 73 (2016)

16. Haller, M., et al.: A generic approach for motion-based video parsing. In: 15th European Signal Processing Conference, pp. 713–717 (2007)

17. Karaman, S., et al.: Hierarchical hidden Markov model in detecting activities of daily living in wearable videos for studies of dementia. Multimed. Tools Appl. **69**(3), 743–771 (2014)

18. Kim, J.G., et al.: Efficient camera motion characterization for mpeg video indexing. In: Proceedings of the IEEE International Conference on Multimedia and Expo, vol. 2, pp. 1171–1174 (2000)

19. Lan, D.J., et al.: A novel motion-based representation for video mining. In: Proceedings of the International Conference on Multimedia and Expo, pp. 469–472 (2003)

20. Liu, Y., et al.: Rushes video summarization using audio-visual information and sequence alignment. In: Proceedings of the 2nd ACM TRECVID Video Summarization Workshop, pp. 114–118 (2008)

21. Lowe, D.G.: Object recognition from local scale-invariant features. In: Proceedings of the 7th IEEE International Conference on Computer Vision, vol. 2, pp. 1150–1157 (1999)

22. Mei, T., et al.: Near-lossless semantic video summarization and its applications to video analysis. ACM Trans. Multimed. Comput. Commun. Appl. **9**(3), 16:1–16:23 (2013)

23. Ngo, C.W., et al.: Video summarization and scene detection by graph modeling. IEEE Trans. Circ. Syst. Video Tech. **15**(2), 296–305 (2005)

24. Nitta, N., et al.: Content analysis for home videos. ITE Trans. Media Tech. Appl. **1**(2), 91–100 (2013)

25. Ojutkangas, O., Peltola, J., Järvinen, S.: Location based abstraction of user generated mobile videos. In: Atzori, L., Delgado, J., Giusto, D. (eds.) MobiMedia 2011. LNICST, vol. 79, pp. 295–306. Springer, Heidelberg (2012). https://doi.org/10.1007/978-3-642-30419-4_25

26. Pan, C.M., et al.: NTU TRECVID-2007 fast rushes summarization system. In: Proceedings of the 1st ACM TRECVID Video Summarization Workshop, pp. 74–78 (2007)
27. Rublee, E., et al.: ORB: an efficient alternative to SIFT or SURF. In: Proceedings of IEEE International Conference on Computer Vision, pp. 2564–2571 (2011)
28. Shi, J., et al.: Good features to track. In: Proceedings of the IEEE Conference on Computer Vision and Pattern Recognition, pp. 593–600 (1994)
29. Wang, G., et al.: Motch: an automatic motion type characterization system for sensor-rich videos. In: Proceedings of the 20th ACM International Conference on Multimedia, pp. 1319–1320 (2012)
30. Xu, J., et al.: Gaze-enabled egocentric video summarization via constrained submodular maximization. In: Proceedings of the IEEE Conference on Computer Vision and Pattern Recognition, pp. 2235–2244 (2015)

A Novel 3D Human Action Recognition Framework for Video Content Analysis

Lianglei Wei[1], Yirui Wu[2], Wenhai Wang[1], and Tong Lu[1(✉)]

[1] National Key Lab for Novel Software Technology,
Nanjing University, Nanjing, China
gnwll199206@163.com, wangwenhai362@163.com, lutong@nju.edu.cn
[2] College of Computer and Information, Hohai University, Nanjing, China
wuyirui@hhu.edu.cn

Abstract. Understanding the meanings of human actions from 3D skeleton data embedded videos is a new challenge in content-oriented video analysis. In this paper, we propose to incorporate temporal patterns of joint positions with currently popular Long Short-Term Memory (LSTM) based learning to improve both accuracy and robustness. Regarding 3D actions are formed by sub-actions, we first propose Wavelet Temporal Pattern (WTP) to extract representations of temporal patterns for each sub-action by wavelet transform. Then, we define a novel Relation-aware LSTM (R-LSTM) structure to extract features by modeling the long-term spatio-temporal correlation between body parts. Regarding WTP and R-LSTM features as heterogeneous representations for human actions, we next fuse WTP and R-LSTM features by an Auto-Encoder network to define a more effective action descriptor for classification. The experimental results on a large scale challenging dataset NTU-RGB+D and several other datasets consisting of UT-Kinect and Florence 3D actions for 3D human action analysis demonstrate the effectiveness of the proposed method.

Keywords: Video analysis · 3D action recognition
Long short-term memory

1 Introduction

Recently, a large number of videos embedded with 3D skeleton data have emerged especially with the development of RGB-D camera, i.e. Kinect and Intel Realsence, making 3D human action recognition a new challenge in content-oriented video analysis. Based on the obtained 3D skeleton data, many existing action recognition methods use hand-crafted features such as HOG [3] and Cuboids [10]. Recently, Recurrent Neural Networks (RNNs) [8,12] have achieved promising performance in 3D action recognition with the variant structure of neural nets to handle sequential data of body joints. However, utilizing a RGB-D camera for action recognition may still suffer from the robust problem due to

© Springer International Publishing AG 2018
K. Schoeffmann et al. (Eds.): MMM 2018, Part I, LNCS 10704, pp. 42–53, 2018.
https://doi.org/10.1007/978-3-319-73603-7_4

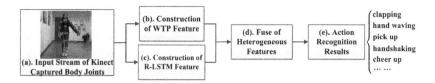

Fig. 1. The framework of the proposed method.

the fact that recognized skeletons are not always accurate especially considering illumination, noise and occlusion variations. In fact, most of the previous methods require a reliable input stream for action recognition, which is not suitable to deal the stream in real-life scenario [6].

In this paper, we propose a novel method for robust 3D action recognition by exploiting temporal patterns and spatio-temporal relations of body joints. To cope with the noisy input of RGB-D camera, we incorporate additional and useful information from temporal patterns and spatio-temporal relations of joints for robust recognition results. The method achieves accurate recognition results on the most popular dataset for 3D actions, which proves that our idea improves the robustness of 3D action recognition. There are three major contributions in this paper:

- Introduction of the WTP feature based on temporal patterns in time-frequency domain, which is invariant to translations of the human body and robust to noises or temporal misalignment;
- Introduction of the R-LSTM feature based on joint relations in spatio-temporal domain, which considers the modeling and retaining of relation factors;
- A highly-efficient fusing method is further introduced to support the fusion between hand-crafted features, namely, the proposed WTP feature and R-LSTM feature.

2   Related Work

There are plenty of works related to understanding human actions in content-oriented video analysis. In this section, we limit our review to the more recent RNN-based and LSTM-based approaches. HBRNN [4] applies bidirectional RNNs in a novel hierarchical fashion. They divided the entire skeleton into five major groups of joints and each group was fed into a separated bidirectional RNN. Because of the disadvantage of RNN-based–vanishing gradient problem, LSTM, a special kind of RNN by using a gating mechanism over an internal memory cell to learn long-term and short term dependencies in sequential input data, has been used in human action recognition. Veeriah et al. [13] proposed a differential gating scheme for the LSTM neural network, which emphasizes on the change in information gain caused by the salient motions between the successive frames. ST-LSTM [2] proposed a tree structure to represent topology of human body and added a trust gate to improve the accuracy. These LSTM-based methods just use one stream to deal with input data. [15] proposed a novel two-stream RNN architecture to model both temporal dynamics and spatial configurations for skeleton based action recognition.

All the methods mentioned above have the same characteristics that they handle the input data directly using LSTM architecture. Shahroudy et al. [12] separated the memory cell to part-based sub-cells and pushed the network towards learning the long-term context representations individually for each part. However, they reduce the relationship between each part of human bodies. In this paper, inspired by [13], we take the difference between the current frame and the previous one as the input value to reduce impact of body parts. We also add the relationship calculation between each part in LSTM and combine traditional handcraft WTP features with automatic learned LSTM features to improve the accuracy.

3   The Proposed Method

In this section, we propose a novel method to explore temporal patterns and spatio-temporal relations of body joints for robust and accurate action recognition. Figure 1 gives the overview of the proposed method, which consists of the following steps: (a) inputting the stream of body joints from a real scene, (b) the construction of WTP feature to represent the patterns of each sub-action, (c) the construction of R-LSTM feature to represent the spatio-temporal relations of body joints, (d) the fusion of WTP and R-LSTM features by Auto-Encoder (AE) network to define a more discriminative representation of an action, and (e) recognizing actions with various kinds of labels. For each human, we utilize Kinect v2.0 to capture body actions. Note that a Kinect v2.0 device tracks 25 body joints, where each joint i has 3D coordinates $j_i^t = [x_i^t, y_i^t, z_i^t]$ at time t. These coordinates are normalized so that actions are invariant to the initial body orientation or body size. To ensure the size of proposed features to be the same, we utilize bag of key poses [1] to sample the same number of key frames for each video. By this way, we achieve a set of positions of body joints $J = \{j_i^t | t = 1...n_k, i = 1...25\}$ for one action, where n_k is defined as the number of key frames.

3.1   Construction of WTP Feature

This section gives a detailed description of our proposed WTP feature, which represents the actions by temporal patterns. It is true that human actions have specific temporal structures [16]. In other words, one action may contain several consecutive sub-actions. For example, the "drink water" action may consist of two sub-actions, namely, "raise the cup" and then "drink". By modeling the temporal relationship of sub-actions, we can distinguish between similar actions. Based on this idea, we propose the WTP feature to adaptively divide each action into combinations of sub-actions by Dynamic Time Warping (DTW) [5] based hierarchy clustering at first, and then utilize 2D-wavelet transform to extract patterns of sub-actions in the time-frequency domain, which is shown in Fig. 2.

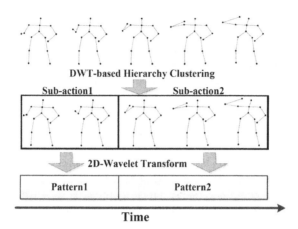

Fig. 2. The construction of WTP feature consists of two parts: DTW-based hierarchy clustering and 2D-wavelet transform.

Different from [16] which adopts pyramids to mechanically divide each action into sub-actions, we suppose that actions can be represented as short-time sequences formed by key frames. In other words, we adopt key frames as the basic components of action. Furthermore, we suppose sub-actions as clusters of key frames which are near in distance. This is true for many types of actions, such as the "drink water" and "pick up", where the latter one can be represented as "bend the body" and "pick". Even though the constructed sub-actions share less sematic meanings, we still argue the components near in distance can be regarded as functional parts to represent the inherent meanings of actions. Therefore, we should model temporal relationship of action with sub-actions. Based on such hypothesis, we do hierarchy clustering to iteratively aggregate the components, i.e. key frames, to form sub-actions. Since the actions are a temporal trajectories of body joints, we use DTW to calculate the distance between two components. Any two nearby components which own the lowest distance will be emerged so that we can construct a cluster tree from bottom to top. We adaptively decide the number of clusters n_s (the number of sub-actions) by maximizing silhouette value and a preset upper-bound of n_s. We thus get a set of disjoint sub-actions $S = \{s_j | j = 1...n_s \wedge s_j \in J\}$.

Regarding sub-action as a signal where joint positions vary with time, wavelet transform helps transform sub-action into time-frequency domain with different scales. We thus apply 2D-Wavelet transform, represented as $\varphi()$, to extract low-frequency pattern of sub-actions with scales varying from 1 to n_l, where n_l represents the total level number. In other words, we will abandon high-frequency coefficients part for levels from 1 to n_l during transform. We adopt the low-frequency parts as temporal patterns for sub-actions due to the fact that the low-frequency part is often the fundamental part for the temporal sequence. After extracting, we concatenate the transformed patterns in all scales to form WTP feature:

$$F_w = [\varphi_1(s_j), ..., \varphi_{n_l}(s_j) | j = 1...n_s] \tag{1}$$

Note that each level of wavelet transform adopts the strategy of half down-sampling on results computed by last level. In other words, the size of levels decrease in half for all sub-actions. Since the action is set to the determined size n_k, the size of F_w will be determined as $(n_k + 1/2 \cdot n_k + ... + (1/2)^{n_l} \cdot n_k)$.

3.2   Construction of R-LSTM Feature

In this subsection, we aim to learn the R-LSTM features for action recognition by our proposed LSTM-based model. LSTM networks have shown tremendous potential in action recognition tasks, which inspires us to learn the highly non-linear feature representation from LSTM to discriminate among various types of actions. In other words, we aim to extract features from the proposed R-LSTM, which is trained as a multi-label classifier assigning labels to the input stream of body joints.

Recall that a typical LSTM unit consists of an input gate i, a forget gate f, an input modulation gate g, an output gate o, an output state h and an internal memory cell state c. By utilizing the gating mechanism, the unit can learn and memorize a complex representation for long-term dependencies at memory cell c among the input sequence data. More detailed, the representation in c is constructed as a combination of former memory information after forgetting and new information generated from input, i.e. $c^t = f^t \odot c^{t-1} + i^t \odot g^t$ at time t, where $\odot$ denotes element-wise multiplication. Instead of keeping the long-term memory of the entire body's motion in the cell, Shahroudy et al. [12] proposed a part-aware LSTM model, which keeps the context of each body part independently. In this way, the output gate will be determined by memory of body parts instead. The idea of keeping memory on body parts is intuitive due to the fact that body joints move together in groups, i.e. the form of body parts. The modeling of interaction between body parts thus helps improve the recognition rate of actions.

We then propose R-LSTM to model the difference relationship between different body parts. But, not all of the body parts are all useful for a certain human action due to the fact that some body part points changes less than others. Inspired by this situation, we add the difference values between front and rear frame as additional input data to reduce the impact of silent body part. In summary, we further model the information of spatio-temporal relation between body parts with the difference values of positions of body parts. It's true that human's actions are consistent in magnitude and frequency. In other words, there will be a trend in the varying position values. By formulating trends of actions by descriptors of difference values of positions and keeping them in

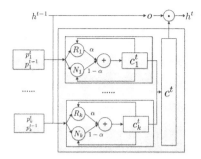

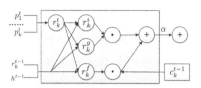

Fig. 3. The structure of R-LSTM unit, where R and N denote the relation-aware part and typical LSTM part, respectively.

Fig. 4. The structure of our relation-aware part R in R-LSTM unit.

memory cell, the output of R-LSTM unit will be more convinced and robust, since the memorized treads can act as inherent patterns of spatio-temporal values of positions to improve the accuracy of recognition. We show the structure of our proposed R-LSTM in Fig. 3. Note that we split the structure of R-LSTM to relation-aware part R and typical LSTM part N, where R is built to describe the spatial relation between body parts. We separate human body joints into five parts $P = \{p_k | k = 1...K\}$, i.e. a torso, two hands and two legs, where K is defined as the number of body parts and p_k consists of body joints j_i which belongs to part k. The formulations for R-LSTM thus can be written as follows:

$$\begin{pmatrix} n_k^i \\ n_k^f \\ n_k^g \end{pmatrix} = \begin{pmatrix} Sigm \\ Sigm \\ Tanh \end{pmatrix} \left(W_k^n \begin{pmatrix} p_k^t \\ p_k^t - p_k^{t-1} \\ h_k^{t-1} \end{pmatrix} \right) \tag{2}$$

$$c_k^t = (\alpha r_k^f + (1-\alpha)n_k^f) \odot c_k^{t-1} + \alpha(r_k^i \odot r_k^g) + (1-\alpha)(n_k^i \odot n_k^g) \tag{3}$$

$$o = Sigm(W_o \cdot (p_1^t, \cdots, p_K^t, r_1^t, \cdots, r_K^t, h^{t-1})^T) \tag{4}$$

$$h^t = o \odot Tanh(c_1^t, \cdots, c_K^t)^T \tag{5}$$

where T refers to transpose operation for matrix, W_k^n and W_o represent the learned weight matrices, and α is a preset weight for relation-aware part R. Essentially, Eq. 2 represents that in the typical LSTM part N, input gate n_k^i, forget gate n_k^f and input modulation gate n_k^g corresponding to the kth body part are determined by the positions p_k^t, the difference of positions $p_k^t - p_k^{t-1}$ between time t and $t-1$ and former output state h_k^{t-1}. Equation 3 describes the keeping information of the internal memory cell c_k^t is a combination of former memory after forgetting, information generated from the spatial relation of body parts and information generated from input. Meanwhile, Eq. 4 computes the output based on positions p_k^t, difference of positions of body parts r_k^t and former output state h^{t-1}, which is determined by output o and internal memory cell state c_k in Eq. 5.

We then describe the structure of our relation-aware part R in Fig. 4, which can be formulated as follows:

$$r_k^t = \bigcup_{i=1}^{K} tanh(W_k^i p_k^t - p_i^t), where\ i \neq k \tag{6}$$

$$\begin{pmatrix} r_k^i \\ r_k^f \\ r_k^g \end{pmatrix} = \begin{pmatrix} Sigm \\ Sigm \\ Tanh \end{pmatrix} \left(W_k^r \cdot \begin{pmatrix} r_k^t \\ r_k^t - r_k^{t-1} \\ h_k^{t-1} \end{pmatrix} \right) \tag{7}$$

where $\bigcup$ represents the concatenate operation and W_k^r is a learned weight matrix. We notice that Eq. 6 utilizes the weighted difference between the kth body part and other body parts to form the spatio-temporal relation descriptor r_k^t. Meanwhile, r_k^t is adopted to construct the input gate r_k^i, forget gate r_k^f and input modulation gate r_k^g of relation-aware part in Eq. 7. The constructed r_k^i, r_k^f and r_k^g will affect the internal memory of R-LSTM as illuminated in Eq. 3. After constructing R-LSTM network, we extract the features of softmax as our proposed R-LSTM feature F_l, which represents the spatio-temporal relation of body parts.

3.3   Fusion of Heterogeneous Features

In this subsection, we propose to fuse them to define a more discriminative feature for recognition of human actions by regarding constructed WTP and R-LSTM features as heterogeneous features. We fuse such heterogeneous features due to the fact that object usually have heterogeneous representations. By fusing different representations of objects, we learn their correlations at a "mid-level" [9] to help improve the robustness and correctness of recognition.

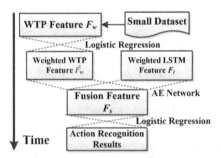

Fig. 5. The fusion model is constructed by Auto-Encoder Network. Before fusing, we adopt logistic regression to assign pre-fused weights for WTP feature.

Inspired by work [18] which fuses multimodal data, i.e. RGB and depth, to learn a shared representation for gesture segmentation and recognition, we generate two different kinds of features from raw skeleton data, i.e. WTP feature

F_w and R-LSTM feature F_l, to fuse the final feature. Different from [18] which uses a 3DCNN and a stacked RBMs/DBN to represent features before fusion, we adopt R-LSTM and WTP instead, and the structure of which is shown in Fig. 5. To speed up fusion, we argue that the "pre-fused" weights are directly used as initializations for AE network due to the consistence of the output in former steps and fusing step, i.e. assigning labels to human actions. Afterwards, the joint training adjusts the parameters to handle the heterogeneity and produces a more reliable estimate from the heterogeneous data. Therefore, we directly initialize the weights ω_l(the weights of R-LSTM) of the layers from the previously trained R-LSTM feature F_l. For hand-crafted WTP feature F_w, we use a logistic regression (LR) model to assign pre-fused weights ω_w(the weights of WTP) and reduce dimensions. Note that the LR model is trained to assign human action category labels with a small dataset D. In fact, the idea of adopting LR for classification help transform the weighting process to be one fully-connected layer, which is similar to the spirit of full-connected layer of LSTM. We thus fuse the weights and features of WTP and R-LSTM in a more reasonable manner. Afterwards, we jointly fine-tune the AE network. The whole process of generating fusion feature F_s thus can be defined as

$$\{\tilde{F}_w(e_i), \omega_d\} = f_\tau(F_w(e_i); D) \tag{8}$$

$$F_s(e_i) = f_\mu(\omega_d, F_l(e_i), \omega_l, \tilde{F}_w(e_i)) \tag{9}$$

where function $f_\tau()$ and $f_\mu()$ represents the LR and AE network and $\tilde{F}_w$ refers to the WTP feature after dimensionality reduction. Note that we keep $\tilde{F}_w$ and F_l to be same in dimensions for equal representations. The training of AE network ends when the validation error rate stops decreasing. During experiments, we find our fusing model can end in less than 10 epochs, which proves the efficiency of our fusing model by adopting pre-fused weights. After fusing, we apply F_s in a LR model to get the label of action as $L = f_\tau(F_s(e_i))$.

4   Experiments

We evaluate our method on three datasets, i.e. NTU RGB+D dataset [12], UT-Kinect dataset [19] and Florence 3D actions datset [11]. The proposed method is implemented with Keras architecture and runs on a Laptop (2.6 GHz 4-core CPU, 16 GB RAM, Nvidia GTX 960M and Windows 64-bit OS) for all the experiments. In order to retain more information on each body part, we repeat shoulder joints and hip joints. So each action has more than 8 joints. Our R-LSTM model includes two parts: R-LSTM layer and softmax layer. In R-LSTM layer, the parameter α is assigned 0.3 and the optimizer is RMSprop and the learning rate is 0.01. We choose the optimum of α by experiments. In detail, we randomly choose 500 action sequences from our datasets, i.e., NTU, Florence 3D and UTK, to determine the optimal value. We plot a graph for recognition rate verses different values. According to the experiments, the value for α is finally selected as 0.3. We follow the guidance of dataset to perform experiments

Table 1. Experimental results on NTU RGB+D dataset

Method	Cross subject	Cross view
Proposed	**73.8%**	**80.9%**
WTP	70.1%	77.5%
R-LSTM	69.6%	70.5%
Du et al. [4]	59.1%	64.0%
Liu et al. [8]	69.2%	77.7%
Shahroudy et al. [12]	62.9%	70.3%
Hu et al. [7]	60.2%	65.2%

Table 2. Experimental results on UT-Kinect dataset

Method	Accuracy
Proposed	93.0%
WTP	89.3%
R-LSTM	90.4%
Zhu et al. [20]	87.9%
Liu et al. [8]	**97.0%**
Xia et al. [19]	90.9

and evaluations with our method. For NTU RGB+D dataset, we adopt cross subject, i.e. half subjects for training and the other half for testing, and cross-view, i.e. two viewpoints for training and the other one is for testing, to be our evaluation methods. We perform 2-fold cross validation on Florence 3D actions dataset, while we follow the leave-one-out-cross-validation protocol illuminated by UT-Kinect dataset.

Tables 1, 2 and 3 give the detailed statistics of our method and other competing methods on NTU RGB+D, UT-Kinect and Florence actions, respectively. In the tables, WTP and R-LSTM represent the detection results by only adopting proposed WTP and R-LSTM features for classification. According to the fuse results from three datasets, we conclude that fusion helps improve recognition accuracy greatly. We calculate that fusion increases the average accuracy from 79.6% by WTP and 79.7% by R-LSTM to 84.8% by the proposed method. This is intuitive since robustness for detection is highly increased by adopting both temporal patterns and spatio-temporal relation features, other than using only one kind of feature. Moreover, the increase in accuracy proves the correctness and effectiveness of our fusion architecture.

We find that WTP and R-LSTM achieve inconsistent performance dealing with different datasets. For example, WTP achieves 77.5% on cross-view accuracy of NTU RGB+D dataset, which is much higher than 70.5% achieved by R-LSTM. Meanwhile, LSTM gets 88.3% on Florence 3D actions Dataset, which is much higher than 81.5% achieved by WTP. We conclude that this is due to the different action categories contained in each dataset. More detailed, the action categories in Florence 3D actions dataset are likely in shape of joints trajectories, such as "drink", "answer phone" and "check time". WTP can not deal with the slight changes in actions since the main focus of WTP is to distinguish temporal pattern in a global manner, while R-LSTM keeps information of spatial relations between each frame which helps distinguish slight variances. On the contrary, keeping information between frames makes it easy to confuse between locally plausible actions, which results in a lower accuracy by R-LSTM compared with WTP.

Table 3. Experimental results on Florence actions dataset

Method	Accuracy
Proposed	91.3
WTP	81.5
R-LSTM	88.3
Vemulapalli et al. [14]	90.9
Anirudh et al. [2]	89.7
Wang et al. [17]	**91.6**

Fig. 6. Action recognition examples of the proposed method on NTU RGB+D, UT-Kinect, Florence 3D actions and our captured action sequences. Note that action recognition results are given under double quotes.

Jointly learning WTP and R-LSTM leads to the consistent and high accuracy performance achieved on the three datasets, which demonstrates the effectiveness and generality of the proposed method. More detailed, Our method achieves the highest 73.8% and 80.9% on the challenging NTU RGB+D dataset, the second highest 93.0% on UT-Kinect dataset and the almost equally highest 91.3% on Florence 3D actions dataset. By incorporating temporal pattern and spatio-temporal relation, our method even outperforms several full LSTM method in accuracy. For example, the accuracy on NTU RGB+D dataset by proposed method is average 77.4% compared with average 73.5% achieved by Liu et al. [8]. This proves the effectiveness of incorporating temporal pattern to improve recognition accuracy in a global manner. However, we find the proposed method is low in accuracy for Florence 3D actions dataset and UT-Kinect dataset, LSTM needs quantity of training examples. However, these two datasets are small ones with only 200 and 215 action sequences compared to NTU RGB-D which consists of 56000 action sequences. Besides the quantitative experimental results, several detection examples on three datasets are shown in Fig. 6, where the first and second row show the results of three datasets and our captured action sequences, respectively.

5   Conclusions

In this paper, we propose a robust 3D action recognition method by jointly learning the temporal patterns and spatio-temporal relations of body joints. We first propose WTP to model temporal patterns in time-frequency domain, which adaptively divides action into sub-actions and extracts convinced representations in temporal patterns for sub-actions. The proposed R-LSTM is then proposed to model the strong dependency between body parts in spatio-temporal domain. Regarding WTP and R-LSTM features as heterogeneous representations for actions, we finally fuse both features to define a robust and discriminative descriptor for action recognition. We believe that our proposed method can be utilized in many vision-based applications, such as ill health and computer-human interaction.

Acknowledgments. This work was supported by the Natural Science Foundation of China under Grant 61672273, Grant 61272218, and Grant 61321491, the Science Foundation for Distinguished Young Scholars of Jiangsu under Grant BK20160021, the Science Foundation of JiangSu under Grant BK20170892, the Fundamental Research Funds for the Central Universities under Grant 2013/B16020141, and the open Project of the National Key Lab for Novel Software Technology in NJU under Grant KFKT2017B05.

References

1. Alexandros, C., Padilla-Lopez, J., Flórez-Revuelta, F.: Fusion of skeletal and silhouette-based features for human action recognition with RGB-D devices. In: Proceedings of the ICCVW, pp. 91–97 (2013)
2. Anirudh, R., Turaga, P.K., Su, J., Srivastava, A.: Elastic functional coding of human actions: from vector-fields to latent variables. In: Proceedings of the CVPR, pp. 3147–3155 (2015). https://doi.org/10.1109/CVPR.2015.7298934
3. Dalal, N., Triggs, B.: Histograms of oriented gradients for human detection. In: Proceedings of the CVPR, pp. 886–893 (2005). https://doi.org/10.1109/CVPR.2005.177
4. Du, Y., Wang, W., Wang, L.: Hierarchical recurrent neural network for skeleton based action recognition. In: Proceedings of the CVPR, pp. 1110–1118 (2015), https://doi.org/10.1109/CVPR.2015.7298714
5. Eamonn, K., Ann, R.C.: Exact indexing of dynamic time warping. Knowl. Inf. Syst. **7**(3), 358–386 (2005)
6. Ho, E.S.L., Chan, J.C.P., Chan, D.C.K., Shum, H.P.H., Cheung, Y., Yuen, P.C.: Improving posture classification accuracy for depth sensor-based human activity monitoring in smart environments. CVIU **148**, 97–110 (2016). https://doi.org/10.1016/j.cviu.2015.12.011
7. Hu, J., Zheng, W., Lai, J., Zhang, J.: Jointly learning heterogeneous features for RGB-D activity recognition. In: Proceedings of the CVPR, pp. 5344–5352 (2015). https://doi.org/10.1109/CVPR.2015.7299172

8. Liu, J., Shahroudy, A., Xu, D., Wang, G.: Spatio-temporal LSTM with trust gates for 3D human action recognition. In: Leibe, B., Matas, J., Sebe, N., Welling, M. (eds.) ECCV 2016. LNCS, vol. 9907, pp. 816–833. Springer, Cham (2016). https://doi.org/10.1007/978-3-319-46487-9_50

9. Ngiam, J., Khosla, A., Kim, M., Nam, J., Lee, H., Ng, A.Y.: Multimodal deep learning. In: Proceedings of the ICML, pp. 689–696 (2011)

10. Scovanner, P., Ali, S., Shah, M.: A 3-dimensional sift descriptor and its application to action recognition. In: Proceedings of the MM, pp. 357–360 (2007). http://doi.acm.org/10.1145/1291233.1291311

11. Seidenari, L., Varano, V., Berretti, S., Bimbo, A.D., Pala, P.: Recognizing actions from depth cameras as weakly aligned multi-part bag-of-poses. In: Proceedings of the CVPRW, pp. 479–485 (2013). https://doi.org/10.1109/CVPRW.2013.77

12. Shahroudy, A., Liu, J., Ng, T., Wang, G.: NTU RGB+D: a large scale dataset for 3D human activity analysis. In: Proceedings of the CVPR, pp. 1010–1019 (2016), http://doi.ieeecomputersociety.org/10.1109/CVPR.2016.115

13. Veeriah, V., Zhuang, N., Qi, G.: Differential recurrent neural networks for action recognition. In: Proceedings of the ICCV, pp. 4041–4049 (2015). https://doi.org/10.1109/ICCV.2015.460

14. Vemulapalli, R., Arrate, F., Chellappa, R.: Human action recognition by representing 3D skeletons as points in a lie group. In: Proceedings of the CVPR, pp. 588–595 (2014). https://doi.org/10.1109/CVPR.2014.82

15. Wang, H., Wang, L.: Modeling temporal dynamics and spatial configurations of actions using two-stream recurrent neural networks. CoRR abs/1704.02581 (2017). http://arxiv.org/abs/1704.02581

16. Wang, J., Liu, Z., Wu, Y., Yuan, J.: Learning actionlet ensemble for 3D human action recognition. IEEE Trans. PAMI **36**(5), 914–927 (2014). https://doi.org/10.1109/TPAMI.2013.198

17. Wang, P., Yuan, C., Hu, W., Li, B., Zhang, Y.: Graph based skeleton motion representation and similarity measurement for action recognition. In: Leibe, B., Matas, J., Sebe, N., Welling, M. (eds.) ECCV 2016. LNCS, vol. 9911, pp. 370–385. Springer, Cham (2016). https://doi.org/10.1007/978-3-319-46478-7_23

18. Wu, D., Pigou, L., Kindermans, P., Le, N.D., Shao, L., Dambre, J., Odobez, J.: Deep dynamic neural networks for multimodal gesture segmentation and recognition. IEEE Trans. PAMI **38**(8), 1583–1597 (2016). https://doi.org/10.1109/TPAMI.2016.2537340

19. Xia, L., Chen, C., Aggarwal, J.K.: View invariant human action recognition using histograms of 3D joints. In: Proceedings of the CVPRW, pp. 20–27 (2012). https://doi.org/10.1109/CVPRW.2012.6239233

20. Zhu, Y., Chen, W., Guo, G.: Fusing spatiotemporal features and joints for 3D action recognition. In: Proceedings of the CVPRW, pp. 486–491 (2013)

Adaptive Image Representation Using Information Gain and Saliency: Application to Cultural Heritage Datasets

Dorian Michaud[1,2(✉)], Thierry Urruty[1],
François Lecellier[1], and Philippe Carré[1]

[1] CNRS, Univ. Poitiers, XLIM, UMR 7252, 86000 Poitiers, France
`dorian.michaud@univ-poitiers.fr`
[2] Quadra Informatique, 68 Rue du Docteur Eloy, 59133 Phalempin, France

Abstract. Recently, the advent of deep neural networks showed great performances for supervised image analysis tasks. However, image expert datasets with little information or prior knowledge still need indexing tools that best represent the expert wishes. Our work fits in this very specific application context where only few expert users may appropriately label the images. Thus, in this paper, we consider small expert collections with no associated relevant label set, nor structured knowledge. In this context, we propose an automatic and adaptive framework based on the well-known bags of visual words and phrases models that select relevant visual descriptors for each keypoint to construct a more discriminating image representation. In this framework, we mix an information gain model and visual saliency information to enhance the image representation. Experiment results show the adaptiveness and the performance of our unsupervised framework on well-known "generic" datasets and also on a cultural heritage expert dataset.

Keywords: Cultural heritage collection
Content Based Image Retrieval · Information gain · Visual saliency

1 Introduction

Lately, "expert image datasets", which are of interest for expert end-users (e.g. digital curators, historians, numismatists, clinicians, etc.), are digitalised for preservation. Such datasets can either have quite heterogeneous contents (historic dataset showing persons, buildings, etc.), or very specific contents (e.g. images of old coins). More than the cost of it, the problem is that only few experts can label the images with the concepts of importance for them. This excludes the use of crowd-based ground-truthing tools, as such datasets are not associated to any exploitable ground truth.

This paper focuses on multimedia information retrieval for cultural heritage image datasets which has become a topic of major interest for experts

© Springer International Publishing AG 2018
K. Schoeffmann et al. (Eds.): MMM 2018, Part I, LNCS 10704, pp. 54–66, 2018.
https://doi.org/10.1007/978-3-319-73603-7_5

and researchers. In this specific applicative context, with no prior knowledge on those small expert datasets, we limit the scope of this paper to Content-Based Image Retrieval (CBIR), and more particularly the image representation. In the last decade, the CBIR evolved from the well known Csurka et al. Bags of Visual Words model (BoVW) [6] to deep neural networks that showed great performances for complex image analysis tasks. Indeed, Convolutional Neural Networks (CNN) outperform results obtained with "classical" schemes [18,30]. However, one of the main objectives of CBIR is still to obtain an image representation which is discriminative and compact.

In this paper, we present our framework, which aims at combining automatically the information from various descriptors to have a better image representation. The main idea of our proposal is to adapt the selection of visual features for each image keypoint. To strengthen the discriminative power of keypoints, we introduce two strategies in our framework. First, a psycho-visual methodology is used to discard irrelevant keypoints before starting the indexation and is also used during the signature construction step. This process gives more importance to salient keypoints and discredits the others. Then, a statistical approach is used to select for each keypoint the combination of local descriptors providing the best Information Gain (IG) with respect to the dataset. IG models have proven their usefulness in the Information Retrieval field [26]. They increase the importance of a term within a document (in our case, an image) by weighting each visual feature by a value that evolves with the number of occurrences within the dataset.

Another contribution of our proposal is its efficiency. Indeed, our framework reduces the number of used keypoints using the visual saliency information. Furthermore, the obtained image signatures are sparser, which reduces the retrieval complexity.

To evaluate the performance of our contribution, we first compare results obtained on well-known "generic" datasets. And we also evaluate our approach on a cultural heritage dataset: ROMANE 1K. It is a collection of 1010 images of Romanesque art with heterogeneous content (especially paintings and sculptures). We compare our performance against the BoVW, a signature concatenation-based approach and other deep learning based methods.

This article is structured as follows: Sect. 2 presents the state of the art. It describes BoVW, BoVP and selected improvements, and CNN based literature. Section 3 gives an overview of our proposal. Section 4 itemises the related experiments and discusses the findings of our study. Finally, Sect. 5 concludes and gives some perspectives.

2   Related Works

In this section, we first present the BoVW model, few inspired improvements and Bags of Visual Phrases model methods. We also present Convolutional Neural Network (CNN) and transfer learning approaches which are booming methods and provide impressive results in CBIR field.

Inspired by the Information Retrieval field, Csurka et al. [6] introduced the classical BoVW model. The main idea of this methodology is to cluster descriptors of image patches and use this clustering to obtain a high-dimensional visual vocabulary. This vocabulary is used to construct the image signatures. The first step is the detection and the description of image patches. Several descriptors can be used as SIFT, DAISY, HOG, ... [3,4]. A quantisation vector algorithm is then used to assign descriptors to a set of predetermined clusters, i.e. the visual vocabulary. By counting number of patches assigned to each cluster, a histogram of the visual words occurrences is constructed. More recently, Jégou et al. [14] have proposed the VLAD representation. This approach can be seen as an accumulation of distances between keypoints descriptors and the different cluster centres. Delhumeau et al. in [7] proposed an extension of this method by using PCA for every part of VLAD vector. A hierarchical VLAD was also proposed by Eggert et al. in [8]. Other methods focus on efficiency like Bags of Visual Phrases (BoVP) model which is an extension of BoVW model. The BoVP model groups the keypoints to better represent small regions and to preserve the geometry of objects inside images. Many ways exist to construct phrases: using sliding window [5], grouping the keypoints with their nearest neighbours [21], or by regions [24]. Finally, with the BoVP model, the image is represented by a histogram of visual phrases that is proved to be more discriminative than the BoVW model however computationally more expensive.

Lately, deep convolutional neural networks provide great performances in a lot of computer vision and image processing tasks [18,30]. This innovative approach in this field is based on the work of LeCun et al. [19] which proposed the first modern CNN architecture. Alex Krizhevsky et al. in [17] presented a deep CNN called AlexNet. This model achieved a top-5 error of 15.4% in the ImageNet Large-Scale Visual Recognition Challenge (ILSVRC) 2012. It is trained on ImageNet [25] data, which contained over 15 million annotated images from over 22,000 categories. The network consists of convolutional layers, max-pooling layers, dropout layers (5 for each of them), and 3 fully connected layers and it was used for classification with 1000 possible categories. Data augmentation and dropout used in AlexNet are part of numerous recent literature frameworks mentioned below. Another model, GoogLeNet, proposed by Szegedy et al. in [27] stands out from the usual CNN. Indeed, GoogLeNet, was one of the first CNN model that does not use the classical sequential structure. The authors proposed a new module, Inception, which does not stack convolutive and pooling layers on top of each other but proceeds these operations in parallel. GoogLeNet achieved a top-5 error of 6.7% in ILSVRC 2015. Microsoft Research Asia proposed during the same challenge the ResNet model which consists of a very deep CNN of 152 layers in [13]. This model outperformed by achieving a top-5 error of 3.6%. Faced with the excellent performances offered by these models, researchers approach this field in different ways. Instead of recreating new models of CNN, several authors have proposed to adapt them to specific problems [10,16,23]. In [23], Pittaras et al. proposed to compare three different fine-tuning strategies in order to investigate the best way to transfer the parameters of popular deep

CNNs. Transfer learning approaches allow to adapt a network trained for one task to another more specific one. In the field of image retrieval, recent papers obtained pretty good results on well-known datasets like SPoC [29] and Neural Codes [1] proposed by Babenko Yandex et al.

The drawback of these methods is the amount of training data needed to adapt and tune the numerous parameters. In our context with no prior knowledge on small expert datasets, they are inapplicable in their entirety. Thus, we keep BoVW and BoVP representations in our scenario. However, we can extract deep features for image retrieval by using a pre-trained model. It provides a feature vector, which can be processed whether as a local feature combined with BoVW or simply as a global feature. In [22], Picard et al. showed the weaknesses of these models on cultural heritage datasets (average mAP of 25%). Their results show the urgent need of new framework that performs in the context of expert dataset.

Our framework uses ideas from BoVW and BoVP models and includes two particular models. A psychovisual one, to make sparse signatures by discarding irrelevant keypoints, and a statistical one, based on IG models to enhance the role of performing descriptors.

3   Proposed Method

In this section, we propose an overview of our CBIR framework and detail our scientific contributions. Our main objective is to create an image signature that ensures an effective and efficient retrieval. To do so, we take advantage of Information Gain and visual saliency models to automatically and locally adapted selection of visual features. The keypoints and visual words from multiple vocabularies are selected according to the IG relevance with respect to their vocabulary and their importance for the human visual system. Indeed, combining those two models gives a better characterisation of each image keypoint with respect to the saliency information and the most informative visual words from multiple visual features. Figure 1 gives an overview of the proposed framework, and following subsections detail the different steps.

3.1   Pre-processing Steps

Our approach requires three pre-processing information: (i) the visual vocabulary by visual features, (ii) the IG values for each vocabulary and (iii) the visual saliency computation for each image of the dataset:

(i) Like BoVW and BoVP models, our method is based on a vocabulary learning step, detailed in Sect. 2. We first choose a set of nd local descriptors (LD) to have a robust image representation. Therefore, we need nd visual words vocabularies (one by descriptor). To construct the visual vocabularies, the choice of the learning dataset is crucial because it has a real influence on results. To compare our results with the baseline and to respect our specific context, we choose a small dataset with sufficient diversity: PASCAL-VOC2012 [9].

(ii) We also need to compute the nd sets of IG values, i.e. the IG values of all visual words in each vocabulary. IG values are computed on the indexed dataset to improve the vocabulary quality according to the discriminative power of words. Thus, for a specific dataset, the visual words are better distinguished.

(iii) The last pre-processing step is the Visual Saliency computation. Keypoints with higher saliency value play a more important role in the retrieval process, and thus, saliency information enhances the discriminative words and consequently the overall performance of our image representation [28]. We need saliency for two different processes: to discard irrelevant keypoints and to weight the image signature.

3.2   Signature Construction

The construction of the image signature is based on an adaptive selection of visual words by keypoint according to their IG values and on a visual saliency based weighting scheme. The first step consists in localisation, selection and description of keypoints. We use a dense grid to select the set of keypoints KP_i of an image i. With this scheme, we ensure that an image i is described in its entirety and that the number of keypoints and their location are normalised before extracting the nd local descriptors. In our previous work [11], we have shown than using a dense grid based keypoint selection gives too many keypoints with meaningless information. Reducing the number of keypoints by selecting the more salient one has shown interesting results. Thus, we applied this strategy and reduced, as recommended in our study, 50% of the less salient keypoints (mostly background keypoints). Note that, the feature extraction process, without this step, takes twice as long to compute. The remaining keypoints better represent salient objects. They can be described by both classical and deep features.

The next step is the selection of relevant visual words for each descriptor. For each keypoint p, the $K * nd$ nearest visual words are extracted. They form a set of pre-selected visual words. Our contribution is to select visual words in this set by using an IG model. Indeed, a thresholding is done according to the IG values previously computed. We extract the N most informative visual words among this set. For example, on Fig. 1, we choose to set to two the number of selected visual words by descriptor for each keypoint and the final number of selected visual words ($K = 2$ and $N = 2$). On Fig. 1, $kp2$ is represented by (vw_a5, vw_a3), (vw_b3, vw_b5), and $(vw_{nd}1, vw_{nd}3)$ respectively for $descr_a$, $descr_b$, and $descr_{nd}$. Among this set of chosen words, the two more relevant in terms of IG values are selected. Indeed, as vw_a3 and $vw_{nd}1$ ones have higher IG values, they will be included in the image signature.

Another contribution consists in including a visual saliency based weighting scheme during the signature construction. In this step, the saliency information is used to weight the histogram of visual words occurrences h_i. We include the saliency value of keypoint $VS_i(p)$ using the following formula:

$$h_i(vw \leftarrow p) = 1 + VS_i(p). \qquad (1)$$

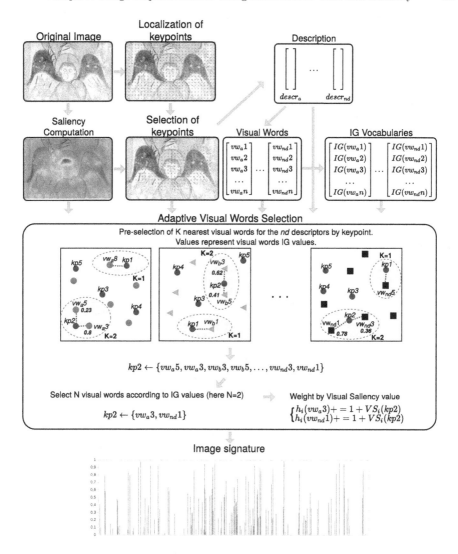

Fig. 1. Overview of our approach.

This scheme allows to give more importance to keypoints with a higher saliency value. Finally, we obtain sparser histogram as the signature of each image of the indexed dataset due to keypoints and visual words selection.

3.3 Retrieval Process

The search step is similar to the indexing one. The query signature is computed similarly to the aforementioned process. Thus, the query and all images in the corpus are represented as histograms of visual words occurrences. Then, the retrieval process computes the similarity between the query signature and each image signature of the dataset by using a distance measure. In our previous work, $L1$, $L2$, and χ^2 distances were studied. Due to better performance during these tests, we select χ^2 distance for this study.

4   Experimental Results

This section presents the datasets used to evaluate our work and explains our technical choices. Experiments are divided in two parts: application to generic datasets (Sect. 4.3) and to a cultural heritage dataset (Sect. 4.4).

4.1   Experimental Setup

Three image datasets were considered as test datasets:

INRIA Holidays [15]: this dataset is a collection of 1491 images, 500 of them are query images, and the remaining 991 are the corresponding relevant images. The evaluation on Holidays is based on mean average precision score (mAP).

UK Benchmark (UKB) [20]: the set consists of 2550 groups of 4 images (10200 images). The 4 images of the same group represent the same object with different points of view. To measure the performance, classically, it is necessary to count how many of the top-4 images belong to the query group. But for comparison purpose, we transform the score value @4 to AP.

ROMANE 1K: we introduce this collection of 1010 images of Romanesque art extracted from the whole ROMANE dataset [2]. It brings together photographs of sculptures, paintings, manuscripts... (e.g. Fig. 2). The dataset contains 10 categories (which contains between 40 and 200 images) and images may belong to several categories. To evaluate the precision, a score value @10, @20, or @30 is computed and transformed to AP. This score is calculated by counting how many of the top images contain at least one of the query categories.

(a)   (b)   (c)   (d)

Fig. 2. Sample images extract from ROMANE 1K: angel (a), dog (b), horse (c) and musician (d).

4.2   Technical Choices

Feature Extraction. We select four well-known local descriptors to represent images in terms of colour, texture, shape and edge: SIFT, LBP, HOG and Colour Moment Invariants (CMI). All descriptors are initially extracted along a common dense grid. To complete this set of common local descriptors, we extract 2,048d deep features on small patches centred on the same set of keypoints in order to benefit the recent literature improvement in CBIR [17].

Vocabulary Construction. In our experiments, we have studied different sizes of visual words vocabulary for each descriptor (100d, 250d, 500d, 1,000d). Our tests have shown that the size of 1,000d is the more adapted for our applicative context. Those vocabularies are learned on Pascal VOC2012 [9] to evaluate our approach on the two selected "generic" datasets and on other images of ROMANE for ROMANE 1K.

Information Gain Model. For this first study, we select TF-IDF [26] as IG model, as it is one of the most commonly used and known in the literature. Note that other IG might give better performance on specific datasets, but it is not in the scope of this paper. TF-IDF model measures the importance of words in a corpus. It is a product of term frequency and inverse document frequency. The term frequency is the number of occurrences of a word w in the document. The $tfidf$ value of a word w is obtained by Eq. 2.

$$tfidf(w) = tf(w).idf(w), \text{ with } idf(w) = log(\frac{|D|}{\{d_j : t_i \, \epsilon \, d_j\}}). \qquad (2)$$

$|D|$ denotes the document cardiniality in a dataset and $\{d_j : t_i \, \epsilon \, d_j\}$, the number of documents which contain word w. This methodology can be transferred to image retrieval by considering images as documents and visual words as words.

Visual Saliency. As stated before, the saliency in our framework is used in two different ways. In our experiments, we select the GBVS model [12] mostly because of its literature performance in many applicative contexts.

4.3   Evaluation on Generic Benchmark Datasets

A first preliminary study on the generic datasets, UKB and Holidays, has shown the differences between the BoVW model and our framework using $K = 1$ and $1 \leq N \leq 4$. We observed that, as soon as we have $N > 1$, our framework outperforms significantly. We notice an average improvement of +5% to +10% on Holidays, and +10% to +15% on UKB. We have also observed that including saliency in the framework gives higher performance. We obtain a gain of +4.8% on average. It highlights the importance of keypoints which describe salient objects for a CBIR system.

Table 1 shows the different results of this study for a vocabulary size of 1000 for both generic datasets. The first line of Table 1 gives the concatenation results of the 4 local descriptors from BoVW with the deep features (Deep-f). It can be seen as the baseline approach. The next 4 lines give performance results of recent literature approaches including complex deep feature models. Then, the following 6 lines present the results of our framework. It presents our best results without including deep features. Last 5 lines give our performance including the deep features as another local descriptor with N between 1 and 5.

Table 1. Results obtained with deep features on UKB and Holidays for a vocabulary size of 1000. Bold results highlight the highest accuracy with respect to the dataset and * indicates the second one.

Methodologies	UKB	Holidays
Concat-signatures (with Deep-f)	0.80	0.64
CNN [27]	0.78	0.64
VLAD [14]	0.795	0.556
Neural codes [1]	0.822	0.789*
SPoC [29]	**0.912**	**0.802**
Best proposal (without Deep-f)	0.81	0.68
Proposal $N = 1$ (with Deep-f)	0.79	0.67
Proposal $N = 2$ (with Deep-f)	0.83	0.67
Proposal $N = 3$ (with Deep-f)	0.84*	0.68
Proposal $N = 4$ (with Deep-f)	0.83	0.70
Proposal $N = 5$ (with Deep-f)	0.80	0.68

The first observation is that the addition of deep features in our framework brings a gain of accuracy. However, the gain is not as high as we expected (between +2% and +3%).

To outline these comparisons, our approach, which uses IG and visual saliency model to select discriminant features by keypoint (including deep features), provides better results than the signature concatenation-based approach, VLAD and CNN. On Holidays dataset, we observe that our method outperforms VLAD and Neural Codes but is lower than SPoC. And on UKB dataset, SPoC and Neural Codes approach obtain higher results than ours.

The next experiments evaluate our approach for cultural heritage dataset.

4.4   Application to Cultural Heritage Dataset

In this section, we present our evaluation study in our specific context, i.e. an expert cultural heritage datasets. We introduce ROMANE 1K dataset to evaluate our proposal. We use as comparison baselines the BoVW model for the selected local descriptors and the CNN deep features. Results are summarised in Table 2.

Our first observation is that our results confirm Picard et al. [22] conclusion: CNN does not provide an outstanding precision on expert cultural heritage

Table 2. Results on ROMANE 1K (bold values represent the highest accuracy)

Method	CNN [27]	BoVW				Ours for K=1			
		SIFT	CMI	HOG	LBP	N=1	N=2	N=3	N=4
@10	0.289	0.291	0.304	0.282	0.267	0.240	0.263	0.302	**0.308**
@20	0.225	0.242	0.244	0.233	0.220	0.201	0.219	0.246	**0.251**
@30	0.202	0.220	0.215	0.210	0.200	0.183	0.199	0.217	**0.225**

dataset. Indeed, the classical BoVW model has better results using SIFT or CMI descriptors. In this specific context, our approach provides the highest accuracy. For $K = 1$ and $N = 4$, we obtain a gain of precision about 6.2% for @10, 10.4% for @20 and 10.2% for @30. Our methodology outperforms CNN and BoVW but the accuracy remains quite low. This can be explained by the proximity of certain categories. Indeed, Table 3 shows the confusion matrix obtained with our method for $K = 1$ and $N = 4$ for the apostle category. Values on this table represent the number of images retrieved for each category by considering all images in Apostle category as queries.

Table 3. Confusion matrix for apostle category

	Apostle	Angel	Horse	Beef	Dragon	Book	Soldier	Shield	Musician	Dog
Apostle	1932	1344	277	365	120	166	374	53	58	293

For this category, images of apostles are mostly retrieved. But, a lot of images of angels are also retrieved. Samples of those two categories are given in Fig. 3 to illustrate the possible confusion between categories, even for the expert.

Fig. 3. Two similar images from categories angel (left) and apostle (right)

We also tried to use deep features as another local descriptor, but in this context of cultural heritage which is very specific, the method does not provide satisfying results.

4.5 Discussion

In this section, we discuss the results of our experiments on both "generic" and "expert" datasets. Due to our specific context of small expert datasets, we limit this approach to small vocabularies for all local visual features. Note that, no pre or post processes to improve the overall accuracy have been applied (as data augmentation or automatic query expansion).

On "generic" datasets, our approach which uses IG and visual saliency models to select discriminant features by keypoint (including deep features) provides better results than BoVW concatenation-based approach, VLAD and CNN transfer learning based approach. However, new methodologies as SPoC, based on neural network or deep learning remain higher than our proposal. They use complex models with lots of parameters to tune with deep learning strategies. In our context with no prior knowledge on small expert datasets, this type of approach is unusable. However, we note that in spite of being a simple model, our performance are on par with or not far from recent literature approaches. On an expert cultural heritage dataset, our methodology outperforms CNN and BoVW (without deep features as local descriptor) but the accuracy remains quite low. This can be explained by the difficulty to distinguish certain categories, even for an expert user. On this type of data, the use of deep features does not provide gain in precision. Indeed, CNN transfer learning based approaches provide poor accuracy with specific collections as cultural heritage datasets because they are learnt on ImageNet [25] which is a collection of "generic" images. Furthermore, Romane dataset has not enough data to train a whole CNN model. It shows again the importance of the learning dataset for complex deep learning approaches.

5 Conclusion

In this paper, we propose to adapt the discriminative power of CBIR models for a specific context of cultural heritage dataset. Based on the well-known Bags of Visual Words and Bags of Visual Phrases models, we propose an automatic and adaptive framework that selects relevant visual descriptors for each keypoint to construct the image representation. The visual saliency information is firstly used to discard irrelevant keypoints by computing a threshold on the image. To construct the image signature, an Information Gain model is used to nuance the importance of all visual descriptors locally and the visual saliency weights the salient visual words. The main contribution of such framework is to discredit the keypoints and their visual features which are not discriminative.

To evaluate our method, we have compared our performance against the BoVW, a signature concatenation-based approach, VLAD, and other deep learning based methodologies. On well-know datasets, our method outperforms BoVW, VLAD, CNN, and signature concatenation-based approach. For one of them, it also outperforms Neural Codes although SPoC still higher in this context. Our approach provides significant results too and outperforms CNN and BoVW approaches on a new cultural heritage dataset: ROMANE 1K. On this cultural heritage collection, we obtain a gain of accuracy about 10,4% compared to CNN, showing the possibility to improve the precision with an unsupervised adaptive approach. This paper highlights the potential of our method and opens up reflections in the area of CBIR for a specific context as cultural heritage.

Our future work will focus on the refinement of the small vocabularies used in the framework. Being at the beginning of the workflow, the vocabulary construction step is crucial in our context as it may improve greatly the final result. We will also investigate semi interactive indexing approaches that would help the global selection of words in the framework. Finally, we will also focus on discriminating categories that are visually closed.

References

1. Babenko, A., Slesarev, A., Chigorin, A., Lempitsky, V.: Neural codes for image retrieval. In: Fleet, D., Pajdla, T., Schiele, B., Tuytelaars, T. (eds.) ECCV 2014 Part I. LNCS, vol. 8689, pp. 584–599. Springer, Cham (2014). https://doi.org/10.1007/978-3-319-10590-1_38
2. CESCM: Romane dataset (2015). http://baseromane.fr/accueil2.aspx
3. Chatoux, H., Lecellier, F., Fernandez-Maloigne, C.: Comparative study of descriptors with dense key points. In: 23rd International Conference on Pattern Recognition, ICPR 2016, Cancún, Mexico, 4–8 December 2016, pp. 1988–1993 (2016)
4. Chen, Q., Song, Z., Dong, J., Huang, Z., Hua, Y., Yan, S.: Contextualizing object detection and classification. IEEE Trans. Pattern Anal. Mach. Intell. **37**(1), 13–27 (2015)
5. Chen, T., Yap, K.H., Zhang, D.: Discriminative soft bag-of-visual phrase for mobile landmark recognition. IEEE Trans. Multimed. **16**(3), 612–622 (2014)
6. Csurka, G., Dance, C.R., Fan, L., Willamowski, J., Bray, C.: Visual categorization with bags of keypoints. In: Workshop on Statistical Learning in Computer Vision, ECCV, pp. 1–22 (2004)
7. Delhumeau, J., Gosselin, P.H., Jégou, H., Pérez, P.: Revisiting the VLAD image representation. In: ACM Multimedia, Barcelona, Spain (2013)
8. Eggert, C., Romberg, S., Lienhart, R.: Improving VLAD: hierarchical coding and a refined local coordinate system. In: 2014 IEEE International Conference on Image Processing (ICIP), pp. 3018–3022 (2014)
9. Everingham, M., Van Gool, L., Williams, C.K.I., Winn, J., Zisserman, A.: The PASCAL Visual Object Classes Challenge 2012 (VOC2012) Results (2012)
10. Gando, G., Yamada, T., Sato, H., Oyama, S., Kurihara, M.: Fine-tuning deep convolutional neural networks for distinguishing illustrations from photographs. Expert Syst. Appl. **66**, 295–301 (2016)
11. Gbehounou, S.: Image database indexing: emotional impact evaluation. Theses, Université de Poitiers, November 2014
12. Harel, J., Koch, C., Perona, P.: Graph-based visual saliency. In: Advances in Neural Information Processing Systems, pp. 545–552 (2006)
13. He, K., Zhang, X., Ren, S., Sun, J.: Deep residual learning for image recognition. In: 2016 IEEE CVPR (2016)
14. Jégou, H., Douze, M., Schmid, C., Pérez, P.: Aggregating local descriptors into a compact image representation. In: 2010 IEEE Conference on Computer Vision and Pattern Recognition (CVPR), pp. 3304–3311 (2010)

15. Jégou, H., Douze, M., Schmid, C.: Hamming embedding and weak geometric consistency for large scale image search. In: Forsyth, D., Torr, P., Zisserman, A. (eds.) ECCV 2008 Part I. LNCS, vol. 5302, pp. 304–317. Springer, Heidelberg (2008). https://doi.org/10.1007/978-3-540-88682-2_24

16. Jung, S.I., Hong, K.S.: Deep network aided by guiding network for pedestrian detection. Pattern Recogn. Lett. **90**, 43–49 (2017)

17. Krizhevsky, A., Sutskever, I., Hinton, G.E.: Imagenet classification with deep convolutional neural networks. In: Proceedings of the 25th International Conference on Neural Information Processing Systems (2012)

18. LeCun, Y., Bengio, Y., Hinton, G.: Deep learning. Nature **521**, 7553 (2015)

19. LeCun, Y., Bottou, L., Bengio, Y., Haffner, P.: Gradient-based learning applied to document recognition. Proc. IEEE **86**(11), 2278–2324 (1998)

20. Nistér, D., Stewénius, H.: Scalable recognition with a vocabulary tree. In: IEEE Conference on Computer Vision and Pattern Recognition, vol. 2 (2006)

21. Pedrosa, G., Traina, A.: From bag-of-visual-words to bag-of-visual-phrases using n-grams. In: SIBGRAPI Conference on Graphics, Patterns and Images, pp. 304–311 (2013)

22. Picard, D., Gosselin, P.H., Gaspard, M.C.: Challenges in content-based image indexing of cultural heritage collections. IEEE SP Mag. **32**(4), 95–102 (2015)

23. Pittaras, N., Markatopoulou, F., Mezaris, V., Patras, I.: Comparison of fine-tuning and extension strategies for deep convolutional neural networks. In: Amsaleg, L., Guðmundsson, G.Þ., Gurrin, C., Jónsson, B.Þ., Satoh, S. (eds.) MMM 2017 Part I. LNCS, vol. 10132, pp. 102–114. Springer, Cham (2017). https://doi.org/10.1007/978-3-319-51811-4_9

24. Ren, Y., Benois-Pineau, J., Bugeau, A.: A comparative study of irregular pyramid matching in bag-of-bags of words model for image retrieval. In: 6th International conference on Image and Signal Processing, ICISP 2014 (2014)

25. Russakovsky, O., Deng, J., Su, H., Krause, J., Satheesh, S., Ma, S., Huang, Z., Karpathy, A., Khosla, A., Bernstein, M., Berg, A.C., Fei-Fei, L.: ImageNet large scale visual recognition challenge. IJCV **115**(3), 211–252 (2015)

26. Salton, G., Buckley, C.: Term-weighting approaches in automatic text retrieval. Inf. Process. Manag. **24**, 513–523 (1988)

27. Szegedy, C., Liu, W., Jia, Y., Sermanet, P., Reed, S., Anguelov, D., Erhan, D., Vanhoucke, V., Rabinovich, A.: Going deeper with convolutions. In: 2015 IEEE Conference on Computer Vision and Pattern Recognition (CVPR) (2015)

28. Wu, Y., Liu, H., Yuan, J., Zhang, Q.: Is visual saliency useful for content-based image retrieval? Multimed. Tools Appl. **76**, 1–24 (2017)

29. Yandex, A.B., Lempitsky, V.: Aggregating local deep features for image retrieval. In: 2015 IEEE International Conference on Computer Vision, pp. 1269–1277 (2015)

30. Zagoruyko, S., Komodakis, N.: Wide residual networks. In: Proceedings of the British Machine Vision Conference, BMVC, York (2016)

AGO: Accelerating Global Optimization for Accurate Stereo Matching

Peng Yao[1,2], Hua Zhang[1,2], Yanbing Xue[1,2(✉)],
and Shengyong Chen[1,2]

[1] Key Laboratory of Computer Vision and System (Ministry of Education),
Tianjin University of Technology, Tianjin, China
yp19880120@sina.com,
{hzhang,Xueyb0718,csy}@tjut.edu.cn
[2] Tianjin Key Laboratory of Intelligence Computing and Novel Software
Technology, Tianjin University of Technology, Tianjin, China

Abstract. In stereo matching, global algorithms could produce more accurate disparity estimation than aggregated ones. Unfortunately, they remain facing prohibitively high computational challenges while minimizing an energy function. Although various computationally tractable optimizers such as *Belief Propagation* (BP), *Graph Cut* (GC) and *Dynamic Programming* (DP) exist, they still time-consumed and perform a relative higher energy. On one hand, too many intermediate parameters are required for constructing the energy function. In fact, they are trivial, difficult to compute and inevitably bring noises because of their approximate representations. That signifies a simplified energy function structure with fewer intermediate parameters may not only accelerate the running time but also provide greater result while utilizing same optimizer. On the other hand, optimizers are usually designed artificially and also generate approximate solutions. Based on this observation, a suboptimal energy is probably obtained. To alleviate these limitations, an *Accelerating Global Optimization* (AGO) stereo matching algorithm is proposed in this paper. Integrating the key ideas of *Two-Step Global Optimization* (TSGO), the modeled energy function of AGO possesses fewer intermediate parameters. What's more, a refinement term is augmented into the message passing formula of *Sequential Tree-Reweighted* (TRW-S) optimizer to lower down the energy. Performance evaluations on Middlebury *v.2 & v.3* stereo data sets demonstrate that the proposed AGO outperforms than other *five* challenging stereo algorithms; and also performs better on Microsoft *i2i* stereo videos. At last, thanks to the simple energy function model of AGO; it shows a faster execution time.

Keywords: Stereo matching · Energy function · Simplified structure
Refinement term · Faster execution time

1 Introduction

Establishing dense correspondence between multiple images is one of the traditional and still unsolved topics in the field of computer vision. When it comes to the case of using *two* images taken at the same scene, it becomes the well-known stereo matching

© Springer International Publishing AG 2018
K. Schoeffmann et al. (Eds.): MMM 2018, Part I, LNCS 10704, pp. 67–80, 2018.
https://doi.org/10.1007/978-3-319-73603-7_6

problem. In terms of literatures in [1–3], researchers had divided stereo algorithms into *two* categories: aggregated and global algorithms. Both of them are enforced by a subset or all of the *four* stages: matching cost computation; cost aggregation; disparity computation; and disparity refinement (post-processing).

Aggregated ones, such as Adaptive Supported Weight (ASW) [4], Geodesic Stereo (GS) [5], Guided Filter (GF) [6], Histogram Aggregation (HA) [7, 8], Accelerating Cost Filter (ACF) [9], Weighted Cost Propagation with Smoothness Prior (WCPSP) [10] and recently proposed Cross-Scale Cost Aggregation (CSCA) [11, 12] are all perform matching cost computation at first and then implement cost aggregation with a local or non-local framework. After that, a Winner-Takes-All (WTA) strategy is employed for disparity computation which selects the corresponding disparity value of the minimum aggregated cost for each pixel. These algorithms have been reported to provide superior results and reflect their higher time efficiency.

Global ones, or called as *Energy Minimization* algorithms always omit the stage of cost aggregation by directly formulate an explicit smoothness term and minimize a predefined energy function. They usually yield much greater results than aggregated ones but inevitably face the bottleneck of computational complexity. Fundamentally, minimizing an energy function is a *NP-hard* problem, so researchers have focused on various approximate optimization approaches. The *two* most celebrated optimizers are BP and GC. The same thoughts also have been employed into stereo matching and some significant progresses were emerged [13–17]. Besides, Semi-Global Matching (SGM) [18] and its most recently extended work which named as Mesh Stereo (MS) [19] were also achieve effective solutions.

No matter what category stereo matching algorithm it is, some disparity refinement strategies such as *Left-Right Cross-check* (LRC), *Occlusion Filling* (OF) and *Weighted Median Filter* (WMF) are widely adopted for attaining final refined results.

TSGO stereo algorithm [20] draws a new connection between both of them and cleverly combines the advantages respectively: better results in occluded regions for aggregated ones and higher accuracy for global ones. Unifying the *unary potential* which is computed by **MRF** *Fully Connected Model* (FCM) (represents the aggregated algorithm) into a standard energy function with **MRF** *Locally Connected Model* (LCM). Then the energy function of TSGO was solved by a faster optimizer, named as TRW-S [21]. It is based on BP and much improves the computational efficiency than traditional ones.

In this paper, our contributions mainly focusing on how to mitigate the following *two* weaknesses on account of TSGO:

(1) As classical global algorithms, too many intermediate parameters are required for constructing the energy function model. They are computed for building (*unary & binary*) potential terms and highly related. However, for obtaining these parameters are trivial and time-consumed. Especially for the highly related intermediate parameters, the errors may be inevitably introduced and accumulated because of their approximate representations by *Probability & Statistics*.

According to this observation, we innovatively model the energy function with a fewer intermediate parameters structure to alleviate the problem of computational bottleneck and noise-perturbation.

(2) Compared with GC, BP can be applied to any function of energy minimization problem. Yet the drawbacks are obvious: It usually finds a solution with higher energy than GC; BP does not always converge, in other words, it usually traps into a loop. TRW-S has perfectly solved the problem of mis-convergence, but needs further refinement for alleviating the intrinsic problem of relative higher energy. Essentially, TRW-S yields an approximate solution which signifies errors are inevitably introduced and accumulated while minimizing the energy function.

For mitigating this weakness, a refinement term is designed and augmented into the TRW-S message passing formula for further optimization. According to the experiments (more details are shown in Sec. 3.1) we can observe that with the modified TRW-S optimizer AGO performs a fairly lower energy than TSGO.

According to the contents we have mentioned above, the basic workflow of AGO can be illustrated in Fig. 1 from input to output. In the figure we visualize the results of initial result u^S (computed by matching cost computation), solution of unary potential $\bar{u}$ (generated by **MRF** FCM with WTA) and the solution of marginal function $\bar{\bar{u}}$ (by solving a standard energy function with **MRF** LCM using modified TRW-S optimizer; it is actually the solution of AGO) in order. In summary, the crux of our presented AGO possesses a simplified energy function structure with fewer intermediate parameters and it is also minimized by a modified TRW-S optimizer. Performance evaluations show that AGO could provide competitive superior results than other *five* most recently challenging stereo matching algorithms on Middlebury *v.2* [1, 22–24] & *v.3* [25, 26] stereo data sets; and also performs better on Microsoft *i2i* [27] stereo videos. Additionally, thanks to the simple energy function structure of AGO; it reflects a faster execution time.

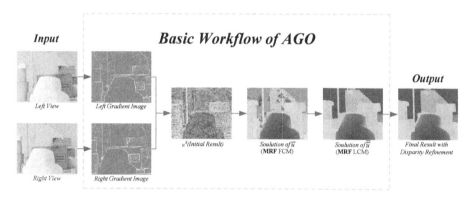

Fig. 1. The basic workflow of AGO stereo matching algorithm from input to output.

2 Proposed Algorithm

2.1 Matching Cost Computation

A linear combination of *color* and *gradient* dissimilarity [28, 29] is widely applied for generating initial matching cost. However, we observe that the color information could bring much noise, especially in textureless regions, various ambient illumination changing environments and *etc.* For each pixel p in color image I, we have to abandon the *color* cue and make the matching cost value $u_p^S(l)$ only relying on *gradient* cue $u_p^G(l)$ to mitigate the adverse effects on disparity l ($l \in L$ and $L \in [0, maxdisp]$):

$$u_p^S(l) = u_p^G(l) \tag{1}$$

Where $u_p^G(l)$ is computed by:

$$u_p^G(l) = \min\left(\left(\sum_{c \in \{r,g,b\}; x_p \in \{x,y\}} \left|g_{c,x_p}^{lf}(x_p) - g_{c,x_p}^{rt}(x_p - l)\right|\right), \ \tau^G\right) \tag{2}$$

Here $\tau^G = 180$, $x_p \in \{x, y\}$ represents the location of pixel p on *Cartesian Coordinates*, $c \in \{r, g, b\}$ denotes the *RGB* channels; and the gradient images (both *left* and *right*: g^{lf} and g^{rt}) are generated by a *6D* vector which is defined by using color image f_c on x and y directions:

$$\begin{pmatrix} g_{c,x}(x,y) \\ g_{c,y}(x,y) \end{pmatrix} = 2 \cdot \begin{pmatrix} f_c(x+1,y) - f_c(x-1,y) \\ f_c(x,y+1) - f_c(x,y-1) \end{pmatrix} + \begin{pmatrix} 1 & 1 \\ -1 & 1 \end{pmatrix}\begin{pmatrix} f_c(x+1,y+1) - f_c(x-1,y-1) \\ f_c(x+1,y-1) - f_c(x-1,y+1) \end{pmatrix} \tag{3}$$

2.2 Simplified MRF Fully Connected Model

After the initial matching cost $u_p^S(l)$ is computed, we further formulate the aggregated algorithm by **MRF** FCM as a *unary potential* like TSGO. It can be calculated by:

$$\bar{u}_p(l) = \sum_{q \in V} \omega(p, q) \cdot u_q(l) \tag{4}$$

For a connected, undirected image graph $G = (V, E)$, where for each node $q \in V$ corresponds to one pixel in I and each edge in E connects a pair of neighbored pixels. Then the adaptive supported weight is represented as:

$$\omega(p, q) = e^{-\frac{|x_p - x_q|^2}{2\sigma_x^2} - \frac{|f_p - f_q|^2}{2\sigma_f^2}} \tag{5}$$

Here we set $\sigma_x = 14$, $\sigma_f = 1.55$; $|x_p - x_q|$, $|f_p - f_q|$ denote the spatial and color dissimilarities between p and q respectively; then for another term $u_q(l)$ of (4) is computed by:

$$u_q(l) = \frac{1}{2}\left(1 + erf\left(4.5 * 10^{-4} \cdot \frac{u_q^S(l) - \theta}{\theta}\right)\right) \tag{6}$$

Where θ is the only intermediate parameter for our proposed algorithm, it is calculated by the following formula on the same image graph $G = (V, E)$:

$$\theta = \frac{1}{|V|} \sum_{q \in V} u_q^S(l) \tag{7}$$

$|V|$ is the total number of graph nodes. Both in formulas (6) and (7), $u_q^S(l)$ equals to the initial matching cost value of which has been yielded by (1).

2.3   Simplified MRF Locally Connected Model

Utilizing the *unary potential* term $\bar{u}_p(l)$ which has been provided by (4), a **MRF LCM** can be performed according to a standard energy function model:

$$E(l) = \sum_{p \in V} \bar{u}_p(l_p) + \sum_{p,q \in N(p)} B_{p,q}(l_p, l_q) \tag{8}$$

The set of edges $N(p)$ denotes the local *four* connected neighbors of pixel p and the *binary potential* term $B_{p,q}(l_p, l_q)$ is determined by:

$$B_{p,q}(l_p, l_q) = \bar{\omega}(p, q) \cdot \bar{\varphi}(|l_p - l_q|) \tag{9}$$

where

$$\bar{\omega}(p, q) = \begin{cases} 2.5/8, & if \quad |f(x_p) - f(x_q)| < 7 \\ 1.25/8, & if \quad 7 \le |f(x_p) - f(x_q)| < 15 \\ 1/8, & if \quad |f(x_p) - f(x_q)| \ge 15 \end{cases} \tag{10}$$

For the term of

$$|f(x_p) - f(x_q)| = \sum_{c \in \{r,g,b\}} |f_c(x_p) - f_c(x_q)| \tag{11}$$

represents the color dissimilarity of p, q in *RGB* color space and

$$\bar{\varphi}(|l_p - l_q|) = \frac{1}{4} \tag{12}$$

2.4   Optimization with Modified TRW-S

Like other global optimization problem on a predefined energy function, solving formula (8) is a *NP-hard* problem, thus approximate minimization optimizers have to be chosen. For TSGO, the authors utilized a TRW-S optimizer, which is based on BP. In short, the *four* connected neighborhood graph with the iterative message passing formula of TRW-S is given by:

$$m^t_{p \to q}(i) = \min_{j \in L} \left(\frac{1}{2} \bar{\bar{u}}^t_p(j) - m^{t-1}_{p \to q}(i) + B_{p,q}(i,j) \right) \tag{13}$$

Where t is the iteration time and:

$$\bar{\bar{u}}^t_p(l) = \bar{u}_p(l) + \sum_{k \in N(p) \backslash \{q\}} m^{t-1}_{k \to p}(l) \tag{14}$$

$N(p)\backslash\{q\}$ represents the *four* connected neighbors of p but excludes q. The same as in [20], the marginal function $\bar{\bar{u}}_p(l)$ uniquely defines the solution of proposed AGO. Hence for each pixel p, the disparity estimation (solution) l_p of AGO could be represented as the minimum (solution) of $\bar{\bar{u}}_p(l)$:

$$l_p = \arg\min_{l \in L} \bar{\bar{u}}_p(l) \tag{15}$$

However, the *message m* in (13) is a vector that has an entry for each allowed disparity and yields an essentially approximate solution. That means with the accumulation of m in formula (14) from neighbors, errors are accumulated into $\bar{\bar{u}}$ ($\bar{u}$ is also an initial and undesirable solution). One effective way to alleviate this problem is to *minus* a term with both $\bar{\bar{u}}$ and m themselves from the message passing formula.

Based on the main idea we have analyzed, the message passing formula of TRW-S with a refinement term can be expressed as:

$$m^t_{p \to q}(i) = \min_{j \in L} \left(\frac{3}{5} \bar{\bar{u}}^t_p(j) - m^{t-1}_{p \to q}(i) - \frac{6}{5} \Delta_r + B_{p,q}(i,j) \right) \tag{16}$$

Where Δ_r denotes the refinement term. Inspired by the original message passing formula of TSGO, we find that this term can be modeled with a form of *minimum difference* between $\bar{\bar{u}}$ and m:

$$\Delta_r = \min_{j \in L} \left(\frac{3}{5} \bar{\bar{u}}^t_p(j) - m^{t-1}_{p \to q}(i) \right) \tag{17}$$

Take (17) into (16) we can know that the proposed refinement term can be seemed as the errors of $\bar{\bar{u}}$.

Especially, in the case of

$$\Delta_r \leq \frac{3}{5} \bar{\bar{u}}^t_p(j) - m^{t-1}_{p \to q}(i) < \frac{6}{5} \Delta_r \tag{18}$$

We assume that the errors of $\bar{\bar{u}}$ are too small to be ignored but the errors of the *binary potential* $B_{p,q}(i,j)$ must take into consideration. For $B_{p,q}(i,j)$, it performs as the smoothness term of energy function model (8), but also with errors for its artificial approximate representation. So in this circumstance the proposed refinement term could be seen as removing the errors of $B_{p,q}(i,j)$ from message passing formula.

3   Experimental Results

In this section, we are interesting to compare our AGO with other *five* most recently challenging stereo matching algorithms: HA [7, 8], ACF [9], WCPSP [10] (as aggregated ones); and MS [19], TSGO [20] (as global ones). All the implementations were implemented on a same PC platform with a *3.60* GHz *Intel Core i7* CPU, *16 GB* RAM and *64-bits* OS. And, they were completely done by *C++* code. That means they could be fairly evaluated both in accuracy & time efficiency. For further proofing the effectiveness, we estimate all the algorithms on Middlebury *v.2* & *v.3* stereo data sets and Microsoft *i2i* stereo videos.

3.1   Iteration-Energy Evaluation

We firstly present a comparison of *Iteration-Energy Evaluation* between TSGO & AGO in Fig. 2. *Four* stereo pairs (*Tsukuba, Venus, Teddy* and *Cones*) from Middlebury *v.2* stereo data set are adopted to evaluate both the *two* algorithms respectively. It can be observed that after certain iterations, stereo results have almost converged (*5* for *Tsukuba* and *Venus, 8* for *Teddy* and *Cones*). Figure 2(a), (b), (c) and (d) have illustrated that AGO (draw in *blue* dash line) provides a faster convergence and much lower energy than TSGO (draw in *magenta* dash line) after the same iterations. Based on the analyses and massive experiments we choose the iteration time as *5* for *Tsukuba* and *Venus, 8* for the others (include Middlebury *v.2* & *v.3* stereo data sets and Microsoft *i2i* stereo videos).

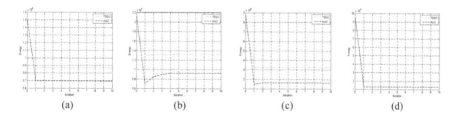

(a)   (b)   (c)   (d)

Fig. 2.   Iteration-energy evaluation between TSGO (draw in *magenta* dash line) and AGO (draw in *blue* dash line). (a) *Tsukuba* (b) *Venus* (c) *Teddy* (d) *Cones*. (Color figure online)

3.2   Middlebury Stereo Data Sets

In this part, we measure our AGO with *five* stereo algorithms on both Middlebury *v.2* & *v.3* stereo data sets. Exactly, we fairly have *three* aggregated and global algorithms for estimating respectively.

Middlebury benchmark [1, 22] is a de facto standard for comparing existing stereo matching algorithms. In this benchmark, *four* stereo pairs (*Tsukuba, Venus, Teddy* and *Cones*) are used to rank more than *160* algorithms. In our experiments, we evaluate not only these *four* stereo pairs but also use "Middlebury 2005" [23] (*6* stereo pairs) and "Middlebury 2006" [24] (*21* stereo pairs) data sets, which involve more complex scenes. Hence, we totally have *31* stereo pairs, which are generally called as Middlebury *v.2* stereo data set. For this data set, we set the error threshold is *1.0* pixel.

Moreover, different from the Middlebury *v.2* stereo data set, a *high-resolution* one, which is Middlebury *v.3* [25, 26] has been released. These new stereo pairs contain more complex scenes and take the effect of rectification error and radiometric changes into account, providing a more challenging benchmark than the previous one. For this data set, we also evaluate the same *six* stereo algorithms on *15* training stereo pairs of the new benchmark, where we use the *quarter size* to estimate and the error threshold is set as *2.0* pixel.

Without disparity refinement. At first, we reveal the detailed error rates of *non-occluded* regions on all *31* Middlebury *v.2* stereo pairs in Table 1. The normal numbers are the percentages of error pixels of initial results and the subscript numbers are the relative rank in each row. It shows that AGO ranks *1* on *17/31* stereo pairs (marked with bold fonts in corresponding rows). The average rank and the average error rates are computed in the last but one and two rows. We can easily conclude that AGO performs best overall accuracy and the best overall rank among all the *six* estimated algorithms. For time efficiency, AGO ranks *four*, but shows much faster than other *two* global ones: TSGO and MS.

Corresponding to Table 1, Fig. 3 visualizes the results of *Bowlilng2*, *Lampshade2* and *Plastic* from Middlebury *v.2* stereo data set. For these classical most challenging stereo pairs, AGO achieves the best results while comparing with aggregated algorithms. Even in the circumstance while comparing with other *two* global algorithms, AGO still shows competitive results.

Then in Table 2 we reveal the detailed quantitive evaluations on Middlebury *v.3* stereo pairs (*quarter size*). In here, we also implement all the same *six* stereo matching algorithms without disparity refinement and error threshold is set as *2.0* pixel. As in Table 1, only the error rates in *non-occluded* regions are measured. Even for this most challenging data set, AGO remains keeping the best performance in accuracy (ranks *1* among *10/15*). For time efficiency, AGO shows *33%* and *2.91* times faster than TSGO and MS respectively, but much slower than aggregated ones. However, the results are well worth the time.

Figure 4 visualizes the competitive results of *Adirondack*, *Piano* and *Playroom* from Middlebury *v.3* stereo data set (*quarter size*) as in Table 2. For this *high-resolution* stereo data set, we can observe that the classical aggregated algorithms provide terrible results; in other words, they become invalid. Even for the most recently challenging stereo matching algorithms TSGO and MS, they also produce inferior results than our proposed AGO.

With disparity refinement. To obtain final results, disparity refinement strategies are also required for stereo matching algorithm. For all the estimated algorithms, here we have implemented them with disparity refinement strategies. Different from former contents, here we also have measured the error rates of *all* pixels (error threshold are *1.0* for Middlebury *v.2* and *2.0* for *v.3* respectively). Tables 3 and 4 simply reveal the average error rates and running time for all the same *six* algorithms. It reflects that with disparity refinement all the results have reached improvements than themselves without it in *non-occluded* regions. Even in this circumstance, our proposed algorithm remains

Table 1. Performance evaluations on all *31* Middlebury *v.2* stereo pairs *without* disparity refinement by *six* algorithms. Error threshold is *1.0* pixel and *non-occluded* regions are estimated.

Stereo pairs	HA	ACF	WCPSP	TSGO	MS	AGO
Tsukuba	2.05_3	4.47_6	3.01_4	1.60_2	3.47_5	$\mathbf{1.31_1}$
Venus	$\mathbf{0.34_1}$	2.21_6	0.86_4	1.16_5	0.64_2	0.85_3
Teddy	7.93_4	9.63_6	$\mathbf{3.71_1}$	8.23_5	7.35_2	7.40_3
Cones	3.05_2	3.70_3	3.95_4	4.18_5	4.47_6	$\mathbf{2.78_1}$
Aloe	7.44_5	8.36_6	$\mathbf{4.04_1}$	5.47_3	6.53_4	4.21_2
Art	10.08_5	9.33_4	8.33_3	7.46_2	11.06_6	$\mathbf{6.40_1}$
Baby1	3.96_5	6.67_6	3.34_4	3.00_3	2.73_2	$\mathbf{2.38_1}$
Baby2	6.13_6	5.86_5	3.21_2	5.48_4	$\mathbf{2.22_1}$	3.73_3
Baby3	3.80_3	6.46_6	$\mathbf{2.58_1}$	5.10_5	4.32_4	3.20_2
Books	10.12_4	12.20_6	$\mathbf{6.42_1}$	10.24_5	8.00_3	7.50_2
Bowling1	18.95_5	44.52_6	11.36_4	8.63_3	$\mathbf{5.00_1}$	6.05_2
Bowling2	9.37_5	16.89_6	5.85_3	6.30_4	5.84_2	$\mathbf{4.99_1}$
Cloth1	1.12_4	0.35_2	0.69_3	2.52_6	1.20_5	$\mathbf{0.22_1}$
Cloth2	5.23_6	3.02_3	2.37_2	5.08_5	4.35_4	$\mathbf{1.95_1}$
Cloth3	2.85_4	$\mathbf{1.39_1}$	1.63_3	3.67_6	3.36_5	1.49_2
Cloth4	1.78_3	2.66_4	1.64_2	3.28_5	3.69_6	$\mathbf{1.06_1}$
Dolls	6.24_3	11.65_6	$\mathbf{4.06_1}$	6.61_4	8.12_5	4.98_2
Flowerpots	15.56_6	13.07_4	13.53_5	11.84_3	$\mathbf{4.20_1}$	6.76_2
Lampshade1	13.91_5	56.53_6	10.31_4	5.60_2	8.96_3	$\mathbf{4.26_1}$
Lamspshde2	21.78_5	43.46_6	7.24_3	9.62_4	4.74_2	$\mathbf{4.08_1}$
Laundry	15.01_5	27.33_6	11.77_3	10.20_2	13.49_4	$\mathbf{9.95_1}$
Midd1	42.10_5	48.40_6	28.72_3	34.74_4	25.89_2	$\mathbf{22.17_1}$
Midd2	40.13_5	49.35_6	35.07_3	35.63_4	$\mathbf{20.99_1}$	22.36_2
Moebius	9.75_2	33.75_6	10.42_4	9.88_3	11.31_5	$\mathbf{7.54_1}$
Monopoly	33.69_5	33.89_6	28.16_4	24.60_3	16.14_2	$\mathbf{15.93_1}$
Plastic	42.64_4	55.90_6	43.24_5	21.01_3	13.50_2	$\mathbf{9.71_1}$
Reindeer	8.97_5	38.00_6	6.11_3	6.19_4	5.81_2	$\mathbf{4.27_1}$
Rocks1	4.16_3	2.26_2	$\mathbf{1.77_1}$	6.60_6	4.58_5	4.16_4
Rocks2	2.51_4	$\mathbf{1.31_1}$	1.33_2	4.46_6	2.72_5	2.44_3
Wood1	6.74_5	23.16_6	2.84_3	2.79_2	3.77_4	$\mathbf{1.90_1}$
Wood2	2.22_3	27.44_6	$\mathbf{0.78_1}$	2.43_5	0.85_2	2.27_4
Avg. error	11.60_5	19.46_6	8.66_3	8.83_4	7.07_2	$\mathbf{5.75_1}$
Avg. rank	4.03_5	5.00_6	2.81_2	3.97_4	3.32_3	$\mathbf{1.71_1}$
Avg. time (s)	2.94_2	5.43_3	$\mathbf{0.41_1}$	14.47_5	84.67_6	11.70_4

keeping competitive results than others. Although the running time increases slightly for all the implementations, AGO still performs a shorter time than TSGO and MS, but slower than aggregated stereo algorithms.

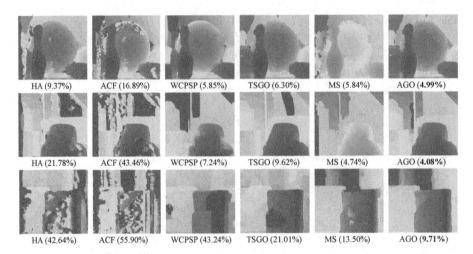

Fig. 3. Results of *Bowling2*, *Lampshade2* and *Plastic* from top to bottom rows by *six* different stereo matching algorithms from Middlebury *v.2* stereo data set. There are no disparity refinement strategies adopted and error threshold is *1.0* pixel. All the error rates in *non-occluded* regions are indicated below for each disparity map.

Table 2. Performance evaluations on *15* Middlebury *v.3* stereo pairs *without* disparity refinement by *six* algorithms. Error threshold is *2.0* pixel and *non-occluded* regions are estimated.

Stereo pairs	HA	ACF	WCPSP	TSGO	MS	AGO
Adirondack	22.74$_5$	22.31$_6$	10.61$_4$	8.35$_3$	3.06$_2$	**2.11$_1$**
ArtL	21.66$_6$	13.42$_5$	10.76$_4$	7.15$_2$	10.57$_3$	**5.93$_1$**
Jadeplant	18.13$_2$	22.72$_4$	26.16$_6$	**17.25$_1$**	23.98$_5$	20.77$_3$
Motorcycle	4.99$_2$	8.07$_6$	5.14$_3$	5.31$_4$	6.04$_5$	**3.48$_1$**
MotorcycleE	21.75$_6$	13.21$_5$	7.81$_4$	6.95$_3$	6.57$_2$	**2.98$_1$**
Piano	21.05$_5$	24.81$_6$	17.50$_3$	18.56$_4$	10.03$_2$	**6.39$_1$**
PianoL	50.95$_6$	46.43$_5$	23.69$_3$	29.36$_4$	19.96$_2$	**19.25$_1$**
Pipes	9.00$_3$	11.91$_4$	12.47$_5$	7.98$_2$	14.71$_6$	**6.61$_1$**
Playroom	27.34$_6$	24.07$_5$	13.16$_4$	13.02$_3$	12.93$_2$	**5.29$_1$**
Playtable	30.16$_4$	31.42$_6$	30.97$_5$	16.66$_3$	**7.58$_1$**	12.06$_2$
PlaytableP	12.99$_5$	13.12$_6$	5.78$_2$	6.77$_3$	7.19$_4$	**5.42$_1$**
Recycle	9.67$_5$	12.22$_6$	4.54$_2$	5.14$_4$	4.84$_3$	**3.99$_1$**
Shelves	38.77$_6$	34.79$_4$	25.60$_2$	34.96$_5$	**25.59$_1$**	26.74$_3$
Teddy	5.99$_6$	5.26$_5$	**3.47$_1$**	4.80$_4$	4.27$_3$	4.02$_2$
Vintage	24.13$_4$	31.07$_6$	25.77$_5$	17.99$_3$	**12.87$_1$**	13.48$_2$
Avg. error	21.29$_6$	20.99$_5$	14.90$_4$	13.35$_3$	11.35$_2$	**9.23$_1$**
Avg. rank	4.73$_5$	5.27$_6$	3.53$_4$	3.20$_3$	2.80$_2$	**1.47$_1$**
Avg. time (s)	6.61$_2$	13.99$_3$	**1.25$_1$**	37.53$_5$	82.11$_6$	28.17$_4$

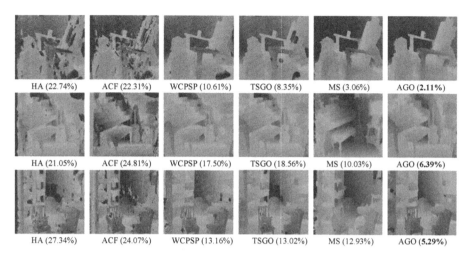

HA (22.74%)	ACF (22.31%)	WCPSP (10.61%)	TSGO (8.35%)	MS (3.06%)	AGO (**2.11%**)
HA (21.05%)	ACF (24.81%)	WCPSP (17.50%)	TSGO (18.56%)	MS (10.03%)	AGO (**6.39%**)
HA (27.34%)	ACF (24.07%)	WCPSP (13.16%)	TSGO (13.02%)	MS (12.93%)	AGO (**5.29%**)

Fig. 4. Results of *Adirondack*, *Piano* and *Playroom* from top to bottom rows by *six* different stereo matching algorithms on Middlebury *v.3* stereo data set. There are no disparity refinement strategies adopted and error threshold is *2.0* pixel. All the error rates in *non-occluded* regions are indicated below for each disparity map.

Table 3. Performance evaluations on all *31* Middlebury *v.2* stereo pairs with disparity refinement. Error threshold is *1.0* pixel.

Algorithms	HA	ACF	WCPSP	TSGO	MS	AGO
Avg. error (non-occ)	11.45	18.57	8.28	7.93	6.84	**4.71**
Avg. error (all)	18.37	25.24	17.12	14.21	14.55	**10.10**
Avg. time (s)	3.17	5.63	**1.92**	16.18	85.95	12.82

Table 4. Performance evaluations on all *15* Middlebury *v.3* training stereo pairs with disparity refinement. Error threshold is *2.0* pixel.

Algorithms	HA	ACF	WCPSP	TSGO	MS	AGO
Avg. errror (non-occ)	19.54	18.31	14.40	13.29	10.96	**9.13**
Avg. error (all)	25.74	22.65	20.66	19.22	**15.30**	15.95
Avg. time (s)	6.66	14.45	**5.90**	40.41	84.26	31.31

Figure 5 illustrates the final results with disparity refinement of *Tsukuba (v.2)*, *Midd1 (v.2)*, *MotorcycleE (v.3)* and *Recycle (v.3)* from Middlebury stereo data sets. According to the exhibited final disparity maps compared with Ground Truth (GT) we conclude that our proposed AGO achieves more excellent results. For *Tsukuba*, it show the greatest performance in foreground (such as the bracket of the lamp) and background. Additionally, for other *three* challenging stereo pairs: *Midd1*, *MotorcycleE* and *Recycle*, our AGO shows more robust in textureless sensitive and exposure problem than other *five* estimated state-of-the-art challenging algorithms.

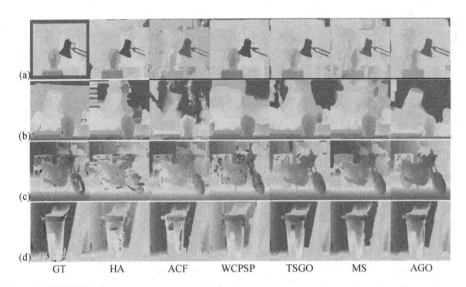

GT   HA   ACF   WCPSP   TSGO   MS   AGO

Fig. 5. Final results with disparity refinement strategies on both Middlebury *v.2 & v.3* stereo data sets by *six* stereo algorithms compared with Ground Truth (GT). (a) *Tsukuba (v.2)*; (b) *Midd1 (v.2)*; (c) *MotorcycleE (v.3)*; (d) *Recycle (v.3)*.

3.3   Stereo Videos

Microsoft *i2i* stereo video data set [27] which contains real world stereo videos. Different from Middlebury *v.2 & v.3* stereo data sets, it performs not only the scenes of urban indoor area but also with peoples. In here, some results of random snapshots from *Antonio* and *Simon* stereo videos are visualized in Fig. 6 respectively. We evaluate the same *six* stereo matching algorithms with disparity refinement too. From the exhibitions we can conclude that the proposed AGO establishes the most smooth disparity maps and has the best performances near foregrounds' depth boundaries and backgrounds' descriptions.

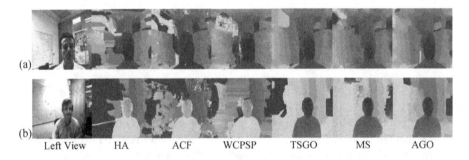

Left View   HA   ACF   WCPSP   TSGO   MS   AGO

Fig. 6. Results of random snapshots are established by using *six* stereo matching algorithms from Microsoft *i2i* stereo video data set. (a) *Antonio*; (b) *Simon*.

4 Conclusions

In this paper, we propose an *Accelerating Global Optimization* (AGO) stereo matching algorithm. It possesses a more simple energy function with fewer intermediate parameters. Additionally, the modeled energy function is also minimized by a modified TRW-S optimizer. Performances evaluations demonstrate that our presented AGO outperforms than other *five* most challenging stereo algorithms both on Middlebury *v.2* & *v.3* stereo data sets; and also performs better on Microsoft *i2i* stereo videos. Lastly, thanks to the simplified energy function structure, the presented AGO shows a much faster execution time than other global algorithms with a relative lower energy. Our future work will focus on how to further improve the energy function and optimizers to attain faster and more accurate disparity estimation.

Acknowledgements. This research has been supported by National Natural Science Foundation of China (U1509207, 61325019, 61472278, 61403281 and 61572357).

References

1. Scharstein, D., Szeliski, R.: A taxonomy and evaluation of dense two-frame stereo correspondence algorithms. Int. J. Comput. Vis. **47**(1), 7–42 (2002)
2. Gong, M., Yang, R., Wang, L., et al.: A performance study on different cost aggregation approaches used in real-time stereo matching. Int. J. Comput. Vis. **75**(2), 283–296 (2007)
3. Tombari, F., Mattoccia, S., Stefano, L., et al.: Classification and evaluation of cost aggregation methods for stereo correspondence. In: IEEE Conference on Computer Vision and Pattern Recognition, pp. 1–8 (2008)
4. Yoon, K.J., Kweon, I.S.: Adaptive support-weight approach for correspondence search. IEEE Trans. Pattern Anal. **28**(4), 650–656 (2006)
5. Hosni, A., Bleyer, M., Gelautz, M., et al.: Local stereo matching using geodesic support weights. In: IEEE International Conference on Image Processing, pp. 2093–2096 (2009)
6. He, K., Sun, J., Tang, X.: Guided image filtering. In: Daniilidis, K., Maragos, P., Paragios, N. (eds.) ECCV 2010. LNCS, vol. 6311, pp. 1–14. Springer, Heidelberg (2010). https://doi.org/10.1007/978-3-642-15549-9_1
7. Min, D., Lu, J., Do, M.N.: A revisit to cost aggregation in stereo matching: how far can we reduce its computational redundancy? In: IEEE International Conference on Computer Vision, pp. 1567–1574 (2011)
8. Min, D., Lu, J., Do, M.N.: Joint histogram based cost aggregation for stereo matching. IEEE Trans. Pattern Anal. **35**(10), 2539–2545 (2013)
9. Helala, M.A., Qureshi, F.Z.: Accelerating cost volume filtering using salient subvolumes and robust occlusion handling. In: Cremers, D., Reid, I., Saito, H., Yang, M.-H. (eds.) ACCV 2014. LNCS, vol. 9004, pp. 316–331. Springer, Cham (2015). https://doi.org/10.1007/978-3-319-16808-1_22
10. Yang, Q.: Local smoothness enforced cost volume regularization for fast stereo correspondence. IEEE Sig. Process. Lett. **22**(9), 1429–1433 (2015)
11. Zhang, K., Fang, Y., Min, D., et al.: Cross-scale cost aggregation for stereo matching. In: IEEE Conference Computer Vision and Pattern Recognition, pp. 407–414 (2014)
12. Zhang, K., Fang, Y., Min, D., et al.: Cross-scale cost aggregation for stereo matching. IEEE Trans. Circuits Syst. Video Technol. **27**(5), 965–976 (2017)

13. Yang, Q., Wang, L., Yang, R., et al.: Real-time global stereo matching using hierarchical belief propagation. In: British Machine Vision Conference, pp. 989–998 (2006)
14. Yang, Q., Wang, L., Yang, R., et al.: Stereo matching with color-weighted correlation, hierarchical belief propagation and occlusion handling. IEEE Trans. Pattern Anal. **31**(3), 492–504 (2008)
15. Yang, Q., Wang, L., Ahuja, N.: A constant space belief propagation algorithm for stereo matching. In: IEEE Conference on Computer Vision and Pattern Recognition, pp. 1458–1465 (2010)
16. Boykov, Y., Veksler, O., Zabih, R.: Fast approximate energy minimization via graph cuts. IEEE Trans. Pattern Anal. **23**(11), 1222–1239 (2001)
17. Taniai, T., Matsushita, Y., Naemura, T.: Graph cut based continuous stereo matching using locally shared labels. In: IEEE Conference on Computer Vision Pattern Recognition, pp. 1613–1620 (2014)
18. Hirschmuller, H.: Stereo processing by semi-global matching and mutual information. IEEE Trans. Pattern Anal. **30**(2), 328–341 (2008)
19. Zhang, C., Li, Z., Cheng, Y., et al.: MeshStereo: a global stereo model with mesh alignment regularization for view interpolation. In: IEEE International Conference on Computer Vision, pp. 2057–2065 (2015)
20. Mozerov, M.G., Weijer, J.: Accurate stereo matching by two-step energy minimization. IEEE Trans. Image Process. **24**(3), 1153–1163 (2015)
21. Kolmogorov, V.: Convergent tree-reweighted message passing for energy minimization. IEEE Trans. Pattern Anal. **28**(10), 1568–1583 (2006)
22. Middlebury Online Stereo Evaluation (v.2) (2002). http://vision.middlebury.edu/stereo/eval/
23. Scharstein, D., Szeliski, R.: Learning conditional random fields for stereo. In: IEEE Conference on Computer Vision and Pattern Recognition, pp. 1–8 (2007)
24. Hirschmuller, H., Scharstein, D.: Evaluation of cost functions for stereo matching. In: IEEE Conference on Computer Vision and Pattern Recognition, pp. 1–8 (2007)
25. Scharstein, D., Hirschmuller, H., Kitajima, Y., et al.: High-resolution stereo datasets with subpixel-accurate ground truth. In: German Conference on Pattern Recognition, pp. 31–42 (2014)
26. Middlebury Online Stereo Evaluation (v.3) (2014). http://vision.middlebury.edu/stereo/eval3/
27. Microsoft i2i Stereo Video (2016). http://research.microsoft.com/enus/projects/i2i/data.aspx
28. Christo, R., Hosni, A., Bleyer, M., et al.: Fast cost-volume filtering for visual correspondence and beyond. In: IEEE Conference on Computer Vision and Pattern Recognition, pp. 3017–3024 (2011)
29. Hosni, A., Christo, R., Bleyer, M., et al.: Fast cost-volume filtering for visual correspondence and beyond. IEEE Trans. Pattern Anal. **35**(2), 504–511 (2013)

An RNN-Based Speech-Music Discrimination Used for Hybrid Audio Coder

Wanzhao Yang[1], Weiping Tu[1,2(✉)], Jiaxi Zheng[1], Xiong Zhang[1],
Yuhong Yang[1,2], and Yucheng Song[1]

[1] School of Computer Science,
National Engineering Research Center for Multimedia Software,
Wuhan University, Wuhan, China
zhao_26@163.com, tuweiping@whu.edu.cn
[2] Research Institute of Wuhan University in Shenzhen, Shenzhen, China

Abstract. Hybrid coders are able to select coding mode for different types of audio data and obtain high coding efficiency in a universal scheme with low bitrate. The selection accuracy is critical to maintain the quality of decoded audio signal and the computational complexity of hybrid coder is also important due to various applications on mobile devices. In this paper, a low complexity coding mode selection method based on Recurrent Neural Networks (RNN) has been investigated to improve the coding performance of the state-of-the-art hybrid coder, AMR-WB+. A constraint is composed on the outputs of RNN by sigmoid function to improve SNR of the decoded audio signal. The experimental results show that the proposed method achieves almost similar quality of decoded audio signal with closed-loop method and comparable complexity with open-loop method in AMR-WB+ coder, outperforming some latest classification methods for this standard.

Keywords: Hybrid audio coder · Recurrent Neural Networks
Coding mode selection

1 Introduction

Hybrid audio coders, such as AMR-WB+ [9], Unified Speech and Audio Coding (USAC) [10] and Enhanced Voice Services (EVS) [11], are based on a switched coding selection design. Compared with one-mode coder, hybrid audio coders are able to classify each segment of input data and provide more flexible coder solution, which meets the demands of diverse types of signals in a universal coding scheme. AMR-WB +, standardized by 3GPP in 2004, is the most classical hybrid coder which compresses speech signal and music signal using the core algorithms of Algebraic Code Excited Linear Prediction (ACELP) and Transform Coding Excitation (TCX), respectively. AMR-WB+ is not only an excellent coder itself, but also plays a key role as a part of USAC scheme which performs well in simplex communication such as typical

W. Tu—This work is supported by National Nature Science Foundation of China (No. 61671335).

K. Schoeffmann et al. (Eds.): MMM 2018, Part I, LNCS 10704, pp. 81–92, 2018.
https://doi.org/10.1007/978-3-319-73603-7_7

broadcast scenarios and multi-media download to mobile devices, while EVS coder, with shorter frame length in coding process, mainly aim at duplex communication such as high-quality multiparty conferencing. Considering a specific hybrid coder, AMR-WB+ is the appropriate one as an experimental subject for its core status, and the improvement in AMR-WB+ is supposed to contribute to USAC scheme as well.

For hybrid coder, it's an issue of crucial importance to select the proper core coding algorithms according to the types of the input signals. There are two methods that have been proposed in AMR-WB+ for coding mode selection. The closed-loop method is done by coding with all possible selection and choosing the one with the highest signal-to-noise ratio (SNR). On the contrast, the open-loop approach discriminates speech from music on the basis of the extracted features from the input signals. Technically, closed-loop method can always acquire the optimal coding selection at the price of computational complexity. Open-loop method is quick enough but the classification accuracy is always disappointing. Compared with fixed coding selection method in closed-loop, it is more feasible to improve open-loop method by using more efficient algorithm of speech-music discrimination.

To make improvements in classifier of open loop methods, many efforts have been made both in features and models. Different kinds of features sets have been tested in [1], concluding that the combination of short-term and long-term features gets the optimum balance between discrimination and computational delay. Perceptual Linear Perception Cepstral Coefficients (PLPCCs) have been used in [2] as one of short-term features and two classifiers have been designed for short-term and long-term features respectively. Although long-term features have outstanding discrimination, they are not cost-efficient in AMR-WB+ because of its restricted structure.

As for the classification models, Gaussian mixture model (GMM) have been successfully applied in the mode selection algorithm for USAC [12]. By reason of strong ability of machine learning and neural network in classification, many machine learning based methods have been used. Decision tree with pruning in [3] has increased the classification accuracy of frame by 6.39% compared with open-loop method in AMR-WB+ (73.41%). In [4], an artificial neural network (ANN) was used, through which a real number was generated and mapped to a certain coding mode by adjusting the threshold to obtain a maximal SNR. The experimental SNR was 13.47 dB, which was slightly better than that of open-loop method (13.39 dB). In addition, many machine learning model such as Multi-Layer Perceptron (MLP) in [5] and Restricted Boltzmann Machine (RBM) in [6] have achieved remarkable classification accuracy, but restricted to defined framework it is difficult for them to play a role in AMR-WB+. Support Vector Machine (SVM) and k-Nearest Neighbor (k-NN) also have been used for music/speech discrimination in [13], but this method can't be used for coding mode selection because the features are extracted from an audio file, not a frame.

In this paper, we propose a speech/music classifier based on Recurrent Neural Network (RNN) for AMR-WB+, only using short-term features calculated inside the coding process and avoiding extra computation load for features extraction. Because of the superiority of making use of sequential information in time, RNN offsets the limitation of short-term features discrimination to a certain extent. Besides, we also statistically analyze the loss of misclassification and properly adjust the threshold of output process in RNN to obtain a better SNR. Given different structure of AMR-WB+ from those of USAC and EVS coders, as well as entirely distinguishing classification reference of these three coders, mode selection methods in USAC and EVS are difficult to be adopted in or compared with those in AMR-WB+. Thus the proposed method is to be compared with method in [4] which uses similar classifier of neural network.

The paper is organized as follows. It begins in Sect. 2 with a brief description of coding mode selection strategy in AMR-WB+. In Sect. 3 the proposed system is presented in terms of feature extraction and neural networks. Finally, in Sect. 4, experiment results are provided and the proposed method is evaluated both in objective and subjective way.

2 AMR-WB+ Coding Mode Selection Strategy

The audio data is divided into super-frames of 1024 samples, and then further divided into segments of 256, 512 or 1024 samples. It is worth mentioning that the frame represents the segment of 256 samples. ACELP is only used for coding 256-sample segments while TCX is applicable for segments with above-mentioned three lengths. So 4 coding modes are available in AMR-WB+, namely, ACELP, TCX256, TCX512 and TCX1024. And there are 26 coding mode permutations for one super-frame.

For closed-loop mode selection, all 26 coding mode permutations are tried for a super-frame, and SNRs of the reconstructed signals are computed for each permutation. The permutation with the highest SNR is decided as the final coding modes for the super-frame. Obviously, closed-loop mode selection method has perfect coding quality while with considerably high computational complexity.

An alternative mode selection method that AMR-WB+ provides to achieve the aim of low complexity is open-loop approach. The open-loop method firstly classifies each 256-sample frame in a super-frame as SPEECH or MUSIC based on features extracted from the input audio data. If there are sequential MUSIC frames within a super-frame, a TCX mode combination with different window lengths will be selected according to segmental SNR, similar to what used in closed-loop method.

The encoding complexity of open-loop method is about 54% and 65% of closed-loop method, with regarding to mono and stereo coding, respectively. However, the quality of reconstructed signals of open-loop approach scores significantly lower than closed-loop one, for the MUSHRA results of open-loop version decreases about 33% with respect to closed-loop version [7].

3 The Proposed Speech/Music Discrimination Method

3.1 System Overview

A speech/music classifier based on RNN is proposed to discriminate each 256-sample frame in a super-frame from speech to music in open-loop mode selection process of AMR-WB+. The reason for adopting a RNN to set up the classifier is that RNNs can use their internal memory to process arbitrary sequences of inputs and capture the dynamics of sequences, which makes them very applicable to classifying mixed audio signals.

Sufficient audio data is used to train a RNN, and the label refers to the coding mode of each frame in closed-loop method. During the regular coding process, features are extracted from each frame as the input of built-in RNN and the output which represents the category of SPEECH or MUSIC is conveyed to subsequent procedure.

3.2 Feature Extraction

Because of the internal sample rate in AMR-WB+, input audio data is always divided into 20 ms length frames with size of 256 samples regardless of the input sample rate. Based on the original scheme, many intermediate variables are calculated which can be used as features of the proposed classifier, instead of designedly calculating extra features which causes additional complexity. The features are extracted as follows.

- Band energy ratio:
  Audio signal is transformed to FFT domain and the magnitude spectrum is non-linearly split into 12 sub-bands. Table 1 lists the proposed split band frequency indices. Then the ratio of each sub-band energy in the whole frequency range is calculated.

Table 1. Split band frequency indices

Index	Frequency	Index	Frequency
1	0–200 Hz	7	1600–2000 Hz
2	200–400 Hz	8	2000–2400 Hz
3	400–600 Hz	9	2400–3200 Hz
4	600–800 Hz	10	3200–4000 Hz
5	800–1200 Hz	11	4000–4800 Hz
6	1200–1600 Hz	12	4800–6400 Hz

- Immittance Spectral Frequencies (ISF)
  ISF are obtained from 16-order linear prediction coefficients to describe the short-term spectrum envelope.
- Sub-bands_flux
  Spectral flux between sub-bands in single frame defined as

$$subband\_flux = \frac{\sum_{i=2}^{12} |energy_m(i) - energy_m(i-1)|}{shortMeanEnergy}, \qquad (1)$$

where

$$shortMeanEnergy = (\sum_{i=1}^{12} energy_m(i) + \sum_{i=1}^{12} energy_{m-1}(i))/2 . \qquad (2)$$

- 200 Hz–4000 Hz energy ratio
  This describes the typical speech signal frequency range which is 200 Hz–4000 Hz.
- High/low energy ratio
  The energy of higher frequency bands (3200 Hz–6400 Hz) is divided by the energy of lower frequency bands (0 Hz–3200 Hz).
- Short-MeanEnergy and long-MeanEnergy
  The mean energy of adjacent two and four frames.
- Zero crossing rate (zcr)
  The rate of sign-changes along a frame signal.
- ISF deviation
  Average short and long time ISF spectral deviation.
- Pitch
  Long-term prediction gain and pitch value of each frame.

The features are normalized by Z-score normalization. Note that the band energy ratio with 12 dimensions is uniformly normalized to keep the correlativity among different sub-bands, and the ISF with 16 dimensions is normalized as the same way.

3.3   Neural Networks

Unlike traditional neural networks in which inputs are independent of each other, RNNs dig the previous input audio frames for information and theoretically map from the entire history of previous inputs to each output. This specialty of RNNs exactly conform to audio data which is a kind of time series meaning the present frame in audio data is always related to the previous frames. A reflection of this relation in discrimination of speech and music is that the long-term features perform better due to the longer time span. RNN in the proposed method replaces and expands the effect of long-term features achieving higher classification accuracy with low computational complexity.

The proposed RNN model starts with 40 units input layer corresponding to 40-dimension features. Then two hidden layers with both 50 units are followed by a full-connection layer with one unit giving the output of RNN. Training datasets are divided as [sample, timesteps, input_dim] liked 3-D tensor, which means the number of feature vectors in each sample is equal to timesteps and the input_dim is the dimension of features (40 in this study). Every hidden layer in RNN is to learn a sequence and output a sequence as well corresponding to the inputs. In general, the value of timesteps is related to rate of networks convergence and depth of learning. Besides, if the value of timesteps is overlarge, RNN cannot acquire information in the most previous steps. However, because of the offline learning in this study, rate of convergence is not the big issue, thus timesteps is set to 1024 due to the best accuracy.

Initialization of kernel weights adopt glorot_uniform method and recurrent weights are initialed by orthogonal method which can partly avoid gradient vanishing and gradient explosion. Activation function for hidden layer is *tanh* and for output layer is sigmoid which ranges the output within 0 and 1 in order to make the category decision based on a threshold. Besides, the technique of dropout is adopted between hidden layers. Units is to be dropped out of the computational process according to a certain probability to avoid overfitting [8]. The probability of dropout in this study is set to 0.5.

4   Experiments

4.1   Datasets

The training datasets consist of recording from British Broadcasting Corporation (BBC) including but not limited to interview programme, entertainment programme and music programme along with nine kinds of music composition (rock, reggae, jazz, pop music, classical, mental, hip-hop, country and blues). In order to explore the performance based on ACELP frames and TCX frames, the datasets are categorized as SPEECH, MUSIC and MIX of an hour in length respectively.

After being coded by closed-loop method, training data is statistically analyzed with results shown in Fig. 1. The coding mode in closed-loop is considerably lopsided with TCX exceeding ACELP in all categories of signals, even accounting for more than 90% in MUSIC. The reason for this lopsidedness is about the specific coding mode selection in AMR-WB+, in which each frame is conclusively to be classified as one of four coding mode: ACELP, TCX256, TCX512, TCX1024. In proposed method, however, each frame is only to be categorized as ACELP or TCX. Therefore, TCX mode in this study contains TCX256, TCX512 and TCX1024 three subclass, consequently leading to the lopsidedness of datasets. However, RNN has difficulty in training such lopsided datasets by only acquiring information from the major category datasets, sequentially weakening the generalization ability of RNN.

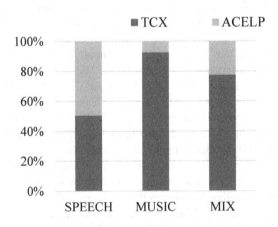

Fig. 1. Statistical analysis of ACELP and TCX frames (Color figure online)

Methods of oversampling such as SMOTE algorithm and undersampling such as EasyEnsemble algorithm are both designed for class-imbalance learning, which generate or prune data based on existing datasets and utilize information of datasets to the full extent. However, due to the easy access to real data (BBC recording), the proposed method extracts frames from extra datasets as supplement to balance training datasets. Meantime the test datasets maintain the class-imbalance for the sake of objectivity.

4.2   Experimental Results

Classification Accuracy and Computational Complexity

After parameter selection and training process, we modified AMR-WB+ reference software code to embed well-trained RNN classifier into open-loop logic and a timer to record time duration of algorithm. The new method is evaluated based on test datasets which are recorded in BBC consisting of half an hour of SPEECH, MUSIC and MIX respectively. The results of classification accuracy and computational complexity are compared with open-loop method in AMR-WB+ shown as Tables 2 and 3.

Table 2. Comparison of mode selection accuracy

	SPEECH	MUSIC	MIX
Open-loop	64.05%	75.75%	74.65%
Proposed method	84.19%	85.06%	83.80%

Table 3. Comparison of computational complexity

	SPEECH	MUSIC	MIX
Closed-loop	126.41 s	128.68 s	151.19 s
Open-loop	78.51 s	66.64 s	86.41 s
Proposed method	76.06 s	76.13 s	80.89 s

The experiments show that the proposed method outperforms the open-loop selection mode by a frame accuracy of 84.19% for SPEECH, 85.06% for MUSIC and 83.80% for MIX. The accuracy for entire datasets is 84.62% which outperforms other classifier for frames embedded in AMR-WB+, such as [3] based on decision tree with accuracy of 79.80%.

Specifically, the open-loop method has better performance with respect to MUSIC dataset due to the intrinsic imbalance. Whereas for SPEECH, which has similar distribution of ACELP and TCX, the accuracy of open-loop method is just beyond 60%. However, the proposed method performs well in three kinds of datasets due to the sufficient learning in all datasets. As for computational complexity, proposed method has the comparable result with that of open-loop method, even has slightly higher speed when deal with SPEECH and MIX dataset.

Objective Performance Evaluation

In AMR-WB+ coder, SNR is used to evaluate the quality variation. With higher SNR, the synthesized audio signal brings into lesser noise and has a better quality. However, due to the fact that classification accuracy cannot directly reflect the SNR, some experiments about threshold of RNN outputs have been conducted.

Considering the subsequent logic of open-loop method, TCX frames are to further categorized as TCX25, TCX512 or TCX1024 according to a half closed-loop method which is shown as Table 4 [9]. Four coding modes have been indexed as follows:0-ACELP; 1-TCX256; 2-TCX512; 3-TCX1024.

Table 4. Possible mode combination selected in TCXS

Selected mode combination after open-loop mode selection (TCX = 1 and ACELP = 0)	Possible mode combination in the final (ACELP = 0, TCX256 = 1, TCX512 = 2 and TCX1024 = 3)	
(0,1,1,1)	(0,1,1,1)	(0,1,2,2)
(1,0,1,1)	(1,0,1,1)	(1,0,2,2)
(1,1,0,1)	(1,1,0,1)	(2,2,0,1)
(1,1,1,0)	(1,1,1,0)	(2,2,1,0)
(1,1,0,0)	(1,1,0,0)	(2,2,0,0)
(0,0,1,1)	(0,0,1,1)	(0,0,2,2)
(1,1,1,1)	(1,1,1,1)	(1,1,2,2)
(1,1,1,1)	(2,2,1,1)	(2,2,2,2)
(1,1,1,1)	(3,3,3,3)	

The coding mode of a super-frame is the combination of the above-mentioned four fundamental modes. If a frame is labeled with 0, then the coding mode is settled, whereas if two successive frames, which are the first or last half part of this super-frame, are labeled with 1, the TCX512 is to be tried and the mode with higher SNR is selected. And if four frames are all labeled with 1, the TCX1024 is to be tried and the best coding mode is selected in the same way.

For the reason of different processing logic aiming at ACELP and TCX, misclassifications about ACELP and TCX in proposed method are supposed to produce different effect. We quantify this effect by using segmental SNR as follows.

$$SEGSNR_i = 10\log_{10}\left[\frac{\sum_{n=0}^{N-1}\left[x_w^i(n) \cdot x_w^i(n)\right]}{\sum_{n=0}^{N-1}\left[x_w^i(n) - \hat{x}_w^i(n)\right]^2}\right], \quad (3)$$

where $SEGSNR_i$ is segmental SNR of the i th computational unit and N is the length of it, which is 64 under the present setting. $x_w(n)$ denotes the original audio signal after perceptual weighting and $\hat{x}_w(n)$ denotes the synthesized audio signal. Then the average segmental SNR of each frame is calculated as

$$SEGSNR = \frac{1}{N_F} \sum_{i=0}^{N_F-1} SEGSNR_i \,, \tag{4}$$

where N_F is the number of units in a frame which is 4 in this study. Regardless of the real classification, each frame is then coded as ACELP and TCX respectively and the segmental SNR is calculated, thus we can define the loss of misclassification for each frame as follows:

$$Cost_{frame} = \left| SEGSNR^0 - SEGSNR^1 \right| \,, \tag{5}$$

where $SEGSNR^b$ is the segmental SNR of a frame coded as b category ($b = 0 \; or \; 1$). Combine the testing audio signal with the coding mode (0 or 1) obtained in closed-loop method, average loss for 0 and 1 is calculated as

$$Cost^m = \begin{cases} \dfrac{1}{N} \sum_{frame=1}^{N} \left(Cost_{frame} \cdot \overline{Mode}_{frame} \right) & (m = 0) \\ \\ \dfrac{1}{N} \sum_{frame=1}^{N} \left(Cost_{frame} \cdot Mode_{frame} \right) & (m = 1) \end{cases} \,, \tag{6}$$

where N is the number of frames.

Since only the relatively extreme conditions are to be considered to explore the loss of two coding mode, only SPEECH and MUSIC datasets are experimented. The results are shown in Table 5.

Table 5. Cost of SNR in speech and music datasets

	SPEECH	MUSIC
$Cost^0$	1.6906	0.4430
$Cost^1$	2.0906	2.7212

The same conclusion can be obtained from SPEECH and MUSIC datasets that loss brought about by misclassification of ACELP is less than that of TCX. Therefore, under the premise of high accuracy of classification in RNN, the precision about ACELP is crucial to the SNR between original signal and synthesized signal. Under the circumstances of unavoidable error rate, more ACELP frames are hoped to be wrongly classified as TCX rather than the misclassification of TCX frames due to the less loss of ACELP frames. The outputs of RNN is constrained by sigmoid function from 0 to 1 and a threshold (0.5 by default) is set to decide the category y based on the sigmoid return value s:

$$y(s) = \begin{cases} 0 & \text{if } s < threshold \\ 1 & \text{if } s > threshold \end{cases} \tag{7}$$

Therefore, proper threshold can be chosen to improve the SNR with acceptable accuracy decline. The thresholds from 0.1 to 0.9 have been experimented on SPEECH, MUSIC and MIX datasets which is shown as Fig. 2.

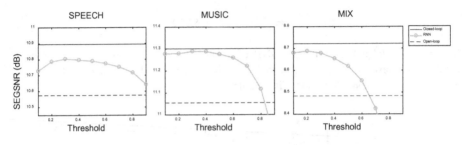

(a)   SEGSNR with variable threshold in SPEECH, MUSIC and MIX

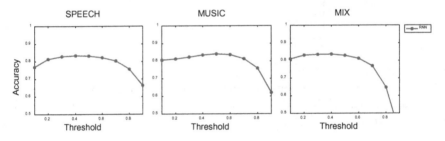

(b)   Accuracy with variable threshold in SPEECH, MUSIC and MIX

Fig. 2. SEGSNR and accuracy with variable threshold in SPEECH, MUSIC and MIX

Overall, the SNR of proposed method is very close to that of closed-loop especially on MUSIC dataset. As for SPEECH datasets, open-loop and closed-loop SEGSNR is 10.58 dB and 10.90 dB; those of MUSIC datasets is 11.05 dB and 11.30 dB; and those of MIX datasets is 8.48 dB and 8.72 dB. With the variation of threshold, proposed method SEGSNR changes between that of open-loop and closed-loop, which gets maximal SEGSNR of 10.80 dB, 11.29 dB and 8.69 dB in three datasets respectively, and has similar trend to discrimination accuracy. For SPEECH and MUSIC datasets, SEGSNR gets the maximal value when threshold is 0.3 which is not the case of maximal accuracy. By using RNN-based method, the SNR is almost up to standard of closed-loop, outperforming ANN-based method in [4] which is slightly better than open-loop. In order to evaluate experimental results, we divide SNR promotion by SNR gap between open-loop and closed-loop methods. Thus we get the normalized promotion of ANN-based method in [4] which is 15.69%. By comparison, proposed method in this study gets 66.11% in SPEECH, 91.35% in MUSIC and 85.94% in MIX.

Due to the priority of SNR compared with classification accuracy as for coding quality, threshold is set to be 0.3 during the subsequent subjective experiment.

Subjective experiment.

The proposed method was evaluated subjectively by using a MUSHRA test methodology. Four MPEG standard series es01, sc01, si01, sm01 were used in the test with the same bit rates (24 kbit/s). All samples were mono with a sampling frequency of 32 kHz. In each of the four experiments, listeners had to rate five versions for each test series: the original as hidden reference; the anchor filtered with a 3.5 kHz low-pass filter; the AMR-WB+ using closed-loop method; the AMR-WB+ using open-loop method; and the proposed RNN-based method.

There are 12 subjects from 20 to 30 years old participating in the subjective evaluation. In order to familiarize the participants with test process, each participant was suggested firstly to conduct a training process and listen to any of the audio sequences as often as desired. The results are shown in Fig. 3. The conclusion is that the proposed method obviously outperforms open loop method in all four series. But with the imperfection of half-closed loop logic after classification, there exists a gap between proposed method and the closed loop method.

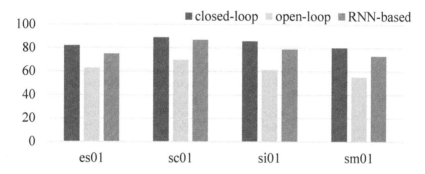

Fig. 3. The subjective evaluation results of sound quality based on MUSHRA method

5 Conclusion

An RNN-based classifier is proposed to improve the coding mode selection in AMR-WB+. The experimental results indicate that the proposed classifier reaches satisfactory accuracy with 84.19% for SPEECH, 85.06% for MUSIC and 83.80% for MIX which is remarkably better than open-loop method in AMR-WB+. At the same time the algorithm complexity is similarly high-efficient as open-loop method.

However, the classification accuracy in open-loop method of AMR-WB+ does not completely match the SNR which is calculated to evaluate the quality of decoded audio signal because of the two-stage mode selection scheme. To resolve this problem, we investigated the loss of misclassification for each frame and proposed a constraint on the outputs of RNN by sigmoid function. Test results show that SNR in our method exceeds that in open-loop method and the reference method using neural network as well. By normalizing the gap of SNR between open-loop and closed-loop methods, reference method gets a SNR promotion of 15.69% whereas our method gets 66.11% in SPEECH, 91.35% in MUSIC and 85.94% in MIX respectively. The promotion of our method was also found in subjective experiment. The RNN-based method has more efficient trade-off between classification accuracy and computational complexity.

References

1. Wang, J., Wu, Q., Deng, H.: Real-time speech/music classification with a hierarchical oblique decision tree. In: IEEE International Conference on Acoustics, Speech and Signal Processing, pp. 2033–2036 (2008)
2. Fuchs, G.: A robust speech/music discriminator for switched audio coding. In: 23rd European Signal Processing Conference, pp. 569–573 (2015)
3. Kim, J., Kim, N.: Improved frame mode selection for AMR-WB+ based on decision tree. IEICE Trans. Inf. Syst. **91**(6), 1830–1833 (2008)
4. Wang, M., Lee, M.: A neural network based coding mode selection scheme of hybrid audio coder. In: IEEE International Conference on Wireless Communications, Networking and Information Security, pp. 107–110 (2010)
5. Khan, M., Al-Khatib, W., Moinuddin, M.: Automatic classification of speech and music using neural networks. In: ACM International Workshop on Multimedia databases, pp. 94–99 (2004)
6. Pikrakis, A., Theodoridis, S.: Speech-music discrimination: a deep learning perspective. In: 22nd European Signal Processing Conference, pp. 616–620 (2014)
7. 3GPP TR 26.936: 3rd Generation Partnership Project; Technical Specification Group Services and System Aspects; Performance Characterization of Audio Codecs (Release 14) (2017)
8. Srivastava, N., Hinton, G., Krizhevsky, A.: Dropout: a simple way to prevent neural networks from overfitting. J. Mach. Learn. Res. **15**(1), 1929–1958 (2014)
9. ETSI TS 126 290: Digital cellular telecommunications system (Phase 2+); Universal Mobile Telecommunications System (UMTS); Audio codec processing functions; Extended Adaptive Multi-Rate - Wideband (AMR-WB+) codec; Transcoding functions (Release 6) (2005)
10. ISO/IEC 23003-3, Information Technology – MPEG Audio Technologies – Part 3: Unified Speech and Audio Coding, ed. 1, International Organization for Standardization (2011)
11. GPP TS 26.441: 3rd Generation Partnership Project; Technical Specification Group Services and System Aspects; Codec for Enhanced Voice Services (EVS); General Overview (Release 14) (2017)
12. Lee, S., Kim, J., Lee, I.: Speech/audio signal classification using spectral flux pattern recogniton. In: IEEE Workshop on Signal Processing Systems, pp. 232–236 (2012)
13. Khonglah, B., Sharma, R., Mahadeva, S.: Speech vs music discrimination using empirical mode decomposition. In: National Conference on Communications, pp. 1–6 (2015)

Co-occurrent Structural Edge Detection
for Color-Guided Depth Map Super-Resolution

Jiang Zhu, Wei Zhai, Yang Cao[✉], and Zheng-Jun Zha

Department of Automation, University of Science and Technology of China,
Hefei 230027, China
{zj130129,wzhai056}@mail.ustc.edu.cn, {forrest,zhazj}@ustc.edu.cn

Abstract. Although RGBD cameras can provide depth information in real scenes, the captured depth map is often of low resolution and insufficient quality compared to the color image. Typically, most of the existing methods work by assuming that the edges in depth map and its corresponding color image are more likely to occur simultaneously. However, when the color image is rich in detail, the high-frequency information which is non-existent in the depth map will be introduced into the depth map. In this paper, we propose a CNN-based method to detect the co-occurrent structural edge for color-guided depth map super-resolution. Firstly, we design an edge detection convolutional neural network (CNN) to obtain the co-occurrent structural edge in depth map and its corresponding color image. Then we pack the obtained co-occurrent structural edges and the interpolated low-resolution depth maps into another customized CNN for depth map super-resolution. The presented scheme can effectively interpret and exploit the structural correlation between the depth map and the color image. Additionally, recursive learning is adopted to reduce the parameters of the customized CNN for depth map super-resolution and avoid overfitting. Experimental results demonstrate the effectiveness and reliability of our proposed approach by comparing with the state-of-the-art methods.

Keywords: Co-occurrent structural edge
Depth map super-resolution · Convolutional neural network (CNN)
Recursive learning

1 Introduction

In recent years, with the development of affordable and portable depth sensors (e.g. ASUS Xtion Pro, Time-of-Flight (TOF) cameras, etc.), depth maps have been exploited popularly in a variety of real world applications, such as human-computer interaction, driver assistance, virtual reality and 3D scene reconstruction. However, depth map acquired from these depth sensors such as Kinect suffers from limited resolution and low quality due to the reflection, scattering and abortion of the structure light. Thus, to facilitate the use of depth information, we often need to recover a high-resolution (HR) depth map from its low-resolution (LR) version.

© Springer International Publishing AG 2018
K. Schoeffmann et al. (Eds.): MMM 2018, Part I, LNCS 10704, pp. 93–105, 2018.
https://doi.org/10.1007/978-3-319-73603-7_8

Despite the significant improvement in RGBD cameras, the quality of depth map is still insufficient when compared with the color image. Therefore, various methods [1–5] have been proposed to use a pre-aligned high resolution intensity image (color image or grayscale image) to help improve the quality of depth map in the upsampling process. The majority of these methods are based on the assumption that there is a co-occurrence of edges in RGBD images. While in reality, this assumption is not always valid. For instance, when the color image is rich in detail (as shown in Fig. 1), the high frequency component such as texture edges are likely to be introduced into depth map, which results in undesirable artifacts in the depth map.

Over the last few years, benefiting from the available of large training data and powerful GPU computation, deep convolutional neural networks (CNNs) have achieved great success in various low-level vision tasks such as super-resolution [6,7], denoising [8], dehazing [9] and de-raining [10]. More recently, Riegler et al. [11] proposed a deep Primal-Dual Network method which combines the advantages of deep CNN and variational methods for depth map super-resolution. Li et al. [12] proposed a learning-based joint filter based on CNNs. Their method takes both color image and depth map into consideration and naturally tackles the inconsistent structure problem. However, these CNN-based methods usually pack interpolated depth maps and the intensity images into a network for depth map super-resolution. Despite impressive results achieved by these approaches, *how to exploit the structural correlation between depth map and its corresponding color image more accurately to further improve the quality of depth map?* - largely remains to be studied.

In this paper, we propose a CNN-based method for color-guided depth map super-resolution. Our goal is to explicitly exploit the structural correlation of RGBD images, and then we can apply the correlation to further improve the quality of depth map. To achieve this goal, we need to overcome the following challenges. (1) It is obvious that there are only part of the edges in RGBD images that satisfy the aforementioned assumption. For depth map super-resolution, what are the helpful edges of color image to its corresponding depth map and how to exclude the redundant edges, such as the texture edges? (2) After obtaining the co-occurrence of the depth map and the color image, how to interpret this relatinship and exploit it to implement depth map super-resolution (3) To improve the performance of the customized deep CNN for depth map super-resolution, one possible solution is to increase the depth of the network by adding convolutional layers. However, this will lead to high computational consumption and may cause overfitting.

To address the aforementioned challenges, we propose a two-step CNN-based framework including two deep CNNs for color-guided depth map super-resolution. The first edge detection CNN is used to describe and establish the structural correlation of RGBD images. It can extract the co-occurrent structural edges in RGBD images. The input of this network is color images and the ground truth edges of HR depth map are used as the label. The second CNN packs the obtained co-occurrent structural edges and the interpolated LR depth maps into the network for depth map super-resolution. Figures 2 and 3 illustrates the details of our proposed two networks. Our proposed approach has the following advantages:

(1) We present an edge detection CNN to describe and establish the structural correlation of RGBD images. It can effectively extract the co-occurrent structural edges in depth map and its corresponding color image.
(2) A deep CNN is customized for depth map super-resolution. To reduce the parameters of this CNN and avoid overfitting, recursive learning is adopted to increase network depth without increasing the number of parameters. It significantly improves convergence speed and boosts the performance of the CNN.
(3) The proposed two-step CNN-based framework can not only interpret and establish the structural correlation between the depth map and the color image, but also tackle texture transfer problem. It outperforms the state-of-the-art methods for color-guided depth map super-resolution.

2   Proposed Method

2.1   The Structural Correlation of RGBD Images

The color image and its associated depth map provide complementary information of the same scene. However, they have strong correlation in structures as can be seen in Fig. 1(a) and (b). The homogeneous regions of color image are more likely to have similar depth value in the associated depth map and the abrupt transition in depth map usually bring about the abrupt transition in its corresponding color image.

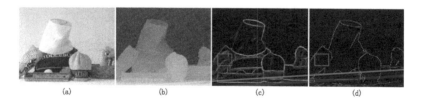

Fig. 1. Middl scene. (a) Color image. (b) Depth map. (c) Edge of (a). (d) Edge of (b). (Color figure online)

There are plenty of edges in RGBD images are consistent with each other as shown in Fig. 1(c) and (d). In the vast majority of cases, the depth map is smoother than its associated color image, and thus texture edges in color images are non-existent in depth map (the region highlighted with a red rectangle in Fig. 1(c) and (d)). These texture edges will cause texture transfer in depth map. For depth map super-resolution, the helpful edges of color image are those which co-exist in RGBD images. The color image is normally of high quality and its edge is sharper than the depth map. Thus we need from HR color image to find out the co-occurrent structural edges in RGBD images and exploit them to tackle texture transfer problem for depth map super-resolution.

2.2   Network Architecture for Co-occurrent Structural Edge Detection

In order to obtain co-occurrent structural edge in RGBD images, we design a CNN for co-occurrent structural edge detection. In particularly, it can describe and establish the correlation of RGBD images. The structural edge dataset are labeled by annotators with their knowledge and some of the labeled structural edges may be non-existent in the depth map. Therefore the label of structural edge datasets is not suitable for the co-occurrent structural edge detection. Ground truth depth edge not only contains the co-occurrent structural edges, but also contains the other edges which are benefit for depth map super-resolution. Hence, we use the ground truth depth edge as label of the designed CNN. In this way, the correlation between depth map and color image is established.

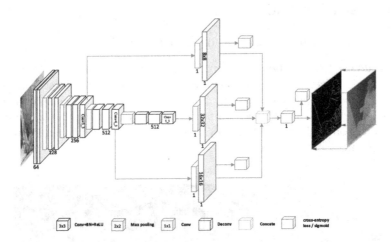

Fig. 2. Architecture of the COSED network for co-occurrent structural edge detection.

The deep CNN can generate perceptually multi-level features and the convolutional features in CNNs gradually change from low-level visual feature to high-level semantic feature with the increasing network depth. The output of higher convolution layer lacks many critical edges and the fine details such as textures usually appear in the lower convolution layers. From such observations, in order to avoid using the details of color image, therefore we try to combine intermediate and higher convolutional features for structural edge detection.

Inspired by most of the existing edge detection work [13,14] in deep learning, we modify VGG16 [15] network as the following and make it suitable for the co-occurrent structural edge detection:

(1) Batch normalization (BN) is added between convolution (*conv*) layer and Rectified Linear Unit (ReLU) in the VGG16 network. Because the batch normalization can speed up training and boost the performance of the network.

(2) We remove the 5th pooling (*pool5*) layer and all the fully connected layers of VGG16 network. The fully connected layers do not align with our holistic edge detection network and the *pool5* layer will further produce smaller feature maps which adds to the disadvantage of edge localization.

(3) The side outputs of *conv3_3*, *conv4_3* and *conv5_3* are connected to a 1×1 *conv* layer, then a deconvolution (*deconv*) layer is used to upsample the corresponding feature maps.

(4) A *cross-entropy loss/sigmoid* layer [13] is added to each *deconv* layer. As we can seen in HED [13] that deep supervision is important for edge detection.

(5) We concatenate all of the *deconv* layers and use a 1×1 *conv* layer to fuse these feature maps. Finally, a *cross-entropy loss/sigmoid* layer is also connected to the fusion output.

Our proposed CNN for co-occurrent structural edge detection is referred to as COSED. Figure 2 shows the details of this network. We combine the intermediate and higher features to exclude texture edges in color image. Consequently, our COSED can effectively exploit the structural correlation of RGBD images.

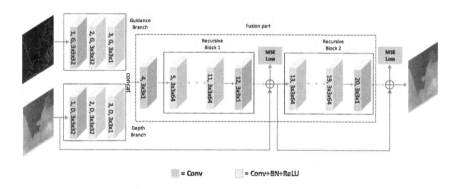

Fig. 3. Our DSRCN network architecture for depth map super-resolution.

2.3 The Proposed Architecture for Depth Map Super-Resolution

After we got the co-occurrent structural edges, then another customized CNN packs the obtained edges and the interpolated low-resolution depth maps into the network for depth map super-resolution. The customized CNN for depth map super-resolution is referred to as DSRCN and the details of our DSRCN are shown in Fig. 3. As we can see that our DSRCN consists of three components: guidance branch, depth branch and fusion part. Most of the existing CNN-based methods [7,16] for image super-resolution don't use pooling to widen the receptive field. Inspired by these works, we set the depth of our fully convolution network (all the kernel size of the *conv* layers is 3×3) to 20 and the receptive field of our DSRCN is 41×41. There are two types of layers in our DSRCN. (1) Conv: We use the *conv* layer as the first layer of guidance and depth branch for feature extraction. The fourth layer and the last layer of each recursive block are also the *conv* layer. (2) Conv+BN+ReLU: It's used for all of the remaning layers in our DSRCN.

The depth map and the obtained co-occurrent structural edge have different data distribution. Directly using the depth map and the obtained structural edge as the input of our DSRCN will bring great interference to the results of depth map super-resolution. To overcome this problem, we first extract the features of the depth map and the obtained co-occurrent structural edge separately. Moreover, edge is one of the basic image features, thus only a few *conv* layers are needed to extract their features before fusion. According to the structure of SRCNN [6], we set the number of *conv* layers to 3 for guidance branch and depth branch.

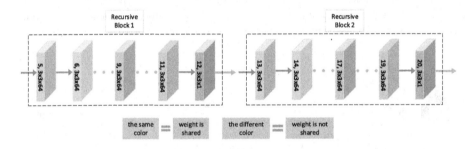

Fig. 4. The structure of our recursive blocks.

Our DSRCN is a deep CNN and overfitting is very likely. Therefore we adopt the residual learning and recursive learning to avoid overfitting and boost the performance of our DSRCN. The skip-connection is added from input and the output of our first recursive block to the corresponding output of each recursive block respectively, so that our network can learn residual mapping. The recursive learning can be seen in DRCN [7]. DRCN has a recursive layer (up to 16 recursions) and all the recursions are supervised to avoid exploding or vanishing gradients. However, their training takes a lot of time (about 6 days) to converge. To reduce training time, we adopt the recursive block which consists of 7 layers of Conv+BN+ReLU and 1 layer of Conv. Our recursive block is a group of different *conv* layers and it can effectively extract different features. We set the number of the recursive blocks to 2 in our DSRCN and Fig. 4 shows the structure of our recursive block. Unlike the DRCN which shares weights among the *conv* layers, the weight set of *conv* layers is not shared in the same recursive blocks. But over all, the weight set is shared among different recursive blocks. It can be seen in Fig. 4 that the weight set of the i-th $(i = 5, 6, ..., 12)$ *conv* layer in recursive block 1 and the *(i+8)-th conv* layer in the recursive block 2 is shared. In our DSRCN, all the outputs of the recursive blocks are supervised.

2.4 Loss Function Definition

Objective function of COSED: The training dataset of our network is denoted as $S = \{(X_n, Y_n), n = 1, ..., N\}$. X_n is the input color image and $Y_n = \{y_j^{(n)}, j = 1, ..., |X_n|\}, y_j^{(n)} \in \{0, 1\}$ is the corresponding ground truth binary depth edge. Then we use the following class-balanced cross-entropy loss function [13] to train our COSED:

$$\ell(\mathbf{W}) = -\beta \sum_{j \in Y_+} log P(y_j = 1|X; \mathbf{W}) - (1 - \beta) \sum_{j \in Y_-} log P(y_j = 0|X; \mathbf{W}). \quad (1)$$

$$\beta = \frac{|Y_-|}{|Y_+| + |Y_-|}, 1 - \beta = \frac{|Y_+|}{|Y_+| + |Y_-|}. \quad (2)$$

Where the $\mathbf{W}$ is the parameters of our network. The class-balancing weight β is used to automatically handle the imbalance between positive classes and negative classes. Y_+ and Y_- denote the edge and non-edge sets of the ground truth Y, respectively. The probability $P(\cdot)$ is obtained by using a sigmoid fuction $\sigma(\cdot)$ on the activations of the output of our network.

Objective function of DSRCN: For the training process of our DSRCN, we use a mean square error (MSE) as the loss function :

$$L(\Theta) = \frac{1}{2N} \sum_{i=1}^{N} \|F(D_i, E_i; \Theta) - D_i^{GT}\|^2. \quad (3)$$

Denote F and Θ as the network mapping function and the network parameter set respectively. Where D_i is the input interpolated LR depth map, E_i is the obtained co-occurrent structural edge by COSED, D_i^{GT} is the ground truth HR depth map, and N represents the number of training samples.

A combined loss function: Our COSED and DSRCN have several loss functions. We denote them as L_i $(i \in \{1, 2, ..., n\}$, n is the number of loss functions). Then a combined loss function consists of these loss functions is referred to as L_{final}. Furthermore, L_{final} is the final loss function to minimize and it can be represented as the following:

$$L_{final} = s_1 \times L_1 + s_2 \times L_2 + ... + s_n \times L_n. \quad (4)$$

The s_i $(i \in \{1, 2, ..., n\})$ is the assigned weight value. However, we don't show details about the process in the Figs. 2 and 3. Because this process can be automatically implemented in the deep learning framework.

3 Experiments and Analysis

In this section, we introduced the experimental settings and conducted a series of experiments to demonstrate the rationality and effectiveness of our proposed COSED and DSRCN.

3.1 Experimental Settings

Parameter setting: For the training of COSED, we initialized our network by using the VGG16 model which was pre-trained on ImageNet [17]. SGD algorithm was adopted to train our COSED. Mini-batch size was 20 and the base learning rate was set to $1e - 6$ which was gradually decayed for every 5000 iterations. We set the momentum and weight decay to 0.9 and 0.0004 respectively. The other parameters setting of our COSED were shown in the Fig. 2. Holistic image was used during the training and testing stage. For the training of DSRCN, we split training images into 50×50 patches with the stride of 25. The mini-batch size was 128, the momentum was set to 0.9, and weight decay was 0.0005. Adam algorithm was adopted to train our DSRCN. The base learning rate varied from $1e - 4$ to $1e - 6$ and we padded zeros for all of the *conv* layers to make the output of our DSRCN had the same size as the input image. The Fig. 3 illustrated the remaining parameters of our DSRCN.

Training and testing data: For co-occurrent edge detection, the dataset which was provided by Riegler et al. [11] contained 5000 RGBD images. The dataset [11] were randomly divided into three parts. 4000, 500 and 500 RGBD images were used for training, validation and testing respectively. The ground truth depth map edge was obtained by using Canny edge detector and we used it as the label of COSED. For depth map super-resolution, We collected 55 RGBD images and 30 RGBD images from MPI-Sintel dataset [18] and Middlebury dataset [19,20] respectively. 65, 17 and 3 RGBD images were used for training, validation and testing respectively. Firstly, color images were inputted to COSED, and then we obtained the co-occurrent structural edges. Next, we packed the obtained edge and LR depth map (interpolation to HR depth map by bicubic firstly) into DSRCN. We also used the dataset provided by Riegler et al. [11] to train our DSRCN and evaluated our results on the challenging ToFMark dataset [4].

Data augmentation: In order to get more training data, the training images were rotated with 90°, 180°, 270° and flipped horizontally. After that, we obtained 7 additional augmented versions of original image.

We implemented all of the experiments by using *caffe* [21]. Training our COSED and DSRCN roughly takes 28 h and 22 h respectively, with a Titan Xp GPU.

3.2 Network Properties

In this subsection, we studied network properties, including the effectiveness of recursive learning, different structural edges and the number of recursive blocks in our DSRCN. All the comparison experiments of depth map super-resolution were evaluated on Middlebury dataset with the zooming factor 8.

Recursive learning: To demonstrate the significance of recursive learning in DSRCN, two contrasting experiments were carried out, one with and the other without recursive learning. The performance curve was shown in Fig. 5(a). We can see that recursive learning improved the convergence speed and accuracy compared to without recursive learning.

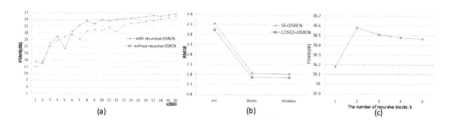

Fig. 5. The comparing results of our network properties and all of the results were evaluated on the 3 noise-free testing images from Middlebury dataset.

Different structural edges: To figure out the effect of different structural edges for guiding depth map super-resolution, we used the structural edges which were extracted by COSED and SE [22] respectively as the input to train two different models. Then we referred to them as COSED+DSRCN and SE+DSRCN respectively. As shown in Fig. 5(b), our COSED+DSRCN produced superior results than SE+DSRCN in the term of RMSE.

The number of recursive blocks: We studied the performance of DSRCN with increasing the number of recursive blocks. Five models were trained with different numbers of recursive blocks: 1, 2, 3, 4 and 5. It illustrated in Fig. 5(c) that the performance of our DSRCN hadn't improved when the number of recursive blocks was over 2. The number of recursive blocks was set to 2 as our DSRCN already achieved its capacity with the depth.

3.3   The Results of Co-occurrent Structural Edge Detection

Before evaluating the detected edges of our COSED, we used Piotr's Structured Forest [22] matlab toolbox to do the standard non-maximum suppression (NMS) and edge thinning. Then we compared the edge detection results of our COSED with the SE [22] and Fig. 6 showed the visual inspection results. In general, the edges which were detected by our COSED contained less textures. Our COSED can more effectively extract the co-occurrent structural edge than the SE. As shown in Fig. 5(b), we used the edges which were detected by COSED and SE respectively to guide depth map super-resolution. Our COSED can achieve better results than SE for depth map super-resolution as it can suppress a substantial part of the texture edges.

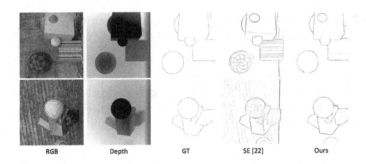

Fig. 6. The co-occurrent structural edge detection results by different methods.

3.4 The Results of Depth Map Super-Resolution

Noise-free Middlebury dataset: Following the experimental setting of DJF [12], we conducted experiments for depth map super-resolution with the noise-free LR depth map on four zooming factors, i.e. 2, 4, 8, 16. We trained a single model for each zooming factor. The comparison experimental results on the 3 noise-free testing images, Art, Books and Moebius with the state-of-the-art methods in terms of RMSE were summarized in Table 1. Our DSRCN achieved better performance with different zooming factors in terms of RMSE. In Fig. 7, we gave the visual results with zooming factor 8. It can be seen that our DSRCN can generate more sharper edges than other methods. The visual results of Park et al. [2], TGV [4] and DJF [12] have some artifacts around the edge region.

Table 1. Experimental results (RMSE) on the 3 noise-free test images

	Art				Books				Moebius			
	×2	×4	×8	×16	×2	×4	×8	×16	×2	×4	×8	×16
Bilinear	2.83	4.15	6.03	8.93	1.12	1.67	2.39	3.53	1.02	1.53	2.21	3.18
Bicubic	2.57	3.85	5.52	8.37	1.01	1.56	2.25	3.35	0.91	1.38	2.04	2.95
Park et al. [2]	2.83	3.51	4.17	6.26	1.09	1.53	1.99	2.76	1.06	1.35	1.81	2.38
TGV [4]	3.03	3.79	4.79	7.12	1.29	1.62	1.99	2.94	1.13	1.46	1.91	2.63
DJF [12]	2.77	3.69	4.92	7.72	1.11	1.71	2.16	2.91	1.04	1.52	1.99	2.95
Ours	**1.21**	**2.25**	**4.02**	**6.17**	**0.52**	**1.04**	**1.66**	**2.67**	**0.54**	**0.96**	**1.65**	**2.47**

ToFMark: The ToFMark dataset [4] consists of three different real scenes. To evaluate our DSRCN on it, we followed the experimental setting of Riegler et al. [11] and trained our DSRCN. We compared our experimental results with several state-of-the-art methods and our DSRCN achieved better performance in terms of RMSE (in mm) in Table 2. It can be obviously seen from the Fig. 8 that our DSRCN tackled texture transfer more effectively and produced sharper edges than the state-of-the-art methods, e.g. TGV [4] and Riegler et al. [11].

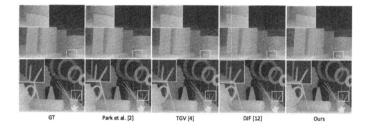

Fig. 7. Depth super-resolution results by different methods with zooming factor 8.

Table 2. Quantitative results on the ToFMark dataset.(RMSE in mm)

	NN	Bilinear	He et al. [1]	TGV [4]	Riegler et al. [11]	Ours
Books	30.46	29.11	27.11	24.01	23.74	**23.61**
Devil	27.53	25.34	23.45	23.19	**20.47**	20.65
Shark	38.21	36.34	33.26	29.89	28.81	**28.69**

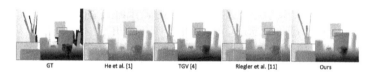

Fig. 8. The evalution results of depth map super-resolution on TOFMark.

4   Conclusion

In this paper, we proposed a two-step CNN-based framework including two deep CNNs for color-guided depth map super-resolution, in which the recursive learning is adopted. The first CNN, COSED is used to describe and establish the structural correlation between depth map and its corresponding color image. Our COSED can effectively extract the co-occurrent structural edge in RGBD images. The second CNN, DSRCN packs the obtained structural edges and interpolated LR depth maps into the network for depth map super-resolution. Moreover, the recursive learning is adopted to reduce the parameters of our DSRCN and avoid overfitting. It could speed up the training and boost depth map super-resolution performance. The experimental results demonstrated that our proposed method can not only effectively exploit the structural correlation between the depth map and the color image, but also apply it to further improve the quality of depth map for depth map super-resolution.

Acknowledgments. This work is supported by the Natural Science Foundation of China (61472380, 61622211, 61472392).

References

1. He, K., Sun, J., Tang, X.: Guided image filtering. In: Daniilidis, K., Maragos, P., Paragios, N. (eds.) ECCV 2010. LNCS, vol. 6311, pp. 1–14. Springer, Heidelberg (2010). https://doi.org/10.1007/978-3-642-15549-9_1
2. Park, J., Kim, H., Tai, Y.W., Brown, M.S., Kweon, I.: High quality depth map upsampling for 3D-TOF cameras. In: IEEE International Conference on Computer Vision, pp. 1623–1630. IEEE (2011)
3. Zhang, J., Cao, Y., Zha, Z.J., Zheng, Z., Chen, C.W., Wang, Z.: A unified scheme for super-resolution and depth estimation from asymmetric stereoscopic video. IEEE Trans. Circuits Syst. Video Technol. **26**(3), 479–493 (2016)
4. Ferstl, D., Reinbacher, C., Ranftl, R., Ruether, M., Bischof, H.: Image guided depth upsampling using anisotropic total generalized variation. In: IEEE International Conference on Computer Vision (ICCV), December 2013
5. Zhu, J., Zhang, J., Cao, Y., Wang, Z.: Image guided depth enhancement via deep fusion and local linear regularization. In: IEEE International Conference on Image Processing (ICIP) (2017)
6. Dong, C., Loy, C.C., He, K., Tang, X.: Image super-resolution using deep convolutional networks. IEEE Trans. Pattern Anal. Mach. Intell. **38**(2), 295–307 (2016)
7. Kim, J., Kwon Lee, J., Mu Lee, K.: Deeply-recursive convolutional network for image super-resolution. In: Proceedings of the IEEE Conference on Computer Vision and Pattern Recognition, pp. 1637–1645 (2016)
8. Zhang, K., Zuo, W., Chen, Y., Meng, D., Zhang, L.: Beyond a Gaussian denoiser: residual learning of deep CNN for image denoising. IEEE Trans. Image Process. **PP**(99), 1 (2017)
9. Cai, B., Xu, X., Jia, K., Qing, C., Tao, D.: Dehazenet: an end-to-end system for single image haze removal. IEEE Trans. Image Process. **25**(11), 5187–5198 (2016)
10. Fu, X., Huang, J., Ding, X., Liao, Y., Paisley, J.: Clearing the skies: a deep network architecture for single-image rain removal. IEEE Trans. Image Process. **26**(6), 2944–2956 (2017)
11. Riegler, G., Ferstl, D., Rüther, M., Horst, B.: A deep primal-dual network for guided depth super-resolution. In: British Machine Vision Conference (2016)
12. Li, Y., Huang, J.B., Narendra, A., Yang, M.H.: Deep joint image filtering. In: European Conference on Computer Vision (2016)
13. Xie, S., Tu, Z.: Holistically-nested edge detection. In: Proceedings of the IEEE International Conference on Computer Vision, pp. 1395–1403 (2015)
14. Yang, J., Price, B., Cohen, S., Lee, H., Yang, M.H.: Object contour detection with a fully convolutional encoder-decoder network. In: Proceedings of the IEEE Conference on Computer Vision and Pattern Recognition, pp. 193–202 (2016)
15. Simonyan, K., Zisserman, A.: Very deep convolutional networks for large-scale image recognition. arXiv preprint arXiv:1409.1556 (2014)
16. Mao, X., Shen, C., Yang, Y.: Image restoration using very deep convolutional encoder-decoder networks with symmetric skip connections. In: Proceedings of Advances in Neural Information Processing Systems (2016)
17. Deng, J., Dong, W., Socher, R., Li, L.J., Li, K., Li, F.F.: Imagenet: a large-scale hierarchical image database. In: IEEE Conference on Computer Vision and Pattern Recognition, pp. 248–255 (2009)
18. Butler, D.J., Wulff, J., Stanley, G.B., Black, M.J.: A naturalistic open source movie for optical flow evaluation. In: Fitzgibbon, A., Lazebnik, S., Perona, P., Sato, Y., Schmid, C. (eds.) ECCV 2012. LNCS, vol. 7577, pp. 611–625. Springer, Heidelberg (2012). https://doi.org/10.1007/978-3-642-33783-3_44

19. Scharstein, D., Pal, C.: Learning conditional random fields for stereo. In: IEEE Conference on Computer Vision and Pattern Recognition, pp. 1–8. IEEE (2007)
20. Scharstein, D., Hirschmüller, H., Kitajima, Y., Krathwohl, G., Nešić, N., Wang, X., Westling, P.: High-resolution stereo datasets with subpixel-accurate ground truth. In: Jiang, X., Hornegger, J., Koch, R. (eds.) GCPR 2014. LNCS, vol. 8753, pp. 31–42. Springer, Cham (2014). https://doi.org/10.1007/978-3-319-11752-2_3
21. Jia, Y., Shelhamer, E., Donahue, J., Karayev, S., Long, J., Girshick, R., Guadarrama, S., Darrell, T.: Caffe: convolutional architecture for fast feature embedding. In: ACM International Conference on Multimedia, pp. 675–678. ACM (2014)
22. Dollár, P., Zitnick, C.L.: Fast edge detection using structured forests. IEEE Trans. Pattern Anal. Mach. Intell. **37**(8), 1558–1570 (2015)

Collision-Free LSTM for Human Trajectory Prediction

Kaiping Xu, Zheng Qin$^{(\boxtimes)}$, Guolong Wang, Kai Huang,
Shuxiong Ye, and Huidi Zhang

School of Software, Tsinghua University, Beijing 10084, China
{xkpl3,qingzh,wanggll6,huang-kl5,
ysxl5,zhdl6}@mails.tsinghua.edu.cn

Abstract. Pedestrians have an intuitive ability for navigation to avoid obstacles and nearby pedestrians. If we want to predict future positions of a pedestrian, we should know how the pedestrian adjust his direction to avoid collisions. In this work, we present a simple and effective framework for human trajectory prediction to generate the future sequence based on pedestrian past positions. The method, called Collision-Free LSTM, extends the classical LSTM by adding Repulsion pooling layer to share hidden-states of neighboring pedestrians. The model can learn both the temporal information of trajectories and the interactions between pedestrians, which is in contrast to traditional methods using hand-crafted features such as Social forces. The experiments results on two public datasets show that our model can achieve state-of-the-art performance with assessment metrics.

Keywords: Human trajectory prediction · Social force · Deep learning

1 Introduction

In real-world scenarios, when people walk in a crowd, such as promenade, market, and sidewalk, they will obey biological habits and social conventions. Pedestrians navigate their trajectories to avoid collision and keep reasonable interspace with the fellows. For instance, one would get around the front crowd from left side, avoid contacting pedestrians, and respect personal distance on the pavement. The problem of trajectory prediction mainly works for anticipating the future trajectory of the pedestrians based on a sequence of past positions. It can be applied in many fields including intelligent traffic engineering, vehicle automatic driving and human-computer interaction. However, trajectory prediction is a challenging problem that requires early detecting human motions and understanding subtle interactions among people in complex nature.

Giannotti et al. [1] proposed the problem "trajectory patterns", which represents descriptions of frequent behaviors in terms of both space and time. Lee et al. [2] explored the partition-and-group framework for clustering trajectories. Morris and Trivedi [3] evaluated different similarity measures and clustering methodologies to catalog their strengths and weaknesses for the trajectory learning. Ballan et al. [4] introduced a Dynamic Bayesian Network which exploits the scene specific knowledge for trajectory prediction. With reference to their researches, the machine learning

© Springer International Publishing AG 2018
K. Schoeffmann et al. (Eds.): MMM 2018, Part I, LNCS 10704, pp. 106–116, 2018.
https://doi.org/10.1007/978-3-319-73603-7_9

methods have some effect on the performance of results achieved. However these approaches do not consider human natural attributes influencing on final performance.

Some advances in the literature address that social factors can improve performance. Social factors include one pedestrian's destination, desired speed, and repulsion from other individuals. Pioneering work by Helbing and Molnar [5] proposed a pedestrian motion model with social factors, which generated attractive and repulsive forces between pedestrians. Many similar methods were followed to human interactions [6, 7] and activity understanding [8–12]. In addition, some works explored human features and attributes to improve tracking and forecasting. Alahi et al. [13] proposed a social affinity feature by learning human trajectories from their relative positions within the crowd, while Yi et al. [14] explored human attributes to improve predicting in dense crowds.

One of these works limitations is that they utilize hand-crafted features to model human activities and interactions for specific scenarios. Hand-crafted features only capture simple interactions and hardly understand more complex scenarios. The other is that they are concerned with instant interactions among humans. They do not consider long-term temporal information and could not anticipate interactions occurring in the distant future.

Recently Recurrent Neural Networks (RNN) have achieved great successful in sequence prediction tasks, especially, the variant models such as Long Short Term Memory (LSTM) [15] and Gated Recurrent Units (GRU) [16]. Alahi et al. [17] proposed a trajectory prediction framework which connects LSTM cells corresponding to nearby pedestrians in the scene at the particular time frame. They explored a Social pooling layer which allows the LSTM of spatially proximal sequences to share their hidden-states. However, the Social LSTM only consider every neighboring pedestrian has same degree of influence. The model is not sufficient to capture the complex navigational information.

In this work, we propose a data-driven architecture based on LSTM for human trajectory prediction in the future which constructs instinctive collision-free of the pedestrians in an unsupervised manner. We address a Repulsion function to calculate different degrees of pedestrians influence with each other, and explore a Repulsion pooling to share the neighboring hidden-states in different directions within a certain space. Collision-Free LSTM (CF-LSTM) proposed can automatically learn multiple sequences in the form of trajectory information from neighboring pedestrians when outputting the predicting sequence. Our model achieves some competitive results on ETH [18] and UCY [19] datasets.

2 Our Method

2.1 Problem Formulation

The problem assumes that each scene needs first preprocess to obtain the spatial coordinates of all pedestrians at each time frame. This preprocessing can follow method in [20]. At any time frame t, the xy-coordinates of the ith pedestrian on the trajectory is defined as (x_i^t, y_i^t). The trajectories we observed are the positions of all pedestrians in a certain space from time 1 to T_{obs} and the task we are interested in is to predict their positions from time instants $T_{obs} + 1$ to T_{pred}. We can consider this as a sequence generation problem, where the input sequence is the spatial positions of the pedestrians in a certain space and the output sequence is the predicted future trajectory of the pedestrian interested.

2.2   Collision-Free LSTM

Pedestrians navigating their trajectories rely on the visual perception of distances or obstacle speeds resulting in instantaneous changing of the speed or the direction within the speed, and result from repulsive and attractive forces with the acceleration. Also, some models are defined in discrete time and are driven by collision avoidance [21, 22]. We explore a novel LSTM based on collision-free model for the trajectory prediction problem as showed in Fig. 1. We set one LSTM to represent a pedestrian in the scene. The LSTMs learn the hidden-states from each pedestrian to predict their positions.

Particularly, different distance have different degrees of the influence between individuals (i.e. a pedestrian walking nearest to the person has greater influence than the others). We develop Repulsion pooling to limit the neighboring LSTMs and address Repulsion function to understand and represent different pedestrian influences from a certain set of observations corresponding to one interested. Pedestrian1 and pedestrian3 have different hidden-states of LSTM (h1 and h3) on pedestrian2, as illustrated in Fig. 1 left.

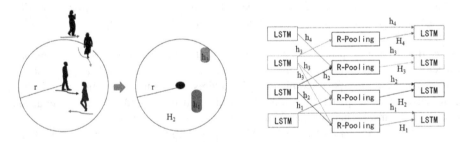

Fig. 1. Overview of Collision-Free LSTM model. The right shows the details on our Repulsion pooling (R-Pooling) for pedestrian2 (in black). The left shows that the LSTMs connect every neighbor in the scope through a Repulsion pooling (R-Pooling). The trajectories of pedestrian 2 of interest are in the scope of the circle of with a radius of r. Different positions have different repulsion influences on pedestrian2 within the circle.

Repulsion function. Pedestrians navigate their paths to avoid collision by the behavior of neighboring persons. The direction model is a simple and effective approach of the pedestrian navigation model. It is based on a Repulsion function depending on the distances with the neighbors [23].

$$R(s) = a \ \exp((l - s)/D) \tag{1}$$

where parameter a quantifies the amplitude of the repulsion with the neighboring pedestrians in the model, and the parameter D calibrates the distance for the repulsion. The other parameters meaning in the function are presented in Fig. 2.

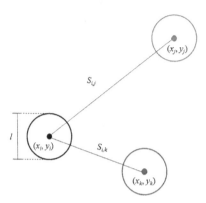

Fig. 2. Notations used in the function. (x_i, y_i) refers to pedestrian i position. l refers to the pedestrian size. $s_{i,j} = \sqrt{(x_i - x_j)^2 + (y_i - y_j)^2}$.

Repulsion pooling. We address Repulsion pooling in Fig. 1, which can share the status information of all pedestrians in the certain space. The LSTM receives information from the pooling layer that collects the hidden-states of the pedestrian neighbors. During the information collected, the networks try to capture spatial information within the circles of pooling. The pooling details is following.

Firstly, we set direction dimension to be N and hidden-state dimension of LSTM to be Q. The hidden-state $H_{i,n}^t$ denotes the social influence at time t in the scene for the pedestrian i corresponding to the direction n. Then we construct the social hidden-state tensor H_i^t with direction dimension of N in a certain space. The Repulsion pooling is shown in Fig. 3.

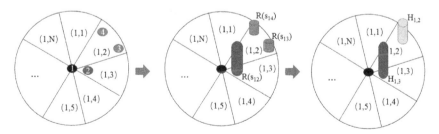

Fig. 3. Repulsion pooling of pedestrian1 (in black). We pool the hidden-states of neighbors (in orange, green and red) in sector (1,2) and sector (1,3) respectively. Different distances have different repulsion forces on pedestrian1 in step 2. The last step shows the social hidden-states for the pedestrian1 in different directions. (Color figure online)

$$H_{i,n}^t = \sum_{j \in M_{i,n}} \mathbf{1}_{i,n}[x_j^t, y_j^t] R(s_{i,j}) h_j^{t-1}$$

$$H_i^t = [H_{i,1}^t, H_{i,2}^t, \cdots, H_{i,N}^t]$$

$$(2)$$

where h_j^{t-1} refers to the hidden-state of the LSTM corresponding to neighbor j at time $t-1$. $\mathbf{1}_{i,n}[x,y]$ is a function to judge if (x,y) is in sector(i,n) representing area of pedestrian i in the direction of n. $M_{i,n}$ denotes the set of neighbors in the sector(i,n).

We transfer the xy-ordinates into r_i^t and the social hidden-state tensor into c_i^t. The encoding function LSTM of the sequence at time t, as following.

$$r_i^t = \phi(x_i^t, y_i^t; W_r)$$

$$c_i^t = \phi(r_i^t, H_i^t; W_c)$$

$$h_i^t = \text{LSTM}(h_i^{t-1}, c_i^t; W_l)$$

$$(3)$$

where $\phi(\cdot)$ refers to the transfer function with ReLU [24] nonlinearity. W_r and W_c are transfer weights, and W_l denotes the LSTM weights.

Position prediction. We use hidden-state at time $t-1$ to predict the distribution of the trajectory position $(\hat{x}, \hat{y})_i^t$ at the next time t. This work is assumed to be a Gaussian distribution, including the mean $\mu_i^t = (\mu_i^t, \mu_i^t)$, standard deviation $\sigma_i^t = (\sigma_i^t, \sigma_i^t)$ and correlation coefficient ρ_i^t. We predict these parameters by a $5 \times Q$ weight matrix W_p.

$$(\hat{x}, \hat{y})_i^t \sim \mathcal{N}(\mu_i^t, \sigma_i^t, \rho_i^t)$$

$$[\mu_i^t, \sigma_i^t, \rho_i^t] = W_p h_i^t$$

$$(4)$$

Collision-Free LSTM learns the parameters by minimizing the negative log- Likelihood loss L_i, which represents the trajectory of pedestrian i.

$$L_i = - \sum_{t=T_{obs}+1}^{T_{pred}} \log(\text{P}(x_i^t, y_i^t | \mu_i^t, \sigma_i^t, \rho_i^t))$$

$$(5)$$

The model is trained by minimizing all trajectory losses in the training dataset. The Repulsion pooling in our model does not need any extra parameters. The hidden-states of multiple LSTMs are combined by the pooling, and shared back-propagation in a scene at every time instant. We stress that it is different from the traditional LSTM.

3   Experiments

3.1   Datasets and Implementations Details

The experiments were conducted on two publicly available pedestrian trajectory datasets: UCY [19] and ETH [18]. The UCY dataset consists of around 786 pedestrians in three different sets (UCY, ZARA-01 and ZARA-02). ETH dataset contains two sets

(ETH and Hotel) with 750 pedestrians. These datasets contain thousands of nonlinear walking trajectories, and cover some complex group behaviors such as couples walking together, groups interleaving, and groups combining and dispersing in certain scenarios. The data contain tagged location information, including scene obstacles, destination and pedestrian group information. Our experiments follow cross validation scheme using four training sets and one testing set, which is repeated for all five sets.

We summarize the number of tags in different datasets as shown in Table 1. The video frame rate of all datasets is 25 fps. Average trajectory density is 30 per frame in the scene.

Table 1. The number of tags in the datasets

Dataset	Frame	Pedestrian	Destination	Group	Obstacle
UCY	541	434	4	297	16
ZARA-01	866	148	4	91	34
ZARA-02	1052	204	4	140	34
ETH	1448	360	5	243	44
Hotel	1168	390	4	326	25

We set direction dimension N to be 12 and neighboring circle radius r to be 16. The Collision-Free LSTM hidden-state dimension Q is 140. About Repulsion function, we follow the parameters setting scheme [23], where coefficient a is set to 5, distance D set to 0.1 and pedestrian size l set to 0.3. For our model, we initialize the learning rate as 0.001 and use RMS-prop as the optimizer [25]. The model is implemented in TensorFlow [26] with a single NVIDIA Tesla K40 GPU.

3.2 Results and Analysis

In this work, we select three error metrics [17] for trajectory prediction accuracy as following: Average displacement error (ADE), Final displacement error (FDE) and Average non-linear displacement error (NL-ADE). ADE refers to the mean square error (MSE) over all estimated points of every trajectory and the true points. FDE means the distance between the predicted final destination and the true final destination at the T_{pred} time. NL-ADE is the MSE for the non-linear regions of a trajectory, which can evaluate all the errors during the non-linear turns in every trajectory.

We set $(\hat{x}_i^t, \hat{y}_i^t)$ to be predicted position of the trajectory i at t time, (x_i^t, y_i^t) to be observed position of the trajectory i at t time, and n to be the number of trajectories in the testing set.

1. *Average displacement error (ADE)*:

$$ADE = \frac{\sum_{i=1}^{n} \sum_{t=T_{obs}+1}^{T_{pred}} \left[(\hat{x}_i^t - x_i^t)^2 + (\hat{y}_i^t - y_i^t)^2 \right]}{n(T_{pred} - (T_{obs} + 1))} \quad (6)$$

2. *Final displacement error (FDE):*

$$FDE = \frac{\sum\limits_{i=1}^{n} \sqrt{(\hat{x}_i^{T_{pred}} - x_i^{T_{pred}})^2 + (\hat{y}_i^{T_{pred}} - y_i^{T_{pred}})^2}}{n} \qquad (7)$$

3. *Average non-linear displacement error (NL-ADE):*

$$NL-ADE = \frac{\sum\limits_{i=1}^{n} \sum\limits_{t=T_{obs}+1}^{T_{pred}} I(\hat{x}_i^t, \hat{y}_i^t)\left[(\hat{x}_i^t - x_i^t)^2 + (\hat{y}_i^t - y_i^t)^2\right]}{\sum\limits_{i=1}^{n} \sum\limits_{t=T_{obs}+1}^{T_{pred}} I(\hat{x}_i^t, \hat{y}_i^t)} \qquad (8)$$

where,

$$I(\hat{x}_i^t, \hat{y}_i^t) = \begin{cases} 1 & \text{if } \frac{d^2 \hat{y}_i^t}{d\hat{x}_i^{t2}} \neq 0 \\ 0 & \text{else} \end{cases}$$

In our experiments, we observed 8 frames of the trajectories, and predicted next 12 frames of the trajectories. We use observe positions from 1st to 8th frame and predicted positions in Eq. (3) from 9th to 20th frame.

We compare our model with the state-of-art methods, Social Force (SF) based on social grouping factors [12], Linear trajectory avoidance (LTA) based on collision avoidance energy [12], Traditional LSTM (LSTM) without shared pooling, Social-LSTM (S-LSTM) with Social pooling [17]. The performance of all the methods is shown in Table 2.

When comparing performance of our model against the others, especially, Social LSTM, experimental results show CF-LSTM outperforms them in the most of data sets. Repulsion function of our model calculates different social force with different distance of neighboring pedestrians, hence Repulsion pooling can capture the neighbor interactions sensitively comparing to Social pooling. The hidden-states of our model is capable of representing the neighbors influence well and improving the human trajectory prediction obviously. Particularly, all of the error metrics are more significant in the UCY sets as they have the heavier trajectory density, more complex motion patterns and more intersecting trajectories than the ETH sets.

In the case of ETH, the intent of pedestrians to reach the destination is predominant. Temporal information influences the prediction of final destination hardly. Final displacement error (FDE) of Social Force get minimum and the performance is best.

Average non-linear displacement error (NL-ADE) of LSTM is better than Linear trajectory avoidance (LTA) and Social Forces (SF), because it can predict non-linear trajectory curves. However, its ADE and FDE are not as good as theirs, since LSTM does not consider the interactions between pedestrians.

Table 2. The results of all the methods

Metric	Dataset	SF	LTA	LSTM	S-LSTM	CF-LSTM
ADE	UCY	0.48	0.51	0.52	0.27	**0.24**
	ZARA-01	0.40	0.37	0.43	0.22	**0.21**
	ZARA-02	0.40	0.40	0.51	0.25	**0.19**
	ETH	0.41	0.54	0.60	0.50	**0.35**
	Hotel	0.25	0.38	0.15	0.11	**0.09**
	Average	0.39	0.44	0.44	0.27	**0.18**
NL-ADE	UCY	0.54	0.57	0.31	0.16	**0.11**
	ZARA-01	0.41	0.39	0.24	0.13	**0.09**
	ZARA-02	0.39	0.41	0.30	0.16	**0.10**
	ETH	0.49	0.70	0.28	0.25	**0.23**
	Hotel	0.38	0.49	0.09	0.07	**0.05**
	Average	0.44	0.51	0.24	0.15	**0.10**
FDE	UCY	0.78	0.95	1.25	0.77	**0.75**
	ZARA-01	0.60	0.66	0.93	**0.48**	0.51
	ZARA-02	0.68	0.72	1.09	0.50	**0.48**
	ETH	**0.59**	0.77	1.31	1.07	1.04
	Hotel	0.37	0.94	0.33	**0.23**	0.25
	Average	0.60	0.74	0.98	0.61	**0.51**

In any case, we can see that Collision-Free LSTM and Social LSTM achieve the smaller errors than LSTM. It is evident on the results of experiments on UCY data sets. This shows shared pooling have the advantage of capturing complex interactions of high dense pedestrians.

In Fig. 4, we show the predicted results of SF model, S-LSTM model and our CF-LSTM model on ZARA-01 of UCY datasets. Figure 4(d),(e) and (f) illustrate that our proposed model has better predictions in crowded areas. Since we train a deep sequence to sequence model, which can learn different patterns of influences from each neighboring pedestrians cluster with Repulsion pooling. From Fig. 4(a) to (f), we demonstrate how our model predicts the trajectories in order to avoid collisions. In the last row of Fig. 4, we show some failure predicted examples. The main reason of deviation trajectories on Ground Truth is that the pedestrians change the destination suddenly. The predicted trajectories do not match Ground Truth, however, our method still gives plausible trajectories avoiding collision with neighboring humans.

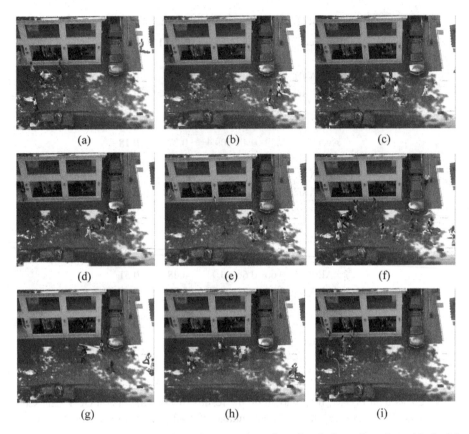

Fig. 4. Qualitative results. We show the examples of predicted the trajectories with Social Forces (in blue), S-LSTM (in green) and our method (in red). Ground Truth is in yellow. (Color figure online)

4   Conclusion

In this work, we have presented a novel deep learning model for human trajectory prediction. We formulate traditional LSTM framework in sequence to sequence into Collision-Free LSTM between the LSTMs with a Repulsion pooling layer. Our model shares the hidden-state of each trajectory at every time instant and successfully predicts the trajectory through learning the multiple sequences from the neighboring pedestrians. Our model achieves state-of-the-art performance on two challenging publicly available datasets. Future work will extend the model to more complex scenes where pedestrians, bicycles and vehicles are crossing each other.

References

1. Giannotti, F., Nanni, M., Pinelli, F., Pedreschi, D.: Trajectory pattern mining. In: Proceedings of the 13th ACM SIGKDD International Conference on Knowledge Discovery and Data Mining, pp. 330–339. ACM (2007)
2. Lee, J.G., Han, J., Whang, K.Y.: Trajectory clustering: a partition-and-group framework. In: Proceedings of the 2007 ACM SIGMOD International Conference on Management of Data, pp. 593–604. ACM (2007)
3. Morris, B., Trivedi, M.: Learning trajectory patterns by clustering: experimental studies and comparative evaluation. In: 2009 IEEE Conference on Computer Vision and Pattern Recognition, CVPR 2009, pp. 312–319. IEEE (2009)
4. Ballan, L., Castaldo, F., Alahi, A., Palmieri, F., Savarese, S.: Knowledge transfer for scene-specific motion prediction. In: Leibe, B., Matas, J., Sebe, N., Welling, M. (eds.) ECCV 2016. LNCS, vol. 9905, pp. 697–713. Springer, Cham (2016). https://doi.org/10.1007/978-3-319-46448-0_42
5. Helbing, D., Molnar, P.: Social force model for pedestrian dynamics. Phys. Rev. E **51**(5), 4282 (1995)
6. Koppula, H.S., Saxena, A.: Anticipating human activities using object affordances for reactive robotic response. IEEE Trans. Pattern Anal. Mach. Intell. **38**(1), 14–29 (2016)
7. Pellegrini, S., Ess, A., Van Gool, L.: Improving data association by joint modeling of pedestrian trajectories and groupings. In: Daniilidis, K., Maragos, P., Paragios, N. (eds.) ECCV 2010. LNCS, vol. 6311, pp. 452–465. Springer, Heidelberg (2010). https://doi.org/10.1007/978-3-642-15549-9_33
8. Choi, W., Savarese, S.: A unified framework for multi-target tracking and collective activity recognition. In: Fitzgibbon, A., Lazebnik, S., Perona, P., Sato, Y., Schmid, C. (eds.) ECCV 2012. LNCS, vol. 7575, pp. 215–230. Springer, Heidelberg (2012). https://doi.org/10.1007/978-3-642-33765-9_16
9. Choi, W., Savarese, S.: Understanding collective activities of people from videos. IEEE Trans. Pattern Anal. Mach. Intell. **36**(6), 1242–1257 (2014)
10. Leal-Taixe, L., Fenzi, M., Kuznetsova, A., Rosenhahn, B., Savarese, S.: Learning an image-based motion context for multiple people tracking. In: Proceedings of the IEEE Conference on Computer Vision and Pattern Recognition, pp. 3542–3549 (2014)
11. Mehran, R., Oyama, A., Shah, M.: Abnormal crowd behavior detection using social force model. In: 2009 IEEE Conference on Computer Vision and Pattern Recognition, CVPR 2009, pp. 935–942. IEEE (2009)
12. Yamaguchi, K., Berg, A.C., Ortiz, L.E., Berg, T.L.: Who are you with and where are you going? In: 2011 IEEE Conference on Computer Vision and Pattern Recognition (CVPR), pp. 1345–1352. IEEE (2011)
13. Alahi, A., Ramanathan, V., Fei-Fei, L.: Socially-aware large-scale crowd fore-casting. In: Proceedings of the IEEE Conference on Computer Vision and Pattern Recognition, pp. 2203–2210 (2014)
14. Yi, S., Li, H., Wang, X.: Understanding pedestrian behaviors from stationary crowd groups. In: Proceedings of the IEEE Conference on Computer Vision and Pattern Recognition, pp. 3488–3496 (2015)
15. Hochreiter, S., Schmidhuber, J.: Long short-term memory. Neural Comput. **9**(8), 1735–1780 (1997)
16. Chung, J., Gulcehre, C., Cho, K., Bengio, Y.: Empirical evaluation of gated recurrent neural networks on sequence modeling. arXiv preprint arXiv:1412.3555 (2014)

17. Alahi, A., Goel, K., Ramanathan, V., Robicquet, A., Fei-Fei, L., Savarese, S.: Social LSTM: human trajectory prediction in crowded spaces. In: Proceedings of the IEEE Conference on Computer Vision and Pattern Recognition, pp. 961–971 (2016)
18. Pellegrini, S., Ess, A., Schindler, K., Van Gool, L.: You'll never walk alone: modeling social behavior for multi-target tracking. In: 2009 IEEE 12th International Conference on Computer Vision, pp. 261–268. IEEE (2009)
19. Lerner, A., Chrysanthou, Y., Lischinski, D.: Crowds by example. In: Computer-Graphics Forum, vol. 26, pp. 655–664. Wiley Online Library (2007)
20. Luber, M., Stork, J.A., Tipaldi, G.D., Arras, K.O.: People tracking with human motion predictions from social forces. In: 2010 IEEE International Conference on Robotics and Automation (ICRA), pp. 464–469. IEEE (2010)
21. Van den Berg, J., Lin, M., Manocha, D.: Reciprocal velocity obstacles for real-time multi-agent navigation. In: 2008 IEEE International Conference on Robotics and Automation, ICRA 2008, pp. 1928–1935. IEEE (2008)
22. Fiorini, P., Shiller, Z.: Motion planning in dynamic environments using velocity obstacles. Int. J. Robot. Res. **17**(7), 760–772 (1998)
23. Tordeux, A., Chraibi, M., Seyfried, A.: Collision-free speed model for pedestrian dynamics. In: Knoop, V., Daamen, W. (eds.) Traffic and Granular Flow 2015, pp. 225–232. Springer, Cham (2016)
24. Nair, V., Hinton, G.E.: Rectified linear units improve restricted Boltzmann machines. In: Proceedings of the 27th International Conference on Machine Learning (ICML 2010), pp. 807–814 (2010)
25. Dauphin, Y., de Vries, H., Bengio, Y.: Equilibrated adaptive learning rates for non-convex optimization. In: Advances in Neural Information Processing Systems, pp. 1504–1512 (2015)
26. Abadi, M., Barham, P., Chen, J., Chen, Z., Davis, A., Dean, J., Devin, M., Ghemawat, S., Irving, G., Isard, M., et al.: Tensorflow: a system for large-scale machine learning. In: Proceedings of the 12th USENIX Symposium on Operating Systems Design and Implementation (OSDI), Savannah, Georgia, USA (2016)

Convolution with Logarithmic Filter Groups for Efficient Shallow CNN

Tae Kwan Lee, Wissam J. Baddar, Seong Tae Kim,
and Yong Man Ro[(✉)]

Image and Video Systems Laboratory, School of Electrical Engineering, KAIST,
Daejeon, South Korea
{ltk010203,wisam.baddar,stkim4978,ymro}@kaist.ac.kr

Abstract. In convolutional neural networks (CNNs), the filter grouping in convolution layers is known to be useful to reduce the network parameter size. In this paper, we propose a new logarithmic filter grouping which can capture the nonlinearity of filter distribution in CNNs. The proposed logarithmic filter grouping is installed in shallow CNNs applicable in a mobile application. Experiments were performed with the shallow CNNs for classification tasks. Our classification results on Multi-PIE dataset for facial expression recognition and CIFAR-10 dataset for object classification reveal that the compact CNN with the proposed logarithmic filter grouping scheme outperforms the same network with the uniform filter grouping in terms of accuracy and parameter efficiency. Our results indicate that the efficiency of shallow CNNs can be improved by the proposed logarithmic filter grouping.

Keywords: Shallow convolutional neural network (CNN)
Nonlinear logarithmic filter groups · Classification tasks
CNN parameter efficiency

1 Introduction

Recently, convolutional neural networks (CNNs) have shown state-of-the-art performance in various classification tasks [1–6], including face recognition [2], facial expression recognition [5, 6], and object classification (e.g. ILSVRC [1, 3, 4]). The increase in performance is largely due to the increased non-linearity in the model and abstractions that allow representation of more complex objects or classes [1].

In constrained conditions, such as embedded systems or mobile devices, networks with smaller parameters are needed due to the limitations of memory and computing power [7]. Therefore, having a CNN classification model small in size, and robust in performance can save memory, and energy in mobile applications. Recently, it has been shown that a reasonably good performance can be achieved with shallower networks for smaller classification tasks (with small number of outcomes) [8, 9]. Nonetheless, model parameters and computational complexity could still be improved in shallower networks.

Several research efforts have recently shown that the parameters in the CNNs could be reduced while maintaining the performance [7, 10–14]. Some approaches make use

© Springer International Publishing AG 2018
K. Schoeffmann et al. (Eds.): MMM 2018, Part I, LNCS 10704, pp. 117–129, 2018.
https://doi.org/10.1007/978-3-319-73603-7_10

of the redundancies in spatial dimensions of filters by factorization of convolutions or low-rank approximations, etc. [10, 12–14]. Another approach introduces the concept of filter grouping [11]. The filter grouping divides a full convolution layer into smaller convolutions with uniform channel size which in sum have the same input and output feature dimensions compared to the full convolution [11]. The method reduces model parameters in deep CNNs while maintaining the performance and enhancing the computation speed [11]. [7] can be seen as an extreme version of [11], where the standard convolution is decomposed into depth-wise and point-wise convolutions. Such methods remove network redundancies in CNNs effectively. However, applying filter grouping in [11] directly to shallow CNNs could degrade the performance of the classification. Moreover, we cannot guarantee whether the uniform filter grouping successfully reflects the nonlinear nature within shallow CNNs.

In this paper, we propose a novel logarithmic filter grouping for a shallow CNN model in general classification tasks (see Fig. 1). Our network develops the proposed logarithmic filter grouping and residual identity connections [1] to reduce parameters in shallow networks while minimizing the performance loss (classification performance loss). The proposed logarithmic filter grouping is devised considering the nonlinear characteristic of filters which resembles the human perception of physical stimuli [15]. Identity connections are incorporated with the proposed filter grouping to encode residual mappings in the shallow CNNs. We show that our compact CNN model with the proposed logarithmic filter grouping shows better classification performance and improved parameter efficiency compared to the uniform filter grouping. The contributions of this paper can be summarized by the following:

1. We propose a new filter grouping which introduces the concept of nonlinear logarithmic filter grouping. The logarithmic filter grouping is devised based on the CNN filters' nonlinear characteristics. By using the proposed filter grouping, the

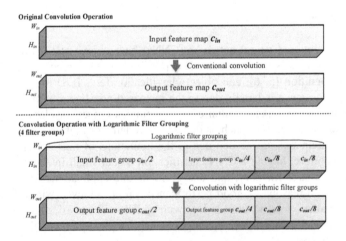

Fig. 1. Overview of the proposed nonlinear logarithmic filter grouping in a convolution layer. H_{in}, W_{in}, H_{out}, W_{out} denote the input and output feature map size. c_{in} is total number of input channels, c_{out} is that of output channels for the convolution layer.

parameters in convolution layers can be reduced while improving classification performance compared to the uniform filter grouping. Further residual identity shortcut is employed to incorporate with the proposed filter grouping for building efficient shallow CNN model.

2. We devise a compact CNN for general classification tasks based on the proposed filter grouping. The model has smaller parameters compared to a baseline compact CNN model with the same depth. At the same time, the proposed CNN architecture with the proposed filter grouping minimizes the performance loss compared to the baseline compact model on different classification tasks (Facial expression recognition using Multi-Pie dataset [16] and object classification using CIFAR-10 dataset [17]).

2   Related Works

2.1   Hierarchical Filter Groups

Typical convolution filters in CNNs have full connections between the input and output feature maps. If the input feature map has c_{in} channels and the output feature map has c_{out} channels, the filter dimension is $h \times w \times c_{in} \times c_{out}$. This means that the height of the filter is h, the width is w, the channel depth is c_{in}, and there are c_{out} filters of corresponding shapes.

The work in [11] applies filter groups manually to disconnect the connectivity between the input and output feature maps. For example, if n filter groups are applied, n uniform filter groups with c_{out}/n filters are used. Each filter group has a dimension of $h \times w \times c_{in}/n$, i.e. total filter dimension becomes $h \times w \times c_{in}/n \times c_{out}$. Total parameters required for this convolution layer is n times smaller than that of the original full convolution layer.

The degree of grouping n is also reduced by half as the network goes deeper. This 'root topology' exploits the idea that deeper layers need more filter dependencies, such that simpler features are combined to produce more complex features. [11] uses this hierarchical filter group concept to reduce parameters in deep convolutional networks, yet maintaining the performance.

2.2   Residual Network

Residual network is an example of a very deep neural network. When a neural network becomes deeper, vanishing gradients problem arises which drops the performance of the network [1]. Layers in residual networks are composed of residual module $F(\cdot)$ and a skip connection bypassing $F(\cdot)$. The identity skip connection allows efficient back-propagation of errors, and resolves the vanishing gradient problem [1].

Apart from conveying gradients effectively, identity skip connections have another important role of encoding residual mapping. The authors in [1] showed through careful experiments that residual mapping with the identity skip connection is better than plain network in both training easiness and performance.

Identity skip connections are utilized in our model to take advantage of the effectiveness of residual mapping. However, because the proposed network is shallow, we assume that the vanishing and exploding gradient problems (addressed in deep CNNs) are insignificant. Our experiments show that residual mapping is not only effective in deep networks, but also useful for enhancing the performance of shallower networks.

2.3 Filter Factorization

In [12], simple techniques were used to reduce the parameters in convolution filters. $n \times n$ convolution was decomposed into $n \times 1$ and $1 \times n$ convolution. For example, factorizing 3×3 convolution filters into 3×1 and 1×3 convolution filters saves 33% of parameters [12].

3 Proposed Method

In this section we present nonlinear logarithmic filter grouping and residual identity connections in the shallow CNN architecture.

3.1 Nonlinear Logarithmic Filter Grouping in Convolution Layers

It is known that human perception is nonlinearly related to external stimuli [15], and is formulated by Weber-Fechner law. The law states that the degree of subjective sensation is proportional to the logarithm of the stimulus intensity, and it can be used to explain auditory and visual systems in humans [19, 20].

We apply this concept of nonlinear perception relation to the aforementioned hierarchical filter groups. In CNNs, convolution filters are supposed to be learned to deliver best responses for input images (or maps). In our method, filters are grouped nonlinearly to assign each filter group with different capacity (e.g., the number of filter or channel size) (refer to Fig. 1). We expect this nonlinear filter grouping could capture the nonlinear nature in the filter distribution (example shown in Fig. 2).

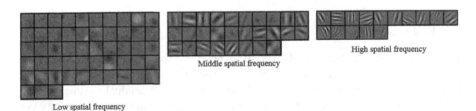

Middle spatial frequency

High spatial frequency

Low spatial frequency

Fig. 2. Filter distribution of the first convolutional layer of AlexNet in the viewpoint of spatial frequency [18]. Note that CNN filters are not distributed uniformly and they could not be grouped linearly into low, middle and high spatial frequency filter categories. Among 96 filters in the first convolution layer, the number of filters of each spatial frequency filter category is approximately 53, 28, and 15, which shows a logarithmic like distribution with an approximate base number 2.

Figure 2 shows the nonlinear distribution of the spatial frequency of filters in AlexNet. The nonlinear nature may also contain phase, color distributions etc. In this paper, we consider the number of filters along the spatial frequency to show the nonlinear nature of filters. As shown in Fig. 2, CNN filters are not distributed uniformly. Instead, they show a nonlinear distribution. In the first convolution layer of AlexNet, among 96 filters in that convolution layer, the numbers of filters of three filter categories (low, middle and high spatial frequency filter categories) are approximately 53, 28, and 15, respectively.

Typical filter grouping for reducing parameters divides the original full convolution filters into n filter groups with identical channel size [11]. Our nonlinear filter grouping divides the full convolution filters into filter groups with different channel sizes according to nonlinear grouping.

The proposed nonlinear filter grouping uses logarithmic scales with base number 2 to decide the size of each filter group in a convolution layer. A convolution layer has input and output channel depth of c_{in} and c_{out}. If the number of filter groups is n, then the set of filter shapes of a convolution layer with the logarithmic filter grouping would be

$$\left\{ h \times w \times \frac{c_{in}}{2^i} \times \frac{c_{out}}{2^i} \middle| i = 1, 2, 3, \ldots, n-2, n-1, n-1 \right\}, \qquad (1)$$

where h and w are height and width size of filters, respectively. When the input and output channel depth are identical, denoted by c, all logarithmic filter group sizes in a convolution layer are uniquely defined by c and n, for given filter size h and w. Channel depth of each filter group would be

$$\left[\frac{c}{2^1}, \frac{c}{2^2}, \frac{c}{2^3}, \ldots, \frac{c}{2^{n-2}}, \frac{c}{2^{n-1}}, \frac{c}{2^{n-1}} \right] \qquad (2)$$

We denote Eq. (2) as g, which is the filter group size array.

If the value of n is too large to divide the filter groups in logarithmic scale (e.g. $n = 16$ and $c = 128$), we divide the selected filter groups into 2 filter groups with identical size. This process is repeated to create n filter groups. Table 1 shows nonlinear logarithmic filter grouping scheme (with different filter group number n and the filter group size array g) in shallow CNN networks (3 convolution layers), which are evaluated in the experiments. In Table 1, we show three types of Filter grouping scheme (called Logarithmic-4, Logarithmic-8, and Logarithmic-16) which are deployed to shallow (3 convolution layers) CNNs.

3.2   Convolution Module with Logarithmic Filter Grouping

To build efficient shallow CNN, we employ residual identity connection on top of the nonlinear logarithmic filter grouping. When the target feature map and the feature map from identity shortcut have the same dimension, shortcut connection is the identity connection. When the channel depth of both feature maps are different, shortcut connection with 1×1 convolution could be used, but it is proven less effective [1].

Table 1. Nonlinear logarithmic filter grouping scheme for shallow (3 convolution layers) CNNs for experiment. Note that the logarithmic filter grouping is performed in convolution layer 2 and 3. Layer 2 and layer 3 have channel depths of 128 and 256, respectively.

Filter grouping scheme	Layer index	Filter group number (n)	Filter group size array (g)
Logarithmic-4	Layer 2	4	[64, 32, 16, 16]
	Layer 3	2	[128, 128]
Logarithmic-8	Layer 2	8	[64, 32, 16, 8, 4, 2, 1, 1]
	Layer 3	4	[128, 64, 32, 32]
Logarithmic-16	Layer 2	16	[32, 16, 16, 8, 8, 8, 8, 4, 4, 4, 4, 4, 2, 1, 1]
	Layer 3	8	[128, 64, 32, 16, 8, 4, 2, 2]

We denote 'logarithmic group convolution module' which consists of one 1×1 convolution layer and one $m \times m$ convolution layer to incorporate the residual identity shortcut into the shallow CNN. The 1×1 convolution expands the channel depth of the feature maps before the $m \times m$ convolution to equalize the input and output feature map dimension. This way identity shortcut connection can be applied. In addition, the 1×1 convolution learns a combination of the filter groups of the previous convolution layer [11].

In this paper, without loss of generality, we further reduce filter coefficients by factorization. We factorize the $m \times m$ convolution into $1 \times m$ and $m \times 1$ distinct convolutions. Filter grouping is applied to these $1 \times m$ and $m \times 1$ convolutions. ReLU activation function is used after each factorized convolution to increase the non-linearity in the network, and all activation functions are kept within the shortcut bypassing the convolution layers. General description of a logarithmic group convolution module is in Fig. 3.

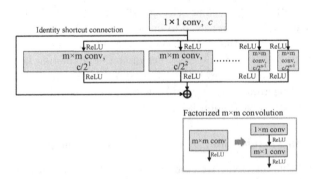

Fig. 3. Example of a logarithmic group convolution module with filter group number n. c indicates the output channel depth. The channel size of each filter group follows the general rule shown in Eq. (2)

4 Experiments

We demonstrate the effectiveness of the proposed logarithmic filter grouping in two different classification tasks. One is facial expression recognition (FER) using Multi-PIE dataset, and the other is object classification using CIFAR-10 dataset.

In order to evaluate the proposed logarithmic filter grouping, we devise compact CNN models which use the proposed logarithmic group convolution module in convolution layers. The shallow network structure we used in experiment was 3 convolution layers-CNN. We applied the filter grouping into 2nd and 3rd convolution layer with the filter grouping scheme seen in Table 1. Figure 4 is an example of the shallow CNN which employs Logarithmic-8 scheme in Table 1.

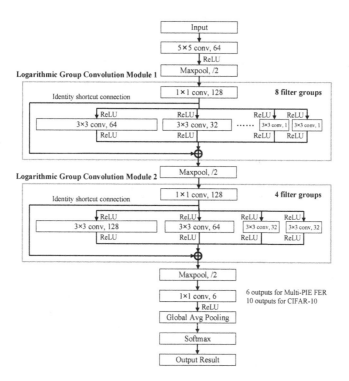

Fig. 4. Example of the shallow CNN model used in experiments, which employed the proposed logarithmic group convolution module ($L = 3$, $n = 8$, Logarithmic-8 in Table 1). Note that factorized convolutions are used for the 3×3 convolutions within the logarithmic group convolution modules.

The CNN is composed of three parts. First part is a convolution layer of filter size 5×5 that expands the channel depth to 64. Second part is convolution modules with filter groups. A 3×3 convolution is used for each module (i.e. 1×3 and 3×1 convolutions), and each module has 128 and 256 output channel depth respectively.

Max pooling layers are used to decrease spatial resolution of feature maps. Third part is the classification layer. Instead of a fully connected layer, 1×1 convolution with global average pooling is used as suggested in [21], and a final softmax layer performs classification.

There are three hyperparameters in this network. One is the number of layers L. We regard one convolution module as one layer in experiments. Another hyperparameter is the filter group number n. Filter group number indicates the degree of grouping in one convolution module. Here, we follow the filter group number decision rule which is shown effective in [11], which is reducing the degree of grouping by half as the depth increases. The other hyperparameter is the filter group size array g, which denotes the size of each filter group. This is used to define the nonlinear filter grouping scheme described in Eq. (2).

4.1   Experiment for FER

Dataset. The database we used in the experiments for FER is Multi-PIE dataset, which is originally a face recognition dataset containing more than 750,000 images of 337 subjects in 20 illumination conditions taken from 15 different angles [16]. The dataset contains six facial expressions (neutral, smile, squint, disgust, surprise, scream), and we selected 20,676 images for training and 5,224 images for testing, total 25,900 images. Facial regions were aligned according to the eye centers, cropped and resized to 64×64 pixels. For facial alignment, landmark detection method described in [22] was used.

Training images were augmented using rotation ($[-7°,-5,-3°,-1°,1°,3°,5°,7°]$), translation ($[-3,3]$ with 1 pixel step) and scaling ($[0.90,1.10]$ with 0.05 step) The total augmented training images are 640,956 images. 5,224 test images were used for testing the trained network. For data preprocessing, each channel of the cropped input images was normalized to have a zero mean and unit variance.

Training Details. In training the shallow network, all networks were trained using Adam optimizer [23]. Parameters for the optimizer were set to default values as suggested in [23] (beta1 = 0.9, beta2 = 0.999, epsilon = 10^{-8}). Learning rate was kept constant to 0.0001 throughout the learning process, and the model was trained for 30 epochs with mini batch size of 128. For loss, standard cross entropy loss was used.

Evaluation of Multi-PIE FER result. The results of Multi-PIE FER on the proposed shallow CNN are presented in Table 2.

The baseline network of the experiment has the same compact structure (i.e., same layer depth, factorized convolution and global average pooling for a compact network) as in Fig. 4, but without filter grouping and residual identity shortcut in convolution modules. In shallow CNN, it is observed that the FER accuracy decreases compared to that of the no filter grouping as the degree of uniform filter grouping increases. This shows that applying filter groups to shallow networks could achieve smaller parameters while degrading the performance. The question is: Can the proposed logarithmic filter grouping reduce the performance degradation?

Table 2. Total parameter size of the compact CNNs and associated classification accuracy (%) on Multi-PIE FER dataset. Uniform-n uses uniform filter grouping with filter group number n in the convolution modules and Logarithmic-n uses nonlinear logarithmic group convolution modules with the grouping scheme defined in Table 1. Uniform-n w/o shortcut has the same network structure as Uniform-n, but without residual identity shortcut. Among filter grouping schemes, the best performance is indicated in **bold**, and the best parameter efficiency is in blue. Note that logarithmic-8 shows small 0.2% accuracy drop compared to uniform-4, while having 53,000 (20%) less parameters than uniform-4. Also, logarithmic-4 presents similar performance to the baseline while having 50% less parameters compared to the baseline.

Filter grouping scheme	Classification accuracy on Multi-PIE FER (%)	Accuracy drop (%)	Total Parameters
Uniform-4 w/o shortcut	86.54	0.48	268,480
Uniform-8 w/o shortcut	85.18	1.84	157,888
Uniform-16 w/o shortcut	84.67	2.35	102,592
Uniform-4	86.81	0.21	268,480
Uniform-8	85.70	1.32	157,888
Uniform-16	85.13	1.89	102,592
Logarithmic-4	**86.98**	**0.04**	**277,696**
Logarithmic-8	86.59	0.43	215,236
Logarithmic-16	86.20	0.82	190,036
No filter grouping (baseline)	87.02	-	543,616

The results in Table 2 indicate that the networks with the logarithmic filter grouping show better classification accuracy than those with the uniform filter grouping when the filter group numbers are the same. For example, logarithmic-8 achieved about 0.9% higher accuracy compared to uniform-8. This might seem natural as more parameters are used for networks with logarithmic filter groups. However, when comparing logarithmic-8 to uniform-4, we can observe that logarithmic-8 has 53,000 fewer parameters than uniform-4, yet shows modest 0.2% drop in performance. 53,000 parameters take about 10% of the baseline parameter. Regarding uniform-4 has already reduced half of the parameters from the original baseline network, we can still further reduce 10% of the total parameters in the shallow network with a reasonably small loss in performance.

Logarithmic-4 also shows improved accuracy and it presents similar performance compared to the baseline while having 50% less parameters. Logarithmic-4 and 16 both showed improved performance, but considering the number of parameters the accuracy increase is not as large as logarithmic-8. Logarithmic-4 uses the logarithmic filter grouping only in layer 2 according to the grouping scheme we defined, and this might not be enough to reflect the nonlinearity in all filters in the network. Adding to this, it can be interpreted that the filter nonlinearity of the shallow network trained with Multi-PIE FER dataset is best represented by the filter grouping scheme of logarithmic-8.

The residual identity shortcut is also shown to be effective in the shallow CNN. For all networks with uniform filter grouping, the accuracy increased when convolution module with identity shortcut was used.

4.2   Experiment for Object Classification

Dataset. CIFAR-10 dataset [17] contains color images of different objects, with 32×32 pixels each. There are 10 classes, and the training and test sets consist of 50,000 and 10,000 images. Each class has 6,000 images. We followed the standard data augmentation scheme used in [1, 21, 24–26] for training: images are padded by 4 pixels on each side, and a random 32×32 crop is sampled from the padded image or its horizontal flip. For testing, we used the 10,000 test images without alterations.

Training Details. Adam optimizer was used with the same parameters as in FER experiment with different learning rate. Learning rate was kept constant to 0.001 until 100 epochs, and halved at 100 epochs, dropped down to 0.0001 at 140 epochs, and halved at 160 epochs and kept constant up to 180 epochs. Mini batch size of 128 was used and standard cross entropy loss was also used.

Table 3. Total parameter size of the compact CNNs and associated classification accuracy (%) on CIFAR-10 dataset. Each network has the same structure as described in Table 2. Number of parameters of each network is increased by 1024 due to the additional 4 classes in CIFAR-10 compared to Multi-PIE FER. Among filter grouping schemes, the best performance is indicated in **bold**, and the best parameter efficiency is in blue. Note that logarithmic-8 shows better performance than uniform-4, while having 20% less parameters than uniform-4.

Filter grouping scheme	Classification accuracy on CIFAR-10 (%)	Accuracy drop (%)	Total Parameters
Uniform-4 w/o shortcut	85.27	1.79	269,504
Uniform-8 w/o shortcut	84.24	2.82	158,912
Uniform-16 w/o shortcut	83.19	3.87	103,616
Uniform-4	85.53	1.53	269,504
Uniform-8	84.54	2.52	158,912
Uniform-16	83.97	3.09	103,616
Logarithmic-4	85.62	1.44	278,720
Logarithmic-8	**85.79**	**1.27**	**216,260**
Logarithmic-16	85.09	1.97	191,060
No filter grouping (baseline)	87.06	-	544,640

Evaluation of CIFAR-10 Result. The results of CIFAR-10 object classification experiment displayed similar trend shown in FER experiment. The results are presented in Table 3.

Similar to the Multi-PIE FER result, the classification accuracy of CIFAR-10 drops as the degree of uniform filter grouping increases. Also, as shown before, the residual identity shortcut redeems the decreased accuracy due to filter grouping. The increase in accuracy is about 0.3% for all uniform-4, 8 and 16 networks which is similar amount compared to the previous experiment.

Overall, networks with the logarithmic filter grouping outperform networks with the uniform filter grouping, and the general improvement is larger than that of Multi-PIE FER. One noticeable observation is that the accuracy of logarithmic-8 is even better than uniform-4, while having 53,000 fewer parameters. Also, logarithmic-8 has slightly better performance compared to logarithmic-4. This result supports the idea that whilst having less parameter than logarithmic-4, logarithmic-8 better represents the nonlinear nature in the network trained with CIFAR-10.

5   Conclusion

We proposed a new filter grouping method which adapts the nonlinear logarithmic filter grouping. The logarithmic filter grouping divides the convolution layer filters in logarithmic sizes, and this grouping scheme reflects the nonlinear nature in filter distribution. To apply the proposed method to shallow CNN structure, we devised a shallow network with logarithmic group convolution modules. This module allows us to use both logarithmic filter grouping and residual identity shortcut in the shallow CNN.

To validate the effectiveness of our method in shallow networks, the suggested shallow CNN with three different logarithmic filter grouping schemes were tested with Multi-PIE FER and CIFAR-10 object classification. The results showed that all networks with the logarithmic filter grouping schemes outperformed the same networks with uniform filter grouping in both experiments. From the parameter point of view, the logarithmic filter grouping could further reduce the number of parameters while maintaining or enhancing the performance compared to the uniform filter grouping. The residual identity shortcut is also shown effective in the shallow CNN, presenting slight increase in performance compared to networks with no identity shortcuts.

The proposed logarithmic filter grouping and shallow CNN can help reducing network sizes for mobile applications with constrained conditions. Further work on deciding different nonlinear filter grouping schemes may help increasing the efficiency of shallow CNNs even more. As a future work, we are going to apply the proposed logarithmic filter grouping to deep networks to show its usefulness in parameter reduction for deep networks.

Acknowledgment. This work was supported by Institute for Information & communications Technology Promotion(IITP) grant funded by the Korea government(MSIT) (No.2017-0-00111, Practical technology development of high performing emotion recognition and facial expression based authentication using deep network).

References

1. He, K., Zhang, X., Ren, S., Sun, J.: Deep residual learning for image recognition. In: Proceedings of the IEEE Conference on Computer Vision and Pattern Recognition, pp. 770–778 (2016)
2. Taigman, Y., Yang, M., Ranzato, M.A., Wolf, L.: DeepFace: closing the gap to human-level performance in face verification. In: Proceedings of the IEEE Conference on Computer Vision and Pattern Recognition, pp. 1701–1708 (2014)
3. Szegedy, C., Liu, W., Jia, Y., Sermanet, P., Reed, S., Anguelov, D., Erhan, D., Vanhoucke, V., Rabinovich, A.: Going deeper with convolutions. In: Proceedings of the IEEE Conference on Computer Vision and Pattern Recognition, pp. 1–9 (2015)
4. Szegedy, C., Ioffe, S., Vanhoucke, V., Alemi, A.A.: Inception-v4, Inception-ResNet and the impact of residual connections on learning. In: AAAI, pp. 4278–4284 (2017)
5. Baddar, W.J., Kim, D.H., Ro, Y.M.: Learning features robust to image variations with siamese networks for facial expression recognition. In: Amsaleg, L., Guðmundsson, G.Þ., Gurrin, C., Jónsson, B.Þ., Satoh, S. (eds.) MMM 2017. LNCS, vol. 10132, pp. 189–200. Springer, Cham (2017). https://doi.org/10.1007/978-3-319-51811-4_16
6. Kim, D.H., Baddar, W., Jang, J., Ro, Y.M.: Multi-objective based spatio-temporal feature representation learning robust to expression intensity variations for facial expression recognition. IEEE Trans. Affect. Comput. (2017)
7. Howard, A.G., Zhu, M., Chen, B., Kalenichenko, D., Wang, W., Weyand, T., Andreetto, M., Adam, H.: MobileNets: efficient convolutional neural networks for mobile vision applications. arXiv preprint arXiv:1704.04861 (2017)
8. Ba, L.J., Caruana, R.: Do deep nets really need to be deep? In: Proceedings of the 27th International Conference on Neural Information Processing Systems, Montreal, Canada, pp. 2654–2662. MIT Press (2014)
9. McDonnell, M.D., Vladusich, T.: Enhanced image classification with a fast-learning shallow convolutional neural network. In: 2015 International Joint Conference on Neural Networks (IJCNN), pp. 1–7. IEEE (2015)
10. Kim, Y.-D., Park, E., Yoo, S., Choi, T., Yang, L., Shin, D.: Compression of deep convolutional neural networks for fast and low power mobile applications. arXiv preprint arXiv:1511.06530 (2015)
11. Ioannou, Y., Robertson, D., Cipolla, R., Criminisi, A.: Deep roots: improving CNN efficiency with hierarchical filter groups. arXiv preprint arXiv:1605.06489 (2016)
12. Szegedy, C., Vanhoucke, V., Ioffe, S., Shlens, J., Wojna, Z.: Rethinking the inception architecture for computer vision. In: Proceedings of the IEEE Conference on Computer Vision and Pattern Recognition, pp. 2818–2826 (2016)
13. Jaderberg, M., Vedaldi, A., Zisserman, A.: Speeding up convolutional neural networks with low rank expansions.
14. Lebedev, V., Ganin, Y., Rakhuba, M., Oseledets, I., Lempitsky, V.: Speeding-up convolutional neural networks using fine-tuned CP-decomposition. arXiv preprint arXiv: 1412.6553 (2014)
15. Fechner, G.: Elements of Psychophysics. vol. I. (1966)
16. Gross, R., Matthews, I., Cohn, J., Kanade, T., Baker, S.: Multi-pie. Image Vis. Comput. **28**, 807–813 (2010)
17. Krizhevsky, A., Hinton, G.: Learning multiple layers of features from tiny images (2009)
18. Krizhevsky, A., Sutskever, I., Hinton, G.E.: ImageNet classification with deep convolutional neural networks. In: Advances in Neural Information Processing Systems, pp. 1097–1105 (2012)

19. Yost, W.A.: Fundamentals of Hearing: An Introduction. Academic Press, Cambridge (1994)
20. Shen, J.: On the foundations of vision modeling: I. Weber's law and Weberized TV restoration. Phys. D: Nonlinear Phenom. **175**, 241–251 (2003)
21. Lin, M., Chen, Q., Yan, S.: Network in network. arXiv preprint arXiv:1312.4400 (2013)
22. Asthana, A., Zafeiriou, S., Cheng, S., Pantic, M.: Incremental face alignment in the wild. In: Proceedings of the IEEE Conference on Computer Vision and Pattern Recognition, pp. 1859–1866 (2014)
23. Kingma, D., Ba, J.: Adam: a method for stochastic optimization. arXiv preprint arXiv:1412.6980 (2014)
24. Huang, G., Sun, Y., Liu, Z., Sedra, D., Weinberger, K.Q.: Deep networks with stochastic depth. In: Leibe, B., Matas, J., Sebe, N., Welling, M. (eds.) ECCV 2016. LNCS, vol. 9908, pp. 646–661. Springer, Cham (2016). https://doi.org/10.1007/978-3-319-46493-0_39
25. Larsson, G., Maire, M., Shakhnarovich, G.: FractalNet: ultra-deep neural networks without residuals. arXiv preprint arXiv:1605.07648 (2016)
26. Srivastava, R.K., Greff, K., Schmidhuber, J.: Training very deep networks. In: Advances in Neural Information Processing Systems, pp. 2377–2385 (2015)

Cost-Sensitive Deep Metric Learning for Fine-Grained Image Classification

Junjie Zhao and Yuxin Peng[(⊠)]

Institute of Computer Science and Technology, Peking University, Beijing, China
{zhaojunjie,pengyuxin}@pku.edu.cn

Abstract. Fine-grained image classification aims to classify hundreds of subcategories which belong to the same basic-level category. The confusion degrees among different subcategories are extremely different, and we should focus on learning the difference among the confusing subcategories. However, current methods treat all subcategories by equal cost, which causes the learned model good power for classifying subcategories that are not easy to confuse, but limited power for confusing ones. For addressing the above problem, we propose a cost-sensitive deep metric learning (CDML) approach, which integrates confusion driven deep metric learning and weighted softmax for learning the difference among the confusing subcategories. *Confusion driven deep metric learning* is proposed to focus on learning the difference among subcategories with small variance emphatically via triplet loss. The sampled ratio for triplets between two subcategories is adaptively and automatically set by confusing degrees, where the confusing subcategories are over-sampled for improving the ability to distinguish them. *Weighted softmax* is proposed to learn more discriminative features for easily mis-classification subcategories, which are assigned with high weights on them according to their mis-classification rates. Comparing with state-of-the-art methods on the CUB-200-2011 dataset, our CDML approach achieves the best classification accuracy.

Keywords: Fine-grained image classification · Cost-sensitive
Deep metric learning · Weighted softmax

1 Introduction

Fine-grained image classification is very important with wide applications, such as image search, biological conservation and medical image analysis. Compared with the basic-level image classification, fine-grained image classification is more difficult, which aims at recognizing hundreds of subcategories belonging to the same basic-level categories, such as recognizing 200 subcategories belonging to bird [1]. Its main challenge is the small variance among different similar subcategories, as shown in Fig. 1. For example, the *Caspian Tern* and the *Common Tern* are different subcategories with similarity in color and pose, which is extremely difficult to distinguish even for human beings.

© Springer International Publishing AG 2018
K. Schoeffmann et al. (Eds.): MMM 2018, Part I, LNCS 10704, pp. 130–141, 2018.
https://doi.org/10.1007/978-3-319-73603-7_11

Fig. 1. Samples of variance among different subcategories. The subcategories on both sides of green arrows are similar with each other, while those on both side of red arrows are dissimilar with each other. (Color figure online)

Over the past years, many methods for fine-grained image classification have been proposed. Early methods [2–4] mainly pay attention to the discriminative hand-crafted features design. Berg and Belhumeur [2] propose a part-based one-vs-one features to learn a diverse set of highly discriminative intermediate features. Xie *et al.* [3] extend the Bag-of-Features model via introducing hierarchical structure learning and geometric phrase pooling to make full use of the part information and train a robust model. With the rapid development of deep learning, many CNN-based methods [5–7] are proposed and achieve good performance recently. Branson *et al.* [7] propose to generate an estimate of object's pose, and then extract features for image patches from multiple layers of a deep convolutional network. Lin *et al.* [8] propose a deep LAC framework integrating three networks, where localization network provides part position, alignment network outputs pose-aligned part images and classification network learns the final classifier via pose-aligned parts. However, these methods rely on the annotations of object or parts, which are the heavy labor consuming. Weakly supervised setting, meaning that neither object nor parts annotations are used in training or testing phase, is adopted in most current methods, while these methods still achieve promising performance. He and Peng [9] and Simon and Rodner [10] mainly pay attention to learning discriminative object and part detectors automatically, which obtain approximate effect with utilizing the object and parts annotations. While Lin *et al.* [11] and Wang *et al.* [12] focus on the structures of networks to learn more discriminative feature representations without using object or parts in their proposed methods.

However, the confusion degrees among different subcategories are extremely different, for example, it is more confusing for *Fish Crow* and *American Crow* than *American Crow* and *Common Tern*. Considering that the small variance among different subcategories only exists in a few subsets of all subcategories, it is vital to learn the highly confusing and easily mis-classification subcategories with more costs, which helps learn more information about these subcategories and improve the ability to distinguish them. However, current methods treat all subcategories by equal cost, which leads the learned model good power for classifying subcategories that are not easy to confuse, but limited power for the confusing ones. For addressing the above problem, this paper proposes a cost-sensitive deep metric learning (CDML) approach for fine-grained image classification. The main contributions of our CDML approach can be summarized as follows:

- **Confusion driven deep metric learning.** There are only a few subsets of all subcategories are extremely similar to distinguish, which mainly causes the difficulty to classify. Therefore, we propose a confusion driven deep metric learning via triplet loss to enhance the distinguish ability of the model for these confusing subcategories. These confusing subcategories are over-sampled, where the sampled ratios for triplets are adaptively and automatically set by their confusing degrees, which improves the ability to distinguish these confusing subcategories.
- **Weighted softmax.** Considering that some subcategories are easier to be incorrectly classified than the others, the weighted softmax is proposed to focus on learning the discriminative features for easily mis-classification subcategories. These mis-classification subcategories are assigned with high weights on them, which enhances representation ability of the learned model to these hard subcategories and reduces their mis-classification probability.

The rest of this paper is organized as follows: Sect. 2 presents cost-sensitive deep metric learning (CDML) approach, and Sect. 3 shows the experimental results and analyses. Finally, Sect. 4 concludes this paper.

2   Cost-Sensitive Deep Metric Learning

2.1   Overview

In this section, we present our cost-sensitive deep metric learning (CDML) approach for fine-grained image classification. An overview of our proposed CDML approach is shown as Fig. 2. Our CDML approach first generates a confusion matrix, and then learns the discriminative feature representations via deep metric learning and weighted softmax. It consists of two main components: (1) Confusion driven deep metric learning. It focuses on the difference between highly similar and confusing subcategories, which utilizes triplet tuples to measure the relationship of these subcategories, and the confusing subcategories are over-sampled for improving the ability to distinguish them. (2) Weighted softmax. It enhances the representations ability of the learned model to easily mis-classification subcategories, where the harder subcategories are assigned with higher weights according to their mis-classification rates for putting more costs on them.

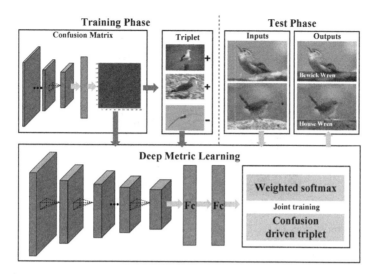

Fig. 2. An overview of our proposed CDML approach. Our CDML first generates a confusion matrix, and then jointly learns confusion driven triplet and weighted softmax. Confusion driven deep metric learning enhances to distinguish the difference between two confusing subcategories, while weighted softmax puts more costs and learn more discriminative feature representations to the easily mis-classification subcategories.

2.2   Confusion Driven Deep Metric Learning

Confusion Analysis. Small variance among different subcategories only exists in a few subsets of all subcategories, which causes these subcategories more confusing to distinguish than others. It is vital to learn the highly confusing and easily mis-classification subcategories, which helps learn more discriminative and subtle features. In order to obtain the confusion degrees among different subcategories, we calculate the confusion matrix. Confusion matrix, known as an error matrix, shows more clear results of correct and incorrect classification for each subcategory. Each row of the matrix corresponds to a ground truth label, while each column represents the prediction score.

In order to obtain the confusion matrix $C \in R^{k \times k}$, where k is the amount of subcategories L, and C_{ij} donates the probability that images labeled L_i are classified to L_j, we first partition the original training set into two parts: new training set and validation set. Then, CNN model is fine-tuned on the new training set and test on the validation set. Finally, confusion matrix C is calculated based on the predicted results of validation set as follow:

$$C_{ij} = \frac{card(\{I_k \mid gt(I_k) = L_i, p(I_k) = L_j, I_k \in V\})}{card(\{I_k \mid gt(I_k) = L_i, I_k \in V\})}, \tag{1}$$

where, $gt(I_k)$ and $p(I_k)$ donate the ground truth and predicted subcategories for image I_k, $card(\cdot)$ donates the count of elements, and V donates the validation set. The confusion matrix on CUB-200-2011 [1] dataset is shown in Fig. 3, and

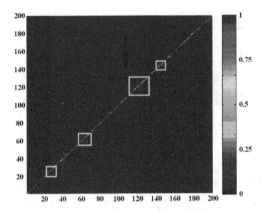

Fig. 3. Confusion matrix on CUB-200-2011 dataset. Subcategories in the yellow square are similar and confused with each other. (Color figure online)

we can observe that only a few subsets of all subcategories are extremely similar to distinguish, while others not. It is natural to learn emphatically for these similar and confusing subcategories.

Confusion Driven Deep Metric Learning. As illustrated in Fig. 2, our CDML approach proposes the confusion driven deep metric learning to learn the difference among highly confusing subcategories emphatically. All triplet tuples are donated as $T = \{<T_i^o, T_i^+, T_i^->\}_i^t$, where T_i^o and T_i^+ are two images belonging to the same subcategories, while T_i^- is from another different subcategory, and t is the number of triplet tuples. Given a triplet tuple $T_i = <T_i^o, T_i^+, T_i^->$, the triplet loss function requires the distance of subcategories pair $<T_i^o, T_i^+>$ be smaller than the pair $<T_i^o, T_i^->$ by a margin m, and minimizes the following triplet regularization term to achieve this requirement:

$$\mathcal{J}(<T_i^o, T_i^+, T_i^->) = \max(0, m + d(\phi(T_i^o), \phi(T_i^+)) - d(\phi(T_i^o), \phi(T_i^-)), \quad (2)$$

$$d(\phi(T_i^o), \phi(T_i^+)) = ||\phi(T_i^o) - \phi(T_i^+)||^2, \quad (3)$$

$$d(\phi(T_i^o), \phi(T_i^-)) = ||\phi(T_i^o) - \phi(T_i^-)||^2, \quad (4)$$

where $|| \cdot ||^2$ donates the L_2-norm distance, and $\phi(\cdot)$ donates the learned feature via CNN model. Then, to focus on learning the difference among similar and confusing subcategories, the number of sampled triplet tuples between two different subcategories is adaptively and automatically set by their confusion degrees. Given the total amount of triplet tuples t, we just need to obtain the triplet distribution matrix $M \in R^{k*k}$, where M_{ij} donates the probability of the triplet tuples made up of the two subcategories L_i and L_j, and the final number of triplet tuples for L_i and L_j is $t * M_{ij}$. The detailed process for calculating M is shown in Algorithm 1, where the confusing subcategory pairs are over-sampled for improving the ability to distinguish them, while other subcategory pairs are sampled normally to ensure the model can also distinguish them.

Algorithm 1. Triplet Distribution Matrix

Input: Confusion matrix C, the number of subcategories k.
Output: Triplet distribution matrix M.
1: Initialize $M = C$.
2: Set $M = M + \epsilon$ to ensure that the sampled triplet tuples can cover all subcategory pairs, where $\epsilon = \min(M)/2$ in our experiments.
3: Get the principal diagonal element of confusion matrix $E = diag(M_{11}, M_{22}, ..., M_{kk})$.
4: Set $M = M - E$ to avoid three images of triplet tuple belonging to the same subcategories.
5: **for** $i = 1 : k$ **do**
6:     **for** $j = 1 : k$ **do**
7:         Set $M_{ij} = \frac{M_{ij}}{\sum_{l=1}^{n} M_{il}}$ to normalize M and avoid the number of some subcategories being too less to learn the feature representations.
8:     **end for**
9: **end for**
10: **return** M.

2.3 Weighted Softmax

Considering that some subcategories are easier to be incorrectly classified than the others, which can be also observed in Fig. 3, it is important to learn the discriminative features for easily mis-classification subcategories. Therefore, we propose the weighted softmax to enhance the representation ability for these hard subcategories with more costs according to the mis-classification rates.

Given the output value of the last fully-connected layer $f(I_i, L_i)$ for image I_i and subcategory L_i, the original softmax loss function is defined as the sum of negative log-likelihood over training images set I and subcategories L:

$$softmax(I, L) = \frac{1}{n} \sum_{i=1}^{n} -log(s_i^{(L_i)}), \tag{5}$$

$$s_i^{(L_i)} = \frac{e_{f(I_i, L_i)}}{\sum_{j=1}^{k} e_{f(I_i, L_j)}}, \tag{6}$$

where n donates the number of training images. The softmax loss can effectively measure the gap between the predicted subcategories and the labeled subcategories. However, it pays equally attention to all subcategories, which causes the learned features limited power for those easily mis-classification subcategories. Therefore, we propose a weighted softmax loss to handle the problem. First, we get the mis-classification probability $W \in R^k$ of the subcategories:

$$W_i = \sum_{j=1, j \neq i}^{k} C_{ij}. \tag{7}$$

And, the weighted softmax loss is defined as follow:

$$weighted\_softmax(I, L) = \frac{1}{n} \sum_{i=1}^{n} -W_i * log(s_i^{(L_i)}) \tag{8}$$

$$s_i^{(L_i)} = \frac{\frac{1}{k} * e_{f(I_i, L_i)}}{\sum_{j=1}^{k} M_{ij} * e_{f(I_i, L_j)}}. \tag{9}$$

Our proposed weighted softmax loss can enhance the representation ability to the easily mis-classification subcategories via putting more costs to these hard subcategories than others.

Finally, our proposed CDML jointly optimizes confusion driven deep metric learning and weighted softmax, where confusion driven deep metric learning pays attention to distinguish confusing subcategories, while weighted softmax enhances the representation ability of the model for the easily mis-classification subcategories.

3 Experiments

Experiments are performed on widely-used CUB-200-2011 [1] dataset for fine-grained image classification. More than 10 state-of-the-art methods are compared to verify the effectiveness of our CDML approach.

3.1 Dataset and Evaluation Metric

CUB-200-2011 [1] dataset is competitive and widely-used for fine-grained image classification. The dataset contains 11788 images of 200 different bird subcategories, which consists of 5994 images for training and 5794 images for test. There are roughly 30 training and test images for each subcategory. All images are annotated with image-level subcategory labels, object bounding boxes and part landmarks. We use the weakly supervised setting in the experiments, meaning only image-level subcategory label is used in the training and test phases of our CDML approach.

Accuracy is adopted to evaluate the classification performance of our CDML approach and compared methods. Accuracy is a widely-used evaluation metric for fine-grained image classification [13,14], which is defined as follow:

$$Acc = \frac{card(R_a)}{card(R)}, \tag{10}$$

where $card(R)$ donates the size of test set, and $card(R_a)$ donates the amount of correctly classified images in test phase.

Table 1. Comparisons with state-of-the-art methods on CUB-200-2011 dataset.

Method	Train annotation		Test annotation		Accuracy (%)	Net
	Object	Parts	Object	Parts		
Our CDML approach					84.88	VGGNet
STN [18]					84.10	GoogleNet
Bilinear-CNN [11]					84.10	VGGNet&VGG-M
Multi-grained [12]					81.70	VGGNet
NAC [10]					81.01	VGGNet
PIR [14]					79.34	VGGNet
TL atten [13]					77.90	VGGNet
MIL [19]					77.40	VGGNet
MTL-H [20]					76.66	VGGNet
NASA [21]					75.36	VGGNet
IFVVA [4]					50.59	
Coarse-to-fine [22]	✓		✓		82.90	VGGNet
PG alignment [23]	✓		✓		82.80	VGGNet
VGG-BGLm [24]	✓		✓		80.40	VGGNet
Webly-supervised [25]	✓	✓			78.60	AlexNet
PN-CNN [7]	✓	✓			75.70	AlexNet
Part-based R-CNN [26]	✓	✓			73.50	AlexNet
Deep LAC [8]	✓	✓	✓		84.10	AlexNet
PS-CNN [27]	✓	✓	✓		76.20	AlexNet
Part-based R-CNN [26]	✓	✓	✓	✓	76.37	AlexNet
POOF [2]	✓	✓	✓	✓	73.30	
GPP [3]	✓	✓	✓	✓	66.35	

3.2   Details of Implementation

We apply the widely-used 19-layer VGGNet [15] with batch normalization [16] as the basic CNN model. First, we pre-train the CNN model on 1.3M images of ImageNet 1k dataset [17]. Then, we use training set to fine-tune the pre-trained CNN model, and use validation set, which is half of the original training set, to generate confusion matrix. Finally, training and validation sets are used to fine-tune the pre-trained CNN model via jointly optimizing the proposed confusion driven deep metric learning and weighted softmax.

3.3   Comparisons with State-of-the-Art Methods

We present the classification performance of our CDML approach in Table 1, as well as the compared state-of-the-art methods. For comparing fairly and clearly, the detailed usage of object and parts annotations in both training and test phases are listed, as well as the type of used CNN model.

Early methods [2,3] mainly choose hand-crafted features to train a classifier, but not achieve good classification performance. The usage of CNN models improves the performance for fine-grained image classification dramatically.

Many CNN-based methods [10] pay attention to learning discriminative object and part detectors, and other methods [11,18] focus on the structures of networks to learn more discriminative feature representations. However, these methods pay equally attention to all subcategories, which causes the learned model good power for classifying subcategories that are not easy to confuse but limited power for confusing ones. Our CDML approach proposes a confusion driven deep metric learning, which can learn the difference among similar and easily confusing subcategories and enhance the distinguish ability for them.

In addition, some methods [12] are proposed to learn multiple granularity descriptors to focus on learning the difference among different subcategories belonging to the same coarse-grained subcategory in the taxonomic tree. However, these methods adopt external prior knowledge, such as the taxonomic tree. Our CDML approach puts more costs on the easily mis-classification subcategories via the weighted softmax, which helps achieve more discriminative representation ability to the hard subcategories and better classification performance.

Moreover, compared with those strongly supervised methods which use the annotations of object [22,23] or even parts [8,25], our CDML approach achieves better classification performance due to the effectiveness of jointly optimizing the confusion driven deep metric learning and weighted softmax.

3.4   Effectiveness of Components

Our CDML approach mainly consists of two components: confusion driven deep metric learning and weighted softmax. The classification performance of the components in our CDML approach are presented in Table 2. "Baseline" denotes the result without utilizing confusion driven deep metric learning and weighted softmax. From Table 2, we can observe that:

- Confusion driven deep metric learning improves the classification accuracy via over-sampling the triplets between the confusing subcategories and learning the difference among them emphatically, which benefits to distinguish the highly confusing subcategories. It improves 1.41% compared with the result of "Baseline" on CUB-200-2011 dataset.
- Weighted softmax enhances the representation ability to the easily mis-classification subcategories and improves the classification performance via putting more costs on the hard subcategories. It improves 1.20% compared with the result of "Baseline".
- Jointly optimizing the confusion driven deep metric learning and weighted softmax can regularize and boost the two tasks to ensure feature representations discriminative, which improves 1.04% improvement compared with the confusion driven deep metric learning and 1.35% improvement compared with the weighted softmax. And the final classification performance is also shown in Fig. 4.

Table 2. Performance of components in our CDML approach.

Method	Accuracy (%)
CDML (Ours)	**84.88**
Confusion driven deep metric learning (Ours)	83.74
Weighted softmax (Ours)	83.53
Baseline	82.33

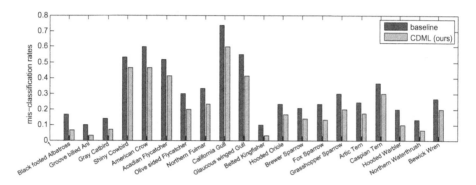

Fig. 4. Classification results of 20 subcategories on CUB-200-2011 dataset. Y-coordinate donates the mis-classification rate, while the shorter bar is the better.

4   Conclusion

In this paper, the cost-sensitive deep metric learning (CDML) approach has been proposed for fine-grained image classification. First, our CDML approach generates a confusion matrix only using training data. Then, our CDML approach proposes the confusion driven deep metric learning for improving the ability to model the difference among the similar and confusing subcategories emphatically. Simultaneously, the weighted softmax is proposed to enhance the representation ability of the model for the easily mis-classification subcategories. Finally, the above two components are jointly optimized to regularize and boost each other, and it achieves the improvement for fine-grained image classification. The future work lies in two aspects: first, we intend to update the confusion matrix automatically in our approach; second, we will experiment on more datasets and apply CDML to other applications like image search to further verify its effectiveness.

Acknowledgments. This work was supported by National Natural Science Foundation of China under Grant 61771025 and Grant 61532005.

References

1. Wah, C., Branson, S., Welinder, P., Perona, P., Belongie, S.: The Caltech-UCSD Birds-200-2011 Dataset (2011)
2. Berg, T., Belhumeur, P.: Poof: part-based one-vs.-one features for fine-grained categorization, face verification, and attribute estimation. In: Proceedings of the IEEE Conference on Computer Vision and Pattern Recognition (CVPR), pp. 955–962 (2013)
3. Xie, L., Tian, Q., Hong, R., Yan, S., Zhang, B.: Hierarchical part matching for fine-grained visual categorization. In: Proceedings of the International Conference on Computer Vision (ICCV), pp. 1641–1648 (2013)
4. Xie, L., Wang, J., Zhang, B., Tian, Q.: Incorporating visual adjectives for image classification. Neurocomputing **182**, 48–55 (2016)
5. Zhao, B., Wu, X., Feng, J., Peng, Q., Yan, S.: Diversified visual attention networks for fine-grained object classification. IEEE Trans. Multimedia (TMM) **19**(6), 1245–1256 (2017)
6. He, X., Peng, Y.: Fine-graind image classification via combining vision and language. In: Proceedings of the IEEE Conference on Computer Vision and Pattern Recognition (CVPR), pp. 5994–6002 (2017)
7. Branson, S., Van Horn, G., Belongie, S., Perona, P.: Bird species categorization using pose normalized deep convolutional nets, arXiv:1406.2952 (2014)
8. Lin, D., Shen, X., Lu, C., Jia, J.: Deep LAC: deep localization, alignment and classification for fine-grained recognition. In: Proceedings of the IEEE Conference on Computer Vision and Pattern Recognition (CVPR), pp. 1666–1674 (2015)
9. He, X., Peng, Y.: Weakly supervised learning of part selection model with spatial constraints for fine-grained image classification. In: Proceedings of the AAAI Conference on Artificial Intelligence (AAAI), pp. 4075–4081 (2017)
10. Simon, M., Rodner, E.: Neural activation constellations: unsupervised part model discovery with convolutional networks. In: International Conference of Computer Vision (ICCV), pp. 1143–1151 (2015)
11. Lin, T.-Y., RoyChowdhury, A., Maji, S.: Bilinear CNN models for fine-grained visual recognition. In: Proceedings of the International Conference on Computer Vision (ICCV), pp. 1449–1457 (2015)
12. Wang, D., Shen, Z., Shao, J., Zhang, W., Xue, X., Zhang, Z.: Multiple granularity descriptors for fine-grained categorization. In: Proceedings of the International Conference on Computer Vision (ICCV), pp. 2399–2406 (2015)
13. Xiao, T., Xu, Y., Yang, K., Zhang, J., Peng, Y., Zhang, Z.: The application of two-level attention models in deep convolutional neural network for fine-grained image classification. In: Proceedings of the IEEE Conference on Computer Vision and Pattern Recognition (CVPR), pp. 842–850 (2015)
14. Zhang, Y., Wei, X.-S., Wu, J., Cai, J., Lu, J., Nguyen, V.-A., Do, M.N.: Weakly supervised fine-grained categorization with part-based image representation. IEEE Trans. Image Process. (TIP) **25**(4), 1713–1725 (2016)
15. Simonyan, K., Vedaldi, A., Zisserman, A.: Deep inside convolutional networks: visualising image classification models and saliency maps, arXiv:1312.6034 (2013)
16. Ioffe, S., Szegedy, C.: Batch normalization: accelerating deep network training by reducing internal covariate shift, arXiv:1502.03167 (2015)
17. Deng, J., Dong, W., Socher, R., Li, L.-J., Li, K., Fei-Fei, L.: ImageNet: a large-scale hierarchical image database. In: Proceedings of the IEEE Conference on Computer Vision and Pattern Recognition (CVPR), pp. 248–255 (2009)

18. Jaderberg, M., Simonyan, K., Zisserman, A., et al.: Spatial transformer networks. In: Neural Information Processing Systems (NIPS), pp. 2017–2025 (2015)
19. Xu, Z., Tao, D., Huang, S., Zhang, Y.: Friend or foe: fine-grained categorization with weak supervision. IEEE Trans. Image Process. (TIP) **26**(1), 135–146 (2017)
20. Dasgupta, R., Namboodiri, A.M.: Leveraging multiple tasks to regularize fine-grained classification. In: Proceedings of the IEEE International Conference on Pattern Recognition (ICPR), pp. 3476–3481 (2016)
21. Luo, C., Meng, Z., Feng, J., Ni, B., Wang, M.: Annotation modification for fine-grained visual recognition. Neurocomputing (2016)
22. Yao, H., Zhang, S., Zhang, Y., Li, J., Tian, Q.: Coarse-to-fine description for fine-grained visual categorization. IEEE Trans. Image Process. (TIP) **25**(10), 4858–4872 (2016)
23. Krause, J., Jin, H., Yang, J., Fei-Fei, L.: Fine-grained recognition without part annotations. In: Proceedings of the IEEE Conference on Computer Vision and Pattern Recognition (CVPR), pp. 5546–5555 (2015)
24. Zhou, F., Lin, Y.: Fine-grained image classification by exploring bipartite-graph labels. In: Proceedings of the IEEE Conference on Computer Vision and Pattern Recognition (CVPR), pp. 1124–1133 (2016)
25. Xu, Z., Huang, S., Zhang, Y., Tao, D.: Webly-supervised fine-grained visual categorization via deep domain adaptation. IEEE Trans. Pattern Anal. Mach. Intell. (TPAMI) (2016)
26. Zhang, N., Donahue, J., Girshick, R., Darrell, T.: Part-based R-CNNs for fine-grained category detection. In: Proceedings of the International Conference on Machine Learning (ICML), pp. 834–849 (2014)
27. Huang, S., Xu, Z., Tao, D., Zhang, Y.: Part-stacked CNN for fine-grained visual categorization. In: Proceedings of the IEEE Conference on Computer Vision and Pattern Recognition (CVPR), pp. 1173–1182 (2016)

Crowd Distribution Estimation with Multi-scale Recursive Convolutional Neural Network

Meng Wei[1], Yu Kang[1,2(✉)], Weiguo Song[1], and Yang Cao[2]

[1] State Key Laboratory of Fire Science,
University of Science and Technology of China, Hefei, China
wmeng211@mail.ustc.edu.cn, {kangduyu,wgsong}@ustc.edu.cn
[2] Department of Automation,
University of Science and Technology of China, Hefei, China
forrest@ustc.edu.cn

Abstract. Crowd distribution estimation has strong demands in surveillance applications, such as overcrowding detection, anomaly detection and traffic monitoring. Although a number of methods have been proposed for crowd counting, it is still a challenging task to estimate an accurate crowd distribution map which reflects the actual spatial intensity of the crowd in a real scene, due to the inhomogeneity of crowd distribution and the uncertainty of observation perspective. To address this problem, this paper proposes a multi-scale recursive convolutional neural network (MRCNN) based framework to map the image to its crowd distribution map. The proposed neural network is trained alternatively with two joint objectives, the estimation of crowd density map and perspective map. Since the scale size and scale variance of crowd are good cues for estimating both crowd density map and perspective map, formulating these two objectives together enables learning a strong feature representation for both tasks. By convolving a perspective-adaptive kernel on the crowd density map, we can generate a pixel-wise crowd distribution map in which the pixel value denotes the actual intensity of the crowd at the corresponding location in the real scene. An extension dataset from Shanghaitech crowd dataset B is introduced for the perspective map learning task, in which 700 images with about 3500 height-annotated pedestrians are labelled. Experimental results on Shanghaitech datasets (both A and B), UCF_CC_50 dataset and UCSD dataset demonstrate the effectiveness and reliability of our proposed approach.

Keywords: Crowd distribution estimation · Crowd counting
Crowd density map estimation · Perspective map estimation
Convolutional neural network

1 Introduction

Crowd density analysis including crowd counting, crowd density estimation and crowd distribution estimation plays an important role in video surveillance,

© Springer International Publishing AG 2018
K. Schoeffmann et al. (Eds.): MMM 2018, Part I, LNCS 10704, pp. 142–153, 2018.
https://doi.org/10.1007/978-3-319-73603-7_12

which can be applied in overcrowding detection, traffic monitoring and public security. Due to severe occlusions, perspective distortions and diverse crowd distributions, crowd density analysis from a single image is still a challenging task.

Generally, the existing crowd density analysis methods mainly focus on crowd counting and crowd density estimation. These methods can be divided to two main categories: detection based and feature based approaches. Detection based methods usually detect independent pedestrians motion, and then count the pedestrians by trajectory-clustering methods [1–3]. These methods work well in low dense crowd, however, the performance drops significantly when occlusion appears. Feature based methods [4] usually extract features from foreground, such as crowd area [5–10], edge count [5, 8, 9] texture [6, 8, 11, 12] or corner points [13], and then predict global count by regression function, such as linear regression and Gaussian process regression. Unfortunately, low level features based methods cannot well represent crowd variation when applied to complex scenes. Recently, deeply learned features [14–19] are applied to overcome the difficulties of crowd counting. These deep learning based methods demonstrate the feasibility of an end-to-end approach to crowd density analysis.

Before crowd distribution estimation, it is important to consider the effects of perspective distortion. The closer the object is to the camera, the larger it appears. Therefore, the features extracted from a foreground pedestrian will account for a smaller portion than the ones extracted from a pedestrian farther away. This makes it important to normalize the features for perspective. To this end, some pre-processing, such as perspective map [8, 20] and geometric factor [7] are involved in previous work. Among several recent deep learning-based successes, Zhang et al. [14] propose a pre-train and fine-tune CNN-based framework, in which a network is first pre-trained for certain scenes and then similar training data is selection to fine-tune the pre-trained network for testing image. However, their method requires the perspective maps of both training images and testing image, which is not usually available in practice. Zhang et al. [15] propose a Multi-column Convolutional Neural Network to extract the features invariable to perspective effect by using filters with adaptive size to people/head to generate ground-truth crowd density map. Their method demonstrates good performance on crowd counting. Unfortunately, the estimated crowd density map cannot reflect the actual spatial distribution of crowd.

This paper aims to develop a method to generate a pixel-wise crowd distribution map where the pixel value denotes the actual intensity of crowd at the corresponding location in the real scene. To achieve this, as shown in Fig. 1, a multi-scale and recursive convolution neural network (MRCNN) based framework is proposed for the estimation of crowd density map and scene perspective map. More specifically, the two tasks share the same multi-scale section of network which consists of three sub-networks with different convolution kernels. Then the recursive convolution parts are introduced to stack the total outputs of all sub-nets, and thus generate the crowd density map and the slope and intercept of perspective map. The crowd distribution map is generated by convolving

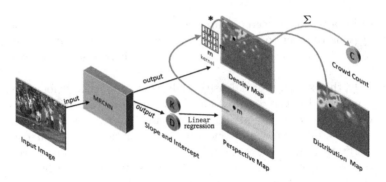

Fig. 1. Illustration of our proposed crowd distribution estimation method.

the crowd density map with a perspective map adaptive kernel. Contributions of this paper are listed as follow:

1. The reason to adopt a two-task learning architecture is rather natural: the scale size and scale variance of crowd are good cues for estimating both crowd counting and perspective map. Therefore, formulating these two objectives together enables learning a strong feature representation for both tasks.
2. The perspective maps for different scenes are generated by a CNN model rather than manual method, and there is no need for extra labels on testing images in our framework. Based on the obtained perspective map, the actual scene crowd distribution map is generated, which is more significant for surveillance applications.
3. An extension dataset from Shanghaitech crowd dataset B is introduced for our perspective learning task. We label 700 images with about 3500 height-annotated pedestrians.

2   Proposed Method

This paper aims to generate a spatial distribution map of the crowd (denotes how many people per unit area in a real scene), rather than just obtaining crowd count or density map. To achieve this, a multi-scale and recursive convolution neural network (MRCNN) based framework is proposed for estimation of crowd density map and perspective map. The crowd count is computed by integration on the crowd density map. And the crowd distribution map is generated by convolving the crowd density map with kernels adaptive to the estimated perspective map.

2.1   Labelled Data for Training

Crowd density map for crowd counting. We adopt crowd density map based method to estimate the crowd count from an input image. This method will use the spatial information in the images instead of only a global number of

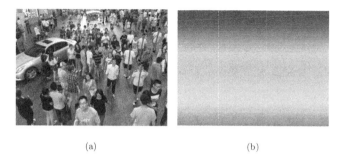

(a)   (b)

Fig. 2. (a) Labelled image. (b) The perspective map. The hot color manifests high value in the perspective map. (Color figure online)

people. The crowd density map contains potential information about the number of pedestrians at arbitrary local regions. We convert each image with labelled pedestrians heads into a crowd density map by blurring annotations with a 2D Gaussian kernel normalized to sum to one, and use the obtained density map as the ground truth of MRCNN. The integration of pixel value is the same as the total number of pedestrians in an image.

Slope and intercept for perspective map estimation. To obtain the crowd distribution map in the actual scene, we need to generate normalized perspective maps for training. As shown in Fig. 2, for each image, we randomly select several adult pedestrians along the view aspect and mark the selected pedestrians with a straight line from head to foot. Then we make a linear regression to obtain the slope and intercept of the selected line under the assumption that all labelled pedestrians are in same height of 175 cm. For simplification, we use the regressed slope and intercept as the ground truth to generate the perspective maps, in which smaller pixel value is given to far objects.

2.2   Network Architecture

An overview of our multi-scale and recursive convolution neural network (MRCNN) is shown in Fig. 3. Due to perspective distortion, pedestrians in different depth have various sizes. In order to extract different scale features of pedestrians, we propose to use multi-scale network to learn corresponding features of different size pedestrians with various size filters. This multi-scale network contains several sub-nets which involve different size filter kernels. Thus, the large filters are more suitable to capture features of large heads and coarse textures, and the small filters are more suitable to capture features of small heads and local details on the contrary. After stacking the total outputs of all sub-nets, we introduce recursive convolution parts [21] to learn the relationships between the multi-scale features and the crowd density map or the slope and intercept of perspective map. The recursive parts enlarge the receptive field of original input image and involve more local crowd information, which significantly boosts the performance of network. Note that the receptive field is

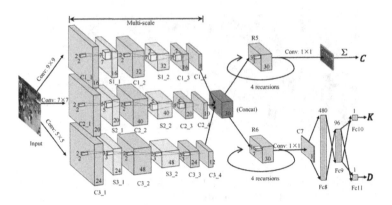

Fig. 3. The structure of our proposed multi-scale and recursive convolution neural network.

extended with every recursion while the number of parameters does not increase due to shared weights. The two tasks, the estimation of crowd density map and perspective map, share the same multi-scale section of network. Since it is necessarily to extract various scale features of heads for density map and acquire relation of pedestrians scale variations for perspective map, sharing the multi-scale features will mutually reinforce to a strong feature representation for both tasks. Nonetheless, two tasks have different recursive part of MRCNN with different shape of convolution kernels. The standard square filters are able to map local features all around to density map while rectangle filters are more useful for mapping features along single direction to perspective map.

As Fig. 3 showed, there are three sub-nets of multi-scale part of MRCNN whose convolution kernels are with different sizes. Excepting the sizes and numbers of convolution kernels, the same network structures are applied to all subnets. Each sub-net has four convolution layers and two Max pooling layers connecting to the first two convolution layers. We use Rectified linear unit (ReLU) activation after each convolution layer. We concatenate the output feature maps of all sub-nets and send them to recursive part of MRCNN. For crowd counting and density map tasks, there are four recursions with same number and size of filters. All recursions share the weights of parameters. We adopt 1×1 size of filters to map the output of recursive part to a single density map. Usually, we calculate the sum of pixel values of density map to obtain the crowd count out of CNN. In order to acquire density map and crowd count more precise, we add sum operation in our MRCNN. The crowd count $C = \sum_p H(p)$, p is the pixel of density map H. The density map H and crowd count C are employed as supervisory signal simultaneously.

To simplify the task of perspective map estimation, we adopt the MRCNN to learn the slope K and intercept D of a linear regression process which generates the perspective map in later step. The linear function describes the relationship between the location and height of labelled pedestrians. The multi-scale part of

MRCNN is the same with counting and density map tasks, however, the recursive parts of two tasks are different in the shape of filters. For crowd counting, we just use standard square filters. For perspective map estimation, we use rectangle filters which are more accommodated to perspective distortion along the vertical direction of image. In order to reduce the parameters, we also generate a single feature map by filters of 1×1. Three fully connected layers are used to map the single feature map to the slope K and intercept D.

For both tasks of crowd counting, density map and and perspective map estimation, we adopt Euclidean loss functions, which are defined as:

$$L_H \left(\Theta\right) = \frac{1}{N} \sum_i^N \left\| F_h \left(X_i; \Theta_h\right) - H_i^2 \right\|, L_C \left(\Theta\right) = \frac{1}{N} \sum_i^N \left\| F_c \left(X_i; \Theta_c\right) - C_i^2 \right\| \quad (1)$$

$$L_K \left(\Theta\right) = \frac{1}{N} \sum_i^N \left\| F_k \left(X_i; \Theta_k\right) - K_i^2 \right\|, L_D \left(\Theta\right) = \frac{1}{N} \sum_i^N \left\| F_d \left(X_i; \Theta_d\right) - D_i^2 \right\| \quad (2)$$

Here Θ is the parameters set of MRCNN and the subscripts h, c, k and d stand for crowd density map, number of people, slope and intercept respectively. N is the number of training images. X_i is the input image. L_H is the loss between the estimated density map $F_h \left(X_i; \Theta_h\right)$ and the ground truth density map H_i. L_C is the loss between the estimated number of people $F_c \left(X_i; \Theta_c\right)$ and the ground truth count C_i. L_K is the loss between the estimated slope $F_k \left(X_i; \Theta_k\right)$ and the ground truth slope K_i. L_D is the loss between the estimated intercept $F_d \left(X_i; \Theta_d\right)$ and the ground truth D_i. Then overall loss function L_1 for density map and crowd count, L_2 for perspective map are defined as:

$$L_1 = L_H + \lambda_1 L_C, L_2 = L_K + \lambda_2 L_D \quad (3)$$

where λ_1 is the weight of count loss, and λ_2 is the weight of intercept loss.

2.3   Crowd Distribution Map Estimation

We can directly generate the crowd density map from the outputs of MRCNN and obtain the crowd count by making an integration on the density map. However, the generated crowd density map only demonstrates the possibility of a pedestrian/head appears at the corresponding location in the scene, and unable to reflect the actual diverse distribution of crowd.

To estimate the spatial distribution of the crowd, the number of pedestrians and unit area are essential. The integration of pixel value at arbitrary local regions in crowd density map stands for the number of people. However, the amount of pixels a unit area occupy on the image are variant because of perspective. We firstly generate the perspective map for each image by the estimated slope K and intercept D. The pixel value of perspective map denotes the number of pixels occupied by one meter at the corresponding location in the actual scene. Therefore, we generate the crowd distribution map by convolving the density map with a filter whose weights are all of one and size vary with respect to the value of perspective map. In the last, the pixel value of the generated crowd distribution map denotes the number of people per unit area in that location. For example, the value of a position in perspective map is m as illustrated in Fig. 1, we use $m \times m$ filter with parameters are all of one to convolute with point in density map at corresponding position. This operation is equal to sum the values around a point in density map with unit area in actual. The value of sum operation is the actual spatial intensity at that position. We use this method to all positions to obtain integrated distribution map of an image.

3   Experiments

The performance of our proposed multi-scale and recursive convolution neural network for crowd distribution estimation is evaluated on Shanghaitech dataset [15], UCF_CC_50 dataset [4] and UCSD dataset [8]. For crowd counting, slop and intercept estimation, we use Mean Absolute Error (MAE) and Mean squared Error (MSE) to quantify the performance of accuracy and robustness of results respectively. The results for density map and crowd counting estimation, crowd perspective map estimation and crowd distribution map estimation are discussed in detail as follows.

3.1   Datasets and Setup

The Shanghaitech dataset [15] contains two subsets. Part A of dataset involves 482 high dense crowd images and Part B of dataset contains 716 busy street images. We select 300 images of Part A and 400 images of Part B as training set and remainder as testing set respectively respect to convention. The UCF_CC_50 dataset [4] is a popular but challenging dataset. This dataset only contains 50 gray images collected from internet. Following the dataset setting convention in [4], we divide the dataset into five subsets randomly and performed 5-fold cross-validation. We also take a single scene into account. The UCSD dataset [8] contains 1200 gray images selected from one surveillance camera of a single scene. This dataset also provides ROI of the scene. Following the dataset setting convention in [8], we adopt frames from 600 to 1400 as training set and a testing set with remainder. We perform data augmentation by cropping 9 overlapping patches from each image. The patches are half size of original images.

For our perspective map learning task, we have labelled 700 images with about 3500 height-annotated pedestrians from Shanghaitech dataset B. The coordinate position of labelled pedestrians are provided. This dataset split into two subsets: 400 images for training and 300 images for testing. Every image has a different perspective map for different scene. The UCSD dataset only have one uniform perspective because of the stationary camera for a single scene. We select and label a pedestrian from sequential frames where the pedestrian appears from bottom to top position of frames. These labelled images will be released in the future.

The proposed MRCNN was trained on the deep learning framework of Caffe [22]. Since the deep recursive architecture was difficult to converge, we adopted adaptive learning rate optimization algorithm Adam for training all tasks. The network was trained by Gaussian initialization with standard deviation of 0.01 as well as momentum set to 0.9 and weight decay set to 0.0005, furthermore, the base learning rate was $1e^-5$ for all tasks. We trained the model for density map and crowd counting firstly, and then used it to fine-tune the model for perspective map estimation. The two tasks shared parameters of multi-scale portion of MRCNN.

3.2 Density Map and Crowd Counting Estimation

The input of MRCNN was gray crowd image and the output was the estimated density map and the number of people in image. Due to the two pooling layers of MRCNN, each dimension of output was 1/4 of input image, therefore, the size of ground truth was also the 1/4 of input image.

Table 1. Comparison of results on various datasets for crowd counting.

Dataset	Shanghaitech				UCF_CC_50		UCSD	
	Part A		Part B					
Method	MAE	MSE	MAE	MSE	MAE	MSE	MAE	MSE
Zhang et al. [14]	181.8	277.7	32.0	49.8	467.0	498.5	1.60	3.31
MCNN [15]	110.2	173.2	26.4	41.3	377.6	509.1	1.07	1.35
Cascaded-MTL [18]	101.3	152.4	20.0	31.1	322.8	**397.9**		
Switch-CNN [19]	**90.4**	**135.0**	21.6	33.4	**318.1**	439.2	1.62	2.10
SS-MRCNN	102.7	157.6	19.8	33.5				
MRCNN	98.9	150.1	**17.3**	**29.8**	319.3	435.3	**1.00**	**1.32**

The quantitative results for crowd counting are showed in Table 1 and qualitative results for crowd density map are showed in Fig. 4(c). We compare our method with 4 existing CNN based methods [14,15,18,19] on three datasets for crowd counting. Our approach achieves the state of the art on Shanghaitech B and UCSD. The results of Shanghaitech A and UCF_CC_50 are also worthy of comparison with existing methods. The experiment results demonstrate that our approach relieves the difficulty of foreground segmentation and is able to work more accurately and robustly for arbitrary perspective scene. The deep convolution and pooling layers of CNN will make the dense images lost the information of extreme small heads, especially on Shanghaitech A and UCF_CC_50 datasets. We also evaluate the performance of our MRCNN with a single supervision MRCNN (SS-MRCNN) of crowd density map in Table 1. Our method outperforms SS-MRCNN because of the supervision of global count. This supervisory signal as a constraint compels the integration of density map closer to global count.

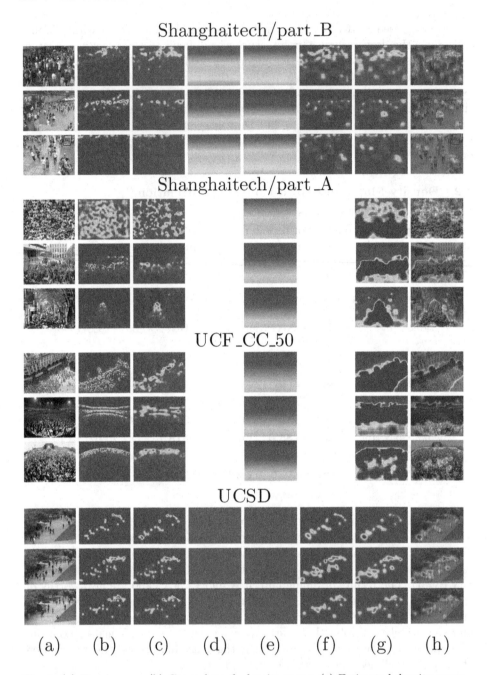

Fig. 4. (a) Test images. (b) Ground-truth density maps. (c) Estimated density maps. (d) Perspective maps generated by Ground-truth slopes and intercepts. (e) Perspective maps generated by estimated slopes and intercepts. (f) Crowd distribution maps generated by Ground-truth density maps and perspective maps. (g) Crowd distribution maps generated by estimated density maps and perspective maps. (h) Qualitative result with estimated crowd density maps (g) on images (a).

3.3 Crowd Perspective Map Estimation

The input of MRCNN was gray crowd image and the output was the estimated slope and intercept of perspective map. The values of annotations were also reduced by 1/4 before generating the ground truth. For our dataset and the UCSD, we used the model of crowd density map to fine-tune the multi-scale part of MRCNN which extracted similar features of pedestrians in crowd for two tasks. And the learning rate of multi-scale part was set to zero. Due to the lack of perspective information of Shanghaitech A and UCF_CC_50, we obtained slope and intercept of images with the model trained on our labelled dataset.

Table 2. Comparison of results on various datasets for perspective map estimation.

Dataset	Method	Slope		Intercept	
		MAE	MSE	MAE	MSE
Our dataset	MPCNN	0.0753	0.0894	2.8553	3.7225
	MRCNN-unshared	0.0626	0.0770	3.7918	4.8375
	MRCNN	**0.0535**	**0.0660**	**2.5728**	**3.3284**
UCSD	MRCNN	**0.0119**	**0.0126**	**0.3518**	**0.3707**

The quantitative results for estimated slope and intercept are showed in Table 2 and qualitative perspective maps are showed in Fig. 4(e). We compare our approach (MRCNN) with the method without recursive part (MPCNN) and the method without sharing parameters of multi-scale section of density map and counting model (MRCNN-unshared) on our dataset. Our MRCNN performs the best because the recursive part enlarges the receptive field and maps the features of pedestrians to the abstraction presentation for perspective. And the rectangle filters in recursive part are beneficial to learn the scale variations. Shared parameters provide prior and strong feature representation for perspective estimation. The performance of UCSD dataset indicates that our model can estimate perspective conversion efficaciously under condition of immobile background.

Subjectively, a larger gap between the size of nearest pedestrian and farthest one, a larger numerical value of slope. From Fig. 4, the gaps between pedestrian of three test images in Shanghaitech A and UCF_CC_50 increase progressively from top to bottom respectively. The slopes estimated by our perspective model for Shanghaitech A are 0.2868, 0.2941 and 0.3264 respectively. The slopes estimated by our perspective model for UCF_CC_50 are 0.2757, 0.3194 and 0.3552 respectively. The consequences demonstrate that our perspective model have learned the tendency of perspective transformation.

3.4 Crowd Distribution Map Estimation

We generate the spatial crowd distribution map with the crowd density map and perspective map as described in Sect. 2.3. Fig. 4(b) and (g) show the qualitative results of crowd density map and crowd distribution map, respectively. As can be seen, the top regions of density map in Fig. 4(b) tend to have higher value, which might be not consistent with the actual crowd distribution due to perspective effect. As the contrast, the heat value in Fig. 4(g) is adaptive to perspective map. It demonstrates that our proposed method can well describe the diverse distribution of crowd.

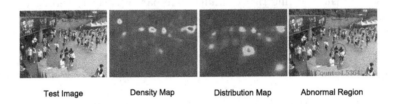

Test Image   Density Map   Distribution Map   Abnormal Region

Fig. 5. Illustration of our crowd distribution map for abnormal detection.

In fact, the crowd distribution map can also be tremendously beneficial to the crowd abnormal detection. As can be seen in Fig. 5, the crowd density map only reflects the probability of pedestrians in the test image, while the crowd distribution map can reflect the actual spatial intensity of the crowd directly. Depending on the crowd distribution map, we can obtain the location of the most dense region of crowd (the region inside the red circle of Fig. 5) and the number of pedestrians in that region automatically. We discover that the most heat region appeared because of crowd gathering, which is abnormal for crowd and is caution for surveillance.

4   Conclusion

In this paper, we propose a multi-scale and recursive convolution neural network based framework for crowd distribution estimation. The proposed neural network is jointly trained for two tasks, the estimation of the crowd density map and scene perspective map. Formulating these two objectives together enables learning a strong feature representation for both tasks simultaneously. In addition, for our training task on crowd perspective map estimation, we have labelled 700 images with about 3500 height-annotated pedestrians from Shanghaitech dataset B. This dataset is a good supplement for crowd perspective map estimation. Experimental results on various datasets demonstrate that our proposed method outperforms the state of the art methods in terms of crowd counting. More importantly, our method can provide the spatial crowd distribution map, which is more substantial for surveillance applications.

Acknowledgments. This work is supported by the Natural Science Foundation of China (61472380).

References

1. Brostow, G.J., Cipolla, R.: Unsupervised bayesian detection of independent motion in crowds. In: CVPR (2006)
2. Rabaud, V., Belongie, S.: Counting crowded moving objects. In: CVPR (2006)
3. Cheriyadat, A.M., Bhaduri, B.L., Radke, R.J.: Detecting multiple moving objects in crowded environments with coherent motion regions. In: CVPR (2008)
4. Idrees, H., Saleemi, I., Seibert, C., Shah, M.: Multi-source multi-scale counting in extremely dense crowd images. In: CVPR (2013)
5. Davies, A.C., Yin, J.H., Velastin, S.A.: Crowd monitoring using image processing. Electron. Commun. Eng. J. **7**(1), 37–47 (1995)
6. Marana, A.N., Costa, L.D.F., Lotufo, R.A., Velastin, S.A.: Estimating crowd density with minkowski fractal dimension. In: IEEE International Conference on Acoustics, Speech, and Signal Processing, vol. 6, pp. 3521–3524 (1999)
7. Paragios, N., Ramesh, V.: A MRF-based approach for real-time subway monitoring. In: CVPR (2001)
8. Chan, A.B., Liang, Z.S.J., Vasconcelos, N.: Privacy preserving crowd monitoring: counting people without people models or tracking. In: CVPR (2008)
9. Ryan, D., Denman, S., Fookes, C., Sridharan, S.: Crowd counting using multiple local features. In: Digital Image Computing: Techniques and Applications, pp. 81–88 (2009)
10. Hou, Y.L., Pang, G.K.H.: People counting and human detection in a challenging situation. IEEE Trans. Syst. Man Cybern. Part A Syst. Hum. **41**(1), 24–33 (2011)
11. Rahmalan, H., Nixon, M.S., Carter, J.N.: On crowd density estimation for surveillance. In: Crime and Security, pp. 540–545 (2007)
12. Ma, W., Huang, L., Liu, C.: Advanced local binary pattern descriptors for crowd estimation. In: PACIIA (2008)
13. Albiol, A., Silla, M.J., Mossi, J.M.: Video analysis using corner motion statistics. In: Proceedings of the IEEE International Workshop on Performance Evaluation of Tracking and Surveillance C38 Tools Appl (2010)
14. Zhang, C., Li, H., Wang, X., Yang, X.: Cross-scene crowd counting via deep convolutional neural networks. In: CVPR (2015)
15. Zhang, Y., Zhou, D., Chen, S., Gao, S., Ma, Y.: Single-image crowd counting via multi-column convolutional neural network. In: CVPR (2016)
16. Shang, C., Ai, H., Bai, B.: End-to-end crowd counting via joint learning local and global count. In: ICIP (2016)
17. Oñoro-Rubio, D., López-Sastre, R.J.: Towards perspective-free object counting with deep learning. In: Leibe, B., Matas, J., Sebe, N., Welling, M. (eds.) ECCV 2016. LNCS, vol. 9911, pp. 615–629. Springer, Cham (2016). https://doi.org/10.1007/978-3-319-46478-7_38
18. Sindagi, V.A., Patel, V.M.: CNN-based cascaded multi-task learning of high-level prior and density estimation for crowd counting. In: AVSS (2017)
19. Sam, D.B., Surya, S., Babu, R.V.: Switching convolutional neural network for crowd counting. In: CVPR (2017)
20. Fradi, H., Dugelay, J.: Low level crowd analysis using frame-wise normalized feature for people counting. In: IEEE International Workshop on Information Forensics and Security, pp. 246–251 (2012)
21. Kim, J., Lee, J.K., Lee, K.M.: Deeply-recursive convolutional network for image super-resolution. In: CVPR (2016)
22. Jia, Y., Shelhamer, E., Donahue, J., Karayev, S., Long, J.: Caffe: Convolutional Architecture for Fast Feature Embedding (2014)

Deep Convolutional Neural Network for Correlating Images and Sentences

Yuhua Jia[1](✉), Liang Bai[1](✉), Peng Wang[2](✉), Jinlin Guo[1], and Yuxiang Xie[1]

[1] Science and Technology on Information Systems Engineering Laboratory,
National University of Defense Technology, Changsha 410073, China
jiayuhua11@outlook.com, xabpz@163.com, gjlin99@gmail.com, yxxie@nudt.edu.cn
[2] National Laboratory for Information Science and Technology,
Department of Computer Science and Technology, Tsinghua University,
Beijing 100084, China
pwang@tsinghua.edu.cn

Abstract. In this paper, we address the problem of image sentence matching and propose a novel convolutional neural network architecture which includes three modules: the visual module for composing fragmental features of images, the textual module for composing fragmental features of sentences, and the fusional module for encoding features of image and sentence fragments jointly to generate final matching scores of image sentence pairs. Different with previous fragment level models, the proposed method represents fragments of images as feature maps generated by CNN, which is more reasonable and effective. By allowing independent and specialized fragmental feature representations to be leveraged for each modality like image or text, the proposed method is flexible in interlinking the intermediate fragmental features to generate a joint abstraction of two modalities, which provides better matching scores. Extensive evaluations on two benchmark datasets have validated the competitive performance of our approach compared to the state-of-the-art bidirectional image sentence retrieval approaches.

Keywords: Image sentence matching · Convolutional neural network
Fragment level method

1 Introduction

As a challenging task in coupling computing vision with natural language processing, modeling the correlation between images and sentences has gained increasing research attentions recently. It has great potentials not only for current practical tasks like solving cross-media retrieval, but also for building up towards intelligent machines which can be regarded as a long-term goal. As a practical sub-problem faced in numerous multimedia retrieval tasks, matching images and sentences is the bottleneck of cross-media retrieval due to its difficulty and complexity. As we know, the cross retrieval between images and videos is simple

K. Schoeffmann et al. (Eds.): MMM 2018, Part I, LNCS 10704, pp. 154–165, 2018.
https://doi.org/10.1007/978-3-319-73603-7_13

because a frame of a video can be seen as an image and both of them share similar features. For text and voice, it is also a fact that speech recognition technology is mature enough to bridge the gap between these two modalities. However, matching images and sentences is still far from being well addressed. In the long run, such technique is a step towards the future artificial intelligence through which we can interact with computers in natural languages to carry out more complex tasks with the assistance of computer vision.

Correlating images and sentence based on their expressed semantics is difficult because of the heterogeneity-gap between them and it is widely considered as a basic barrier to match the two modalities. The most important part of modeling the correlation between images and sentences is to capture the semantic correlations by learning a multimodal joint model. While some previous models [1–3] have been proposed to study the global level matching relations between image and sentence by representing them as a global vector, they neglect the local fragments of the sentence and their correspondences to the image content. Fragment level methods [4–7] try to align the fragments of sentence and regions of image to address this problem. However, these methods usually represent fragments of image as objects or instances and it is necessary to extract visual features of these objects or instances respectively which inevitably leads to high complexities.

In this work, we propose a novel end-to-end architecture to tackle the problem of image sentence matching. The proposed method is inspired by the fact that CNN have demonstrated their powerful abilities in learning the visual representation of an image. As the feature map generated by a CNN can represent partial semantics of the corresponding image, it is reasonable to represent the fragments of images as feature maps generated by CNN. Different with previous models, the proposed method represents fragments of images as feature maps generated by CNN, using convolutional method to compose fragmental features of sentences, and finally obtains matching score by encoding features of image and sentence fragments jointly. As independent and specialized fragmental feature representations are allowed for images and texts, the proposed method is flexible to generate a joint abstraction of two modalities by interlinking the intermediate fragmental features.

The key contributions of this work can be summarized as follows:

- An end-to-end trainable system is proposed which composes features of image and sentence fragments and then generates matching score of image and sentence by fusing the intermediate fragmental features of them.
- Feature maps generated by CNN are utilized as fragments of images to build a fragment-level model for image sentence matching, which is shown to be reasonable and advantageous.
- Effectiveness of the proposed model is demonstrated by comprehensive experiments on two public datasets: Flickr8K [18] and Flickr30K [19]. Our experimental results have shown its competitive performance with the state-of-the-art approaches.

2 Related Work

The proposed method is relevant to several fields in natural language processing and computer vision research. The typical research related to the work presented in this paper mainly includes matching images and sentences, which is now described.

Modeling semantic correlation between images and sentences has significant values in multimedia understanding and retrieval. The shared concept across modalities plays an important role in interlinking the interpretations of two modalities. There has been a large body of work resorting to modeling semantic correlation between images and sentences in dealing with various tasks like image captioning, bidirectional image and sentence retrieval and visual question answering, etc.

In image captioning, literatures of [10–14] have focused on generating novel descriptive sentences for a query image. Vinyals et al. [10] presented an end-to-end system that can automatically generate reasonable descriptions in plain English for images based on a CNN as encoder for image representations and a RNN as decoder for generating corresponding sentences. Ghosh et al. [11] used discourse representation structure to gain semantic information for image captions which is further modeled into a graphical structure. Fang et al. [12] used multi-instance learning and traditional maximum-entropy language model for description generation. Most recently, Wang et al. [13] proposed an end-to-end trainable deep bidirectional LSTM model including a deep CNN and two separate LSTM networks for description generation. Word2VisualVec [14] is proposed to project vectorized sentences into a given visual feature space which is advocated as a new shared representation of images and sentences.

In bidirectional image and sentence retrieval, global level matching [1–3] of relations between image and sentence is studied by representing sentence and image as global vectors while fragment level methods [4–7] align the fragments of sentence and regions of image in a finer-grained manner. Socher et al. [1] proposed to employ the semantic dependency-tree recursive neural network (SDT-RNN) to map the sentence into the same semantic space as the image representation, and the association is then measured as the distance in that space. Eisenschtat and Wolf [2] introduced a bidirectional neural network architecture for the task of matching vectors from two data sources. Yan and Mikolajczyk [21] used deep canonical correlation analysis (DCCA) for matching images and texts.

Some other related work which is closer to our motivation in this paper tries to study the local inter-modal correspondences between image and sentence fragments. In [4], Karpathy et al. broke down images and sentences into fragments and then embedded these fragments in a common space. Plummer et al. [5] regarded the objects as fragments of image to collect region-to-phrase (RTP) correspondences for richer image-to-sentence models. Ma et al. [6] proposed multimodal convolutional neural networks which consist of one image CNN encoding the image content, and one matching CNN composing words to different semantic fragments and learning the inter-modal relations between image and the composed fragments of sentence at different levels. Huang et al. [7]

proposed sm-LSTM which selects pairwise instances from image and sentence which are salient and aggregates local similarity measurement. As fragment level methods, these literatures have the same characteristics in representing fragments of image as objects or instances whose visual features need to be extracted respectively. Although this processing is reasonable and interpretable, it highly relies on the sophisticatedly constructed neural networks which are usually more complex and hard to train. Instead, in this paper we represent fragments of images as the feature maps directly generated by a CNN model (i.e., VGG model with 16 weight layers), hence the design complexity of image processing can be significantly reduced.

3 Modeling Image and Sentence Correlation

In this section, a novel convolutional neural network architecture is proposed for image and sentence matching. With this architecture, we aim at learning reasonable matching scores for image and sentence pairs, i.e., assigning semantically similar pairs of image and sentence with higher score values. The proposed model can be trained on a set of images and sentences whose relationships are labeled as relevant or irrelevant.

As illustrated in Fig. 1, the proposed method takes images and sentences as the inputs and generates the corresponding matching scores. The proposed method is advantageous in allowing independent and specialized fragmental feature extractions from both images and sentences, so that it is flexible to encode the intermediate fragmental features at higher-level in order to provide better matching scores. This is achieved by designing the whole architecture with three

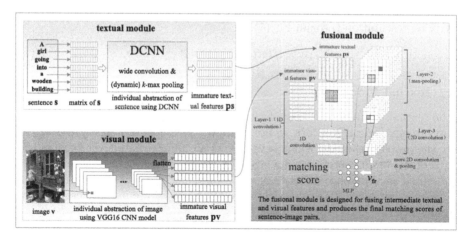

Fig. 1. The framework of proposed method, including visual module for composing fragmental features of images, textual module for composing fragmental features of sentences, and fusional module for generating final matching score of images and sentences.

components. The textual module is responsible for the abstraction of textual data as fragments of sentences. The visual module is responsible to extract the intermediate features of images as visual fragments. Finally, the fusional module combines the above extracted features with a matching convolutional neural network and a multi-layer perceptron (MLP). The matching convolutional neural network in this module is designed for the interaction between fragments of sentences and images generated by textual and visual modules respectively and produces the fusional representation of textual and visual data. Following the matching CNN, MLP produces the final matching scores between images and sentences.

3.1   Visual Module

Inspired by semantic representation using vectors in natural language processing, we utilize feature maps of CNN model in a novel way in visual module. As a remarkable method in solving NLP problems, word2vec [8] is flexible in modeling the high-level semantics of word or sentence with a vector. Similarly, we use a vector to represent partial or entire high-level semantics of an image and in our method, we regard a feature map generated by CNN of an image as the representation of partial visual semantics (i.e., fragment of image) in the given image. The feature map is then flattened to a vector as the representation of visual semantics in a similar manner that a word embedding vector is used as a representation of textual semantics. As illustrated in Fig. 1, VGG [15] (16 weight layers) with all fully-connected layers removed is utilized to generate fragments of an image $\mathbf{v}$. We add an flatten layer to flatten all feature maps of the top max-pooling layer of VGG to vectors, which is then aligned into a matrix $\mathbf{pv}$ as intermediate representation of an image. The functional role of visual module can be summarized as taking image $\mathbf{v}$ as input and generating the matrix representation through Eq. (1):

$$\mathbf{pv} = flatten(VGG(\mathbf{v})) \tag{1}$$

3.2   Textual Module

In the textual module, wide convolutional layers and pooling layers of Dynamic Convolutional Neural Network [9] are employed to model sentences, in order to solve the problem that the width is various at an intermediate layer because the length of the input sentence is not fixed. In the proposed method, a sentence is represented as a sentence matrix $\mathbf{s}$ whose column corresponds to the embedding of a word as $\mathbf{w}_i \in R^d$. The values in each embedding $\mathbf{w}_i$ are parameters that are optimized during the training phase.

$$\mathbf{s} = [\mathbf{w}_1 \ldots \mathbf{w}_s] \tag{2}$$

where the subscript s is the length of the sentence.

As illustrated in Fig. 1, taking sentence matrix $\mathbf{s}$ as the input, textual module generates the intermediate abstraction of a sentence $\mathbf{ps}$ (i.e., fragments of sentence) through a 7 layers structure, including **s** as the first layer, two wide convolution layers, one dynamic k-max pooling layer, one k-max pooling layer, one folding layer and the last flatten layer. The relationships between each consecutive layers are detailed in Fig. 2. In Fig. 2, the wide convolution layers are obtained by wide convolution operation which ensures that all weights in the filter reach the entire sentence, including the words at the margins. A dynamic k-max pooling layer is a k-max pooling operation where k is a function of the length of the sentence and the depth of the network in the textual module. The function is designed as [9]:

$$k_l = \max(k_{top}, [\frac{L - l}{L} s])$$

(3)

where l is the number of the current convolutional layer to which the pooling is applied and L is the total number of convolutional layers in the network, k_{top} is the fixed pooling parameter applied for the folding layer. The k-max pooling operator with $k = k_{top}$ is applied on top of the folding layer to guarantee that the input to the flatten layers is independent of the length of the input sentence. Folding layer is after the convolutional layer and before (dynamic) k-max pooling which is responsible to sum every two rows in a feature map component-wise.

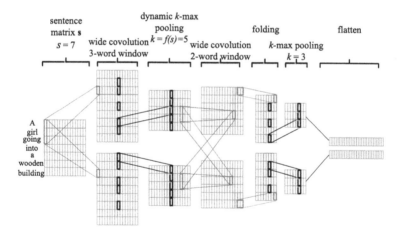

Fig. 2. The architecture of texual module with seven words input sentence. Word embeddings have size of 16. The network has two convolutional layers with two feature maps each. The widths of the filters at the two layers are respectively 3 and 2. The (dynamic) k-max pooling layers have values k of 5 and 3.

3.3 Fusional Module

As we can see from the Fig. 1, the fusional module is composed of a matching convolutional neural network for generating the final fusional representation

$v_{\mathbf{fr}}$ of image and sentence by encoding intermediate textual and visual features jointly and a multi-layer perceptron (MLP) for producing the matching score of image-sentence pair. We designed a 8 layers architecture for fusional module (one for 1D convolution, two for 2D convolution, three for pooling, and two for MLP).

Basically, in Layer-1 of fusional module (shown in Fig. 1), we apply sliding windows to both intermediate features of sentence and image i.e., $\mathbf{ps}$ and $\mathbf{pv}$, and model all possible combinations of them through one-dimensional (1D) convolution. 1D convolution firstly composes different segments of image and sentence respectively and then generates different local matchings of these compositions. For segment i on $\mathbf{ps}$ and segment j on $\mathbf{pv}$, we have the feature map:

$$\mathbf{z}_{i,j}^{(1,f)} \overset{def}{=} \mathbf{z}_{i,j}^{(1,f)}(\mathbf{ps},\mathbf{pv}) = \sigma(\mathbf{w}^{(1,f)}\hat{\mathbf{z}}_{i,j}^{(0)} + b^{(1,f)}) \tag{4}$$

where $\mathbf{z}_{i,j}^{(1,f)}$ is the output of feature map of type-f for location (i,j) in Layer-1 of fusional module, $\mathbf{w}^{(1,f)}$ is parameters for type-f in Layer-1 of fusional module, and $\hat{\mathbf{z}}_{i,j}^{(0)}$ simply concatenates the vectors of image fragments and sentence segments for $\mathbf{ps}$ and $\mathbf{pv}$:

$$\hat{\mathbf{z}}_{i,j}^{(0)} = [\mathbf{ps}_{i:i+k_1-1}^{\mathrm{T}}, \mathbf{pv}_{j:j+k_1-1}^{\mathrm{T}}]^{\mathrm{T}} \tag{5}$$

where k_1 is the width of the window in 1D convolution.

Clearly the 1D convolution preserves the location information about sentence segments. In the following Layer-2, a two-dimensional (2D) max-pooling in non-overlapping 2×2 windows (illustrated in Fig. 1) is carried out.

After Layer-2, we can obtain a low level fusional representation of sentence and image fragments. The next step is to generate a high level fusional representation which encodes the information from both sentence and image fragments. This is performed by employing general 2D convolutions and 2D poolings. General 2D convolution is formulated as:

$$\mathbf{z}_{i,j}^{(l,f)} = \sigma(\mathbf{w}^{(l,f)}\hat{\mathbf{z}}_{i,j}^{(l-1)} + b^{(l,f)}), l = 3, 5, ... \tag{6}$$

where $\hat{\mathbf{z}}_{i,j}^{(l-1)}$ concatenates the corresponding vectors from its 2D receptive field in Layer-$(l-1)$. General 2D pooling layer is followed by 2D convolution layer and this combination can be repeated if necessary. We apply the pooling strategy used in [26] to all pooling layers except for the first pooling layer.

After the final fusional representation $v_{\mathbf{fr}}$ of image and sentence is generated by the matching convolutional neural network, a two layers multi-layer perceptron with $v_{\mathbf{fr}}$ as input are then applied to produce the matching score as Eq. (7):

$$score = \mathbf{w}_s(\sigma(\mathbf{w}_f(v_{\mathbf{fr}} + b_f))) + b_s \tag{7}$$

where $\sigma(\cdot)$ is the ReLu activation function, $\mathbf{w}_f$ and b_f are parameters of the first layer of MLP, $\mathbf{w}_s$ and b_s are parameters of the second layer of MLP.

Table 1. Results comparison in terms of $R@K$ (the higher the better) and Med r (median rank) (the lower the better) on Flickr8K. Values in brackets correspond to performances worse than our proposed method.

Flickr8K								
Model	Image annotation				Image retrieval			
	$R@1$	$R@5$	$R@10$	Med r	$R@1$	$R@5$	$R@10$	Med r
Deep fragment [4]	(0.126)	(0.329)	(0.440)	(14)	(0.097)	(0.296)	(0.425)	(15)
m-RNN [20]	(0.145)	(0.372)	(0.485)	(11)	(0.115)	(0.310)	(0.424)	(15)
DTSN [23]	(0.122)	(0.342)	(0.481)	(12)	(0.091)	(0.285)	(0.432)	(15)
DCCA [21]	(0.179)	(0.403)	(0.519)	(9)	(0.127)	(0.312)	(0.441)	(13)
m-CNNs [6]	(0.248)	0.537	0.671	5	0.203	(0.476)	0.617	5
Our method	**0.271**	**0.526**	**0.653**	**5**	**0.191**	**0.482**	**0.614**	**5**
Bi-LSTM [13]	0.293	0.582	0.696	3	0.197	(0.470)	(0.606)	5
FV (GMM+HGLMM) [22]	0.310	0.593	0.737	4	0.213	0.500	0.648	5

3.4 Implementation Details

Configuration. In implementing our method, we use 50-dimensional word embedding trained with the Word2Vec [8] in the textual module. The value of k_{top} for the top k-max pooling is 5. The widths of the wide convolutional filters in two wide convolution layers are 7 and 5, respectively. The number of feature maps at the first convolutional layer is 6 while the number of maps at the second convolutional layer is 12.

In the visual module, we use VGG [15] (16 weight layers) with all fully-connected layers removed and we borrow the architecture and the original parameters learnt from ImageNet dataset [24] for initialization. In the fusional module, a 3-word window is used in the first 1D convolution layer throughout all experiments. Various numbers of feature maps (typically from 150 to 300) are tested to obtain an optimal performance. We use ReLu as the activation function for all models (both convolution and MLP), which is validated to have better performances than sigmoid-like functions.

Training. To optimize the model parameters, a measure of max-margin objective function is quantified as Eq. (8), in order to force the matching scores of correlated image-sentence pairs to be greater than those of uncorrelated image-sentence pairs:

$$loss(x_i, y_i, y_j, \Theta) =$$
$$\max(0, margin + score(x_i, y_j) - score(x_i, y_i)) \tag{8}$$

where Θ denotes the parameters to be optimized, $margin$ is a hyper parameter to control the penalty of matching scores, (x_i, y_i) denotes the correlated image-sentence pair, and (x_i, y_j) is the randomly sampled uncorrelated image-sentence pair $(i \neq j)$. The notational meanings of x and y vary with the matching tasks: for image retrieval from a query sentence, x denotes a sentence while y denotes a image, and vice versa. It is obvious that the iterative optimization is time-consuming if all irrelevant image-sentence pairs are taken into account. As a result, we use stochastic gradient descent (SGD) with mini-batch (100 200 in sizes) for optimization. In order to avoid over-fitting, early-stopping [16] and dropout (with probability 0.5) [17] are both employed.

During the training process, $margin = 0.5$ is assigned in the max-margin function defined by Eq. (8) to force the semantic similar image-sentence pairs to get higher matching scores. Once the training process is completed, all the training data are discarded and the resulted network is validated on another set of testing dataset on which the image-sentence pairs are scored and sorted.

4 Experiments and Discussions

In this section, the effectiveness of the proposed method is evaluated on two public datasets for two tasks of both image and sentence retrieval.

4.1 Datasets and Evaluation Metrics

Datasets. Two public datasets of Flickr8K [18] and Flickr30K [19] are employed to evaluate our method since both datasets contain images and corresponding descriptive sentences. Flickr8K consists of 8,000 images collected from Flickr, each with 5 sentences describing the image contents while Flickr30K is a larger dataset consisting of 31,783 images also collected from Flickr. Similar to Flickr8K, there are also 5 sentences describing the content of each image in Flickr30K. For Flickr8K dataset, we use the standard training, validation and testing split provided by the database. Meanwhile, the public training, validation and testing split as in [20] is directly used for Flickr30K dataset in our experiments.

Evaluation metrics. The popular metrics recall and median rank score are evaluated for both image and sentence retrieval. Recall $R@K$ stands for the percentage of ground truth among the top K returned results, which is a useful metric of performances especially for search engines and ranking systems. The median rank indicates the position k of the returned list at which a system has a recall of 50%.

4.2 Results and Discussions

We compare our model with some typical models in performing bidirectional image sentence retrieval, including DCCA [21], FV [22], Deep Fragment [4], m-RNN [20], m-CNNs [6], Bi-LSTMV [13] and DTSN [23]. All performances obtained by these models are reported to be the state-of-the-art in the corresponding literatures and the reported metric values are directly compared in this paper. The performances of the proposed method and the other methods on Flickr8K and Flickr30K are shown in Tables 1 and 2 respectively.

Table 2. Results comparison in terms of $R@K$ (the higher the better) and Med r (median rank) (the lower the better) on Flickr30K. Values in brackets correspond to performances worse than our proposed method.

Flickr30K								
Model	Image annotation				Image retrieval			
	$R@1$	$R@5$	$R@10$	Med r	$R@1$	$R@5$	$R@10$	Med r
Deep fragment [4]	(0.142)	(0.377)	(0.513)	(10)	(0.102)	(0.308)	(0.442)	(14)
m-RNN [20]	(0.184)	(0.402)	(0.509)	(10)	(0.126)	(0.312)	(0.415)	(16)
DCCA [23]	(0.167)	(0.393)	(0.529)	(8)	(0.126)	(0.310)	(0.430)	(15)
RTP [5]	0.374	(0.631)	0.743	*	(0.260)	0.560	0.693	*
Bi-LSTM [13]	(0.281)	(0.531)	(0.642)	(4)	(0.196)	(0.438)	(0.558)	(7)
FV (GMM+HGLMM) [22]	0.350	(0.620)	0.738	3	(0.250	(0.527)	(0.660)	5
Our method	**0.327**	**0.635**	**0.729**	**3**	**0.269**	**0.558**	**0.685**	**5**
m-CNNs [6]	0.336	0.641	0.749	3	(0.262)	0.563	0.696	4

As we can see from Tables 1 and 2, our method is competitive and reaches the state-of-the-art performances across different metrics on both datasets. When there are more training instances in Flickr30K, the proposed method performs much better than on Flickr8K. Compared to Deep Fragment [4] and RTP [5] which represent fragments of image as objects or instances, the comparable results achieved by the proposed method demonstrate that feature maps generated by CNN are also promising in representing fragments of image. Breaking down both images and sentences into fragments and then jointly encoding them in our method presents competitive results in both datasets, as it improves or equals the performance of m-CNNs [6] in at least one metric, which instead encodes an image to a vector to interact with different level of sentence fragments.

To fully investigate the performances of the proposed method, extended evaluation is carried out in inter dataset scenarios, i.e., training the model from one dataset but testing on another. The corresponding inter dataset results are shown in Table 3. From the table, our model derived from Flickr30k and tested on Flickr8k shows similar performances as in inner dataset scenarios in Tables 1 and 2. However, the performance is much worse on the other direction, i.e., deriving the model from Flickr8k and testing on Flickr30k. This implies that more training instances are valuable to improve the performance of the proposed model, which is a reasonable phenomenon across many approaches.

4.3   Limitations and Future Work

Though comparable performances can be achieved using the proposed method, it still has much space to be improved: In visual module, a basic CNN architecture VGG is employed to generate fragments of images. Note that there are many CNN models with better capability in image representation e.g. attention model [25], which have great potentials in improving our method. Similarly, the adoption of more optimized structures in the textual module and the fusional module can also improve the whole performance of the proposed method, which benefits from the proposed architecture as it allows fragmental feature extraction and combination to be processed seperatedly. One direction of future work

Table 3. Performance comparison of inter datasets scenario on Flickr8K and Flickr30K.

Image annotation	$R@1$	$R@1$	$R@1$	Med r
Flickr30K to Flickr8K	0.237	0.472	0.598	7
Flickr8K to Flickr30K	0.153	0.361	0.487	12
Image retrieval	$R@1$	$R@1$	$R@1$	Med r
Flickr30K to Flickr8K	0.164	0.436	0.541	9
Flickr8K to Flickr30K	0.104	0.293	0.419	16

is to extend the proposed method to apply more effective image representation CNN models to improve the overall performances.

5   Conclusions

In this work, we introduced a novel fragment level method to solve the task of bidirectional cross-media information retrieval. The proposed method includes three modules, the visual module for representing fragments of images, the textual module for representing fragments of sentences, and the fusional module for generating the final matching scores of image and sentence pairs. In combination with the fragmental abstraction of textual input, this novel representation of image fragments is demonstrated to be reasonable and effective. Experimental results on benchmark datasets have shown that our method is promising in bidirectional image and sentence retrieval and achieves comparable performances among many state-of-the-art models.

Acknowledgements. Thanks to the Natural Science Foundation of China under Grant No. 61571453 and No. 61502264, Natural Science Foundation of Hunan Province, China under Grant No. 14JJ3010, Research Funding of National University of Defense Technology under grant No. ZK16-03-37.

References

1. Socher, R., Karpathy, A., Le, Q.V., et al.: Grounded compositional semantics for finding and describing images with sentences (2013). Nlp.stanford.edu
2. Eisenschtat, A., Wolf, L.: Linking Image and Text with 2-Way Nets (2017)
3. Girshick, R., Donahue, J., Darrell, T., et al.: Rich feature hierarchies for accurate object detection and semantic segmentation. In: Computer Vision and Pattern Recognition, pp. 580–587. IEEE (2013)
4. Karpathy, A., Joulin, A., Li, F.F.: Deep fragment embeddings for bidirectional image sentence mapping. In: Advances in Neural Information Processing Systems, vol. 3, pp. 1889–1897 (2014)
5. Plummer, B.A., Wang, L., Cervantes, C.M., et al.: Flickr30k entities: collecting region-to-phrase correspondences for richer image-to-sentence models. Int. J. Comput. Vis. **123**(1), 74–93 (2017)

6. Ma, L., Lu, Z., Shang, L., et al.: Multimodal convolutional neural networks for matching image and sentence. In: IEEE International Conference on Computer Vision, pp. 2623–2631 (2015)
7. Huang, Y., Wang, W., Wang, L.: Instance-aware Image and Sentence Matching with Selective Multimodal LSTM (2016)
8. Mikolov, T., Chen, K., Corrado, G., et al.: Efficient estimation of word representations in vector space. arXiv preprint arXiv:1301.3781 (2013)
9. Kalchbrenner, N., Grefenstette, E., Blunsom, P.: A convolutional neural network for modelling sentences. Eprint Arxiv, p. 1 (2014)
10. Vinyals, O., Toshev, A., Bengio, S., et al.: Show and tell: a neural image caption generator. Comput. Sci. 3156–3164 (2015)
11. Ghosh, S., Das, N., Goncalves, T., et al.: Representing image captions as concept graphs using semantic information. In: International Conference on Advances in Computing, Communications and Informatics, pp. 162–167 (2016)
12. Fang, H., Gupta, S., Iandola, F., et al.: From captions to visual concepts and back. Eprint Arxiv, pp. 1473–1482 (2014)
13. Wang, C., Yang, H., Bartz, C., et al.: Image captioning with deep bidirectional LSTMs. In: ACM on Multimedia Conference, pp. 988–997 (2016)
14. Dong, J., Li, X., Snoek, C.G.M.: Word2VisualVec: image and video to sentence matching by visual feature prediction. Arxiv (2016)
15. Simonyan, K., Zisserman, A.: Very deep convolutional networks for large-scale image recognition. arXiv preprint arXiv:1409.1556 (2014)
16. Caruana, R., Lawrence, S., Giles, L.: Overfitting in neural nets: backpropagation, conjugate gradient, and early stopping. In: International Conference on Neural Information Processing Systems, pp. 381–387. MIT Press (2000)
17. Hinton, G.E., Srivastava, N., Krizhevsky, A., et al.: Improving neural networks by preventing co-adaptation of feature detectors. Comput. Sci. **3**(4), 212–223 (2012)
18. Hodosh, M., Young, P., Hockenmaier, J.: Framing image description as a ranking task: data, models and evaluation metrics. J. Artif. Intell. Res. **47**(1), 853–899 (2013)
19. Young, P., Lai, A., Hodosh, M., et al.: From image descriptions to visual denotations: new similarity metrics for semantic inference over event descriptions (2014). Nlp.cs.illinois.edu
20. Mao, J., Xu, W., Yang, Y., et al.: Explain images with multimodal recurrent neural networks. arXiv preprint arXiv:1410.1090 (2014)
21. Yan, F., Mikolajczyk, K.: Deep correlation for matching images and text. In: Computer Vision and Pattern Recognition, pp. 3441–3450. IEEE (2015)
22. Klein, B., Lev, G., Sadeh, G., et al.: Fisher vectors derived from hybrid gaussian-laplacian mixture models for image annotation. Eprint Arxiv (2014)
23. Yu, T., Bai, L., Guo, J., Yang, Z., Xie, Y.: A deep two-stream network for bidirectional cross-media information retrieval. In: Chen, E., Gong, Y., Tie, Y. (eds.) PCM 2016. LNCS, vol. 9916, pp. 328–337. Springer, Cham (2016). https://doi.org/10.1007/978-3-319-48890-5_32
24. Russakovsky, O., Deng, J., et al.: Imagenet large scale visual recognition challenge. Int. J. Comput. Vis. **115**(3), 211–252 (2015)
25. Mnih, V., Heess, N., et al.: Recurrent models of visual attention. In: International Conference on Neural Information Processing Systems, pp. 2204–2212. MIT Press (2014)
26. Hu, B., Lu, Z., Li, H., Chen, Q.: Convolutional neural network architectures for matching natural language sentences. In: NIPS 2014 (2014)

Deep Pedestrian Detection Using Contextual Information and Multi-level Features

Weijie Kong[1], Nannan Li[1], Thomas H. Li[2], and Ge Li[1(✉)]

[1] School of Electronic and Computer Engineering, Shenzhen Graduate School,
Peking University, Shenzhen, China
geli@ece.pku.edu.cn
[2] Gpower Semiconductor, Inc., Suzhou, China

Abstract. Recently, Faster R-CNN achieves great performance in deep learning based object detection. However, a major bottleneck of Faster R-CNN lies on the sharp performance deterioration when detecting objects that are small in size or have a similar appearance with their backgrounds. To address this problem, we present a new pedestrian detection approach based on Faster R-CNN, which combines contextual information with multi-level features. The contextual information is embedded by pooling information from a larger area around the original region of interest. It helps pedestrians detection from cluttered backgrounds. The multi-level features can be obtained by pooling proposal-specific features from several shallow but high-resolution layers. These features are more informative for detecting small-size pedestrians. Extensive experiments on the challenging Caltech dataset validate that our approach not only performs better than the baseline of Faster R-CNN but also boosts the detection performance when combined with contextual information and multi-level features. Meanwhile, compared with numerous pedestrian detection approaches, our combined method outperforms all of them and achieves a quite superior performance.

Keywords: Pedestrian detection · Faster R-CNN
Contextual information · Multi-level features

1 Introduction

As a popular topic in computer vision community, pedestrian detection has attracted plenty of attention for decades for its importance in many practical applications, such as video surveillance, tracking, mobile robotics and advanced driver assistance systems (ADAS). During the last decade, numerous methods have been proposed to improve the performance of pedestrian detection.

Recently, taking advantage of convolutional neural networks (CNN), many excellent deep learning models have promoted the object detection performance to a much higher level. As one of the most popular and successful models, Faster R-CNN [1] uses a deep fully convolutional network called Region Proposal Network (RPN) to generate high-quality Region of Interests (RoI), which are fed

© Springer International Publishing AG 2018
K. Schoeffmann et al. (Eds.): MMM 2018, Part I, LNCS 10704, pp. 166–177, 2018.
https://doi.org/10.1007/978-3-319-73603-7_14

Hard Positive Samples   Hard Negative Samples

Fig. 1. Examples of hard positive and hard negative samples of Caltech dataset. These low-resolution samples are less discriminable from backgrounds. It's difficult to discriminate between them.

into the Fast R-CNN [2] detection network to simultaneously classify the object categories and regress the object bounding. Based on this pioneering work, many state-of-the-art detection models are proposed such as SSD [3], YOLO [4], and R-FCN [5].

Since pedestrian detection is a canonical case of the general object detection problem, many models derived from Faster R-CNN have been brought to this problem and taken the Caltech benchmark [6] top ranks [7–10]. Inspired by the great success of Faster R-CNN, we take the pipeline of [1] as the baseline of our work. However, Faster R-CNN has its shortcomings lie in two main aspects.

Firstly, as shown in Fig. 1, compared to general objects, pedestrians are less discriminable from backgrounds. These pedestrians usually appear in low resolution. Meanwhile, backgrounds such as vertical structures, tree trunk, and traffic lights easily bring about hard negative samples. During detecting, Faster R-CNN only uses information abstracted from a RoI close to the object, which is unable to discriminate between possible pedestrians and backgrounds, resulting in the increase of miss-rate. In addition, Faster R-CNN struggles with detecting small objects. For instance, the feature stride of VGG16 [11] last convolutional layer is 16. In a 600×1000 image, the feature scale of a 32×32 pedestrian will be just 2×2 on the last convolutional layer, which is too coarse to detect small objects.

To address the aforementioned limitations of Faster R-CNN, we explore enhancing Faster R-CNN to include two additional information sources to help pedestrian detection. Firstly, we incorporate contextual information. Context is known to be very useful for improving performance on deep learning based detection methods. It enables the detector to look wider around a pedestrian's RoI and makes a better discrimination between backgrounds and possible pedestrians, which helps reduce more false positive errors. Then, we utilize multi-level features which combine deep, coarse information with shallow, fine information to make features more abundant. These combined features can be more informative for detecting small pedestrians. In summary, the main contributions of this work are:

1. We integrate extra contextual information and multi-level features based on Faster R-CNN, which helps to detect pedestrians from cluttered backgrounds and small pedestrians.

2. Through an extensive experimental evaluation on the challenging Caltech pedestrian benchmark, we demonstrate that our approach not only performs better than the baseline of Faster R-CNN, but also boosts the detection performance when combined with contextual information and multi-level features.

3. Compared with numerous pedestrian detection approaches, our combined model yields a competitive result, which achieves a miss-rate of 14.0%.

This paper is organized as follows. Section 2 covers related works. Section 3 describes how to combine Faster R-CNN with contextual information and multi-level features. Section 4 presents the results of our experiments on Caltech dataset. Finally, Sect. 5 concludes this paper.

2   Related Work

In the past years, various efforts have been proposed to improve the performance of pedestrian detection. Current pedestrian detection methods can be generally grouped into two categories. The first category is known as hand-crafted approaches. Dalal and Triggs [12] firstly use the grids of Histograms of Oriented Gradient (HOG) descriptors, which significantly outperforms previous features. After that, most of the HOG based detection methods are proposed. Wang et al. [13] make full use of both HOG feature and LBP feature to handle partial occlusion. Furthermore, Deformable part-based models (DPM) [14] consider the appearance of each part and handle translational movement of parts. Besides, the Integral Channel Features (ICF) [15] and Aggregated Channel Features (ACF) [16] are among the most popular hand-crafted approaches, which efficiently extract features such as local sums, histograms, and Haar features using integral images.

Recently, object detection methods based on CNN have achieved very good performance [1–5]. Some recent works focus on improving the performance of pedestrian detection using CNN and push pedestrian detection results to an unprecedented level. Sermanet et al. [17] use an unsupervised method based on convolutional sparse coding to pre-train CNN for pedestrian detection. Based on Fast R-CNN, Li et al. [7] introduce multiple built-in sub-networks to detect pedestrians with scales from disjoint ranges. Tian et al. [18] improve pedestrian detection by learning high-level features from DNNs of multiple tasks, including pedestrian attribute prediction. Zhang et al. [8] use RPN [1] to generate a set of candidate region proposals and re-scored them with decision forest classifier trained over convolutional features. In [9], Tian et al. handle partial occlusion by training CNN with automatically selected part pool. Fused DNN [10] use a SSD [3] pedestrian candidate generator, a parallel classification network, and a pixel-wise semantic segmentation network to perform the detection.

Unlike the above CNN-based methods, our methods firstly make full use of contextual information and multi-level features together to perform pedestrian detection. It helps to detect pedestrians from cluttered backgrounds and small pedestrians.

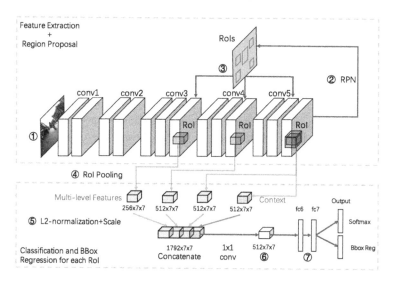

Fig. 2. The architecture of our proposed method. For an image, we extract features based on VGG16 model and generate 2000 RoIs. To evaluate each RoI, we extract contextual information from conv5_3 feature map, and extract multi-level features from several intermediate layers. Contextual information and multi-level features are normalized with L_2-norm, concatenated and compressed to a fixed-length feature descriptor. Finally, these features are fed into two fully-connected layers and produce two outputs: softmax probabilities and bounding-box regression offsets.

3   Proposed Method

In this section, we describe our proposed method. We begin with a brief overview of the entire framework, followed by specific details.

3.1   Framework

The framework of our method is shown in Fig. 2. It consists of two components: a fully convolutional Region Proposal Network (RPN) for proposal generation, and a downstream Fast R-CNN detector taking regions with high foreground likelihood as input. We choose Faster R-CNN not only for its prevalence and state-of-the-art performance, but also generality: our observations should remain mostly effective when similar techniques are applied in other CNN-based pedestrian detectors.

To detect pedestrians, a deep VGG16 model processes an image and generates the hierarchical convolutional feature maps. By performing an RPN on the last feature map conv5_3, we obtain thousands of high-quality region proposals that might contain pedestrians. For each RoI, we first pool contextual information from conv5_3. Then we pool a fixed-length feature descriptor from several layers (conv3_3, conv4_3, and conv5_3) to form the multi-level features. The contextual information and multi-level features are normalized with L_2-norm, concatenated and compressed (1×1 convolution) to produce a fixed-length feature descriptor of size $512 \times 7 \times 7$. Finally, the fixed-length features are fed into two fully-connected layers and produce two sibling output layers.

The first sibling layer outputs softmax probability values, $p = (p_0, p_1)$, over "background" and pedestrian classes. p_0 and p_1 denote the probability values of "background" and pedestrian classes respectively. The second sibling layer outputs the bounding-box regression offsets for pedestrian class, which is denoted as $t = (t_x, t_y, t_w, t_h)$. For each training region proposal, there is a ground-truth class label u and a ground-truth bounding-box regression target v. To jointly train for classification and bounding-box regression, we minimize an objective function using following multi-task loss L on each labeled proposal:

$$L(p, u, t^u, v) = L_{cls}(p, u) + \lambda[u \geq 1]L_{loc}(t^u, v) \tag{1}$$

where $L_{cls} = -logp_u$ is log loss for true class u.

The second task loss L_{loc}, which is defined over the true bounding-box regression targets for class u, $v = (t_x, t_y, t_w, t_h)$, and a predicted tuple (formula) again for class u. The Iverson bracket indicator function $[u \geq 1]$ evaluates to 1 when $u \geq 1$ and 0 otherwise. By convention the catch-all background class is labeled $u = 0$. We ignore the L_{loc} for background RoIs since there is no notion of a ground-truth bounding box. For bounding-box regression, we use the loss:

$$L_{loc}(t^u, v) = \sum_{i \in \{x, y, w, h\}} smooth_L(t_i^u - v_i) \tag{2}$$

where the robust loss $smooth_L(\cdot)$ is defined as:

$$smooth_L(x) = \begin{cases} 0.5x^2 & |x| < 1 \\ |x| - 0.5 & \text{otherwise} \end{cases} \tag{3}$$

The parameter λ controls the balance between the two task losses. The ground-truth regression targets v is normalized to have zero mean and unit variance. By default we set $\lambda = 1$ in all experiments. We use the stochastic gradient descent (SGD) algorithm to calculate the minimization of loss function.

3.2   Context Embedding

Context is known to be useful for improving the performance of deep learning based detection and segmentation tasks. By visualizing the original Faster R-CNN detection results on Caltech testing set, we observe numerous false positive errors. These false positive errors mainly result from backgrounds of vertical structures, tree leaves, or traffic lights. The behind reason is that Faster R-CNN only uses information involved in a RoI close to the object. However, the region around a RoI always contains additional information that may provide visibility over larger ranges, which enables the detector to look wider around a RoI and makes a better discrimination between possible pedestrians and backgrounds.

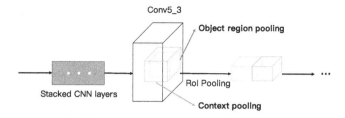

Fig. 3. Contextual information extraction. The green (blue) cubes represent object (context) region pooling. (Color figure online)

This information is known as contextual information. Thus, from the above observation, we hypothesize that adding additional contextual information to Faster R-CNN is helpful to reduce false positive errors. As shown in Fig. 3, in order to gather contextual information on conv5_3, we scale the size of the original proposal box by a factor of 1.5. Specifically, when performing the RoI pooling on conv5_3, we pool from 1.5× larger area than the original proposal region, so that the pooling features contain both original object and contextual information.

3.3   Multi-level Feature Extraction

Faster R-CNN struggles with detecting small objects. It pools from the last convolutional feature map. However, for small pedestrians (50–70 pixels for Caltech), the last feature map always has low resolution (usually with a stride of 16 pixels). When RoI pooling layer is performed on such low-resolution feature map, it will lead to "plain" features caused by collapsing bins. These features are not discriminative on small regions and too coarse for classification of small pedestrians. Thus, in order to detect small pedestrians, the features for region proposal and detection should be more informative and the feature resolution should be more reasonable.

We address this problem by pooling proposal-specific features from several shallow but high-resolution layers to form the multi-level features. For instance, we extract features from RoIs on conv3_3 (of a stride = 4 pixels), conv4_3 (of a stride = 8 pixels) and conv5_3 (of a stride = 16 pixels) and concatenate them together. However, since these features have different scales and norms, they should not be concatenated simply. Naively concatenating features leads to poor performance as the features of larger value will dominate the smaller ones. Thus, inspired by [19], we normalize each individual feature with L_2-norm first, and learn to scale each separately, as described in Sect. 3.4. It makes the training more stable and improves performance. Then we concatenate these normalized features together to form the multi-level features and use a convolutional layer to reduce the final feature to the shape of $512 \times 7 \times 7$, so that it has the correct dimension to feed into the first fully-connected layer (fc6). The convolutional layer is initialized with "Xavier" algorithm [20] and has the filter size of 1×1. In this way, we combine finer, high-resolution features with coarse, low-resolution features for better classification of small pedestrians.

3.4 L_2-normalization and Scale

For a layer with d-dimensional input $\mathbf{x} = (x_1 \ldots x_d)$, we use L_2-norm to normalize it with $\hat{\mathbf{x}} = \mathbf{x}/||\mathbf{x}||_2$, where $||\mathbf{x}||_2 = (\sum_{i=1}^{d} |x_i|^2)^{1/2}$ is the L_2-norm. However, without scaling each input of layer accordingly, simply normalizing the input will change the scale of the layer and will slow down the learning. Thus, it's necessary to learn the scale for each channel by introducing a scaling parameter γ_i, which scales the normalized value by $y_i = \gamma_i \hat{x}_i$. During training, we use back-propagation and chain rule to compute derivatives with respect to scaling factor γ and input data x. We use the implementation of L_2-normalization layer from [19].

4   Experiments

4.1   Dataset for Training and Testing

We choose Caltech dataset [6] to train and test our model. It is one of the most widely used pedestrian datasets. It consists of about 250,000 frames with a total of 350,000 bounding boxes, where 2,300 unique pedestrians are annotated. For all experiments, we train our model on the improved Caltech-10x annotations from [21], which are of higher quality than the original annotations. We train the model with two categories (person and ignore) depending on whether the bounding box is annotated as "ignore". For evaluation, we adopt the original annotations and follow the standard Caltech evaluation [6]: log miss-rate (MR) is averaged over the FPPI (false positives per image) of the range $[10^{-2}, 10^0]$. Unless otherwise specified, all experiments are evaluated on the "reasonable" setup (pedestrians over 50-pixel height with no or partial occlusion).

4.2   Experimental Setup

The whole network is trained on NVIDIA Tesla GPU K80 with 12 GB memory. Both region proposal and object detection networks are trained on a single-scale image. We rescale the images so that their shorter side is 600 pixels. For RPN training, it is performed on the last convolutional layer. An anchor is considered as a positive example if it has an Intersection-over-Union (IoU) greater than 0.7 with one ground truth box, and IoU less than 0.3 is considered as negative. To reduce redundancy proposals, we adopt non-maximum suppression (NMS) with IoU threshold at 0.7, which leaves us about 2000 proposal regions per image. We adopt approximate joint training strategy for sharing features between RPN and Fast R-CNN. We train with a learning rate of 0.001 for 60k mini-batches, and 0.0001 for the next 20k mini-batches. We use a momentum of 0.9 and a weight decay of 0.0005. Other details are as in [1] and we adopt the publicly available code of [1].

After training the Baseline-Faster R-CNN model with above parameter settings, it achieves 20.3% miss-rate, which underperforms on the pedestrian detection task. It is because Caltech dataset contains abounding small pedestrians and original Faster R-CNN fails to handle them. To generate more proposals for small sizes, we first slightly modify Faster R-CNN to generate anchors with 10 scales starting from the scale of 2.0 with a stride of 1.3×. Then we adopt anchors of a single aspect ratio of 2.44 (height to width), which is the average pedestrian aspect ratio of Caltech dataset. With this modification, we reduce the miss-rate from 20.3% down to 18.5%, as shown in Table 1.

4.3 Ablation Experiments

In this subsection, we conduct ablation experiments on the Caltech dataset. We conduct 5 different experiments, each one combined with different extra features. The overall experimental results are presented in Table 1.

Table 1. Combining context with features from different layers. Metric: log-average miss-rate on Caltech benchmark. M: modify the anchor scales and ratio aspects. Ctx: combine with contextual information. C5: combine with features pooled from conv5_3. C4: combine with features pooled from conv4_3. C3: combine with features pooled from conv3_3. ∗: This entry is the unstable result when combine multi-level features without L_2 and scale.

Exp. no.	RoI pooling from	M	Ctx	MR (without L_2 + Scale)	MR (with L_2 + Scale)
1	C5 (baseline)			20.3%	-
2	C5	√		18.5%	18.9%
3	C5	√	√	16.7%	16.4%
4	C5 + C4	√	√	15.0%	14.7%
5	C5 + C4 + C3	√	√	∗15.3%	**14.0%**

Effects of Multi-level Features. To investigate the impact of multi-level features, we first train several Faster R-CNN models with features that are pooled from different layers. These models are combined with contextual information. When concatenating these features, we adopt L_2-normalization and scale operations to make the features from different layers have similar magnitude. As shown in Table 1, we clearly observe that the miss-rate appears to be lower due to more features pooled from different layers are added (C3 & C4). It indicates that multi-level features can improve the detection performance consistently. This is because lower convolution features (C3 & C4) are finer and more high-resolution, which is more informative for detecting small pedestrians.

Effects of Contextual Information. Next, we disentangle the influence of contextual information. For this purpose, we train different multi-level models with context embedding as mentioned in Sect. 3.2. L_2-normalization and scale

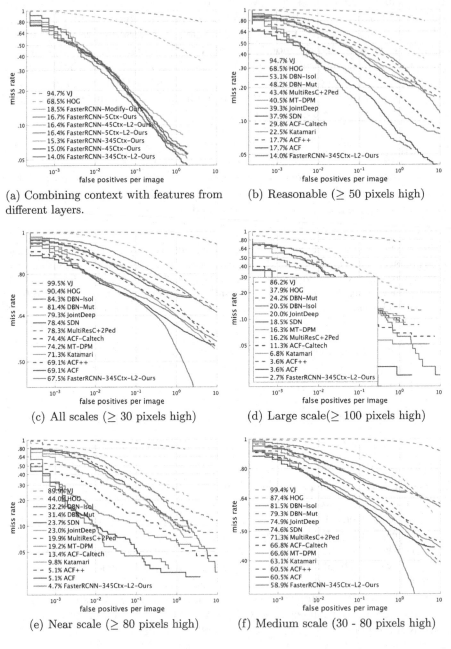

(a) Combining context with features from different layers.

(b) Reasonable (≥ 50 pixels high)

(c) All scales (≥ 30 pixels high)

(d) Large scale(≥ 100 pixels high)

(e) Near scale (≥ 80 pixels high)

(f) Medium scale (30 - 80 pixels high)

Fig. 4. The comparison of our approach for pedestrian detection with recent state-of-the-art methods on Caltech benchmark.

operations are also adopted. Table 1 presents that with context embedding (Exp. 3, Exp. 4 & Exp. 5), it leads the miss-rate to be 16.4%, 14.7% and 14.0% receptively, which are all lower than baseline result (20.3%). It demonstrates that the detection performance has been actually boosted by contextual information. When without L_2-normalization and scale, contextual information still leads to the decrease of miss-rate. Figure 4(a) presents the ROC curves when combining context with features from different layers.

Effects of L_2-normalization and Scale. As mentioned above, our detector pools features from multiple layers and combines them for pedestrian detection. From Table 1 (fourth column), we observe that when adding C3, the result of MR (without L2+Scale) becomes worse. This is because features from different layers always have a much different scale and norm, if we simply concatenate the features from each layer and reduce the dimensionality using a 1×1 convolutional operation, the performance gain is unstable. Thus, it's necessary to normalize each individual feature with L_2-norm first, and then learn to scale each separately, so that features pooled from all layers have similar magnitude. As shown in Table 1 (fifth column), after adopting L_2-normalization and scale, the problem is fixed and leads to a competitive result (14.0%).

4.4 Comparison with State-of-the-Art Methods

We compare our method with hand-crafted models such as VJ, HOG, ACF, MT-DPM, MultiResC + 2Ped, Katamari. And we also compare with deep models including DBN-Isol, DBN-Mut, SDN, and JointDeep. The overall experimental results are depicted in Fig. 4(b)–(f). We can clearly observe that:

1. The proposed method performs significantly better than the baseline detector (Faster R-CNN) on reasonable test set (in Fig. 4(b), our miss-rate is **14.0%**, Faster R-CNN miss-rate is 20.3%).
2. As shown in Fig. 4(c)–(f), the proposed method outperforms all the other state-of-the-art methods on all of the four tests, indicating that our method is an effective way for pedestrian detection, especially in multi-scale cases.
3. As shown in Fig. 4(f), the proposed method performs better than all the other methods on medium test sets (pedestrian of 30–80 pixels high, which contains small scale pedestrians), demonstrating that the proposed detector truly benefits from combining features from multi-levels in the training phase.

5   Conclusion

Based on Faster R-CNN, we have presented a method that combines contextual information with multi-level features for pedestrian detection task. On the one hand, the contextual information, which is gathered by enlarging the original object region scale, helps the detector make a better discrimination between possible pedestrians and backgrounds. On the one hand, the multi-level features, which can be obtained by pooling proposal-specific features from several shallow but high-resolution intermediate layers, are more informative for detecting small-size pedestrians. Extensive experiments validate that the detection performance has been actually boosted by contextual information and multi-level features. Meanwhile, experiments also show that when concatenating features from different level layers, it's necessary to normalize and scale each individual feature. Compared with recent state-of-the-art methods, our combined method achieves a superior result on Caltech dataset.

Acknowledgment. This project was supported by Shenzhen Key Laboratory for Intelligent Multimedia and Virtual Reality (ZDSYS201703031405467), Shenzhen Peacock Plan (20130408-183003656), and National Science Foundation of China (No. U1611461).

References

1. Ren, S., He, K., Girshick, R.B., Sun, J.: Faster R-CNN: towards real-time object detection with region proposal networks. CoRR abs/1506.01497 (2015)
2. Girshick, R.: Fast R-CNN. In: ICCV, pp. 1440–1448 (2015)
3. Liu, W., Anguelov, D., Erhan, D., Szegedy, C., Reed, S., Fu, C.-Y., Berg, A.C.: SSD: single shot multibox detector. In: Leibe, B., Matas, J., Sebe, N., Welling, M. (eds.) ECCV 2016. LNCS, vol. 9905, pp. 21–37. Springer, Cham (2016). https://doi.org/10.1007/978-3-319-46448-0_2
4. Redmon, J., Divvala, S.K., Girshick, R.B., Farhadi, A.: You only look once - unified, real-time object detection. CoRR cs.CV (2015)
5. Dai, J., Li, Y., He, K., Sun, J.: R-FCN - object detection via region-based fully convolutional networks. In: NIPS (2016)
6. Dollar, P., Wojek, C., Schiele, B., Perona, P.: Pedestrian detection: an evaluation of the state of the art. IEEE Trans. Pattern Anal. Mach. Intell. 34(4), 743–761 (2012)
7. Li, J., Liang, X., Shen, S., Xu, T., Yan, S.: Scale-aware fast R-CNN for pedestrian detection. CoRR (2015)
8. Zhang, L., Lin, L., Liang, X., He, K.: Is faster R-CNN doing well for pedestrian detection? In: Leibe, B., Matas, J., Sebe, N., Welling, M. (eds.) ECCV 2016. LNCS, vol. 9906, pp. 443–457. Springer, Cham (2016). https://doi.org/10.1007/978-3-319-46475-6_28
9. Tian, Y., Luo, P., Wang, X., Tang, X.: Deep learning strong parts for pedestrian detection. In: ICCV, pp. 1904–1912 (2015)
10. Du, X., El-Khamy, M., Lee, J., Davis, L.S.: Fused DNN: a deep neural network fusion approach to fast and robust pedestrian detection, October 2016. arXiv.org
11. Simonyan, K., Zisserman, A.: Very deep convolutional networks for large-scale image recognition. CoRR abs/1409.1556 (2014)
12. Dalal, N., Triggs, B.: Histograms of oriented gradients for human detection. In: IEEE Computer Society Conference on Computer Vision and Pattern Recognition, CVPR 2005, vol. 1, pp. 886–893. IEEE (2005)
13. Wang, X., Han, T.X., Yan, S.: An HOG-LBP human detector with partial occlusion handling. In: 2009 IEEE 12th International Conference on Computer Vision, pp. 32–39. IEEE (2009)

14. Felzenszwalb, P.F., Girshick, R.B., McAllester, D., Ramanan, D.: Object detection with discriminatively trained part-based models. IEEE Trans. Pattern Anal. Mach. Intell. **32**(9), 1627–1645 (2010)
15. Dollár, P., Tu, Z., Perona, P., Belongie, S.: Integral channel features (2009)
16. Dollár, P., Appel, R., Belongie, S., Perona, P.: Fast feature pyramids for object detection. IEEE Trans. Pattern Anal. Mach. Intell. **36**(8), 1532–1545 (2014)
17. Sermanet, P., Kavukcuoglu, K., Chintala, S., LeCun, Y.: Pedestrian detection with unsupervised multi-stage feature learning. In: Proceedings of IEEE Conference on Computer Vision and Pattern Recognition, pp. 3626–3633 (2013)
18. Tian, Y., Luo, P., Wang, X., Tang, X.: Pedestrian detection aided by deep learning semantic tasks. In: Proceedings of IEEE Conference on Computer Vision and Pattern Recognition, pp. 5079–5087 (2015)
19. Liu, W., Rabinovich, A., Berg, A.C.: ParseNet: looking wider to see better, June 2015. arXiv.org
20. Glorot, X., Bengio, Y.: Understanding the difficulty of training deep feedforward neural networks. In: Teh, Y.W., Titterington, M. (eds.) Proceedings of 13th International Conference on Artificial Intelligence and Statistics. Proceedings of Machine Learning Research, Chia Laguna Resort, PMLR, Sardinia, Italy, vol. 9, pp. 249–256, 13–15 May 2010
21. Zhang, S., Benenson, R., Omran, M., Hosang, J., Schiele, B.: How far are we from solving pedestrian detection? In: CVPR (2016)

Dual-Way Guided Depth Image Inpainting with RGBD Image Pairs

Hua Yuan, Yuanyuan Zhou, Yun Sheng[✉], and Guixu Zhang

The School of Computer Science and Software Engineering,
East China Normal University, Shanghai 200062, China
ysheng@cs.ecnu.edu.cn

Abstract. Raw depth images acquired by low-cost range imaging sensors, such as Kinect v1 and Kinect v2, usually contain invalid regions without depth information and suffer from noise. Although many approaches are proposed to address the problems, the robustness of these approaches still needs enhancement. This paper introduces a dual-way guided inpainting method with RGBD image pairs to restore the missing depth values of invalid regions and to eliminate noise caused by acquisition apparatus. By leveraging the structural difference between the colour and depth images, the colour image is first segmented with watershed segmentation and then merged under the guidance of the simultaneously captured depth image, followed by inpainting the depth image guided by the merged colour image using Radial Basis Functions (RBFs). The proposed framework of the dual-way guided approach with the RBFs is new for depth image inpainting and outperforms the existing state-of-the-art approaches in the experimental evaluations.

Keywords: Image processing · Multimedia sensor · Guided filtering
Depth image inpainting · RBF

1 Introduction

The advent of low-cost depth sensors, such as Kinect v1 and Kinect v2, has substantially eased the research overhead in 3D reconstruction, gesture recognition, and stereoscopic video capture, *etc.* Nevertheless, raw depth images acquired by these sensors contain some invalid regions where the depth values are missing due to transparent or reflective surfaces, camera joggling, bad lighting, or ranging limit of sensors and usually visualised as black holes. In addition, depth sensors alone produce noise. For simplicity, we call both the invalid regions and noise of depth images invalid pixels in this paper. These invalid pixels limit the direct use of depth images for further applications. Raw depth images must be repaired before any use.

Many methods, which can be grouped into two classes according to source images utilised, have been proposed to cope with raw depth images. One class of methods try to recover the impaired depth images with only consecutive

© Springer International Publishing AG 2018
K. Schoeffmann et al. (Eds.): MMM 2018, Part I, LNCS 10704, pp. 178–189, 2018.
https://doi.org/10.1007/978-3-319-73603-7_15

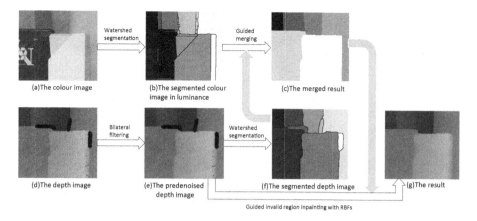

Fig. 1. Illustration of the dual-way guided depth image inpainting method. (Color figure online)

depth frames by taking advantage of their temporal consistency and spatial similarity [16,17]. Nonetheless, because the depth frames have built-in deficiencies caused by the limited working range of sensors or by the object properties, such as reflectance and transparency, or even by inter-frame misalignments, the utility of this class of methods is poor. As the colour sensor coming along with the depth sensor is usually available, the other class of methods make use of the spatial information from both the depth and colour images captured simultaneously [4,6,9]. In fact, all of the aforementioned methods only consider the neighbourhood of invalid regions in the depth and colour images, and would fail if the neighbouring pixels were missing or contaminated. In order to resolve this problem, we insist on preventing those contaminated pixels from being used in filling invalid regions.

In this paper, we propose a dual-way guided depth image inpainting method with RGBD image pairs. In order to inpaint invalid regions more accurately, we resort to valid pixels and meanwhile insulate the contaminated ones. We find that the colour image generally has a higher resolution and clearer object silhouettes, while its corresponding depth image is usually visually more structured. We name this phenomenon structural difference of an RGBD image pair. Moreover, we find that a segmented colour image can help identify the valid pixels from the contaminated ones. Nevertheless, as the colour image often contains complex texture leading to over-segmentation, the segmented colour image needs to be merged first. This merging process can be accomplished under the guidance of the depth image thanks to the structural difference. We name the above guided operations dual-way guided inpainting in order to distinguish it from the extant guided methods, mostly single-way. Therefore, the major contribution of this paper lies in the proposal and implementation of this brand new idea of dual-way guided inpainting which is later experimentally demonstrated in comparison with the existing guided depth inpainting methods. Moreover, another

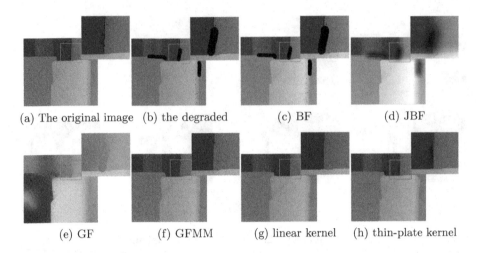

(a) The original image   (b) the degraded   (c) BF   (d) JBF

(e) GF   (f) GFMM   (g) linear kernel   (h) thin-plate kernel

Fig. 2. An inpainting result comparison on '*plastic*'.

major contribution of this paper is that we, for the first time, apply Radial Basis Functions (RBFs) to the inpainting procedure. The RBFs have been broadly employed to resolve the problems in neural networks, pattern recognition, and 3D reconstruction [3], as they are capable of approximating multivariable functions with a unique solution. We use the RBFs to inpaint invalid regions mainly because the RBFs take global account of the distribution of those known depth pixels around invalid regions and learn fast. The RBFs have also been experimentally demonstrated to be an effective means for depth image inpainting.

2   Related Work

In this section, we review the state-of-the-art guided inpainting methods that our work competes with. Guided depth image inpainting has been explored for years [15]. Bilateral Filtering (BF) presented in [1,5] employs both the position and intensity information of the depth image to construct two Gaussian filter kernels. With the aligned colour image available, BF was generalised to Joint Bilateral Filtering (JBF) [10,11,14], where the spatial similarity of the colour image rather than the depth image was calculated. Although many papers have been published to use the information from both the depth image and its aligned colour image, it still remains a tough issue to balance the amounts of information to be used. More specifically, in the conventional single-way guided inpainting approaches, if the colour image weighs too much, the result will be short of credibility; whereas taking too much information from the depth image also hardly produces a trustworthy result. For example, although Guided Filtering (GF) [7] is able to handle both invalid regions and noise, GF depends too much on the colour image to precisely recover the depth image.

Another consideration is how to intelligently select the search region of candidate pixels. For example, Gong *et al.* conducted Guided Filtering via the Fast

Marching Method (GFMM) [6] by introducing a new inpainting model to recover invalid regions in the depth image. Similar to JBF, a geometric distance term, colour similarity term, level set term, and distance term in the normal direction were multiplied into the weighting function in GFMM. They also calculated a colour-similarity term to decide the proceeding order for depth propagation. The guided image filter proposed in [7] was then adopted to further refine the results. However, there are two major problems in GFMM. One is if the neighbourhood of a pixel to be inpainted on the region boundary contained invalid pixels, the resulting inaccuracy would be spread into the whole region by the following propagation process. The other problem in GFMM is that an invalid region would be incorrectly inpainted if the guiding colour image contained too much texture detail. In order to resolve the above problems in the existing guided methods, in this paper, we propose a dual-way guided inpainting method by taking advantage of the structural difference between the colour and depth images.

3   Dual-Way Guided Depth Image Inpainting

The framework of the new inpainting method is illustrated in Fig. 1. Figure 1(a) and (d) show an RGBD image pair, where white Gaussian noise ($\mu = 0.001$, $\sigma = 0.001$) is deliberately added into the depth image to simulate the physical noise caused by a depth sensor itself. Furthermore, some black holes are artificially crafted on the regional boundaries of the depth image to represent the invalid regions whose depth values are missing. The dual-way guided operations are depicted by two shaded arrows. Since the segmented depth image (Fig. 1(f)), after predenoising (Fig. 1(e)), is usually less divided than the watershed segmented colour image (Fig. 1(b)), the segmented depth image can be used to guide merging the over-segmented colour image, which is thought of as the first guided operation, resulting in Fig. 1(c). As the other shaded arrow points, the second guided operation is carried out by inpainting, under the guidance of the merged colour image, the invalid regions of the predenoised depth image with the RBFs, leading to the result shown in Fig. 1(g).

3.1   Depth Guided Segmentation of Colour Image

In the proposed framework, we need to assign each pixel in an invalid region a partition under the guidance of the colour image. To this end, we resort to the well-known watershed segmentation algorithm. Watersheds are composed of pixels with the locally highest gradient values in the image, and the highest gradient values usually occur on edges of the image. The gradient image can be easily achieved by filtering the input image with the 'Sobel' operators in both the vertical and horizontal directions. The original watershed algorithm is sensitive to weak edges due to abundant texture or noise, leading to over-segmentation with unwanted partitions. Hereupon, we provide some betterments.

As discussed previously, apart from the invalid regions, the raw depth image may contain some noise which should be cleared up ahead of the watershed segmentation. The clearance, also called predenoising, is carried out using the edge-preserving bilateral filter, whose result is shown in Fig. 1(e). After predenoising, the watershed algorithm is applied to the depth image.

Algorithm 1. Depth guided segmentation of the colour image

Input: An over-segmented colour image with regions $C = \{C_1, C_2, \ldots, C_l\}$ sorted in area and a similarity threshold ε.

Output: A merged colour image under the guidance of the depth image.

1 **for** $k = 1; k \leq l; k = k + 1$ **do**

2   sample boundary pixels of C_k and in turn compute the similarity term $R(p)$ of each sampling boundary pixel p with its nearest pixel of the neighbouring region;

3   **if** *the corresponding depth value of p is missing* **then**

4        $R(p) = G_{dst}G_{col}$;

5   **else**

6        $R(p) = G_{dst}G_{col}G_{dep}$;

7   **if** $max(R(p)) > \varepsilon$ **then**

8   merge C_k with its neighbouring region of the largest similarity, *i.e.* maximal $R(p)$;

9 **return** the merged colour image.

Similarly, we segment out the colour image with the watershed algorithm. Figure 1(b) shows the segmented result, which, however, appears over-segmented. To deal with the over-segmentation in the colour image, the segmented depth image (Fig. 1(f)) is used to guide merging the segmented colour image.

In our algorithm, colour, depth, and distance similarities dominate the merging of the over-segmented colour image. Of each sampling pixel on the boundary of a single region in the colour image, a regional similarity with its nearest pixel of the neighbouring region is calculated. A single region is only merged with the neighbouring region with the largest regional similarity when satisfying an empirically predefined threshold ε. The regional similarity term around a pixel p on the boundary is calculated by

$$R(p) = \begin{cases} G_{dst}G_{col}G_{dep}, & \text{if } p_d \text{ is valid} \\ G_{dst}G_{col}, & \text{if } p_d \text{ is invalid}' \end{cases} \tag{1}$$

where p_d denotes the corresponding depth value of p. $R(p)$ is evaluated by a geometric distance term G_{dst}, a colour similarity term G_{col}, and a depth similarity term G_{dep} if the depth value is valid, and these terms are defined as

$$G_{dst} = \exp\left(-\frac{\|i - j\|^2}{\sigma_{dst}^2}\right), G_{col} = \exp\left(-\frac{\|I(i) - I(j)\|^2}{\sigma_{col}^2}\right),$$

$$G_{dep} = \exp\left(-\frac{\|D(i) - D(j)\|^2}{\sigma_{dep}^2}\right), \tag{2}$$

where i is the coordinate of the current pixel, and j indexes the neighbourhood of i; I and D symbolize the corresponding pixel values in the colour and depth images, respectively; notations σ_{dst}^2, σ_{col}^2, and σ_{dep}^2 are the variances of corresponding Gaussian functions determined empirically. In our method, G_{dst} gives a pixel geometrically closer to p a higher contribution to $R(p)$; G_{col} ensures that a pixel having similar colour to $I(p)$ contributes more; If p_d is valid, G_{dep} governs the merging of the segmented colour image under the guidance of the depth image. We find such a combination of similarity terms works well for our inpainting scheme. Moreover, this guided merging process is also described with pseudocode in Algorithm 1. As can be seen in Fig. 1, the letter 'N' in the blue book of the colour image is merged into the book region in Fig. 1(c) under the guidance of the depth image.

3.2   Colour Image Guided Invalid Region Inpainting

After the over-segmented colour image is merged, it can be used to guide inpainting invalid regions of the depth image. In this paper we use the RBFs to inpaint the invalid regions under the guidance of the merged colour image because the RBFs take global account of the distribution of those known depth pixels around invalid regions and learn fast. The task of the RBFs is explained as follows:

Given a set of points $\{x_m \in R^d\}$ and its associated function values $\{f_m \in R\}$, find an interpolant $s : R^d \rightarrow R$ such that $s(x_m) = f_m$, where $m = 1, \ldots, N$. Treating depth pixels as the third dimensional data, we have d equal to 2 here. Note that the notation $x_m = (x, y)$ represents the 2D coordinate of a valid pixel with a known depth value in the depth image. N denotes the number of the given points. In this paper, N denotes the number of pixels in the invalid regions. Let δ denote the radial basis function. The problem is to find a set of coefficients $\{\varphi_n\}$ satisfying the equation

$$s(x_m) = \sum_n \varphi_n \delta(||x_m - x_n||) \tag{3}$$

where x_n denotes the neighbourhood of pixel x_m, and $\delta(||x_m - x_n||)$ is the symmetric kernel function. Among the various RBF kernels, the linear and thin-plate kernels are most extensively used, and respectively, expressed as,

$$\delta_{linear}(r) = r, \quad \delta_{thin-plate}(r) = r^2 \log r. \tag{4}$$

Given that the depth values within a segmented region are distributed plainly, it is ready to implement the RBFs to interpolate the invalid regions on the predenoised depth image (Fig. 1(e)) under the guidance of the merged colour image (Fig. 1(c)). For each invalid region, the merged colour image in our method determines the effective regions for evaluating the coefficients of the RBFs. With the evaluated coefficients, the missing depth values in the invalid regions can be interpolated. Figure 1(g) is the recovered result of Fig. 1(d) using the linear kernel. We also test the RBFs with the thin-plate kernel. Comparing the results of using two kernels (Fig. 2(g) and (h)), we find that the linear outperforms the thin-plate with less computational time but a visually better result.

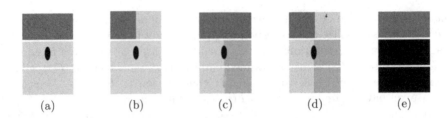

Fig. 3. Case study. In each subfigure, there are three blocks representing the corresponding regions in the colour image, depth image and inpainting result, where the areas in black represent invalid regions to inpaint. (Color figure online)

3.3 Case Study

In this section, we summarise all the possible cases that our colour image guided inpainting scheme in Sect. 3.2 can or cannot deal with. As the sketch maps in Fig. 3 show, most of the cases, except the one in Fig. 3(e), belong to two sets, according to whether or not an invalid region occurs on regional boundaries of the depth image. The set of an invalid region not occurring on the regional boundaries can also be divided into two subsets, according to whether or not the invalid region lies on the corresponding regional boundaries of the colour image, as shown in Fig. 3(a) and (b). Similarly, the set of an invalid region occurring on the region boundaries of the depth image can also be divided into two subsets, as shown in Fig. 3(c) and (d). Our colour image guided inpainting can handle all the above cases properly except the one illustrated by Fig. 3(c). For the case in Fig. 3(c), the program incorrectly determines the effective regions of the RBF for the invalid region, making the RBF interpolation result to the invalid region totally chaotic. Moreover, the block for the colour image in Fig. 3(b) is crafted slightly larger than the depth one in order to illustrate the two colour regions not having been merged in the previous step. Note that we only show the double-region cases in Fig. 3 for the sake of simplicity. However, an invalid region may occur on the boundaries of multiple regions. Such a case can be handled in the same way as those shown in Fig. 3. Moreover, there is an extreme case that a whole invalid region exactly corresponds to a single region in the colour image, as illustrated in Fig. 3(e). Our scheme cannot cope with such a case as well since the effective region of the RBF is void.

4 Experimental Evaluations

We conduct experiments on the RGBD image pairs from the Middlebury dataset [12,13], the in-house dataset acquired by both Kinect v1 and Kinect v2, as well as the RGBD video sequences captured by Kinect v1 [2] and Kinect v2 [8].

On 'plastic' of the Middlebury dataset: Figure 2 shows a comparison between our method and BF, JBF, GF, and GFMM on the deliberately degraded

(a)   (b)   (c)   (d)   (e)

Fig. 4. The depth images inpainted by different methods. The experiments are conducted on '*mask*', '*lampshade1*', '*flowerpot*', '*teddy*', and '*books*'. The first row shows the input colour images, and the aligned input depth images are arranged in the second row. The 3rd-6th rows present, respectively, the results inpainted by BF, JBF, GF, and GFMM. Our results are shown in the last row. (Color figure online)

Table 1. PSNR (in DB) and RMSE (in pixel) values of the results on '*plastic*'

	BF	JBF	GF	GFMM	Ours (thinplate)	Ours (linear)
PSNR	18.645	19.150	11.098	31.626	**33.561**	**34.062**
RMSE	0.117	0.110	0.279	0.0262	**0.0210**	**0.0198**

depth image of '*plastic*'. It is observed that BF cannot properly handle those invalid regions. Even if we increase the size of the filter window, the result is still unacceptable. The result of JBF in Fig. 2(d) depicts that although the guiding colour image helps reconstruct the boundaries of the holes, the redundant texture has done harm to the result. For example, the unwanted stripes in the bottom-left region of the close-up in Fig. 2(d) are the byproduct of the input colour image in Fig. 1(a). Similar to BF, GF also fails to fill the holes because of its characteristic of global filtering, as shown in Fig. 2(e). The result in Fig. 2(f) shows that GFMM only performs well on the invalid regions, while the added Gaussian noise remains intact. Figure 2(g) and (h) are the results of our method, which visually outperform the other competing methods. It can be seen that the RBF interpolation with the thin-plate kernel produces a less acceptable result than the linear kernel and comes with a higher computational complexity. Thus, we use only the linear kernel in the following experiments. Furthermore, in Table 1, we carry out objective comparisons on '*plastic*' with both the Peak Signal to Noise Ratio (PSNR) and Root Mean Square Error (RMSE), two common measures of the denoising effectiveness. The larger the PSNR value and the smaller the RMSE value, the better the algorithm performance. The table shows that our method holds the largest PSNR as well as the smallest RMSE. Moreover, the linear kernel beats the thin-plate once again in the objective evaluations. It is worth noting that in theory there is no groundtruth for the calculation of both the PSNR and RMSE. Instead, we presume that the original depth image shown in Fig. 2(a) is the groundtruth image. Such a strategy has also been adopted by [6].

On five scenarios of the Middlebury dataset: The next group of experiments are conducted on five scenarios of the Middlebury dataset, *mask*, *lampshade1*, *flowerpot*, *teddy*, and *books*. Each scenario contains an RGBD image pair selected with the best shooting condition, where the depth image still possesses some invalid pixels. The experimental results are presented in Fig. 4, showing that our method produces similar results to GFMM, but outperforms the other competitors. Note that the region highlighted by the red rectangle in the 6th row of Fig. 4(b) shows that GFMM produces an incorrect result due to the redundant texture information of the colour image. By contrast, our method is immune to the redundant texture of the colour image thanks to the guidance of the depth image. Furthermore, the region highlighted by the red rectangle in the 7th row of Fig. 4(c) corresponds to the case studied in Fig. 3(e). Neither our method nor the others can properly handle this invalid region.

Fig. 5. The RGBD image pairs captured by both Kinect v1 (the left two images) and Kinect v2 (the right two images).

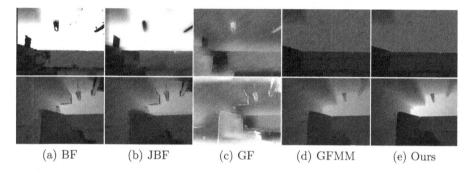

   (a) BF   (b) JBF   (c) GF   (d) GFMM   (e) Ours

Fig. 6. An inpainting comparison on the in-house data (Fig. 5) captured by both Kinect v1 (the first row) and Kinect v2 (the second row).

On the in-house dataset: Our experiments are also conducted on some in-house data shown in Fig. 5, where the depth images contain many invalid pixels. Since the resolutions of the raw depth and colour images captured by Kinects are different, the input colour images must be first aligned with the input depth images using a built-in alignment function of the Kinect SDK. Moreover, because there is no diploid relation between the depth and colour image resolutions in Kinect v2, there are some empty margins in the colour image in Fig. 5. Such a situation may affect the segmentation result of the colour image, but will be offset by our merging procedure. An inpainting comparison among BF, JBF, GF, GFMM, and our method on the images in Fig. 5 is shown in Fig. 6, where our method outperforms the competitors, such as BF, JBF, and GF. Compared with GFMM, our method inpaints the depth images more thoroughly, especially in the tip of the rightmost fluorescent lamp in the first row and the glass in the second row.

On the RGBD video sequences: The last group of experiments are conducted on two publicly accessible RGBD video sequences captured by Kinect v1 [2] and Kinect v2 [8]. Five arbitrary pairs of frames from the two RGBD video sequences are in turn shown in Fig. 7. As can be seen from the second row of Fig. 7, the input depth sequence contains many invalid regions in the person and chairs, which are repaired well by our method in the third row. Similarly, in the fifth row, the input depth video data contain numerous invalid regions in the table,

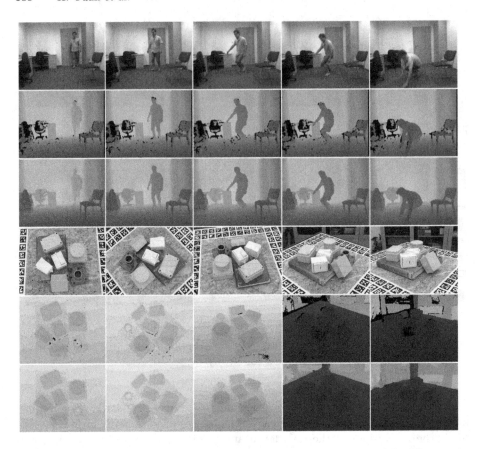

Fig. 7. Experimental results on two RGBD video sequences captured by Kinect v1 (the first three rows) and Kinect v2 (the last three rows).

especially in the cupboard, which are also repaired well in the last row. It is worth noting that all the colour and depth frames evaluated here have been aligned beforehand.

5   Concluding Remarks

By taking advantage of the structural difference of RGBD image pairs we propose a dual-way guided inpainting framework with RBFs to repair contaminated raw depth images. Both the objective and subjective experimental comparisons show that our method recovers the depth images more credibly than the other guided methods. Our method works under the assumption that the depth image is more structured than its colour counterpart, which is a common case usually seen in RGBD image pairs. There are cases where the depth image is relatively more divided than its corresponding colour image, as we studied in Fig. 3(c). However, such cases rarely exist in practice as under such scenarios, the colour change of variant objects in the colour image must be as little as possible; the illumination on every object in the colour image must keep consistent; the depth of the scene must be versatile enough. As for the case in Fig. 3(c), our method cannot properly determine the effective region of RBF interpolation to the invalid region. As a result, this invalid region would be interpolated linearly, if a linear kernel is used, according to the depth values of the surrounding regions of the invalid region, as shown in Fig. 3(c).

References

1. Bae, S., Paris, S., Durand, F.: Two-scale tone management for photographic look. ACM TOG **25**(3), 637–645 (2006)
2. Kepski, M., Kwolek, B.: Human fall detection on embedded platform using depth maps and wireless accelerometer. Comput. Methods Progr. Biomed. **117**(3), 489–501 (2014)
3. Carr, J.C., Beatson, R.K., Cherrie, J.B., Mitchell, T.J., Fright, W.R., McCallum, B.C., Evans, T.R.: Reconstruction and representation of 3D objects with radial basis functions. In: SIGGRAPH 2001, pp. 67–76. ACM (2001)
4. Chen, L., Lin, H., Li, S.: Depth image enhancement for kinect using region growing and bilateral filter. In: Proceedings of 21st ICPR, pp. 3070–3073. IEEE (2012)
5. Durand, F., Dorsey, J.: Fast bilateral filtering for the display of high-dynamic-range images. ACM Trans. Graph. (TOG) **21**(3), 257–266 (2002)
6. Gong, X., Liu, J., Zhou, W., Liu, J.: Guided depth enhancement via a fast marching method. Image Vis. Comput. **31**(10), 695–703 (2013)
7. He, K., Sun, J., Tang, X.: Guided image filtering. IEEE Trans. PAMI **35**(6), 1397–1409 (2013)
8. Hodaň, T., Haluza, P., Obdržálek, Š., Matas, J., Lourakis, M., Zabulis, X.: T-LESS: an RGB-D dataset for 6D pose estimation of texture-less objects. In: IEEE Winter Conference on Applications of Computer Vision (WACV) (2017)
9. Kim, S.-Y., Kim, M., Ho, Y.-S.: Depth image filter for mixed and noisy pixel removal in RGB-D camera systems. IEEE Trans. Consum. Electron. **59**(3), 681–689 (2013)
10. Kopf, J., Cohen, M.F., Lischinski, D., Uyttendaele, M.: Joint bilateral upsampling. ACM TOG **26**(3), 96 (2007)
11. Paris, S., Durand, F.: A fast approximation of the bilateral filter using a signal processing approach. Int. J. Comput. Vis. **81**(1), 24–52 (2009)
12. Scharstein, D., Pal, C.: Learning conditional random fields for stereo. In: Proceedings of CVPR, pp. 1–8. IEEE (2007)
13. Scharstein, D., Szeliski, R.: High-accuracy stereo depth maps using structured light. In: Computer Vision and Pattern Recognition, vol. 1, pp. I–195. IEEE (2003)
14. Tomasi, C., Manduchi, R.: Bilateral filtering for gray and color images. In: Proceedings of ICCV, pp. 839–846. IEEE (1998)
15. Yang, J., Ye, X., Li, K., Hou, C., Wang, Y.: Color-guided depth recovery from RGB-D data using an adaptive autoregressive model. IEEE Trans. Image Process. **23**(8), 3443–3458 (2014)
16. Zhang, G., Jia, J., Wong, T.-T., Bao, H.: Recovering consistent video depth maps via bundle optimization. In: Proceedings of CVPR, pp. 1–8. IEEE (2008)
17. Zhang, G., Jia, J., Wong, T.-T., Bao, H.: Consistent depth maps recovery from a video sequence. IEEE Trans. PAMI **31**(6), 974–988 (2009)

Efficient and Interactive Spatial-Semantic Image Retrieval

Ryosuke Furuta$^{(\boxtimes)}$, Naoto Inoue, and Toshihiko Yamasaki

Department of Information and Communication Engineering,
The University of Tokyo, Tokyo, Japan
{furuta,inoue,yamasaki}@ay-lab.org

Abstract. This paper proposes an efficient image retrieval system. When users wish to retrieve images with semantic and spatial constraints (*e.g.*, a horse is located at the center of the image, and a person is riding on the horse), it is difficult for conventional text-based retrieval systems to retrieve such images exactly. In contrast, the proposed system can consider both semantic and spatial information, because it is based on semantic segmentation using fully convolutional networks (FCN). The proposed system can accept three types of images as queries: a segmentation map sketched by the user, a natural image, or a combination of the two. The distance between the query and each image in the database is calculated based on the output probability maps from the FCN. In order to make the system efficient in terms of both the computation time and memory usage, we employ the product quantization technique (PQ). The experimental results show that the PQ is compatible with the FCN-based image retrieval system, and that the quantization process results in little information loss. It is also shown that our method outperforms a conventional text-based search system.

1 Introduction

With the increase in number of images that have been captured and uploaded to the Internet, the importance of image retrieval system has been increasing. The most widely employed image retrieval systems are based on text. Namely, the query consists of text and relevant images are retrieved. Conventional text-based retrieval systems require tags or captions to be attached to each image in the database. To tackle this problem, many retrieval methods based on machine learning techniques have been proposed, such as caption generation [13,16,26] or the mapping of features into a common latent space between text and images [8, 17]. However, such methods still cannot deal with spatial constraints such as object positions.

To this end, Xu et al. [32] proposed an image retrieval system based on concept maps. A query consists of a canvas, where the textual information is distributed to represent spatial constraints. Although that method can deal with object names and positions simultaneously, it cannot consider object shapes and scales. Recently, a novel image retrieval method has been proposed in which a

© Springer International Publishing AG 2018
K. Schoeffmann et al. (Eds.): MMM 2018, Part I, LNCS 10704, pp. 190–202, 2018.
https://doi.org/10.1007/978-3-319-73603-7_16

query is a canvas with a set of bounding boxes representing semantic and spatial constraints [22]. Although this method can deal with object scales and locations, it still cannot treat object shapes. Moreover, it also cannot take background information into consideration.

In this paper, we propose an efficient image retrieval system based on semantic segmentation. The proposed system can accept three types of queries: a natural image, a segmentation map drawn by the user, and a combination of the two. We employ a fully convolutional network (FCN) [21], which is composed only of convolution and pooling layers. By retrieving images based on the probability maps from the FCN, our system can deal with object scales, shapes, positions, and background information. As shown in Fig. 3, our system also enables users to search for images interactively, by selecting one of the retrieved images as the new query, and adding a partial segmentation map to the new query. To the best of our knowledge, this is the first work to propose an interactive image retrieval system based on semantic segmentation.

In order to make the proposed system efficient in terms of both the search speed and memory usage, we employ the product quantization (PQ) technique [11], which is compatible with our system. Using subjective evaluations in Sect. 4.2, we show that the proposed system provides a superior performance compared with a conventional text-based image retrieval system. Furthermore, in Sect. 4.5 we demonstrate that the PQ makes our system orders of magnitude faster while maintaining the retrieval quality, by quantizing each probability map independently.

2 Related Work

2.1 Semantic Image Retrieval

As pointed out in [22], the majority of early methods for spatial-semantic retrieval extracted low-level features from exemplars [3,19,32]. Inspired by the recent success of convolutional neural networks (CNNs) for image classification, some studies have employed CNNs to learn and extract effective features for image retrieval, where queries consist of images [7] or sketches [20,28–30,33]. The objective of such a method is to retrieve images that have similar appearances, even in cross-modal domains, which differs from our approach.

To capture the context or object topology, some methods have incorporated graphs into the image retrieval, which represent attributes and the relationships between them [14,27]. However, these methods do not enable users to search for images interactively, because users cannot create the graph as a query directly. In contrast, in our method users can draw a segmentation map as a query on the canvas, or even on the natural image.

The most relevant work to ours is in [9], where a query consists of a single source object and a target object sketched by the user. Similar to our method, that one is based on semantic segmentation. However, their objective is to retrieve images considering the interaction between two objects by extracting RAID (relation-augmented image descriptor) features. In contrast, our method uses the probability maps directly for image retrieval.

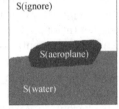

Fig. 1. Interface of the proposed system.   **Fig. 2.** Example of segmentation map.

2.2 Quantization for Efficient Retrieval

Many techniques have been proposed for efficient retrieval, such as binary coding and hashing (summarized in [31]). Product quantization (PQ) [11] is one of the most popular techniques among these, because it is efficient in terms of both computational cost and memory usage. By partitioning the vectors in the database into subvectors and quantizing them using k-means clustering, the approximate distances between the query vector and those in the database can be calculated efficiently via lookup tables. Although variants of PQ have also been proposed and shown superior performances [1,6,15,23,25], in this paper we use the original PQ [11], because of its simplicity and compatibility with our system. Recently, Hinami and Satoh [10] proposed an efficient image retrieval system using an adaptive quantization technique. However, their method is tailored for R-CNN-based object detection, and cannot be applied to semantic segmentation.

3 Proposed Method

3.1 System Overview

Figure 1 presents the interface of the proposed system. The top-left shows the canvas that is treated as the query. The retrieved images are shown in the right area. The proposed system can accept three types of queries: (i) a segmentation map drawn by a user, (ii) a natural image, and (iii) a combination of the two.

(i) Users can easily create a segmentation map with predefined C class labels by drawing it using a mouse input. For example, when the user wants to retrieve images in which a horse is located at the center, he/she chooses the *horse* label and roughly draws its shape at the corresponding location as he/she likes.

(a) Users can draw a segmentation map as a query.

(b) Users can choose an image from the retrieved images as the next query.

(c) Users can add a partial segmentation map to the query image.

Fig. 3. Interactive image retrieval. Query and top five retrieved images are shown.

(ii) Users can also use a natural image as a query. In this case, the proposed system retrieves images that contain objects and backgrounds whose shapes and locations are similar to those of the query image. In addition, the user can choose a query image from the retrieved images shown in the right area.

(iii) In addition, users can draw a partial segmentation map on a natural image. In this case, the proposed system retrieves images by considering both the objects and backgrounds in the query image and those drawn by the user.

3.2 Semantic-Spatial Image Retrieval

We use a fully convolutional network (FCN) trained for C class semantic segmentation to extract spatial-semantic information. The FCN takes an image whose size is $n' \times n'$ as an input, and outputs C probability maps of size $n \times n$. In general, n is smaller than n', because the resolutions of the intermediate feature maps are decreased by pooling layers (the scale difference n'/n depends on which FCN we employ). In this paper, we use DeepLab-v2 [4], which has demonstrated a state-of-the-art performance, and $n' = 8n$ in this case.

Offline Pre-process. Let I^i denote the i-th reference image ($i = 1, \cdots, N$) in the database. We input I^i into the FCN and obtain the C probability maps. The j-th location ($j = 1, \cdots, n^2$) of the c-th probability map ($c = 1, \cdots, C$) has the probability $p_c^i(j)$ that the c-th class label is assigned to that location. The probability is normalized by the final softmax layer in the FCN, and satisfies the following:

$$\forall i,j, \ p_c^i(j) \in [0,1], \ \sum_{c=1}^{C} p_c^i(j) = 1. \tag{1}$$

We reshape this c-th probability map as a vertical vector $\boldsymbol{p}_c^i = [p_c^i(1), \cdots, p_c^i(n^2)]^{\top}$. Furthermore, we vectorize the C probability maps as $\boldsymbol{p}^i = [\boldsymbol{p}_1^{i\top}, \cdots, \boldsymbol{p}_C^{i\top}]^{\top}$. As an offline pre-process, we obtain the probability vectors $\boldsymbol{p}^i$ for all reference images I^i ($i = 1, \cdots, N$) in the database.

When the Query is a Natural Image. We first consider the case that the query consists of a natural image. Given a query image, we input the query image into the FCN and obtain the probability vector $\boldsymbol{p}^{query} \in [0,1]^{n^2 C}$ online. We define the distance between the query image I^{query} and the reference image I^i as the L2 distance between $\boldsymbol{p}^{query}$ and $\boldsymbol{p}^i$:

$$dist(I^{query}, I^i) = ||\boldsymbol{p}^{query} - \boldsymbol{p}^i||^2 = \sum_{c=1}^{C} ||\boldsymbol{p}_c^{query} - \boldsymbol{p}_c^i||^2. \tag{2}$$

By calculating the rankings of the reference images based on the above distance, we can retrieve the images that contain objects whose shapes and locations are similar to those of the query image. In addition, we can consider background information if scene labels such as *sky*, *building*, and *grass* are included in the C class labels.

When the Query is a Segmentation Map Drawn by a User. Next, we consider the case that the query consists of a segmentation map drawn by a user. Let $\boldsymbol{y}$ denote the query segmentation map whose size is $n \times n$, and let $y(j) \in \{0, \cdots, C\}$ be the label assigned to the j-th location. Here, $y(j) = 0$ denotes the *ignore* label, which is assigned when the user does not specify any label at the j-th location. We define the region where the c-th class label is assigned as $S(c)$:

$$S(c) = \{j \mid y(j) = c\}. \tag{3}$$

Figure 2 presents an example of $S(c)$.

Given a query image, we construct a vector $\boldsymbol{q} \in \{0,1\}^{n^2 C}$ as follows:

$$\boldsymbol{q} = [\boldsymbol{q}_1^{\top}, \cdots, \boldsymbol{q}_C^{\top}]^{\top}, \ \boldsymbol{q}_c = [q_c(1), \cdots, q_c(n^2)]^{\top}, \ q_c(j) = \begin{cases} 1 & if \ y(j) = c \\ 0 & otherwise. \end{cases} \tag{4}$$

$\boldsymbol{q}_c$ can be interpreted as the binary probability map for the c-th class, which is calculated from the segmentation map drawn by the user. In $\boldsymbol{q}_c$, a location at which the user has assigned the c-th label has the value 1, and all other locations have the value 0. Using this vector $\boldsymbol{q}$, we define the distance between the query and a reference image as following:

$$dist(\boldsymbol{y}, I^i) = \sum_{c=1}^{C} \mathbf{1}[S(c) \neq \emptyset] ||\boldsymbol{q}_c - \boldsymbol{p}_c^i||^2, \tag{5}$$

where $\mathbf{1}[\cdot]$ is the indicator function, which is 1 if the statement in the blanket is true and 0 otherwise. This indicator function is introduced in order to only consider the labels that the user has specified. The rankings of the reference images are obtained by using the above distance.

When the Query is the Combination of a Natural Image and a Partial Segmentation Map Drawn by a User. In the proposed system, the user can search for images interactively by adding a partial segmentation map y to a natural image I^{query}. In this case, we define a query vector $q = [q_1^\top, \cdots, q_C^\top]^\top$ as follows:

$$q_c = [q_c(1), \cdots, q_c(n^2)]^\top, \quad q_c(j) = \begin{cases} 1 & if \ y(j) = c \\ 0 & if \ y(j) \neq c \wedge y(j) \neq 0 \\ p_c^{query}(j) & if \ y(j) = 0. \end{cases} \quad (6)$$

In q_c, locations at which the user has assigned the c-th label have the value 1. The locations where other labels are assigned have the value 0, and all other locations have the value $p_c^{query}(j)$. Similarly to the above cases, we define the distances between the query and the reference images as follows:

$$dist(y, I^i) = ||q - p^i||^2 = \sum_{c=1}^{C} ||q_c - p_c^i||^2. \quad (7)$$

By calculating the rankings using Eq. (7), we can consider both the objects in the query image and those drawn by the user.

3.3 Product Quantization for Efficient Retrieval

In Sect. 3.2, we introduced image retrieval based on semantic segmentation, which considers spatial-semantic information. However, storing the long vectors $p^i \in [0, 1]^{n^2 C}$ is memory consuming, because of the dimensions of $n^2 C = 64^2 \times 60 = 245,760$ in our setting in Sect. 4. In addition, the naive computation of Eqs. (2), (5) or (7) is slow. Therefore, we employ PQ [11] in order to make the system efficient in terms of both the computational time and memory usage. We show that the approximate values of Eqs. (2), (5) and (7) can be efficiently computed by applying PQ.

Offline Pre-process. We partition the vector p^i into M distinct subvectors $u_1^i, \cdots, u_M^i$, and quantize them independently, i.e., $f_1(u_1^i), \cdots, f_M(u_M^i)$. Following the original PQ technique [11], we learn the quantizer f_m ($m = 1, \cdots, M$) using k-means. We perform k-means on the set of vectors $\{u_m^i \mid i = 1, \cdots, N\}$ and obtain K centroids $\mathcal{A}_m = \{a_{m,k} \mid k = 1, \cdots, K\}$. The quantizer f_m is the mapping function to the nearest centroids:

$$f_m(u_m^i) = \underset{a_{m,k} \in \mathcal{A}_m}{\arg \min} ||u_m^i - a_{m,k}||^2. \quad (8)$$

When we set $M = C$, this quantization process corresponds to partitioning $\boldsymbol{p}^i$ into each probability map $\boldsymbol{p}_c^i(= \boldsymbol{u}_m^i)$ and quantizing these. If the probability maps are independent of each other, this is the optimal setting of M, because this partitioning results in no information loss. In our experiments, we assume that they are almost independent, and set $M = C$. We show that PQ with this setting does not decrease the retrieval quality in Sect. 4.5.

Online Search. By using PQ, we can efficiently compute the approximate value of Eq. (2) as follows:

$$dist(I^{query}, I^i) = ||\boldsymbol{p}^{query} - \boldsymbol{p}^i||^2 = \sum_{m=1}^{M} ||\boldsymbol{u}_m^{query} - \boldsymbol{u}_m^i||^2 \qquad (9)$$

$$\approx \sum_{m=1}^{M} ||\boldsymbol{u}_m^{query} - f_m(\boldsymbol{u}_m^i)||^2. \qquad (10)$$

Because $f_m(\boldsymbol{u}_m^i)$ is the mapping function to the nearest centroid, as shown in Eq. (8), we can efficiently compute Eq. (10) for all reference images by constructing a lookup table of the distances between the query subvector $\boldsymbol{u}_m^{query}$ and each of the centroids. Similarly, Eq. (7) can be also computed efficiently using the lookup table.

There is a further benefit of setting $M = C$. Namely, we can efficiently compute Eq. (5) by approximating as follows:

$$dist(\boldsymbol{y}, I^i) = \sum_{c=1}^{C} \mathbb{1}[S(c) \neq \emptyset]||\boldsymbol{q}_c - \boldsymbol{p}_c^i||^2 \qquad (11)$$

$$\approx \sum_{c=1}^{C} \mathbb{1}[S(c) \neq \emptyset]||\boldsymbol{q}_c - f_c(\boldsymbol{p}_c^i)||^2. \qquad (12)$$

Similarly, we can construct a lookup table of the distances between the query subvector $\boldsymbol{q}_c$ and each of the centroids. To exploit this approximation, we set $M = C$ in Sect. 4.

4 Experimental Results

4.1 Implementation Details

As the FCN, we used DeepLab-v2 [4] implemented on the Caffe library [12], which is publicly available. We trained this network on the trainval set of the PASCAL-Context Dataset [24], which contains 5,105 images with groundtruth pixel-level labels. This is a dataset for $60(= C)$ class semantic segmentation, where a variety of classes are included, such as *car*, *building*, *sky*, and *road*. We denote the set of 60 class names as $\mathcal{C}$. Similarly to [4], we employed poly-learning, where the learning rate started at 2.5×10^{-4} and was multiplied by

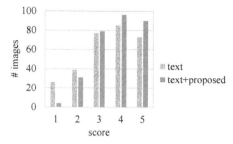

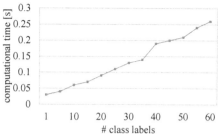

Fig. 4. Histogram of scores.

Fig. 5. Computational time versus number of class labels.

$(1 - (\frac{iter}{max\_iter})^{power})$ at each iteration. We set the max_iter to 20,000, $power$ to 0.9, momentum to 0.9, and weight decay to 5.0×10^{-4}. We used the pixel-wise softmax cross-entropy between the groundtruth label and the predicted score. The input size is $n' \times n' = 512 \times 512$, and the output size is $n \times n = 64 \times 64$. We implemented the user interface and PQ on MATLAB, and set $K = 256$.

4.2 Subjective Evaluation

We conducted subjective evaluation tests to verify the efficacy of the proposed system. As the database, we used the MSCOCO2014 training set [18], which contains 82,783 images. Each image has five caption annotations written by Amazon Mechanical Turk workers.

We compared the following two methods.

Text-based retrieval. The user can input a set of words as a query. The rankings of images are simply calculated based on the number of words in the captions that are the same as the query words.

Text+proposed system. The user can input both a set of words and the three types of images described in Sect. 3.1 as a query. Given the input, we first obtain the rankings in a similar manner to the text-based retrieval method above. Subsequently, we sort the images that have the same rank based on the distance in Eq. (10) or (12). When the user does not input any images on the canvas, this system is equivalent to the text-based retrieval method above. In contrast, when the user does not input query words, the ranking is calculated simply based on the distance in Eq. (10) or (12).

The procedure of the test is as follows.

1. We used the MSCOCO2014 validation set, which has 202,654 captions, to construct a caption set $\mathcal{T}$. We picked up the captions that contain three or more class names in $\mathcal{C}$, and there consequently remained 2,896 captions.
2. We randomly chose a caption from $\mathcal{T}$, and asked subjects to imagine an image that the caption describes.

3. We asked subjects to choose ten images that they think are similar to the imagined image using the text-based and text+proposed systems, respectively. Subjects could make queries and search for images any number of times.
4. We showed the twenty chosen images in random order, and asked subjects to assign relevance scores from 1 to 5 to the each image. A score of 5 indicates the highest relevance, and 1 the lowest.
5. Steps 2–4 were repeated three times.

The number of subjects was ten, and their ages were 21–26. Figure 4 presents the histograms of the scores. We observe that the number of images scored as 1 using the text+proposed system is significantly lower than that for the text-based system. Accordingly, the number of images scored as 4 and 5 increased when using the text+proposed system. This is reasonable, because the text-based system cannot deal with semantic-spatial information, such as the shapes and locations of objects that subjects imagine. The average score of the all 300 images for the text-based system is 3.5, and that of the text+proposed system is 3.8. There is a significant difference ($p < 0.01$) between these according to the Student's t-test.

4.3   Computational Time Analysis

Using the 82,783 images in the MSCOCO train set, we analyze the computational time required to calculate the ranking and sorting based on Eq. (10) or (12) with PQ. Because we set $M = C$, the size of lookup table for computing Eq. (10) is $C \times K$, where M is the quantization level, C is the number of classes, and K is the number of centroids. The average computational time for Eq. (10) and sorting for all 82,783 images was about 0.3 s on a machine with an Intel Core i7-6600U and 12GB RAM, which is sufficiently fast for real application.

When the query consists of a segmentation map drawn by a user, the size of the lookup table required for Eq. (12) depends on the number of classes the user specifies (*i.e.*, $|\mathcal{C}'|$ where $\mathcal{C}' = \{c \mid S(c) \neq \emptyset\}$). Figure 5 shows the computational time versus $|\mathcal{C}'|$ for all 82,783 images. The computational time increases linearly as $|\mathcal{C}'|$ becomes large. However, even when the user specifies all classes (*i.e.*, $|\mathcal{C}'| = 60$), the computational time is only 0.26 sec, which is sufficiently fast.

We could not measure the computational time without PQ, because we could not store 82,783 vectors of length $n^2C = 245,760$ on the RAM.

4.4   Qualitative Evaluation

Figure 6 shows some examples of the retrieved images with the proposed system on the MSCOCO2014 train set. We observe that the proposed system successfully performs retrieval considering the spatial-semantic contexts of the query images.

Fig. 6. Examples of retrieved images using the proposed method on the MSCOCO2014 train set. Query and top five images are shown.

4.5 Performance for Structured Retrieval

We used the rPascal and rImageNet datasets [27], which contain 1,895 and 3,354 images, respectively. The rPascal dataset contains 50 query images, and each query image has 180 reference images on average. The rImageNet dataset contains 50 query images, with 305 reference images per query on average. Both datasets contain relevance score annotations for each pair of query and reference images. Using these datasets, we evaluated the performance of the proposed method for structured retrieval. Similarly to [27], we used the normalized discounted cumulative gain (nDCG).

Figure 7a and b show the results of the proposed method with various values of K (the number of centroids) and without PQ. We observe that the search speed is enhanced without degrading the search accuracy.

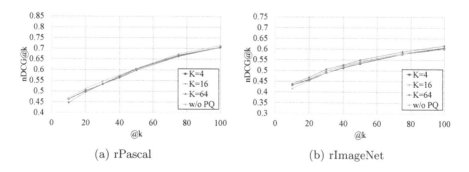

(a) rPascal

(b) rImageNet

Fig. 7. nDCG of the proposed method with various numbers of centroids (K).

Figure 8a and b present comparisons with other methods on rPascal and rImageNet, respectively. The proposed method is significantly inferior to Attribute-Graph [27], which is reasonable, because that method is tailored for structured retrieval and ours is not. Although the proposed method performs worse than other methods on rPascal, it shows a competitive performance with other methods except for Attribute-Graph [27] on rImageNet.

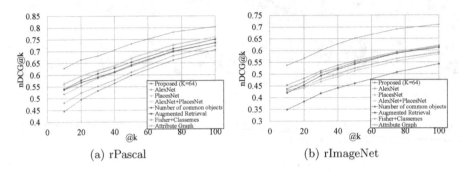

(a) rPascal   (b) rImageNet

Fig. 8. Comparison of nDCG. Except for the proposed method, the plots are from [27]. *Augmented Retrieval, Fisher+Classemes,* and *Attribute Graph* indicate [2,5,27], respectively.

Table 1 presents a comparison of the computational time with and without PQ on the rPascal and rImageNet datasets. PQ makes the computation orders of magnitude faster, especially when K is small. When K is large, PQ is not as effective. However, this is because the numbers of reference images are extremely small (180 and 305, respectively). We believe that PQ will be more effective when the dataset size is large.

Table 1. Comparison of the computational times [s] with and without PQ.

	rPascal	rImageNet
$K = 4$	0.006	0.006
$K = 16$	0.016	0.016
$K = 64$	0.054	0.055
w/o PQ	0.079	0.135

5   Conclusion

In this paper, we have proposed an efficient and interactive image retrieval system using FCN and PQ. The FCN is used to treat spatial-semantic information, and PQ is applied for efficient computation and memory usage. The experimental results showed that the proposed system is effective in reflecting the intentions of users. It was also shown that PQ is compatible with the proposed system, and makes it considerably faster while maintaining the retrieval quality. The limitation of the proposed method is that it cannot treat new classes that are not included in the training dataset of semantic segmentation.

Acknowledgement. This work was partially supported by the Grants-in-Aid for Scientific Research (no. 26700008 and 16J07267) from JSPS, JST-CREST (JPMJCR1686), and Microsoft IJARC core13.

We would like to thank Nikita Prabhu and R. Venkatesh Babu for providing their data.

References

1. Babenko, A., Lempitsky, V.: Additive quantization for extreme vector compression. In: CVPR (2014)
2. Cao, X., Wei, X., Guo, X., Han, Y., Tang, J.: Augmented image retrieval using multi-order object layout with attributes. In: ACMMM (2014)
3. Cao, Y., Wang, H., Wang, C., Li, Z., Zhang, L., Zhang, L.: Mindfinder: interactive sketch-based image search on millions of images. In: ACMMM (2010)
4. Chen, L.C., Papandreou, G., Kokkinos, I., Murphy, K., Yuille, A.L.: DeepLab: semantic image segmentation with deep convolutional nets, atrous convolution, and fully connected CRFs. IEEE TPAMI (2017). http://ieeexplore.ieee.org/document/7913730
5. Douze, M., Ramisa, A., Schmid, C.: Combining attributes and fisher vectors for efficient image retrieval. In: CVPR (2011)
6. Ge, T., He, K., Ke, Q., Sun, J.: Optimized product quantization for approximate nearest neighbor search. In: CVPR (2013)
7. Gordo, A., Almazán, J., Revaud, J., Larlus, D.: Deep image retrieval: learning global representations for image search. In: Leibe, B., Matas, J., Sebe, N., Welling, M. (eds.) ECCV 2016. LNCS, vol. 9910, pp. 241–257. Springer, Cham (2016). https://doi.org/10.1007/978-3-319-46466-4_15
8. Gordo, A., Larlus, D.: Beyond instance-level image retrieval: leveraging captions to learn a global visual representation for semantic retrieval. In: CVPR (2017)
9. Guerrero, P., Mitra, N.J., Wonka, P.: RAID: a relation-augmented image descriptor. ACM TOG **35**(4), 46:1–46:12 (2016)
10. Hinami, R., Satoh, S.: Large-scale R-CNN with classifier adaptive quantization. In: Leibe, B., Matas, J., Sebe, N., Welling, M. (eds.) ECCV 2016. LNCS, vol. 9907, pp. 403–419. Springer, Cham (2016). https://doi.org/10.1007/978-3-319-46487-9_25
11. Jegou, H., Douze, M., Schmid, C.: Product quantization for nearest neighbor search. IEEE TPAMI **33**(1), 117–128 (2011)
12. Jia, Y., Shelhamer, E., Donahue, J., Karayev, S., Long, J., Girshick, R., Guadarrama, S., Darrell, T.: Caffe: convolutional architecture for fast feature embedding. In: ACMMM (2014)
13. Johnson, J., Karpathy, A., Fei-Fei, L.: DenseCap: fully convolutional localization networks for dense captioning. In: CVPR (2016)
14. Johnson, J., Krishna, R., Stark, M., Li, L.J., Shamma, D., Bernstein, M., Fei-Fei, L.: Image retrieval using scene graphs. In: CVPR (2015)

15. Kalantidis, Y., Avrithis, Y.: Locally optimized product quantization for approximate nearest neighbor search. In: CVPR (2014)
16. Karpathy, A., Fei-Fei, L.: Deep visual-semantic alignments for generating image descriptions. In: CVPR (2015)
17. Kim, G., Moon, S., Sigal, L.: Ranking and retrieval of image sequences from multiple paragraph queries. In: CVPR (2015)
18. Lin, T.-Y., Maire, M., Belongie, S., Hays, J., Perona, P., Ramanan, D., Dollár, P., Zitnick, C.L.: Microsoft COCO: common objects in context. In: Fleet, D., Pajdla, T., Schiele, B., Tuytelaars, T. (eds.) ECCV 2014. LNCS, vol. 8693, pp. 740–755. Springer, Cham (2014). https://doi.org/10.1007/978-3-319-10602-1_48
19. Liu, C., Wang, D., Liu, X., Wang, C., Zhang, L., Zhang, B.: Robust semantic sketch based specific image retrieval. In: ICME (2010)
20. Liu, L., Shen, F., Shen, Y., Liu, X., Shao, L.: Deep sketch hashing: fast free-hand sketch-based image retrieval. In: CVPR (2017)
21. Long, J., Shelhamer, E., Darrell, T.: Fully convolutional networks for semantic segmentation. In: CVPR (2015)
22. Long Mai, H.J., Lin, Z., Fang, C., Brandt, J., Liu, F.: Spatial-semantic image search by visual feature synthesis. In: CVPR (2017)
23. Matsui, Y., Yamasaki, T., Aizawa, K.: Pqtable: fast exact asymmetric distance neighbor search for product quantization using hash tables. In: ICCV (2015)
24. Mottaghi, R., Chen, X., Liu, X., Cho, N.G., Lee, S.W., Fidler, S., Urtasun, R., Yuille, A.: The role of context for object detection and semantic segmentation in the wild. In: CVPR (2014)
25. Norouzi, M., Fleet, D.J.: Cartesian k-means. In: CVPR (2013)
26. Ordonez, V., Han, X., Kuznetsova, P., Kulkarni, G., Mitchell, M., Yamaguchi, K., Stratos, K., Goyal, A., Dodge, J., Mensch, A., et al.: Large scale retrieval and generation of image descriptions. IJCV 119(1), 46–59 (2016)
27. Prabhu, N., Venkatesh Babu, R.: Attribute-graph: a graph based approach to image ranking. In: ICCV (2015)
28. Qi, Y., Song, Y.Z., Zhang, H., Liu, J.: Sketch-based image retrieval via siamese convolutional neural network. In: ICIP (2016)
29. Sangkloy, P., Burnell, N., Ham, C., Hays, J.: The sketchy database: learning to retrieve badly drawn bunnies. ACM TOG 35(4), 119 (2016)
30. Wang, F., Kang, L., Li, Y.: Sketch-based 3D shape retrieval using convolutional neural networks. In: CVPR (2015)
31. Wang, J., Zhang, T., Sebe, N., Shen, H.T., et al.: A survey on learning to hash. IEEE TPAMI (2017). http://ieeexplore.ieee.org/document/7915742/
32. Xu, H., Wang, J., Hua, X.S., Li, S.: Image search by concept map. In: SIGIR (2010)
33. Yu, Q., Liu, F., Song, Y.Z., Xiang, T., Hospedales, T.M., Loy, C.C.: Sketch me that shoe. In: CVPR (2016)

Evaluation of Visual Content Descriptors for Supporting Ad-Hoc Video Search Tasks at the Video Browser Showdown

Sabrina Kletz[✉], Andreas Leibetseder, and Klaus Schoeffmann

Institute of Information Technology, Alpen-Adria University (AAU),
9020 Klagenfurt, Austria
{sabrina,aleibets,ks}@itec.aau.at

Abstract. Since 2017 the Video Browser Showdown (VBS) collaborates
with TRECVID and interactively evaluates Ad-Hoc Video Search (AVS)
tasks, in addition to Known-Item Search (KIS) tasks. In this video search
competition the participants have to find relevant target scenes to a given
textual query within a specific time limit, in a large dataset consisting of
600 h of video content. Since usually the number of relevant scenes for
such an AVS query is rather high, the teams at the VBS 2017 could find
only a small portion of them. One way to support them at the interactive
search would be to automatically retrieve other similar instances of an
already found target scene. However, it is unclear which content descriptors should be used for such an automatic video content search, using a
query-by-example approach. Therefore, in this paper we investigate several different visual content descriptors (CNN Features, CEDD, COMO,
HOG, Feature Signatures and HOF) for the purpose of similarity search
in the TRECVID IACC.3 dataset, used for the VBS. Our evaluation
shows that there is no single descriptor that works best for every AVS
query, however, when considering the total performance over all 30 AVS
tasks of TRECVID 2016, CNN features provide the best performance.

Keywords: Video Browser Showdown · Ad-Hoc Video Search
TRECVID · Video retrieval · Similarity search · Content descriptors

1 Introduction

After the last three decades we have reached the Zettabyte era, where approximately 47% of the world's population is online and CISCO highlights that
monthly video traffic will take an individual more than 5 million years to watch
the tremendous amount of video content [6,18]. The reason behind is the fact that
various devices facilitate the recording of high-quality images and videos as well
as easily sharing of multimedia content online via social media. On YouTube,
more than 300 h of videos[1] are uploaded every minute, which certainly contributes to the immense amount of traffic data. But in addition to YouTube,

---

[1] YouTube Company Statistics 2016, www.statisticbrain.com/youtube-statistics
(accessed September 1, 2017).

© Springer International Publishing AG 2018
K. Schoeffmann et al. (Eds.): MMM 2018, Part I, LNCS 10704, pp. 203–215, 2018.
https://doi.org/10.1007/978-3-319-73603-7_17

there are numerous other examples for growing video archives in terms of amount and diversity such as broadcast archives, personal video collections as well as surveillance or medical video archives. However, the challenge is not just the transmission but also the retrieval of video contents.

Over the recent years, video retrieval evaluation benchmarks and showcases such as TRECVID [22] and the Video Browser Showdown (VBS) [7,21], have been instrumental in advancing research on content-based video retrieval. As opposed to TRECVID, the VBS is a live video retrieval competition that evaluates interactive video search tools [19] in a competitive setting and in front of the conference audience. The participating teams have to solve visual and textual search tasks on a shared dataset, which is known as the TRECVID IACC.3 dataset[2]. The video search tasks simulate two different visual information retrieval situations: *Known-Item Search* (KIS) and *Ad-Hoc Video Search* (AVS). The KIS task refers to a situation, where users have detailed knowledge of a specific target scene and want to find it, but do not know where to look for it. On the other hand, the AVS task simulates a scenario, where users want to find as many scenes as possible, according to a given textual query. One example of such a query would be: *"Find all shots showing palm trees."* The AVS has recently started as a task in the VBS 2017 and is promoted in collaboration with TRECVID. While some queries are taken from the previous TRECVID contest and evaluated according to their ground truth, other queries are issued and judged by a live evaluation committee on site. However, although the previous VBS competition has shown that teams were able to find at least one correct scene for AVS queries, they struggled with finding many instances. One reason was that simple concept-based search (e.g., in a textual index created from automatic concept detections) did not work well for the AVS queries – this is also confirmed by the results of TRECVID 2016 for the automatic AVS, which achieved rather low performance in general (see Sect. 2). For the scenario tested by the VBS this means that users had to browse through long result lists after firing the textual query and could hardly find more than one relevant shot in a few minutes.

In this paper, we focus on content-based similarity search for finding more instances of a relevant shot, which is already found during an AVS run. This shot can then be used as an example query for the search of further similar examples. However, it is unclear which content descriptor works best for such a query-by-example approach in the underlying dataset of VBS and TRECVID AVS. Therefore, in this paper we investigate several different visual content descriptors (CNN Features, Feature Signatures, CEDD, COMO, HOG as well as Dynamic Feature Signatures, 3D-HOG and HOF) for their achievable performance at similarity search, when using the TRECVID 2016 AVS queries as a basis. More specifically, we evaluate the achievable performance in terms of mean average precision (MAP) for each descriptor and discuss the obtained results.

---

[2] TRECVID video data, http://www-nlpir.nist.gov/projects/tv2016/tv2016.html#data.

The remaining sections of this paper are organized as follows: Sect. 2 summarizes the different systems that participated in the VBS 2017 and gives an overview of the TRECVID Ad-Hoc Video Search task as well as the achieved automatic performance at TRECVID 2016. Section 3 comprises the experimental setup, including the video dataset and the different visual content descriptors used for our evaluation, which is presented in the following Sect. 4. Finally, Sect. 5 concludes the achieved results.

2   Related Work

In the Video Browser Showdown (VBS) 2017, several teams presented video browsing tools with different content-based similarity search approaches [4,10, 14–17,20] pursuing the same goal of finding specific target scenes, which either are textually described or visually shown. Regardless of the given task, each of these tools support different combinations of search strategies including query-by-text, query-by-example, or query-by-sketch. Although for AVS, concept-based search (query-by-text) is the most promising approach, the results can be further restricted by visual filters (e.g., some color-based descriptors) as indicated by [10]. In case one relevant scene has been found already, this specific example can be further used for additional search queries with a query-by-example approach. However, these visual or concept search strategies always require video content dependent approaches for extracting useful semantic and visual features.

The top three ranking teams [4,17,20] that attended the AVS task not only use semantic features for concept-based searches but also visual features, specifically for filtering the initial retrieval results. Among them are global color information, for example, obtained by extracting color histograms or determining dominant colors [10,17] as well as local color information, described by properties such as fuzzy color histograms, color moments or MPEG-7 Descriptors [14,17]. When considering object search, some teams integrate histograms of oriented gradients (HOG) [16,20] and edge histograms [4,16] for characterizing detailed scenes where objects are visible. Furthermore, for describing actions, only a few teams use global motion histograms to describe motion patterns [17,20]. Besides the possibility to search for color similarity, motion as well as objects, teams also improve upon their concept-based search results by using state-of-the-art CNN features, extracted from last fully-connected layer of the deep neural network architecture (e.g., AlexNet or GoogleNet trained on ImageNet) [4,15,20].

In contrast to VBS, the TRECVID AVS task is composed of two individual sub-categories: manually assisted and automatic search based on different textual query topics (see Table 1). While for manually assisted submissions the predefined query phrases can be re-formulated by humans before feeding them to their system, automatic runs are required to operate on the unmodified terms. Competing teams can either choose to participate in both sub-tasks or potentially skip either one. All submissions from the 2016 challenge were evaluated using an approved measure for estimating the performance of a competing system called the *mean extended inferred average precision* (xinfAP) [24]. According to Awad

Table 1. Overview of the 30 different query topics, and the number of judged examples, evaluated at TRECVID 2016 and VBS 2017

Query Nr.	Shots containing	Count
501	a person playing guitar outdoors	106
502	a man indoors looking at camera where a bookcase is behind	349
503	a person playing drums indoors	580
504	a diver wearing diving suit and swimming under water	41
505	a person holding a poster on the street at daytime	194
506	the 43rd president George W. Bush sitting down talking with people indoors	477
507	a choir or orchestra and conductor performing on stage	267
508	one or more people walking or bicycling on a bridge during daytime	82
509	a crowd demonstrating in a city street at night	171
510	a sewing machine	19
511	soldiers performing training or other military maneuvers	259
512	palm trees	219
513	military personnel interacting with protesters	221
514	soldiers performing training or other military maneuvers	468
515	a person jumping	198
516	a man shake hands with a woman	33
517	a policeman where a police car is visible	71
518	one or more people at train station platform	103
519	two or more men at a beach scene	261
520	any type of fountains outdoors	156
521	a man with beard talking or singing into a microphone	278
522	a person sitting down with a laptop visible	281
523	one or more people opening a door and exiting through it	125
524	a man with beard and wearing white robe speaking and gesturing to camera	39
525	a person holding a knife	154
526	a woman wearing glasses	386
527	a person drinking from a cup, mug, bottle, or other container	46
528	a person wearing a helmet	1015
529	a person lighting a candle	9
530	people shopping	41
30		6649

et al. [1], systems for manually assisted tasks at best yielded a mean xinfAP of just below 0.18 and an overall median value of 0.043. Automatic submissions resulted in even lesser values: slightly above 0.05 at the highest with a cumulative median xinfAP of 0.024. Since in this work we focus on evaluating visual content descriptors instead of textual phrases, we are limited to a conceptual rather than a direct comparison. Finally, since all of the VBS approaches' precise performance results to the best of our knowledge have not been made public, only the participating teams have acquired some insight about the applicability of their individual methodologies. This work's baseline comparison, therefore, could represent a much needed general guideline for choosing task-specific descriptors.

3   Experimental Setup

In this section, we outline the setup of our experimental evaluation, comprising a description of the video dataset as well as the individual visual content descriptors that are finally extracted and used to assess the performance of similarity search.

3.1 Video Data

We base our evaluations on the TRECVID IACC.3 dataset, as used for the AVS task, and evaluate the achievable performance according to the combined ground truth from TRECVID AVS and VBS 2017[3]. In 2016, TRECVID prepared the IACC.3 video dataset with various metadata for the AVS task, which comprises 600 h of video content amounting to a total of 144 GB. The same video collection is also used as dataset in the VBS competition. The dataset consists of 4,593 videos chosen from one of the largest digital libraries in order to build a collection for large-scale video retrieval benchmarking. The selected videos are provided under various Creative Commons licenses and were originally gathered from the tremendous data compilation of the Internet Archive[4]. Compared to each other the videos considerably differ in genre (e.g., interviews, cartoons for kids or how-to tutorials), resolution as well as frame rate and duration.

Every single TRECVID video is provided with shot boundary references, which split the entire dataset (4,593 videos) into 335,944 smaller video clips (mastershots) and for any task these constitute the participating teams' submission pool as well as the basis for the conference committee's judgments. Within the 2016 challenge, the video clips were judged according to 30 textual concepts and the ground truth consisted of the concept (query number), the submitted mastershots, the corresponding video and the degree of judgment: *not in the judged sample, shot contains the concept, shot doesn't contain the concept*. For comparisons between keyframe-based and shot-based descriptors, we only consider ground truth mastershots that are longer than one second. This restriction leaves us with a total of 186,630 remaining video clips and 6,649 evaluated clips.

Table 1 shows an overview of all evaluated query topics and the number of judged mastershots. Each topic is considered individually meaning that retrieval results are assumed to be binary: any shot can either be assigned to a specific concept or not. Overall the amount of judged mastershots per query varies from as low as 9 (query 529: "a person lighting a candle") up to 1015 shots (query 528: "a person wearing a helmet") indicating a rather uneven distribution. This can partially be attributed to some concepts being much more common than others – for example the occurrence of "a sewing machine" (query 510 with 19 shots) intrinsically seems to be a much less likely event than "a man indoors looking at camera where a bookcase is behind" (query 502 with 349 judged shots). However, the judged shots of some other contained queries are not as foreseeable: seemingly equally common concepts like "a person playing guitar outdoors" (query 501) and "a person playing drums indoors" (query 503) strongly differ in their corresponding judged mastershot counts (106 versus 580). Such considerations of course are strongly dataset and judgment effort dependent, yet, they as well simply underline the need for continuing ground truth improvements.

In order to highlight visual differences across the individual queries as well as within them, Fig. 1 shows three judged examples for each concept listed in

---

[3] TRECVID extra Ad-Hoc video search judgments, www-nlpir.nist.gov/projects/tv2016/pastdata/extra.avs.qrels.tv16.xlsx.

[4] Internet Archive, www.archive.org.

Fig. 1. Overview of the 30 Ad-Hoc search concepts: three examples per query number. (Color figure online)

Table 1. Clearly the evaluated queries are nonrestrictive to color, as can be observed when regarding dissimilarities such as grayscale clips appearing among vividly colored shots. However, there are a few concepts that allow for some conjectures about dominant tints: for instance, typical outdoor scenes like queries 501, 518 or 520 often contain large portions of blue sky. Similarly, blue water surfaces that are likely to appear in ground truths for queries 504 or 512 share the same notion. Another observation is the predominant appearance of people within the mastershot ground truths, which indeed can be attributed to the overall composition of queries, as most of them mention persons performing various actions. Accordingly, at least from an interpretative point of view, considering distinctive facial features as well as tracking motion information seem to be promising approaches for increasing retrieval performance. Finally, several query concepts can yield scenes involving very specific textures such as grainy concrete (e.g. queries 508, 514), wavy sand (e.g. queries 512, 519) or reflective glass (e.g. 518, 523).

3.2 Visual Content Descriptors

In the literature, different content descriptors are proposed for different applications and ranges from the extraction of color, texture, and shape over motion features. For this reason, we selected content descriptors that were used by actual systems at the Video Browser Showdown and, on the other hand, dynamic descriptors that partly extend static content descriptors. For keyframe-based descriptors, we use the middle frames as keyframe for each video clip and extract CNN Features, Feature Signatures [3], Color and Edge Directivity Descriptor (CEDD) [5], Color and Moment-Based Descriptor (COMO) [23] and the histogram of oriented gradients (HOG) [8]. Furthermore, we extract for the entire video clip Dynamic Feature Signatures [12], 3D volumes of histogram of oriented gradients (3D-HOG) and histogram of optical flow (HOF) [9,13].

CNN Features have been shown to improve not only performance on classification tasks but also enhance retrieval effectiveness [2]. The features resulting in the fully-connected layers of deep neural network architectures are commonly used as visual content descriptors for image retrieval [11]. We extract CNN Features from the GoogLeNet architecture (i.e., Inception-v3) trained with 1,000 classes from ImageNet, as used for the ImageNet Large Scale Visual Recognition Challenge (ILSVRC). Notice that the neural network is used as a fixed feature extractor and we extract the last fully-connected layer of GoogLeNet, which results in a 1024-dimensional feature vector that is also known as neural codes.

Signature-based descriptors are commonly known as adaptive-binning histograms and are obtained by aggregating local color and texture information [3,4]. We use two different variants of signature-based descriptors: Feature Signatures, which are extracted from single keyframes, and flow-based Dynamic Feature Signatures, which are extracted from entire video shots. In general, for a set of random sample points, each point is described by its position, Lab color values, as well as contrast and entropy, which results in a 7-dimensional feature vector per samplepoint. All extracted features are then clustered using k-means. In addition to keyframe-based Feature Signatures, the flow-based Dynamic Signatures expand spatial position information within one keyframe with movement between adjacent frames [12].

Color and texture features are an important component in distinguishing visual similarity and are extensively used in image retrieval. The authors in [3,23] compare several content descriptors with their proposed approaches (Feature Signatures, COMO and CEDD). Taking into account the retrieval effectiveness of these descriptors, which differ only slightly in the UKBench dataset, we compare additionally those two suggested descriptors that build on the HSV color space and fuzzy linking systems. The CEDD descriptor comprises color and texture information represented as 144-dimensional feature vector per keyframe. The features are extracted block-wise and for each block, a 24-bin fuzzy linking histogram is calculated and classified into one of 6 different texture types by their edge orientations. In contrast to CEDD, the COMO descriptor exchanges the edge classification component with Hu-Moments to be invariant against rotation, scaling, and translation.

The Histograms of Oriented Gradients (HOG) descriptor has shown good performance for human detection tasks [8,9,13]. The descriptor is computed on a dense grid and is based on counting contours to capture occurrences of gradient orientations for describing objects. Local object appearance and shape are described by the distribution of local edge directions. This descriptor is also used in combination with videos, but instead of extracting HOG from a single keyframe, the video is represented in so-called 3D volumes and the histograms are extracted by combining spatiotemporal histogram of oriented gradients. In contrast to counting local orientation of gradients, the Histograms of Optical Flow (HOF) descriptor is only based on describing occurrences of displaced motion direction between adjacent frames. All of these descriptors result in a varying number of vectors depending on the spatial resolution and temporal frame rate. We used it as a global descriptor by resizing the resolution to a fixed frame size and for the video volume, we used a fixed number of uniformly sampled frames.

4   Evaluation Results

This section provides an overview of retrieval performance results with respect to the TRECVID IACC.3 video dataset, the TRECVID-VBS ground truth and the different visual content descriptors: CNN, FS, DFS, CEDD, COMO, HOG, 3D-HOG and HOF. We extracted the descriptors and evaluated the query-by-example approach with the focus on a user that has already found one example of a specific target scene and want to find other similar instances. For the retrieval performance comparisons, we measure the Mean Average Precision (MAP) for each query topic individually and determine the overall performance for each descriptor by the arithmetic average MAP (AA-MAP).

4.1   Retrieval Measure

The query-by-example approach allows users to formulate their search by using an example (image/shot) to find other similar instances. For the retrieval performance comparisons, we are interested in measuring how many returned results are similar to the query example. For this reason we determine the Average Precision (AP) for each element in the ground truth. As can be seen from Table 1, for each query topic the third column contains the number of relating ground truth shots provided from the last TRECVID retrieval evaluation (see Subsect. 3.1). For example this means that for query 501: "a person playing guitar outdoors" 106 AP values are calculated and arithmetically averaged. In the end, we get the Mean Average Precision (MAP) for each of the 30 query topics, which is defined as follows:

$$MAP = \frac{1}{|Q|} \sum_{q \in Q} AP(q) \quad \text{and} \quad AP = \frac{1}{|R|} \sum_{r \in R} P@r$$

For every query $q \in Q$ within a topic, the similarity is computed to all elements in the ground truth (i.e., to all $186,630$ shots) and a ranked result list is created. For each relevant item $r \in R$ in this result list, the precision P at the corresponding position in the ranking is computed, added up and an average of the AP values is obtained (which is the MAP per topic). The MAP values of all topics are further arithmetically averaged, in order to obtain the AA-MAP as an overall performance measure for all topics.

4.2 Similarity Measure

The degree of similarity between a query and all other elements in the dataset is obtained by calculating the distance among their feature vectors. Since feature vectors of the CNN, CEDD, COMO, HOG, 3D-HOG, and HOF descriptors have a fixed length for each element (e.g., keyframe/shot), we measure the similarity by using the Euclidean distance. In the case of the signature-based descriptors, we use the Signature Matching Distance (SMD) because signatures consist of different numbers of feature vectors per element and therefore, they need a special distance metric [3]. As evaluated in [12], we calculate the distance using the asymmetric query variant. For finding similar signatures, we choose the nearest neighbor strategy with the Euclidean distance as a base distance.

4.3 Retrieval Performance

The visual content descriptors detailed in Sect. 3.2 are evaluated in order to determine their usefulness in characterizing each of the 30 query topics listed in Table 1. The retrieved results are listed in Table 2, which compares query-specific MAP values among descriptors (rows). CNN features overall yield the best results, as for 26 topics they consistently achieve higher MAPs than other approaches, albeit at about half of the queries they are closely followed by static feature signatures with a mere MAP difference of 0.0001–0.0086. They even slightly outperform CNN features in 3 out of the 4 remaining topics: "a person jumping" (query 515), "a person drinking from a cup, mug, bottle, or other container" (query 527) and "people shopping" (query 530). 3D-HOG as well manages to marginally outperform CNN on one single query (527) and accordingly shares a tied position with FS. The CEDD descriptor achieves the best results for the topic 504 ("a diver wearing diving suit and swimming under water").

In contrast to topics such as 506 ("the 43rd president George W. Bush sitting down talking with people indoors"), where the MAP scores across all approaches seem to vary greatly (0.0076–0.1499), there are several topics seemingly almost equally suitable for all approaches: e.g. topic 516 with the topic of looking for "a man shake hands with a woman" (0.0306–0.0325) or topic 530 inquiring for "people shopping" (0.0248–0.0294) all descriptors seem to show very similar performance. Lastly, when regarding the average MAP values over all topics (AA-MAP), it becomes apparent that all descriptors influence the retrieval results in comparison to chance results (0.0012) and indeed CNN features seem to be most suitable for all queries (0.0448), followed by static feature signatures (0.0348) and the according to its individual MAP performance rather surprising third best descriptor: dynamic feature signatures (0.0316).

An interesting observation is that there are a few topics where CNN Features perform extraordinarily well (502, 506, 507, 510, 524, and 529), which is especially surprising for the latter three topics, which have relatively few ground truth instances (510:19, 524:39, 529:9). Also static and dynamic feature signatures work very well for a few of these topics (particularly 506, 524, and 529), whereas the other descriptors achieve much lower (except for 529, which seems

Table 2. Evaluation results (MAPs) of visual content descriptors for individual Ad-hoc search concepts.

Query Nr.	CNN	FS	DFS	CEED	COMO	HOG	3D-HOG	HOF	RANDOM
501	0.0434	0.0256	0.0230	0.0202	0.0171	0.0155	0.0141	0.0134	0.0006
502	0.1003	0.0233	0.0242	0.0230	0.0238	0.0190	0.0177	0.0149	0.0019
503	0.0413	0.0171	0.0141	0.0127	0.0134	0.0068	0.0054	0.0053	0.0032
504	0.0337	0.0350	0.0330	0.0396	0.0351	0.0261	0.0261	0.0259	0.0003
505	0.0175	0.0110	0.0100	0.0101	0.0099	0.0081	0.0082	0.0083	0.0011
506	0.1499	0.1293	0.1116	0.0668	0.0655	0.0341	0.0201	0.0076	0.0026
507	0.0922	0.0857	0.0755	0.0660	0.0491	0.0540	0.0290	0.0061	0.0015
508	0.0249	0.0210	0.0196	0.0186	0.0184	0.0175	0.0176	0.0164	0.0005
509	0.0485	0.0245	0.0268	0.0143	0.0149	0.0135	0.0132	0.0133	0.0010
510	0.1005	0.0789	0.0661	0.0774	0.0773	0.0699	0.0684	0.0607	0.0002
511	0.0255	0.0179	0.0149	0.0101	0.0115	0.0129	0.0119	0.0100	0.0014
512	0.0235	0.0163	0.0156	0.0146	0.0144	0.0145	0.0149	0.0115	0.0012
513	0.0139	0.0098	0.0096	0.0083	0.0082	0.0088	0.0090	0.0094	0.0012
514	0.0131	0.0083	0.0068	0.0063	0.0058	0.0077	0.0070	0.0062	0.0026
515	0.0172	0.0194	0.0169	0.0128	0.0088	0.0085	0.0093	0.0072	0.0011
516	0.0325	0.0323	0.0312	0.0307	0.0307	0.0306	0.0306	0.0306	0.0003
517	0.0431	0.0345	0.0284	0.0230	0.0228	0.0214	0.0204	0.0175	0.0004
518	0.0289	0.0224	0.0183	0.0186	0.0183	0.0193	0.0167	0.0144	0.0006
519	0.0211	0.0185	0.0122	0.0099	0.0091	0.0142	0.0108	0.0060	0.0015
520	0.0170	0.0118	0.0105	0.0095	0.0093	0.0103	0.0094	0.0085	0.0009
521	0.0181	0.0156	0.0131	0.0122	0.0105	0.0093	0.0081	0.0070	0.0016
522	0.0485	0.0242	0.0203	0.0201	0.0210	0.0170	0.0159	0.0127	0.0016
523	0.0191	0.0117	0.0115	0.0098	0.0102	0.0103	0.0097	0.0091	0.0007
524	0.0923	0.0882	0.0877	0.0591	0.0635	0.0561	0.0413	0.0318	0.0003
525	0.0260	0.0259	0.0230	0.0143	0.0160	0.0105	0.0103	0.0087	0.0009
526	0.0144	0.0093	0.0089	0.0085	0.0086	0.0069	0.0063	0.0055	0.0021
527	0.0268	0.0270	0.0267	0.0244	0.0250	0.0260	0.0270	0.0255	0.0003
528	0.0391	0.0269	0.0237	0.0144	0.0148	0.0118	0.0103	0.0080	0.0055
529	0.1433	0.1431	0.1372	0.1378	0.1388	0.1277	0.1277	0.1113	0.0001
530	0.0285	0.0294	0.0275	0.0264	0.0255	0.0248	0.0258	0.0252	0.0003
AA-MAP	0.0448	0.0348	0.0316	0.0273	0.0266	0.0238	0.0214	0.0179	0.0012

to work well with all descriptors). However, there are also several topics that seem to be very difficult for similarity search with all descriptors ($MAP < 0.02$), including CNN features: 505, 513, 514, 515, 520, 521, 523, and 526. When looking at Table 1 the reason for that seems to be the rather generous formulation of the queries, with many relevant examples that are not necessarily visually similar. On the other side, the different descriptors do not work as human intuition might expect. For example, for "a person jumping" (515), "a sewing machine" (510), or "any type of fountains outdoors" (520) one could expect dynamic descriptors to work well, which is not the case. Similarly, for "palm trees" (512) or "two or more men at a beach scene" (519) we could assume color-based descriptors to achieve well results, which is also not true for the tested data.

5   Conclusion

Utilizing the TRECVID IACC.3 dataset together with the combined ground truth of TRECVID 2016 and VBS 2017, consisting of video scenes portraying 30 individual query topics, we have evaluated the performance of eight different visual content descriptors. CNN features overall outperform the other methodologies, yet, static and dynamic feature signatures as well achieve promising performance results, while the other tested content descriptors achieve quite low results. Color-based features as anticipated work moderately well when expected query results involve distinct color schemes. For future work we plan on evaluating further features as well as further investigating CNNs: it would, for instance, be interesting to compare this works' results to the performance achieved when training a new network from scratch using TRECVID data.

Acknowledgement. This work is supported by the Alpen-Adria University Klagenfurt and Lakeside Labs GmbH, Klagenfurt, Austria and funding from the European Regional Development Fund and the Carinthian Economic Promotion Fund (KWF) under grant KWF 20214 u. 3520/26336/38165.

References

1. Awad, G., Fiscus, J., Michel, M., Joy, D., Kraaij, W., Smeaton, A.F., Quénot, G., Eskevich, M., Aly, R., Ordelman, R.: TRECVID 2016: evaluating video search, video event detection, localization, and hyperlinking. In: Proceedings of TRECVID (2016)
2. Babenko, A., Slesarev, A., Chigorin, A., Lempitsky, V.: Neural codes for image retrieval. In: Fleet, D., Pajdla, T., Schiele, B., Tuytelaars, T. (eds.) ECCV 2014. LNCS, vol. 8689, pp. 584–599. Springer, Cham (2014). https://doi.org/10.1007/978-3-319-10590-1_38
3. Beecks, C., Kirchhoff, S., Seidl, T.: Signature matching distance for content-based image retrieval. In: Proceedings of 3rd International ACM Conference on Multimedia Retrieval (2013)
4. Blažek, A., Lokoč, J., Kuboň, D.: Video hunter at VBS 2017. In: Amsaleg, L., Guðmundsson, G.Þ., Gurrin, C., Jónsson, B.Þ., Satoh, S. (eds.) MMM 2017. LNCS, vol. 10133, pp. 493–498. Springer, Cham (2017). https://doi.org/10.1007/978-3-319-51814-5_47
5. Chatzichristofis, S.A., Boutalis, Y.S.: CEDD: color and edge directivity descriptor: a compact descriptor for image indexing and retrieval. In: Gasteratos, A., Vincze, M., Tsotsos, J.K. (eds.) ICVS 2008. LNCS, vol. 5008, pp. 312–322. Springer, Heidelberg (2008). https://doi.org/10.1007/978-3-540-79547-6_30
6. Cisco: The Zettabyte Era: Trends and Analysis. Technical report, Cisco (2017). http://tinyurl.com/cisco-trends-2017
7. Cobârzan, C., Schoeffmann, K., Bailer, W., Hürst, W., Blažek, A., Lokoč, J., Vrochidis, S., Barthel, K.U., Rossetto, L.: Interactive video search tools: a detailed analysis of the video browser showdown 2015. Multimedia Tools Appl. **76**(4), 5539–5571 (2017)

8. Dalal, N., Triggs, B.: Histograms of oriented gradients for human detection. In: Proceedings of IEEE Computer Society Conference on Computer Vision and Pattern Recognition, vol. I, pp. 886–893. IEEE (2005)

9. Dalal, N., Triggs, B., Schmid, C.: Human detection using oriented histograms of flow and appearance. In: Leonardis, A., Bischof, H., Pinz, A. (eds.) ECCV 2006. LNCS, vol. 3952, pp. 428–441. Springer, Heidelberg (2006). https://doi.org/10.1007/11744047_33

10. Hürst, W., Ching, A.I.V., Schoeffmann, K., Primus, M.J.: Storyboard-based video browsing using color and concept indices. In: Amsaleg, L., Guðmundsson, G.Þ., Gurrin, C., Jónsson, B.Þ., Satoh, S. (eds.) MMM 2017. LNCS, vol. 10133, pp. 480–485. Springer, Cham (2017). https://doi.org/10.1007/978-3-319-51814-5_45

11. Joe Yue-Hei, N., Fan, Y., Davis, L.S.: Exploiting local features from deep networks for image retrieval. In: Proceedings of IEEE Conference Workshop on Computer Vision and Pattern Recognition, pp. 53–61 (2015)

12. Kletz, S., Schoeffmann, K., Münzer, B., Primus, J.M., Husslein, H.: Surgical action retrieval for assisting video review of laparoscopic skills. In: Proceedings of ACMMM Conference Workshop on Educational and Knowledge Technologies (2017)

13. Laptev, I., Marszałek, M., Schmid, C., Rozenfeld, B.: Learning realistic human actions from movies. In: Proceedings of 26th IEEE Conference on Computer Vision and Pattern Recognition (2008)

14. Lu, Y.-J., Nguyen, P.A., Zhang, H., Ngo, C.-W.: Concept-based interactive search system. In: Amsaleg, L., Guðmundsson, G.Þ., Gurrin, C., Jónsson, B.Þ., Satoh, S. (eds.) MMM 2017. LNCS, vol. 10133, pp. 463–468. Springer, Cham (2017). https://doi.org/10.1007/978-3-319-51814-5_42

15. Moumtzidou, A., et al.: VERGE in VBS 2017. In: Amsaleg, L., Guðmundsson, G.Þ., Gurrin, C., Jónsson, B.Þ., Satoh, S. (eds.) MMM 2017. LNCS, vol. 10133, pp. 486–492. Springer, Cham (2017). https://doi.org/10.1007/978-3-319-51814-5_46

16. Nguyen, V.-T., Ngo, T.D., Le, D.-D., Tran, M.-T., Duong, D.A., Satoh, S.: Semantic extraction and object proposal for video search. In: Amsaleg, L., Guðmundsson, G.Þ., Gurrin, C., Jónsson, B.Þ., Satoh, S. (eds.) MMM 2017. LNCS, vol. 10133, pp. 475–479. Springer, Cham (2017). https://doi.org/10.1007/978-3-319-51814-5_44

17. Rossetto, L., Giangreco, I., Tănase, C., Schuldt, H., Dupont, S., Seddati, O.: Enhanced retrieval and browsing in the IMOTION system. In: Amsaleg, L., Guðmundsson, G.Þ., Gurrin, C., Jónsson, B.Þ., Satoh, S. (eds.) MMM 2017. LNCS, vol. 10133, pp. 469–474. Springer, Cham (2017). https://doi.org/10.1007/978-3-319-51814-5_43

18. Sanou, B.: World in 2016: ICT Facts and Figures. Technical report, International Telecommunication Union (ITU) (2017). http://tinyurl.com/itu-facts-2016

19. Schoeffmann, K., Hudelist, M.A., Huber, J.: Video interaction tools: a survey of recent work. ACM Comput. Surv. 48(1), 14:1–14:34 (2015)

20. Schoeffmann, K., Primus, M.J., Muenzer, B., Petscharnig, S., Karisch, C., Xu, Q., Huerst, W.: Collaborative feature maps for interactive video search. In: Amsaleg, L., Guðmundsson, G.Þ., Gurrin, C., Jónsson, B.Þ., Satoh, S. (eds.) MMM 2017. LNCS, vol. 10133, pp. 457–462. Springer, Cham (2017). https://doi.org/10.1007/978-3-319-51814-5_41

21. Schoeffmann, K.: A user-centric media retrieval competition: the video browser showdown 2012–2014. IEEE MultiMedia 21(4), 8–13 (2014)

22. Smeaton, A.F., Over, P., Kraaij, W.: Evaluation campaigns and TRECVid. In: Proceedings of 8th ACM International Workshop on Multimedia Information Retrieval, p. 321. ACM Press (2006)

23. Vassou, S.A., Amanatiadis, A., Christodoulou, K., Chatzichristoos, S.A.: CoMo: a compact composite moment-based descriptor for image retrieval. In: Proceedings of 15th International Workshop on Content-Based Multimedia Indexing (2017)
24. Yilmaz, E., Kanoulas, E., Aslam, J.A.: A simple and efficient sampling method for estimating AP and NDCG. In: Proceedings of 31st Annual International ACM SIGIR Conference on Research and Development in Information Retrieval, p. 603. ACM Press (2008)

Find Me a Sky: A Data-Driven Method for Color-Consistent Sky Search and Replacement

Saumya Rawat[(✉)], Siddhartha Gairola, Rajvi Shah, and P. J. Narayanan

Center for Visual Information Technology, KCIS, IIIT Hyderabad, Hyderabad, India
saumya.rawat@students.iiit.ac.in

Abstract. Replacing overexposed or dull skies in outdoor photographs is a desirable photo manipulation. It is often necessary to color correct the foreground after replacement to make it consistent with the new sky. Methods have been proposed to automate the process of sky replacement and color correction. However, many times a color correction is unwanted by the artist or may produce unrealistic results. We propose a data-driven approach to sky-replacement that avoids color correction by finding a diverse set of skies that are consistent in color and natural illumination with the query image foreground. Our database consists of ~1200 natural images spanning many outdoor categories. Given a query image, we retrieve the most consistent images from the database according to L_2 similarity in feature space and produce candidate composites. The candidates are re-ranked based on realism and diversity. We used pre-trained CNN features and a rich set of hand-crafted features that encode color statistics, structural layout, and natural illumination statistics, but observed color statistics to be the most effective for this task. We share our findings on feature selection and show qualitative results and a user-study based evaluation to show the effectiveness of the proposed method.

1 Introduction

With the ubiquity of smart phone cameras, photography has become a democratized hobby with millions of photos uploaded to social media platforms like Instagram, Flickr, Facebook every day. Along with this comes the need for sharing perfect photographs, however, the captured shots are often unattractive due to undesirable backgrounds, occlusions, poor lighting or exposure, motion blur, lack of smile, presence of eye blinks, etc. In recent years, many methods are proposed for a number of automatic photo enhancements. This paper focuses on the problem of automatic sky-replacement.

Sky is often the hardest part of the scene to perfect in outdoor photography. Depending upon the geographic location and weather conditions, sky could persistently be gray and dull, or too bright. Even when the sky is perfect blue with white

---

S. Rawat and S. Gairola— Both authors have contributed equally to this work.

Project page: https://cvit.iiit.ac.in/research/projects/cvit-projects/findmeasky.

K. Schoeffmann et al. (Eds.): MMM 2018, Part I, LNCS 10704, pp. 216–228, 2018.
https://doi.org/10.1007/978-3-319-73603-7_18

clouds and looks beautiful to the naked eye, it most often gets washed out in a single exposure shot captured with a standard smart-phone camera. Professional outdoor photographers often prefer the golden hour (when sun is closer to the horizon) or use specifically designed filters and polarizers to overcome this problem. Multi-exposure (HDR) photography can alleviate this problem to some extent, however, not much can be done if at the time of capture sky is just dull (Fig. 1).

Fig. 1. For a query image with a dull sky (left), examples of consistent (middle) and inconsistent (right) sky replacements. (Color figure online)

Professional digital artists, perfect the bad-sky photographs by manually replacing the original sky with a desirable one and performing a series of inter-active corrections to make the sky and the foreground consistent with each other while keeping the final composite 'plausible'. This is a non-trivial and time consuming edit that is too cumbersome for a naïve user to perform. Recently, [9] proposed an automatic method for sky-replacement that performs semantic-aware color transform on the foreground to achieve natural looking composites. However, color-correction is not always desirable. Hence, we propose a different approach to sky-replacement that avoids or minimizes the need for post-replacement color corrections.

Our approach is data-driven and centered around the idea of 'compatible' sky-search. Given a query image with a problematic sky, our method first finds images with similar foregrounds and natural illumination. It then creates candidate composites by replacing the query image sky with the retrieved image skies and ranks the composites based on realism and diversity. The user is finally presented with the top-k candidate composites as replacement outcomes without color transfer thereby retaining the natural color composition of the foreground in the original image. We demonstrate the effectiveness of our method with qualitative results and a comprehensive user study. Figure 2 summarizes the proposed system with a block diagram.

For retrieving compatible yet useful images, we curated a dataset of 1246 outdoor images spanning many outdoor categories with interesting skies from ADE20K dataset [18] and the dataset of [10]. To achieve compatible sky-search, we use an ensemble of hand-crafted features such as Color Statistics (Correlated Color Temperature (CCT), Luminance, and Saturation histograms), GIST [5], Bag of Words [8], and natural illumination statistics [4] (represented as a probability map of sun position in the sky); as well as CNN features (pre-trained). These features encode rich information about color distribution, structural layout, semantics, and natural illumination. We finally select the color statistical features, as we found based on an ablation study that the composites produced using the retrieval results with these features were most realistic. We evaluate the composite images using RealismCNN [19] – a discriminative model trained to predict realism of an image. Section 3 explains the data collection, feature selection, and re-ranking based on realism and diversity in detail.

To summarize, our contributions are the following, (i) We present a novel pipeline for compatible-search based sky-replacement that is a useful alternative or prelude to automatic color transfer based methods. (ii) We curated a large database of outdoor images with interesting skies and evaluated usefulness of a large number of features for this task. Our findings along with the database would be useful to the community for future research in this direction.

2   Related Work

Automatic Sky-Search and Sky-Replacement: Tao et al. [9] proposed an interactive search system using a set of semantic sky attributes (category, layout, richness, horizon, etc.) and showed how it can be used for controllable sky replacement. However the sky segmentation and consequently horizon detection introduce errors in sky replacement. Tsai et al. [10] proposed a data-driven sky search scheme based on semantic layout of the input image. To re-compose the stylized sky with the original foreground naturally, an appearance transfer method is developed to match statistics locally and semantically. However, the color transfer algorithm is linked with label matching between the source and the target which adds both complexity and a limitation on the kind of source images that can be used. Also, color transfer may be undesirable and may introduce artefacts in the foreground regions. In contrast, we do not rely on similar sky replacement methods and also do not need to use appearance transfer methods.

Realistic Image Composition: Much work has been done for realistic image composition [14] and for evaluating realism of composites [13,15]. Lalonde and Efros [3] propose an object insertion technique that searches for objects that are consistent with the input photograph in terms of camera orientation, lighting, resolution, etc. and uses feature based assessment of composite realism. Xue et al. [16] determine the key statistical measures that influence the realism of a composite and then adjust these in a given query composite automatically using a data-driven algorithm. In this work, we leverage the implicit correlation between background and foreground regions in natural images for compatible sky-search that lead to more realistic composites.

3   Proposed System

The motivation behind our sky replacement method is to find naturally consistent yet interesting skies for a query image. Our system is based on the following hypothesis. Given two images, (i) if their foreground regions are similar

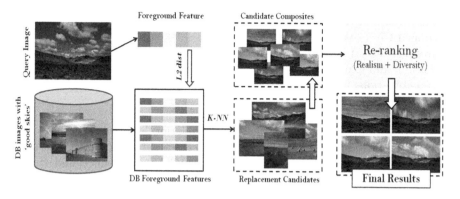

Fig. 2. An overview of our sky-replacement pipeline. Candidate composites are created using skies from database images with most similar foregrounds. Final composites are re-ranked to maximize realism and diversity of the presented set.

(in color, layout, and semantic makeup), and (ii) if the estimated natural illumination (predicted positions of the sun in the sky) is similar, swapping their skies would lead to highly realistic composites that wouldn't need foreground color correction. This hypothesis is validated with experiments (discussed later). We first curate a database of outdoor images with interesting and aesthetically appealing skies along with their foreground masks. We represent each database image with image features corresponding to its foreground region and illumination. Similarly, given a query image (and its foreground mask), we compute its foreground features and natural illumination. For each query, we retrieve the top-K nearest neighbor images from the database based on the L_2 distance in feature space and use the sky regions in these images as viable candidates for replacement. We evaluate all candidate composites for realism and diversity and re-rank the candidates to provide most realistic yet diverse alternatives to the query image. This procedure is outlined in Fig. 2.

3.1   Database Collection

The database of 1246 images used with the proposed system consists of 415 Flickr images with diverse skies (collected by [10]) and 831 outdoor images curated from the ADE20K Dataset [18]. ADE20K dataset consists of $\sim$ 22K images with 150 semantic categories like sky, road, grass. The images with sky category were first filtered to a set of $\sim$ 6K useful images for which the sky region made >40% of the total image. These images were manually rated between 1 to 5 for interestingness and aesthetic appeal of the skies by two human raters and only the images with average scores higher than 3 were added to the final database.

3.2   Feature Representation

To find images with a similar foreground make-up and illumination, we performed experiments with a rich set of hand-crafted and pre-trained CNN features and found the feature based on color statistics to be equal or more effective than pre-trained CNN features for this task. In this section, we briefly introduce the features used for (i) foreground representation, and (ii) natural illumination representation, and explain the ablation on effectiveness of individual features and their combinations in the next section.

Foreground Features

Color Statistics: Xue et al. [16] studied the relation between the background and foreground regions for realistic composition using various 2D statistical measures and identified correlated color temperature (CCT), luminance, and saturation to be the most significant measures in determining realism of a composite. We use this finding and represent the image foreground using histograms of these color statistics computed at every pixel (using [12]).

Bag of Visual Words and GIST: Hand-crafted features such as Bag of visual words (BoW) [8] and GIST have been popularly used for measuring object-level and scene-level similarities between images. For our task, BoVW features are computed by quantizing densely extracted local descriptors (like SIFT) from foreground region of an image into a large visual vocabulary and building a normalized histogram of these word occurrences. GIST features are designed to capture spatial envelope of the scene and use histogram representation of gabor filter responses applied at multiple scales and orientations. We use VLFeat library [11] to extract BoW and GIST features.

Pre-trained CNN Features: Image descriptors computed using convolutional neural networks (CNNs) pre-trained on large data such as ImageNet have proven to be very effective for a number of visual understanding tasks. The success of these features can be attributed to implicit learning of spatial layout and object semantics at later layers of the network from very large datasets. We use two different pre-trained networks, (i) VGG19 architecture [7] trained on ILSVRC-2012 (ImageNet) dataset, and (ii) VGG16 architecture trained on Places205 dataset [17], and extract two variants of CNN features. With both architectures, we use the output of FC7 (fully-connected) layer (4096 dim.) as feature representation. Between these two, ImageNet pre-trained CNN features performs better. We did not fine-tune these networks for our task due to lack of labeled data.

Illumination Features

Sun Position and Visibility: Apart from foreground similarity, images with illumination similar to the query would be better candidates for sky replacement. We compare the sun position in the sky estimated using [4]. This method estimates a probability distribution over sun position in the sky (azimuth and zenith angles) and visibility using a combination of weak cues (sky pixel intensities, cast shadows on ground, vertical surface shading) and a data-driven prior.

Fig. 3. An overview of the sky replacement step.

3.3   Candidate Search and Composition

Candidate Search: The query and the candidates are compared using a combination of foreground distance (d_{fg}) and the sun position distance (d_{il}) as follows,

$$d(I_q, I_c) = d_{fg}(I_q, I_c) + \alpha\, d_{il}(I_q, I_c) \tag{1}$$

Foreground features are compared using L_2 distance. For comparing illumination, instead of comparing two probability distributions, we directly compute the angular distance (zenith and azimuth) between the query and the candidate images. If the highest probability is below 0.5, the parameter α is 0, we do not consider the illumination distance as reliable and discard it otherwise α is 1. Distances are normalized between 0 and 1.

Composition: The database images are stored with an alpha mask corresponding to the sky/foreground segmentation. We assume the availability of alpha mask for query image also. [10] explain an automatic method to obtain accurate sky segmentation. Alternatively a semi-automatic method [6] can be used to obtain a reliable alpha mask for the query image. Given the query and the candidate images with corresponding segmentation masks, we first crop the tightest rectangle consisting only of the sky pixels from the candidate image and scale it to match the size of the maximum bounding rectangle of the query image. We then replace the query image sky patch by the scaled candidate sky patch as illustrated in Fig. 3 and perform laplacian pyramid based blending [1] along the seam to reduce composition artifacts.

3.4   Feature Selection Based on Composite Realism

Given a query, the ideal feature is the one that yields candidate images with most suitable skies for replacement. Suitability of an image for this task is determined by perceived realism and aesthetic appeal of the final composite. These properties are highly subjective and hence obtaining ground-truth rankings/ratings for a large number of query images requires extensive human annotation effort. Recently, [19] trained a discriminative model to predict realism of an image (RealismCNN). While, this is not an accurate indicator of 'goodness' of a candidate for our task, it is a useful alternative to validate usefulness of the features in absence of any ground-truth/baseline. We created a validation set of 100 query images for this ablation study. For each query, we retrieved the top-100 candidates using L_2 distance of the five foreground features and also using a combination of foreground and sun position distances. This leads to 100 composites per query per feature (100K composites per feature). Using the predictive model of [19], we obtain a realism score for each composite.

Figure 4 shows the running average of realism scores for incremental subsets of top-K composites (10%, 20%, ..., 100%). As discussed before, our hypothesis is that using skies of images with most similar foregrounds and/or illumination would lead to most realistic composites. If this hypothesis is valid, with increase in value of K, average realism score of the top-K composites should be decreasing. This trend can be observed for all features, validating our hypothesis. Among all foreground features, color statistics feature yields the highest average realism scores, CNN feature is a close second (ImageNet pre-trained). We study the effect of these two features combined with illumination feature (sun positions) as per Eq. 1. While the average scores drop for combined illumination and color features, these features are helpful to avoid physically implausible composites. But since the performance is significantly lower we finally only use color statistic features for finding the suitable candidate skies.

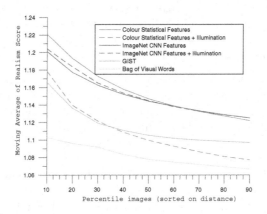

Fig. 4. Ablation study: running average of realism scores for composites sorted on feature distances

3.5   Re-ranking for Realism and Diversity

While the candidates obtained using feature based distances are compatible and the resulting composites are realistic, presenting all composites to the user is unnecessary and often undesirable. Many composites can potentially be redundant if the replaced sky is similar to the query and/or to other composites. We propose to select a small and diverse subset of highly realistic composites. To achieve this, the composites are re-ranked based on the realism score (RealismCNN) and a diversity measure. This is done by casting this problem to a max-sum diversification objective and optimizing this objective using a facility dispersion algorithm as proposed by [2].

For relevant and diverse retrieval, we wish to select a subset that maximizes total relevance ($\sum w$) and total dissimilarity ($\sum d$). Consider U is the set of all candidate composites for a query image I_q and $S \subseteq U$ is the desired subset. The bi-criteria objective ($f(S)$) that achieves this can be given by Eq. 2 [2] (where $\lambda > 0$ is a trade-off parameter).

$$f(S) = (k-1) \sum_{u \in S} w(u) + 2\lambda \sum_{u,v \in S} d(u,v) \tag{2}$$

$$d'(u,v) = w(u) + w(v) + 2\lambda d(u,v) \tag{3}$$

To recast the objective as *max-sum dispersion* (that maximizes sum of all pairwise distances in the subset S), [2] introduces a new pairwise distance given in Eq. 3. For our task, we want the composite to be realistic and the sky regions to have comparable aspect ratios hence, (i) relevance w for each composite is a product of it's min-max normalized realism score and the scale factor (i.e. scaling applied to the candidate sky patch), and (ii) the dissimilarity d is the L_2 distance between two *sky regions* in color feature space.

4   Results and Discussion

Our system is implemented in MATLAB with binary bindings for realism evaluation and blending. Currently, the code is not optimized for performance and takes around a minute to produce 100 candidates for a query image, of which, we show the top-4. To evaluate the effectiveness of our method, we show qualitative results for a few query images and discuss findings of the user-study based evaluation conducted for a larger query set.

Qualitative Results: Figure 5 illustrates the 4 best composites for the query images on the top. The query images shown include a variety of scene types and configurations such as aerial/ground shots, presence/absence of foreground objects (person, tower), dull/interesting skies. It can be seen that for all queries, the composites are diverse, natural looking, and aesthetically appealing. Figure 6 shows the usefulness of the re-ranking algorithm. The images before re-ranking have similar backgrounds to the input image. But after re-ranking we get images which are both diverse and relevant. Figure 8 compares the results from the given pipeline and the results given by [10]. The comparison clearly shows that our method produce results which are similar in aesthetic appeal. Figure 7 depicts the failure of the color transfer techniques used by [10] as the specularity and reflection from the roofs in the houses is clearly visible. There is no need for such correction in our method as it chooses skies that are already compatible with the foreground of the input image.

User-Study Evaluation: To assess the performance of our replacement system, we conducted a user study where we asked the users to rate groups of images

Fig. 5. Example results of our diverse and compatible sky-replacement system

Table 1. Statistics on user preferences

	Min	Max	Mean	Median
$\mathcal{R}_q > $ all $\mathcal{R}_c$	0%	52%	12.72%	8.6%
Any $\mathcal{R}_c \geq \mathcal{R}_q$	48.48%	100%	87.32%	91.4%
Any $\mathcal{R}_c > \mathcal{R}_q$	10.5%	81.67%	43.38%	43.31%

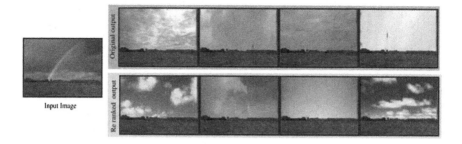

Fig. 6. Example illustrating the efficacy of the re-ranking.

Fig. 7. Failure of colour transfer methods in the in-house implementation of [10] as compared with our method which chooses skies that are already compatible with the foreground.

based on their naturalness and aesthetic appeal. Each group included a query image and top-3 composites in a randomized (and anonymous) fashion. The user study was conducted for a set of 30 query groups and each group was rated by at least 40 participants. The participants belonged to age group 20 to 35 and had varying degrees of photography and composition expertise, with a larger segment self-identifying as amateur or casual photographers. Each image was rated between scores 1 to 5 which correspond to 'very bad', 'bad', 'okay', 'good', and 'very good' descriptions. In absolute terms, the median score (across users and queries) for the original image is 2.82 (below 'okay') while for the composites, it is 3.12 (above 'okay') indicating that the composites were perceived to be equally or more attractive than the original images, Relatively, 83.33% of the times at least one out of three composites received a rating strictly higher than the query image indicating preferable aesthetic appeal of the composites. We also report statistics on the fraction of times a query image I_q is rated $>, =, <$ any of the composite images I_c in Table 1. It shows user agreement for various cases, e.g. for the criteria any $\mathcal{R}_c > \mathcal{R}_q$ (where $\mathcal{R}_i$ is rating of an image i), the worst performing query set (column corresponding to min) 10.5% users agree, the best set has 81.67% users in agreement, and on average over all query sets

Fig. 8. Comparison with existing state of the art method, [10]. We tested our model on the same input image, the results obtained are just as aesthetically appealing using a completely different pipeline.

43.38% users agree. The survey results clearly indicate merit in our replacement system.

Failure Cases: Figure 9 shows a few cases where our pipeline fails. Figure 9(i) illustrates that like any composition system, success of our system also assumes accurate segmentation and incorrect segmentation can lead to inconsistent composites. In case of scenes with specular surfaces like in (ii–iii), inconsistent reflection of the sky can lead to unnatural looking compositions.

Fig. 9. Failure cases, from left, (i) segmentation error, (ii) inconsistent sky reflection in water, (iii) bright (sun) spot, (iv) better composition achieved with use of illumination map.

5   Conclusions

In this paper, we proposed a data-driven method that given a query image produces interesting and realistic composites with different skies without using color transfer as a post-processing step. To achieve interesting replacements, we curated a new dataset of outdoor images with interesting skies. To achieve realism without color transfer, we proposed a foreground similarity hypothesis and validated it using a realism prediction model. We also experimented with a variety of image based features for this task and observed color statistical features to be very effective. We further showed a re-ranking technique to achieve both realism and diversity in the final subset presented to the user. The effectiveness of our method is evaluated by conducting a thorough user study. In future, we would like to explore an unsupervised learning based alternative to our selection pipeline and also explore generative formulation of sky-replacement problem.

References

1. Burt, P.J., Adelson, E.H.: A multiresolution spline with application to image mosaics. ACM Trans. Graph. **2**(4) (1983)
2. Gollapudi, S., Sharma, A.: An axiomatic approach for result diversification. In: Proceedings of ACM WWW (2009)
3. Lalonde, J.-F., Efros, A.A.: Using color compatibility for assessing image realism. In: Proceedings of IEEE ICCV (2007)
4. Lalonde, J.-F., Efros, A.A., Narasimhan, S.G.: Estimating natural illumination from a single outdoor image. In: Proceedings of IEEE ICCV (2009)
5. Oliva, A., Torralba, A.: Modeling the shape of the scene: a holistic representation of the spatial envelope. Int. J. Comput. Vis. **42**(3) (2001)
6. Rother, C., Kolmogorov, V., Blake, A.: "Grabcut": interactive foreground extraction using iterated graph cuts. ACM Trans. Graph. **23**(3) (2004)
7. Simonyan, K., Zisserman, A.: Very deep convolutional networks for large-scale image recognition. CoRR, abs/1409.1556 (2014)
8. Sivic, J., Zisserman, A.: Video Google: a text retrieval approach to object matching in videos. In: Proceedings of IEEE ICCV (2003)
9. Tao, L., Yuan, L., Sun, J.: Skyfinder: attribute-based sky image search. ACM Trans. Graph. **28**(3) (2009)
10. Tsai, Y.-H., Shen, X., Lin, Z., Sunkavalli, K., Yang, M.-H.: Sky is not the limit: semantic-aware sky replacement. ACM Trans. Graph. **35**(4) (2016)
11. Vedaldi, A., Fulkerson, B.: VLFeat - an open and portable library of computer vision algorithms. In: ACM MM (2010)
12. Wågberg, J.: OptProp: Matlab Toolbox for Calculation of Color Related Optical Properties: Version 2.1. FSCN-rapport (2007)
13. Wang, D., Jia, W., Li, G., Xiong, Y.: Natural image composition with inhomogeneous boundaries. In: Ho, Y.-S. (ed.) PSIVT 2011. LNCS, vol. 7088, pp. 92–103. Springer, Heidelberg (2011). https://doi.org/10.1007/978-3-642-25346-1_9
14. Wang, J., Cohen, M.F.: Image and video matting: a survey. Found. Trends. Comput. Graph. Vis. **3**(2) (2007)
15. Wong, B.Y., Shih, K.T., Liang, C.K., Chen, H.H.: Single image realism assessment and recoloring by color compatibility. IEEE Trans. Multimedia **14** (2012)

16. Xue, S., Agarwala, A., Dorsey, J., Rushmeier, H.: Understanding and improving the realism of image composites. ACM Trans. Graph. **31**(4) (2012)
17. Zhou, B., Khosla, A., Lapedriza, À., Torralba, A., Oliva, A.: Places: an image database for deep scene understanding. CoRR, abs/1610.02055 (2016)
18. Zhou, B., Zhao, H., Puig, X., Fidler, S., Barriuso, A., Torralba, A.: Scene parsing through ade20k dataset. In: Proceedings of IEEE CVPR (2017)
19. Zhu, J.-Y., Krähenbühl, P., Shechtman, E., Efros, A.A.: Learning a discriminative model for the perception of realism in composite images. In: Proceedings of IEEE ICCV (2015)

Font Recognition in Natural Images via Transfer Learning

Yizhi Wang, Zhouhui Lian$^{(\boxtimes)}$, Yingmin Tang, and Jianguo Xiao

Institute of Computer Science and Technology, Peking University,
Beijing, People's Republic of China
lianzhouhui@pku.edu.cn

Abstract. Font recognition is an important and challenging problem in areas of Document Analysis, Pattern Recognition and Computer Vision. In this paper, we try to handle a tougher task that aims to accurately recognize the font styles of texts in natural images by proposing a novel method based on deep learning and transfer learning. Major contributions of this paper are threefold: First, we develop a fast and scalable system to synthesize huge amounts of natural images containing texts in various fonts and styles, which are then utilized to train the deep neural network for font recognition. Second, we design a transfer learning scheme to alleviate the domain mismatch between synthetic and real-world text images. Thus, large numbers of unlabeled text images can be adopted to markedly enhance the discrimination and robustness of our font classifier. Third, we build a benchmarking database which consists of numerous labeled natural images containing Chinese characters in 48 fonts. As far as we know, it is the first publicly-available dataset for font recognition of Chinese characters in natural images.

1 Introduction

Font recognition is an important and challenging problem in areas of Document Analysis, Pattern Recognition and Computer Vision. Automatic font recognition can greatly improve the efficiency of many people's work. First and foremost, it helps people (not limited to designers) to know what their favorite font styles are in the text in images they see. Besides, font producers can use it to find copyright infringements by automatic font identification. Moreover, font recognition is useful in improving the accuracy and speed of character recognition systems. Actually, it is a specific problem of object detection and classification, in which deep neural networks [1–5] have made great success. As we know, methods based on deep neural network demand large-scale training data and thus time-consuming manual labeling is typically required. Unlike other object detection and classification tasks, the real-world font annotations are extremely hard to get because large numbers of experts are needed to identify the fonts of texts in images. This problem can be resolved to some extends by synthesizing high-quality images with texts in different fonts. However, there still exist domain mismatch problems between synthesized and real-world text images. In

K. Schoeffmann et al. (Eds.): MMM 2018, Part I, LNCS 10704, pp. 229–240, 2018.
https://doi.org/10.1007/978-3-319-73603-7_19

this paper, we put emphasis on how to synthesize high-quality text images of different fonts and how to conduct effective learning from massive unlabeled images without supervision.

Up to now, many algorithms have been proposed for font recognition, such as modified quadratic discriminant functions (MQDF) [6], wavelet feature descriptors [7], the texture descriptor based on fractal geometry [8], Gaussian mixture models [9], local binary patterns (LBPs) [10], local feature embedding (LFE) [11] and sparse features [12] etc. However, these traditional methods based on hand-crafted features are not able to satisfactorily deal with noisy data.

Recently, neurodynamic models have been presented for solving font recognition problem. The DeepFont system proposed in [13] employs a Convolutional Neural Network (CNN) architecture to recognize the font of English text lines. In addition to synthetic data augmentation, a Stacked Convolutional Auto-Encoder (SCAE) trained with unlabeled real-world text images is also utilized to reduce overfitting. Another system reported in [14] is specifically designed to handle the Chinese Character Font Recognition (CCFR) task. They considered CCFR as a sequence classification problem and developed a 2-D long short-term memory (2DLSTM) model to capture a character's trajectory and identify its font style. Although these recently-developed methods could markedly outperform traditional methods, they also have their own shortcomings. For instance, the system proposed in [13] can only deal with alphabetic language systems, such as English, that consist of small number of different characters. For hieroglyph like Chinese with more than 6000 different characters whose geometric structures are often quite complicated, through experiments we found that the SCAE does not work well. For real-world images, the method developed by Tao et al. [14] may fail to capture characters' trajectories especially when they are under complicated background and appear with various special effects.

Based on above-mentioned reasons, we select Chinese as one of the text languages in our experiment and propose a transfer learning algorithm to make use of unlabeled text images. Also, our system aims to recognize the font of texts in natural images, instead of synthetic text images adopted in [14]. Moreover, our method can be applied to any other language systems. Experiments conducted on publicly-available databases demonstrate the effectiveness of our system for font recognition in natural images.

2   Overview of the System

As shown in Fig. 1, the proposed font recognition system can be built as follows. First, we employ our engine to synthesize huge amounts of natural images containing texts in various fonts and styles and meanwhile information of each text line's font and location is also recorded. Then, by using the location information we train a text localizer to automatically detect texts in images collected from internet. Thus, we have both labeled synthetic text images and unlabeled real-world text images. Afterwards, our initial font classifier base on Convolutional Neural Networks (CNNs) can be obtained by training on labeled synthetic

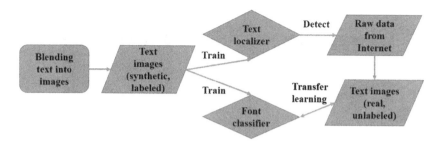

Fig. 1. The pipeline of our font recognition system.

text images. Finally, the proposed transfer learning algorithm is implemented to make use of unlabeled data and improve the classifier's performance on recognizing fonts of texts in natural images. Details of each step in our system will be explained explicitly in the following sections.

3 Synthesizing Text Images

The synthetic text image datasets such as the one described in [13] only contain word-level image regions and simple backgrounds. Thus they are unsuitable to train text detectors and font classifiers for natural images. The method proposed in [15] for generating synthetic text images naturally blends texts in existing natural scenes, using off-the-shelf deep learning and segmentation techniques to align texts to the geometry of a background image and respect scene boundaries. Inspired by the idea of this method, we develop a new system to generate synthetic text images with texts in different fonts and styles in cluttered conditions. As long as we get the TTF (True Type Font) or OTF (Open Type Font) files of some fonts, we can generate nearly real text images in these fonts automatically, along with the font label and location of each character.

3.1 Blending Texts into Images

As shown in Fig. 2, texts can be naturally blended into a given image by using our system. As we know, texts tend to be contained in well-defined regions in real-world images, instead of crossing strong image discontinuities. For this reason, we segment the image into contiguous regions based on the cues of local color and texture information using the approach presented in [16]. After obtaining segmentation regions, we choose suitable candidates from them for placing texts. Suitable regions should not be too small, should not have an extreme aspect ratio, or have surface normal orthogonal to the view direction.

In natural images, texts are typically painted on top of surfaces. In order to achieve a similar effect in our synthetic data, we need to calculate the local surface normal of the region where we are going to put the text. To get the local

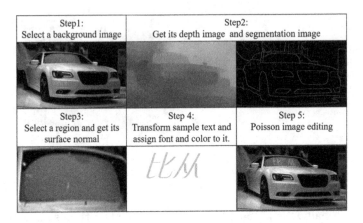

Fig. 2. Main steps to blend texts into a background image.

surface normal of each contiguous region, we need to obtain a dense pixel-wise depth map, which can be estimated by the CNN model proposed in [17].

Next, the text sample is assigned with a color and a font. The font is chosen randomly from a font list. With this font's library file we can render the glyphs of text. Then the text is assigned with a color which matches well with the background color. Finally, the text is transformed according to the local surface orientation and is blended into the scene using Poisson image editing [18].

Note that, here we record the font type for each character instead of its content. In our experiment, the text's font is chosen randomly from one of the fonts mentioned in Sect. 6. Beyond that, we introduce more data augmentations to single character images to make them possess more visually similar appearance to real-world data. Details are discussed in the following section.

3.2   Text and Image Source

We employ news corpora of different languages, including Arabic, Bangla, Chinese, Japanese, Korean and English, as our text source. Each time we randomly select some words from the corpus and blend them into a background image.

The background image for blending text can neither be too simple nor too complex. To cover common scenes in our daily lives, we select images from Open Images, an open dataset with 9 million URLs to images that were uploaded by users and have been annotated with labels spanning over 6000 categories. We pick about 30,000 images from the dataset with the labels such as "person" and "natural scenes" instead of "street" etc. whose backgrounds are too cluttered. Some samples of synthetic images are shown in Figs. 3 and 4.

3.3   Data Augmentation

The synthetic texts generated by the above method are painted on flat surfaces and match well with the background color. As a matter of fact, texts photographed in natural scenes may be blurred or in uneven illumination. To increase the diversity of our synthetic dataset, we apply some augmentation processing to those synthetic text images, including rotation, changing contrast and brightness, GaussianBlur, adding Gaussian noise, and shearing. The parameter of each effect is selected randomly within certain range and these effects are stacked on one image.

Arabic   Bangla   Chinese   English   Japanese   Korean

Fig. 3. Texts in different languages blended into natural images.

Fig. 4. Blending Chinese texts in different fonts into natural images.

4   Text Detection and Font Recognition

To recognize the fonts of texts in natural images, we first need to accurately localize texts and then correctly identify its font style. Since text spotting techniques have been extensively studied in the last few years [15,19,20], our work does not focus on this problem. The synthetic images with text location labels are utilized to train a CTPN (Connectionist Text Proposal Network) [20] as our text localizer, which detects text lines by finding and grouping a sequence of fine-scale text proposals.

The font recognition methods employed in this paper are patch-based CNN models, the same as [13]. We first extract square patches from a word image, and send them to the convolutional neural network. Each extracted patch, whose side length equals the word image's height, contains one or more characters from the word image. For each patch, the network outputs a vector with each element corresponding to the probability it belongs to each font. We average all vectors to determine the final classification result of the word image. Our font classifiers are constructed by modifying two famous CNN models (see Fig. 5), i.e., AlexNet and VGG16, proposed in [1,2], respectively.

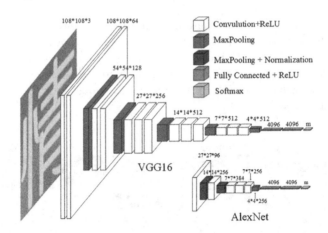

Fig. 5. An illustration of two modified CNN models for font recognition. A 108 * 108 image patch is put into a network and the network ouputs a m-dimensional probability vector (m represents the number of font classes). AlexNet is a lightweight network with fast training speed while VGG16 is a much deeper and more complex network. As we can see, VGG16 has more convolutional layers and smaller convolution strides than AlexNet.

5   Boosting Accuracy via Transfer Learning

Due to the domain mismatch between synthetic data and real-world data, there still exist a lot of text images that can not be classified correctly. Thus, we want to exploit more information from unlabeled real-world text images. Fortunately, real-world text images are easy to obtain from internet. For example, when we type keywords like "text images" in a search engine, we can get large numbers of images with texts in various kinds of fonts.

The proposed transfer learning algorithm aims to further improve the performance of font recognition for real-world text images by making use of the knowledge we gain from the synthesized data. The key idea of our method is to try to assign the unlabeled text images with correct tags by using our initial font classifiers. Then, these newly-labeled texts images can be adopted with our synthetic images to train our CNN-based classifiers again to make them more robust and effective.

It is worthy of noting that how we label text images whose font categories are out of the range we consider. Since some of them have similar font styles, we should label them with the most similar fonts included in our font list. Meanwhile, we discard those images whose font styles are very different against the fonts that we are interested in.

The problem to be addressed can be formulated as follows. Assume that the unlabeled dataset is composed of n text lines (a text line contains one or more words), let x^i be the ith text line of our dataset. The text line x^i contains $t(i)$ extracted patches and each patch in x^i is denoted by x_j^i ($1 \leq i \leq n$, $1 \leq j \leq t(i)$). Our m-class font classifier takes a single patch as input. After feeding a patch x_j^i into our pre-trained classifier, we get the probability distribution $P\left(x_j^i\right) = \left(P_1\left(x_j^i\right), P_2\left(x_j^i\right), ..., P_m\left(x_j^i\right)\right)$, in which $P_k\left(x_j^i\right)$ means the probability of x_j^i belonging to the font f_k $(1 \leq k \leq m)$, and $\sum_{k=1}^{m} P_k\left(x_j^i\right) = 1$. The classification result of x_j^i is $L_p\left(x_j^i\right) = \arg\max_k P_k\left(x_j^i\right)$. For a given text line, we intend to predict each patch's most probable font or discard it based on the above-mentioned analyses.

Intuitively, the font type of patch image x_j^i can be labeled according to the classification result $L_p\left(x_j^i\right)$. If $P_{L_p\left(x_j^i\right)}\left(x_j^i\right)$ is smaller than a threshold, we discard this patch. However, our pre-trained CNN classifier may make mistakes when handling real-world images it has never seen before. If we label these unknown images with inaccurate classification results, the classifier would be incorrectly supervised which often results in a decline in its performance. **Typically, text images possess a property that characters (or words) in one text line are usually in the same font style.** On account of this, the font labels of patches in one text line identified by the classifier are supposed to be identical. If the labels are not identical, it means that our pre-trained classifier fails to adapt new data. Through a statistical analysis of all patches' classification results in the same text line, we select a representative font style to relabel them. In this manner, the probability of making mistake can be greatly reduced.

Our method is designed as follows: for each font f_k $(1 \leq k \leq m)$, we define two variables to estimate how likely this entire text line x^i is in font f_k. The first variable is $A\left(k\right) = \sum_{j=1}^{t(i)} 1\left\{L_p\left(x_j^i\right) = k\right\}$, meaning the times that label k appears in the predicted labels of patches in x^i. The other one is $B\left(k\right) = \sum_{j=1}^{t(i)} P_k\left(x_j^i\right)$, denoting the probability of x^i belonging to font f_k accumulated by patches in the text line. We use A as the first sort key and B as the second sort key to rank these fonts $(f_1, f_2, ..., f_m)$ $(f_k$ ranks ahead if $A\left(k\right)$ or $B\left(k\right)$ is higher). Let the font ranking first be f_l, if $B\left(l\right) \geq th * t\left(i\right)$ $(th$ is set to 0.4 here), we assign the label of each patch in text line x^i with f_l. The method is actually a voting procedure to decide a text line's font. As a general rule, in turn-based games the player wining more rounds wins the game. The pseudo code of this method is shown in Algorithm 1.

Lastly, these newly-labeled texts images are combined with synthetic images to fine-tune our initial font classifiers, which is a relearning process for the font classifiers to correct their mistakes made in the first stage. As a result, the parameters of our classifiers can be further optimized and become more adaptable to real-world images.

6   Experiments

6.1   Font Recognition of Chinese Text Images

To measure the performance of our font recognition method, we need to collect real-world text images containing characters in various font styles as our test dataset. We cooperate with Founder Electronics, one of the world's largest

---

Algorithm 1. Predicting Labels for Unlabeled Text Images

Input The font label list $(f_1, f_2, ..., f_m)$, the unlabeled patches set $T = \{x_j^i | 1 \leq i \leq n, 1 \leq j \leq t(i)\}$, the pre-trained font classification function P.

Output The most probable font $L\left(x_j^i\right)$ for each patch x_j^i.

1: **for** $i = 1 \to n$ **do**
2:     **for** $j = 1 \to t(i)$ **do**
3:         $\left(P_1\left(x_j^i\right), P_2\left(x_j^i\right), ..., P_m\left(x_j^i\right)\right) \leftarrow P\left(x_j^i\right)$
4:         $L_p\left(x_j^i\right) \leftarrow \arg\max_k P_k\left(x_j^i\right)$
5:     **end for**
6:     **for** $k = 1 \to m$ **do**
7:         $A(k) \leftarrow \sum_{j=1}^{t(i)} 1\left\{L_p\left(x_j^i\right) = k\right\}$
8:         $B(k) \leftarrow \sum_{j=1}^{t(i)} P_k\left(x_j^i\right)$
9:     **end for**
10:    $sortedlist \leftarrow sort(f_1, f_2, ..., f_m), sortkey(A, B)$
11:    $f_l \leftarrow sortedlist[0]$
12:    **if** $B(l) \geq th * t(i)$ **then**
13:        **for** $j = 1 \to t(i)$ **do**
14:            $L\left(x_j^i\right) \leftarrow f_l$
15:        **end for**
16:    **end if**
17: **end for**

Chinese font producer, to build a large-scale database for font recognition in natural images, named **VFRWild-CHS**[1]. Specifically, the VFRWild-CHS dataset consists of 816 text images captured in natural scenes, from which 6,827 single Chinese character images in 48 fonts are extracted and labeled. As we can see from Fig. 6, the noisy backgrounds and special effects added artificially make it quite difficult to locate the characters and recognize their font styles.

We prepare three different datasets to train our font classifier. The first dataset, denoted as Syn_Simple, consists of simple synthetic character images with no augmentations (black characters rendered in white background images). The second dataset, denoted as Syn_Blend, is composed of single Chinese character images cropped from synthetic images generated by our text image synthesizing method without data augmentations. Sample images of these two datasets are shown in Fig. 7. We apply the augmentation methods mentioned in Sect. 3.3 to Syn_Blend and get a larger dataset Syn_Blend_Aug. Detailed information of these datasets is described in Table 1. Besides, we build a database consisting of more than 200,000 unlabeled images which are collected from internet (See Fig. 8).

We compare the performance of our classifiers on the test set which are trained on the above-mentioned training datasets, respectively. Through our experiments, we find that compared to Syn_Simple, the synthetic text images generated by our method can significantly improve the classification performance on our test dataset. As it can be observed from Table 2, the accuracy of our

---

[1] http://www.icst.pku.edu.cn/zlian/FRWild.

Fig. 6. Examples of single Chinese character images cropped from text images in our test dataset.

Fig. 7. The Left images (in Dataset Syn_Blend) are synthetic characters generated by our method. The right images (in Dataset Syn_Simple) are corresponding blank-background and no-special-effect characters.

Fig. 8. Some text lines detected by the our text localizer. These images come from Internet and have some special effects and manual designs our synthetic images don't have.

Table 1. Comparison of all datasets adopted in our experiment

Name	Source	Label?	Purpose	Size	Class
VFRWild-CHS	Real	Y	Test	6,827	48
Syn_Simple	Syn	Y	Train	324,624	48
Syn_Blend	Syn	Y	Train	474,757	48
Syn_Blend_Aug	Syn	Y	Train	670,873	48
Unlabeled dataset	Real	N	Train	229,044	N/A

The unlabeled dataset consists of text line images. The others consist of single Chinese character images.

classifier based on AlexNet and VGG16 is very low when trained with Syn_Simple, but improves considerably when trained with Syn_Blend and Syn_Blend_Aug. The result is reasonable because the images in Syn_Blend and Syn_Blend_Aug look more natural than images in Syn_Simple. To sum up, the method mentioned in Sect. 3 is an effective solution to recognize fonts of texts in natural images.

Next, we would like to verify the effectiveness of our transfer learning scheme. As shown in Table 2, our transfer learning algorithm further improves the classifier's performance. On the contrary, if we directly label each character with the predicted result given by the initial classifiers (discard it if the classification probability is lower than th), we witness a decline in classification accuracy: AlexNet top-1 70.30%, VGG16 top-1 83.03% in our experiment. This demonstrates the effectiveness of the proposed transfer learning scheme in font recognition tasks.

Table 2. Our method's performance on VFRWild-CHS

Accuracy Method Model	SS	SB	SBA	TL
AlexNet(top-1)	13.85%	69.30%	71.14%	77.75%
AlexNet(top-5)	46.80%	90.75%	91.12%	93.93%
VGG16(top-1)	34.21%	81.93%	84.83%	87.68%
VGG16(top-5)	53.68%	95.22%	96.14%	97.53%

SS, SB and SBA denote our proposed methods trained on Syn_Simple, Syn_Blend and Syn_Blend_Aug datasets, respectively. TL denotes transfer learning.

6.2   Comparison with Other Methods

We compare the performance of our methods with other recently-proposed approaches on VFRWild-CHS. LFE (local feature embedding) introduced in [11] is a representative traditional method which fuses handcrafted local features. DeepFont F introduced in [13] uses synthetic text images with traditional augmentations to train a convolutional neural network. These two methods, along with our SBA method, are supervised learning methods. DeepFont CAEFR [13] and our transfer learning method are both semi-supervised methods exploiting unlabeled real-world images.

For comparative analysis, we employ **the same network architecture** as [13], which is very similar to AlexNet. The difference is that we utilize methods introduced in Sects. 3 and 5 to synthesize training data and exploit unlabeled data. As shown in Table 3, our method outperforms other methods. The VFRWild-CHS dataset features noisy backgrounds and distortions, which can not be properly handled by methods of [11,13]. Results shown here verify the effectiveness and generality of our methods.

Table 3. Comparison of different methods' performance on VFRWild-CHS

Methods	Accuracy	
	TOP-1	TOP-5
LFE [11]	32.65%	60.69%
DeepFont F [13]	50.26%	72.93%
SBA (ours)	**70.97%**	**91.05%**
DeepFont CAEFR [13]	55.58%	76.21%
TL (ours)	**77.68%**	**93.97%**

7   Conclusion

In this paper, we developed a new system for accurate font recognition in natural images. One major advantage of our system is that time-consuming and costly font annotations for images in the training dataset can be avoided. On the one hand, by blending text into background images and implementing data augmentations, the synthesized text images look more real and thus large-scale high-quality training data can be automatically constructed for our CNN based font classifiers. On the other hand, the introduction of our transfer learning algorithm exploits a large corpus of unlabeled real-world images and thereby significantly improves the capacity and accuracy of classification. Experimental results on a publicly-available database we built demonstrated that considerable good performance of font recognition in natural images can be obtained by using our system.

Acknowledgements. This work was supported by National Natural Science Foundation of China (Grant No.: 61472015, 61672043 and 61672056), Beijing Natural Science Foundation (Grant No.: 4152022), National Language Committee of China (Grant No.: ZDI135-9), and Key Laboratory of Science, Technology and Standard in Press Industry (Key Laboratory of Intelligent Press Media Technology).

References

1. Krizhevsky, A., Sutskever, I., Hinton, G.E.: Imagenet classification with deep convolutional neural networks. In: Advances in Neural Information Processing Systems, pp. 1097–1105 (2012)
2. Simonyan, K., Zisserman, A.: Very deep convolutional networks for large-scale image recognition. arXiv preprint arXiv:1409.1556 (2014)
3. Girshick, R., Donahue, J., Darrell, T., Malik, J.: Rich feature hierarchies for accurate object detection and semantic segmentation. In: Proceedings of the IEEE Conference on Computer Vision and Pattern Recognition, pp. 580–587 (2014)
4. Girshick, R.: Fast R-CNN. In: Proceedings of the IEEE International Conference on Computer Vision, pp. 1440–1448 (2015)
5. Ren, S., He, K., Girshick, R., Sun, J.: Faster R-CNN: towards real-time object detection with region proposal networks. In: Advances in Neural Information Processing Systems, pp. 91–99 (2015)

6. Kimura, F., Takashina, K., Tsuruoka, S., Miyake, Y.: Modified quadratic discriminant functions and the application to Chinese character recognition. IEEE Trans. Pattern Anal. Mach. Intell. **1**, 149–153 (1987)
7. Ding, X., Chen, L., Wu, T.: Character independent font recognition on a single Chinese character. IEEE Trans. Pattern Anal. Mach. Intell. **29**(2), 195–204 (2007)
8. Moussa, S.B., Zahour, A., Benabdelhafid, A., Alimi, A.M.: New features using fractal multi-dimensions for generalized Arabic font recognition. Pattern Recogn. Lett. **31**(5), 361–371 (2010)
9. Slimane, F., Kanoun, S., Hennebert, J., Alimi, A.M., Ingold, R.: A study on font-family and font-size recognition applied to Arabic word images at ultra-low resolution. Pattern Recogn. Lett. **34**(2), 209–218 (2013)
10. Tao, D., Jin, L., Zhang, S., Yang, Z., Wang, Y.: Sparse discriminative information preservation for Chinese character font categorization. Neurocomputing **129**, 159–167 (2014)
11. Chen, G., Yang, J., Jin, H., Brandt, J., Shechtman, E., Agarwala, A., Han, T.X.: Large-scale visual font recognition. In: Proceedings of the IEEE Conference on Computer Vision and Pattern Recognition, pp. 3598–3605 (2014)
12. Song, W., Lian, Z., Tang, Y., Xiao, J.: Content-independent font recognition on a single Chinese character using sparse representation. In: 2015 13th International Conference on Document Analysis and Recognition (ICDAR), pp. 376–380. IEEE (2015)
13. Wang, Z., Yang, J., Jin, H., Shechtman, E., Agarwala, A., Brandt, J., Huang, T.S.: Deepfont: identify your font from an image. In: Proceedings of the 23rd ACM International Conference on Multimedia, pp. 451–459. ACM (2015)
14. Tao, D., Lin, X., Jin, L., Li, X.: Principal component 2-D long short-term memory for font recognition on single Chinese characters. IEEE Trans. Cybern. **46**(3), 756–765 (2016)
15. Gupta, A., Vedaldi, A., Zisserman, A.: Synthetic data for text localisation in natural images. In: Proceedings of the IEEE Conference on Computer Vision and Pattern Recognition, pp. 2315–2324 (2016)
16. Arbeláez, P., Pont-Tuset, J., Barron, J.T., Marques, F., Malik, J.: Multiscale combinatorial grouping. In: Proceedings of the IEEE Conference on Computer Vision and Pattern Recognition, pp. 328–335 (2014)
17. Liu, F., Shen, C., Lin, G.: Deep convolutional neural fields for depth estimation from a single image. In: Proceedings of the IEEE Conference on Computer Vision and Pattern Recognition, pp. 5162–5170 (2015)
18. Pérez, P., Gangnet, M., Blake, A.: Poisson image editing. ACM Trans. Graph. (TOG) **22**, 313–318 (2003). ACM
19. Jaderberg, M., Simonyan, K., Vedaldi, A., Zisserman, A.: Reading text in the wild with convolutional neural networks. Int. J. Comput. Vis. **116**(1), 1–20 (2016)
20. Tian, Z., Huang, W., He, T., He, P., Qiao, Y.: Detecting text in natural image with connectionist text proposal network. In: Leibe, B., Matas, J., Sebe, N., Welling, M. (eds.) ECCV 2016. LNCS, vol. 9912, pp. 56–72. Springer, Cham (2016). https://doi.org/10.1007/978-3-319-46484-8_4

Frame-Based Classification of Operation Phases in Cataract Surgery Videos

Manfred Jüergen Primus[1(✉)], Doris Putzgruber-Adamitsch[2],
Mario Taschwer[1], Bernd Münzer[1], Yosuf El-Shabrawi[2], Laszlo Böszörmenyi[1],
and Klaus Schoeffmann[1]

[1] Alpen-Adria Universität Klagenfurt, Klagenfurt, Austria
{juergen.primus,mt,bernd,laszlo,ks}@itec.aau.at
[2] Klinikum Klagenfurt am Wörthersee, Klagenfurt, Austria
{doris.putzgruber-adamitsch,yosuf.el-shabrawi}@kabeg.at

Abstract. Cataract surgeries are frequently performed to correct a lens opacification of the human eye, which usually appears in the course of aging. These surgeries are conducted with the help of a microscope and are typically recorded on video for later inspection and educational purposes. However, post-hoc visual analysis of video recordings is cumbersome and time-consuming for surgeons if there is no navigation support, such as bookmarks to specific operation phases. To prepare the way for an automatic detection of operation phases in cataract surgery videos, we investigate the effectiveness of a deep convolutional neural network (CNN) to automatically assign video frames to operation phases, which can be regarded as a single-label multi-class classification problem. In absence of public datasets of cataract surgery videos, we provide a dataset of 21 videos of standardized cataract surgeries and use it to train and evaluate our CNN classifier. Experimental results display a mean F1-score of about 68% for frame-based operation phase classification, which can be further improved to 75% when considering temporal information of video frames in the CNN architecture.

Keywords: Medical multimedia · Deep learning · Video analysis
Surgical workflow analysis

1 Introduction

Cataract is known as clouding of the eye's lens, a defect that often occurs in the course of aging. It affects the human visual system and has a tremendous negative impact on the patient's quality of life. This condition can be treated with a surgical procedure during which the natural lens is removed and an artificial lens is implanted, which usually results in a noticeable improvement of vision. Cataract surgery is by far the most frequently performed surgical procedure in the medical specialty of ophthalmology and one of the most frequently performed procedures across all specialties world-wide. It therefore follows broadly accepted

© Springer International Publishing AG 2018
K. Schoeffmann et al. (Eds.): MMM 2018, Part I, LNCS 10704, pp. 241–253, 2018.
https://doi.org/10.1007/978-3-319-73603-7_20

common rules and can be called a *quasi-standardized procedure*. Cataract surgery is usually performed in local anesthesia within 5 to 10 min, unless complications occur. High-volume surgeons usually operate several cataract surgeries within a single day. The surgeon looks at the patient's eye through an optical microscope for appropriate visualization and magnification. Furthermore, surgical microscopes usually have an additional optical system with a mounted camera to acquire a video signal. This video stream is displayed on a monitor and can also be recorded on a digital medium.

The facts that (1) a video signal is inherently available without any additional effort, (2) the course of action is well standardized, and (3) the procedure is frequently performed, make this specific domain an interesting subject of medical multimedia research. One of the fundamental problems in this field is automatic understanding of the surgical workflow and, in particular, temporal segmentation of a video into surgical phases. Such an automatic segmentation can greatly support surgeons in coping with their potentially huge video archives. It may even open the door for a comprehensive video documentation, which is not widely used yet due to the lack of video organization and navigation support. Beyond that, real-time processing methods may even support surgeons during the procedure in order to recognize or prevent adverse events. Such situations could be identified by detecting deviations from the surgical process model, causing the system to immediately alert the surgeon and provide context-sensitive assistance.

In this paper, we address the problem of differentiating between surgical phases in cataract surgery videos with a frame-based classification approach. Each video frame is classified separately as belonging to one of multiple operation phases. The task can therefore be considered as a multi-class single-label classification problem. The proposed frame-based classifier may be used to build an automatic operation phase detection system in future work. As underlying classification framework we use deep convolutional neural networks (CNN), which have proven to be very expedient for similar tasks with other types of surgery videos [5], but—to the best of our knowledge—have not been applied to ophthalmic surgery videos before. In addition to applying a CNN to a raw dataset of cataract surgery videos, we propose and evaluate two data preprocessing methods that aim at improving classification performance: (1) training data purification and balancing, and (2) adding temporal information of video frames. Since public datasets of cataract surgery videos are not yet available, we created such a dataset with ground-truth annotations to evaluate our proposed approach and provide it for public use by the scientific community.

Although acquiring videos from cataract surgeries and performing frame classification might seem to be a straightforward task, we encountered numerous challenges. They mainly relate to the strong domain specificity of ophthalmic videos, which require thorough analysis and adaptations of established techniques. For example, the visual appearance can vary considerably due to different individual preferences of surgeons regarding positioning of the microscope in terms of angle, zoom level, and light configuration. These settings can also change during a procedure. Moreover, the video camera that is mounted at the secondary optics is independent of the main optics and therefore needs to be adapted separately by an assistant in case the surgeon changes settings. If this is not done properly, the video quality can be considerably impaired. Another major challenge in this domain is the necessity to incorporate highly skilled domain experts, i.e. experienced surgeons. Their knowledge about the specific characteristics and semantics of the videos is essential. However, as they only can spare a limited amount of time, it is crucial to provide appropriate annotation tools to extract their expert knowledge as efficiently as possible.

The contributions of this paper are: (1) We propose to apply convolutional neural networks (CNN) to frame-based operation phase classification of cataract surgery videos and obtain promising results; (2) we show that classification performance of our approach can be further improved by (a) dataset purification and balancing and (b) adding temporal information of video frames as input to the CNN; (3) we provide a novel public dataset containing video recordings of 21 cataract surgeries and corresponding ground-truth annotations in terms of operation phase boundaries.

2   Related Work

We focus on related work concerning image understanding techniques applied to recorded videos of surgeries. Video recordings in the medical domain can primarily be found in the context of endoscopic or microscopic surgery. Literature in this field is mostly concerned with classification of instruments, actions, anatomy, and surgical workflow.

Early methods focus on hand-crafted features and similarity measures to detect and recognize instruments used in endoscopy. Speidel et al. [9] used images captured by a stereo endoscope and segment the potential shaft region based on saturation, brightness and amount of reddish color. The tip of the instrument is segmented with the help of a Bayesian classifier, before the instrument is recognized based on the normalized contour and distances to 3D representations of each instrument.

A bag-of-visual-words representation of SIFT-, SURF-, and ORB-features was used to train a support vector machine (SVM) for recognizing instruments and operation phases in cholecystectomy surgeries (i.e. removal of the gallbladder) [6,7]. The authors improved their approach by segmenting the image area into parts where an instrument might show up and parts that only show tissue. For classification only the potential instrument area was used.

Petscharnig and Schöffmann [4] proposed the use of transfer learning based on the AlexNet CNN architecture for frame-based classification of actions and anatomy in gynecologic surgery videos. In follow-up work [5] they showed that a GoogLeNet CNN model trained from scratch outperformed their AlexNet-model as well as an SVM classifier using off-the-shelf AlexNet features. Their best performing network achieved an F1-score of 85%.

Twinanda et al. [11] trained a CNN called EndoNet based on the AlexNet architecture for the classification of operation phases of cholecystectomy surgeries. The authors concatenated the FC7 layer of the AlexNet architecture with the subsequent output layer to a new fully connected layer. A refinement of classifications was achieved using a hierarchical hidden Markov model.

In the field of cataract surgeries, Lalys et al. [3] used visual information such as histograms, texture, and shape for the classification of surgical tasks using an SVM. The classified images were aligned to already annotated recordings using a hidden Markov model and dynamic time warping. Charriere et al. [1] used a Bayesian network and two conditional random fields for classification of operation phases in cataract surgery videos.

Quellec et al. [8] introduced a method that divides cataract surgeries into ten phases. Each phase is divided into an action phase—where the surgical task is performed—and an idle phase—where almost nothing happens in the operation area, because the next step is prepared out of the microscope's sight or instruments are exchanged. Recorded videos were used to learn the differences between action phases and idle phases. A conditional random field was used to align phases of new videos to existing ones.

Previous multimedia research in the domain of cataract surgeries used the strict sequential order of the surgical workflow to detect phase transitions and did not yet employ CNNs. In contrast, our work addresses the classification of single frames of cataract surgery videos using newly trained CNNs. The major advantage of this approach is that it can be easily extended to additional classes pertaining to optional operation phases, out-of-order phases, or complications.

3   Cataract Surgery Dataset

Cataract surgery can be divided in eleven phases, which are: 1. Incision, 2. Viscous agent injection I, 3. Rhexis, 4. Hydrodissection, 5. Phacoemulsification, 6. Irrigation and aspiration, 7. Capsule polishing, 8. Viscous agent injection II, 9. Lens implant setting-up, 10. Viscous agent removal, 11. Tonifying and antibiotics. This is the standardized sequence of a cataract surgery without complications. Still, it can happen that some steps are repeated. E.g. incisions (done in the first phase) need to be widened for the implantation of the artificial lens. It can also be necessary to moisten the operation area in some cases. Representative keyframes of the standardized phases are shown in Fig. 1.

The dataset, which we use for training and evaluation of CNN models, has been kindly provided by the ophthalmologic department of our medical partner. It consists of 21 single video recordings of cataract surgeries performed by four different surgeons and following closely the standardized surgical procedure. Videos containing optional phases (e.g. "moistening" to moisturize dry eyes, or "blue vision" to facilitate the *Rhexis* phase and avoid complications) are not considered in this work.

The videos are recorded using MPEG-2 with a resolution of 720 × 576 pixels. The bitrate is about 6 Mb/s with a framerate of 25 frames per second. The average length of a recording of a cataract surgery is 6 min and 52 s with a standard deviation of 2 min and 38 s. The videos contain also irrelevant parts before the first phase and after the last phase. This is due to the fact that the

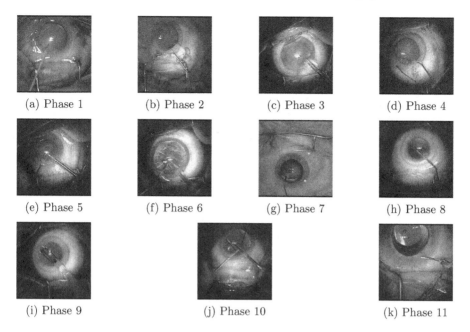

(a) Phase 1	(b) Phase 2	(c) Phase 3	(d) Phase 4
(e) Phase 5	(f) Phase 6	(g) Phase 7	(h) Phase 8
(i) Phase 9	(j) Phase 10		(k) Phase 11

Fig. 1. Example images for each phase of a cataract surgery (Color figure online)

recording is started some seconds before the surgery starts and stopped a few seconds after the operation has ended. These parts of the videos are not used for training and evaluation of our CNN models. All phases including the transitions have been annotated by a surgeon according to the standardized workflow model of cataract surgeries.

Table 1 shows the distribution of video frames per operation phase in the cataract surgery video dataset, which is extremely unbalanced due to different durations of operation phases. The longest phase (phase 5) takes approximately one third of the surgery's duration, whereas phases 2 and 8 represent the shortest phases. Since phases 2 and 8 are identical with respect to both visual appearance and semantics (viscous agent injection), they are treated as a single class for classification purposes. The numbers of frames in the merged phases 2 and 8 sum up to roughly 5% of all video frames. The smallest class is then represented by phase 1 (4.19%).

Figure 1 shows example images from each phase. Typically, the pupil is wide opened and the iris is very small. The lens can appear in a reddish color, if light is reflected directly from the choroid or rather gray in case of very dense cataract or a vitreous hemorrhage. The position of the lens is not always centralized, which may affect analysis methods in a negative manner. Instruments appear typically from the left or from the right or from both sides. A cataract surgery uses a small set of instruments. Moreover, most of the instruments are used for a specific action and they are therefore characteristic for a phase.

Table 1. Distribution of video frames in the cataract surgery video dataset

Nr.	Phase	Absolute number of frames	Relative number of frames (in percent)
1	Incision	8, 896	4.19
2	Viscous agent injection I	5, 303	2.50
3	Rhexis	16, 602	7.81
4	Hydrodissection	11, 998	5.65
5	Phacoemulsification	67, 293	31.67
6	Irrigation and aspiration	28, 704	13.51
7	Capsule polishing	9, 654	4.54
8	Viscous agent injection II	4, 953	2.33
9	Lens implant setting-up	13, 868	6.53
10	Viscous agent removal	32, 888	15.48
11	Tonifying and antibiotics	12, 328	5.80
	Total:	212, 487	100.0

Every phase consists of alternating action and idle periods. This fact has been exploited by Quellec et al. [8] to segment a cataract surgery video based on the occurrence of idle phases. The surgeon uses the instrument(s) belonging to a certain phase in the action period. The instrument can still be visible in the idle period. It can also be changed to the instrument that belongs to the next phase during this idle period. In that case no instrument is visible. This behavior can not be handled directly by a CNN architecture. However, the appearance of an eye changes during a cataract surgery with respect to texture and color, which can be modeled by a CNN.

The anonymized dataset including annotations is available under ftp://ftp-itec.aau.at/pub/datasets/ovid/cat-21/.

4   Frame-Based Classification of Cataract Surgery Videos

We propose to apply a convolutional neural network (CNN) to classify frames of cataract surgery videos with respect to the operation phase (class) the video frame belongs to. In an effort to obtain more effective classification models, we consider three different preprocessing techniques applied to the training dataset, leading to different CNN models: (1) basic training dataset (no preprocessing), (2) manually filtered ("purified") and automatically balanced dataset, and (3) the purified and balanced dataset with additional temporal information of each video frame. Details of these preprocessing techniques and the corresponding experimental setup will be described in Sects. 4.1, 4.2, and 4.3, respectively.

The CNN is trained from scratch based on the GoogLeNet architecture [10]. This neural network was designed and trained for the 1000-class ImageNet

Challenge (ILSVRC) and used to classify everyday images. The GoogLeNet architecture has 27 layers consisting of 5 pooling layers and 22 layers with parameters that include a modular structure involving nine inception modules, each using 1×1 convolutions for dimensionality reduction. The input of the network are $224 \times 224 \times 3$ sized RGB images shifted by a mean image. The prediction of the 1000 classes is done using a linear layer with softmax loss. To adapt the network architecture for prediction of ten phases of cataract surgery, we decreased the number of output neurons to 10. Otherwise the GoogLeNet architecture remains unchanged.

Training of CNN models is performed using the CAFFE framework [2]. The video frames are fed into a Lightning Memory-Mapped Database (LMDB), which is used as input for the CNN. The solver uses *Adam* as gradient-based optimization method provided by CAFFE. As base learning rate we use 0.001; momentum 1 and momentum 2 are set to 0.9 and 0.999, respectively. The training batch size is set to 64 images.

4.1 Basic Cataract-Surgery-Phase CNN

For the basic cataract surgery phase CNN model we partitioned the dataset described in Sect. 3 into a training and an evaluation subset. Out of the 21 videos in the dataset, 17 videos were chosen randomly for training. The remaining four videos are used for the evaluation of the CNN model. To train this first CNN model, we use the annotated videos of the training set as they are and split the videos into phases according to annotations without further refinement.

Table 2 shows the distribution of video frames in the resulting training and evaluation datasets. Phases *incision, irrigation and aspiration,* and *tonifying*

Table 2. Full videos are randomly sampled for either training or evaluation dataset.

Nr.	Phase	Absolute number of frames		Relative number of frames (in percent)	
		Train.	Eval.	Train.	Eval.
1	Incision	6,642	2,254	3.78	6.09
2+8	Viscous agent injection I + II	8,522	1,734	4.86	4.69
3	Rhexis	13,594	3,008	7.75	8.13
4	Hydrodissection	9,570	2,428	5.45	6.56
5	Phacoemulsification	54,679	12,614	31.16	34.09
6	Irrigation and aspiration	26,000	2,704	14.82	7.31
7	Capsule polishing	8,223	1,431	4.69	3.87
9	Lens implant setting-up	11,787	2,081	6.72	5.62
10	Viscous agent removal	27,498	5,390	15.67	14.57
11	Tonifying and antibiotics	8,973	3,355	5.11	9.07
	Total:	175,488	36,999	100.0	100.0

and antibiotics have a large difference in the relative number of frames between training and evaluation datasets. This can be explained by the large variation in the duration of these phases. For example, phase *irrigation and aspiration* has an average duration of 55 s with a standard deviation of 40 s. All four *irrigation and aspiration* phases occurring in videos of the evaluation dataset have a duration below the average duration of this phase. Similar observations can be made for the other deviations.

The 175,488 images of the training dataset are center-cropped to a square shape and downsized to 256 × 256 pixels. This preparation reduces the size of the LMDB and the training time. Furthermore, we shuffle images before writing them into the LMDB to avoid feeding the CNN with a group of similar pictures when the LMDB is read sequentially. At training time we use the data augmentation methods provided by the CAFFE framework to vary the input on every training iteration (epoch): random mirroring and random cropping to the required size of 224 × 224 pixels.

4.2   Purified and Balanced Cataract-Surgery-Phase CNN

The first preprocessing method of the training dataset consists of manual purification followed by automatic balancing of the dataset. Purification takes care to reduce the variation of data within each class (operation phase). Each phase is characterized by the presence of certain instruments. During a phase there are also short periods, where these instruments are not visible. During manual purification, we identify all frames where none of these instruments are visible, and remove them from the training dataset. Table 3 shows that in total 44,004 images have been removed from the original training dataset.

Table 3. Purified training dataset of cataract surgery videos

Nr.	Phase	Absolute number of frames	Relative number of frames (in percent)
1	Incision	3,279	2.49
2+8	Viscous agent injection	3,780	2.87
3	Rhexis	11,772	8.95
4	Hydrodissection	5,970	4.54
5	Phacoemulsification	49,986	38.02
6	Irrigation and aspiration	22,049	16.77
7	Capsule polishing	5,307	4.04
9	Lens implant setting-up	5,541	4.21
10	Viscous agent removal	17,447	13.27
11	Tonifying and antibiotics	6,353	4.83
	Total:	131.484	100.0

It is interesting that some phases are affected less than others from purification. Phases *incision*, *viscous agent injection*, and *lens implant setting-up* lose approximately half of their samples, which can be explained as follows. In phase *incision* the surgeon performs two incisions, which are done within seconds. Between them and the end of the phase no instrument is visible. After the viscous agent is injected in phase eight, the lens implant setting-up is prepared, resulting in several seconds when no instrument is visible. The main instrument in phase *lens implant setting-up* is the cartridge for the lens, which is visible for approximately half of the phase. The least affected phase is *phacoemulsification*, where only 8.6% of the images are dropped, because during the whole phase the phacoeomulsification-tip is visible except at the end of the phase when instruments are changed.

Purification makes the training dataset even more unbalanced, especially if we compare phase *incision* with 2.5% of the training images and phase *phacoemulsification* with more than 38% of the training images. This unbalanced dataset strongly increases the likelihood to classify in favor of the majority class. To overcome this problem we apply either random sampling (to video frames of large classes) or three data augmentation techniques (to frames of small classes): (1) simple copying, (2) rotation, and (3) scaling.

In detail, we choose 12,000 as uniform sample size for each phase. This means that larger classes are randomly reduced and smaller classes are extended with randomly chosen data augmentation techniques. For example, the phase *phacoemulsification* is reduced to one quarter of the original size, whereas phase *incision* is extended four-fold with artificially modified images.

To ensure that each available image is used for training, all images of the classes are copied in a first step. As long as a class has too many samples, one sample is randomly chosen and deleted. If the class has too few samples, we choose one of three data augmentation methods randomly and apply it to one randomly chosen (unmodified) image of the class. These steps are repeated until a uniform distribution of 12,000 images per class is achieved.

For rotation and scaling we randomly choose values for the rotation angle and the scaling factor. The angle for the rotation is constrained to the range $[-10°, +10°]$. The rotation introduces an empty area in the image, which is eliminated by cropping the image to a maximum-sized square whose corners hit these areas. Finally, the rotated image is resized to 256×256 pixels again. For scaling we select a square with a randomly chosen length between 246 and 156 pixels. We center-crop the image to this square and scale the resulting image up to a size of 256×256 pixels.

4.3   Timestamp-Based Cataract-Surgery-Phase CNN

For the third CNN model we extend each of the video frames with time information: the ratio of the frame number and the total number of frames in the video (relative timestamp). To feed timestamps into the CNN, we add a fourth "color channel"[1] to each image that contains this time information. Figure 2 shows that for most of the phases the starting time is well distinguishable. Temporal information of video frames is therefore expected to improve the classification performance of the trained CCN model.

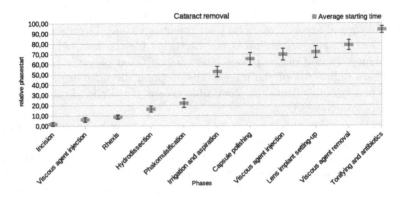

Fig. 2. Relative starting time of operation phases in surgery videos

5   Evaluation

As evaluation dataset we use the four randomly selected videos mentioned in Sect. 4.1. It consists of 36,999 samples. The detailed distribution of video frames can be seen in Table 1.

For a given (preprocessed) training dataset, the CNN is trained for 50 epochs and the CNN model resulting from each epoch is kept for subsequent model selection. From the 50 resulting CNN models, only the best performing model (with respect to accuracy on the training dataset) is selected for final evaluation.

Table 4 structures the results in three quality measures: Precision, Recall, and F1-score (harmonic mean). In each of the table sections we see among each other the results of the three CNN-models: *Basic CNN* (Sect. 4.1), *balanced CNN* (Sect. 4.2), and *time-based CNN* (Sect. 4.3). It can be seen that each refinement improves the average performance of the network in terms of precision, recall, and F1-score clearly.

The *time-based CNN* shows problems with precision for phase 2+8 compared to other phases, where it performs similar or better than the other two CNN models. Figure 3c shows that *time-based CNN* tends to confuse phases 2 and 8 with neighboring phases 3 and 9, respectively.

A considerable performance gain can be achieved in terms of recall for the *balanced CNN* and the *time-based CNN*. Again, the *time-based CNN* outperforms both other networks for all phases but 1, 9, and 11, where it performs only slightly worse.

---

[1] This decision is due to restrictions of the CAFFE framework, which does not easily allow adding inputs to fully connected layers of the CNN.

Table 4. Classification results. Bold numbers indicate best performance within a phase.

Phase numbers											
CNN-Type	1	2+8	3	4	5	6	7	9	10	11	Average
Precision											
Basic CNN	**0.87**	0.24	0.61	0.70	0.73	0.55	0.61	0.62	**0.83**	0.76	0.65
Balanced CNN	0.38	**0.59**	**0.89**	0.66	0.89	**0.68**	**0.72**	0.39	0.75	0.90	0.69
Time-based CNN	0.65	0.37	0.82	**0.75**	**0.96**	**0.68**	0.71	**0.76**	0.75	**0.91**	**0.74**
Recall											
Basic CNN	0.06	0.54	0.55	0.43	0.93	0.48	0.33	0.62	0.63	0.75	0.53
Balanced CNN	**0.80**	0.49	0.56	0.45	0.91	0.57	0.51	**0.67**	0.83	**0.88**	0.67
Time-based CNN	0.72	**0.55**	**0.69**	**0.54**	**0.95**	**0.80**	**0.79**	0.50	**0.84**	0.85	**0.72**
F1-score											
Basic CNN	0.11	0.33	0.58	0.53	0.82	0.51	0.43	**0.62**	0.72	0.76	0.59
Balanced CNN	0.52	**0.54**	0.69	0.54	0.90	0.62	0.60	0.49	**0.79**	**0.89**	0.68
Time-based CNN	**0.69**	0.44	**0.75**	**0.62**	**0.95**	**0.73**	**0.75**	0.60	**0.79**	0.88	**0.73**

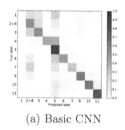
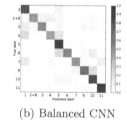
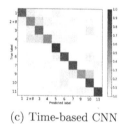

(a) Basic CNN   (b) Balanced CNN   (c) Time-based CNN

Fig. 3. Confusion matrices for the basic CNN, balanced CNN, and time-based CNN

Looking at the F1-score we see that the *time-based CNN* shows a similar performance or outperforms the *balanced CNN* and the *basic CNN* in all cases except one (phase 2+8). In the absence of similar studies in the area of frame-based classification of ophthalmic surgery videos, we can compare our work only with results for frame-based classification of other types of surgery videos [4–6], where the authors achieve F1-scores of 0.51, 0.69, and 0.85.

Figure 3 visualizes the improvement in classification performance for *balanced CNN* and *time-based CNN* in comparison to *basic CNN*. The *basic CNN* has many false positive predictions for phase 5, which is overrepresented in the training dataset. There are also a lot of false positive predictions for phase 2+8. The confusion matrices also show that all CNN models have problems with the classification of phase 6.

6   Conclusion

In this paper, we examined frame-based classification of operation phases in cataract surgery videos using different CNN models. Along with this paper we provide a dataset of 21 video recordings of cataract surgeries that have been annotated by our medical partner. In particular we trained three CNN models based on the GoogLeNet-architecture. The basic CNN model was trained with a dataset that took the annotated phases directly as classes. For a second approach the dataset was modified manually by removing images where no instrument was visible. This dataset was additionally balanced using different data augmentation techniques. Temporal information of video frames was added for training the third CNN model.

The evaluation showed that the classification performance can be improved significantly with a cleaned, balanced dataset and temporal information. In future work this CNN model can be extended for classification of various optional operation phases as well as for detection of complications. The development of such a neural network model enables also further automatic tools like keyframe selection for documentation, video summarization, or operation planning.

Acknowledgement. This work was supported by Universität Klagenfurt and Lakeside Labs GmbH, Klagenfurt, Austria and funding from the European Regional Development Fund and the Carinthian Economic Promotion Fund (KWF) under grant KWF-20214 U. 3520/26336/38165.

References

1. Charrière, K., Quellec, G., Lamard, M., Martiano, D., Cazuguel, G., Coatrieux, G., Cochener, B.: Real-time analysis of cataract surgery videos using statistical models. Multimed. Tools App. **76**, 1–19 (2016)
2. Jia, Y., Shelhamer, E., Donahue, J., Karayev, S., Long, J., Girshick, R., Guadarrama, S., Darrell, T.: Caffe: convolutional architecture for fast feature embedding. In: Proceedings of the 22nd ACM International Conference on Multimedia, pp. 675–678. ACM (2014)
3. Lalys, F., Riffaud, L., Bouget, D., Jannin, P.: A framework for the recognition of high-level surgical tasks from video images for cataract surgeries. IEEE Trans. Biomed. Eng. **59**(4), 966–976 (2012)
4. Petscharnig, S., Schöffmann, K.: Deep learning for shot classification in gynecologic surgery videos. In: Amsaleg, L., Guðmundsson, G.Þ., Gurrin, C., Jónsson, B.Þ., Satoh, S. (eds.) MMM 2017. LNCS, vol. 10132, pp. 702–713. Springer, Cham (2017). https://doi.org/10.1007/978-3-319-51811-4_57
5. Petscharnig, S., Schöffmann, K.: Learning laparoscopic video shot classification for gynecological surgery. Multimed. Tools App. 1–19 (2017)
6. Primus, M.J., Schoeffmann, K., Böszörmenyi, L.: Instrument classification in laparoscopic videos. In: 2015 13th International Workshop on Content-Based Multimedia Indexing (CBMI), pp. 1–6. IEEE (2015)
7. Primus, M.J., Schoeffmann, K., Böszörmenyi, L.: Temporal segmentation of laparoscopic videos into surgical phases. In: 2016 14th International Workshop on Content-Based Multimedia Indexing (CBMI), pp. 1–6. IEEE (2016)
8. Quellec, G., Lamard, M., Cochener, B., Cazuguel, G.: Real-time segmentation and recognition of surgical tasks in cataract surgery videos. IEEE Trans. Med. Imaging **33**(12), 2352–2360 (2014)

9. Speidel, S., Benzko, J., Krappe, S., Sudra, G., Azad, P., Peter, B.: Automatic classification of minimally invasive instruments based on endoscopic image sequences. In: SPIE Medical Imaging, pp. 72610A (2009)
10. Szegedy, C., Liu, W., Jia, Y., Sermanet, P., Reed, S., Anguelov, D., Erhan, D., Vanhoucke, V., Rabinovich, A.: Going deeper with convolutions. In: IEEE Conference on Computer Vision and Pattern Recognition, pp. 1–9 (2015)
11. Twinanda, A.P., Shehata, S., Mutter, D., Marescaux, J., de Mathelin, M., Padoy, N.: Endonet: a deep architecture for recognition tasks on laparoscopic videos. IEEE Trans. Med. Imaging **36**(1), 86–97 (2017)

High-Precision 3D Coarse Registration Using RANSAC and Randomly-Picked Rejections

Jong-Hee Back, Sunho Kim, and Yo-Sung Ho[✉]

Gwangju Institute of Science and Technology, 123 Cheomdangwagi-ro, Buk-gu,
Gwangju 61005, Republic of Korea
{jongheeback, sunhokim, hoyo}@gist.ac.kr

Abstract. A point cloud registration is an essential process of finding a spatial transformation between two point clouds in computer vision. The Iterative Closest Point (ICP) algorithm is one of the most widely used registration methods. Since the ICP algorithm is a locally optimal registration method, it is not guaranteed to converge to an exact solution because of local-minimum problem. In addition, the ICP algorithm is a time-consuming task. Because the ICP algorithm is performed repeatedly to find the best transformation, it tends to be slow. For those reasons, a coarse registration, which helps point clouds align fast and exactly, is needed before fine alignment. This paper provides a 3D coarse registration method to solve the local-minimum problem in the ICP algorithm. First of all, an initial matching is computed by performing feature extraction using Fast Point Feature Histogram (FPFH) feature which establishes good initial correspondences. Since these correspondences are not accurate yet, we need to reject outlier correspondences. Inlier correspondences are picked out through two rejection methods, RANSAC rejection and Randomly-picked rejection we propose. With these organized correspondences, a transformation matrix between point clouds is obtained. As a result, it is helpful to avoid the local-minimum problem in the ICP algorithm. Moreover, it is quite efficient to register point clouds with noise and large transformations.

Keywords: Point cloud registration · 3D coarse registration
Initial correspondence matching · Outlier rejection method

1 Introduction

A point cloud registration is an important process to find a spatial transformation between two point clouds. It is being utilized to a wide range of fields in computer vision or robotics such as simultaneous localization and mapping (SLAM) [1–3], 3D reconstruction [6–8, 10], etc.

The Iterative Closest Point (ICP) algorithm [13–15] is one of the most widely used registration methods in computer vision. In the algorithm, a transformation is updated iteratively in the direction of minimizing an error metric between one cloud and the other transformed cloud. Therefore, we can compute a proper transformation matrix which is 3-by-3 rotation matrix and 3-by-1 translation vector. However, the ICP

© Springer International Publishing AG 2018
K. Schoeffmann et al. (Eds.): MMM 2018, Part I, LNCS 10704, pp. 254–266, 2018.
https://doi.org/10.1007/978-3-319-73603-7_21

algorithm has two kinds of problems we should deal with. Since the ICP algorithms is a locally optimal registration method, it is not guaranteed to converge to an exact solution without an initial transformation that is close to the exact solution. In other words, it will be difficult to find an exact transformation if there are two point clouds with large transformation. The second problem is that the ICP algorithm is a time-consuming task. Since the ICP algorithm is performed repeatedly to find the best transformation matrix, it tends to be slow. For those reasons, a coarse registration, which helps point clouds align fast and exactly, is needed. Thanks to a coarse registration, a local-minimum problem can be fixed and two point clouds can be aligned fast and exactly through the low iteration of the ICP.

In this paper, we propose a 3D coarse registration method to solve the local-minimum problem in the ICP algorithm. In order to compute an initial matching, we use Fast Point Feature Histogram (FPFH) [5] features. FPFH is a feature which provides quite good initial correspondences. Nevertheless, these correspondences we obtain are still limited to find an accurate transformation. Through RANSAC [4] rejection and a proposed mechanism comparing a correlation between three correspondences randomly, inlier correspondences are picked out. The proposed outlier rejection mechanism, which is called Randomly-picked rejection method, is a method to find highly-correlated three pairs of correspondences repeatedly. RANSAC rejection is a strong rejection method that makes our algorithm more efficient. With these organized correspondences, a transformation matrix between two point clouds can be computed. As a result, it is helpful to solve local-minimum problem in the ICP algorithm. It also saves much time and trouble before fine registration such as the ICP algorithm. Even though there is some noise in point clouds, these point clouds are almost aligned. Moreover, our algorithm has quite good performance in the case of point clouds with large transformation.

2 Related Works

An extensive study of the point cloud registration has been made. Generally, there are two types of methods to register point clouds, local method and global method. The global method is a method to find the globally optimal alignment, and local method is a method to calculate the transformation iteratively in the direction of minimizing an error metric by making use of optimization theory.

The Iterative Closest Point (ICP) algorithm [13–15], which is used widely, is one of the local registration methods. The most typical ICP algorithm is point-to-plane ICP [15]. This method is a popular algorithm employed to register, but it is still limited to find an accurate transformation since incorrect pairs of correspondences have a large effect on the result and a local-minimum problem exists. Recently, several good ICP methods such as Generalized ICP [13] and EM-ICP [14] have been proposed. Besides, there are many approaches to perform robust registration based on Gaussian Mixture Model (GMM) [17].

There are a variety of global methods in order to solve the local-minimum problem. The feature-based methods, which set up highly-accurate correspondences making use of 3D local descriptors such as Fast Point Feature Histograms (FPFH) [5] and Intrinsic

Shape Signatures (ISS) [16] and estimate a transformation matrix, have been proposed. Zhou [6] proposed a fast registration method that initial matching using FPFH was performed and optimization based on Geman-McClure estimator was done. Yang [7] introduced Go-ICP which was a global registration method based on BnB searching scheme. Recently, correspondence propagation method [9] to find exact correspondences globally was introduced.

3   Proposed Approach

Figure 1 presents the flowchart of the proposed coarse registration method. After uniform down-sampling of point cloud P and Q, an initial matching using FPFH is computed. The role of uniform down-sampling is to reduce the computational complexity of several processes such as feature detection, RANSAC rejection, etc. Next, two outlier rejection algorithms, which are RANSAC rejection and Randomly-picked rejection, are performed. A transformation matrix can be computed by using several pairs of the inlier correspondences we obtain through two rejection methods. This is the whole algorithm of coarse registration and more accurate transformation can be found by the process of fine alignment. We use point-to-plane ICP [15] as the fine alignment. We focus on three main processes of the proposed method in detail.

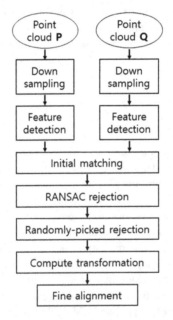

Fig. 1. Flowchart of the proposed registration method.

3.1   Uniform Down-Sampling

There are a lot of points in point cloud $\mathbf{P}$ and $\mathbf{Q}$. If we perform a registration method using all points, it might be time-consuming. That's the advantage of uniform down-sampling. Let $\mathbf{P}_s = \{p_1, p_2, \cdots, p_m\}$ be the points of sampled point cloud $\mathbf{P}$ and $\mathbf{Q}_s = \{q_1, q_2, \cdots, q_n\}$ be the points of sampled point cloud $\mathbf{Q}$. The important thing is that proper sampling rate should be set. If a lot of points in a point cloud are removed, it can cause bad result due to a lack of information. On the contrary, the algorithm might be slow if the points in a point cloud are hardly sampled. Figure 2 is the result of uniform down-sampling of a point cloud. We use a library function called UniformSampling which is included in Point Cloud Library (PCL) [18].

Fig. 2.   Uniform down-sampling

3.2   Feature Detection

An initial matching using FPFH feature [5] is performed. FPFH, which reduces the computational complexity and retains highly efficient performance, provides quite good initial correspondences. In order to get FPFH features of points in point clouds, surface normals are required. After obtaining FPFH features of each point cloud based on the surface normals, we can establish initial correspondences. Let $M = \{(p_k, q_t), \ldots, (p_r, q_s)\}$ be the initial correspondences using FPFH features. Figure 3 represents a part of the initial correspondences. There are a lot of good correspondences in Fig. 3, however bad pairs of correspondences can be found.

Fig. 3.   Initial correspondences M using FPFH

3.3 Correspondence Rejection

As shown in Fig. 3, inaccurate correspondences exist in the initial correspondences *M*. By rejecting outlier correspondences, it is possible to find exact transformation matrix. That's the reason why the correspondence rejection method is needed. We use two rejection methods, RANSAC rejection [4] and Randomly-picked rejection that we propose.

Before the process of Randomly-picked rejection, RANSAC rejection method plays the primary role of eliminating bad correspondences. RANSAC is widely used because of its high performance.

Randomly-picked rejection we propose is an outlier rejection method to find three highly-correlated correspondences repeatedly. Figure 4 represents a principle of Randomly-picked rejection method. The right picture in Fig. 4 is the example of unselected correspondences due to the unsatisfied condition.

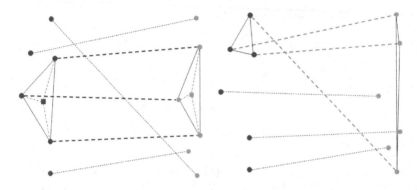

Fig. 4. A principle of randomly-picked rejection method.

First of all, three correspondences in the initial correspondence set *M* are selected randomly and two matrices are formed as below.

$$V = [P_a, P_b, P_c], U = [Q_a, Q_b, Q_c] \tag{1}$$

where matrix *V* and *U* are 3×3 matrices which consist of three column vectors. The P_k is a 3-by-1 coordinate column vector of point p_a in point cloud **Ps**. The Q_k is the same type as the P_k. Next, the average of three points in each matrix is computed and matrix *V1* and *U1* are calculated as below.

$$P_{avg} = \frac{P_a + P_b + P_c}{3}, Q_{avg} = \frac{Q_a + Q_b + Q_c}{3} \tag{2}$$

$$V_1 = [P_a - P_{avg}, P_b - P_{avg}, P_c - P_{avg}], U_1 = [Q_a - Q_{avg}, Q_b - Q_{avg}, Q_c - Q_{avg}] \tag{3}$$

With these matrices, we can compute the matrix V_2 and U_2 which mean the correlation information of three points in each matrix.

$$V_2 = V_1^T V_1, U_2 = U_1^T U_1 \tag{4}$$

We decide whether those correspondences are proper or not by comparing the matrix V_2 and U_2. Given the complexity, we only compare the sign of each corresponding element by using bit operation as shown in Fig. 5 below. The simple idea to filter bad correspondences realizes the fast algorithm without using special cost function.

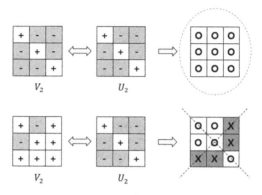

Fig. 5. A process of bad correspondences filtering

Finally, three correspondences are selected if the condition is satisfied and go back to the first step. There are a few things to be aware of. Duplicated correspondence is not allowed and the minimum number of correspondence should be decided. Additionally, it is important to repeat this mechanism properly. If the number of repetition is large, it takes several times. If the number of repetition is small, biased information tends to be obtained.

Figure 6 represents the performance of outlier rejection methods. With these organized correspondences, the accurate transformation matrix can be obtained.

Fig. 6. The result of two rejection algorithms

Since the number of inlier correspondences is more than the number of outlier correspondences, a probability to select three bad correspondences is relatively low. Even though three bad correspondences are chosen, the majority of the picked correspondences are good correspondences, so it does not have a big influence on the result. Therefore, a globally optimal transformation can be computed.

4   Experimental Results

We explain a variety of experimental results in order to verify the performance of our proposed method. The algorithm has been implemented using Point Cloud Library (PCL) which is C/C++ based [18] in Microsoft Visual C++ 2013. All experiments were performed using a PC with Intel Xeon E5630 CPU clocked at 2.53 GHz.

4.1   Robustness to Noise

In order to verify robustness to noise, we test our method on Aim@shape repository (Bimba, Dancing Children, and Chinese dragon), Stanford bunny[1], and the Berkeley angel [11] which are experimented in [6]. We made use of the results of other methods which are tested in [6] for an accurate comparison of performance. There are 25 partially overlapping point clouds with $\sigma = 0.0025$ and 0.005 respectively. σ is the standard deviation of the Gaussian distribution which means noise.

Table 1 shows average root mean square error (RMSE) values of point clouds with $\sigma = 0.0025$ and 0.005 which represents a widely-used measure to check how accurate two point clouds are aligned. The lower RMSE value is, the better the performance is.

$$RMSE = \sqrt{\frac{1}{N} \sum_{i=1}^{N} \left(Rp_i - \hat{p}_i\right)^2} \tag{5}$$

In our method, the sampling rate is set to 0.03 and the number of iterations is fixed to 500. RANSAC threshold is set to 0.2.

Table 1. Average of 25 RMSE values in the case of $\sigma = 0.0025$ and 0.005

Method	$\sigma = 0.0025$	$\sigma = 0.005$
GoICP [7]	0.06513	0.07624
GoICP-Trimming [7]	0.07624	0.08659
Super4PCS [10]	0.02191	0.02730
CZK [8]	0.01326	0.07319
Fast Global Registration [6]	0.00742	0.01407
Proposed method	**0.00394**	**0.00771**

---

[1] https://graphics.stanford.edu/data/3Dscanrep/.

In Table 1, two average RMSE values of the proposed method are lower than other methods. Despite the presence of quite strong noise such as $\sigma = 0.005$, the proposed method has a good performance.

Figure 7 represents the visualized results of the proposed method. The right-hand column in Fig. 7 means input point clouds before alignment. After performing coarse registration, two point clouds are almost converged as shown in the center column of the picture in Fig. 7. Thanks to coarse registration, fine alignment such as point-to-plane ICP algorithm, is done fast. The right-hand column in Fig. 7 is the results of the final alignment is performed.

Fig. 7. The results of proposed registration method in the case of $\sigma = 0.005$

Table 2 represents performance comparison between using only RANSAC and using RANSAC and Randomly-picked rejection method. For greater accuracy, a coarse alignment process is excluded and experiment is performed according to the RANSAC threshold. As shown in Table 2, outliers RANSAC cannot reject are removed through Randomly-picked rejection. Only Randomly-picked rejection spends less time compared to RANSAC. In Table 2, RS means RANSAC and RS + RP represents RANSAC and Randomly-picked rejection method.

Table 2. Performance comparison between RANSAC and RANSAC + Randomly-picked

RANSAC threshold	$\sigma = 0.0025$				$\sigma = 0.005$			
	RS		RS + RP		RS		RS + RP	
	RMSE	Time	RMSE	Time	RMSE	Time	RMSE	Time
0.2	0.01618	0.144	**0.01500**	0.156	0.02790	0.587	**0.02641**	0.597
0.4	0.05279	0.046	**0.04341**	0.056	0.12913	0.132	**0.12653**	0.143
0.6	0.08134	0.025	**0.07882**	0.034	0.15086	0.048	**0.13451**	0.061
0.8	0.07693	0.017	**0.06831**	0.027	0.18512	0.027	**0.15828**	0.039

4.2 Execution Time

Table 3 shows the running time of proposed method and Fast Global Registration [6] method. In [6], Fast Global Registration is overwhelmingly faster than the other point cloud registration methods such as Go-ICP [7], Super 4PCS [10], etc. Therefore, we compare the execution time of our method with Fast Global Registration. The measured time unit is seconds. The time of feature detection process is not included in the measured time of Fast Global Registration in Table 3. However, it does not seem to have a significant effect on the results.

Table 3. Comparison with running time of Fast Global Registration

Method	$\sigma = 0.0025$	$\sigma = 0.005$
Fast Global Registration [6]	1.1369	**1.1500**
Proposed method	**1.0753**	2.7798

In the case of $\sigma = 0.0025$, our method is faster than [6]. However, since the speed of our method depends on the number of initial correspondences, our method is slower than [6] even considering the time of feature detection process in [6].

Actually, rejection method we propose takes so little time that it does not have a large effect on total running time of registration method. Figure 8 represents execution time of each process in the proposed method. The blue part occupying the widest area in Fig. 8 means RANSAC rejection, and the purple part means feature detection process. The black part which looks black line above blue part is the rejection method that accounts for about 1% of the total running time. Other processes such as normal estimation represent the mint color part. The speed of our method depends on the number of initial correspondences. Especially, RANSAC rejection method is largely affected by the number of initial correspondences. Additionally, the number of initial correspondences depends on the number of down-sampled points. To sum up, sampling rate affects the running time and performance like RMSE. That's why it is important to set the sampling rate properly.

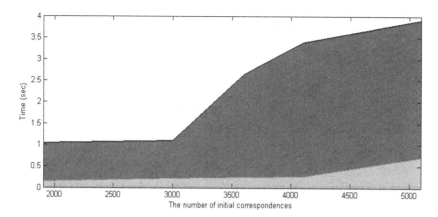

Fig. 8. Execution time of each process in proposed method (Color figure online)

4.3   Ability to Solve Local-Minimum Problem in the Case of RGB-D Data

As mentioned above, the ICP algorithm has a local-minimum problem. In addition, it is easy to converge to a strange place without the accurate pairs of correspondences. We test whether to solve the local-minimum problem using RGB-D data. Figure 9 Represents two frames of ICL-NUIM dataset [12].

For the experiment, the sampling rate is set to 0.04 and the number of iterations is fixed to 500. RANSAC threshold is set to 0.3. One image in Fig. 9 is largely transformed to the other. Without coarse registration, a local-minimum problem such as the left side of the picture in Fig. 10 is encountered. With wrong pairs of correspondences, this problem cannot be solved. By using our method making use of globally-picked correspondences, two point clouds from Fig. 9 can be registered clearly as shown in the right side of the picture in Fig. 10 below. Even though one image is transformed largely, a local-minimum problem can be solved easily. Figure 11 is the result of reconstruction using only eight frames of ICL-NUIM dataset.

Fig. 9. Two images for testing large transformation

Fig. 10. The result of proposed method solving local-minimum problem

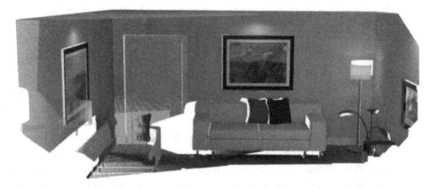

Fig. 11. 3D Reconstruction using the eight RGB-D data

4.4 Discussion

Through experiments, as shown above, we present that our method has quite good performance while maintaining fast execution time. Unfortunately, there are some limitations to our algorithm. In order to achieve good performance and fast running time, the sampling rate should be decided properly. Second, RANSAC rejection method is a highly-efficient algorithm, but it is a time-consuming task. The proposed rejection method must be more efficient if a fast rejection method with comparatively good performance is involved. If two things are dealt with, our method will get better performance.

5 Conclusion

In this paper, we have presented 3D coarse registration method which uses two outlier rejection methods, RANSAC based method, and Randomly-picked rejection method. In order to speed up, uniform down-sampling is performed. Initial matching is computed using FPFH feature. Through two outlier rejection methods, we obtain quite accurate pairs of correspondences. By using organized correspondences, a transformation matrix is computed. The point-to-plane ICP which is widely used ICP algorithm is utilized as a fine registration.

We present that our method has good performance through various experiments. Our method works rather efficiently in the case of point clouds with noise compared with other registration methods. In addition, we observe that local-minimum problem is solved fast in RGB-D data. We also discuss some drawbacks that need to be addressed. Nevertheless, our algorithm can be applied to various fields that require point cloud registration like SLAM and 3D reconstruction. Specifically, our method can be used with other fine registration methods. If those fine registration methods have superior performance, it might be better than before.

Acknowledgements. This research was partially supported by the 'Brain Korea 21 Plus Project' of the Ministry of Education & Human Resources Development, Republic of Korea (ROK) [F16SN26T2205], and partially supported by the 'Cross-Ministry Giga Korea Project' of Ministry of Science, ICT and Future Planning, Republic of Korea (ROK). [GK17C0100, Development of Interactive and Realistic Massive Giga – Content Technology].

References

1. Kerl, C., Sturm, J., Cremers, D.: Dense visual SLAM for RGB-D cameras. In: Proceedings of the International Conference on Intelligent Robot Systems (IROS) (2013)
2. Izadi, S., Kim, D., Hilliges, O., Molyneaux, D., Newcombe, R., Kohli, P., Shotton, J., Hodeges, S., Freeman, D., Davison, A., Fitzgibbon, A.: KinectFusion: real-time 3D reconstruction and interaction using a moving depth camera. In: Proceedings of ACM Symposium on User Interface Software and Technology (2011)
3. Endres, F., Hess, J., Engelhard, N., Sturm, J., Cremers, D., Burgard, W.: An evaluation of the RGB-D SLAM system. In: ICRA (2012)
4. Fischler, M.A., Bolles, R.C.: Random sample consensus: a paradigm for model fitting with applications to image analysis and automated cartography. Commun. ACM **24**(6), 381–395 (1981)
5. Rusu, R.B., Blodow, N., Beetz, M.: Fast point feature histograms (FPFH) for 3D registration. In: ICRA, pp. 3212–3217 (2009)
6. Zhou, Q.-Y., Park, J., Koltun, V.: Fast global registration. In: Leibe, B., Matas, J., Sebe, N., Welling, M. (eds.) ECCV 2016. LNCS, vol. 9906, pp. 766–782. Springer, Cham (2016). https://doi.org/10.1007/978-3-319-46475-6_47
7. Yang, J., Li, H., Campbell, D., Jia, Y.: Go-ICP: a globally optimal solution to 3D ICP point-set registration. IEEE TPAMI **38**(11), 2241–2254 (2016)
8. Choi, S., Zhou, Q.Y., Koltun, V.: Robust reconstruction of indoor scenes. In: CVPR (2015)
9. Lei, H., Jiang, G., Quan, L.: Fast descriptors and correspondence propagation for robust global point cloud registration. IEEE Trans. Image Process. **26**(8), 3614–3623 (2017)
10. Mellado, N., Aiger, D., Mitra, N.J.: Super4PCS: fast global pointcloud registration via smart indexing. In: Computer Graphics Forum. 33(5), pp. 205–215. Wiley Online Library (2014)
11. Kolluri, R., Shewchuk, J.R., O'Brien, J.F.: Spectral surface reconstruction from noisy point clouds. In: Proceedings of the 2004 Eurographics/ACM SIGGRAPH Symposium on Geometry processing, pp. 11–21 (2004)

12. Handa, A., Whelan, T., McDonald, J., Davison, A.J.: A benchmark for RGB-D visual odometry, 3D reconstruction and SLAM. In: ICRA, pp. 1524–1531 (2014)
13. Segal, A.V., Haehnel, D., Thrun, S.: Generalized-ICP. In: Proceedings of Robotics: Science and Systems, pp. 26–27 (2009)
14. Granger, S., Pennec, X.: Multi-scale EM-ICP: a fast and robust approach for surface registration. In: Heyden, A., Sparr, G., Nielsen, M., Johansen, P. (eds.) ECCV 2002. LNCS, vol. 2353, pp. 418–432. Springer, Heidelberg (2002). https://doi.org/10.1007/3-540-47979-1_28
15. Low, K.L.: Linear least-squares optimization for point-to-plane ICP surface registration. Technical report, TR-04-004. University of North Carolina (2004)
16. Zhong, Y.: Intrinsic shape signatures: a shape descriptor for 3D object recognition. In: ICCV Workshops, pp. 689–696 (2009)
17. Jian, B., Vemuri, B.C.: Robust point set registration using Gaussian mixture models. IEEE TPAMI 33(8), 1633–1645 (2011)
18. Rusu, R.B., Cousins, S.: 3D is here: point cloud library (PCL). In: ICRA, pp. 1–4 (2011)

Image Aesthetic Distribution Prediction with Fully Convolutional Network

Huidi Fang[1], Chaoran Cui[2(✉)], Xiang Deng[1], Xiushan Nie[2], Muwei Jian[2], and Yilong Yin[1(✉)]

[1] School of Computer Science and Technology, Shandong University, Jinan, China
huidif@163.com, dxcvai@gmail.com, ylyin@sdu.edu.cn
[2] School of Computer Science and Technology,
Shandong University of Finance and Economics, Jinan, China
{crcui,niexsh,jianmuwei}@sdufe.edu.cn

Abstract. Image aesthetics assessment emerges as a hot topic in recent years for its potential in numerous applications. In this paper, we propose to quantify the image aesthetics by a distribution over multiple quality levels. The distribution representation can effectively characterize the disagreement among users' aesthetic perceptions regarding the same image. We realize an end-to-end framework of aesthetic distribution prediction with fully convolutional network, which accepts input images of arbitrary sizes. In this way, we circumvent the requirement of fixed-sized inputs from prevalent convolutional neural network, and thereby avoid the risk of impairing the intrinsic aesthetic appeal of images. Experiments on two benchmark datasets well verified the effectiveness of our approach in both scenarios of aesthetic distribution prediction and aesthetic label prediction.

Keywords: Image aesthetics assessment · Label distribution learning
Fully convolutional network

1 Introduction

Image aesthetics assessment aims to automatically measure whether an image looks beautiful in human's perception, and has recently received increasing attention due to its wide range of applications. For example, it is expected that modern image search engines would rank results not only by topical relevance but also by aesthetic quality [11]; when dealing with similar images of the same scene or object, it may be acceptable to single out those aesthetically pleasing ones and only retain them for cost-effective storage [30]; image aesthetics assessment could also be deployed in photo cameras to make real-time suggestions on photographing [25].

With the rapid development of pattern recognition and computer vision technologies, image aesthetics assessment is typically cast as a classification or regression problem, where each image is assigned *a single label* (i.e., category or score)

© Springer International Publishing AG 2018
K. Schoeffmann et al. (Eds.): MMM 2018, Part I, LNCS 10704, pp. 267–278, 2018.
https://doi.org/10.1007/978-3-319-73603-7_22

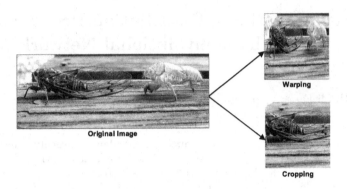

Fig. 1. Example of fitting an image to the fixed size via warping or cropping.

indicating its aesthetic quality level. Recent research advances mainly range from using low-level visual features to systematically learning deep representations for image aesthetics [7]. However, as the saying goes, *"beauty is in the eye of the beholder"*; aesthetics is essentially a subjective human perception, and different people may have different ideas about the beauty of the same image. In light of this, a single label is insufficient to characterize the disagreement among users' aesthetic perceptions.

In this paper, we propose to use a distribution to depict the aesthetic quality of an image. Each component of the distribution indicates the probability of users assigning a specific quality level to that image. The form of distribution offers advantages in two aspects: (1) Distinguished from a single label, a distribution quantifies the uncertainty in the process of aesthetic evaluation, so that the disagreement among users' aesthetic perceptions can be effectively captured; (2) Depending on practical needs, a distribution can be easily converted to a category or score with its numerical characteristic, such as the expectation and variance. This ensures that the traditional tasks of aesthetic classification and ranking can be smoothly performed with the distribution representation as well.

Following the idea of label distribution learning [12], we seek to learn a mapping from an image instance to its distribution over multiple aesthetic quality levels. Recently, convolutional neural network (CNN) has brought in revolutions to a variety of applications in the field of computer vision, including image classification [15], object detection [27], and semantic segmentation [21]. However, a critical issue of using CNN for image aesthetics assessment lies in its requirement of a fixed input size (e.g., 224×224). Generally, the input images have to be fitted to the fixed size via warping or cropping [22], which may bring about the geometric distortion or the loss of the entire content. More importantly, as shown in Fig. 1, fitting an image to the fixed size could cause severe damage to its intrinsic aesthetic appeal, and thereby affect the efficacy of the subsequent process of aesthetics assessment.

To address the above challenge, we propose to realize image aesthetic distribution prediction with fully convolutional network (FCN) [21,29], which is a variant of CNN adapting the fully connected layers into the convolutional layers. This is based on the intuition that the neurons in both fully connected layers and convolutional layers perform dot product operations, and their functional form is identical. As pointed in [14], the fixed-size constraint of CNN comes only from the fully connected layers; the convolutional layers operate convolution with a filter in a sliding-window manner and do not require a fixed-sized input. Therefore, FCN allows for arbitrary-sized input images by using the fully convolutional architecture. It is worth noting that, through skillfully designing the shape and number of filters in the convolutional layers, we can directly fine-tune FCN with the pre-trained model weights of CNNs. In this way, our model is much more tractable and efficient to train.

The main contributions can be summarized as follows:

- We investigate the problem of image aesthetics assessment from a new perspective of learning the distribution over quality levels. Our approach is able to characterize the disagreement among users' aesthetic perceptions.
- We build the framework of aesthetic distribution prediction upon FCN. Our approach is able to efficiently accept images with arbitrary sizes and avoid impairing their intrinsic aesthetic appeal.
- We evaluate our approach in both scenarios of distribution prediction and label prediction for image aesthetics assessment. The results demonstrate the promise of our approach in comparison with the state-of-the-art methods.

The remainder of the paper is structured as follows. Section 2 reviews the related work. Section 3 details the proposed framework of image aesthetic distribution prediction with fully convolutional network. Experimental results and analysis are reported in Sect. 4, followed by the conclusion and future work in Sect. 5.

2 Related Work

In this section, we first review the existing literature on image aesthetics assessment. We then present a brief overview of fully convolutional network.

2.1 Image Aesthetics Assessment

Image aesthetics assessment has drawn numerous research attention in recent decades due to its potential in various applications. Prior studies have predominantly cast it as a classification or regression problem, and focused on the challenge of designing appropriate features. As the early efforts, many handcrafted features were proposed based on the intuitions about human's aesthetic perceptions or the photographic rules. For example, Datta et al. [5] designed 56 visual features such as the indictors of colorfulness, rule of thirds, and depth of field, to discriminate between aesthetically pleasing and displeasing images. Some high-level describable attributes from the perspectives of layout, content, and illumination of images were also extracted to predict the perceived aesthetic quality [8,24]. Tang et al. [30] and Tian et al. [31] considered that different types of images are related to different aesthetic evaluation criteria, and designed features in different ways according to the variety of image content. Instead of extracting features from the whole image, Luo and Tang [23] first identified the focus subject area of an image, and then formulated a number of high-level semantic features based on this subject and background division. In [25], generic image descriptors, including the Bag-of-Visual-Words and the Fisher Vector, were used to assess aesthetic quality, and shown to achieve competitive or even better performance than traditional handcrafted features.

With the rise of deep learning in recent years, CNN has been widely applied to learn aesthetic features automatically, and obtained the state-of-the-art performance. Lu et al. [22] developed a double-column CNN to capture both global and local characteristics of images, and employed the style and semantic attributes of images to further boost the aesthetics categorization performance. Dong et al. [9] adopted the activations of the penultimate layer of AlexNet [18] pre-trained on ImageNet [6] as aesthetic features, based on which a SVM classifier was then trained. Kao et al. [16] proposed a multi-task CNN framework by exploiting the semantic recognition as a related task to assist the aesthetics assessment. To compensate the influence of fitting an input image to a fixed size, the above methods carried out a preprocessing of segmenting the image into multiple regions, and then jointly feeding them into the network [9,22]. In contrast, our work leverages the FCN architecture and is able to directly accept images with arbitrary sizes.

Distinguished from most existing works relying on a single label, our work quantifies the image aesthetics using a distribution over multiple quality levels. The most similar work to ours is [34], where the authors viewed the aesthetic distribution as a structure and solved the problem via structured learning. However, there is no intuitive way to define the auxiliary compatibility function measuring how well a possible aesthetic distribution fits for an image. In our study, we consider label distribution learning as a more rational approach to this issue. We achieve this purpose with multivariate support vector regression in our previous work [3], while here we utilize deep neural networks to realize an end-to-end solution.

2.2 Fully Convolutional Network

FCN was originally introduced for semantic segmentation in images [21]. Before that, Springenberg et al. [29] proposed to replace not only fully connected layers by 1-by-1 convolutions, but also pooling layers by convolutional layers with increased stride. The new architecture consisting solely of convolutional layers yields competitive or state of the art performance on several object recognition datasets. One advantage of FCN is that it can take inputs of arbitrary sizes and produce semantic maps of corresponding size for efficient pixelwise inference and learning. Recently, research efforts have achieved remarkable successes with FCN for various tasks, such as object tracking [1], saliency detection [33], and action estimation [32]. To the best of our knowledge, we are the first to apply FCN for image aesthetics assessment.

3   Framework

In this section, we first formulate the problem of aesthetic distribution learning. Then, we present the fully convolutional architecture that accepts inputs of arbitrary sizes. Finally, we illustrate the implementation details of our framework.

3.1   Deep Aesthetic Distribution Learning

Instead of assigning an image a single label (i.e., category or score), which is a common strategy used in previous works, we apply a distribution to represent the aesthetic quality of an image. As discussed earlier, a distribution representation can effectively characterize the disagreement among users' aesthetic perceptions. Formally, we denote an input image by $\mathbf{x} \in \mathbb{R}^{w \times h \times d}$, where w, h, and d are the width, height, and number of color channels of the image, respectively. Following the idea of label distribution learning [12], our goal is to directly predict a distribution vector $\hat{\mathbf{y}} \in \mathbb{R}^{|\mathcal{L}|}$ for $\mathbf{x}$, where $\mathcal{L} = \{l_1, l_2, \ldots, l_c\}$ denotes the set of c predefined aesthetic quality levels. The j-th element $\hat{y}_j$ of $\hat{\mathbf{y}}$ indicates the probability of users perceiving $\mathbf{x}$ as being at the quality level of l_j.

In this paper, we utilize deep neural networks to realize an end-to-end framework for aesthetic distribution learning. Assume that $\mathbf{a} = \phi(\mathbf{x}; \boldsymbol{\theta})$ is the c-dimensional vector of activations of the last layer in the network, where $\boldsymbol{\theta}$ is the parameter of the framework. We use a softmax function to turn these activations into a probability distribution, that is,

$$\hat{y}_j = \frac{\exp(a_j)}{\sum_{k=1}^{c} \exp(a_k)} . \tag{1}$$

We learn the model parameter $\boldsymbol{\theta}$ in a supervised manner. Typically, a training set is available in the form of $\mathcal{D} = \{(\mathbf{x}^1, \mathbf{r}^1), (\mathbf{x}^2, \mathbf{r}^2), \ldots, (\mathbf{x}^n, \mathbf{r}^n)\}$, where $\mathbf{r}^i$ is a c-dimensional rating vector of the image instance $\mathbf{x}^i$, whose element r_j^i denotes the number of users rating $\mathbf{x}^i$ with the quality level of l_j. In the following, we shall omit the superscript i for notational simplicity. Therefore, the ground-truth aesthetic distribution $\mathbf{y}$ associated with $\mathbf{x}$ can be approximately estimated by

$$y_j = \frac{r_j}{\sum_{k=1}^{c} r_k} . \tag{2}$$

In our study, we choose the Kullback-Leibler (KL) divergence [10] as the loss function to penalize the deviation of the predicted distribution $\hat{\mathbf{y}}$ from the ground-truth distribution $\mathbf{y}$, then the best parameter $\boldsymbol{\theta}^*$ is determined by

$$\boldsymbol{\theta}^* = \arg\min_{\boldsymbol{\theta}} \sum_{j=1}^{c} y_j \ln \frac{y_j}{\hat{y}_j} = \arg\min_{\boldsymbol{\theta}} - \sum_{j=1}^{c} y_j \ln \hat{y}_j . \tag{3}$$

We resort to mini-batch stochastic gradient descent (SGD) for solving the minimization problem.

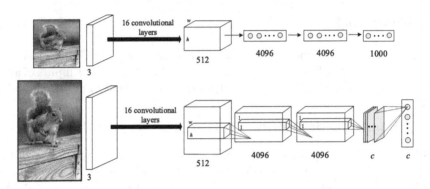

Fig. 2. The architecture comparison between VGG19 (top row) and FCN-VGG19 (bottom row).

3.2   Network Architecture

Nowadays, CNN is the most commonly used deep learning model in the area of computer vision. However, CNN requires an input image to be fitted to a fixed size, and hence may cause severe damage to the intrinsic aesthetic appeal of that image. In order to circumvent this problem, we adopt FCN as the backbone of our model, which directly operates on an input image of arbitrary size.

Generally, CNN mainly consists of two types of layers: the convolutional layers and the fully connected layers. The convolutional layers operate convolution with a filter in a sliding-window manner and do not require a fixed-sized input. In contrast, the fully connected layers demand a fixed-length vector as the input, which essentially leads to the fixed-size constraint of CNN. Inspired by this, we realize FCN by replacing the fully connected layers by the convolutional layers, and thus endow the network with the ability to accept arbitrary-sized inputs.

To be specific, we adapt the VGG19 [28] network into the fully convolutional architecture. The original VGG19 network consists of 16 convolutional layers, which are divided into 5 blocks and each block is followed by one max-pooling layer, as well as 3 fully connected layers, where the first two layers have 4096 dimensions and the third contains 1000 dimensions. We keep all convolutional layers unchanged, and replace the first fully connected layer by a $w \times h$ convolutional layer with 4096 filters, where w and h are the width and height of the feature maps output by the last pooling layer in VGG19, respectively. Then, we convert the second and third fully connected layer to the 1×1 convolution layers with 4096 and c filters, respectively. As previously mentioned, c denotes the number of the predefined aesthetic quality levels. After such a stack of convolution layers, the network can generate one feature map for each corresponding aesthetic quality level. Lastly, we append a global average pooling layer on the top of these feature maps. This layer takes the average of each feature map, and the resulting vector is fed into the softmax function (see Eq. (1)). It has been demonstrated that the global average pooling layer makes the feature maps easier to interpret, and is also less prone to overfitting [19]. We term the new adapted network FCN-VGG19. Figure 2 illustrates the architecture comparison between VGG19 and FCN-VGG19.

One thing worth noting is that even though the architecture of FCN-VGG19 is quite different from that of VGG19, the pre-trained weights of VGG19 on the large dataset (e.g., ImageNet) can still be reused to fine-tune FCN-VGG19. The reason lies in that the number of weights of the first and second fully connected layers in VGG19 is identical to that of their corresponding convolutional layers in FCN-VGG19. Therefore, only by reshaping the pre-trained weights of VGG19 from matrices to tensors (except for the last fully connected layer), we can reuse them to initialize the weights of FCN-VGG19. In this way, FCN-VGG19 is much more tractable and efficient to train.

3.3   Implementation Details

Multi-size Training. Theoretically, FCN-VGG19 is expected to be applied on images of any sizes. However, to leverage contemporary deep learning libraries, the images in one epoch (or one mini-batch) of SGD algorithm need to have the same size. Under this circumstance, we adopt a multi-size training strategy [14] to simulate the scenario of varying input sizes. Specifically, we counted the aspect ratios of the images in the training set, and found two dominant and representative aspect ratio values: 1.0 and 1.5. Then, we chose 224 as the image scale, and further considered two predefined sizes, i.e., 224×224 and 224×336. All images in the training set were resized to both sizes. During training, we iteratively trained one epoch over the images of one size, and then switched to the other sized images for the next epoch. Note that the above multi-size strategy is for training only. At the testing stage, it is straightforward to apply FCN-VGG19 on images of any sizes.

Data Augmentation. To further reduce the overfitting problem, we generated the horizontal reflection of each image and thereby doubled the size of our training set. Note that since our model allows for the input images of arbitrary sizes, we did not apply the means of cropping and warping for data augmentation, which maintains the original content of images as much as possible.

Optimization. We trained both VGG19 and FCN-VGG19 with the mini-batch SGD algorithm under the framework of Keras [2]. Note that the last fully connected layer in VGG19 needs to be changed from 1000 dimensions to c dimensions in our case. Based on the pre-trained weights over ImageNet, we fine-tuned VGG19 with the batch size of 64 and FCN-VGG19 with that of 32. We initially set the learning rate and momentum coefficient as 10^{-3} and 0.9, respectively. For VGG19, we decreased the learning rate by a factor of 0.1 when the loss on validation set stopped declining for 10 epochs; while for FCN-VGG19, we reduced the learning rate by a factor of 0.1 after each 20 epochs. We used the normal initialization [13] to initialize the weights of the last layer in both VGG19 and FCN-VGG19. All biases were initialized with zero.

4   Experiments

In this section, we report a series of experiments to evaluate our approach in both scenarios of aesthetic distribution prediction and aesthetic label prediction. All experiments have been implemented in Python or Matlab, and tested on a workstation equipped with 12-core 3.50 GHz Intel Xeon processor and 64 GB RAM.

4.1   Datasets

To ensure the comparability and fairness of empirical results, our experiments were conducted on two benchmark datasets for aesthetic visual analysis, i.e., AVA [26] and CUHKPQ [30]. Both datasets are collected from a website of online digital photography contest[1].

AVA. The AVA dataset contains about 255,530 images, and each image receives an average of 210 aesthetic ratings ranging from 1 to 10 scale. The provider of AVA does not release the images but rather their web links. We successfully downloaded 255,420 images, and the links of the others are invalid due to the update of the website. We randomly picked out 70% of the images for training, 10% for validation, and the remaining for testing.

CUHKPQ. The CUHKPQ dataset consists of 17,690 images, which are grouped into 7 categories, i.e., "animal", "architecture", "human", "landscape", "night", "plant", and "static". Each image is labeled as either high or low aesthetic quality by at least 8 out of 10 independent viewers. We randomly and evenly divided the high and low quality images in each category into training and test set.

4.2   Aesthetic Distribution Prediction

We first set up the experiment in the scenario of aesthetic distribution prediction for images. As there is no rating distribution information available on CUHKPQ, this experiment was only conducted on AVA. We compared our proposed FCN-VGG19 model against several state-of-the-art methods for label distribution learning [12], namely, AA-kNN, AA-BP, and SA-IIS. For these methods, we took the 4096-dimensional activations from the penultimate layer of VGG19 model pre-trained on ImageNet as the image feature representations. In addition, VGG19 trained with fixed-sized input images was also included for comparison. We evaluated each method by measuring the average distance or similarity between the predicted and ground-truth aesthetic distributions of test images. Specifically, four distance and two similarity metrics were adopted, i.e., Chebyshev distance (Cheb), Clark distance (Clark), Euclidean distance (Euc), Kullback-Leibler distance (KL), cosine coefficient similarity (Cosine), and intersection similarity (Intersec).

---

[1] http://www.dpchallenge.com/.

Table 1. Results of aesthetic distribution prediction on AVA. ↓ indicates the value in terms of the corresponding metric is the smaller the better, while ↑ indicates the contrary.

Metric	AA-kNN	AA-BP	SA-IIS	VGG19	FCN-VGG19
Cheb ↓	0.113	0.108	0.233	0.102	**0.096**
Clark ↓	1.396	1.350	1.575	1.320	**1.283**
Euc ↓	0.172	0.166	0.304	0.155	**0.144**
KL ↓	0.176	0.160	0.390	0.138	**0.120**
Cosine ↑	0.918	0.923	0.807	0.935	**0.944**
Intersec ↑	0.793	0.797	0.685	0.813	**0.827**

Table 1 displays the empirical results of different methods on AVA. It is clearly shown that FCN-VGG19 outperforms the other competitors in all evaluation metrics. For example, the maximum relative increases are 69.2% and 20.7% in terms of KL and Intersec, whereas the minimum gains still reach 13.0% and 1.72%, respectively. Such results verify the efficacy of our approach for aesthetic distribution prediction. Besides, the following important observations can be made from Table 1:

- All three conventional algorithms (i.e., AA-kNN, AA-BP, and SA-IIS) for label distribution learning substantially fall behind both the deep network models of VGG19 and FCN-VGG19. This implies the potential of deep learning techniques in the task of label distribution learning.
- FCN-VGG19 consistently achieves better performance than VGG19, which points clearly to the importance of keeping the input size intact for image aesthetics assessment.

4.3   Aesthetic Label Prediction

As stated in Introduction, a distribution representation can also be easily converted to a single label with its numerical characteristic. Therefore, we further evaluated our approach in the traditional task of image aesthetic classification. Due to the lack of aesthetic category on AVA, we only carried out this experiment on CUHKPQ. Moreover, in order to verify the generalization ability of our approach, we conducted a cross-set evaluation as suggested by [4]. That is, we trained VGG19 and FCN-VGG19 models on AVA, and directly tested them on CUHKPQ. Given a test image, the expectation of its rating was estimated with the predicted aesthetic distribution, which was used to indicate the confidence of the image belonging to the high quality category. Also, we introduced several existing aesthetic classification algorithms as the baselines, including the methods of Ke et al. [17], Marchesotti et al. [25], and Lo et al. [20]. For these methods, CUHKPQ was used for both training and testing.

Figure 3 plots the ROC curves for the classification performance of different methods. As expected, our proposed FCN-VGG19 model still obtains the best

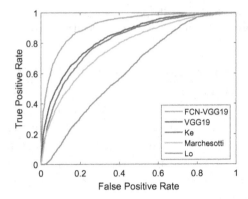

Fig. 3. ROC curves for the classification performance of different methods on CUHKPQ.

performance. More precisely, the AUC value achieved by FCN-VGG19 is 0.920, and much higher than the values of 0.840, 0.820, 0.776, and 0.630 for VGG19, Ke, Marchesotti, and Lo, respectively. The observation suggests that our approach, while specialized for aesthetic distribution learning, still emerges as a highly effective tool for image aesthetic classification. Furthermore, even though implemented without training on CUHKPQ, FCN-VGG19 is remarkably superior to its contenders. The finding confirms the good generalization capability of our approach in real applications.

5   Conclusions and Future Work

In this paper, we have investigated the problem of image aesthetics assessment from a new perspective of predicting the distribution of multiple quality levels. Our approach is hence able to capture the disagreement among users' aesthetic perceptions regarding the same image. An end-to-end framework of distribution learning is developed based on fully convolutional network, and it is capable of efficiently processing input images with arbitrary sizes. Extensive experiments are conducted on two benchmark datasets in comparison with state-of-the-art methods. The results have verified the effectiveness of our approach in both scenarios of distribution prediction and label prediction for aesthetics assessment. In the future, we plan to explore a richer context for image aesthetics assessment. Intuitively, aesthetics assessment is coupled with the identification of semantic content of images. We shall leverage the information of object categorization and scene understanding to enhance the accuracy of image aesthetics assessment.

Acknowledgements. This work is supported by the National Natural Science Foundation of China (61573219, 61671274, 61701281), NSFC Joint Fund with Guangdong under Key Project (U1201258), China Postdoctoral Science Foundation (2016M592190), Shandong Provincial Natural Science Foundation (ZR2017QF009), and the Fostering Project of Dominant Discipline and Talent Team of Shandong Province Higher Education Institutions.

References

1. Bertinetto, L., Valmadre, J., Henriques, J.F., Vedaldi, A., Torr, P.H.S.: Fully-convolutional siamese networks for object tracking. In: Hua, G., Jégou, H. (eds.) ECCV 2016. LNCS, vol. 9914, pp. 850–865. Springer, Cham (2016). https://doi.org/10.1007/978-3-319-48881-3_56
2. Chollet, F., et al.: Keras. https://github.com/fchollet/keras (2015)
3. Cui, C., Fang, H., Deng, X., Nie, X., Dai, H., Yin, Y.: Distribution-oriented aesthetics assessment for image search. In: Proceedings of the 40th International ACM SIGIR Conference on Research and Development in Information Retrieval, pp. 1013–1016 (2017)
4. Cui, C., Shen, J., Ma, J., Lian, T.: Social tag relevance learning via ranking-oriented neighbor voting. Multimedia Tools Appl. **76**(6), 8831–8857 (2017)
5. Datta, R., Joshi, D., Li, J., Wang, J.Z.: Studying aesthetics in photographic images using a computational approach. In: Leonardis, A., Bischof, H., Pinz, A. (eds.) ECCV 2006. LNCS, vol. 3953, pp. 288–301. Springer, Heidelberg (2006). https://doi.org/10.1007/11744078_23
6. Deng, J., Dong, W., Socher, R., Li, L.J., Li, K., Fei-Fei, L.: Imagenet: a large-scale hierarchical image database. In: Proceedings of the IEEE Conference on Computer Vision and Pattern Recognition, pp. 248–255 (2009)
7. Deng, Y., Loy, C.C., Tang, X.: Image aesthetic assessment: an experimental survey. IEEE Sig. Process. Mag. **34**(4), 80–106 (2017)
8. Dhar, S., Ordonez, V., Berg, T.L.: High level describable attributes for predicting aesthetics and interestingness. In: Proceedings of the IEEE Conference on Computer Vision and Pattern Recognition, pp. 1657–1664 (2011)
9. Dong, Z., Shen, X., Li, H., Tian, X.: Photo Quality assessment with DCNN that understands image well. In: He, X., Luo, S., Tao, D., Xu, C., Yang, J., Hasan, M.A. (eds.) MMM 2015. LNCS, vol. 8936, pp. 524–535. Springer, Cham (2015). https://doi.org/10.1007/978-3-319-14442-9_57
10. Gao, B.B., Xing, C., Xie, C.W., Wu, J., Geng, X.: Deep label distribution learning with label ambiguity. IEEE Trans. Image Process. **26**(6), 2825–2838 (2017)
11. Geng, B., Yang, L., Xu, C., Hua, X.S., Li, S.: The role of attractiveness in web image search. In: Proceedings of the 19th ACM International Conference on Multimedia, pp. 63–72 (2011)
12. Geng, X.: Label distribution learning. IEEE Trans. Knowl. Data Eng. **28**(7), 1734–1748 (2016)
13. Glorot, X., Bengio, Y.: Understanding the difficulty of training deep feedforward neural networks. In: Proceedings of the International Conference on Artificial Intelligence and Statistics, pp. 249–256 (2010)
14. He, K., Zhang, X., Ren, S., Sun, J.: Spatial pyramid pooling in deep convolutional networks for visual recognition. In: Fleet, D., Pajdla, T., Schiele, B., Tuytelaars, T. (eds.) ECCV 2014. LNCS, vol. 8691, pp. 346–361. Springer, Cham (2014). https://doi.org/10.1007/978-3-319-10578-9_23
15. He, K., Zhang, X., Ren, S., Sun, J.: Deep residual learning for image recognition. In: Proceedings of the IEEE Conference on Computer Vision and Pattern Recognition, pp. 770–778 (2016)
16. Kao, Y., He, R., Huang, K.: Deep aesthetic quality assessment with semantic information. IEEE Trans. Image Process. **26**, 1482–1495 (2017)
17. Ke, Y., Tang, X., Jing, F.: The design of high-level features for photo quality assessment. In: Proceedings of the IEEE Conference on Computer Vision and Pattern Recognition, pp. 419–426 (2006)

18. Krizhevsky, A., Sutskever, I., Hinton, G.E.: Imagenet classification with deep convolutional neural networks. In: Proceedings of the Advances in Neural Information Processing Systems, pp. 1097–1105 (2012)
19. Lin, M., Chen, Q., Yan, S.: Network in network. arXiv preprint arXiv:1312.4400 (2013)
20. Lo, K.Y., Liu, K.H., Chen, C.S.: Assessment of photo aesthetics with efficiency. In: Proceedings of the 21st International Conference on Pattern Recognition, pp. 2186–2189 (2012)
21. Long, J., Shelhamer, E., Darrell, T.: Fully convolutional networks for semantic segmentation. In: Proceedings of the IEEE Conference on Computer Vision and Pattern Recognition, pp. 3431–3440 (2015)
22. Lu, X., Lin, Z., Jin, H., Yang, J., Wang, J.Z.: Rating image aesthetics using deep learning. IEEE Trans. Multimedia 17(11), 2021–2034 (2015)
23. Luo, Y., Tang, X.: Photo and video quality evaluation: focusing on the subject. In: Forsyth, D., Torr, P., Zisserman, A. (eds.) ECCV 2008. LNCS, vol. 5304, pp. 386–399. Springer, Heidelberg (2008). https://doi.org/10.1007/978-3-540-88690-7_29
24. Marchesotti, L., Murray, N., Perronnin, F.: Discovering beautiful attributes for aesthetic image analysis. Int. J. Comput. Vis. 113(3), 246–266 (2015)
25. Marchesotti, L., Perronnin, F., Larlus, D., Csurka, G.: Assessing the aesthetic quality of photographs using generic image descriptors. In: Proceedings of the IEEE International Conference on Computer Vision, pp. 1784–1791 (2011)
26. Murray, N., Marchesotti, L., Perronnin, F.: AVA: a large-scale database for aesthetic visual analysis. In: Proceedings of the IEEE Conference on Computer Vision and Pattern Recognition, pp. 2408–2415 (2012)
27. Ren, S., He, K., Girshick, R., Sun, J.: Faster R-CNN: towards real-time object detection with region proposal networks. In: Proceedings of the Advances in Neural Information Processing Systems, pp. 91–99 (2015)
28. Simonyan, K., Zisserman, A.: Very deep convolutional networks for large-scale image recognition. arXiv preprint arXiv:1409.1556 (2014)
29. Springenberg, J.T., Dosovitskiy, A., Brox, T., Riedmiller, M.: Striving for simplicity: the all convolutional net. arXiv preprint arXiv:1412.6806 (2014)
30. Tang, X., Luo, W., Wang, X.: Content-based photo quality assessment. IEEE Trans. Multimedia 15(8), 1930–1943 (2013)
31. Tian, X., Dong, Z., Yang, K., Mei, T.: Query-dependent aesthetic model with deep learning for photo quality assessment. IEEE Trans. Multimedia 17(11), 2035–2048 (2015)
32. Wang, L., Qiao, Y., Tang, X., Van Gool, L.: Actionness estimation using hybrid fully convolutional networks. In: Proceedings of the IEEE Conference on Computer Vision and Pattern Recognition, pp. 2708–2717 (2016)
33. Wang, L., Wang, L., Lu, H., Zhang, P., Ruan, X.: Saliency detection with recurrent fully convolutional networks. In: Leibe, B., Matas, J., Sebe, N., Welling, M. (eds.) ECCV 2016. LNCS, vol. 9908, pp. 825–841. Springer, Cham (2016). https://doi.org/10.1007/978-3-319-46493-0_50
34. Wu, O., Hu, W., Gao, J.: Learning to predict the perceived visual quality of photos. In: Proceedings of the IEEE International Conference on Computer Vision, pp. 225–232 (2011)

Improving the Quality of Video-to-Language Models by Optimizing Annotation of the Training Material

Laura Pérez-Mayos[1]([⊠]), Federico M. Sukno[1], and Leo Wanner[1,2]

[1] Department of Information and Communication Technologies,
Pompeu Fabra University, Barcelona, Spain
{laura.perezm,federico.sukno,leo.wanner}@upf.edu
[2] Catalan Institute for Research and Advanced Studies (ICREA), Barcelona, Spain

Abstract. Automatic video captioning is one of the ultimate challenges of Natural Language Processing, boosted by the omnipresence of video and the release of large-scale annotated video benchmarks. However, the specificity and quality of the captions vary considerably, having an adverse effect on the quality of the trained captioning models. In this work, we address this issue by proposing automatic strategies for optimizing the annotations of video material, removing annotations that are not semantically relevant and generating new and more informative captions. We evaluate our approach on the MSR-VTT challenge with a state-of-the-art deep learning video-to-language model. Our code is available at https://github.com/lpmayos/mcv_thesis.

Keywords: Video-to-language · Video captioning
Video understanding · Text annotation optimization
Semantic sentence similarity

1 Introduction

Video has become omnipresent, and the analysis of the semantics of video has a large variety of applications, including scene understanding, accessibility improvement and information retrieval. Automatically describing videos in terms of natural language is one of the ultimate challenges of video understanding, given the difficulties of video interpretation and abstractive natural language summarization. Many state-of-the-art models focus on the generation of captions of short-term videos. In this context, Microsoft has released Microsoft Research - Video to Text (MSR-VTT)[24], a large-scale annotated video benchmark that contains 41.2 h of recordings. The annotation consists of 20 Mechanical Turk captions per video, resulting in 200K captions-video pairs in total.

However, as shown in Fig. 1, the specificity and quality of the captions vary considerably. For example, in the second video all five captions have different subjects (*A child, A girl, Children, People, A group of people*), and while some

© Springer International Publishing AG 2018
K. Schoeffmann et al. (Eds.): MMM 2018, Part I, LNCS 10704, pp. 279–290, 2018.
https://doi.org/10.1007/978-3-319-73603-7_23

of them describe general actions like *cooking* and *make food*, others are more specific, like *putting her finger into a plastic cup containing an egg*. Notice how some captions are syntactically incorrect, like the first caption of the first video, which is missing determinants. Furthermore, the dataset contains misspelled words and captions wrongly assigned to other videos. This variation in specificity and quality is likely to have a negative influence on the quality of the trained models. In this work, possible automatic strategies for optimizing the annotations of video material are explored and the consequences of this optimization are analyzed with a state-of-the-art deep learning video-to-language model. First, we propose different semantic similarity measures based on Sense Embeddings to remove non-semantically related descriptions. Then, we present a data augmentation strategy that exploits the high number of captions per video offered by MSR-VTT, based in the combination of subjects and predicates.

1. A woman giving speech on news channel.
2. Hillary Clinton gives a speech.
3. Hillary Clinton is making a speech at the conference of mayors.
4. A woman is giving a speech on stage.
5. A lady speak some news on TV.

1. A child is cooking in the kitchen.
2. A girl is putting her finger into a plastic cup containing an egg.
3. Children boil water and get egg whites ready.
4. People make food in a kitchen.
5. A group of people are making food in a kitchen.

Fig. 1. MSR-VTT Dataset examples: two video samples represented with four frames, with five human-labeled captions out of 20.

2   Related Work

As described in [18], MSR-VTT dataset presents several challenges, including noisy text data and high variation in sentence length. This is a common problem when compiling datasets, especially for those that require human annotation. Furthermore, it is not unusual that captions for different videos end up mixed together in the compilation process, resulting in noisy datasets. To our knowledge there does not exist any literature tackling this specific issue. For the case of multiple annotation sentences, like MSR-VTT dataset, we already have the sentences describing a video clustered together, all in the same language, and therefore we do not have to detect similar sentences across text, nor translate them or summarize them. However, tools and techniques on automatic translation and summarization can be very useful to solve the challenges presented by this kind of datasets, as they can be seen as semantic distance problems.

2.1 Semantic Similarity Models

There exist several semantic measures, some relying only on raw text (distributional measures) and some relying on knowledge sources (i.e. WordNet-based [15]). Word embeddings represent a new branch of corpus-based distributional semantic models which leverages neural networks to model the context in which a word is expected to appear, capturing both syntactic and semantic information. They are vector space models representing words as real-valued vectors in a low-dimensional space, and are traditionally obtained by computing a term-document occurrence matrix on large corpora. More recently, supervised processes have been used to generate Word embeddings, based on neural networks [4,8,14,16,21].

While word embeddings have been successfully applied to several NLP tasks, including semantic similarity measuring [2,14,25,26], they are by their very nature unable to capture polysemy, as different meanings of a word are fused into a single representation. Additionally, their learning does not take advantage of structured knowledge, as it relies on massive corpora only. In [13], Iacobacci, Pilehvar, and Navigli address both issues by proposing a multi-faceted approach that transforms word embeddings to the sense level and leverages knowledge from a large semantic network for effective semantic similarity measurement. The authors rely on BabelNet [17] as underlying sense inventory, which merges multiple lexical resources as WordNet and Wikipedia, providing a high coverage of domain-specific terms and named entities and a rich set of relations.

Three semantic text similarity metrics are presented in [12], combining POS tagging, Latent Semantic Analysis and WordNet knowledge, and considering only the semantics of a word and not its lexical category (i.e. the verb *marry* should be semantically similar to the noun *wife*). More recently, a novel metric for semantic assessment of abstractive summaries has been presented in [23], based upon a weighted composition of the level of agreement, contradiction, topical neutrality, paraphrasing and ROUGE score. It correlates maximally with human evaluation of summaries, but has not been designed to evaluate shorter sentences like video captions.

2.2 Sentence Fusion

Sentence fusion was introduced by Barzilay and McKeown [3] as a novel text-to-text generation technique for synthesizing common information across documents, statistically combining common phrases into a sentence, and it can be used as a method to generate new data by combining captions of the same video.

A popular strategy for fusion relies on merging the dependency trees of input sentences to produce an output sentence. Most of the works rely on the use of integer linear programming, both supervised [9,20] and unsupervised [7,11]. In [9], Elsner and Santhanam present a system for fusing sentences which are drawn from the same source document but have different content, by merging dependency graphs. In [20], the authors recover the highest scoring output fusion under an n-gram factorization. In [11], Filippova and Strube formulate the fusion task as an optimization problem, aligning the dependency trees of a group of related sentences and building a dependency graph, to then compress it to a new tree. Bing et al. [5] propose a framework that first constructs a poll of concepts and facts represented by phrases from the input documents, and then generates new sentences by selecting and merging informative phrases. In [7], Cheung and Penn increase the range of possible summary sentences by allowing the combination of dependency subtrees from any sentence from the source text.

Furthermore, compression techniques for sentence clusters generate output sentences as high-scoring paths in weighted bigram graphs [6,10,22], aiming at producing sentences as short as possible.

3   Method

All Video-to-language models participating in the 2016 MSR-VTT challenge rely on deep learning, taking advantage of the available features. However, none of them performs any work with the captions. Working with raw captions containing syntactic errors and semantically unrelated descriptions is likely to induce the learning of a poor language model, having a negative influence in the generated captions. In this work, we aim at improving the performance of video-to-language models by optimizing the annotation of the training material, focusing on removing semantically unrelated captions, and in building new annotations to boost the training process.

3.1   Removing Outliers from the Dataset

In [13], the authors present a method to obtain continuous representation of individual word senses, *sense embeddings*, and propose SensEmbed to measure semantic similarity. Unlike word embeddings, their predecessor, sense embeddings are able to model the different meanings of a word, and they take advantage of existing semantic resources, leveraging knowledge from a large semantic network for effective semantic similarity measurement. We propose the use of SenseEmbed to detect those captions less semantically related to all the others.

Let us define $C_V = \{C_1, C_2, ..., C_n\}$ as the set of captions of a video V, $C_a = \{t_1^a, t_2^a, ..., t_m^a\}$ as the set of tokens of caption a, and $S_t = \{s_1^t, s_2^t, ..., s_o^t\}$ as the set of senses of token t. We first propose a somewhat *naive* approach to the use of sense embeddings to measure the semantic similarity among the captions of a video, using them to create a caption embedding which can be projected into a common space where it is possible to measure the distance of the different caption embeddings to their centroid, determining which captions are far away and are good candidates to be removed from the training set. To create those caption embeddings, we simply add the sense embeddings of the first sense s_1 of all the tokens t of the caption C_a, where a token is any word or group of words which can be associated with a sense in the sense repository (Eq. 1). In this way, each token contributes to the final embedding.

$$emb(C_a) = \sum_{i=1}^{m} SensEmbed(s_1^{t_i^a}) \tag{1}$$

Notice that we use the first sense for the sake of simplicity: if two sentences contain the same token, it would be represented by the same SensEmbed, as we consider that it is very improbable that two sentences of the same video contain the same token with different meanings. An alternative to choosing the first sense would be performing Word Sense Disambiguation. However, it would significantly increase the system complexity and execution time.

This approach presents a major problem: those sentences which contain more tokens are somehow difficult to compare with those with fewer tokens, even though they may share a common root. For example, consider the sentences *Two girls playing* and *Two girls playing in a nice green garden on a sunny day*. Even though they share a common subject and the first argument of the predicate that intuitively should place them much closer, those sentences are likely to get projected far away, as all the tokens present in the second sentence and missing in the first are probable to add a lot of weight in the final embedding.

To avoid the drawback of the first approach, we propose a global similarity measure that indicates for a given caption how similar it is with respect to all other captions, relying on the use of the sense embeddings of the tokens of the captions, and using SensEmbed as similarity measure. Given two captions, we propose to compute their similarity as the fraction of tokens in the first caption with a similar enough correspondence in the second caption (Eq. 2). To measure how similar two tokens are we rely on the word similarity algorithm proposed in [13], using the *closest* strategy shown in Eq. 3, where S_{t_i} corresponds to the set of senses of token i and $\tau(s_1, s_2)$ corresponds to the Tanimoto distance (Eq. 4), a generalization of Jaccard similarity for real-valued vectors in $[-1, 1]$.

$$S(C_k, C_p) = \frac{1}{m_k} \sum_{i=1}^{m_k} (1| \max_{t_j \in C_p} Sim_{closest}(t_i^k, t_j^p) > t_{h1}) \tag{2}$$

$$Sim_{closest}(t_1, t_2) = \max_{\substack{s_1 \in S_{t_1} \\ s_2 \in S_{t_2}}} \tau(s_1, s_2) \tag{3}$$

$$\tau(s_1, s_2) = \frac{s_1 \cdot s_2}{\|s_1\|^2 + \|s_2\|^2 - s_1 \cdot s_2} \tag{4}$$

Having a measure of similarity between each pair of captions, it is possible to compute a global caption similarity as the mean of the similarity of each caption to all others (Eq. 5). Using those global similarities we can rank the captions of any video, removing those that are not similar enough to the others.

$$S(C_k) = \frac{1}{n} \sum_{i=1}^{n} S(C_k, C_i) \tag{5}$$

Notice that $S(C_k, C_p)$ is not necessarily equal to $S(C_p, C_k)$, as for a token t_l^k in C_k the most similar token in C_p could be t_m^p, while for t_m^p the most similar token in C_k could be t_n^k, and it could happen that $Sim_{closest}(t_l^k, t_m^p) > t_{h1}$ while $Sim_{closest}(t_m^p, t_n^k) < t_{h1}$. However, it is possible to force the similarity between captions to be symmetrical by averaging their similarities (Eq. 6).

$$S_{sym}(C_k, C_p) = \frac{1}{2}(S(C_k, C_p) + S(C_p, C_k)) \tag{6}$$

3.2 Augmenting the Dataset

Inspired by the data augmentation strategies for image datasets used in the Convolutional Neural Networks literature, in which images are flipped and cropped to generate new training images, and relying on the presence of multiple annotation sentences for each video, we propose a data augmentation method that consists in the combination of subjects and predicates of different captions. Let us define $C_V = \{C_1, C_2, ..., C_n\}$ as the set of captions of a video V, each one composed of a subject and a predicate: $C_i = \{subj_i, pred_i\}$. We define the set of subjects of the captions of a video V as: $subj_V = \{subj_1, subj_2, ..., subj_n\}$, and the set of predicates as $pred_V = \{pred_1, pred_2, ..., pred_n\}$.

Then, we define the set of new training captions C_{V_a} as the combination of all subjects and all predicates of the captions of a video. However, not all subjects and predicates are combinable, the newly generated captions must be syntactically correct and humanly comprehensible (i.e. captions *A child is cooking in the kitchen* and *People make food in a kitchen*, or captions *Table tennis is being played by two men* and *Two men play ping pong in a large stadium*, are not combinable). Thus, we add two constraints to ensure that their numbers match and the similarity between their subjects is above a certain threshold (Eq. 7), defining this similarity as done in Eq. 2 but applying it just to the subjects.

$$C_{V_a} = \{(subj_i, pred_j) \subset C_{V_a} | S(subj_i, subj_j) > t_h; num(subj_i) = num(subj_j)\} \tag{7}$$

4 Experiments

In this work, we train and evaluate our models on the MSR-VTT dataset [24], a new large-scale video benchmark for video understanding, which has boosted the research on video-to-language translation, providing 10,000 clips (41.2 h) of approximately 14.8 s each, 200K natural language descriptions (20 captions per video) by AMT workers and well-defined categories. We use the Caption-Guided Visual Saliency model described in [19], publicly available[1], and we rely on Sense Embeddings [13] to measure the semantic similarity between tokens and sentences. Our code is available at https://github.com/lpmayos/mcv_thesis.

---

[1] https://visionlearninggroup.github.io/caption-guided-saliency.

4.1 Removing Outliers from the Dataset

Experiment 1. Captions Distance Using Caption Embeddings. The main idea is to create an embedding to represent each video caption, in order to project all the embeddings of the captions of a video in the same space and remove those far away from the centroid. We define the embedding of a caption a as the sum of the SensEmbed of the first sense of each token in the caption, as shown in Eq. 1. Figure 2 shows the data distribution of the distances to the respective centroids of the captions of all the videos. A total of 1263 captions were removed from the training set applying an outliers threshold defined as 1.5 times the distance to the upper quartile of the data distribution boxplot[2].

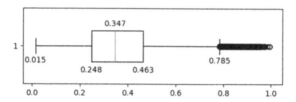

Fig. 2. Experiment 1. Data distribution of the distances to the respective centroids of the captions of all the videos.

Experiment 2. Captions Similarity Ranking (non-Symmetrical). The goal is to compute a captions similarity ranking, in order to discard those captions whose similarity to all the others is below a certain threshold. Let us define the similarity between two captions as the fraction of the tokens in the first caption that have a similar enough correspondence in the second caption (Eq. 2). Token similarity is computed as the implementation of the word similarity measure described in Algorithm 1 of [13] using the *closest* strategy (Eq. 3). Then, a global caption similarity is computed as the mean of the similarity of each caption to all others (Eq. 5), and the ones below a certain threshold t_{h2} are discarded. Threshold t_{h1} has been determined experimentally, and the outliers

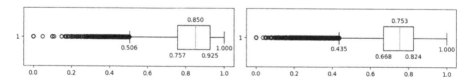

Fig. 3. Data distribution of the similarity measures of the captions of all the videos for experiment 2 (left) and experiment 3 (right).

---

[2] Note that $1.5xIQR$, the interquartile range, is a standard definition for suspected outliers.

threshold t_{h2} has then been defined as 1.5 times the distance to the lower quartile of the data distribution boxplot (Fig. 3, left). A total of 1543 captions were removed from the training set.

Experiment 3. Captions Similarity Ranking (symmetrical). Again, the goal is to compute a captions similarity ranking to discard then those captions whose similarity to all the others is below a certain threshold. The approach is exactly the same, but before computing the global similarities of the captions using Eq. 5, the similarity between captions is forced to be symmetrical as shown in Eq. 6. A total of 2790 captions were removed from the training set applying an outliers threshold defined as 1.5 times the distance to the lower quartile of the data distribution boxplot (Fig. 3, right).

Experiments Sample. Table 1 offers a sample of the distance/similarity metrics computed by each of the experiments on one of the videos of the MSR-VTT training set (Fig. 4). For each experiment, it shows the measure of distance (experiment 1) or similarity (experiments 2 and 3) of each caption respect all the others, underlined if it will be removed because of the selected outliers threshold. Notice how captions that are clearly misplaced in the dataset, i.e. *The site was very informative*, and captions lacking references to the human actors and their actions, i.e. *The beginning of a tech show*, are selected to be removed.

Fig. 4. Sample frames of video 24 of the MSR-VTT training set.

4.2   Experiment 4. Augmenting the Dataset

The goal is to generate a bigger training set by combining subjects and predicates of the initial training sentences, as expressed in Eq. 7. We work with the training and validation sets of the MSR-VTT dataset, and we rely on the outliers-free annotations generated by experiment 2. We use the parsing web service provided by TALN research group, which returns the parsed captions in *conll format*. We use the similarity measure and the threshold used in experiment 2, as previous experiments show this approach as the most promising. As an example, for video 3742 of the training set 8 new captions are generated, i.e. *A person is using scissors to cut paper* or *Someone is cutting and folding a sheet of paper*, while 11 are discarded given that they don't meet the required constraints, i.e. *A paper tube is explaining something* or *A paper tube is cutting paper with scissors*.

Table 1. Removing outliers from the dataset. Experiments sample (repeated captions removed).

Caption	Exp. 1	Exp. 2	Exp. 3
The site was very informative	0.826	0.475	0.193
An advertisement of software	0.648	0.575	0.378
Two men and standing beside each other	0.453	0.55	0.485
Two people are talking to each other	0.349	0.7	0.535
An introduction for a how to use linux tutorial	0.808	0.512	0.333
Two overweight men talking and one of the men drives a car	0.279	0.616	0.595
Two men promote their linux class	0.437	0.56	0.535
There is a man who met another man in this video and he is also travelling in a car	0.537	0.453	0.485
The beginning of a tech show	0.791	0.4	0.297
Two men stand together and talk while opening credits to a show appear intermittendly	0.45	0.585	0.606
Guys showcasing technology for people	0.616	0.662	0.472
Two men star in how to linux	0.366	0.563	0.487
The video is a trailer for some tv show	0.654	0.68	0.447
People are hosting show	0.603	0.825	0.525
Two men are talking	0.273	0.6	0.453
A man is driving a car	0.609	0.6	0.371
A clip with a heavy man talking to the camera	0.494	0.6	0.488
Two men discuss linux options with their computers	0.354	0.625	0.581
Two men are talking to each other about something	0.334	0.575	0.43

5 Results

To study how the different experiments influence video captioning, we retrain the Caption-Guided Visual Saliency model with the newly generated caption sets, and we evaluate them on the MSR-VTT test set by executing the Microsoft COCO Caption Evaluation that computes the well known Bleu, Meteor, Rouge-L and CIDEr metrics for each of the generated sentences and its 20 reference sentences, keeping the best result. Table 2 offers the results of the quantitative evaluation for all the experiments (higher is better). Note that these metrics are known to perform more poorly when used to evaluate the quality of individual sentence variations rather than sentences within a corpus [1].

As it was done in the MSR-VTT Challenge, we carry out a human evaluation of the first three systems on a random subset of 10 test videos. A total of 14 participants were asked to rank the captions generated by the different systems from 0 to 10 with respect to the following criteria: **Coherence** (to judge the logic

Table 2. Quantitative evaluation results.

Experiment	CIDEr	Bleu 1	ROUGE_L	METEOR
Original training set	0.38	0.77	0.58	0.27
Experiment 1	0.39	0.77	0.58	0.26
Experiment 2	0.39	0.77	0.58	0.27
Experiment 3	0.37	0.77	0.58	0.26
Experiment 4	0.35	0.76	0.57	0.26

and readability of the sentence), **Correctness** (to judge if the sentence is valid for the video), **Relevance** (to judge if the sentence contains the most relevant and important objects/actions/events in the video clip) and **Helpful for blind** (to judge how helpful would the sentence be for a blind person to understand what is happening in this video clip). Results are shown in Table 3. To evaluate the data augmentation experiment, we carry out a second human evaluation on a subset of 10 videos, with 24 participants (Table 4). Results of both evaluations show that all four metrics improve with the elimination of outliers, even if that means training with less data, suggesting that video-to-language models are indeed sensible to wrong data. Furthermore, the results seem to indicate that training with bigger training sets without outliers improves the language model.

Table 3. Qualitative evaluation results (mean ± standard deviation).

Experiment	Coherence	Correctness	Relevance	Helpful for blind
Original training set	7.46 ± 3.22	4.09 ± 3.22	3.74 ± 2.92	3.32 ± 2.97
Experiment 1	7.59 ± 3.34	3.99 ± 3.36	3.98 ± 3.09	3.71 ± 3.12
Experiment 2	7.79 ± 3.22	4.49 ± 3.51	4.31 ± 3.40	3.98 ± 3.48
Experiment 3	7.54 ± 3.37	3.78 ± 3.34	3.71 ± 3.01	3.31 ± 3.10

Table 4. Qualitative evaluation results II (mean ± standard deviation).

Experiment	Coherence	Correctness	Relevance	Helpful for blind
Original training set	8.21 ± 2.51	4.77 ± 3.10	4.31 ± 2.75	3.91 ± 2.80
Experiment 4	8.46 ± 2.20	6.33 ± 2.84	5.63 ± 2.66	5.02 ± 2.82

6   Conclusions

Video-to-language datasets are not optimal, they contain typos and misplaced captions. To overcome this problem, either we develop strategies to automatically improve those datasets, or we think on better ways of obtaining them. In this work, we investigate automatic strategies for optimizing the annotations of video material, proposing three different strategies to remove annotations that are not semantically relevant and a data augmentation method. We test our experiments on the MSR-VTT dataset using the Caption-Guided Visual Saliency model, and we offer quantitative and qualitative results. Results seem to indicate that, indeed, video-to-language models are able to learn better language models when they are trained without outliers, improving in all four evaluated metrics, even though if the clean training sets are smaller than the original ones. Thus, the use of SenseEmbeddings has proven useful to measure how similar two captions are. Moreover, experiments on data augmentation over outliers-free training sets suggest that augmenting the training sentences once the outliers have been removed can benefit the learning of a better language model.

Acknowledgment. This work is partly supported by the Spanish Ministry of Economy and Competitiveness under the Ramon y Cajal fellowships, and the Kristina project funded by the European Union Horizon 2020 research and innovation programme under grant agreement No 645012. The Titan X GPU used for this research was donated by the NVIDIA Corporation.

References

1. Awad, G., et al.: Trecvid 2016: evaluating video search, video event detection, localization, and hyperlinking. In: Proceedings of TRECVID, vol. 2016 (2016)
2. Baroni, M., Dinu, G., Kruszewski, G.: Don't count, predict! a systematic comparison of context-counting vs. context-predicting semantic vectors. In: ACL, vol. 1, pp. 238–247 (2014)
3. Barzilay, R., McKeown, K.R.: Sentence fusion for multi-document news summarization. CL **31**(3), 297–328 (2005)
4. Bengio, Y., et al.: A neural probabilistic language model. JMLR **3**, 1137–1155 (2003)
5. Bing, L., et al.: Abstractive multi-document summarization via phrase selection and merging. arXiv preprint arXiv:1506.01597 (2015)
6. Boudin, F., Morin, E.: Keyphrase extraction for n-best reranking in multi-sentence compression. In: NAACL (2013)
7. Cheung, J.C.K., Penn, G.: Unsupervised sentence enhancement for automatic summarization. In: EMNLP, pp. 775–786 (2014)
8. Collobert, R., Weston, J.: A unified architecture for natural language processing: deep neural networks with multitask learning. In: Proceedings of the 25th ICML, pp. 160–167. ACM (2008)
9. Elsner, M., Santhanam, D.: Learning to fuse disparate sentences. In: Proceedings of the Workshop on Monolingual Text-To-Text Generation, pp. 54–63. ACL (2011)
10. Filippova, K.: Multi-sentence compression: finding shortest paths in word graphs. In: Proceedings of the 23rd ICCL, pp. 322–330. ACL (2010)
11. Filippova, K., Strube, M.: Sentence fusion via dependency graph compression. In: Proceedings of the CEMNLP, pp. 177–185. ACL (2008)
12. Han, L., et al.: UMBC_EBIQUITY-CORE: semantic textual similarity systems. In: * SEM@ NAACL-HLT, pp. 44–52 (2013)

13. Iacobacci, I., Pilehvar, M.T., Navigli, R.: SensEmbed: learning sense embeddings for word and relational similarity. In: ACL, vol. 1, pp. 95–105 (2015)
14. Mikolov, T., et al.: Efficient estimation of word representations in vector space. arXiv preprint arXiv:1301.3781 (2013)
15. Miller, G.A.: WordNet: a lexical database for English. Commun. ACM **38**(11), 39–41 (1995)
16. Mnih, A., Hinton, G.: Three new graphical models for statistical language modelling. In: Proceedings of the 24th ICML, pp. 641–648. ACM (2007)
17. Navigli, R., Ponzetto, S.P.: BabelNet: building a very large multilingual semantic network. In: Proceedings of the 48th Annual Meeting of the ACL, pp. 216–225. ACL (2010)
18. Ramanishka, V., et al.: Multimodal video description. In: Proceedings of the 2016 ACM on Multimedia Conference, pp. 1092–1096. ACM (2016)
19. Ramanishka, V., et al.: Top-down visual saliency guided by captions. In: arXiv preprint arXiv:1612.07360 (2016)
20. Thadani, K., McKeown, K.: Supervised sentence fusion with single-stage inference. In: IJCNLP, pp. 1410–1418 (2013)
21. Turian, J., Ratinov, L., Bengio, Y.: Word representations: a simple and general method for semi-supervised learning. In: Proceedings of the 48th Annual Meeting of the ACL, pp. 384–394. ACL (2010)
22. Tzouridis, E., Nasir, J.A., Brefeld, U.: Learning to summarise related sentences. In: COLING, pp. 1636–1647 (2014)
23. Vadapalli, R. et al.: SSAS: semantic similarity for abstractive summarization. In: Proceedings of the IJCNLP (2017)
24. Xu, J., et al.: MSR-VTT: A large video description dataset for bridging video and language. In: Proceedings of the IEEE Conference on CVPR, pp. 5288–5296 (2016)
25. Yu, M., Dredze, M.: Improving lexical embeddings with semantic knowledge. In: ACL, vol. 2, pp. 545–550 (2014)
26. Zou, W.Y., et al.: Bilingual word embeddings for phrase-based machine translation. In: EMNLP, pp. 1393–1398 (2013)

Iterative Active Classification of Large Image Collection

Mofei Song, Zhengxing Sun$^{(\boxtimes)}$, Bo Li, and Jiagao Hu

State Key Laboratory for Novel Software Technology,
Nanjing University, Jiangsu, China
szx@nju.edu.cn

Abstract. To efficiently and accurately classify a large image collection, this paper proposes a novel interactive system by incorporating active learning, online learning and user intervention. Given an image collection, our system iteratively alternates the interactive annotation and verification until all the images are classified. The main advantage is that it provides faster interactive classification rates than alternative approaches. Our system achieves this goal by a unified active learning algorithm that selects the images to be annotated or verified, which requires a probability model for simulating the time cost of human input during manual intervention. To assist manual annotation and verification, we generate the classification hypothesis of the selected images using a conditional random field (CRF) framework, which combines the cues from an online learned classifier and pairwise similarities of unlabeled images. Experimental results demonstrated the effectiveness of the method.

Keywords: Image classification · Online learning · Active learning

1 Introduction

With the rapid development of portable camera and smart phone, it is common that a person can collect thousands of live photos. To ease the searching and management of these images, a classification tool is required to categorize them in accord with users' preferences. Though there are many image classification methods, they mainly focus on generating a classifier for automatic prediction based on a predefined taxonomy [2,5,11,16]. As no learning is perfect, the prediction generated by these classifiers cannot be always reliable. Another challenging problem is that different people usually have different taxonomies. The offline training mode employed by most existing methods cannot be applicable to these personalized applications, since it is impractical to pre-label large images specially to train a customized classifier. Therefore, it demands novel ways to classify a given image collection flexibly in a user-adaptive way.

To address this issue, an effective way is human-machine collaboration [6,7]. These methods classify the given collection group by group through interleaving automatic classification, manual refinement and incremental training iteratively.

© Springer International Publishing AG 2018
K. Schoeffmann et al. (Eds.): MMM 2018, Part I, LNCS 10704, pp. 291–304, 2018.
https://doi.org/10.1007/978-3-319-73603-7_24

Thus, all parts of image classification pipelines are integrated into a cohesive framework, from image collection and annotation to classifier learning and inference. By putting human in the loop, every prediction of the classifier is explicitly confirmed or refined by the user to ensure the accuracy, and the classifier is allowed to capture the user's intent of categorization gradually along the iterative process. However, since the training images are limited in the early stage, learning a reliable classifier is usually a long-term process. This increases a heavy effort from the user, who has to fix many incorrect predictions of the classifier during manual refinement. To solve this problem, our idea is to introduce active learning [10] to select more valuable images for human operation in the early iterations. We expect to expedite the learning of the classifier by training these images first, and the classifier can then make more accurate predictions on the unclassified images to reduce the user effort.

In this paper, we develop an interactive image classification tool that utilizes active learning to maximize the interactive classification efficiency. Existing image categorization methods based on active learning [8, 15, 19] usually ask the user to label the image one by one, and their goal is to tune the classifier with the highest accuracy in the fewest labeled images. Different from these methods, we classify the images group by group, and focus on the end-goal of generating the accurate classification of all the data in the least amount of time. Our active classification system provides two types of manual tasks: annotation and verification. The annotation asks the user to label the images one by one with any tag, while the verification allows the user to confirm the predictions and indicate the outliers among the results. By alternating annotation and verification, the given image collection can be fast and accurately classified as an iterative manner.

To maximize the classification efficiency, a vital problem is to select which images to be annotated or verified for the current iteration. To solve it, we propose an active learning algorithm that formulates it as a unified combination optimization problem. We define the objective function as the ratio between the number of classified images and the total time spent by the user. The expected value of the function is measured by estimating the cost of each manual operation, such as annotating a certain image, or selecting the outlier. The optimal annotation or verification set is therefore iteratively constructed by maximizing the expected efficiency for each iteration. The selected images are then shown to the user and waits for interactive annotation or verification.

After obtaining the user feedback, a classifier is learned by soft confidence-weighted learning method incrementally [18] as new classified images are produced. The classifier can quickly infer the likelihood that any image belongs to each object category. When classifying the unclassified images, a more precise prediction can be generated by jointly exploiting the learned classifier and the pairwise similarity between the images. This is achieved by optimizing a conditional random field over a k-nearest neighbor graph of all the unclassified images in the input collection.

We evaluate our system on several public image repositories across multiple users, and compare our method to other interactive image classification methods.

The result shows that it can classify the collection faster than state-of-the-art approach. The experiment of user study shows that our tool provides a flexible way for the novice users to classify large image collection freely with very light user supervision.

Contribution. Our work builds on the existing body of research on image classification in the following ways: first, we develop a novel interactive system for efficient and accurate classification of large image collections. This is achieved by combining active learning, online learning and user assistance into a unique framework. Second, we propose an explicit classification efficiency model for incremental multi-class classification, which is optimized by dynamic image selection for manual annotation and verification. Third, we design a classification prediction algorithm that exploits the classifier and the pairwise distance between the images, which improves the reliability of the automatic prediction significantly.

2   Overview

Our active classification framework produces free and accurate per-image labels of image collection while minimizing the user effort. It starts without any pre-labeled sample or pre-trained classifier. The input to our system is an unlabeled image set. The output is several disjoint groups of images labeled by the corresponding semantic tags. Figure 1 illustrates the overall architecture of our system.

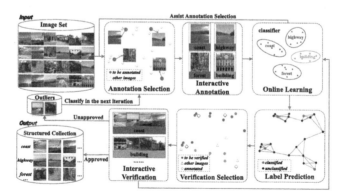

Fig. 1. The framework of our method.

Our approach iteratively alternates between annotation and verification until all the images are classified. The annotation aims to label the images that are vital to improve the classifier, while the verification provides a much cheaper way for classifying large image collection. At each iteration we address four problems: choosing the images to be annotated or verified, interactive annotation or verification, updating the classifier by the new classified images and predicting the labels of the remaining images.

Annotation/verification selection. The key new aspect of our system is that it dynamically chooses the images for each human task with the goal of maximizing the classification efficiency. To enable the dynamic selection, we define a unified objective function as the ratio between the classified images and expended human time. Since the labels of images are not known in advance, measuring the value of the function is non-trivial. Thus, the system only obtains the approximate efficiency measurement according to the prediction of the classifier. The active selection can then be performed by an optimal subset searching process to maximize the expected efficiency. This image selection step is performed twice in each iteration: first to choose which images to be annotated, and second, after interactive annotation, online learning and label prediction, to select which images to be verified.

Interactive annotation/verification. To obtain human input, we design two intuitive interfaces for each task respectively. For the annotation task, the selected images are shown as a list and labeled one by one. Our system also predicts several possible labels for each image to assist human task, and the users can select the required label if the correct label appears in the list. As shown in Fig. 2(a), the users can simply confirm, select among the suggestion list, or type the label according to the requirement. For the verification task, the selected images are grouped according to their predicted categories for manual confirmation. The users are asked to indicate the outliers in each group, and all the outliers can be classified in the subsequent sessions. In Fig. 2(b), the highlighted images are the outliers indicated by the users, and other images are positively confirmed without any operation.

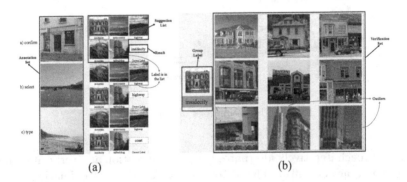

(a)   (b)

Fig. 2. User interface. (a) annotation interface; (b) verification interface.

Online learning. To fit our progressive classification process, our system uses soft confidence-weighted learning to train and update the classifier incrementally. This allows our system to evolve to novel classes and training data without retraining the classifier from scratch. The training phase starts after some new classified images are generated from the interactive annotation/verification. To avoid catastrophic forgetting in online learning, we randomly sample some previously classified images and combine them into the current batch of training data.

Label Prediction. When making classification hypothesis, we predict the labels of all the unlabeled images over a k-nearest neighbor graph. The inference leverages the prediction of the classifier and the image-to-image similarity jointly to generate a consolidated classification. This novel combination is made possible with efficient CRF formulation where the nodes are all the unclassified images. Our CRF data term is defined based on the output of the classifier, and the pairwise term is derived from the similarity between the images of the collection.

3 Annotation and Verification Selection

To maximize the classification efficiency, we develop an effective algorithm for selecting images to be annotated or verified in each iteration. Our selection method is inspired with recent 3D region annotation method [21]. However, their approach annotates only one class of region at one time, and their selection strategy is mainly applicable to the binary classification problem. In contrast, we classify multiple categories of images simultaneously by extending it for multiclass setting. Similar to their method, we measure the efficiency as the ratio between the classified images N^m and time investment T^m at the end of the mth iteration. As the exact value of N^m and T^m cannot be determined before human input is obtained, N^m and T^m are treated as random variables with respect to annotation and verification sets A^m, V^m. Thus, the probabilistic efficiency model is defined as $E^m(A^m, V^m) = N^m(A^m, V^m)/T^m(A^m, V^m)$. Based on this utility function, we propose an effective optimization framework to select the annotation and verification set. In this section, we first introduce probabilistic efficiency model, then describe the optimal annotation and verification selection successively.

3.1 Probabilistic Efficiency Model

As all variables at the previous iteration are known, we only need to measure the expected increased value at mth iteration. To measure the expected N^m, we should compute the expected number of new classified images from the annotation and verification respectively. For the annotation, the number of new classified images is obviously the size of the annotation set. For the verification, the number of images relies on the probability of the user executing positive confirmation. Thus, the expected N^m is

$$N^m = N^{m-1} + |A^m| + \sum_{i=1}^{|V^m|} p_i^p \tag{1}$$

Where, p_i^p is the probability of the user positively confirming the ith image in V^m. The expected T^m is measured by adding the expected time costs of interactively finishing annotation and verification tasks:

$$T^m = T^{m-1} + \sum_{i=1}^{|A^m|} \tau_i^A + \sum_{i=1}^{|V^m|} \tau_i^V \tag{2}$$

Where, τ_i^A and τ_i^V are the expected time costs of annotating and verifying the ith image in A^m and V^m respectively.

To compute τ_i^A and τ_i^V, we simulate the time cost of every human operation, and then compute the weighted average according to the probability of the user executing each operation. Given the image to be annotated, there are three optional operations: confirming, selecting or typing the label. For the verification task, the user can confirm the image or indicate it as the outlier. Thus, the expected cost τ_i^A and τ_i^V are

$$\begin{aligned} \tau_i^A &= p_i^c \tau_i^c + p_i^s \tau_i^s + (1 - p_i^c - p_i^s)\tau_i^t \\ \tau_i^V &= p_i^p \tau_i^p + (1 - p_i^p)\tau_i^n \end{aligned} \tag{3}$$

Where, $\tau_i^c = 1.5\,\text{s}$, $\tau_i^s = 4.0\,\text{s}$ and $\tau_i^t = 5.0\,\text{s}$ are the times required to confirm the top label, select the other label from the suggestion list, and type a label for the ith image x_i of A^m respectively. $\tau_i^p = 0.4\,\text{s}$ and $\tau_i^n = 1.2\,\text{s}$ are the times required to positively confirm the ith image and negatively reject the one in the V^m respectively. All the times are average values estimated through user study. Besides, p_i^c and p_i^s are the probabilities of the user executing the label confirmation and selection respectively.

Our remaining challenge is to compute all the probabilities p_i^c, p_i^s and p_i^p. This depends on the output of the classifier. Given an image x_i, the classifier outputs the probability of the image belonging to each category, which is represented by a sorted probability distribution vector $c_i = \{c_{i1}, c_{i2}, ..., c_{il}\}(c_{i1} \geq c_{i2} \geq ... \geq c_{il})$. As the image x_i might belong to a new category, we cannot directly use c_i to estimate these three probabilities. Accordingly, we introduce novelty detection to predict whether the image belongs to a new category (as described in Sect. 3.2), and the probability of the ith image belonging to a new category is denoted by c_i^{novel}. Thus, p_i^c, p_i^s and p_i^p are

$$\begin{aligned} p_i^c &= (1 - c_i^{novel})c_{i1} \\ p_i^s &= (1 - c_i^{novel}) \sum_{j=2}^{NL} c_{ij} \\ p_i^p &= c_{i1} \end{aligned} \tag{4}$$

Where, NL is the length of the suggestion list (in our system, $NL = 5$). When computing p_i^p, we do not introduce the novelty probability. The reason is that the verification tends to select the images from the known categories while the annotation tends to choose the novel ones.

3.2 Annotation Selection

During one iteration, the classifier changes due to the incremental training by the labeled annotation set. To distinguish the two states, we indicate the initial classifier as C_{pre} and the updated classifier as C_{post}. This variation brings a challenging problem when selecting the annotation set, since computing N^m and T^m requires to know the exact classifier C_{post} before the labeling result of the annotation set is determined. To solve it, we perform a pseudo-labeling algorithm on A^m and update the classifier C_{pre} by the pseudo-labeled A^m. A virtual classifier $\hat{C}_{post}$ is then produced to realize the approximate evaluation of N^m and T^m.

Objective computation by pseudo-labeling A^m. Pseudo-labeling of unlabeled data is usually assigned by picking up the class which has the maximum predicted probability [13]. This strategy cannot be applicable to our system, since it is common that the unlabeled images belongs to an unknown category of the classifier during our iterative process. To solve it, we realize pseudo-labeling by combining the classifier and novelty detection. Novelty detection is a binary decision task to determine for each image a_i^m in A^m whether it belongs to the known categories or not. If the image a_i^m is judged to belong to a novel category, we label it by a stochastic new tag. Otherwise, we annotate it by the label which has the largest predicted probability of the classifier.

To realize novelty detection, we implement and extend the recent method proposed by Vinokurov and Weinshall [17]. It lies the training of an ensemble of classifiers, each trained to discriminate known from novel classes based on some partition of the training data into presumed-known and presumed-novel classes. However, the previous method judges the novelty only by the ambiguity of the classifier's prediction, which might not be very reliable. Accordingly, we increase another frequently-used criteria [1]: checking whether the distance between the sample and the known class is large enough. To compute the two cues of one unlabeled image, we search its nearest labeled image and use their distance as distance criteria, and compute the ratio between the second best and the best probability distribution in the classifier's output as ambiguity criteria.

Based on the novelty detection and the classifier, we realize the pseudo-labeling of A^m to update the classifier C_{pre} to $\hat{C}_{post}$ by online learning (Sect. 4). We can then use the virtual classifier $\hat{C}_{post}$ to compute the optimal verification set as described in Sect. 3.3. Therefore, annotation set selection can be performed by generating several candidate sets and selecting the one with the best efficiency.

Selecting Annotation Set. The set A^m is selected by maximizing the efficiency: $A^m = \arg\max_A E^m(A, V^m)$. At each iteration, we choose a fixed number of images for annotation ($|A^m| = 0.005N$). Obviously, this is an optimal sub-set selection problem, which is NP-Hard. To make it tractable, we first sample the the most representative images according to the clustering of the unlabeled images. This makes a much limited search set D (in our system, $|D| = 2|A^m|$). Then, having constructed D, we perform a beam search strategy to search the best solution by evaluating $E^m(A^m, V^m)$.

To construct the limited set D, we first exclude the images that are likely to belong to the known class, since these images are less contributive to the predictions on unlabeled images. To realize it, we sort all the unlabeled images according to their novelty scores in ascending order and eliminate the top 10% images. A k-means clustering is then performed on the remaining images to generate $2|A^m|$ clusters. D is created by selecting the image that is nearest to the center for each cluster.

With the set D, the annotation selection is realized by beam search, which is a heuristic search technique. The basic idea is to keep b candidate solutions at each iteration as the best partial solutions seen thus far, where b is the predefined beam width (in our system, $b = |A^m|$). Let Ω_k denote the set of solutions at iteration k. Initially, every solution includes one image. To realize the initializa-tion, we compute $E^m(\{x_j\}, V^m)$ for each $x_j \in D$, sort the list $\{x_j\}$ in decreasing order of the expected efficiency, and reserve all $\{x_j\}$ that are in the top-b list to construct Ω_0. At every iteration $k > 0$, we extend every solution Ω_{k-1}^l by adding one image $\hat{x} \in D$ in a breadth-first fashion. All the extended solutions are sorted in decreasing order of their expected efficiencies, and Ω_k is created by pruning the ones that are not in the top-b list. The iterative searching terminates until the size of every solution in Ω_k reaches $|A^m|$, and the top element in Ω_k is the selected annotation set that maximizes the efficiency.

3.3 Verification Selection

Our verification selection is the same as that of active region annotation [21], which is performed by maximizing the same objective function: $V^m = \arg\max_V E^m(A^m, V)$ with a fixed constant A^m. Since our system only ben-efits from positive verification, we only choose the images that are the most reliable to be predicted by the current classifier. The classifier can be the vir-tual classifier generated by the pseudo-labeling of A^m or the true classifier after the actual annotation. To select V^m, we first sort the unlabeled images accord-ing to the probability distribution derived from CRF inference (Sect. 5), and then iteratively add images to V^m in the order until the expected efficiency $E^m(A^m, V^m)$ stops increasing.

4   Online Learning

The learning starts when the interactive annotation or verification is done. To support incremental multi-class setting naturally, we adopt a one-versus-all set-ting and maintain a set of M soft confidence-weighted (SCW) binary classifiers

$\{(\mu^i, \Sigma^i)\}_{i=1}^M$ initialized with $(\mu_0 = 0, \Sigma_0 = \mathbf{I})$. Each SCW binary classifier corresponds to a multivariate Gaussian distribution with mean vector μ^i and covariance matrix Σ^i [18]. To avoid catastrophic forgetting in online learning, we randomly sample one image per class from the previously classified images and merge them into the current batch of training set. By retraining these images, the historic information of the previous data can be preserved in the updated classifier.

After generating the training set, we use SCW to update the classifier by traversing this set in a stochastic order. Given a training sample (x_t, y_t), the algorithm updates the weighted distribution by choosing a new weight distribution closest in the KL divergence sense to satisfy the margin constraint. The problem is formulated as

$$
\begin{aligned}
(\mu_{t+1}, \Sigma_{t+1}) = \arg \min_{(\mu, \Sigma)} D_{KL}((\mu, \Sigma) \| (\mu_t, \Sigma_t)) \\
+ C l^\phi(\mu, \Sigma, x_t, y_t)
\end{aligned}
\tag{5}
$$

where $D_{KL}(\cdot \| \cdot)$ is the KL distance, and

$$
l^\phi(\mu, \Sigma, x_t, y_t) = \max\{0, \phi \sqrt{x_t^T \Sigma x_t} - y_t \mu \cdot x_t\}
\tag{6}
$$

is a loss function for penalizing the violation of the margin constraint, and the parameter C controls this trade-off between conservativeness and aggressiveness. The optimization can be solved by online passive-aggressive algorithm [18].

5   Label Prediction

In this section, we provide a detailed description of our label prediction method based on CRF framework. Our solution is to optimize a global objective that links similar images across the input collection. In this way, the labels of the unlabeled images can be jointly optimized to achieve a more satisfactory classification, compared with using the stand-alone classifier. The label space is denoted by L, which corresponds to the output of the classifier. The variable set is $\mathcal{L} = \{l_i\}$, where $l_i \in L$ is the category label of the image x_i in the collection X. The CRF objective function has the following form:

$$
\min_{\mathcal{L}} \sum_{i=1}^{|X|} \phi_i(l_i) + \sum_{(x_i, x_j) \in \mathcal{X}} \varphi_{ij}(l_i, l_j)
\tag{7}
$$

Where, $\mathcal{X}$ is a graph structure that connects each image to its 10 nearest neighbors. The unary potentials $\phi_i(l_i)$ encourages the label of each image to be similar to the prediction of the classifier:

$$
\phi_i(l_i) = -log(c_i(l_i))
\tag{8}
$$

Where, $c_i(l_i)$ is the probability distribution of the image x_i belonging to the category with label l_i, which is derived from the classifier. The pairwise potentials $\varphi_{ij}(l_i, l_j)$ penalize inconsistent predictions for similar images:

$$
\varphi_{ij}(l_i, l_j) = \mu(l_i, l_j) \alpha(x_i, x_j)
\tag{9}
$$

Where, $\mu(l_i, l_j)$ is the label compatibility term, if $l_i = l_j$, $\mu(l_i, l_j) = 0$, otherwise, $\mu(l_i, l_j) = 1$. The weight $\alpha(x_i, x_j)$ adjusts the strength of the pairwise term based on the similarity of x_i and x_j and is defined in terms of the feature distance. Objective 7 is optimized using TRW-S [9].

6   Results

In this section, we describe the experimental results and demonstrate the effectiveness and efficiency of our classification approach. The experiment environment is Intel(R) Core(TM) i5-2400 3.10 GHz with 8 GB of memory.

Dataset. The method is evaluated on four image sets: UIUC-Sports event dataset [14], MIT Scene 15 Dataset [12], Caltech 101 [4], PASCAL Visual Object Classes 2007 [3]. According to the study of previous interactive classification approach [7], we represent each image by the AlexNet architecture [11] for its discriminative ability.

The Evaluation of Annotation Selection. To compare our annotation selection, we randomly choose 2100 images from Scene15. We compare our annotation selection method to the following baseline methods: random selection (ran.) and representative sampling (rep.). To realize representative sampling, we use the method based on k-means clustering [20]. After annotating the images selected by these methods, we learn different classifiers respectively to compare their accurate rates with a uniform test set. The test set is constituted by all the unlabeled images excluding the images that are selected by the three methods. Since representative sampling requires an initial classifier, we choose the second iteration to test the improvement of the classifier, and the first iteration is performed by our selection method. The statistics show that the prediction accuracy increases from 13.8% (before training) to 18.8% (ran.), 26.8% (rep.), and 29.2% (ours) respectively, demonstrating that our active selection achieves the best performance. Besides, we investigate the distribution of the prediction confidences derived from different classifiers. Figure 3 shows our method achieves the best improvement, since the bin from 0.9–1.0 has more correct predictions and less incorrect ones than other methods. Meanwhile, we measure the computation time of the selection, which takes no more than 5 s.

Comparison to Alternative Methods. The most closely related works are interactive streaming image classification (ISIC) [7] and PicMarker [6]. To compare the efficiency, we selected the two image sets from the user studies of these two methods as the evaluation sets, which are both from Scene15. We then performed two user studies, where we recruited some participants to classify two image sets based on their own requirements respectively. After all the users completed the classification tasks, we recorded the interactive process and the invested timing. For the first user study, we asked 12 users to classify the same

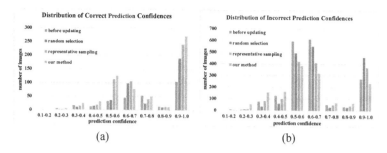

Fig. 3. The distribution of prediction confidences. A good distribution should place more correct predictions into the bin with higher confidences. (a) correct; (b) incorrect.

400 images in the user study of ISIC. Figure 4(a) shows the user effort required by the 12 users, and the average timing is 385.8 s. According to the report of [7], the average timing is 656.3 s. Thus, our method can classify the collection 1.7 times faster than ISIC. For the second user study, we asked 6 users to classify the same 538 images in the user study of PicMarker. As shown in Fig. 4(b), the timing required by these users are almost similar, and the average timing is 456.7 s. This would have taken 1.2 times longer with PicMarker, and their average timing is 561 s. Similar to these two methods, different users generate different and reasonable classification results. This proves that our method can ease the user burden and adapt to diverse demands of real users. From the user study, we also achieve the average timing of every operation in the user sessions. After statistics, we use conservatively rounded averages: $\tau_i^c = 1.5$ s, $\tau_i^s = 4.0$ s, $\tau_i^t = 5.0$ s, $\tau_i^p = 0.4$ s and $\tau_i^n = 1.2$ s. These average timings are used to estimate our utility function and simulate the invested time in the following experiment.

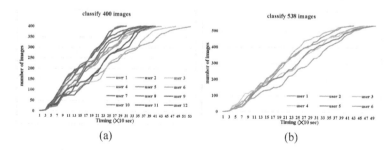

Fig. 4. This figure illustrates the number of classified images (y-axis) as people spend more time providing input (x-axis). (a) classify the images of ISIC; (b) classify the images of PicMarker.

Evaluating Design Choices. In this experiment, we compare our method with all components and alternatives with one of our choices disabled. We run the following variants: (a) no active selection: we use random selection to choose the images to be annotated. (b) no retraining: we only use the images of the current iteration as the incremental training data and do not retrain the historic data. (c) no CRF: we use the stand-alone classifier to predict the label of the unclassified image. We run our method and the variants on the four image sets. To construct the evaluation set, we randomly choose 1200 images from the these four sets respectively. We then simulate the human feedback according to the ground truth, and all the classification results are therefore 100% accuracy. To compare these methods, we estimate total timing based on the average timings from the user study. Figure 5 shows the user effort required by each method. As we can see from this evaluation, our method with all components achieves significant performance boost, while incorporating CRF plays the most significant role.

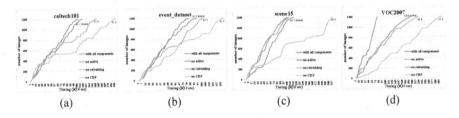

(a)   (b)   (c)   (d)

Fig. 5. This figure illustrates the number of classified images (y-axis) as people spend more time providing input (x-axis). (a) Caltech101; (b) Event dataset; (c) Scene15; (d) VOC2007.

7   Conclusion

In this paper, we propose a novel interactive system for efficient and accurate classification of large image collections. This method incorporates active learning, online learning and user intervention into a cohesive framework. Besides the introduction of this idea, our research contributions include an active learning algorithm to choose the images for annotation and verification that minimize the expected time of classifying the whole collection, and a conditional random field framework to improve the reliability of automatic classification prediction. Experimental results demonstrated the effectiveness of the proposed method. Future work will introduce more promising feature representation and extend our method for hierarchical classification.

Acknowledgment. This work is supported by the National High Technology Research and Development Program of China (2007AA01Z334), National Natural Science Foundation of China (61321491, 61272219, 61021062 and 61100110), Project (No. ZZKT2013A12) supported by Key Projects Innovation Fund of State Key Laboratory, Jiangsu Planned Projects for Postdoctoral Research Funds (1601014A).

References

1. Bodesheim, P., Freytag, A., Rodner, E., Kemmler, M., Denzler, J.: Kernel null space methods for novelty detection. In: Proceedings of the IEEE Conference on Computer Vision and Pattern Recognition, pp. 3374–3381 (2013)
2. Dosovitskiy, A., Fischer, P., Springenberg, J.T., Riedmiller, M., Brox, T.: Discriminative unsupervised feature learning with exemplar convolutional neural networks. IEEE Trans. Pattern Anal. Mach. Intell. **38**(9), 1734–1747 (2016)
3. Everingham, M., Van Gool, L., Williams, C.K.I., Winn, J., Zisserman, A.: The PASCAL Visual Object Classes Challenge 2007 (VOC 2007) Results. http://www.pascal-network.org/challenges/VOC/voc2007/workshop/index.html
4. Fei-Fei, L., Fergus, R., Perona, P.: Learning generative visual models from few training examples: an incremental bayesian approach tested on 101 object categories. Comput. Vis. Image Underst. **106**(1), 59–70 (2007)
5. He, K., Zhang, X., Ren, S., Sun, J.: Deep residual learning for image recognition. In: Proceedings of the IEEE conference on computer vision and pattern recognition, pp. 770–778 (2016)
6. Hu, J., Sun, Z., Li, B., Wang, S.: PicMarker: data-driven image categorization based on iterative clustering. In: Lai, S.-H., Lepetit, V., Nishino, K., Sato, Y. (eds.) ACCV 2016. LNCS, vol. 10114, pp. 172–187. Springer, Cham (2017). https://doi.org/10.1007/978-3-319-54190-7_11
7. Hu, J., Sun, Z., Li, B., Yang, K., Li, D.: Online user modeling for interactive streaming image classification. In: Amsaleg, L., Guðmundsson, G., Gurrin, C., Jónsson, B.Þ., Satoh, S. (eds.) MMM 2017. LNCS, vol. 10133, pp. 293–305. Springer, Cham (2017). https://doi.org/10.1007/978-3-319-51814-5_25
8. Joshi, A.J., Porikli, F., Papanikolopoulos, N.: Multi-class active learning for image classification. In: IEEE Conference on Computer Vision and Pattern Recognition, CVPR 2009, pp. 2372–2379. IEEE (2009)
9. Kolmogorov, V.: Convergent tree-reweighted message passing for energy minimization. IEEE Trans. Pattern Anal. Mach. Intell. **28**(10), 1568–1583 (2006)
10. Krishnakumar, A.: Active learning literature survey. Technical reports, University of California, Santa Cruz. 42 (2007)
11. Krizhevsky, A., Sutskever, I., Hinton, G.E.: Imagenet classification with deep convolutional neural networks. In: Advances in Neural Information Processing Systems, pp. 1097–1105 (2012)
12. Lazebnik, S., Schmid, C., Ponce, J.: Beyond bags of features: spatial pyramid matching for recognizing natural scene categories. In: 2006 IEEE Computer Society Conference on Computer Vision and Pattern Recognition, vol. 2, pp. 2169–2178. IEEE (2006)
13. Lee, D.H.: Pseudo-label: the simple and efficient semi-supervised learning method for deep neural networks. In: Workshop on Challenges in Representation Learning, ICML, vol. 3, p. 2 (2013)
14. Li, L.J., Fei-Fei, L.: What, where and who? Classifying events by scene and object recognition. In: IEEE 11th International Conference on Computer Vision, ICCV 2007, pp. 1–8. IEEE (2007)
15. Li, X., Guo, Y.: Adaptive active learning for image classification. In: Proceedings of the IEEE Conference on Computer Vision and Pattern Recognition, pp. 859–866 (2013)
16. Russakovsky, O., Deng, J., Su, H., Krause, J., Satheesh, S., Ma, S., Huang, Z., Karpathy, A., Khosla, A., Bernstein, M., et al.: Imagenet large scale visual recognition challenge. Int. J. Comput. Vis. **115**(3), 211–252 (2015)

17. Vinokurov, N., Weinshall, D.: Novelty detection in multiclass scenarios with incomplete set of class labels. arXiv preprint arXiv:1604.06242 (2016)
18. Wang, J., Zhao, P., Hoi, S.C.H.: Exact soft confidence-weighted learning. In: ICML (2012)
19. Wang, K., Zhang, D., Li, Y., Zhang, R., Lin, L.: Cost-effective active learning for deep image classification. IEEE Trans. Circuits Syst. Video Technol. (2016)
20. Xu, Z., Yu, K., Tresp, V., Xu, X., Wang, J.: Representative sampling for text classification using support vector machines. In: Sebastiani, F. (ed.) ECIR 2003. LNCS, vol. 2633, pp. 393–407. Springer, Heidelberg (2003). https://doi.org/10.1007/3-540-36618-0_28
21. Yi, L., Kim, V.G., Ceylan, D., Shen, I., Yan, M., Su, H., Lu, A., Huang, Q., Sheffer, A., Guibas, L., et al.: A scalable active framework for region annotation in 3D shape collections. ACM Trans. Graph. (TOG) **35**(6), 210 (2016)

Learning to Index in Large-Scale Datasets

Amorntip Prayoonwong, Cheng-Hsien Wang, and Chih-Yi Chiu[(✉)]

National Chiayi University, No. 300 Syuefu Rd., Chiayi City 60004, Taiwan
{s1040463,s1050468,cychiu}@mail.ncyu.edu.tw

Abstract. In this paper, we present a novel ranking scheme that learns the nearest neighbor relation embedded in the index structure. Given a query point, a direct way to rank clusters of the index structure is based on their Euclidean distances to the query from near to far. However, the data quantization loss will inevitably impair the index accuracy. To address this problem, the proposed method ranks clusters based on the nearest neighbor probabilities of clusters rather than their Euclidean distances. We present two algorithms for offline training and online indexing that leverage the deep neural networks to learn the neighborhood relation. The proposed method can replace the distance-based ranking scheme and can be integrated with other nearest neighbor search methods to boost their retrieval accuracy. Experiments on one million and one billion datasets demonstrate a promising result of the proposed ranking scheme.

Keywords: Nearest neighbor search · Deep neural networks
Nearest neighbor graph · Residual vector quantization · Index structures

1 Introduction

Searching nearest neighbors (NN) in a large-scale dataset has posed great challenges and attracted active interests recently. As an exhaustive approach is prohibitive, numerous approximate algorithms are proposed to address the tradeoff issue between search accuracy, computation efficiency, and memory occupancy.

One solution is to generate compact codes to replace the original data in NN search. In general, research on compact code generation has two main trends: data quantization and binary embedding. In data quantization, a set of centroids is generated by some clustering technique, and each data point is assigned to its nearest centroid. For binary embedding, each data point is transformed into a binary pattern through a set of hashing functions. With the compact code representation, the memory and computation load can be reduced. Furthermore, by compiling the compact codes in a codebook, we can build an index structure to accelerate NN search. Thereby we rank and traverse the codes for a given query to retrieve NN candidates; the far away reference data can be filtered out promptly.

Unfortunately, the inevitable information loss between the original data points and their representative codes will impair the index accuracy. Figure 1(a) gives an example of a 2-dimensional Euclidean space with three clusters **A**, **B**, and **C**. Let a, b, and c be the centroids of the respective clusters, and q be the query point. The Euclidean distances between the query and centroids are denoted as $\|\overline{qa}\|$, $\|\overline{qb}\|$, and $\overline{\|qc\|}$ shown

K. Schoeffmann et al. (Eds.): MMM 2018, Part I, LNCS 10704, pp. 305–316, 2018.
https://doi.org/10.1007/978-3-319-73603-7_25

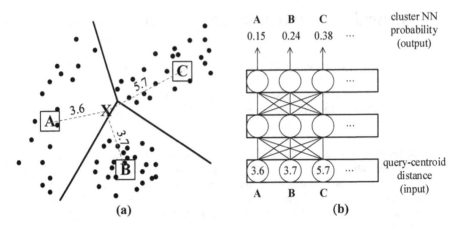

Fig. 1. (a) A 2-dimensional Euclidean space, where **A**, **B**, and **C** are the clusters, *a*, *b*, and *c* are the centroids of the respective clusters, and *q* is the query. Dash lines indicate the Euclidean distances between the query and centroids. (b) The DNN architecture used in the proposed method to learn the neighborhood relation in the local space.

with dash lines. Since $\overline{\|qa\|} < \overline{\|qb\|} < \overline{\|qc\|}$, the priority to traverse the clusters is **A** > **B** > **C**. Notice that the traversal priority does not reflect the NN distribution among clusters well. In fact, cluster **C** contains more relevant data closer to the query than the other clusters; it should be visited earlier so that more true positives can be retrieved. However, existing NN search methods mainly rely on the distance-based scheme to rank clusters. By following the conventional cluster pruning [19], cluster **C** may not be visited if we only traverse the top one or two ranked clusters, and those relevant data indexed in cluster **C** are unable to be found.

In this paper, we propose a novel method that learns the neighborhood relation embedded in the index structure to rank the cluster traversal order for any given query. The idea behind the proposed method is that the cluster ranking is determined by clusters' NN probabilities rather than their centroid distances to the query. For example in Fig. 1(a), cluster **C** has most of NNs (in a certain radius) with respect to query *q*, i.e., the highest NN probability, and therefore its traversal priority should be at the top rank. To predict of cluster NN probabilities, we leverage the deep neural networks (DNN) to train a nonlinear function of query-centroid distances, as shown in Fig. 1(b). More precisely, the query is represented by its local query-centroid distances as DNN input, and the neighborhood relation is described by the cluster NN probabilities as DNN output. Eventually the clusters are ranked based on the predicted NN probabilities and traversed to retrieve NN candidates accordingly. The contributions of the proposed method are highlighted as follows:

- Two algorithms for offline training and online indexing are developed for learning to index. They employ the DNN architecture to capture the neighborhood relation for predicting clusters' NN probabilities.

- The proposed ranking scheme is served as a first-stage (coarse) filter that can replace the distance-based ranking scheme. It can be integrated with other NN search methods to boost their retrieval accuracy.
- Experiments on one million and one billion datasets show a promising result to support our claim that the neighborhood relation can be learned and utilized to improve NN search.

The remainder of this paper is organized in the following. In Sect. 2, we discuss related work about NN search techniques. Section 3 presents the proposed learning to index method. In Sect. 4, we demonstrate the experimental results in large-scale datasets. Finally, conclusion remarks are given in Sect. 5.

2   Related Work

The conventional grid-based and tree-based index structures are widely used techniques for vector space partitioning and indexing [5, 22, 24]. Its performance is easily degenerated in high-dimensional spaces and large-scale datasets. Lejsek et al. proposed the NV-tree that is built by using the combination of data projections, and data can be fetched efficiently with a single disk read [17]. Muja and Lowe presented the priority search k-means tree algorithm that is effective for matching high-dimensional features [21]. However, it required all tree nodes loaded in memory for fast computation, and thus consume considerable amount of memory space.

Binary embedding provides the most compact data representation. Numerous binary embedding methods, including data independent (e.g., LSH [8] and kernelized LSH [16]) and data dependent (e.g., spectral hashing [27, 28], ITQ [10], k-means hashing [12], and boosted complementary hashing [18]) methods, have been proposed recently. Although binary embedding enables an efficient NN search in the Hamming space, it suffers imprecise distance computation.

Product quantization (PQ) is an efficient lossy compression technique for high-dimensional vector spaces [13]. PQ decomposes each vector into several sub-vectors and encoded by individual codebooks; the vector is represented by a concatenation of codewords. Some works like optimized PQ [9] and Cartesian k-means [23] generalize PQ by finding an optimal transformation of the dataset.

PQ-based methods try to decompose the data space into orthogonal subspaces. On the other hand, some works develop an alternative approach that approximates each vector by the sum of codewords instead of concatenation. For example, residual vector quantization (RVQ) first quantizes original vectors and then iteratively quantizes the residuals [1, 6, 25, 26]. Additive quantization is a generalized PQ without making the orthogonal subspace assumption [3]. Tree quantization constructs the coding tree and codebooks through integer programming-based optimization to minimize the quantization error [2].

Inverted file system with asymmetric distance computation (IVFADC) is a framework that is designed to handle billion-scale datasets efficiently [13]. It employs k-means for coarser quantization and then utilizes PQ for residual quantization. Asymmetric distance computation (ADC) is applied for fast Euclidean distance computation via inverted table lookup [11]. The inverted multi-index (IMI) is a multi-dimensional index table, where cell centroids are constructed by the product of codebooks [4]. A multi-sequence algorithm is employed to traverse IMI. Since a large number of cells provides very dense partitioning of the space, IMI can reach a high recall by traversing only a small fraction of the dataset. PQTable is proposed to accelerate the exhaustive PQ search by using the entries of multiple hash tables as a PQ code for indexing [20]. Multi-index voting adopts a voting mechanism to efficiently traverse across multiple hash tables and effectively collect high-quality candidates [7]. Locally optimized product quantization (LOPQ) is a modified IVFADC that uses separate local PQ codebooks for data compression [15]. As local codebooks can model the local data distribution more precisely, the accuracy of LOPQ is better than that of IVFADC.

3 Learning to Index

Suppose that we have a reference dataset of N s-dimensional real-valued vectors $D = \{d_n \in \{\mathbf{R}\}^s | n = 1, 2, \ldots, N\}$. We construct an index structure of M clusters $\{C_m | m = 1, 2, \ldots, M\}$ with a codebook $\{u_m | m = 1, 2, \ldots, M\}$ via k-means clustering. The mth cluster C_m is associated with its centroid u_m and an inverted list L_m, which contains indices of reference data indexed in the mth cluster:

$$L_m = \{n | Z(d_n) = u_m\}, \tag{1}$$

where function $Z(d_n)$ returns the nearest centroid of d_n. Given a query q, a typical way to utilize the index structure is retrieving the top-R ranked clusters whose centroids are nearest to q. Denote the top-R ranked clusters as $\{C_{m_1}, C_{m_2}, \ldots, C_{m_R}\}$, and the index subscripts are expressed by:

$$\{m_1, m_2, \ldots, m_R\} = \operatorname{argmin}_{m \in \{1, 2, \ldots, M\}} (\|q - u_m\|, R), \tag{2}$$

where function $\operatorname*{argmin}_{b}(A, k)$ returns the k arguments indexed by b of the minima in set A, $\| \cdot \|$ denotes the Euclidean distance. C_{m_r} is the rth-nearest distance cluster to q. These clusters are traversed sequentially to retrieve NN candidates from their inverted lists. The indexing process is usually served as a coarse filter and widely adopted in existing NN search methods. As we mentioned earlier, however, the quantization loss exhibited in the index structure will degrade the candidate quality.

To address this issue, we learn to model the neighborhood relation embedded in the index structure. The neighborhood relation is modeled as a nonlinear function f that maps Euclidean distances to the predicted NN distribution over clusters, where the predicted NN distribution is denoted as a list of probabilities $\{p_{C_1}, p_{C_2}, \ldots, p_{C_M}\}$, where p_{C_m} represents the predicted probability of NNs appearing in the mth cluster C_m:

$$\{p_{C_1}, p_{C_2}, \ldots, p_{C_M}\} = f(\|q - u_1\|, \|q - u_2\|, \ldots, \|q - u_M\|). \tag{3}$$

The top-R clusters are re-ranked based on their predicted NN probabilities instead of Euclidean distances:

$$\{m'_1, m'_2, \ldots, m'_R\} = \text{argmax}_{m \in \{1, 2, \ldots, M\}}(p_{C_m}, R). \tag{4}$$

$C_{m'_r}$ represents the rth-largest probability cluster to q. The re-ordered traversal sequence determined by NN probabilities can better reflect the neighborhood relation between the query and clusters, and thus improve the candidate quality.

We present two algorithms in the following subsections. The first algorithm describes the offline training process that builds a DNN model to learn the neighborhood relation for each cluster. The second algorithm states the online index and search process that employs trained DNN models to retrieve high quality NN candidates.

3.1   Training

The training dataset contains a set of T queries $Q = \{q^{(1)}, q^{(2)}, \ldots, q^{(T)}\}$. The tth query $q^{(t)}$ is associated with the ground truth of K NNs, denoted as $G^{(t)} = \{g_1^{(t)}, g_2^{(t)}, \ldots, g_K^{(t)}\}$, where $g_k^{(t)}$ is the kth NN of $q^{(t)}$. Define the similarity between $q^{(t)}$ and C_m by the inverse of their Euclidean distance:

$$x_m^{(t)} = \frac{1}{1 + \|q^{(t)} - C_m\|} \tag{5}$$

Denote the true NN probability distribution among all M clusters as $Y^{(t)} = \{y_1^{(t)}, y_2^{(t)}, \ldots, y_M^{(t)}\}$, where $y_m^{(t)}$ is defined as the number of NNs stored in C_m divided by the number of points stored in C_m:

$$y_m^{(t)} = \frac{\left| \left\{ k \middle| Z\left(g_k^{(t)}\right) = C_m, g_k^{(t)} \in G^{(t)} \right\} \right|}{|C_m|} \tag{6}$$

where $| \cdot |$ denotes the cardinality of the set. Consequently, the tth training data $\{q^{(t)}, G^{(t)}\}$ can be represented as $\left\{ \left(x_1^{(t)}, x_2^{(t)}, \ldots, x_M^{(t)}\right), \left(y_1^{(t)}, y_2^{(t)}, \ldots, y_M^{(t)}\right) \right\}$, where the first parenthesis contains the query similarities of the M clusters, and the second parenthesis contains the true NN probabilities of the M clusters.

We learn the neighborhood relation of each individual cluster. That is, each cluster has a corresponding DNN model to characterize its local property. For the mth cluster C_m, we construct its nearest neighbor graph, which is represented as an id list of L nearest clusters (including itself) [22]. Denote the nearest neighbor graph as $nng(C_m) = \{nng(C_m, 1), nng(C_m, 2), \ldots, nng(C_m, L)\}$, where $nng(C_m, l)$ is the lth nearest cluster of C_m.

Let Ω_m be the DNN model of C_m. Ω_m contains one input layer, h hidden layers, and one output layer. Each layer has L units and is regular densely-connected. The input layer receives the query similarity feature of the L nearest clusters of C_m:
$X^{(t)}_{nng(C_m)} = \left(x^{(t)}_{nng(C_m,1)}, x^{(t)}_{nng(C_m,2)}, \ldots, x^{(t)}_{nng(C_m,L)}\right)$, where $x^{(t)}_{nng(C_m,l)}$ is the similarity of cluster $C_{nng(C_m,l)}$ with respect to query $q^{(t)}$. The output layer predicts L NN probabilities corresponding to the L nearest clusters of C_m, denoted as $P^{(t)}_{nng(C_m)} = \left(p^{(t)}_{nng(C_m,1)}, p^{(t)}_{nng(C_m,2)}, \ldots, p^{(t)}_{nng(C_m,L)}\right)$. Based on the loss between the predicted NN probability distribution $P^{(t)}_{nng(C_m)}$ and the true NN probability distribution $Y^{(t)}_{nng(C_m)} = \left(y^{(t)}_{nng(C_m,1)}, y^{(t)}_{nng(C_m,2)}, \ldots, y^{(t)}_{nng(C_m,L)}\right)$, we compute the error derivative with respect to the output of each unit, which is backward propagated to each hidden layer for weight adjustment. The whole training dataset $\{q^{(t)}, G^{(t)} | t = 1, 2, \ldots, T\}$ is used to learn the DNN model of a cluster, and M DNN models are trained for M clusters in total.

The proposed method builds the local DNN model of a cluster based on its L neighboring clusters. An alternative approach is to build a global DNN model that includes all M clusters. In the global DNN model, each layer has M units. Since M is greater than L, the global DNN model becomes a wider network. It introduces more parameters to be learned in the global DNN model, and hence increases the chance of overfitting and generalization error. Besides, the wider network takes a longer time for feedforward prediction.[1] The local DNN models will be more effective in neighborhood relation learning and more efficient for NN search applications.

3.2 Indexing and Search

Given the query q, we make a soft assignment that assigns q to multiple clusters. We first calculate the Euclidean distances between the query and all centroids $\{\|q - u_m\| \, | m = 1, 2, \ldots, M\}$, and then retrieve the top-R ranked clusters $\{C_{m_1}, C_{m_2}, \ldots, C_{m_R}\}$ according to Eq. (2). For the rth ranked cluster C_{m_r}, denote its nearest neighbor graph as $nng(C_{m_r}) = \{nng(C_{m_r}, 1), nng(C_{m_r}, 2), \ldots, nng(C_{m_r}, L)\}$. We compute the list of similarities between q and the nearest clusters of C_{m_r} through Eq. (5), represented by $X_{nng(C_{m_r})} = \left(x_{nng(C_{m_r},1)}, x_{nng(C_{m_r},2)}, \ldots, x_{nng(C_{m_r},L)}\right)$. Let Ω_{m_r} be the DNN model of C_{m_r}. $X_{nng(C_{m_r})}$ is fed as the input of Ω_{m_r} to output the prediction of the NN probability distribution $P_{nng(C_{m_r})} = \left(p_{nng(C_{m_r},1)}, p_{nng(C_{m_r},2)}, \ldots, p_{nng(C_{m_r},L)}\right)$. We aggregate the predicted results from the R soft-assigned clusters to generate the final prediction for the NN probability of the mth cluster C_m:

$$p_{C_m} = \sum_{r=1}^{R} \sum_{l=1}^{L} \left\{p_{nng(C_{m_r},l)} \, | nng(C_{m_r}, l) = C_m\right\}, \tag{7}$$

---

[1] The time complexities taken in prediction for the local and global DNN models are about $O(L^2)$ and $O(M^2)$, respectively.

Consequently, the top-R clusters are re-ranked according to Eq. (4).

The re-ranked clusters are traversed sequentially to collect NN candidates from the associated inverted lists. To refine the candidate quality further, we adopt the multi-stage RVQ method [1, 6], where multiple quantizers are concatenated sequentially to approximate the quantization errors of preceding stages. Each quantizer has its corresponding codebook. Let $U^{(1)} = \left\{u_m^{(1)} | m = 1, 2, \ldots, M^{(1)}\right\}$ be the first-stage codebook of quantizer $Z^{(1)}$ that partitions the s-dimensional real-valued space into $M^{(1)}$ clusters, where $u_m^{(1)}$ is the mth centroid of $B^{(1)}$. The residual, known as the quantization error, of the reference data d_n is expressed as:

$$e_n^{(1)} = d_n - Z^{(1)}(d_n). \tag{8}$$

Based on the residual vectors $\left\{e_n^{(1)} | n = 1, 2, \ldots, N\right\}$, we apply a clustering algorithm (e.g., k-means clustering) to partition the residual space into $M^{(2)}$ subclusters to generate the second-stage quantizer $Z^{(2)}$ and its codebook $B^{(2)} = \left\{u_m^{(2)} | m = 1, 2, \ldots, M^{(2)}\right\}$. The codebooks for succeeding stages can be created in the same manner. Assume that we have S stages; the total number of subclusters created by multi-stage RVQ is therefore $\prod_{s=1}^{S} M^{(s)}$. That is, multi-stage RVQ provides $\prod_{i=1}^{S} M^{(S)}$ distinct quantization values with S codebooks. The reference data d_n is identified by the product index set $I = I_1$ $I_2 \times \ldots \times I_S$ and approximated as:

$$d_n \approx Z^{(1)}(d_n) + Z^{(2)}\left(e_n^{(1)}\right) + \cdots + Z^{(S)}\left(e_n^{(S-1)}\right). \tag{9}$$

We utilize multi-stage RVQ to extract the list of candidate subclusters for refinement. At the first stage, we retrieve the top-$R^{(1)}$ clusters by the proposed re-ranking method and Eq. (4), denoted as $C^{(1)} = \left\{C_{m_1'}^{(1)}, C_{m_2'}^{(1)}, \ldots, C_{m_{R^{(1)}}'}^{(1)}\right\}$. For $C_{m_r'}^{(1)} \in C^{(1)}$, we then find the top-$R^{(2)}$ subclusters $C^{(2)} = \left\{C_{m_1'}^{(2)}, C_{m_2'}^{(2)}, \ldots, C_{m_{R^{(2)}}'}^{(2)}\right\}$ from $B^{(2)}$, where

$$\left\{m_1', m_2', \ldots, m_{R^{(2)}}'\right\} = \operatorname*{argmax}_{m \in \{1, 2, \ldots, M^{(2)}\}} \left(\left\|q - \left(u_{m_r'}^{(1)} + u_m^{(2)}\right)\right\|, R^{(2)}\right), \tag{10}$$

where $u_m^{(2)} \in B^{(2)}$ and $u_{m_r'}^{(1)}$ is the centroid of $C_{m_r'}^{(1)}$. The process is repeated until it reaches the S-stage and finds subclusters $\tilde{C}^{(S)} = \left\{\tilde{C}_1^{(S)}, \tilde{C}_2^{(S)}, \ldots, \tilde{C}_{R^{(S)}}^{(S)}\right\}$. In total $\prod_{s=1}^{S} R^{(s)}$ subclusters are collected as the candidate subcluster set. The reference data indexed in the candidate subclusters are reconstructed according to their index sets, and asymmetric distances between the reconstructed values and query q are computed. Finally, the candidate data are sorted based on their asymmetric distances and output as NN search result in response to q.

4 Experimental Result

4.1 Dataset

We examined our proposed method on two benchmarks: SIFT-1M and SIFT-1B [14]. SIFT-1M contains one million 128-dimensional SIFT descriptors [17] and 10,000 queries, each of which provide 100 NNs (that have the smallest Euclidean distances to the query) as the ground truth, whereas SIFT-1B contains one billion SIFTs and 10,000 queries vectors, each of which provides 1,000 NNs. We applied principal component analysis (PCA) on these datasets and map to a lower-dimensional space to produce the reference datasets. Consequently the 128-dimensional SIFTs were transformed to 32-dimensional PCA-compressed vectors.

4.2 Implementation

We employed a 3-stage RVQ process to construct the index structure of the reference datasets. The codebook of each stage had 256 centroids of clusters $\left(M^{(1)} = M^{(2)} = M^{(3)} = 256\right)$, which are generated by k-means clustering. The first stage codebook was generated based on the 32-dimensional PCA-compressed vectors of SIFTs. The second and third stage codebooks were generated based on the quantization residuals of the preceding stages. In total we produced $256^3 = 16,777,216$ subclusters at the third stage for indexing reference data. Note that the average number of SIFTs indexed per subcluster in the SIFT-1M dataset was about 0.06, whereas that in the SIFT-1B was about 59.6. The data distribution of the SIFT-1M dataset was sparse; most of subclusters were empty.

At the first stage, each cluster C_m had a nearest neighbor graph containing 30 nearest clusters of C_m ($L = 30$). The DNN model Ω_m was a 3-layer architecture: $I_1 - H_2 - H_3 - O_4$, where I_1 was the input layer with 30 units representing the similarities of the nearest clusters of C_m, H_2 and H_3 were hidden layers with 30 units that were fully connected with the preceding layers, and O_4 is the output layer with 30 units corresponding to the probabilities of the nearest clusters of C_m. The hyperbolic tangent and softmax were used as the activation functions, and cross entropy was used as the loss function.

In NN search, we made a soft assignment of the query to the top-5 ranked clusters at the first stage. The 3-stage RVQ process was applied to traverse the index structure. The numbers of clusters traversed at the three stages were 5, 15, and 30, respectively $\left(R^{(1)} = 5, R^{(2)} = 15, R^{(3)} = 30\right)$; in total $5 \cdot 15 \cdot 30 = 2,250$ subclusters at the third stage are retrieved as the candidate NN set.

We implemented three methods, including proposed, baseline, and ideal, for comparison. These methods represented different cluster ranking strategies used at the first stage RVQ. The baseline method ranked clusters according to their Euclidean distances to the query. The proposed method transformed the Euclidean distances to the predicted NN probabilities of the query through the learning mechanism for cluster ranking. The ideal method was based on the actual NN probabilities of clusters. In other words, the ideal method looked the answer in advance to select the clusters that contain the most NNs of the query; the performance was regarded as the upper bound.

These methods were implemented by C++. Programs were run on a PC using Windows 10, with an Intel Core i7 Processor 3.4 GHz (only one thread was used), 256 KB L2 cache, and 64 GB memory.

4.3   Result

We first demonstrate the top-1 recall, which reflects that the correctness of the first NN in the ground truth is retrieved in response to the query. Figure 2 shows the results of the SIFT-1M and SIFT-1B datasets. The X-axis represents the number of clusters we retrieved at the first stage RVQ, whereas the Y-axis represents the top-1 recall. The proposed method exhibits an approximate accuracy to the ideal method. Through the learning mechanism, the proposed method greatly improves the baseline method that ranks clusters by Euclidean distances about 20% when 5 clusters retrieved. The error bars on curves represent 95% confidence intervals. Since there is no overlap between the baseline and proposed methods (except for the 1 retrieved cluster), it indicates the improvement is statistically significant.

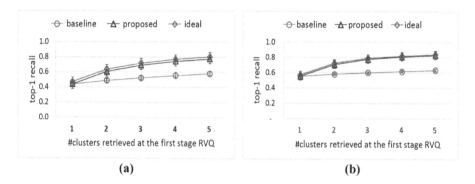

Fig. 2. Top-1 recall of (a) the SIFT-1M dataset and (b) the SIFT-1B dataset.

Figure 3 plots the precision-recall graphs. The X-axis represents the top-100 recall (the ratio of the first 100 NNs of the ground truth in the retrieved set) and top-1,000 recall (the ratio of the first 1,000 NNs of the ground truth in the retrieved set) for the SIFT-1M and SIFT-1B datasets, respectively. The Y-axis represents the precision. For the SIFT-1M dataset, since its data distribution is sparse, the search process retrieves less NN candidates than that in the SIFT-1B dataset. It thus induces a lower recall rate and a higher precision rate in the SIFT-1M dataset.

Figure 4 shows the top-1 recall vs. run time under different numbers of retrieved clusters for the proposed method. Run time represents the average time spent to response a given query. The growth is linearly proportional to the number of retrieved clusters. Note that the SIFT-1M dataset takes a longer run time than the SIFT-1B dataset. This is because there are many empty subclusters in the SIFT-1M dataset. In order to increase the recall, when an empty subcluster is traversed, we skip it and find the next nearest "non-empty" subcluster for replacement. As the SIFT-1M dataset has a

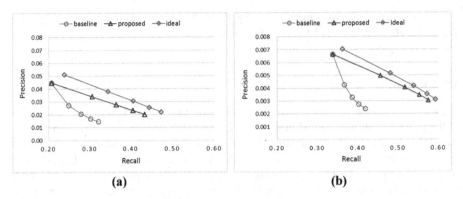

Fig. 3. The precision-recall graphs of (a) the SIFT-1M dataset and (b) the SIFT-1B dataset.

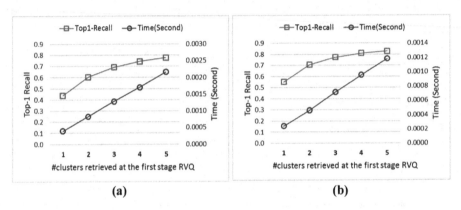

Fig. 4. Top-1 recall vs. run time for (a) the SIFT-1M dataset and (b) the SIFT-1B dataset.

sparse data distribution in the index structure, we have to spend more time to find non-empty subclusters during the search process.

5 Conclusion

In this paper, we propose a novel ranking scheme that learns the neighborhood relation embedded in the index structure. The proposed method ranks clusters based on the nearest neighbor probabilities of clusters rather than their Euclidean distances with respect to the given query. The ranking scheme leverages the DNN architecture to learn the neighborhood relation. It can replace the distance-based ranking scheme and can be integrated with other nearest neighbor search methods to boost their retrieval accuracy. Experiment results support that the proposed method is effectual to alleviate the quantization problem in NN search.

Acknowledgements. This work is supported by the Ministry of Science and Technology, Taiwan, under grant MOST 106-2221-E-415-019-MY3.

References

1. Babenko, A., Lempitsky, V.: Efficient indexing of billion-scale datasets of deep descriptors. In: Proceedings of IEEE International Conference on Computer Vision and Pattern Recognition, Las Vegas, USA, pp. 2055–2063 (2016)
2. Babenko, A., Lempitsky, V.: Tree quantization for large-scale similarity search and classification. In: Proceedings of IEEE International Conference on Computer Vision and Pattern Recognition, Massachusetts, USA, pp. 4240–4248 (2015)
3. Babenko, A., Lempitsky, V.: Additive quantization for extreme vector compression. In: Proceedings of IEEE International Conference on Computer Vision and Pattern Recognition, Ohio, USA, pp. 931–938 (2014)
4. Babenko, A., Lempitsky, V.: The inverted multi-index. In: Proceedings of IEEE International Conference on Computer Vision and Pattern Recognition, Rhode Island, USA, pp. 3069–3076 (2012)
5. Blott, S., Weber, R.: A simple vector-approximation file for similarity search in high-dimensional vector spaces (1998)
6. Chen, Y., Guan, T., Wang, C.: Approximate nearest neighbor search by residual vector quantization. Sensors **10**(12), 11259–11273 (2010)
7. Chiu, C.Y., Liou, Y.C., Prayoonwong, A.: Approximate asymmetric search for binary embedding codes. ACM Trans. Multimed. Comput. Commun. Appl. **13**(1), 3:1–3:25 (2016)
8. Datar, M., Immorlica, N., Indyk, P., Mirrokni, V.S.: Locality-sensitive hashing scheme based on p-stable distribution. In: Proceedings of Symposium on Computational Geometry, New York, USA, pp. 253–262 (2004)
9. Ge, T., He, K., Ke, Q., Sun, J.: Optimized product quantization for approximate nearest neighbor search. In: Proceedings of IEEE International Conference on Computer Vision and Pattern Recognition, Colorado, USA, pp. 2946–2953 (2011)
10. Gong, Y., Lazebnik, S.: Iterative quantization: a procrustean approach to learning binary codes. In: Proceedings of IEEE International Conference on Computer Vision and Pattern Recognition, Colorado, USA, pp. 817–824 (2011)
11. Gordo, A., Perronnin, F., Gong, Y., Lazebnik, S.: Asymmetric distances for binary embeddings. IEEE Trans. Pattern Anal. Mach. Intell. **36**(1), 33–47 (2014)
12. He, K., Wen, F., Sun, J.: K-means hashing: an affinity-preserving quantization method for learning binary compact codes. In: Proceedings of IEEE International Conference on Computer Vision and Pattern Recognition, Portland, USA (2013)
13. Jégou, H., Douze, M., Schmid, C.: Product quantization for nearest neighbor search. IEEE Trans. Pattern Anal. Mach. Intell. **33**(1), 2481–2488 (2011)
14. Jégou, H., Tavenard, R., Douze, M., Amsaleg, L.: Searching in one billion vectors: re-rank with source coding. In: Proceedings of IEEE International Conference on Acoustics, Speech and Signal Processing, Prague, Czech Republic, pp. 861–864 (2011)
15. Kalantidis, Y., Avrithis, Y.: Locally optimized product quantization for approximate nearest neighbor search. In: Proceedings of IEEE International Conference on Computer Vision and Pattern Recognition, Ohio, USA, pp. 2329–2336 (2014)
16. Kulis, B., Grauman, K.: Kernelized locality-sensitive hashing for scalable image search. In: Proceedings of IEEE International Conference on Computer Vision, Kyoto, Japan, pp. 2130–2137 (2009)

17. Lejsek, H., Jónsson, B.Þ., Amsaleg, L.: NV-Tree: nearest neighbors at the billion scale. In: Proceedings of ACM International Conference on Multimedia Retrieval, Trento, Italy (2011)
18. Liu, X., Deng, C., Mu, Y., Li, Z.: Boosting complementary hash tables for fast nearest neighbor search. In: Proceedings of AAAI Conference on Artificial Intelligence, San Francisco, USA, pp. 4183–4189 (2017)
19. Lowe, D.G.: Distinctive image features from scale-invariant keypoints. Int. J. Comput. Vis. 60(2), 91–110 (2004)
20. Matsui, Y., Yamasaki, T., Aizawa, K.: PQTable: fast exact asymmetric distance neighbor search for product quantization using hash tables. In: Proceedings of IEEE International Conference on Computer Vision, Santiago, Chile, pp. 1940–1948 (2015)
21. Muja, M., Lowe, D.G.: Scalable nearest neighbor algorithms for dimensional data. IEEE Trans. Pattern Anal. Mach. Intell. 36(11), 2227–2240 (2014)
22. Nistér, D., Stewénius, H.: Scalable recognition with a vocabulary tree. In: Proceedings of IEEE International Conference on Computer Vision and Pattern Recognition, New York, USA (2006)
23. Norouze, M., Fleet, D.: Cartesian k-means. In: Proceedings of IEEE International Conference on Computer Vision and Pattern Recognition, Portland, USA (2013)
24. Silpa-Anan, C., Hartley, R.: Optimized KD-trees for fast image descriptor matching. In: Proceedings of IEEE International Conference on Computer Vision and Pattern Recognition, Anchorage, USA (2008)
25. Wang, J., Li, S.: Query-driven iterated neighborhood graph search for large scale indexing. In: Proceedings of ACM International Conference on Multimedia, New York, USA, pp. 179–188 (2012)
26. Wei, B., Guan, T., Yu, J.: Projected residual vector quantization for ANN search. IEEE Multimed. 21(3), 41–51 (2014)
27. Weiss, Y., Torralba, A., Fergus, R.: Spectral hashing. In: Proceedings of Advances in Neural Information Processing Systems, vol. 21, pp. 1753–1760 (2009)
28. Weiss, Y., Fergus, R., Torralba, A.: Multidimensional spectral hashing. In: Fitzgibbon, A., Lazebnik, S., Perona, P., Sato, Y., Schmid, C. (eds.) ECCV 2012. LNCS, vol. 7576, pp. 340–353. Springer, Heidelberg (2012). https://doi.org/10.1007/978-3-642-33715-4_25

Light Field Foreground Matting Based on Defocus and Correspondence

Jianshe Zhou[1], Tuya Naren[1], Xianyu Chen[2,3], Yike Ma[2], Jie Liu[1(✉)], and Feng Dai[2]

[1] Beijing Advanced Innovation Center for Imaging Technology,
Capital Normal University, Beijing 100048, China
liujie@cnu.edu.cn
[2] Key Laboratory of Intelligent Information Processing of Chinese Academy
of Sciences, Institute of Computing Technology, CAS, Beijing 100190, China
[3] Graduate University of Chinese Academy of Sciences, Beijing 100190, China

Abstract. Foreground matting is an elementary image processing problem. It is challenged especially in the case of complicated background. Recently, light field camera has been employed to help improve computer vision algorithms. Light field image can record angular information of rays, which enable us to analyses the 3D scene from the aspects of defocus and correspondence. In this paper, we develop an improved light field algorithm to separate the foreground automatically and accurately. Focal stack and epipolar plane image generated from light field are used to calculate focusness cue and correspondence cue. We then use k-means to integrate all the cues of regions with an ensemble vote and get a hierarchical region boundary. Finally, markov random field is used to assign foreground labels to regions. We show that our light field matting method can overcome the camouflage color or cluttered background problem. Our algorithm is evaluated on a public light field dataset. Compared to some state-of-the-art segmentation algorithms based on two dimension images, our method outputs a more accurate result.

Keywords: Light field · Foreground matting · K-means · MRF

1 Introduction

Foreground matting separates the objects foreground from a scene view. It is usually used in image editing, visual tracking and image recognition algorithm. In this paper, we propose a matting algorithm based on light field to overcome problems in some special scenes, like complex or camouflage background. Light field image contains many redundant pixels sampled from different view, so it can be used to extract many useful assistant image, such as refocused image, 3D image and depth map.

Until now, we just have few of matting algorithm based on light field. Some make use of the refocusing features [4], while others use correspondence in multi-view [5]. Inspired by [21], we use both these two cues to assistant segmentation. We know that refocused image gets focusness precisely, while correspondence excels at estimating regions with complex texture and noise. Therefore, utilizing these two features we may

© Springer International Publishing AG 2018
K. Schoeffmann et al. (Eds.): MMM 2018, Part I, LNCS 10704, pp. 317–328, 2018.
https://doi.org/10.1007/978-3-319-73603-7_26

promote the segmentation precision in the complex and ambiguous scene. Besides we use k-means to classify the image regions and then generate a hierarchical region boundary by borrowing the idea from ensemble method. Based on the classification result, we can calculate the region distance that fit in the markov random field (MRF) and finally get the matting result.

We evaluate our algorithm on a public light field dataset, Light Field Saliency Dataset (LFSD). Most images in this dataset have separable objects and are suitable for foreground matting. We also compare our algorithm with the state-of-the-art algorithm, and our algorithm outperform them in F-measure.

2 Related Works

2.1 Traditional Methods

There are already many existing algorithms that solve the 2D matting problem. They consider color, texture or focusness as prior [10, 18, 20, 23]. [6] builds a Gaussian model for foreground and utilizes bayesian possibility method to choose alpha. Focusness is another useful prior to extract foreground. In this field, the early work is based on edge detection. In-focus edges are detected and linked to form a closed region using sober operation. [22] Then region-based methods arise because of their robustness and accuracy. Kim calculates fourth order moment in a local window for all pixels. Then morphological filters select seeds to initiate a region merging procedure [11]. Garf improves robustness of Kim's method by evaluating region relevance [9]. Li applies bilateral and morphological filters to saliency maps [13]. Zhang calculates fuzzy membership values for region classification [25]. There are also algorithms using active contour [16] and machine learning [14] to separate foreground. Some methods also conduct the matting technique in video sequences, like [19, 28]. [28] use three cameras to capture video of one scene in different depth of field then generate a trimap for matting estimation. In summary, the shortcoming of these two dimension algorithms is that they need user guidance or certain type images, like low depth of field images or extra image captured by multi-camera.

2.2 Light Field Algorithms

Light field camera provides more information than traditional pin-hole camera. There are some works based on light field calculating depth map or reconstructing scenes, but only a few of them are concerned about light field matting. [5] pioneered the use of light field images to solve matting problem. They built Gaussian mixture model to generate color sample sets for background and foreground respectively, and then constrain the matting loss function with non-local epipolar plane image (EPI) smoothness term. But this method only analyzes the EPI in light field and ignores the refocused feature of light field. Besides matting, [24] calculated the disparity according to the EPI, then introduced random forest to do the segmentation. [15, 26] calculate weighted average of refocused image of different depth, and then use focusness measure as an extra cue to generate saliency map. [4] extract the focusness measure and proposed a focusness distance in graph model to obtain foreground regions, avoiding complicated depth map refinement.

In this paper, we try to exploit both refocused image and EPI in the matting at the same time. k-means is introduced to generate region boundary for MRF. And finally, we use focusness, depth and region boundary in the MRF and output matting result.

3 Epipolar Plane Image and Refocused Image

Light field is analyzed mainly from two aspects, the epipolar plane image and refocused images. These two features can be easily obtained from raw light field data.

3.1 Epipolar Plane Image

Light field is represented in the form of four-dimension ray space, including two spatial dimensions (x, y) and two angular dimensions (s, t). If we sample pixels along axis (x, s) or (y, t), the image is made up of regular line patterns, as showed in Fig. 1. The slope of a line corresponds to the scene depth of a scene point. This kind of image is called epipolar plane image, aka EPI. We use a structure tensor method from [2, 8] to resolve slope of line in EPI. Structure tensor evaluates the local depth by finding the main eigenvectors of the local patch in Fourier domain.

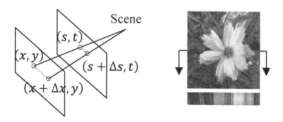

Fig. 1. Illustrations of epipolar plane image.

3.2 Refocused Image

Refocused image is the other cue that can assist matting. In the paper [17], rays in four-dimension light field can be rearranged and render low depth of field images. If we focus rays on planes at different depth, we will get a focal stack, as Fig. 2. When the

Fig. 2. Two layers from the focal stack and their corresponding focusness map.

pixel is in-focus in a certain layer, depth of the scene points equals to depth of that layer. It requires us to measure focusness of a pixel. Frequency responses of DCT and harmonic variance can well model focusness in images [12]. Since focusness is related to the focus plane of low depth-of-field image, depth that can maximize the focusness is the distance between the camera and the scene point.

4   Light Field Matting

Generally, our algorithm consists of three steps. Firstly, we generate regions to deal with the missing depth or missing focusness in the image. This simple but efficient processing method can lead to great improvement of matting result. In the second step, we extract both color and depth features for every region. The k-means cluster is implemented to generate a hierarchical region boundary. Finally, we view every region as a node in a graph model, then we solve the MRF energy model to obtain the matting result.

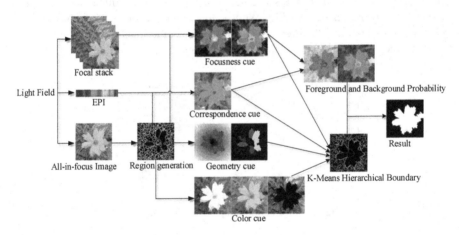

Fig. 3. Pipeline of our algorithm

4.1   Region Generation

We segment the all-in-focus image into small regions. Pixels have similar color inside regions. All the following sections are based on these regions, which will increase the robustness of the algorithm. Some scenes have a large area of unique color, like sky or wall. These areas show little disparity in different views. It will lead to the failure of detecting the focusness or calculating the slope in the EPI. In this case, it is necessary to find these areas and propagate the right focusness to them.

Initializing Regions. Small initial regions are generated by Simple Linear Iterative Clustering (SLIC) [1] on all-in-focus image. SLIC only has two parameters, i.e. number of regions and compact degree. After running SLIC on the all-in-focus image, the initial region looks near square and is compact. However, the large area of the same color is also segmented into pieces, which is not fit for the continued processing.

Merging Initial Regions. We calculate a gradient map of all-in-focus image by utilizing the gradient method in [7]. The gradient method is running in CIE Lab color space, whose color distribution is more even than that in RGB space. We then mark pixels whose gradient is below a threshold G_{th} and group these pixels by 4-connection criterion. The large area of marked pixels identifies an object. Some marked pixels do not link to any other pixels. We regard these pixels as outliers and they do not represent any objects. These pixels groups are smaller than 0.5% of the image size, and they will be filtered out while other groups are labelled with subsequent number. We denote these pixels group as region $\{S_i\}, i = 1, 2, \cdots, I$, where I is the region number. The whole flow is showed in Fig. 4.

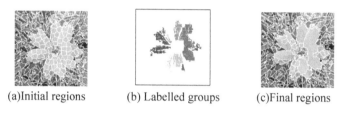

(a)Initial regions   (b) Labelled groups   (c)Final regions

Fig. 4. Illustration of region generation

4.2   Region Generation

The region arrangement can be assigned to all layer of the focal stack.

$$\forall i \in I, \forall j \in J, \quad \text{contour}(S_i) = \text{contour}\left(S_i^{(j)}\right) \tag{1}$$

Here J is the layer number of focal stack. Although the edge of defocus object is blur, the region arrangement does not affect the location of objects. So the region assignment is feasible (Fig. 3).

Based on these regions, we then extract features using focusness cues, EPI depth cue, color cues and region geometry cues. Both focusness cues and EPI depth cue are three dimensional cues, which have an implicit real-world position information. And color cues are the general useful cues. Region geometry cues includes area property and position property of regions, because we assume that the matting object is located in the center of the image and large regions usually belong to the background. When we get these features, they are then clustered in k-means, and we generate a region distance according to the cluster result.

Focusness Cue. Focusness has the three-dimension information of the scene. As we mentioned in Sect. 3.2, a pixel in different refocused image have various focusness but its focusness will reach the maximum at the depth of the real scene point. This focusness cue aims at finding the actual depth of the pixel. Since the dataset already provides the refocused image, so we use layer indexes of each refocused image to measure their depth. By calculating from two aspects, we can derive two focusness features based on regions from the layer indexes.

The first one is weighted average focusness of region,

$$C_{af}(S_i) = \frac{1}{\sum_{j=1}^{J} F\left(S_i^{(j)}\right)} \sum_{j=1}^{J} F\left(S_i^{(j)}\right) \left(\frac{J-j+1}{J}\right)^{\alpha} \qquad (2)$$

Parameter α controls the contrast of foreground and background layer index. It uses focusness as a possibility, then C_{af} is the expectation of the region depth index.

The second focusness feature is the weighted histogram focusness of region. In the first step, we count the layer index corresponding to maximum focusness for every pixel.

$$h(S_i) = \left\{ j | j = \text{argmax}_j \, F^{(j)}(x,y), (x,y) \in S_i \right\} \qquad (3)$$

The $h(S_i)$ is a histogram of maximum focusness of pixels within region S_i. It is assumed that the reliability of focusness can be improved by the statistics. Define $t(S_i, j)$ as the number of pixels that maximize on the jth layer. Then $t(S_i, j)$ satisfies $\sum_{j=1}^{J} t(S_i, j) = card(h(S_i))$ and the weighted histogram focusness of region is

$$C_{hf}(S_i) = \frac{1}{\sum_{j=1}^{J} t(S_i, j)} \sum_{j=1}^{J} t(S_i, j) \left(\frac{J-j+1}{J}\right)^{\alpha} \qquad (4)$$

Correspondence Cue. Depth obtained from EPI essentially equals to find disparity of correspondence in different views. The correspondence cue a high reliability when pixels are located at the edge of objects or pixels have a texture neighborhood. Since the reliability of the estimated depth, the certainty measure λ, is calculated, we use certainty measure to weigh the EPI depth. This part of EPI depth values are aggregated by weighted average function.

$$C_d(S_i) = \frac{1}{\sum_{(x,y) \in S_i} \lambda(x,y)} \sum_{(x,y) \in S_i} D(x,y)\lambda(x,y) \qquad (5)$$

Color Cue. Color cue is the common visual cue of all image processing algorithms. It can separate objects of different color. Those regions group pixels that have similar color. To find a color that can represent the region, we only need to average colors within regions. The color cue is

$$C_{r,g,b}(S_i) = \frac{1}{\varphi(S_i)} \sum_{(x,y) \in S_i} RGB(x,y) \qquad (6)$$

where $\varphi(S_i)$ is the pixel number of region S_i, standing for the area of region S_i.

Geometry Cue. Geometry cue includes area property and position property of regions. The area cue can prevent k-means to group a large region and some small regions into one typed. Then the large region can be classified into foreground or background individually.

$$C_a(S_i) = \varphi(S_i) \tag{7}$$

The position cue compensates for space inconsistency of k-means. k-means clusters the sample points in its feature space. Two regions that are close to each other in feature space, are not always adjacent in the image. We assume that the foreground is probably located at center of the image. So we use the relative Manhattan position to the center as the feature. It is represented by

$$C_p(S_i) = \|\boldsymbol{p}(S_i) - \boldsymbol{p}\|_2 \tag{8}$$

where $\boldsymbol{p}(S_i)$ is the average center position of region S_i and $\boldsymbol{p}$ is the center of the whole image.

4.3 Hierarchical Boundary

After calculating all region cues, we introduce k-means to cluster regions and generate a hierarchical region boundary, which measures difference between regions. For every region, we have a sample vector that is

$$\boldsymbol{x} = (C_{af}, C_{hf}, C_d, C_r, C_g, C_b, C_a, C_p). \tag{9}$$

All components of the vector are map to interval between 0 and 1 for normalization. So, the k-means runs in an eight-dimension feature space.

However, k-means is an unstable algorithm because its cluster centers initialize randomly. To overcome the above limitation and make our algorithm an automatic one, we build an ensemble model by repeatedly running the k-means in N times with different initial points for each cluster number k, where $k \in [2, K_{max}]$. The K_{max} is the max cluster number we set for k-means in repeated running. So finally, we have $N(K_{max} - 1)$ clusterred results. We aggregate all the results in the ensemble vote with equal weight, which is

$$B(S_{i1}, S_{i2}) = \sum_{k=2}^{K_{max}} \sum_{n=1}^{N} T(l_{nk}(S_{i1}) \neq l_{nk}(S_{i2})) \tag{10}$$

where K_{max} is the number of max clusters we set, N is the repeated time of k-means, n means the nth running with a given k and $l_{nk}(S_i)$ is the nth region cluster result of region S_i when the cluster number is set to k. The function $T(\cdot)$ stands for boolean function, which returns one if the inside expression is true; otherwise, zero. The boundary value $B(S_{i1}, S_{i2})$ measures difference between two regions S_{i1} and S_{i2}. It counts the number of time when regions S_{i1} and S_{i2} are in the same cluster among $N(K_{max} - 1)$ results. If we choose several thresholds to draw a binary map of $B(S_{i1}, S_{i2})$, we will get a hierarchical result, as showed in Fig. 5. We can also calculate the similar between regions as

$$B'(S_{i1}, S_{i2}) = N(K_{max} - 1) - B(S_{i1}, S_{i2}) \tag{11}$$

and we use $B'(S_{i1}, S_{i2})$ in the next section as weights between nodes.

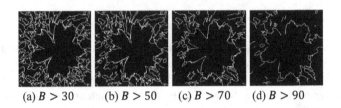

(a) $B > 30$ (b) $B > 50$ (c) $B > 70$ (d) $B > 90$

Fig. 5. For $N = 10$ and $K_{max} = 11$, the boundary can be turn into binary map with thresholds.

4.4   Foreground Matting and Optimization

Notice that k-means cannot determine whether a region belongs to foreground or background specifically. Thus, based on the segmentation result, we utilize MRF to label foreground and background. The energy function [3] is

$$E(L) = \sum_{i \in I} L_c(S_i) + \sum_{i1, i2 \in I} L_w(S_{i1}, S_{i2}) T(L(S_{i1}) \neq L(S_{i2})) \tag{12}$$

where $T(\cdot)$ stands for boolean function. As for data term L_c, it should be the cost of assigning either foreground or background labels to regions.

$$L_c(S_i) = \begin{cases} C_{af}(S_i) + C_{hf}(S_i) + C_d(S_i), & L(S_i) = 0 \\ 3 - C_{af}(S_i) - C_{hf}(S_i) - C_d(S_i), & L(S_i) = 1 \end{cases} \tag{13}$$

The smooth term $L_w(\cdot, \cdot)$ enforces the smoothness of foreground parts, which measures similarity of two regions. Besides, we introduce a parameter β to balance these two terms. The mapping is described as

$$L_w(S_{i1}, S_{i2}) = \beta B'(S_{i1}, S_{i2}) \tag{14}$$

Our goal is to minimize the global energy $E(L)$ and then we get the final foreground matting result.

5   Evaluation

5.1   Experiments

We evaluate our algorithm on the public light field dataset [15], LFSD. The dataset contains 100 pieces of light field images, including raw images files and refocused images, and it has a variety of scenes. Though originally used for saliency detection, it suits for foreground matting because most images in this dataset have one or many interested objects that are close to the camera. It is also challenging. Some foreground objects in the dataset have similar color with background or the background is cluttered. Considering not all images in the dataset are suitable to implement foreground matting, we choose 77 images, which have a foreground, among 100 pieces. In the super pixel step, we set the generated regions number to 300 and the gradient threshold $G_{th} = 1$. The window size in focusness calculation is set as 8. A large window size would slow down the focusness extraction and reduce the accuracy while a small one would not make focusness extraction failed. The parameter α in focusness cue is $\alpha = 3$. This parameter controls the contrast of the foreground and background. In the hierarchical boundary step, we set $N = 10$ and $K_{max} = 11$. This value is a trade-off because both N and K_{max} have no significant affect in result when they are large enough, but they will take lots of time if they are large.

Other matting algorithms use their default settings to process the light field dataset. These two-dimension matting algorithms are not designed for light field originally, so their input is still a low-depth-of-field image. We choose a refocused image, which is blur background and sharp foreground, as their inputs. They will perform well when the background is blur enough.

The output of our algorithm is a 0/1 label map. Thus, we use F-measure to calculate the accuracy of a single matting result, comparing the result with ground truth in the dataset. The ground truth label map is matted by human [15]. Each image chosen in the dataset are used to evaluate the algorithm. Then every image will have one F-measures score. To show performance of the algorithm on this dataset, we compute the average of all F-measures and get an overall score. A high score represents the better performance.

5.2   Results

We compare our algorithm with six different methods, include [4, 9, 11, 13, 16, 27].

As we can see from Fig. 6, our algorithm outperforms the other method in a large scale. Our result exceeds the second one 9%, which means the matting result is more

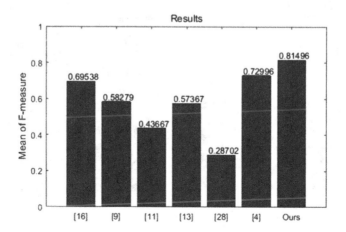

Fig. 6. Comparison of different algorithms.

accuracy in some complex scenes. In Fig. 7, the final matting result show that our algorithm extracts the foreground more accurately. Even though the foreground has small components, our algorithm still separates it from the background. Other methods do not consider large smooth regions in foreground. Some areas of foreground with one color will be mistaken for background. In addition, in scenes that the foreground is close to the camera, our algorithm can recognize it easily. But if the objects are all far away the camera and have little disparity between views, we algorithm will not get enough information for matting. And background of some images in our dataset are not blur enough, which also affect the performance of those low-depth-of-field algorithm.

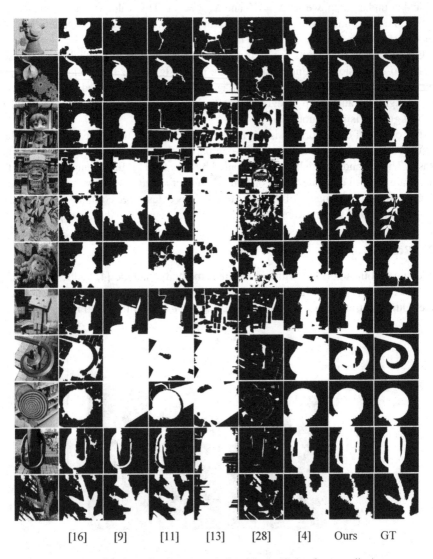

      [16]   [9]   [11]   [13]   [28]   [4]   Ours   GT

Fig. 7. Visual result of compared algorithms. (Color figure online)

Cluttered background also makes it hard to detect foreground. Since our algorithm explores the 3D information of the scene, it avoids the interference of background.

6   Conclusions

In this paper, a light field matting algorithm is proposed to separate the foreground from cluttered and camouflage scene. Both refocused image and epipolar plane image are explored to assist the algorithm. We calculate coarse depth without optimization. Depth map is not our final goal, so we pass over the depth refinement. We then use k-means to calculate a boundary between regions by repeating it and get a hierarchical region boundary. Finally, MRF is used to assign foreground labels to regions. We evaluate our algorithm evaluated on a public light field dataset. In comparison, our method outputs a more accurate result. In the future, we will apply light field camera to more computer vision problem.

Acknowledgments. This work is supported by Beijing Advanced Innovation Center for Imaging Technology (BAICIT-2016009), National Nature Science Foundation of China (61371194, 61672361, 61402440, 61771458, 61702479), Beijing Natural Science Foundation (4152012) and the Key Research Program of the Chinese Academy of Sciences, Grant NO. KFZD-SW-407.

References

1. Achanta, R., Shaji, A., Smith, K., Lucchi, A., Fua, P., Süsstrunk, S.: SLIC superpixels compared to state-of-the-art superpixel methods. IEEE Trans. Pattern Anal. Mach. Intell. **34**, 2274–2281 (2012)
2. Bigun, J., Granlund, G.H.: Optimal orientation detection of linear symmetry. In: Proceedings of the IEEE First International Conference on Computer Vision, pp. 433–438 (1987)
3. Boykov, Y., Kolmogorov, V.: An experimental comparison of min-cut/max-flow algorithms for energy minimization in vision. IEEE Trans. Pattern Anal. Mach. Intell. **26**, 1124–1137 (2004)
4. Chen, X., Dai, F., Ma, Y., Zhang, Y.: Automatic foreground segmentation using light field images. In: 2015 Visual Communications and Image Processing, VCIP 2015, pp. 1–4 (2016)
5. Cho, D., Kim, S., Tai, Y.-W.: Consistent matting for light field images. In: Fleet, D., Pajdla, T., Schiele, B., Tuytelaars, T. (eds.) ECCV 2014. LNCS, vol. 8692, pp. 90–104. Springer, Cham (2014). https://doi.org/10.1007/978-3-319-10593-2_7
6. Chuang, Y.Y., Curless, B., Salesin, D.H., Szeliski, R.: A Bayesian approach to digital matting. In: 2001 IEEE Computer Society Conference on Computer Vision and Pattern Recognition, vol 2, pp. 264–271 (2001)
7. Garcia Ugarriza, L., Saber, E., Vantaram, S.R., Amuso, V., Shaw, M., Bhaskar, R.: Automatic image segmentation by dynamic region growth and multiresolution merging. IEEE Trans. Image Process. **18**, 2275–2288 (2009)
8. Wanner, S., Goldluecke, B.: Globally consistent depth labeling of 4D light fields. In: 2012 IEEE Conference on Computer Vision Pattern Recognition, pp. 41–48 (2012)
9. Graf, F., Kriegel, H.P., Weiler, M.: Robust segmentation of relevant regions in low depth of field images. In: Proceedings - International Conference on Image Processing, ICIP, pp. 2861–2864 (2011)

10. He, K., Rhemann, C., Rother, C., Tang, X., Sun, J.: A global sampling method for alpha matting. In: CVPR 2011, pp. 2049–2056. IEEE (2011)
11. Kim, C.: Segmenting a low-depth-of-field image using morphological filters and region merging. IEEE Trans. Image Process. **14**, 1503–1511 (2005)
12. Li, F., Porikli, F.: Harmonic variance: a novel measure for in-focus segmentation. In: Proceedings of the British Machine Vision Conference 2013, pp. 33.1–33.11. British Machine Vision Association (2013)
13. Li, H., Ngan, K.N.: Unsupervised video segmentation with low depth of field. IEEE Trans. Circuits Syst. Video Technol. **17**, 1742–1751 (2007)
14. Li, H., Ngan, K.N.: Learning to extract focused objects from low DOF images. IEEE Trans. Circuits Syst. Video Technol. **21**, 1571–1580 (2011)
15. Li, N., Ye, J., Ji, Y., Ling, H., Yu, J.: Saliency detection on light field. In: 2014 IEEE Conference on Computer Vision and Pattern Recognition (CVPR), pp. 2806–2813 (2014)
16. Mei, J., Si, Y., Gao, H.: A curve evolution approach for unsupervised segmentation of images with low depth of field. IEEE Trans. Image Process. **22**, 4086–4095 (2013)
17. Ng, R., Levoy, M., Brédif, M., Duval, G., Horowitz, M., Hanrahan, P.: Light field photography with a hand-held plenoptic camera. Comput. Sci. Tech. Rep. **20**, 1–11 (2005)
18. Rhemann, C., Rother, C., Gelautz, M.: Improving color modeling for alpha matting. In: Proceedings on the British Machine Vision Conference 2008, pp. 115.1–115.10 (2008)
19. Joshi, N., Matusik, W., Avidan, S., Pfister, H., Freeman, W.T.: Exploring defocus matting. IEEE Comput. Graph. Appl. **27**, 43–52 (2007)
20. Varnousfaderani, E.S., Rajan, D.: Weighted color and texture sample selection for image matting. IEEE Trans. Image Process. **22**, 4260–4270 (2013)
21. Tao, M.W., Hadap, S., Malik, J., Ramamoorthi, R.: Depth from combining defocus and correspondence using light-field cameras. In: Proceedings of the IEEE International Conference on Computer Vision, pp. 673–680 (2013)
22. Tsai, D.-M., Wang, H.-J.: Segmenting focused objects in complex visual images Pattern Recogn. Lett. **19**, 929–940 (1998)
23. Wang, J., Cohen, M.F.: Optimized color sampling for robust matting. In: Proceedings of the IEEE Computer Society Conference on Computer Vision Pattern Recognition, pp. 1–8 (2007)
24. Wanner, S., Straehle, C., Goldluecke, B.: Globally consistent multi-label assignment on the ray space of 4D light fields. In: Proceedings of the IEEE Computer Society Conference on Computer Vision Pattern Recognition, pp. 1011–1018 (2013)
25. Zhang, C., Zhang, H.: An unsupervised approach to determination of main subject regions in images with low depth field. In: Proceedings of the 2008 IEEE 10th Workshop on Multimedia Signal Processing, MMSP 2008, pp. 650–653 (2008)
26. Zhang, J., Wang, M., Gao, J., Wang, Y., Zhang, X., Wu, X.: Saliency detection with a deeper investigation of light field. In: IJCAI International Joint Conference on Artificial Intelligence, pp. 2212–2218 (2015)
27. Zhang, K., Lu, H., Wang, Z., Zhao, Q., Duan, M.: A fuzzy segmentation of salient region of interest in low depth of field image. In: Cham, T.-J., Cai, J., Dorai, C., Rajan, D., Chua, T.-S., Chia, L.-T. (eds.) MMM 2007. LNCS, vol. 4351, pp. 782–791. Springer, Heidelberg (2006). https://doi.org/10.1007/978-3-540-69423-6_76
28. McGuire, M., Matusik, W., Pfister, H., Hughes, J.F., Durand, F.: Defocus video matting. ACM Trans. Graph. **24**, 567 (2005)

LOCO: Local Context Based Faster R-CNN for Small Traffic Sign Detection

Peng Cheng, Wu Liu$^{(\boxtimes)}$, Yifan Zhang, and Huadong Ma

Beijing Key Laboratory of Intelligent Telecommunication Software and Multimedia,
Beijing University of Posts and Telecommunications, Beijing 100876, China
{Peng_C,liuwu,bkyifanleo,mhd}@bupt.edu.cn

Abstract. Given the tremendous attention on autonomous driving technology, traffic sign detection is increasingly important to guide the driving of the vehicles. However, the existed object detection methods cannot be directly employed as they always ignore the small objects. Different from general targets, the small objects only occupy a few pixels in images, which makes it hard to extract the discriminative features from them. In this paper, we propose a LOcal COntext based Faster R-CNN (LOCO) approach for traffic sign detection, which utilizes the regional proposal network for proposal generation, and local context information surrounding proposals for classifying. More importantly, a local context layer is designed to automatically extract the discriminative information from the regions around the proposal objects. The evaluations on two public real-world datasets demonstrate that our approach can significantly outperform the state-of-the-art methods.

Keywords: Traffic sign detection · Small object · Local context
Faster R-CNN · Autonomous driving

1 Introduction

Recently, the autonomous driving technology attracts massive researches as its huge application values. Undoubtedly, traffic sign detection is an extremely important research problem in autonomous driving. Its task is to detect the traffic signs, which can be further recognized by sign recognition to guide the driving of the vehicles. Although we have witnessed several breakthroughs in the traditional field of object detection, few of them can be directly employed in the traffic sign detection [22]. In the main object detection competitions such as PASCAL VOC [4] and COCO [15], the target objects typically occupy a large proportion of image. Differently, in traffic sign detection task, the target may only occupy a very small fraction. As an typical example of autonomous driving shown in Fig. 1, the traffic signs might be only 30×15 pixels in a 1280×720 pixels image.

These differences make the traffic sign detection become a very challenging problem. Firstly, the fewer pixels are available for these small target objects, the

© Springer International Publishing AG 2018
K. Schoeffmann et al. (Eds.): MMM 2018, Part I, LNCS 10704, pp. 329–341, 2018.
https://doi.org/10.1007/978-3-319-73603-7_27

(a) The common traffic signs and lights.   (b) The traffic signs and lights in the real-world autonomous driving views.

Fig. 1. Traffic sign and traffic lights, which are all significant objects in autonomous driving usually, only occupy a small fraction of the image. Compared with the bounding box of each object fills on nearly 20% of an image in PASCAL VOC and ImageNet ILSVRC, A typical traffic-sign might be just 0.2% of the image [32].

fewer features can be extracted. Thus it is much harder to detect them. Secondly, detecting the small objects indubitably needs more computation complexity to detect more possible regions than big object. Actually, not just traffic sign detection, many detection tasks, such as object detection in aerial photos, are also obstructed by the small targets.

In existed object detection methods, the state-of-the-art detectors, such as Faster R-CNN [21] and R-FCN [3], achieve aggressive performance on many benchmark object detection datasets. They can accurately detect objects such as vehicles, persons, animals, and buildings. However, they are both failed at detecting small objects such as traffic signs. The main reasons are that in the ROI-pooling layer, it builds features from the last convolution layer, which usually has a overall stride of 16. Given a typical 64×64 pixels traffic sign ROI region in an image, its output in the last convolution layer only contains 4×4 pixels, which is insufficient to encode informative features. As the above reasons, the traffic signs detection attracts massive research in recent years [8,12,14,29,31,32]. In particular, Zhu et al. [32] collect a large-scale realistic traffic-sign benchmark dataset named Tsinghua-Tencent 100K Dataset, which covers real-world conditions, with large variations in such aspects as illuminance and weather conditions. They also propose a benchmark multi-class network for traffic sign detection on their dataset.

In this paper, we propose a local context based Faster R-CNN approach to detect the small traffic signs. When humans detect the small objects, they usually try to find them by the local context information from the surrounding areas of these small objects. For example, as shown in Fig. 1, the traffic light or sign is usually on the top of a vertical pole or suspended on a horizontal pole. Therefore, the poles become local context information of the traffic signs. Motivated by the human beings, to utilize these context information, we propose a local context layer in the original Faster R-CNN network, which can extract features from both horizontal and vertical areas surrounding small objects. Moreover, we concatenate these features and apply 1×1 convolution for dimensionality reduction. Finally, the new features are sent to R-CNN network for classification. To comprehensively evaluate the proposed approach, we compare it with many state-of-the-art methods on two large-scale benchmark datasets: Tsinghua-Tencent 100K and BDCI16-TSDAD2 dataset. They are all collected from the real-world surveillance or autonomous driving situation. The results demonstrate that our approach achieves the highest accuracy for traffic sign detection compared with state-of-the-art methods, i.e., Faster R-CNN, R-FCN, and multi-class network in [32].

The contribution of this paper can be concluded as follows:

– We propose a local context based Faster R-CNN framework to detect the small objects in the image, especially for the traffic sign detection in autonomous driving application.
– In the framework, a local context layer is designed to extract more discriminative features from the regions around the target objects.
– The evaluations on the traffic-sign detection dataset in the wild and the real-world autonomous driving dataset demonstrate that the proposed method can significantly outperform the state-of-the-art methods.

2   Related Work

2.1   Object Detectors

Due to the high accuracy of CNNs [17,18] in many computer vision and multimedia task, they were naturally applied to object detection. Among them, *OverFeat* [23] proposes a network that can determine an object's localization as well as its category by extracting features through CNN. In R-CNN [7], Girshick et al. propose a strategy for object detection in two stages: (1) object proposals are generated category-independent by *selectivesearch* [27] or *EdgeBoxes* [33], which is time consuming; (2) a deep CNN is applied to extract features for each candidate proposal generated in the first stage, then the features are sent to a Support Vector Machine (SVM) for classification. In the second stage, the proposals are calculated by CNN independently. As there are many overlaps among these proposals, this stage brings many repeated calculations. To solve this problem, the spatial pyramid pooling network (SPP-NET) is proposed in [9] to calculate a convolutional feature map for the entire image, which greatly speeds up R-CNN.

Unlike [7,9], Fast R-CNN [6] employs a *softmax* layer to replace the SVM classifier, which achieves higher accuracy by updating all network layers while training. To improve the object proposal speed, Faster R-CNN [21] proposes regional proposal networks (RPNS) to generate object proposals through convolutional feature maps. By sharing the full image convolutional features with the detection network, RPNS saves a lot of computing time. This allows Faster R-CNN to achieve a frame rate at 5 fps. Based on Faster RCNN, Dai et al. [3] propose a fully convolutional network which could achieve comparable accuracy to Faster R-CNN at faster running time. Moreover, [11] evaluate many different object detection methods, which demonstrates the existed state-of-the-art detectors cannot well detect the small objects. In addition, [5] proposed an object detection framework in Low-Resolution images via sparse representation.

2.2   Traffic Sign Detection

As traffic sign detection is a basic problem in the field of autonomous driving, various methods [8, 12–14, 20, 24, 28, 29, 31, 32] have been proposed to address this challenging task. Recently, convolutional neural network approaches have shown its aggressive performance in this task. Sermanet and LeCun [24] try to extract multi-stage features for classifier to recognize traffic signs. Wu et al. [29] detect traffic signs through CNN with fixed and learnable layers. The fixed layer can locate the borders of traffic signs, and the learnable layers can increase the accuracy of detection. Jin et al. [12] propose hinge loss for CNN training, which can benefit traffic sign detection. Zang et al. [31] employ cascaded CNNs to reduce negative samples of ROI for traffic sign recognition, which can achieve competitive results compared with conventional CNN. In particular, Zhu et al. [32] create a large traffic-sign benchmark named Tsinghua-Tencent 100K, and train end-to-end CNNs for traffic signs detection and classification. They also propose a state-of-the-art method named multi-class network on their dataset.

3   Our Approach

In this section, we will introduce the framework of the proposed method. First of all, as the state-of-the-art performance in object detection, the basic theories of Faster R-CNN and R-FCN are reviewed. Then based on these basic Region based CNN, we describe how to use the proposed LOCO to solve the challenges of detecting traffic signs which only occupy small fraction of an image.

3.1   Region Based Detectors

Faster R-CNN. Faster R-CNN is a particularly influential method in object detection. Half of the submissions to the COCO object detection server before November 2016 are reported to be based on the Faster R-CNN system. Moreover, a number of works [1, 2, 10, 16, 19, 25, 26, 30] are proposed based on Faster R-CNN. Faster R-CNN [21] consists of two stages. In the first stage, the RPNS is implemented as a fully convolutional network to predict the conditional localization and score of being an object. According to the scores, the proposals are selected among bounding boxes with respect to reference boxes (anchors) of multiple size. In the second stage, the features of the proposals generated from the first stage are cropped from the feature extractor by ROI-pooling layer. Then

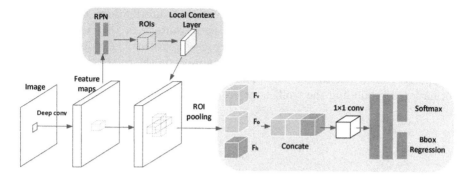

Fig. 2. Our proposed LOcal COntext based Faster R-CNN (LOCO) framework.

fully connected layers are attached to predict the class and class-specific box refinement for each proposal. In addition, the two stages have a multi-task loss, one is for bounding box regression, and the other is a softmax for classification (Fig. 2).

R-FCN. R-FCN [3] is another typical method after Faster R-CNN, which follows the two-stage object detection strategy that consists of region proposal and region classification. Compared to Faster R-CNN, R-FCN is a fully convolutional network which adopts a position-sensitive cropping method. In stage 1, the RPNS in R-FCN is the same as Faster R-CNN. In stage 2, the original ROI-pooling layer is replaced by a position-sensitive ROI-pooling layer on the top of R-FCN. The layer shepherds information from position-sensitive score maps. The score maps encode the position information by a bank of specialized convolutional layers. It is shown that the R-FCN with ResNet101 can achieve comparable accuracy to Faster R-CNN at faster running times.

Limitations. Although the Faster R-CNN and R-FCN achieve the state-of-the-art performance in general object detection, they both ignore the small targets like traffic signs. As we introduced, the small targets like traffic signs cannot be extracted enough features to be discriminated from other small objects. More worse, the existed ROI-pooling layers, which are employed to normalize the different ROI features in the two networks, make them easily ignore the small targets. For example, both VGG-16 and ResNet101 models use ROI-pooling from the "conv5" layer, which has a overall stride of 16. However, when the size of traffic sign in the original image is less than 16×16, its ROI-pooling region is less than 1 pixel in the last convolution layer even if the proposed region is correct. It is impossible to detect the object based on only one pixel.

3.2 LOCO

In order to solve the above problems, we need to extract more information from the ROI-pooling layer. As we introduced, when humans detect the small objects, they always try to find more effective local context information. Therefore, in the proposed LOCO network, we try to take advantage of the context information around traffic signs to extract more useful features. According to the observation, we can find that traffic signs are always on the top of a vertical pole or suspended on a horizontal pole. Thus, the vertical and horizontal context information surrounding the traffic signs can be utilized to localize them.

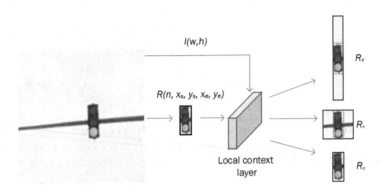

Fig. 3. The proposed local context layer can automatically learn more discriminative features from the original traffic sign.

Therefore, we add a new local context layer to capture more local context information in the original Faster R-CNN framework, which can be found in the Fig. 3. In this framework, the detection takes place in two main stages. The first stage is also a typical RPNS. For an image $I(w, h)$, the RPNS network generates many ROIs as proposal regions by the features extracted from the last convolution layer. One original ROI is presented by $R_o = (x_s, y_s, x_e, y_e)$, where (x_s, y_s) and (x_e, y_e) is the start and end points of the rectangle.

In the second stage, we add the novel local context layer, which vertically and horizontally expands the original ROIs generated from RPNS, respectively. The vertical context ROI is

$$R_v = (x_s, max(0, y_s - w_v \times (y_e - y_s)),$$
$$x_e, min(h, y_e + w_v \times (y_e - y_s))). \tag{1}$$

The horizontal context ROI is

$$R_h = (max(0, x_s - w_h \times (x_e - x_s)), y_s,$$
$$min(w, x_e + w_h \times (x_e - x_s)), y_e). \tag{2}$$

In our network, the w_v and w_h are both nearly to 1 according to the training. One local context example can be found in the Fig. 3. We can find that the R_v region automatically captures the horizontal pole which supports the traffic light.

Next, the context regions R_h, R_v and R_o are sent to the standard ROI pooling operation for cropping and pooling features from the last convolution layer (i.e., conv5 layer). Thus we can get the features F_h, F_v, and F_o through ROI pooling. Obviously, F_h, F_v and F_o have the same channel C, as they are operated on the same convolution layer. To make use of local context information, we concatenate F_h, F_v, and F_o. Thus we get a $3 \times C$ channel feature, which contains information inside and surrounds the ROI. Then a C dimension and 1×1 size convolution layer is added into the network to compress the channel size of the concatenated tensor to the original one, i.e., the same number as the channel size of the last convolution feature map. Then we send the new C channel feature into full connection layer for classifying. The detail training parameters can be found in the experiments[1].

4   Experiments

4.1   Tsinghua-Tencent 100K Dataset

We evaluate our method on the Tsinghua-Tencent 100K [32] Dataset[2]. It contains 30,000 traffic sign instances in 10,000 panoramas. Its image resolution is 2048×2048. There are 6,088 images for training and 3,055 images for testing. This dataset covers large variations in illuminance and weather conditions. In the meanwhile, different sizes of objects have been shown in this dataset, including 3,270 small object (area $\leq 32 \times 32$ pixels), 3,829 medium objects (32×32 pixels $\leq$ area $\leq 96 \times 96$ pixels), and 599 large objects (area $\geq 96 \times 96$ pixels). Thus we know that most targets are less than 96×96 pixels, which means only 0.2% of a 2048×2048 pixel image.

Zhu et al. [32] applied a traffic sign detector by modifying the OverFeat framework. Their network branches into two streams after layer 6, one is for bounding box regression and the other is an object classifier. Besides, data augmentation is applied for traffic signs, they rotated it randomly and scaled it randomly within a specific range. Furthermore, a random perspective distortion was added for traffic signs and they blended images without traffic signs in the transformed template. Benefit from this, Zhu et al. [32] achieves a distinguished performance in their Tsinghua-Tencent 100K dataset.

Implement details and results. In the experiment, to verify the effectiveness of our method in localizing traffic signs, we treat all traffic-signs as one category during training and testing. We evaluate the performance of different methods by mean Average Precision (mAP) as usual. Unlike [32], we train and test images at the scale of 1280×1280 and 1820×1820. Differently, Zhu et al. [32] take the original image of resolution 2048×2048 as input, which is time consuming for training and testing. We set $N = 2$ so that each SGD mini-batch is constructed from 2 images. Both foreground objects and background examples are selected

---

[1] Please download our method in "https://github.com/CPFLAME/LOCO".

[2] "Tsinghua-Tencent 100K dataset," http://cg.cs.tsinghua.edu.cn/traffic-sign.

from the ROIs in 2 images. As in Faster R-CNN, the rest of the mini-batch is filled with negative samples if the foreground objects are less than 128 (i.e. 50% of the ROIs in a minibatch), we set $N = 2$ to make sure there are enough positive samples for training.

In particular, as adopted by Zhu et al. [32], no data augmentation has been applied. We set $RPN_{min} = 5$ in Faster R-CNN and our proposed LOCO (the default one is 16). RPN_{min} indicates that both height and width of proposals generated by RPNS need to be greater than it. We find that Faster R-CNN and LOCO do not perform well while training and testing with the default RPN_{min}, so a smaller RPN_{min} is adapted to make sure that small object candidates would not be filtered.

In the experiment, we compare our method with the original Faster R-CNN based on VGG16 network and the detection network proposed in [32]. We set the Jaccard similarity coefficient to 0.5 as normal for evaluation. Our network and Faster R-CNN are both trained 15 epoches on the training data. The base learning rate was initialized with 0.001 at a factor of 0.1 decrease after 6 epoches.

Table 1. Comparisons of detection performance for different methods on Tsinghua-Tencent 100K Dataset.

Method	Image scale	mAP
Faster R-CNN [21]	1280 × 1280	0.748
Faster R-CNN [21]	1820 × 1820	0.858
Zhu et al. [32]	2048 × 2048	0.887
LOCO	1280 × 1280	0.857
LOCO	1820 × 1820	**0.891**

As seen in Table 1, with tuning parameters for fitting the Tsinghua-Tencent 100K Dataset, Faster R-CNN reaches 0.748 mAP by taking 1280×1280 images as input in this dataset. A higher resolution by simply increasing the scale of input images to 1820 × 1820 results in higher mAP at 0.857. The detection network proposed by Zhu et al. [32] reaches 0.887 mAP, note that data augmentation has been applied and the size of the input image is 2048 × 2048. Moreover, our proposed LOCO outperforms the highes mAP (0.891) without any data augmentation, which demonstrate that the proposed LOCO method can well utilize the local context information around the objects to extract more useful features for small object detection. Finally, our LOCO at 1820 × 1820 image scale also shows a comparable result.

4.2 Real-World Traffic Signs Detection Dataset for Autonomous Driving

To make our results more convincing, we also evaluate our method on a traffic sign detection dataset, named BDCI16-TSDAD2 dataset. The dataset is firstly introduced by UISEE[3] to support the Traffic Sign Detection for Autonomous Driving of 2016 competition[4]. In this dataset, the street images are taken by a drive recorder inside a moving vehicle. Besides, the traffic signs are usually less than 50×50 pixels in the dataset, which bring lots of challenge to locate those small object in a 1280×720 pixels frame. There are $36,000$ real-world images from different scenes, lighting, and orientations. More than 393 teams use the dataset in the competition. However, as we do not have the groundtruth of the test dataset, we cannot compare with them directly.

The Comparison of Different Methods. In the experiments, object detection accuracy is measured by mAP, which is the actual metric for object detection. We take $13,500$ images for training and $23,000$ images for testing. As [3] shows that a lower stride for the same layer brings better performance, we re-scale the images such that their shorter side is $s = 1000$ pixels (the default $s = 600$). On the re-scaled images, the stride of the last convolution layer in VGG16 nets is 16 pixels. It is ~11.5 pixels on a typical image before resizing. We set training iterations to $200,000$ so that there are about 15 epoches for training data. The learning rate is initially set to 0.001, and then decreased by a factor of 0.1 after $80,000$ iterations.

During fine-tuning, each SGD mini-batch is constructed from $N = 1$ image. We set minibatch size for RPNS training to 256 and minibatch size for box classifier training to 128. We take 50% of the ROIs from object proposals that have intersection over union (IoU) overlap with a groundtruth bounding box of at least 0.7. These ROIs comprise the examples labeled with a foreground object class. The remaining ROIs are sampled from object proposals that have a maximum IoU with groundtruth of 0, which are set as the background examples.

In our experiments, we compare our method with the original Faster R-CNN with VGG16 network and R-FCN with ResNet-101 network. Because of the limitation of GPU's memory, we do not use ResNet101 network in Faster RCNN and LOCO. Besides, we also give the multi-scale testing process. Following [10], multi-scale testing is an efficient way to improve the performance of object detection. We resize the image in each testing iteration such that the shorter side is $\{600, 800, 1000, 1200\}$ pixels. It means that we will detect an image for 4 times at different scale. Thus we can get four results from an image.

The Tables 2 and 3 show the performance of all methods with and without multi-scale testing. First of all, due to the more representative high-level features extracted by ResNet101, R-FCN can perform better than the Faster R-CNN method. However, as the proposed LOCO networks can utilize the local context information to extract more effective information, our method achieves the best performance. The examples in Fig. 4 also demonstrate the performance of LOCO. Compared with faster R-CNN and R-FCN, the LOCO not only detect more traffic signs than other methods, but also achieve higher precision.

From the results on two public datasets, all the methods perform much better in Tsinghua-Tencent 100K Dataset. The reason is that the BDCI16-TSDAD2

---

[3] "UISEE," http://www.uisee.com.
[4] "2016 CCF BDCI," http://www.wid.org.cn.

Table 2. Performance of Faster R-CNN with VGG16, R-FCN with ResNet101, and our method with VGG16 on BDCI16-TSDAD2 dataset.

Method	Feature extractor	mAP
Faster R-CNN [21]	VGG16	0.512
R-FCN [3]	ResNet-101	0.547
LOCO	**VGG16**	**0.566**

Table 3. Comparisons of detectors using multi-scale testing on BDCI16-TSDAD2 dataset.

Method	Feature extractor	mAP
Faster R-CNN [21]	VGG16	0.539
R-FCN [3]	ResNet-101	0.570
LOCO	**VGG16**	**0.591**

(a) Faster R-CNN   (b) R-FCN   (c) LOCO

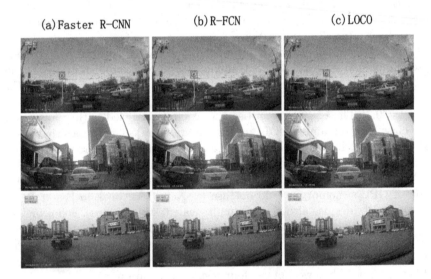

Fig. 4. Examples of traffic signs detected by different methods: (a) Faster R-CNN; (b) R-FCN; and (c) our LOCO.

dataset is more complexity. Tsinghua-Tencent 100K Dataset focuses on the scene in wild and BDCI16-TSDAD2 dataset focuses on the scene in the crowded city which has more interference factors. There are more diverse lighting conditions and targets (including traffic lights, traffic signs and etc.) in BDCI16-TSDAD2 dataset. Moreover, the traffic lights are less structured than traffic signs at different shooting angles, i.e., traffic lights look quite different from the profile and the front. It is more difficult to detect traffic lights than traffic signs. Nonetheless, our proposed LOCO shows its aggressive performance in different scenes.

5   Conclusions

This paper presents a novel local context based Faster R-CNN approach to effectively solve the problem of traffic sign detection for autonomous driving. Different from big objects such as humans, vehicle, animal and buildings, the traffic signs only contain a few pixels in the images. Therefore, it is very hard to detect them because of few discriminative features. To solve it, in the proposed framework, a local context layer is designed to automatically extract more discriminative information from the regions around the traffic signs, which can take advantage of the local context information to accurately detect the small objects. The results on two public datasets, Tsinghua-Tencent 100K dataset and real-world autonomous driving dataset, demonstrate that the proposed method can significantly outperform the state-of-the-art methods. In the future, we will try to extend the proposed framework to detect more small objects, such as objects in aerial photos. Moreover, deeper network structure will be implemented in our framework to improve the performance.

Acknowledgement. This work is partially supported by the Funds for International Cooperation and Exchange of the National Natural Science Foundation of China (No. 61720106007), the National Natural Science Foundation of China (No. 61602049), the Beijing Training Project for the Leading Talents in S&T (ljrc 201502), the NSFC-Guangdong Joint Fund (U1501254), and the Fundamental Research Funds for the Central University (No. 2016RCGD32).

References

1. Bell, S., Zitnick, C.L., Bala, K., Girshick, R.: Inside-outside net: detecting objects in context with skip pooling and recurrent neural networks. In: IEEE CVPR, pp. 2874–2883 (2016)
2. Dai, J., He, K., Sun, J.: Instance-aware semantic segmentation via multi-task network cascades. In: IEEE CVPR, pp. 3150–3158 (2016)
3. Dai, J., Li, Y., He, K., Sun, J.: R-FCN: object detection via region-based fully convolutional networks. In: NIPS, pp. 379–387 (2016)
4. Everingham, M.: The Pascal visual object classes (VOC) challenge. Int. J. Comput. Vis. **88**, 303–338 (2010)
5. Fang, W., Chen, J., Liang, C., Wang, X., Nan, Y., Hu, R.: Object detection in low-resolution image via sparse representation. In: He, X., Luo, S., Tao, D., Xu, C., Yang, J., Hasan, M.A. (eds.) MMM 2015 Part I. LNCS, vol. 8935, pp. 234–245. Springer, Cham (2015). https://doi.org/10.1007/978-3-319-14445-0_21
6. Girshick, R.: Fast R-CNN. In: IEEE ICCV, pp. 1440–1448 (2015)
7. Girshick, R., Donahue, J., Darrell, T., Malik, J.: Rich feature hierarchies for accurate object detection and semantic segmentation. In: IEEE CVPR, pp. 580–587 (2014)
8. Haloi, M.: A novel pLSA based traffic signs classification system. CoRR 1503.06643 (2015)
9. He, K., Zhang, X., Ren, S., Sun, J.: Spatial pyramid pooling in deep convolutional networks for visual recognition. IEEE Trans. Pattern Anal. Mach. Intell. **37**, 1904–1916 (2015)

10. He, K., Zhang, X., Ren, S., Sun, J.: Deep residual learning for image recognition, pp. 770–778 (2016)
11. Huang, J., Rathod, V., Sun, C., Zhu, M., Korattikara, A., Fathi, A., Fischer, I., Wojna, Z., Song, Y., Guadarrama, S., Murphy, K.: Speed/accuracy trade-offs for modern convolutional object detectors. CoRR 1611.10012 (2016)
12. Jin, J., Fu, K., Zhang, C.: Traffic sign recognition with hinge loss trained convolutional neural networks. IEEE Trans. Intell. Transp. Syst. **15**, 1991–2000 (2014)
13. Le, T.T., Tran, S.T., Mita, S., Nguyen, T.D.: Real time traffic sign detection using color and shape-based features. In: Nguyen, N.T., Le, M.T., Świątek, J. (eds.) ACIIDS 2010 Part II. LNCS (LNAI), vol. 5991, pp. 268–278. Springer, Heidelberg (2010). https://doi.org/10.1007/978-3-642-12101-2_28
14. Li, J., Liang, X., Wei, Y., Xu, T., Feng, J., Yan, S.: Perceptual generative adversarial networks for small object detection. CoRR 1706.05274 (2017)
15. Lin, T.-Y., Maire, M., Belongie, S., Hays, J., Perona, P., Ramanan, D., Dollár, P., Zitnick, C.L.: Microsoft COCO: common objects in context. In: Fleet, D., Pajdla, T., Schiele, B., Tuytelaars, T. (eds.) ECCV 2014 Part V. LNCS, vol. 8693, pp. 740–755. Springer, Cham (2014). https://doi.org/10.1007/978-3-319-10602-1_48
16. Liu, W., Anguelov, D., Erhan, D., Szegedy, C., Reed, S., Fu, C.-Y., Berg, A.C.: SSD: single shot multibox detector. In: Leibe, B., Matas, J., Sebe, N., Welling, M. (eds.) ECCV 2016 Part I. LNCS, vol. 9905, pp. 21–37. Springer, Cham (2016). https://doi.org/10.1007/978-3-319-46448-0_2
17. Liu, W., Ma, H., Qi, H., Zhao, D., Chen, Z.: Deep learning hashing for mobile visual search. EURASIP J. Image Video Process. **2017**, 17 (2017)
18. Liu, W., Mei, T., Zhang, Y., Che, C., Luo, J.: Multi-task deep visual-semantic embedding for video thumbnail selection. In: IEEE Conference on Computer Vision and Pattern Recognition, pp. 3707–3715 (2015)
19. Ma, H., Liu, W.: Progressive search paradigm for internet of things. IEEE MultiMed. (2017)
20. Ma, H., Liu, L., Zhou, A., Zhao, D.: On networking of internet of things: explorations and challenges. IEEE Internet Things J. **3**(4), 441–452 (2016)
21. Ren, S., He, K., Girshick, R.B., Sun, J.: Faster R-CNN: towards real-time object detection with region proposal networks. In: NIPS, pp. 91–99 (2015)
22. Schauerte, B., Stiefelhagen, R.: How the distribution of salient objects in images influences salient object detection. In: IEEE ICIP, pp. 74–78 (2013)
23. Sermanet, P., Eigen, D., Zhang, X., Mathieu, M., Fergus, R., LeCun, Y.: OverFeat: integrated recognition, localization and detection using convolutional networks. CoRR 1312.6229 (2013)
24. Sermanet, P., LeCun, Y.: Traffic sign recognition with multi-scale convolutional networks. In: IJCNN, pp. 2809–2813 (2011)
25. Shrivastava, A., Gupta, A.: Contextual priming and feedback for faster R-CNN. In: Leibe, B., Matas, J., Sebe, N., Welling, M. (eds.) ECCV 2016 Part I. LNCS, vol. 9905, pp. 330–348. Springer, Cham (2016). https://doi.org/10.1007/978-3-319-46448-0_20
26. Shrivastava, A., Gupta, A., Girshick, R.B.: Training region-based object detectors with online hard example mining. In: IEEE CVPR, pp. 761–769 (2016)
27. Uijlings, J.R.R., van de Sande, K.E.A., Gevers, T., Smeulders, A.W.M.: Selective search for object recognition. Int. J. Comput. Vis. **104**, 154–171 (2013)
28. Wei, T., Zhou, A., Zhang, X.: Facilitating robust 60 GHz network deployment by sensing ambient reflectors. In: 14th USENIX Symposium on Networked Systems Design and Implementation, NSDI 2017, Boston, MA, USA, 27–29 March 2017, pp. 213–226 (2017)

29. Wu, Y., Liu, Y., Li, J., Liu, H., Hu, X.: Traffic sign detection based on convolutional neural networks. In: IJCNN, pp. 1–7 (2013)
30. Zagoruyko, S., Lerer, A., Lin, T.Y., Pinheiro, P.O., Gross, S., Chintala, S., Dollér, P.: A multipath network for object detection. arXiv preprint arXiv:1604.02135 (2016)
31. Zang, D., Zhang, J., Zhang, D., Bao, M., Cheng, J., Tang, K.: Traffic sign detection based on cascaded convolutional neural networks. In: SNPD, pp. 201–206 (2016)
32. Zhu, Z., Liang, D., Zhang, S., Huang, X., Li, B., Hu, S.: Traffic-sign detection and classification in the wild. In: CVPR, pp. 2110–2118 (2016)
33. Zitnick, C.L., Dollár, P.: Edge boxes: locating object proposals from edges. In: Fleet, D., Pajdla, T., Schiele, B., Tuytelaars, T. (eds.) ECCV 2014 Part V. LNCS, vol. 8693, pp. 391–405. Springer, Cham (2014). https://doi.org/10.1007/978-3-319-10602-1_26

Multi-hypothesis-Based Error Concealment for Whole Frame Loss in HEVC

Yongfei Zhang[1(✉)] and Zhe Li[2]

[1] Beijing Key Laboratory of Digital Media, School of Computer Science
and Engineering, Beihang University, Beijing 100191, China
yfzhang@buaa.edu.cn
[2] Shandong Province Key Laboratory of Wisdom Mine Information
Technology, Shandong University of Science and Technology,
Qingdao 266590, China

Abstract. In video transmissions over wired and wireless networks, packet losses occurs frequently due to channel errors and/or network latency, which may result in the whole video frame losses and severe video quality degradation. To address this problem, many error concealment algorithms have been proposed in order to reduce the effect of channel errors. However, most of these algorithms only focus on concealment of a missing block rather than a missing frame, which is far more difficult than the former since intra-frame information are no longer available in concealing the error. In this paper, we propose a practical multi-hypothesis based error concealment algorithm to recover the whole missing frame. This algorithm first reconstructs a motion vector field for each coding tree unit in the lost video frame according to the motion vector relationship between adjacent coding unit levels, and then the lost frame is reconstructed based on the theory of multi-hypothesis using each motion vector in the reconstructed motion vector field. The experimental results show that the proposed algorithm can effectively reconstruct the lost frames and significantly improve the video quality under frame loss.

Keywords: HEVC · Error concealment · Frame loss · Multi-hypothesis

1 Introduction

With the rapid development of network and video coding technology, network video applications are widely used in the everyday life. Despite of the fast improvement in the network bandwidth and video compression efficiency, the current network transmission is still not reliable and the packet losses may occur frequently. Due to the predictive coding used in current video coding standards, such as H.264/AVC [1] and the emerging High Efficiency Video Coding (HEVC) [2], packet losses will result in error propagation and seriously affect the video quality.

To alleviate the corruption of the video frame and especially the error propagation in subsequent frames, many error concealment algorithms [3–6] have been proposed at the decoder side. However, most of them only use the adjacent blocks or frames to

© Springer International Publishing AG 2018
K. Schoeffmann et al. (Eds.): MMM 2018, Part I, LNCS 10704, pp. 342–354, 2018.
https://doi.org/10.1007/978-3-319-73603-7_28

conceal some macro-blocks missing in one frame resulted from the bit error, and they are invalid in case of packet losses because a whole frame is usually encapsulated in a single packet.

The most commonly used error concealment algorithms for the whole frame loss are Frame Copy-based Error Concealment (FCEC) [7] and Motion Compensated Error Concealment (MCEC) [7]. The former simply copies and repeats the previous decoded frame while the latter reconstructs the lost frame by motion compensation using the motion vectors (MVs) of the previous frame. However, both of these two algorithms simply use the temporal correlations between adjacent frames and only work well for motion-smooth scenes.

From the point of the lost frame reconstruction, only the temporal information can be used. That is to say, accurate prediction of the motion vector is the key to reconstruct the lost frame. For this problem, the algorithm of block-based motion vector extrapolation (BMVE) is proposed in [8], which determines the best MV of each block according to its overlapped areas with motion extrapolated macro-blocks. Similarly, [9] proposes the algorithm of pixel-based motion vector extrapolation (PMVE). And [10] proposes a hybrid motion vector extrapolation (HMVE) algorithm which merges previous two methods. These algorithms only use the motion vector information of the previous decoded frames, and they work well for the overlapped areas but they are usually not effective to the un-overlapped areas.

To make full use of the correlation information of the previous decoded frames at the decoder side, Zhao [11] builds multiple estimates of the lost frame using each probable motion vector and integrates them adaptively on the basis of the multi-hypothesis theory (MHME). This algorithm can reconstruct the lost frame better than others, but it needs multiple motion estimation processes at the decoder side, so it is very time-consuming, which prevents it from being used in the real-time practices.

To solve the above problem, this paper first explores the motion vector correlation between adjacent coding unit (CU) levels in HEVC and builds a motion vector prediction model to construct the motion vector field for the coding tree units (CTUs) of the lost frame at the decoder. Second, multiple estimates of the lost frames are restored based on the previously built motion vector prediction model and are then integrated adaptively to obtain the final concealed frame using the multi-hypothesis theory.

The rest of the paper is organized as follows. Section 2 builds a motion vector prediction model and constructs the motion vector field. In Sect. 3, multiple estimates of the lost frame are restored and the weight model of them is introduced to construct the best estimate of the lost frame. Then the experimental results are shown in Sect. 4, and finally the conclusion is drawn in Sect. 5.

2 Motion Vector Field Derivation

The reconstruction of the lost frame at the decoder side is mainly based on the temporal correlation between adjacent frames, which is represented as the motion vector. However, the information of the lost frame is not available at the decoder, which results in that the accurate motion vector can't be achieved. To solve the problem, the motion vector field including several probable motion vectors is introduced.

This section first analyze the motion vector correlation between adjacent CU levels in one CTU, and then build a practical motion vector prediction model for each probable CU using the best motion vector of the CTU. At last, the method of deriving the motion vector field is given.

2.1   Motion Vector Prediction Model

At the encoder side, a CTU may be divided into several CUs which take a size from 8×8 to 64×64 according to the rate-distortion cost minimization criterion. Generally, the divided CUs have different motion vectors in most cases. However, the difference between them is usually very small.

Figure 1 show the difference between adjacent CU levels of the sequences of *BasketBallDrill* and *RaceHorsesC*. From Fig. 1 we can see that the probability of the motion vector difference between adjacent CU levels less than 1 pixel is nearly 100% for the motion smooth sequences like *BasketballDrill* and that is also almost around 80% for the motion rich sequences like *RaceHorsesC*. And the probability increases gradually as the CU level increases. Thus, this strong correlation of motion vector between adjacent CU levels can be used for predicting the motion vector field of the current CTU.

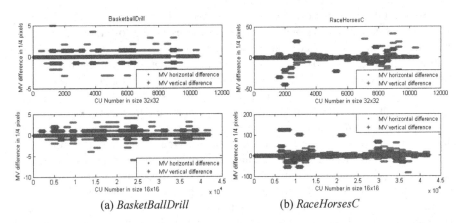

(a) *BasketBallDrill*   (b) *RaceHorsesC*

Fig. 1. MV difference between adjacent CU levels in (a) *BasketBallDrill* and (b) *RaceHorsesC*

Figure 2 shows the correlation between the mean of sub-CUs' MV and CU's MV in various CU sizes. From the figure we can see that they have a distinctive linear relationship. Based on this observation, a linear model can be built to predict the motion vector for each CU level in the CTU with the best motion vector of the CTU, as

$$MV_{pre} = \frac{a}{4}\sum_{i=1}^{4} MV_i' + b,$$ (1)

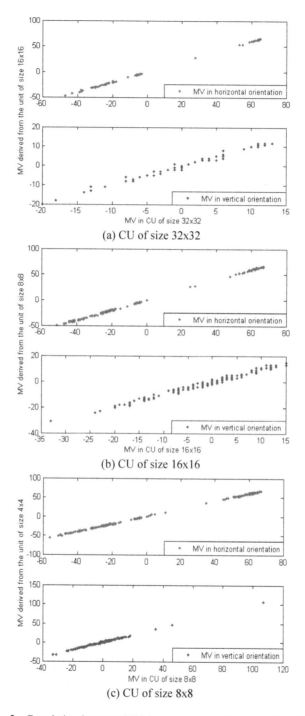

(a) CU of size 32x32

(b) CU of size 16x16

(c) CU of size 8x8

Fig. 2. Correlation between MVs' mean of sub-CUs and MV of CU.

where MV_{pre} is the predicted MV of the current CU, and MV' is the MV of sub-CU. a is the scale factor dependent on the self-correlation of the CU and b is the addictive factor as a constant. The two model parameters a and b can be estimated through curve fitting and the fitted a and b for several typical video sequences are shown in Table 1. As can be seen, the scale factor a is consistently to be around 1 while the addictive factor b is around 0. Most importantly the correlation coefficient R^2 is almost 1, which further verifies the effectiveness of the proposed motion vector prediction model in (1). So both of the model parameters a and b can be empirically set to 1 and 0, respective without losing too much prediction accuracy as shown later while saving the curve fitting process, which further reduces the computational complexity and make the model much more practical for the real-time video decoding.

Table 1. Curve fitting results for model parameter a and b

Sequences	CU sizes	Horizontal MV			Vertical MV		
		a	b	R^2	a	b	R^2
Cactus (1080p)	32 × 32	1.00	0.09	0.99	1.00	0.05	0.99
	16 × 16	1.00	0.05	1.00	1.00	0.03	0.99
	8 × 8	1.00	−0.01	1.00	1.00	0.03	0.99
BasketballDrive (1080p)	32 × 32	1.00	0.01	1.00	1.00	0.07	0.99
	16 × 16	1.00	0.00	1.00	1.00	0.04	1.00
	8 × 8	1.00	0.02	1.00	1.00	0.00	0.99
BQMall (WVGA)	32 × 32	1.00	0.13	1.00	0.98	0.07	0.96
	16 × 16	1.00	0.07	1.00	1.00	0.04	0.98
	8 × 8	1.00	0.00	1.00	1.00	0.00	0.99
BasketballDrill (WVGA)	32 × 32	1.00	0.09	1.00	1.00	0.10	0.99
	16 × 16	1.00	0.05	1.00	1.00	0.05	1.00
	8 × 8	1.00	0.00	1.00	1.00	0.01	1.00
Keiba (WQVGA)	32 × 32	1.00	0.12	1.00	0.99	0.19	0.95
	16 × 16	1.00	0.04	1.00	1.00	0.12	0.99
	8 × 8	1.00	0.01	1.00	1.00	0.00	1.00
BasketballPass (WQVGA)	32 × 32	1.00	0.09	0.94	0.92	0.04	0.79
	16 × 16	1.01	0.04	0.97	0.97	0.03	0.91
	8 × 8	0.98	0.04	0.97	0.99	0.00	0.95

2.2 Motion Vector Field Derivation

In this paper, the motion vector field (MVF) of a CTU includes four types of motion vectors corresponding to blocks of size 4 × 4, 8 × 8, 16 × 16 and 32 × 32 respectively and the motion vector on each pixel can be obtained using the HMVE algorithm [10].

As we know, the best motion vector of the CTU in the lost frame is not available. Hence, the motion vector of the CTU should be estimated before predicting the motion vector field. To get the motion vector in the lost frame conveniently, we also assume that objects move in a constant speed along a straight line in consecutive frames as the assumption in [10, 11]. If the motion vector of each 4×4 block in the lost frame was derived, the total MVF would be estimated according to the model proposed in Sect. 2. A. In this paper, the motion vector of each 4×4 block is extrapolated from the previous decoded frame referring the algorithm proposed in [10].

As depicted in Fig. 3, the B_n block in the lost frame $Frame_n$ corresponding to the B_{n-1} block in the previous frame $Frame_{n-1}$ according to the later motion vector may not place on the regular position. So in the process of deriving the motion vector using the previous frame motion information, some blocks might have more than one referenced MVs and some blocks might have no referenced MV as shown in Fig. 4.

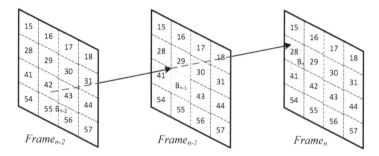

Fig. 3. Motion vector derivation in the lost frame

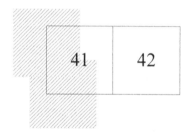

Fig. 4. Diagram of referenced MVs

From above observation, the blocks in the lost frame can be divided into two types:

Type A: blocks which are covered by at least one extrapolated block, for example the 41st block in Fig. 4.

Type B: blocks which are not covered by any of the extrapolated blocks, for example the 42nd block in Fig. 4.

For blocks of type A, we adopt the same extraction algorithm as described in [10] to extract the motion vector. Then, at motion vector selection process, motion vectors of adjacent blocks are considered to eliminate the probable blocking artifact resulted from the weak correlation between non-adjacent blocks in the previous frame. Here, we predict a motion vector using the advanced motion vector prediction (AMVP) algorithm at the HEVC encoder according to the adjacent blocks' motion vectors.

And for blocks of the type B, there is no temporal information available to be used. But we can estimate the MVs using adjacent blocks' motion vectors with AMVP because of the high correlation between adjacent areas.

After deriving the motion vector of each 4×4 block, the motion vector field of each CTU in the lost frame can be estimated using the motion vector prediction model (1).

3   Multi-hypothesis Based Error Concealment

As analyzed in [11], the recovery of the lost frame can't achieve a better performance if only using the limited motion vector information. More information of the previous frames should be applied to reconstruct the lost frame.

According to the motion vectors for various block sizes in the MVF, multiple estimated pictures for the lost frame can be constructed using the corresponding pixels in the previous frame. Then, based on the multi-hypothesis theory, the lost frame can be built using these estimated pictures according to different weights, as can be formulated as

$$\hat{f}_n(x,y) = \sum_k w^k(x,y) \cdot f_n^k(x,y),$$ (2)

where $\hat{f}_n(x,y)$ and $f_n^k(x,y)$ refer to pixels at the location of (x, y) in the reconstructed frame and the kth estimated frame respectively, and $w^k(x,y)$ is the weight which shows the reliability of the estimated pixel value $f_n^k(x,y)$ in the kth estimated frame.

Considering that the weight is responsible of trading off the devotion of each hypothesis to the reconstructed frame, it should reflect the reliability of the hypothesis. The more reliable the estimated pixel value $f_n^k(x,y)$ is, the larger its weight $w^k(x,y)$ should be. However, the current frame doesn't exist so that there is no way to obtain the accurate reliability. Hence, according to the high correlation between adjacent frames, only the information of the previous two frames can be used at the assumption of the object moving along the straight line with a constant speed.

In this paper, the reliability of a 4×4 block is computed from the sum of absolute difference (SAD) between 4×4 blocks which include the co-related pixels. The formula can be described as

$$r^k(bx, by) = \frac{1}{SAD^k(bx, by) + levels_{mvf}},$$ (3)

where

$$SAD^k(bx, by) = \sum_{0 \leq i,j \leq 4} |f_{n-2}(bx \times 4 + 2mv_x + i, by \times 4 + 2mv_y + j)$$

$$-f_{n-1}(bx \times 4 + mv_x + i, by \times + mv_y + j)|.$$ (4)

Here, $levels_{mvf}$ is the levels of the motion vector field, (bx, by) is the coordinate of the current 4×4 block, and (mv_x, mv_y) is the motion vector of the current 4×4 block. Then by normalizing the reliability, the weight for each 4×4 block can be obtained from the formula (5) as follows.

$$w^k(bx, by) = \Psi(r^k(bx, by)), \tag{5}$$

where $\Psi(\cdot)$ is the normalization factor, which makes the weight $w^k(bx, by)$ ranges from 0 to 1.

Specifically to a pixel, the weight $w^k(x, y)$ can be derived from the current 4×4 block, that is to say, the weight of each pixel in one 4×4 block is the same.

4   Experimental Results

In this section, we evaluate the performance of the proposed algorithm with comparisons to state-of-the-art algorithms in term of both subjective/objective video quality and computational complexity.

4.1   Experimental Settings

The proposed algorithm is implemented in the HEVC reference software HM16.0 [12] and performed on a PC with an Intel i3-3100M central processing unit 2.4 GHz and 2.0 GB random access memory. The experimental condition is the low delay main configuration with *IPPP* picture structure, and the intra period and the size of group of picture (GOP) defined in the HEVC is set to 25 and 1 respectively. And six recommended test sequences in the three classes (*B, C, D*) [13] are used to validate the performance of the proposed algorithm. In the experiment, the test QP value is set to 27 and 32 respectively.

To verify the performance of the proposed algorithm for the whole frame loss, four typical error concealment algorithms, including the most commonly used Frame Copy-based Error Concealment (FCEC) [7] and Motion Compensated Error Concealment (MCEC) [7], and the state-of-the-art HMVE [10] and the MHME [11] algorithms, are also implemented in HM16.0. In this experiment, one frame is dropped in each Intra frame period (similar to the group of pictures in H.264/AVC) and the dropped frames will be concealed by above algorithms.

4.2   Performance Evaluation on Subjective/Objective Video Quality

In this subsection, we evaluate the subjective/objective video quality performance of the proposed algorithm in case of P-frame losses and I-frame losses, respectively.

First, we evaluate the performance when P-frames, the 4th P frame (i.e. the 5th frame including the first I frame) in each Intra frame period more specifically, are lost. Table 2 demonstrates the objective video quality of the proposed algorithm with comparisons to the other algorithms, where the peak signal-to-noise ratio (PSNR) is used as the objective measurement. Compared to the conventional FCEC and MCEC

Table 2. Video quality comparison of comparable algorithms

Class	Sequences	QP	PSNR (dB)						Δ (dB)			
			No loss	FCEC	MCEC	HMVE	MHME	Proposed	FCEC	MCEC	HMVE	MHME
B (1080p)	ParkScene	27	37.36	24.33	25.45	26.11	26.64	26.32	1.99	0.87	0.21	−0.32
		32	34.60	24.01	25.12	25.85	26.36	26.03	2.02	0.91	0.18	−0.33
	Cactus	27	36.81	25.24	26.84	28.20	28.78	28.41	2.28	1.57	0.20	**−0.37**
		32	34.75	24.44	25.84	26.21	26.70	26.36	0.92	0.52	0.15	−0.34
C (WVGA)	PartyScene	27	34.78	22.73	23.03	24.13	24.75	24.49	1.76	1.46	0.36	−0.26
		32	31.11	21.81	22.25	22.49	23.03	22.73	0.92	0.48	0.24	−0.30
	BQMall	27	37.08	21.85	23.84	24.27	25.01	24.83	2.98	0.99	**0.56**	−0.18
		32	34.09	21.36	23.27	24.93	25.93	25.65	2.92	**2.38**	0.34	−0.28
D (WQVGA)	BasketballPass	27	38.28	25.03	26.44	27.87	28.35	28.00	2.97	1.56	0.13	−0.35
		32	35.01	24.14	25.63	25.83	26.31	25.97	1.83	0.34	0.14	−0.34
	RaceHorses	27	36.34	19.15	20.08	21.82	22.41	22.05	2.70	1.97	0.23	−0.36
		32	32.80	18.65	19.94	21.55	22.09	21.79	**3.14**	1.85	0.24	−0.30
Avg. Gain									**2.49**	**1.24**	**0.28**	**−0.31**

[7], the proposed algorithm obtains on average 2.49 dB and 1.24 dB gains on average. As compared to the HMVE algorithm [10], the proposed algorithm can achieve up to 0.56 dB and on average 0.28 dB gains. When compared with the MHME algorithm [11], the proposed algorithm results in on average 0.31 dB loss, which is however at a much lower computational complexity, as will be seen in Sect. 4.3.

Figure 5(a), (c) and (e) present the frame-wise PSNR for *Cactus*, *BQMall*, and *RaceHorses* sequences, respectively. As expected, when a P frame is lost, the decoded video quality drops dramatically. More importantly, it will influence the subsequent frames until next I frame due to the motion estimation/compensation-incurred error propagation. We can see from Fig. 5 that the proposed algorithm, together with the HMVE and MHME algorithms, can significantly improve the video quality, as compared to the FCEC and MCEC schemes.

For subjective evaluation, the error-free frame and recovered frames reconstructed by HMVE, MHME and the proposed algorithm are demonstrated in Fig. 6. As for the areas like the shadowed floor in red rectangle, our proposed algorithm and the MHME outperforms the HMVE which yields obvious distortions, while our proposed algorithm achieves the even better performance than MHME with almost no visible distortion. As for the girl's coat areas in blue ellipses, MHME achieves the best recovery results while our algorithm achieves much better results than HMVE. As for the motion-rich areas like the girl's right lower leg, all three algorithms fails to well conceal the losses. However, our proposed algorithm achieves slightly better performance than both HMVE and even MHME algorithm.

Besides P-frame lost shown above, we also evaluate the performance when I frames (except for the first I frame. Otherwise, the whole sequence will fail to decode.) are lost. Figure 5(b), (d) and (f) present the frame-wise PSNR for *Cactus*, *BQMall*, and *RaceHorses* sequences, respectively. As expected, when I frames are lost, the decoded video quality drops dramatically, much severe that when P frames are lost, as shown in Fig. 5(a), (c) and (e). Similarly, the proposed algorithm achieves slightly inferior video quality as compared to the best scheme MHME and much improved video quality as compared to the other three comparable schemes, i.e., HMVE, FCEC and MCEC.

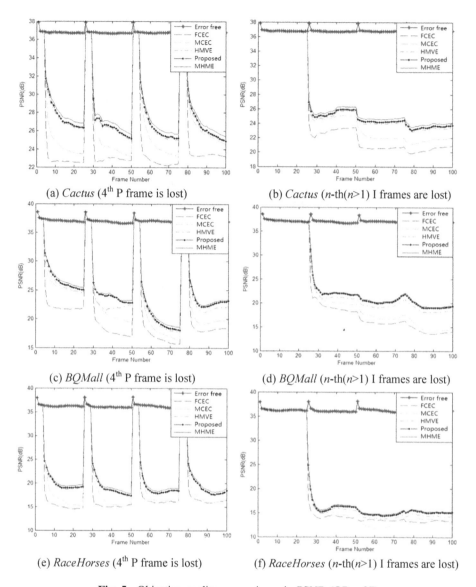

(a) *Cactus* (4th P frame is lost)   (b) *Cactus* (*n*-th(*n*>1) I frames are lost)

(c) *BQMall* (4th P frame is lost)   (d) *BQMall* (*n*-th(*n*>1) I frames are lost)

(e) *RaceHorses* (4th P frame is lost)   (f) *RaceHorses* (*n*-th(*n*>1) I frames are lost)

Fig. 5. Objective quality comparisons in PSNR (QP = 27)

4.3   Performance Evaluation on the Computational Complexity

Table 3 tabulates the computational complexity comparison of the five comparable algorithms for six sequences coded with different QPs. As expected, the FCEC and MCEC work at the least and comparable computational complexity. Since more complicated MV recovery is adopted, HMVE results in about 8.89% overhead as compared to MCEC. As our proposed scheme further constructed the motion vector field and introduces the theory of multi-hypothesis to fully use the multiple recovered

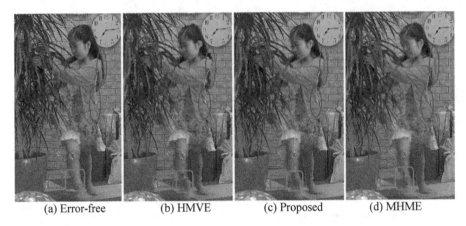

| (a) Error-free | (b) HMVE | (c) Proposed | (d) MHME |

Fig. 6. Subjective quality comparison of Motion area of the reconstructed 5th frame for *PartyScene* sequence. (Color figure online)

Table 3. Complexity comparison of comparable algorithms

Class	Sequences	QP	Time consumption (s)					Δ (%)			
			FCEC	MCEC	HMVE	MHME	Proposed	FCEC	MCEC	HMVE	MHME
B (1080p)	ParkScene	27	10.05	10.09	10.75	15.60	11.21	11.54	11.10	4.28	−28.14
		32	7.43	7.49	8.26	13.06	9.12	22.75	21.76	10.41	−30.17
	Cactus	27	8.79	8.82	9.96	15.39	10.62	20.82	20.41	6.63	−30.99
		32	6.86	6.87	7.53	12.36	8.26	20.41	20.23	9.69	−33.17
C (WVGA)	PartyScene	27	3.11	3.11	3.24	4.46	3.38	8.68	8.68	4.32	−24.22
		32	2.26	2.28	2.47	3.36	2.56	13.27	12.28	3.64	−23.81
	BQMall	27	2.05	2.06	2.20	3.43	2.53	23.41	22.82	15	−26.24
		32	1.58	1.60	1.78	2.66	1.91	20.89	19.38	7.30	−28.20
D (WQVGA)	BasketballPass	27	0.55	0.57	0.62	0.90	0.70	27.27	22.81	12.90	−22.22
		32	0.44	0.47	0.51	0.78	0.56	27.27	19.15	9.80	−28.21
	RaceHorses	27	0.81	0.85	0.90	1.21	0.91	12.35	7.06	1.11	−24.79
		32	0.67	0.69	0.73	1.05	0.77	14.93	11.59	5.48	−26.67
Avg. Gain								18.63	16.44	7.55	−27.24

frames for the final concealment, it introduce about additional 7.55% complexity. However, it achieves much less, up to 33.17% and on average 27.24% more specifically, time-consumption than MHME since the latter needs multiple time-consuming motion estimation processes at the decoder side.

In all, the proposed algorithm achieves much improve video quality that the FCEC, MCEC as well as the HMVE algorithms with slight complexity overhead. Although the gains obtained by the proposed algorithm are slightly lower than that of the MHME algorithm, the complexity of the proposed algorithm is significantly less than that of MHME. Thus, we can conclude that the proposed algorithm achieves a nice tradeoff between the decoded video quality and the computational complexity, which makes it more suitable for practical real-time video applications.

5   Conclusion

This paper has studies the error concealment problem for whole frame loss of HEVC coding streams and proposed a practical multi-hypothesis based error concealment algorithm. The algorithm first built a motion vector prediction model between adjacent coding unit levels to construct the motion vector field easily for a coding tree unit of the lost frame, and then reconstructed the missing frame based on the multi-hypothesis theory using the built motion vector field. Experimental results show that the proposed algorithm achieves a nice tradeoff between the decoded video quality and the computational complexity, which makes it more suitable for practical real-time video applications. As the future work, we will focus on accuracy improvement of the motion vector prediction model and performance decline problem of the following frames after the lost frame.

Acknowledgements. The authors would like to thank the anonymous reviewers for their potential valuable comments and suggestions that would help further improve the presentation of this paper. This work was partially supported by the National Key R&D Program of China (Grant No. 2016YFC0801001), the NSFC Key Project (No. 61632001) and the National Natural Science Foundation of China (No. 61772054, 61502278), Scientific Research Foundation of Shandong University of Science and Technology for Recruited Talents (No. 2015RCJJ067). This paper is partially done when Zhe Li was with Beijing Key Lab of Digital Media, School of Computer Science and Engineering, Beihang University, Beijing, China, 100191.

References

1. Wiegand, T., Sullivan, G.J., Bjontegaard, G., Luthra, A.: Overview of the H.264/AVC video coding standard. IEEE Trans. Circuits Syst. Video Technol. **13**(7), 560–576 (2003)
2. Sullivan, G.J., Ohm, J.-R., Han, W.-J., Wiegand, T.: Overview of the high efficiency video coding (HEVC) standard. IEEE Trans. Circuits Syst. Video Technol. **22**(12), 694–698 (2012)
3. Kumwilaisak, W., Kuo, C.J.: Spatial error concealment with sequence-aligned texture modeling and adaptive directional recovery. J. Vis. Commun. Image Represent. **22**(2), 164–177 (2011)
4. Lin, T., Ding, T., Yang, N., Wu, P., Tung, K., Lai, C., Chang, T.: Video motion vector recovery method using decoding partition information. J. Disp. Technol. **12**(11), 1451–1463 (2016)
5. Hsia, S., Hsiao, C.: Fast-efficient shape error concealment technique based on block classification. IET Image Process. **10**(10), 693–700 (2016)
6. Zhou, J., Yan, B., Gharavi, H.: Efficient motion vector interpolation for error concealment of H.264/AVC. IEEE Trans. Broadcast. **57**(1), 75–80 (2011)
7. Wu, Z., Boyce, J.M.: An error concealment scheme for entire frame losses based on H.264. In: IEEE International Symposium on Circuits and System (ISCAS) (2006)
8. Peng, Q., Yang, T., Zhu, C.: Block-based temporal error concealment for video packet using motion vector extrapolation. In: IEEE International Conference on Communications, Circuits and System and West Sino Expo, pp. 10–14 (2002)
9. Chen, Y., Yu, K., Li, J., Li, S.: An error concealment algorithm for entire frame loss in video transmission. In: IEEE Picture Coding Symposium (PCS) (2004)

10. Yan, B., Gharavi, H.: A hybrid frame concealment algorithm for H.264/AVC. IEEE Trans. Image Process. **19**(1), 98–107 (2010)
11. Zhao, C., Ma, S., Zhang, J., Gao, W.: A highly effective error concealment method for whole frame loss. In: IEEE International Symposium on Circuits and System (ISCAS) (2013)
12. HM Reference Software 16.0. http://hevc.hhi.fraunhofer.de/svn/svn_HEVCSoftware
13. Bossen, F.: Common test conditions and software reference configurations. In: Joint Collaborative Team on Video Coding Meeting, JCTVC-J1100, July 2012

Multi-stream Fusion Model for Social Relation Recognition from Videos

Jinna Lv, Wu Liu, Lili Zhou, Bin Wu[✉], and Huadong Ma

Beijing Key Laboratory of Intelligent Telecommunications Software and Multimedia,
Beijing University of Posts and Telecommunications, Beijing 100876, China
{lvjinna,liuwu,xuanyuanjian,wubin,mhd}@bupt.edu.cn

Abstract. Social relations are ubiquitous in people's daily life. Especially, the widespread of video in social media and intelligent surveillance gives us a new chance to discover the social relations among people. Previous researches mostly focus on the recognition of social relations from texts, blogs, or images. However, these methods are only concentrated on limited social relations and incapable of dealing with video data. In this paper, we address the challenges of social relation recognition by employing a multi-stream model to exploit the abundant multimodal information in videos. First of all, we build a video dataset with 16 categories of social relations annotation according to psychology and sociology studies, named Social Relation In Videos (SRIV), which comprises of 3,124 videos. According to our knowledge, it is the first video dataset for the social relation recognition. Secondly, we propose a multi-stream deep learning model as a benchmark for recognizing social relations, which learns high level semantic information of spatial, temporal, and audio of people's social interactions in videos. Finally, we fuse them with logical regression to achieve accurate recognition. Experimental results show that the multi-stream deep model is effective for social relation recognition on the proposed dataset.

Keywords: Social relation · Video analysis · Deep learning

1 Introduction

Social relations are major part of human daily life, which can be captured via social media, video surveillance and movies. Social relation analysis is helpful for mining hidden semantic information of videos and being beneficial for human's social activities. The task of social relation recognition from videos is to design an effective model that can learn social relation traits of persons in videos, then the goal is to automatically predict which types of social relation they are, as shown in Fig. 1. In the past years, some previous works have recognized social relations from texts, blogs, and images [1,2]. However, few studies have researched social relation recognition in the domain of videos, furthermore, there are still great challenges: (1) lacking annotated video dataset; (2) learning high-level action

© Springer International Publishing AG 2018
K. Schoeffmann et al. (Eds.): MMM 2018, Part I, LNCS 10704, pp. 355–368, 2018.
https://doi.org/10.1007/978-3-319-73603-7_29

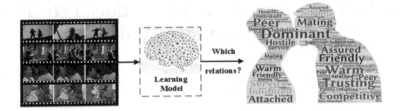

Fig. 1. The sketch of recognizing social relation from videos.

and voice features of social relations from video is difficult; (3) how to make full use of social information in video data with multi-label and multi-class. Thus it becomes crucial to build a video dataset for social relation analysis and design innovative learning models to solve these challenges.

The lack of video dataset is a key problem to hinder the development of social relation recognition from videos. Existing visual datasets are usually for analyzing social relations in images. For example, a photo dataset collected from the web and movies for classification of social relations was released [3], and images datasets were proposed based on social domain theory [5] or psychology [6]. These datasets have shown some successes in analyzing static image features of social relations. However, they are only suitable for image analysis and limited to a handful of adhoc defined classes. In the aspect of models for relationship recognition, many scholars have proposed methods to recognize family member and verify kinship, such as probabilistic model [3], and deep learning model [5,6]. However, they highlight the image features and discount the temporal features of video, such as actions of people, and other valuable cues for social relations. Therefore, to solve this problem, in this paper we build a new dataset for studying social relation from videos based on psychology and sociology studies, and propose a learning model from computer vision point of view.

Firstly, to facilitate future research, we build a benchmark (SRIV), collected from 69 movies and TV dramas. It consists of 3,124 videos, 25 h, which make the dataset scalable for social relation recognition. According to psychology and sociology studies, the videos are classified into Subjective Relations (Sub-Relation) and Objective Relations (Obj-Relation) and labeled by 16 subclasses: eight subclasses in the light of psychological theory in [7] and the other eight subclasses according to the study in [8]. Each video belongs to one or more class, so with this multi-label and multi-class dataset, complicated models can be designed and predicted for learning social relations.

In addition, we propose a benchmark model for social relation recognition on the proposed dataset, which progressively fuses spatial, temporal, and audio deep semantic features to learn social relation traits. First, spatial network is introduced as the baseline to obtain spatial information using RGB frames. Second, a two-stream deep network is adopted to learn video-level social relation representation, in which sequences of short segments are sparsely sampled from the entire video that can tolerate limited training samples. Third, a multi-stream model is proposed, which not only combines spatial and action social traits, but also learns audio features by GoogleNet. Especially, audio features can provide crucial complementary clues to the visual features. For example, when people arguing, the voices of them are always loud, and vice versa. At last, late fusion method using logistic regression is introduced to get the final prediction, moreover, we optimize the network to adapt multi-label problem.

In summary, the contributions of this paper can be concluded as follows:

- We systematically investigate how to recognize the social relations from video. Consequently, we discovery that social relations vary in different areas, which can be generalized as subjective and objective relations. More importantly, the relation traits in video are diversified and needed to be mined.
- We build a Social Relation In Videos (SRIV) dataset with multi-label and multi-class. To the best of our knowledge, this is the first video dataset for social relation recognition.
- A multi-stream deep learning model is proposed as a benchmark on SRIV, which fuses spatial, temporal and audio social features to represent and recognize the social relations.

2 Related Works

Social relation recognition from visual data. Many researchers aim to infer social relations from multimedia [10–14]. Firstly, most of these studies analyzed social relations based on images or texts. For example, Tannisil et al. explored the facial regions and their spatial configurations which contributed to the recognition of people's interactions [10]. Secondly, some researches have exploited models for analyzing people's interaction in the group. For instance, Zurrida et al. investigated verbal and non-verbal cues to model speaker's behavior [11]. Thirdly, the types of social relations of existing studies were still limited and rough. Tran et al. focused on the appearance of each character during movie play and analyzed the characters' relationships [13]. Bojanowski et al. used script and movie to find actors and actions in video [14]. In short, people's position and facial appearance attributes provide effective cues for relation recognition in images. However, relation recognition in video faces the problems that two people being in different images and having sides faces or even backs. Therefore, novel traits learning are urgently needed, such as action, audio, scenes and so on.

Social relation dataset. In recent years, some relation datasets have been released [3,5,6,10]. For example, Zhang et al. proposed a comprehensive dataset from pairs of face images annotated with eight pairwise relations [6]. Dai et al. introduced a photo albums dataset which consisted of 37,107 photos and considered occlusion with other people [3]. Sun et al. released a large scale image dataset that classified social relations into five domains [5]. Tanisik et al. collected an image dataset including 10 human interaction classes [10]. However, there is no video dataset for social relation recognition according to our knowledge.

Therefore, a new video dataset is urgent to provide resources for relation analysis in videos. In addition, most of these datasets focus on familial relations, but social relations are not confined to these [8].

Deep learning models for social relation analysis. In the past years, deep learning has achieved great successes in computer vision [4]. There have been some works focusing on developing effective features to recognize the human relations [5,6,9,10,14,15]. For instance, Zhang et al. introduced a siamese like deep convolutional network to learn relations from pairs of face images [6]. In [5], an end to end deep network based on multiple domain features was proposed, which utilized not only age and head appearance, but also clothing and proximity information. Tanisik et al. proposed a deep model to get face features of people's interactions [10]. In brief, above studies enlighten the problem of relation recognition in image domain. There are also successful ConvNets methods in video analysis [15] and human actions [9,14]. To solve the problem of social relation recognition from videos, it requires efficient deep learning model to mine high-level semantic information. In this work, we proposed a multi-stream deep model to learn multiple cues of social relations.

3   Social Relation in Videos (SRIV) Dataset

3.1   Social Relation Theory

Social relations are formed on multiple bases and some attributes are intrinsic, therefore it can be classified into more than one category. Two-dimensional interpersonal behaviors are constructed according to psychological theory in [7], which divided relations into 16 segments, 8 pairs, such as warm and cold, mistrusting and trusting. However, the author did not consider that the social relation is within the specialization of an academic discipline in [8]. For example, kinship, political authority, affection and sexual attraction may tend to fall with anthropology, sociology, or psychology studies. In addition, office or employment and social connections tend to fall within sociology. Therefore, social relations are difficult to be classified as a whole, and the better way is to classify them according to specific areas.

3.2   SRIV Dataset

In this paper, we derive social relations of the movie and television domain, which can reflect the daily life of people. Moreover, we classify social relations by two classification approaches. One divided method is inspired by the theory in [7], named Subjective Relations (Sub-Relation). As a result, we classify social relations into 8 categories, as shown in the Table 1. In particular, there are some descriptions in the second column referring to the relations [6]. Social relations are always subjective perception, so some relations are easy to distinguish, such as "dominant" and "competitive". Conversely, some are difficult to be completely separated, such as "trusting" and "assured". Therefore,

Table 1. Descriptions of Sub-Relation classes based on [6] and [7].

Relations	Descriptions	Examples
Dominant	One leads or gives advices to the other	Controlling, dictatorial
Competitive	Contest for advancement or quarreling	Critical, ambitious
Trusting	No frowning or doubtful expression	Forgiving, merciful
Warm	Speak in a gentle way, show tender feelings	All-loving, absolving
Friendly	Be helpful, act in a polite way	Cooperative, helpful
Attached	Involved with each other	Lovers
Inhibited	One is shy and bashful	Taciturn, unreponsive
Assured	Positive self-concept, instead of depressed	Confident, arrogant

Table 2. Descriptions of Obj-Relation classes based on [8].

Relations	Subclasses	Examples
Working relation	Supervisor-Subordinate	Teacher-student, leader-subordinate
	Peer	Classmates, colleagues
	Service	Waiter-customer
Kinship relation	Parent-Offspring	Father-child, mother-child
	Mating	Lovers, spouses
	Sibling	Brothers, sisters
Other relation	Friendly	Friends
	Hostile	Enemies, antagonist

another classification method is designed in our dataset, named Objective Relations (Obj-Relation), which divide social relations into three classes: "working", "kinship" and "others", and eight subclasses, as shown in the Table 2. To the best of our knowledge, the dataset is the first one for social relation recognition from videos. More importantly, it is challenging because of variations including actions, illuminations, audio and face angles.

To study the social relations among people from videos, we propose a new dataset, named SRIV. It contains 3,124 videos collected from TV dramas and movies, about 25 h, and each video length is ranging from 5 s to 50 s. The SRIV is divided into 16 classes by two classification approaches, which makes our dataset scalable enough for social relation recognition. Its characters are shown in Fig. 2, besides some samples are shown in Fig. 3. The statistics of the two kinds of classifications are derived from two aspects: the video length and the number of videos per class.

Because of complex scenes and social relations, our dataset can be employed for different relation recognition applications. This also makes SRIV a very challenging dataset. One of the challenges is that characters in video are always with side faces or even with backs, which make it difficult to recognize faces or persons.

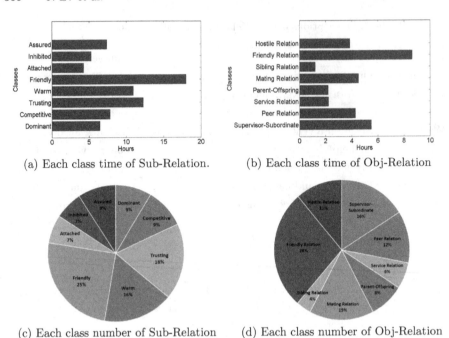

(a) Each class time of Sub-Relation.   (b) Each class time of Obj-Relation

(c) Each class number of Sub-Relation   (d) Each class number of Obj-Relation

Fig. 2. The characters of the proposed SRIV dataset.

Another challenge is that persons have diverse interaction activities with different scenes, viewpoints and illuminations. Therefore, novel learning models are demanded to instead of the traditional methods based on images. Furthermore, multiple labels annotation of our dataset makes researchers capture correlations between them to accurately recognize social relations.

When building the dataset, ten postgraduates were asked to cut out and annotate for each video clip independently. When students intercepting video clips, each clip is guaranteed to contain at least two persons. In addition, each student can skip the uncertain relation label, or he can tag "maybe" for this relation. After manual annotation step, we adopt the relation labels at least three persons labeled which are justified also by the following rule: each video clip has at least one label.

4   Multi-stream Model for Social Relation Recognition

In the analysis of social relation based on image information, researches have collected lots of semantic clues, such as, head or body, location and scale, clothing, proximity and so on. However, it is difficult to extract above features of social relations from videos. For example, relative distance (far, close) is unable to compute due to persons are always in different images, and clothes of the same person are often changed in a movie or daily life. In our paper, we endeavor to

Fig. 3. Each class samples of Obj-Relation in SRIV.

learn social features in videos. Firstly, we introduce a baseline method using a ConvNet based on RGB images of videos to learn clues of social relations, such as video scenes and people representations. Secondly, the action feature is fused by a temporal segment network [9], which is adopted in action classification and achieved successful performance. Furthermore, aiming to adopt multiple high level features of social relations, a multi-stream ConvNet is proposed including spatial, temporal and audio features. Finally, because the dataset is multi-labeled, and there are valuable correlations among different labels, we optimize the architecture to adapt to the multi-label classification.

4.1   Network Architecture

Network architecture is a critical aspect in deep learning. Some studies have demonstrated that the deeper structures and multi-network fused improve learning performance [16,17]. The architecture of the multi-stream model is as shown in Fig. 4, which fuse spatial, temporal, and audio networks to achieve favorable performance of the recognition. Especially, a temporal segment networks is employed [9] for learning spatial and temporal features, in which the Inception with Batch Normalization (BN-Inception) [18] is chosen due to its good balance between accuracy and efficiency. At first, videos are divided into several segments. Following, segments of each video are fed into spatial and temporal networks. Then, all segments are summed, as well predicted scores are computed. More importantly, we adopt GoogleNet to learn audio features using audio spectrums. Furthermore, sigmoid cross entropy loss function is utilized to optimize the multi-label classification. The three networks are learned independently. After prediction scores of each stream are computed, the late fusion method with logistic regression is used to get the final prediction.

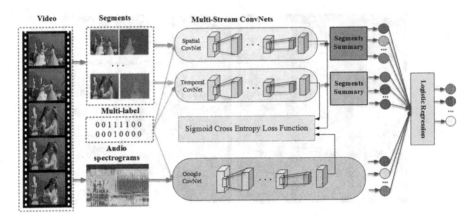

Fig. 4. The architecture of multi-stream model for social relation recognition.

4.2   Segment Sampling and Multi-label Classification

Because last for a few seconds frames are always highly similar and redundant, a sparse temporal sampling strategy is adopted instead of dense temporal sampling. In the model, as shown in Fig. 4, a set of segment proposals are generated $S = \{s_i = (b_i, e_i)\}_{i=1}^{N}$, where N is the segment numbers, and b_i, e_i denote the beginning and ending locations of the ith segment proposal s_i. $(T_1, T_2, ..., T_K)$ is a sequence of segments, and each segment T_K is randomly sampled from S. The sequence of segments is fed into the spatial and temporal networks and produce class scores for all the classes. Then, segments summary combines the outputs, which predicts the probability of each class for the whole video. We introduce sigmoid cross entropy loss function as in Eq. (1) to deal with the multi-label classification.

$$loss = -\frac{1}{N} \sum_{n=1}^{N} [label_n \log(p_n) + (1 - label_n) \log(1 - p_n)]. \tag{1}$$

where $label_n$ is the ground truth of the n-th class, and p_n is the probability of predicted class computed by sigmoid function.

The inputs of spatial network are RGB images resized by 340×256. Stacked optical flow fields as inputs for the temporal stream aiming to capture the motion information. In addition, the inputs of deep audio network are voice spectrums of the video clips. The significant contribution of our model is that audio information is introduced which was not used in previous social relations analysis. We convert audio files into audio spectrograms, in which short-time fourier transformation is adopted to convert the 1-d soundtrack into a 2-d images (time-scale and frequency-scale respectively). Then, we use GoogleNet to learn deep features as a complement of the visual channel.

4.3 Late Fusion Method

In the spatial-temporal network, the segments summary functions are provided. Especially, we choice the evenly averaging method to evaluate all segments scores. After all segments scores are computed, the multi-stream scores are integrated to calculate final perdition scores. More formally, we denote the prediction scores from the multi-streams as $m^i \in \mathbb{R}^C (i = 1, ...I)$ with C is the number of classes and I is the number of streams. A straightforward way of late fusion is to compute the final prediction labels as $pre\_y = H(m^1, m^2, ..., m^I)$. The prediction function H predicts the probability of each relation class for test videos, which can be a linear function or a logistic function. Given there are N test samples, after training and testing in multi-stream network, the prediction scores metric can be represented as:

$$m_n = \left[m_n^{1^T}, \cdots, m_n^{i^T}, \cdots, m_n^{I^T} \right]^T \in \mathbb{R}^{CI}. \tag{2}$$

Aiming to adaptively integrate the prediction scores, we use a like logistic regression to determine the optimal fusion weights W of each class shown as following:

$$W = \arg \min_{w_1, w_2, ..., w_c} \sum_{c=1}^{C} \sum_{n=1}^{N} \log(1 + \exp[(1 - 2y_{n,c}) m_n^T w_c]), \tag{3}$$

where $y_{n,c}$ is the ground-truth label of the $n - th$ test sample for class c, and W is the 3-dimension weights metric for all prediction scores.

5 Experiments

5.1 Implementation Detail

We randomly divide the SRIV dataset into two parts for training and testing respectively. The training set has 2,343 videos and the testing set contains 781 videos. For the spatial and temporal network, the mini-batch stochastic gradient descent algorithm is utilized to learn the network parameters. In our experiment, the batch size of temporal spatial networks is set to 128, the base learning rate is set to 0.001 and decreases to its 0.01 every one epoch. For the audio ConvNet, the batch size is set to 32, the base learning rate is set to 0.01 and decreases to its 0.1 every one epoch, and the max iteration is 3,000. In addition, we initialize network weights with per-train model from GoogleNet [19]. The segment number N is set to 20. For the multi-label learning problem, we compare two methods: (1) turn the multi-label problem into a general classification problem, i.e., a sample of multiple labels is written as multiple samples with single label; (2) modify the network and loss function to learn the correlation between multiple classes, called Mulit-label Learning (ML).

5.2 Evaluation Metrics

We use four evaluation metrics to evaluate the performance of the proposed method in this paper.

F1_micro and F1_macro. These two evaluations are based on label evaluations based on F_1 scores. F_1 of the i-th class is

$$F_1(i) = 2 \times TP(i)/(2 \times TP(i) + FP(i) + FN(i)), \tag{4}$$

where $TP(i)$, $FP(i)$, $TN(i)$ and $FN(i)$ denote the number of correct positive, false positive, true negative, and false negative of the i-th class respectively. As a result, F_{1_macro} and F_{1_micro} are computed as

$$F_{1\_macro} = \frac{1}{C} \sum_{i=1}^{C} F_1(i), \tag{5}$$

$$F_{1\_micro} = 2 \times \sum_{i=1}^{C} TP(i)/(2 \times \sum_{i=1}^{C} TP(i) + \sum_{i=1}^{C} FP(i) + \sum_{i=1}^{C} FN(i)), \tag{6}$$

where C is the number of classes.

Accuracy. To account for the imbalance positive and negative, a balance accuracy is adopted which was proposed in [6]:

$$Accuracy = \frac{1}{2}(\frac{TP}{N_p} + \frac{TN}{N_n}), \tag{7}$$

where N_p and N_n are the number of positive and negative samples.

Subset Accuracy. This evaluation requires that the predicted labels set match exactly with the ground truth set, which is defined as

$$Subaccuracy(h) = \frac{1}{n} \sum_{k=1}^{n} I(h(x_k) = Y_k), \tag{8}$$

where $I(true) = 1$, $I(false) = 0$.

5.3 Results of Social Relation Recognition

The results of our experiments demonstrate the multi-stream model for social relation recognition task achieves the best performance. We first report the performance of the progressive fuse the multiple streams. Then, we compare the results with and without the multi-label learning optimization.

Table 3 shows the comparison results of multi-stream model with evaluation metrics. We can find that regardless of whether using multi-label optimization, our multi-stream fusion method can significantly improve the performances. Spatial network produces a relatively low accuracy 0.6782 and 0.5331, which reflects

Table 3. Performance of individual stream and their fusion on SRIV. (S-T: Spatial-Temporal network; ML: Mulit-label Learning.)

Classifications	Methods	F1_micro	F1_macro	Accuracy	Subaccuracy
Sub-Relation	Spatial	0.709	0.6136	0.6782	0.3219
	S-T	0.7512	0.6302	0.7037	0.4659
	Multi-stream	0.7824	0.6538	0.7206	0.4818
	Spatial (ML)	0.7142	0.6142	0.7089	0.3482
	S-T (ML)	0.7828	0.6449	0.7372	0.4913
	Multi-stream (ML)	**0.8119**	**0.6683**	**0.7436**	**0.5213**
Obj-Relation	Spatial	0.6022	0.4890	0.5331	0.3066
	S-T	0.6528	0.5549	0.5972	0.4902
	Multi-stream	0.6988	0.6278	0.6024	0.5213
	Spatial (ML)	0.6034	0.4894	0.5412	0.3045
	S-T (ML)	0.6605	0.5627	0.6083	0.5026
	Multi-stream (ML)	**0.7019**	**0.6383**	**0.6136**	**0.5291**

the scene features where they are, and relative location information. From the results, we can find it a better way that fuses temporal cues to improve the identification accuracy which increase 3.8% and 12.02%, respectively. It demonstrates that the action information is definitely advantageous for social relation recognition. For example, kiss for mating relation, bow for supervisor-subordinate relation et al. More importantly, after audio features are fused too, the performances are improved again. For example, accuracy achieves 0.7206 (+2.4%) and 0.6024 (+0.8%), sub accuracy achieves 0.4818 (+3.4%) and 0.5213 (+6.3%). Which suggests that audio feature can help to distinguish relations, such as arguments with loud voice and warm relations with soft voice.

Compared with single label learning, the proposed multi-label optimization strategy achieves the best performance, which demonstrates that the proposed multi-stream network can more effectively mine the valuable relevance of social traits among different classes. The performance of multi-label optimization method is average increased by 2.5% and 4.9% in the terms of accuracy and sub accuracy, respectively. However, compared with the results of the Sub-Relation, we can find that the improvement of the Obj-Relation is relatively less. For instance, the performance is improved by 1.1% in terms of F_1, which is lower than 2.5% of the Sub-Relation. In contrast to there always are multiple labels of Sub-Relation in one video, there may be only one label of Obj-Relation. Consider as an illustration, a video has been labeled by "trusting", "friendly", and "warm" of the Obj-Relation, instead only "peer" relation of the Obj-Relation.

Figure 5 shows the recognition performance of the different categories with our multi-stream method. We can see that the results of spatial network can basically identify social relations. This explains that the RGB spatial features can express the elementary characteristics of the people's relation traits.

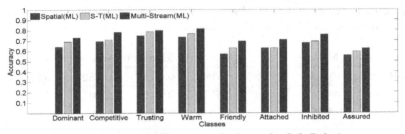

(a) Performance of different methods on the Sub-Relation.

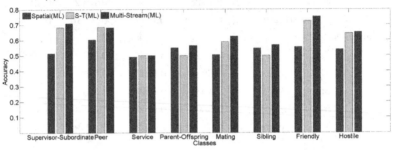

(b) Performance of different methods on the Obj-Relation.

Fig. 5. Social relation prediction performance of each classes.

Specifically, "peer" corresponds to the office scene, similar clothes, and "warm" and "parent-offspring" are always occurred in their house. After action feature is introduced, the accuracy is increased a lot for "supervisor-subordinate" and "friendly" relation traits, which are shown in Fig. 5(b). The reason is that for these relationships, they are often accompanied by actions such as raising hands and hugging. In addition, after fusing audio features, the prediction accuracies of the "competitive" relation is obviously improved. This is because voices of people in these scenes are always loud or noisy. However, some classes have not high accuracy enhancement after integration, because it is visually subtle compared to other relations, such as "peer" and "friendly".

6   Conclusion

In this paper, we first introduce the SRIV that collected from movies and TV dramas, a new video benchmark dataset for social relation recognition. More importantly, the SRIV is built with multi-label and multi-class annotated according to psychology and sociology studies. Our work is the first step towards social relation recognition from videos. We address the main challenges of social relation recognition, an effective benchmark model is proposed, which fuses multi-stream (i.e. spatial, temporal, and audio) networks to learn multiple cues and labels for the problem. Experimental results show that our method achieve good performance. In the future, we will mine more valuable attributes to further improve the recognition performance.

Acknowledgment. This research is supported in part by the National High-tech R&D Program (No. 2015AA050204), the Special Found for Beijing Common Construction Project, the National Natural Science Foundation of China (No. 61602049), and the Fundamental Research Funds for the Central Universities (No. 2016RCGD32).

References

1. Luan, M.N.: Context-aware text representation for social relation aided sentiment analysis. In: WWW, pp. 85–86 (2016)
2. Xiang, L., Sang, J., Xu, C.: Demographic attribute inference from social multimedia behaviors: a cross-OSN approach. In: Amsaleg, L., Guðmundsson, G.Þ., Gurrin, C., Jónsson, B.Þ., Satoh, S. (eds.) MMM 2017. LNCS, vol. 10132, pp. 515–526. Springer, Cham (2017). https://doi.org/10.1007/978-3-319-51811-4_42
3. Dai, Q., Carr, P., Sigal, L., Hoiem, D.: Family member identification from photo collections. In: Applications of Computer Vision, pp. 982–989 (2015)
4. Liu, W., Mei, T., Zhang, Y., Che, C., Luo, J.: Multi-task deep visual-semantic embedding for video thumbnail selection. In: CVPR, pp. 3707–3715 (2015)
5. Sun, Q., Schiele, B., Fritz, M.: A domain based approach to social relation recognition. In: CVPR, pp. 435–444 (2017)
6. Zhang, Z., Luo, P., Loy, C.-C., Tang, X.: Learning social relation traits from face images. In: ICCV, pp. 3631–3639 (2015)
7. Kiesler, D.J.: The 1982 interpersonal circle: a taxonomy for complementarity in human transactions. Psychol. Rev. **90**(3), 185 (1983)
8. Ho, D.Y.: Interpersonal relationships and relationship dominance: An analysis based on methodological relationism. Asian J. Soc. Psychol. **1**(1), 1–16 (1998)
9. Wang, L., Xiong, Y., Wang, Z., Qiao, Y., Lin, D., Tang, X., Van Gool, L.: Temporal segment networks: towards good practices for deep action recognition. In: Leibe, B., Matas, J., Sebe, N., Welling, M. (eds.) ECCV 2016. LNCS, vol. 9912, pp. 20–36. Springer, Cham (2016). https://doi.org/10.1007/978-3-319-46484-8_2
10. Tanisik, G., Zalluhoglu, C., Ikizler-Cinbis, N.: Facial descriptors for human interaction recognition in still images. Pattern Recogn. Lett. **73**, 44–51 (2016)
11. Zurrida, S., Mazzarol, G., Galimberti, V., Renne, G., Bassi, F., Iafrate, F., Viale, G.: Automatic recognition of emergent social roles in small group interactions. IEEE Trans. Multimed. **17**(5), 746–760 (2015)
12. Ramanathan, V., Huang, J., Abu-El-Haija, S., Gorban, A., Murphy, K., Fei-Fei, L.: Detecting events and key actors in multi-person videos. In: CVPR, pp. 3043–3053 (2016)
13. Tran, Q.D., Jung, J.E.: Cocharnet: extracting social networks using character co-occurrence in movies. J. Univers. Comput. Sci. **21**(6), 796–815 (2015)
14. Bojanowski, P., Bach, F., Laptev, I., Ponce, J., Schmid, C., Sivic, J.: Finding actors and actions in movies. In: ICCV, pp. 2280–2287 (2013)
15. Petscharnig, S., Schöffmann, K.: Deep learning for shot classification in gynecologic surgery videos. In: Amsaleg, L., Guðmundsson, G.Þ., Gurrin, C., Jónsson, B.Þ., Satoh, S. (eds.) MMM 2017. LNCS, vol. 10132, pp. 702–713. Springer, Cham (2017). https://doi.org/10.1007/978-3-319-51811-4_57
16. Szegedy, C., Liu, W., Jia, Y., Sermanet, P., Reed, S., Anguelov, D., Erhan, D., Vanhoucke, V., Rabinovich, A.: Going deeper with convolutions. In: CVPR, pp. 1–9 (2015)

17. Wu, Z., Jiang, Y.-G., Wang, X., Ye, H., Xue, X.: Multi-stream multi-class fusion of deep networks for video classification. In: MM, pp. 791–800 (2016)
18. Ioffe, S., Szegedy, C.: Batch normalization: accelerating deep network training by reducing internal covariate shift. In: ICML, pp. 448–456 (2015)
19. Deng, J., Dong, W., Socher, R., Li, L.J., Li, K., Li, F.F.: Imagenet: a large-scale hierarchical image database. In: CVPR, pp. 248–255 (2009)

Multimodal Augmented Reality – Augmenting Auditory-Tactile Feedback to Change the Perception of Thickness

Geert Lugtenberg[1,2], Wolfgang Hürst[1(✉)], Nina Rosa[1],
Christian Sandor[2], Alexander Plopski[2], Takafumi Taketomi[2],
and Hirokazu Kato[2]

[1] Utrecht University, Princetonplein 5, 3584 CC Utrecht, The Netherlands
`geert_lugtenberg@hotmail.com`, `{huerst,N.E.Rosa}@uu.nl`
[2] Nara Institute of Science and Technology, 8916-5,
Takayama, Ikoma, Nara 630-0192, Japan
`{sandor,plopski,takafumi-t,kato}@is.naist.jp`

Abstract. With vision being a primary sense of humans, we often first estimate the physical properties of objects by looking at them. However, when in doubt, for example, about the material they are made of or its structure, it is natural to apply other senses, such as haptics by touching them. Aiming at the ultimate goal of achieving a full-sensory augmented reality experience, we present an initial study focusing on multimodal feedback when tapping an object to estimate the thickness of its material. Our results indicate that we can change the perception of thickness of stiff objects by modulating acoustic stimuli. For flexible objects, which have a more distinctive tactile characteristic, adding vibratory responses when tapping on thick objects can make people perceive them as thin. We also identified that in the latter case, adding congruent acoustic stimuli does not further enhance the illusion but worsens it.

Keywords: Augmented reality · Multimodal AR · Multimodal perception

1 Introduction

Today's hardware for Augmented Reality (AR), such as see-through head-worn displays, allows us to project computer-generated imagery (CGI) into our surroundings at a quality of sometimes stunning realism. Hardware to stimulate other senses than vision and research on perception of these modalities is however relatively lacking, although we do experience our environment based on the integration of multiple senses; for example, auditory-tactile [1, 3, 4, 10], sound [16], smell and taste [13]. An obvious example is the exploration of objects and their material. A table might look like being made of sturdy, solid wood, but when we touch it, we realize that it is just thin synthetic material with the visual texture of wood applied on it. Likewise, picking up an object allows us to feel its weight and texture and thus make a better estimate of its volume. Haptic exploration of real objects, such scratching their surface or tapping them, results in vibrations in the object's material. These vibrations are dependent on certain

© Springer International Publishing AG 2018
K. Schoeffmann et al. (Eds.): MMM 2018, Part I, LNCS 10704, pp. 369–380, 2018.
https://doi.org/10.1007/978-3-319-73603-7_30

properties of the material, some of which we can estimate when we feel or hear the vibrations. We know from elasticity theory [9] that the displacement of a rod or plate that force acts upon depends on the force, elastic modulus of the material, and its thickness. Previous work investigated stiffness perception (i.e., the inverse of elasticity) [3, 17] for virtual objects. In this research, we expand this by looking at real objects in an AR setting and investigate the influence of sound and touch feedback upon haptic exploration of thickness. Our concrete *aim* is to *verify if we can change the perception of thickness when tapping by modulating auditory-tactile feedback*.

To get a better understanding of the relative influence of acoustic and haptic feedback when tapping an object to determine its thickness, we first start by augmenting the auditory modality. In a first experiment, described in Sect. 3, we measure the correctness of discriminating between different thicknesses under varying auditory conditions. In Sect. 4, we discuss a second experiment were we first augment the tactile modality before finally studying multisensory integration, that is, the combined influence of tactile and auditory augmentations for the perception of thickness. Starting with studying sound is motivated by the fact that, compared to haptic hardware solutions, auditory hardware is easier to obtain, can create a rich, realistic sound experience, and is simple to utilize using headphones. Our results, summarized in Sect. 5, show that we can indeed manipulate how people perceive the thickness of a material by adding acoustic or tactile feedback. We also show that when both modalities are present, manipulation only one of them is not sufficient, but both should be presented congruently to achieve the desired effect.

2 Related Work

Previous work in Virtual Reality (VR) aiming to influence the perception of physical properties related to haptic sensations is seeking to mimic real sensations in such virtual environments [3, 15]. These sensations in VR can be 'build from the ground up' whereas real objects have inherited physical properties that are often perceived in a multimodal way. For example, Hachisu et al. [5] add or subtract vibrations to a haptic pen applying force to a material. This augmentation creates the illusion of touching a different material than the real one. This work was the inspiration for our second experiment presented in Sect. 4, where we propose an approach for augmenting vibro-tactile feedback when tapping an object with your finger to estimate its thickness.

Research in multisensory integration, that is, the way in which the human brain combines congruently or incongruently perceived stimuli of different modalities, has shown that we can, for example, get a desired effect of perception of touch by simulation of another, seemingly unrelated modality. A well-known and robust effect is the so-called 'Size-Weight illusion' [2]. Here, the visual indication of size has a cross-modal effect on the perception of weight of two equally heavy objects. We also know that when stroking a surface, 'roughness' can be changed by visual [7, 8] and auditory [4] simulation. The perception of hardness can be influenced by deforming the CGI of a texture that is projected on a surface upon pressing it [6, 14]. In our research, we are interested in similar effects using the modality of sound and tactile stimuli, and if there is a comparable integration effect for the perception of a material's thickness.

3   Experiment 1: Augmented Sound

If we assume that there is no tactile indication of thickness, that is, no noticeable difference when touching a thick or a thin object, then perception of thickness of two visually indistinguishable objects is entirely dependent on what we hear. Therefore, we hypothesize that we can change the perception of thickness solely by modulation of the auditory feedback when tapping it. We summarize this assumption in our first research question:

RQ1: *Can we achieve a different perception of thickness (solid or hollow) of an object when tapping it by solely modifying auditory feedback and otherwise fixed physical properties?*

We approach this problem by measuring the correct identification of a cube-shaped object as 'solid' or 'hollow' in a yes/no-type psychophysical experiment. Figure 1 shows the sound spectrograms of the typical impulse responses of a thick and thin material; plastic, as used in this experiment, and wood, as used in Sect. 4. They illustrate that a long decay of low frequencies is characteristic for thin material, as opposed to a short decay of higher frequencies for bigger, more solid ones. Thus, for our experiment, we generated the needed sounds by resynthesizing the original real-time sound of a tap on a cube and transforming it according to the desired characteristic (Table 1). By resynthesizing, we take the acoustic properties of the material and object (modal models [16]) and the velocity and duration of the tap into account.

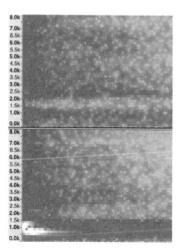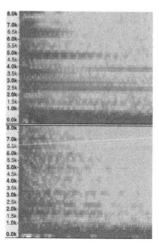

Fig. 1. Spectrograms of impulse responses of plastic cubes (left) and wooden plates (right) show characteristics of thick (top row) and thin (bottom row) material. Sounds originating from thin objects have a high amplitude, shown in white, in the lower frequency range. Furthermore, we see that these high amplitude low frequencies have a longer decay time.

Table 1. Characteristics of thickness in vibrating material

	Avg. amplitude	Frequency range of high amplitudes	Decay time
Thick	Low	1000 Hz	Short
Thin	High	0 Hz–1000 Hz	Long

3.1   Experimental Design and Setup

Used platform. Figure 2 shows the platform used in the first experiment. A Mogges piezoelectric sensor [12] is connected to the Mogees Virtual Studio Technology (VST) plugin running in Cycling'74 Max 6 on a MacBook Pro. This VST plugin transforms the vibrations measured by the piezoelectric sensor in real-time and outputs it as audio signal to the headphones worn by the participant. We used Sehnheiser CX3.00 in-ear headphones, so that earmuffs could be worn over the headphones to cancel out external sounds during the experiment. The used objects are two 3D-printed cubes of a styrenic plastic material that have a Young's Modulus of 2.0–2.6 GPa. The cubes' dimensions are $70 \times 70 \times 70$ mm. The hollow one has walls with a thickness of 2 mm.

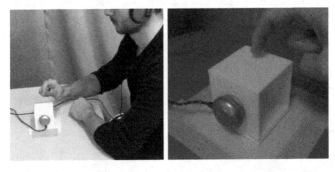

Fig. 2. Setup for experiment 1: (left) Participants tap the top of a solid or hollow cube. There is visually no distinction between the two thicknesses (during the experiment, the opening in the right figure was facing down). The cube is placed in a holder that is firmly attached to a table surface. A piezoelectric sensor is attached to the side of the cube (right) to capture vibrations in the material.

Method and procedure. Before participants enter the examination room, one of the cubes (either hollow or solid) is placed in the holder on the table. Test subjects then read an information sheet before an examiner explains the procedure again verbally. Each participant tests three conditions: no sound augmentation (control), white noise sound (no auditory cues), and resynthesized sound (simulating thin or thick material). The resynthesized sounds are pitched down and up and decay time increased and decreased for the modulation of thin or thick, respectively. The values for pitch and decay are determined subjectively to create a big contrast between sounds for thick and thin.

Participants are asked to tap the cube in front of them on the top side only with the index finger of their dominant hand. They can repeat this tapping action as often as they want before writing down on an answer sheet if they think the cube is hollow or solid. Then, the cube is exchanged with the other model (out of sight of the participant, so they cannot see the thickness of either of the cubes). The order of cubes as well as audio conditions was counterbalanced among all participants.

Thus, given the two independent variables *cube thickness* (solid, hollow) and *tapping sound* (real, static noise, thin, tick), each participant repeats all permutations of these variables one time, resulting in 2 * 4 = 16 trials per participant. The duration of the whole experiment for one person is about 30 min.

Participants. Eight students with ages ranging from 20 to 31 participated in our experiment. They volunteered and were not reimbursed in any way. Their number was motivated by the number of unique permutations of the independent variables. While this sample size is not enough to gain statistical significance, it is sufficient to identify a trend confirming or rejecting our research question RQ1, that is, if sound augmentation is sufficient or if tactile augmentation is needed as well.

3.2   Results and Discussion

Figure 3 shows the results of the experiment. We see that in the control condition, where real sound is heard (*real.hollow* and *real.solid* in the diagram), on average participants estimated the thickness of the cube correctly in 81.25% of the cases (75% for hollow, 87.5% for solid cube). In the conditions where any sound cue is removed by generating static white noise (*static.hollow* and *static.solid*), the correctness for the solid cube stays high (93.75%), but for the hollow one, it drops to 18.75%. This already indicates a strong impact of the hollow tapping sound on thickness perception, whereas the relevance of the solid sound seems less apparent. Looking at the simulated hollow

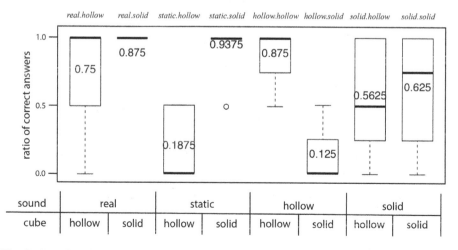

Fig. 3. Boxplot of results of the thickness discrimination task in experiment 1. Mean scores of correctly identifying the cube's real thickness are indicated in red. (Color figure online)

sound (*hollow.hollow* and *hollow.solid*), as expected, we see a high correctness when the hollow sound matches the hollow material (87.5%), but a strong drop when the hollow sound is played upon tapping a solid cube (12.5%). This proves that peoples' perception of thickness can indeed be manipulated by changing the acoustic stimuli. Yet, results for the simulated solid sound (*solid.hollow* and *solid.solid*) are close to chance level (56% for hollow cubes and 63% for solid ones) suggesting that subjects were just guessing. This shows that this sound also has an impact on the perception, because people were not able to make the right choices anymore, but that it is not enough to consistently create the target scenario.

There are two possible explanations for why simulated solid sounds did not have a similar manipulating effect as hollow ones. First, the sound of tapping a solid object is already less significant in real life, whereas real hollow sounds are much more distinctive and meaningful. The fact that we observed a strong drop when comparing real sound feedback to white noise in case of the hollow cube, but none in case of the solid one seems to confirm this. If this assumption is correct, our results would show that we can indeed use audio to manipulate peoples' perception, but only for certain subsets of materials, characteristics, and audio signals. Another reason why results for solid cubes are around chance level could be that the sound sample used in our experiment is just not indicative or distinctive enough to cause a better effect. We can speculate that with a better sound quality we might still be able to achieve the desired effect. Also, if people would compare the solid sound to the hollow one directly, it is likely that they discriminate between the two correctly. To cope with this, we will modify the experimental design for our next experiment by using a two-alternative forced choice task. We will also use pre-recorded audio samples instead of synthesized ones. Further experiments with improved sound quality for solid sounds are left for future work.

In conclusion, we can answer our research question positively, that is, we can indeed achieve a different perception of thickness solely by auditory feedback. Yet, this does not seem to be true for all situations, and the concrete conditions and possible limitations need to be specified by further experimentation.

4   Experiment 2: Auditory-Tactile Feedback

In the introduction, we discussed that human perception is generally based on a combination of simultaneously perceived multimodal stimuli, such as visual, acoustic, and haptic feedback when tapping an object. Experiment 1 showed that acoustic stimuli might be sufficient to change perception under certain conditions. In our second experiment, we want to further focus on the integration between two modalities – sound and tactile feedback – and verify their influence on thickness perception. We summarize our goal in a second research question:

RQ2: *Can we achieve a different perception of thickness (solid or hollow) of an object when tapping it by modifying auditory and tactile feedback and otherwise fixed physical properties?*

For this second experiment, we switched the objects from cubes to larger wooden plates to make the tactile indication of thickness more pronounced. Because using the terms "hollow" and "solid" does not make sense for such an object, and the terms "thick" and "thin" might be too context dependent and be interpreted differently by subjects, we changed the experimental design. With a two-alternative forced-choice (2AFC) psychophysical experiment, subjects are now asked to correctly identify which one of two plates is "thinner" than the other one.

4.1   Experimental Design and Setup

Used platform. Two wooden frames have been constructed to each hold two wooden plates in place. The wooden plates have a dimension of 200 × 200 × <T> mm with <T> being a thickness of either T = 4 mm (thin) or T = 10 mm (thick). Each frame can hold a thin and a thick plate. Two clamps are used to hold the plates in place and preventing inter-resonance. The clamps and the wooden frames are covered with a 9 mm thick polyethylene foam to stop vibrations in the plates from resonating into the underlying surface. The setup is illustrated in Fig. 4(a) and (c). To generate tactile vibrations when users tap on the plates, we have created two tactile sensors/actuators, as shown in Fig. 4(b). They consist of a PVC cylinder with a diameter of 20 mm and a height of 8 mm with a cutout in which the vibro-actuators fit precisely. The vibro-actuators and connected AL-202H Amulech amplifier are per design of the TECHTILE toolkit [11] and can display a range of 1-20000 Hz. A Force Sensitive Resistor (Interlink FSR402) is attached on top of the vibro-actuator and PVC cylinder. Pressure on the FSR is registered by our serially connected software, which measures the tap force approximately between 0 and 50 N. Based on this tap force, the software plays a pre-recorded audio file. Measured latency between moment of impact on the FSR and audio output ranges from 20 ms to 60 ms.

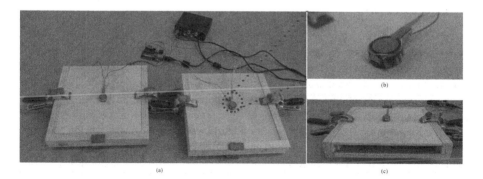

Fig. 4. Setup for experiment 2: (a) two wooden plates are clamped into two wooden frames. Vibration-damping material is attached to places where the wood or clamps touch the underlying surface. In the middle of the plates are Force Sensing Resistors (FSR) that are pasted on top of vibro-tactile actuators as shown in (b). The actuators are connected to an amplifier and together with the FSRs make a serial connection to a computer. (c) shows the back-view of the frames. Both frames can be turned-over to change the thickness of the plates.

Method and procedure. Each participant is tested under the following conditions: tactile stimuli (thin, thick), auditory-tactile stimuli (congruent or discrepant with each other). Under each condition real tactile feedback of the tapped plate is present. The participants are asked to determine the thinner one of the two plates by tapping on the sensors. The two plates presented to the subjects are always of opposed thickness; a thick and a thin one. The thinner one is on the left side in 50% of the cases, but the order is randomized. There are no visual cues indicating the thickness of the plates.

In a preprocessing phase, we recorded the actual tapping sounds used later in the experiment to make them sound more realistic, thus avoiding possible negative influences on the results (cf. discussion of experiment 1 in the preceding section). When capturing the sound snippets, we have also recorded the impact force of the tap and saved it a pair to be played-back during the experiment. In total, we have recorded twelve sound-force pairs of tapping on thick wood, and nine sound-force pairs of tapping on thin wood. The forces of the taps are approximately equally distributed ranging from subjectively 'soft' touch to a 'very hard' tap.

We decided to generate vibro-tactile feedback by modulating a sine wave. Our aim is not to simulate all touch sensations, as this would arguable result in a virtual reality problem. Instead, we add vibratory cues to vibrations in the real material. Frequencies, base amplitude, and decay times for thick and thin vibrations are summarized in Table 2. The decay time represents the total time for an exponential fade-out to zero amplitude of the sine wave. These specific values have been chosen subjectively to have a large contrast in feedback between 'thin' and 'thick'.

Table 2. Tactile vibratory properties

	Base amplitude	Base frequency	Decay time
Thick	0.3	500 Hz	100 ms
Thin	1.0	100 Hz	500 ms

When entering the examination room, subjects are asked to sit on a rotating chair in front of the equipment and read an information sheet. Every participant then undergoes one training round to familiarize them with the auditory and tactile experience, taking particular care on practicing tapping intensity and order. They first had to tap the left plate three times on the sensor; with a soft tap, (place finger upon the sensor; ± 1 N force), a medium tap (± 20 N force), and a hard tap (± 50 N force). During training, participants tap on the plates without any augmentation and are asked with one is thinner. They are then told if they are correct or not. Via in-ear headphones, they are presented with a sample of thick and a sample of the pre-recorded tapping sounds for wood; a 'thin' and a 'thick' one, and must indicate which one 'sounds thinner'.

During the actual test, participants wear additional earmuffs over the in-ear headphones to eliminate external noise. For every condition, they must tap with the index finger of their dominant hand, and start with the left plate, followed by taps on the right one. After this process, they must indicate which plate they think is the thinner one by saying 'left' or 'right', which was logged by the examiner. Then their chair is rotated around, so they are facing the back wall and cannot see the examiner modifying the thickness of the plates for the next round. Every permutation of the independent variables is repeated ten times, resulting in 60 trials per participant and a total duration of about 45 min per subject.

Participants. Ten male students participated in this experiment. Participation was voluntary and subject have not been reimbursed in any way. Due to their length, one participant's nails touched the sensor when tapping it, which creates a very different haptic and auditory feedback. Thus, he was asked to tilt his finger slightly in a way that the nail would not touch the sensor. Data for this subject does not show a noteworthy difference compared to the others. Therefore, we do not expect any impact for the results.

4.2   Results and Discussion

Figure 5 illustrates the results of experiment 2 by showing the mean correctness scores for determining the thinner of the two plates. Labels on the x-axis indicate the different conditions: First, pure tactile where haptic feedback does match the real situation (*Hm*) or does not (*Hn*). They represent the tactile counterpart to the conditions *hollow.hollow*, *static.static* and *hollow.static*, *static.hollow* in experiment 1. These conditions are followed by four others where we have both haptic and acoustic feedback; first where both are congruent and either match the real situation (*HmSm*) or not (*HnSn*), then where they are not congruent, that is, either the sound (*HmSn*) or the tactile feedback (*HnSm*) diverge from the real signals.

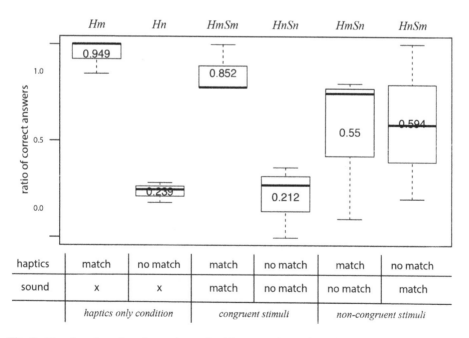

Fig. 5. Boxplot of results of experiment 2 with means shown in red. Labels below the x-axis specify the related conditions. (Color figure online)

Like in experiment 1, we want to verify if a non-matching signal can be used to manipulate the perception of users. We see that this is clearly the case for the pure haptic situation. Like with pure audio feedback in experiment 1, there is a huge drop in correctness from 94.9% to 23.0% when the haptic feedback does not match the real one (*Hn* and *Hm*). A similar decrease appears when we have matching modalities for haptics and sound; correct answers drop from 85.2% when both signals match the real situation (*HmSm*) to 23.9% when they both do not (*HnSn*). Thus, as expected, by representing an opposed signal for both modalities, we can manipulate people's perception in a way to experience the 'wrong', that is opposite characteristic of the material. Yet, if only one of the two modalities do not match (*HnSm*, *HmSn*), results are at chance level (55% and 59.4%). Running a two-way ANOVA with repeated measures and an error term on differences between participants over the data showed a significant effect ($p < 0.1$) of sound on correct discrimination of thickness ($p = 0.0959$) as well as of tactile feedback ($p = 0.0441$). However, an interaction effect between the two was not significant ($p = 0.492$). Normality of the mean data was confirmed using a Shapiro-Wilk test and QQ-normals plot.

Thus, we can positively answer our research question by concluding that perception of thickness can indeed be manipulated by providing opposed haptic and auditory feedback. Yet, this is only the case if both signals are congruent, as our results show that one of the two is not enough to achieve this effect.

5 Conclusion and Future Work

We presented two experiments verifying that we can influence how people perceive certain characteristics of material when tapping on them by manipulating auditory and haptic feedback. In a first initial test, we showed that we could 'trick' people into perceiving the volume of a solid cube as hollow by just changing the auditory feedback. Despite the small sample size, the trend clearly suggests the potential of such an approach. Yet, the results also show that there are limitations to this, since a similar effect could not be achieved for a solid, non-hollow cube. A second experiment confirmed these observations in a similar scenario (estimating the thickness of a wooden plate) and haptic feedback. Again, using different stimuli than the real situation changed the users' perception and experience of it. Yet, it also showed that in a more realistic scenario involving both senses, manipulating one of the stimuli is not sufficient. When manipulating one of them, results were on chance level; neither was the matching one strong enough to let people experience the situation as it is in the real world nor was the non-matching one strong enough to convince them of the opposed characteristic. But when both modalities matched, we are indeed able to manipulate users' perception again.

Our results are a small but important step towards creating a richer, more multimodal augmented reality environment that are not just focused on visual stimuli but embrace all our senses. Alternative applications of our research include a scenario where a single 3D-printed object is presented to users with different characteristics, such as hollow or solid by purely manipulating the multimodal haptic and acoustic feedback. Important areas to explore in future research include studying further characteristics of different materials and utilizing richer and more complex audio and haptic signals. Furthermore, one could explore how adding visual cues could further help in creating these augmented experiences; promising examples include visualizations of different materials, such as wood, marble, porcelain, and combining them with different audio cues or haptic feedback.

References

1. Avanzini, F., Crosato, P.: Integrating physically based sound models in a multimodal rendering architecture. Comput. Anim. Virtual Worlds **17**(3–4), 411–419 (2006)
2. Charpentier, A.: Experimental study of some aspects of weight perception. Archives de Physiol. Norm. Pathol. **3**, 122–135 (1981)
3. DiFranco, D.E., Beauregard, G.L., Srinivasan, M.A.: The effect of auditory cues on the haptic perception of stiffness in virtual environments. In: Proceedings of the ASME Dynamic Systems and Control Division, vol. 61, pp. 17–22 (1997)
4. Guest, S., Catmur, C., Lloyd, D., Spence, C.: Audiotactile interactions in roughness perception. Exp. Brain Res. **146**(2), 161–171 (2002)
5. Hachisu, T., Sato, M., Fukushima, S., Kajimoto, H.: Augmentation of material property by modulating vibration resulting from tapping. In: Proceedings of the International Conference on Human Haptic Sensing and Touch Enabled Computer Applications, pp. 173–180 (2012)
6. Hirano, Y., Kimura, A., Shibata, F., Tamura, H.: Psychophysical influence of mixed-reality visual stimulation on sense of hardness. In: Proceedings of IEEE Virtual Reality, pp. 51–54 (2011)
7. Iesaki, A., Somada, A., Kimura, A., Shibata, F., Tamura, H.: Psychophysical influence on tactual impression by mixed-reality visual stimulation. In: 2008 IEEE Virtual Reality Conference, VR 2008, pp. 265–266. IEEE (2008)
8. Kagimoto, M., Kimura, A., Shibata, F., Tamura, H.: Analysis of tactual impression by audio and visual stimulation for user interface design in mixed reality environment. In: Proceedings of the International Conference on Virtual and Mixed Reality, pp. 326–335 (2009)
9. Landau, L.D., Lifshitz, E.: Theory of Elasticity, vol. 1. Course of Theoretical Physics, vol. 3, p. 109 (1986)
10. Lederman, S.J., Klatzky, R.L., Morgan, T., Hamilton, C.: Integrating multimodal information about surface texture via a probe: relative contributions of haptic and touch-produced sound sources. In: 2002 10th Symposium on Haptic Interfaces for Virtual Environment and Teleoperator Systems, HAPTICS 2002, Proceedings, pp. 97–104. IEEE (2002)
11. Minamizawa, K., Kakehi, Y., Nakatani, M., Mihara, S., Tachi, S.: Techtile toolkit: a prototyping tool for design and education of haptic media. In: Proceedings of the 2012 Virtual Reality International Conference, p. 26. ACM (2012)
12. Mogees Ltd. Mogees pro (2016). http://www.mogees.co.uk/pro. Accessed 15 Sept 2017
13. Narumi, T., Nishizaka, S., Kajinami, T., Tanikawa, T., Hirose, M.: Augmented reality flavors: gustatory display based on edible marker and cross-modal interaction. In: Proceedings of Human Factors in Computing Systems, pp. 93–102. ACM (2011)
14. Punpongsanon, P., Iwai, D., Sato, K.: SoftAR: visually manipulating haptic softness perception in spatial augmented reality. IEEE Trans. Vis. Comput. Graph. **21**(11), 1279–1288 (2015)

15. Rosa, N., Hürst, W., Vos, W., Werkhoven, P.: The Influence of visual cues on passive tactile sensations in a multimodal immersive virtual environment. In: Proceedings of the ACM International Conference on Multimodal Interaction, pp. 327–334 (2015)
16. Van Den Doel, K., Kry, P.G., Pai, D.K.: FoleyAutomatic: physically-based sound effects for interactive simulation and animation. In: Proceedings of ACM Computer Graphics and Interactive Techniques, pp. 537–544 (2001)
17. Wu, W.-C., Basdogan, C., Srinivasan, M.A.: Visual, haptic, and bimodal perception of size and stiffness in virtual environments. ASME Dyn. Syst. Control Div. Publ. DSC **67**, 19–26 (1999)

Parameter Selection for Denoising Algorithms Using NR-IQA with CNN

Jianjun Li[1]([✉]), Lanlan Xu[1], Haojie Li[2], Chin-chen Chang[3], and Fuming Sun[4]

[1] School of Computer, Hangzhou Dianzi University, Hangzhou 310018, China
lijjcan@gmail.com
[2] School of Software, Dalian University of Technology, Dalian 140023, China
[3] Department of Information Engineering and Computer Science,
Feng Chia University, Taichung 40724, Taiwan
[4] School of Software, Liaoning University of Technology, Shenyang 140023, China

Abstract. In order to yield satisfied image after denosing processing, the process of error tracing is nearly necessary for parameter selection. In practice, usually the choice of such parameters is time consuming and empirically dependant when a ground-truth reference is inavailable. Although some successful methods have been proposed in recent research, they still require certain parameters to be set a priori for parameter optimization. These methods tend to be strongly reliant on restrictive assumptions on the signal and noise of input image. In this paper, we propose a framework of parameter selection, which is based on subjective perceptive evaluation and implementated by a well-designed convolutional neural network. The proposed algorithm has the following advantages: (1) consistents with subjective perception, (2) does not require a reference image available, (3) with better capability of robustness and generalization, (4) trims the number of iteration of denosing in parameter selection. Experimental results show that our algorithm outperforms other methods in parameter selection. Our parameter trimming framework saves the computation of iterative image denoising up to 74%.

Keywords: Image denosing · Parameter selection · CNN · NR-IQA
Parameter trimming

1 Introduction

In the digital image processing system, the phase of image preprocessing is of great significance to the success of subsequent tasks such as target detection, recognition and tracking. In many image processing algorithms, the value of parameters can greatly affect the result of image processing. In this paper, we study the parameter selection in image denoising algorithms. Image denoising algorithm is a dilemma. On the one hand, we need to select the optimized parameter that produces the best quality of image. On the other hand, we have to avoid those parameters that may cause noise, blur and so on. The general method for

© Springer International Publishing AG 2018
K. Schoeffmann et al. (Eds.): MMM 2018, Part I, LNCS 10704, pp. 381–392, 2018.
https://doi.org/10.1007/978-3-319-73603-7_31

selecting the best parameter, firstly, is to set a reasonable range for the values of parameters. Then, we can obtain denoised images with different degrees for each candidate parameter. Finally, we adapt an image quality assessment method to evaluate these denoised images and the best quality of image with low noise can be determinated.

In this paper, our study consists of three parts: image quality assessment, image denoising algorithms and parameter selection framework. For image quality assessment, according to whether the reference image is available, it can be divided into three kinds: full-reference image quality assessment (FR-IQA) [1, 2], reduced-reference image quality assessment (RR-IQA) [3] and no-reference image quality assessment (NR-IQA) [4–6]. The first two methods extract the characteristics of the distorted image by comparing with the reference images. These methods are able to accurately measure the distortion degree of the image objectively without involving any subject's judgements. However, since the reference image is not available in many applications, the no-reference image quality evaluation is particularly useful in the real world. Most of no-reference image quality assessment methods are based on the natural scene statistics (NSS) model [6]. Peng Ye et al. [4] proposed a non-reference image quality assessment method based on a dictionary learning. In recent years, deep learning technique has also been applied to no-reference image quality assessment [5] and achieved reasonable results. These methods train model using the human subjective opinion, so the results of the evaluation match human visual perception very well.

Image denoising is a very important part of image processing, and has always been the focus of research. So far, many denoising algorithms have achieved a good denoising effect. Buades et al. [7] proposed a non-local averaging image denoising algorithm which makes image blocks as a unit to find similar areas in the image. The algorithm can better remove the Gaussian noise that exists in image. Dabov [8] proposed the BM3D (Block-Matching and 3D filtering) algorithm which achieves a good denoising effect and therefore there are many researches follow it up. In this paper, we study two denoising algorithms, one is BM3D algorithm and the other is TV denoising algorithm implemented by regular iterations.

Parameter selection frameworks of image processing based on image quality have been proposed in [10,11,18]. However, images quality assessment is performed after the completion of the whole processing of iterative convergence. So choosing an optimum parameter in a certain range requires a very large number of iterations [10,11]. Liang and Weller [18] proposed a parameter selection framework which measures the image quality after each iteration and trimmed iterative process when the parameter unlikely to achieve the best result. The iterative process of one parameter candidate is determined by comparing the convergence trend of this candidate with another one. However, the algorithm is complicated when the range of parameter is large. To solve these problems, we propose a simple parameter selection framework to obtain the optimum parameter of denoising algorithm and reduce the implementation time.

The remainder of this paper is organized as follows. In Sect. 2, we describe our method in detail. Section 3 presents experimental results. Section 4 concludes with a summary of our work.

2 Methodology

2.1 No-Reference Image Quality Assessment

We propose a no-reference image quality assessment method using Convolutional Neural Networks (CNNs). First, we perform a local normalization for a gray image and then sample non-overlapping image patches where the size is 64×64 pixels from normalized image. Our network consists of ten layers: $64 \times 64 - 32 \times 30 \times 30 - 32 \times 15 \times 15 - 96 \times 15 \times 15 - 96 \times 7 \times 7 - 128 \times 7 \times 7 - 128 \times 3 \times 3 - 800 - 800 - 1$. Figure 1 shows the architecture of our network. The first layer is a convolutional layer that filters the input of 64×64 with 32 kernels. Each size of 5×5 with a stride of 2 pixels produces 32 feature maps with size of 30×30. A max pooling layer follows the convolutional layer to reduce each feature map to size of 15×15. The second layer is a convolutional layer consisting of 96 convolutional kernels each size of 3×3 with a padding of 1 pixel. This layer produces 96 feature maps with size of 15×15, followed by a max pooling layer to reduce each feature map with size of 7×7. The next layer is a convolutional layer that contains of 128 kernels with size of 3×3 padding of 1 pixel, producing 128 feature maps with size of 7×7. The sixth layer is a max pooling layer to downsampling each feature map to size of 3×3. The next two layers are fully connected layers with 800 nodes for each. The last layer is also a fully connected layer with one node that outputs the quality score Q. Except for the last fully connected layer, all of the layers are activated through the ReLU activation function. We apply a dropout regularization with a ratio of 0.5 after the second fully connected layers. Finally, we obtain average scores of all of the image patches to represent the entire image quality score.

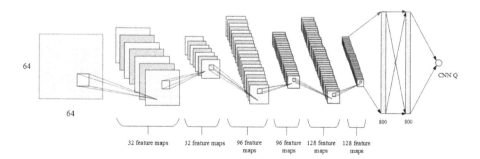

Fig. 1. The architecture of our network.

2.2   Image Denoising Algorithm

Rudin et al. proposed ROF model of Total Variation image denoising [13] which has become one of the most successful methods in image denoising and image restoration. The idea is to model the problem of image denoising as a minimization of the energy function to make the image smooth while the edge can be maintained well. This algorithm solves the contradiction between the restoration of the image detail and the suppression of the noise is better solved accordingly.

Generally, the total variation value of the noisy image is significantly larger than noise free image, so minimizing the total variance can eliminate the noise. Therefore, the ROF model of image denoising can be determined as follows:

$$\arg \min \left\{ \frac{\mu}{2} \|u - f\|_2^2 + \|u\|_{TV} \right\} \tag{1}$$

where $f \in R_d$ is noisy image, u is denoised image. The first term is the fidelity term, making u to retain the information of f as much as possible. The second term is the TV regularizer, which effectively preserve the edge during denoising. μ is the regularization parameter. The larger μ is, the smoother the image will be; the smaller μ is, the worse the effect of noise removal is. Therefore, choosing a suitable μ is crucial to the performance of image denoising. In our work, we consider the isotropic ROF denoising problem:

$$\min_u \left\{ \left\| \sqrt{(\nabla_x u)^2 + (\nabla_y u)^2} \right\|_1 + \frac{\mu}{2} \|u - f\|_2^2 \right\} \tag{2}$$

Split Bregman method [14] is used to solve (2). Suppose $d_x \approx \nabla_x u$ and $d_y \approx \nabla_y u$, then the denoising problem becomes:

$$\min_{u,d_x,d_y} \|(d_x, d_y)\|_2 + \frac{\mu}{2} \|u - f\|_2^2 + \frac{\lambda}{2} \|d_x - \nabla_x u - b_x\|_2^2 + \frac{\lambda}{2} \|d_y - \nabla_y u - b_y\|_2^2 \tag{3}$$

Appling Bregman iteration to (3), the minimization algorithm for the isotropic ROF function:

Initialize: $u^0 = f, d_x^0 = d_y^0 = b_x^0 = b_y^0 = 0$
while $\|u^k - u^{k-1}\|_2 > tol$ **do**
   $u^{k+1} = G(u^k)$
   $d_x^{k+1} = \max(s^k - \frac{1}{\lambda}, 0) \frac{\nabla_x u^k + b_x^k}{s^k}$
   $d_y^{k+1} = \max(s^k - \frac{1}{\lambda}, 0) \frac{\nabla_y u^k + b_y^k}{s^k}$
   $b_x^{k+1} = b_x^k + (\nabla_x u^{k+1} - d_x^{k+1})$
   $b_y^{k+1} = b_y^k + (\nabla_y u^{k+1} - d_y^{k+1})$
end while

---

where $G(u^k)$ represents the results of one Gauss Seidel sweep for the corresponding L2 optimization problem.

2.3 The Framework of Parameter Selection

In order to study the effect of parameter selection based on image quality on denoising results, we denoise the image of *Park* [17] with 25 different parameter values and the values are uniformly sampled from 1 to 49. Figure 2(a) shows the variation of the quality of denoised image during the iterative process of different parameters. In Fig. 2(a), the red curve represents the iterative process with the parameter of 13. It achieves the best denoising effect, therefore it is the optimal parameter for Park image. Figure 2(b) shows the results of evaluating of the denoised image produced by different parameters on SSIM and CNN Q. Because of the train data, a smaller value of CNN Q indicates image quality is better. In Fig. 2(b), it can be observed that the curves of CNN Q and SSIM is just the opposite, which means that the trend of predicted image quality is the same. And it is obvious that the best denoising effect is obtained when parameter is 13.

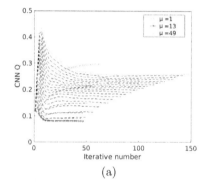 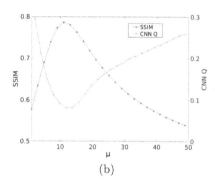

(a)   (b)

Fig. 2. (a): Denoising process of different parameters. (b): The result using SSIM and CNN Q to evaluate the denoised image. (Color figure online)

Image denoising is aimed to produce a clear image that has good visual perception, so we determine whether the algorithm converges on the basis of the change of the denoised image quality with each iteration. Assuming that $D_m = Q(m+1) - Q(m)$, $Q(m)$ represents the quality score of the denoised image produced by the m-th iteration, then the algorithm convergence is presented:

---

if $\max(D_m, D_{m-1}, ..., D_{m-l}) < T_q$ **then**
    Converge
else
    Continue iterating
end if

---

where l is the length of the change of quality score to ensure that the algorithm convergence, and T_q is the permissible change of quality score. If the value of l becomes larger and T_q becomes smaller, the convergence condition is more stringent.

From Fig. 2(a), it can be seen that the denoising algorithm is not monotonous. The image after iterative convergence is not necessarily the best quality image. And it's a waste of time to wait iterative convergence with each parameter. Therefore, we need to determine whether the parameter is the optimal parameter before iterative convergence. Suppose $pre(k) = q(j) + dev(j) * l_{pre}$, $pre(k)$ is the predicted quality value of the parameter k, $q(j)$ is the quality score of denoised image produced by the j-th iteration, $dev(j)$ is the numerical derivative of the j-th iteration, and l_{pre} is the predicted iteration length. Suppose q_{best} is the quality score of denoised image whose visual quality is best. The conditions of an iteration termination are expressed as follows: where t is the count and T is the threshold. The purpose of the parameter selection of the denoising algorithm is to obtain the best quality image. Therefore, the quality of the denoised image produced by each iteration of each parameter is compared with the quality of the best image. The iterative process is terminated when denoised image quality is worse than the q_{best} in consecutive T iterations. However, there may be a dramatic change in the subsequent iterations, we add the comparison criteria $pre(k) < q_{best}$ to prevent miscarriage.

Algorithm 1. parameter selection framework

Require: the noisy image
Ensure: the denoised image, the optimal parameter, the number of iterations.
  for $k =$parameter candidates **do**
    if $q(j) < q_{best}$ **then**
      $q_{best} = q(j)$
      $\mu_{best} = k$
      $t = 0$
    else if $pre(k) < q_{best}$ **then**
      continue iterating
    else
      $t = t + 1$
    end if
    if $t = T$ **then**
      parameter k is terminated
    end if
  end for

---

3 Experiments

3.1 The Performance of No-Reference Image Quality Assessment Method

Database. There are two common image databases used to train and test our CNN model.

LIVE [15]: This is the most commonly used database for evaluating IQA algorithms. The LIVE database consists of 779 distorted images, generated by 5 different types of distortion, with 29 reference images. The five types of distortions are JPEG2000 compression (JP2K), JPEG compression (JPEG), additive white noise (WN), Gaussian blur (Blur) and fast fading channel distortion (FF). We do not use all types of distorted images, only select WN and Blur distorted images. DMOS (Differential mean opinion score) is provided for each image in the database. The value is in range of [0,100], the larger the DMOS value is, the worse the visual quality of the image is.

TID2008 [16]: It contains 1700 distorted images, produced by 25 clear reference images through 17 types of distortions, 4 levels of distortions. We still only test WN and Blur types of distorted images. Each image in the database has a MOS value (Mean Opinion Score). The range of MOS values is [0,9]. The larger the MOS value is, the better the visual quality of the image is.

Evaluation Result. In order to evaluate the performance of our proposed NR-IQA algorithm, we adopt the two correlation coefficients between the predicted score and the subjective score of the image: (1) The Pearson Correlation Coefficient (LCC) is used to measure the linear relationship between the two variables. (2) Spearman Rank Order Correlation Coefficient (SROCC) is used to measure the monotonic relationship between two variables. The values of LCC and SROCC close to 1 indicate that the image quality predicted by the algorithm has a high correlation with human subjective opinion.

We train our CNN model on the LIVE database and test the performance of model on the TID2008 database. Our training data is WN and blur types of distortion images from the LIVE database. By default, all results reported are averaged from 100 train-test iterations. In each iteration, we randomly select 80% distorted images as the training set and the remaining 20% as the validation set. In order to verify the generalization ability of our proposed method, we test the model on two distortions (WN, blur) on TID2008 database. Table 1 is the result of experiments on validation set and test set.

Table 1. The result of experiments on validation set and test set

	LCC	SROCC
Validation	0.966	0.957
Test	0.916	0.901

3.2   Parameter Selection of Image Denoising Algorithm

In order to study the performance of the proposed parameter selection framework, we apply it to the ROF denoising model. First, two images are denoised with different parameter candidates and we observe the denoising results. The two images are distorted images of WN type from the CSIQ database [17] which is the image quality assessment database. Figures 3 and 4 shows the denoised process for *Prak* image and *Fisher* image with different parameters.

Then, we optimize the parameters of BM3D algorithm. The *Boat* image and *House* image (as shown in Fig. 5) are used to show the improvement of denoising effect comparing with default parameter after the original image suffers different variance of Gaussian noise whose range is [0.01, 0.1]. Figures 6 and 7 show the result of BM3D denoising algorithm using SSIM and CNN. In our experiment, we use default parameter $\mu = 30$ and optimize the parameter in the range of 1 to 40. Figures 6 and 7 demonstrate that parameter selection for BM3D improves the performance distinctly.

We examine the effect of the parameter selection framework on the denoising process. In our work, we set $T_q = 0.001, l = 5, l_{pre} = 5$, and $T = 10$ to achieve good performance which verified by experiment. We measure the quality of denoised image after each iteration for each parameter candidates. In our experiments, the predicted quality value of image is in the range [0,1] and its value close to 0 indicates better quality. Figures 8 and 9 show the difference between denoising process without or with parameter selection. From Figs. 8 and 9, it is obviously that the number of iterations is significantly reduced when using parameter selection framework. Moreover, the best μ is the same as the best μ from denoising process without parameter selection framework.

(a)   (b)   (c)   (d)

Fig. 3. (a) Noisy image; (b) denoising result with $\mu = 1$; (c) denoising result with $\mu = 13$; (d) denoising result with $\mu = 35$.

In order to show the advantages of the parameter selection framework intuitively, we make statistics on the data generated by denoising experiments on some images. Table 2 is the result of the comparison of the two algorithms. We name the denoising process without parameter selection framework and denoising process with parameter selection framework as A and B respectively. Clearly, our proposed algorithm can accurately find the optimal parameters from 25 values of candidates. More importantly, it saves implementation time dramatically.

Fig. 4. (a) Noisy image; (b) denoising result with $\mu = 1$; (c) denoising result with $\mu = 11$; (d) denoising result with $\mu = 49$.

Fig. 5. (a) Boat image; (b) House image.

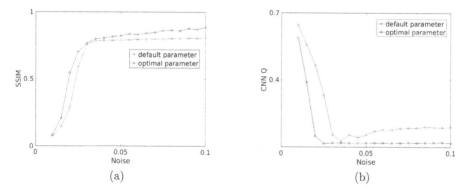

Fig. 6. Boat image, (a) image quality is evaluated by SSIM; (b) image quality is evaluated by our CNN model.

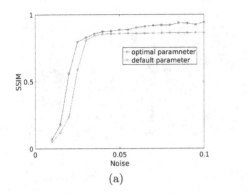
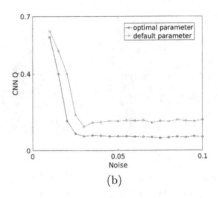

(a)   (b)

Fig. 7. House image, (a) image quality is evaluated by SSIM; (b) image quality is evaluated by our CNN model.

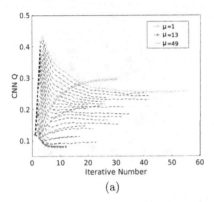
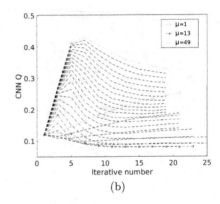

(a)   (b)

Fig. 8. Park image [17], (a) image denoising without parameter selection (b) image denoising with parameter selection.

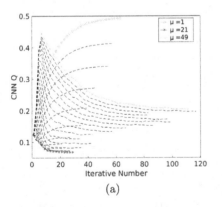
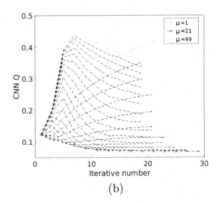

(a)   (b)

Fig. 9. Pepper image, (a) image denoising without parameter selection (b) image denoising with parameter selection.

Table 2. Performance of our parameter selection framework

	μ_{best} of A	μ_{best} of B	Iterations of A	Iterations of B	Reduced iteration
Park	13	13	658	259	60.7%
Fisher	11	11	932	238	74.5%
Pepper	21	21	709	245	65.4%
Man	11	11	707	217	69.3%
Cameraman	13	13	1063	274	74.2%
Barbara	13	13	817	235	71.2%

4 Conclusion

In this paper, we present a novel parameter selection framework based no-reference image quality assessment. We propose a CNN network to accurately evaluate the image quality, which is consistent with human subjective opinion. We apply our proposed parameter selection framework to BM3D denoising algorithm and Total Variation image denoising whose denoising process is iterative. For BM3D algorithm, we achieve better denoising effect by optimizing parameters. And it is verified that the iteration numbers of denoising process is significantly reduced by parameter selection. Meanwhile, we can accurately find the best parameters from a bunch of parameter candidates. We only study the effect of the parameter selection framework on the denoising algorithm in this paper. We will continue to verify the advantage of parameter selection in other image processing algorithms in the future work.

References

1. Wang, Z.: Image quality assessment: from error visibility to structural similarity. IEEE Trans. Image Process. **13**, 600–612 (2004). A Publication of the IEEE Signal Processing Society
2. Zhang, L.: FSIM: a feature similarity index for image quality assessment. IEEE Trans. Image Process. **20**, 2378–2386 (2011). A Publication of the IEEE Signal Processing Society
3. Tao, D.: Reduced-reference IQA in contourlet domain. IEEE Trans. Syst. Man Cybern. Part B Cybern. **39**, 1623–1627 (2009). A Publication of the IEEE Systems Man & Cybernetics Society
4. Doermann, D.: Unsupervised feature learning framework for no-reference image quality assessment. In: IEEE Conference on Computer Vision and Pattern Recognition, pp. 1098–1105. IEEE, Providence (2012)
5. Kang, L., Ye, P., Li, Y., Doermann, D.: Convolutional neural networks for no-reference image quality assessment. In: IEEE Conference on Computer Vision and Pattern Recognition, pp. 1733–1740. IEEE Computer Society, Columbu (2014)
6. Mittal, A., Moorthy, A.K., Bovik, A.C.: No-reference image quality assessment in the spatial domain. IEEE Trans. Image Process. **21**, 4695–4708 (2012)

7. Buades, A., Coll, B., Morel, J.M.: A non-local algorithm for image denoising. In: IEEE Computer Society Conference on Computer Vision and Pattern Recognition, pp. 60–65. IEEE Computer Society, San Diego (2005)

8. Dabov, K.: Image denoising by sparse 3-D transform-domain collaborative filtering. IEEE Trans. Image Process. **16**, 2080–2095 (2007). A Publication of the IEEE Signal Processing Society

9. Elad, M., Aharon, M.: Image denoising via sparse and redundant representations over learned dictionaries. IEEE Trans. Image Process. **15**, 3736–3745 (2006)

10. Herraiz, J.L., Gabarda, S., Cristobal, G.: Automatic parameter selection in PET image reconstruction based on no-reference image quality assessment. In: Nuclear Science Symposium and Medical Imaging Conference, pp. 3371–3374. IEEE, Anaheim (2012)

11. Zhu, X., Milanfar, P.: Automatic parameter selection for denoising algorithms using a no-reference measure of image content. IEEE Trans. Image Process. **19**, 3116–3132 (2010)

12. Liang, H., Weller, D.S.: Comparison-based image quality assessment for selecting image restoration parameters. IEEE Trans. Image Process. **25**, 5118–5130 (2016)

13. Rudin, L.I., Osher, S., Fatemi, E.: Nonlinear total variation based noise removal algorithms. In: Eleventh International Conference of the Center for Nonlinear Studies on Experimental Mathematics: Computational Issues in Nonlinear Science: Computational Issues in Nonlinear Science, North-Holland, Los Alamos, pp. 259–268. Elsevier (1992)

14. Goldstein, T., Osher, S.: The split Bregman method for L1-regularized problems. Soc. Ind. Appl. Math. **2**, 323–343 (2009)

15. Sheikh, H.R., Wang, Z., Cormack, L., Bovik, A.C.: LIVE image quality assessment database release 2. http://live.ece.utexas.edu/research/quality

16. Ponomarenko, N.: TID2008 - a database for evaluation of full-reference visual quality assessment metrics. Adv. Mod. Radioelectron. **10**, 30–45 (2004)

17. Larson, E.C., Chandler, D.M.: Most apparent distortion: full-reference image quality assessment and the role of strategy. J. Electron. Imaging **19**, 011006 (2010)

18. Liang, H., Weller, D.S.: Regularization parameter trimming for iterative image reconstruction. In: Asilomar Conference on Signals, Systems and Computers, pp. 755–759. IEEE, Pacific Grove (2015)

Real-Time Polyps Segmentation for Colonoscopy Video Frames Using Compressed Fully Convolutional Network

Itsara Wichakam, Teerapong Panboonyuen, Can Udomcharoenchaikit, and Peerapon Vateekul[✉]

Department of Computer Engineering, Chulalongkorn University, Bangkok, Thailand
{itsara.w,teerapong.pan,can.u}@student.chula.ac.th,
peerapon.v@chula.ac.th

Abstract. Colorectal cancer is one of the leading causes of cancer death worldwide. As of now, colonoscopy is the most effective screening tool for diagnosing colorectal cancer by searching for polyps which can develop into colon cancer. The drawback of manual colonoscopy process is its high polyp miss rate. Therefore, polyp detection is a crucial issue in the development of colonoscopy application. Despite having high evaluation scores, the recently published methods based on fully convolutional network (FCN) require a very long inferring (testing) time that cannot be applied in a real clinical process due to a large number of parameters in the network. In this paper, we proposed a compressed fully convolutional network by modifying the FCN-8s network, so our network is able to detect and segment polyp from video images within a real-time constraint in a practical screening routine. Furthermore, our customized loss function allows our network to be more robust when compared to the traditional cross-entropy loss function. The experiment was conducted on CVC-EndoSceneStill database which consists of 912 video frames from 36 patients. Our proposed framework has obtained state-of-the-art results while running more than 7 times faster and requiring fewer weight parameters by more than 9 times. The experimental results convey that our system has the potential to support clinicians during the analysis of colonoscopy video by automatically indicating the suspicious polyps locations.

Keywords: Colonoscopy · Polyp detection
Video frame segmentation · Real-time detection
Convolutional network

1 Introduction

Colorectal cancer (CRC), also known as colon cancer, is a very serious health issue. It can be fatal if not treated early; it is one of the leading causes of cancer deaths worldwide [1]. Colonoscopy is a very important procedure which medical professionals employ to visually examine and diagnose colorectal cancer without

© Springer International Publishing AG 2018
K. Schoeffmann et al. (Eds.): MMM 2018, Part I, LNCS 10704, pp. 393–404, 2018.
https://doi.org/10.1007/978-3-319-73603-7_32

causing a large surgical incision. The outcome of the diagnosing is dependent on clinicians' experiences as well as their mental and physical conditions [1], the screening procedure might be impaired by his/her exhaustion. Polyps miss rate is a critical problem. A comprehensive study shows that 22% of 1,650 polyps are missed at the screening round [2]. It is not uncommon that a clinician might miss smaller polyps and might have to re-perform the whole procedure to detect the polyps.

Polyp found in colonoscopy should be removed before it transforms to a malignant polyp. Polyp detection is one of the most important tasks in the development of computer-aided detection (CAD) system. An automated CAD system for polyp detection can speed up the examination time and improve the diagnosis outcome. Therefore, it would be very beneficial to introduce an automated CAD system for regular CRC screening routine.

In recent years, convolutional networks (ConvNet) have achieved state-of-the-art performance in various domains [3–5]. Despite the additional difficulty of having limited amount of labeled data, ConvNet models have been successfully applied to a variety of medical analysis tasks, by resorting to aggressive data augmentation techniques [6,7]. More precisely, ConvNet models have excelled at semantic segmentation tasks in medical analysis, such as the MICCAI 2015 Endoscopic Vision Challenge [1], where the top entries are built on ConvNet. However, some of the methods reported in [1] are not sufficiently described. Surprisingly, to the best of our knowledge, we associate this with the lack of large publicly available annotated databases, which are needed in order to train and validate such networks.

The development of colonoscopy application has been an active research area for over a decade. In the polyp image segmentation task, there are many issues that can cause limited detection performance. Although the most recent fully convolution approaches for semantic segmentation have shown promising segmentation performance on natural images datasets [8], the results for polyp segmentation are still limited as it fails to detect many polyps. In previous research, researchers have employed a traditional fully convolutional network (FCN); however, the classification time is too long [9]. For real-time image segmentation video sequences, scene segmentation requires a classification time that must be less than 40 ms for video recorded at 25 frames per second [9]. Unfortunately, all previously published deep learning based approaches cannot fulfill this requirement.

In this paper, we aim to speed up inference time for polyp segmentation while maintaining the accuracy of the model. We have initialized the weights using pre-trained weights from VGG-16 [4] model trained on ImageNet [10] for the accuracy improvement. A compressed FCN (C-FCN) architecture has been modified by removing the bottleneck fully-connected layers. In addition, our network has been compressed for faster inference time. Moreover, our customized loss function allows our network to be more robust when compared to the traditional cross-entropy loss function in this problem. We customized a loss function by computing the loss score from polyp class only and ignored the other classes.

The experiment was conducted on publicly CVC-EndoSceneStill database [9] consists of 912 image frames of 44 sequences from 36 patients. Our proposed framework has obtained state-of-the-art results while running more than 7 times faster and requiring fewer weight parameters by more than 9 times.

This paper is organized as follows: Sect. 2 describes related work; our proposed methods are presented in Sect. 3; dataset used in this study is stated in Sect. 4; experimental results and discussions are presented in Sects. 5 and 6, respectively; finally, we conclude our work in Sect. 7.

2   Related Work

Image Segmentation algorithms are often formulated to solve structured pixel-wise labeling problems, and ConvNet-based algorithms are state-of-the-art supervised learning algorithms for modeling and extracting latent feature hierarchies.

A prior application of deep neural networks to medical image segmentation is reported by [9]. Here, the authors take on the task of segmenting stacks of colonoscopy video frames, using a ConvNet such as FCN architecture. To segment an entire stack, the classifier is applied to each pixel of every slice in a sliding window manner by extracting a patch around the pixel. Improvements in deep learning based techniques over other hand-crafted techniques have been illustrated. Those successes have been attractive enough to draw attention of researchers in the field of computational medical imaging to investigate the potential of deep learning in medical images acquired with CT, MRI, and X-ray; for example, the variety of ConvNet-based medical image segmentation methods is due to different attempts at addressing difficulties specific to medical images [6].

Long et al. [8] proposed an adapted contemporary classification network incorporating Alex, VGG-16 and Google networks into a full ConvNet. In this method, some of the connections are skipped: pooling-3 (FCN-8s), pooling-4 (FCN-16s), and pooling-5 (FCN-32s). The skip connections technique reduces the potential gradient vanishing problem and has shown improvements in performance ranging from 20 to 62.2 percents in the experiments tested using PASCAL VOC 2012 dataset. Vázquez et al. [9] proposed the best baselines on the CVC-EndoSceneStill dataset (polyp data set which used in this paper) by training standard FCN for semantic segmentation and significantly outperforming, without any further post-processing, prior results in endoluminal scene segmentation.

In our paper, FCN-8s is selected as the reference model, since it is the top-rank architecture as reported in Long et al. [8] and Vázquez et al. [9].

3   Proposed System

For real-time polyps segmentation, we propose a network called "Compressed Fully Convolutional Network (C-FCN-8s)"—a lightweight ConvNet architecture for real-time polyps segmentation in colonoscopy video frames. There are three main contribution in our network: (*i*) the FCN-8s network compression, (*ii*) pre-trained weight initialization, and (*iii*) the loss function customization.

3.1 Compressed Fully Convolutional Network

Figure 1 shows network architectures of VGG-16 [4], FCN-8s (baseline) [8], and our network (C-FCN-8s). Both baseline and our network are designed for image segmentation; they are modified based on VGG, which is a network designed for image classification tasks. VGG-16 comprising of five feature extraction blocks, the first two blocks consists of a stack of two convolutional layers followed by one max-pooling layer. The last three blocks each consists of three convolutional layers followed by one max-pooling layer each. Each block has the number of feature maps: 64, 128, 512, 512, and 512, respectively. Two fully-connected (FC) layers have 4096 dimensions each. All layers are followed by ReLU nonlinearity except the classification layer which has linear activation and feeds to a softmax function.

In the original FCN-8s architecture (baseline), it is modified from VGG-16 to support an image segmentation task. Its fully connected (FC) layers have been transferred to convolutionalized layers. Each FC layer is transformed into $7 \times 7 \times 4096$ dimensions by 1×1 convolution through a process called *convolutionalization*. Although FCN-8s shows high segmentation performance, it is extremely slow due to a large number of parameters in the convolutionalized layers.

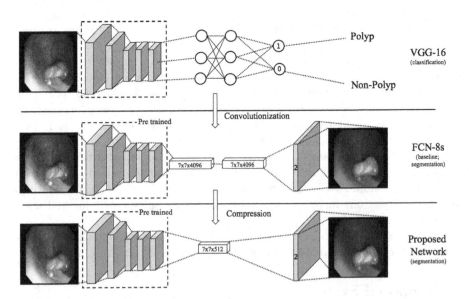

Fig. 1. Overview of our compressed network which is compressed from the original FCN-8s [8] based on VGG-16 [4] architecture.

Our proposed model aims to reduce a computational time by compressing the convolutionalized layers in FCN-8s [8] architecture. In the classification model, e.g. the VGG-16 which is a base architecture of FCN networks, removal of the FC layers only contributed to 1% of floating point operations (FLOP) [11]. In contrast, for the fully convolutional-like model, the number of FLOP significantly decreased due to a high number of parameters required in the upsampling connections between the convolutionalized layer and the up-sampling layer. Therefore, it is reasonable to compress the model by removing two convolutionalized layers as shown in Fig. 1. This reduces the number of trainable weights significantly.

Although, the FCN-8s model can obtain a promising accuracy in the task of polyp segmentation, its classification time is too long and it is unable to segment polyp in a video recorded at a high frame rate in real-time. For this reason, in our proposed system, we discard the FC layers (refers to the VGG-16 architecture) and its corresponding dropout which are the bottleneck in the FCN-8s network.

3.2 Pre-trained Weights

It is usual to initialize parameters in a network using random numbers. Unfortunately, it requires a large number of training examples and very long training time to obtain an accurate network. To solve this issue, we adapt the concept of "transfer learning" that applies pre-trained weight parameters from other models, mostly trained on natural images such as ImageNet [10] dataset, to initialize a neural network. Transfer learning outperforms random weight initialization as reported in the literature. Two recently published research fine-tuned a pre-trained Google's Inception v3 model on medical images. Their results yielded specialists' level in various medical imaging analysis tasks [12,13].

In preliminary experiments, we observed that the use of pre-trained weights led to a better performance. For both FCN-8s and our compressed networks, pre-trained weights of VGG-16 trained on ImageNet is used as initialized weights. Note that we transfer pre-trained weights to our compressed network only weights from the first five blocks, while weights on the remaining layers are randomly initialized.

3.3 Custom Loss Function

Normally, cross-entropy loss is widely used as a loss function. To ensure an accuracy of the network, the imbalanced training strategy aims to alleviate an imbalanced issue on the number of background class. Since the number of non-polyp pixels is large compared to that of the polyp ones. In most recent studies, the performance of segmentation algorithm has been measured in different ways [1,9]. In the field of medical image analysis, the most common evaluation metric is dice score which is computed as follow:

$$Dice(P(classes), T(classes)) = \frac{2 \times (P(classes) \cap T(classes))}{P(classes) \cup T(classes)} \tag{1}$$

where P is the prediction of the model and T is the actual target class. Loss function of dice score is computed by $1 - Dice$. Due to a large number of non-polyp pixels, background class (0) is extremely influential to the loss value during the learning phase. Therefore, we compute the loss value by only using the loss score from polyp class (1) and ignore the loss score from non-polyps class as follows:

$$Dice(P(polyp), T(polyp)) = \frac{2 \times (P(polyp) \cap T(polyp))}{P(polyp) \cup T(polyp)} \qquad (2)$$

In our preliminary experiments, we found that this loss function yielded a better performance than the standard cross-entropy loss. A major advantage of computing the loss value using polyp class only is that the network is forced to learn the feature associated with polyp regions.

4   Experimental Setup

4.1   Dataset

CVC-EndoScenceStill [9] dataset is composed of 912 video frames obtained from 44 video sequences taken from 36 patients. This dataset consists of two subsets; (i) CVC-ColonDB contains 300 images frame acquired from difference 13 patients. (ii) CVC-ClinicDB contains 612 image frames acquired from difference 23 patients. Colonoscopy video frames are provided with its corresponding handmade pixel-wise annotation. Table 1 summarizes the dataset used in this study.

Table 1. Summary of CVC-EndoSceneStill database

Database	nPatients	nSequences	nFrames	Resolution
CVC-ColonDB	13	13	300	500×574
CVC-ClinicDB	23	31	612	384×288
CVC-EndoSceneStill	36	44	912	500×574 & 384×288

4.2   Experimental Study and Design

Data split. The dataset is divided into three groups at patient level following the information provided by the data owner [9]. The training set is comprised of 547 frames (60%), the validation set contains 183 frames (20%), and the testing set is consist of 182 frames (20%). All frames are rescaled down to 224×224 using bilinear interpolation function.

Metrics. Intersection over Union (IoU) metric, which is the standard evaluation metric in medical image segmentation, is reported in this study. We computed the IoU for polyp class following the reference's [9] formula. Moreover, we also evaluated using widely use metrics such as, Dice score, F1 score, Precision (Pr) score and Recall (Re) score. To be more precise, we evaluated the experimental results based on metrics given by the Pascal VOC challenge [9,14] and determined that a polyp is detected if it has a high percentage of overlapping area with its corresponding ground truth.

Training strategy. Training strategies described in this section were used for all experiments. For each (R, G, and B) channel, mean subtraction was applied to the frames before they are fed to the network. We apply random rotation (up to $180°$), translation (random x and y shift from the center, maximum shift is 20%), shear intensity (up to 0.2), zoom (range from -0.8 to 1.2), zeros-padding (used for pixels outside the boundaries), horizontal flip, and vertical flip. The learning rate was initialized at $1e^{-3}$ and was reduced by a factor of 10 if the training loss did not decrease for 10 epochs. The models were trained using stochastic gradient descent with a batch size of 16, momentum of 0.9 and weight decay $5e^{-4}$. In order to prevent the overfitting problem, the training was halted when the validation dice coefficient did not increase for 50 epochs. Keras library with Tensorflow as backend was chosen for this study. All experiments were done using a single GeForce GTX 1080Ti GPU card.

5 Results

The results in this section were evaluated using the provided testing set as shown in Table 2. Our proposed system yielded a mean IoU score for polyps class of 69.36%, while the baseline system obtained a mean IoU score of 69.67%. Furthermore, we found no significant differences in evaluation scores on the FCN-8s and C-FCN-8s models based on paired t-tests.

Table 2. Results of detection performance in terms of IoU, Dice, F1, precision, and recall comparing between baseline (FCN-8s) and our method (C-FCN-8s). The last row refers to the p-value of paired t-test; no significant difference was found in any metrics.

Architecture	IoU	Dice	F1	Precision	Recall
FCN-8s	69.67	95.99	79.27	88.09	78.91
C-FCN-8s	69.36	95.94	78.61	88.48	78.14
P-value	0.67	0.54	0.33	0.51	0.38

Table 3 summarizes the testing time along with the number of parameters in the networks (required memory capacity). Note that the testing time constraint for video image segmentation must be less than 40 milliseconds per frame. At the inferring stage, our compressed network only requires 8 ms to segment polyps in each frame (conforming to the time constraint), while original FCN-8s network takes 59 milliseconds per frame. Moreover, our compressed network is three times faster—in the same environment settings—during the training stage.

Table 3. Results in terms of time and memory efficiency comparing between baseline (FCN-8s) and our method (C-FCN-8s). For time efficiency, there are training time and testing time. For memory efficiency, *nParams* refers to the number of trainable parameters of the networks (in million). The last row refers to a percentage of time and space reduction by the compressed network.

Architecture	Testing per frame (milliseconds)	Training per epoch (seconds)	nParams (million)	Memory (MB)
FCN-8s	59	23	134.2	1074.27
C-FCN-8s	8	7	14.7	117.84
% of reduction	86.44%	69.57%	89.05%	89.03%

Other than a huge improvement in terms of time, the results in Fig. 3 have shown that our compressed networks still maintain a competitive detection rate to the baseline, where the results of both models are almost identical. The most interesting aspect of this figure is that our proposed system yielded 80% detection rate as same as the level of baseline model when the overlap degree with ground truth is 50% which is the standard threshold for the detection performance. This means that our polyp miss rate is only 20%.

Figure 2 shows that our compressed network converges faster after a few epochs. Moreover, our compressed network is more robust on unseen data than

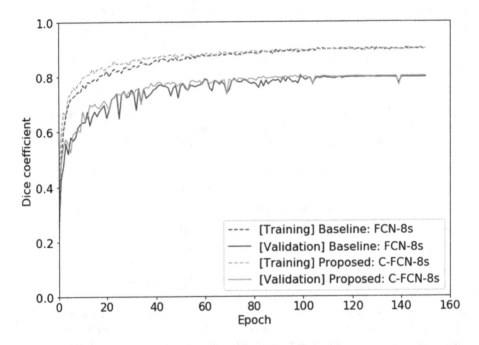

Fig. 2. Training monitor: each solid lines represents dice score for polyp class validated on validation data. Likewise, each dashed line represents dice score monitored on training data.

the FCN-8s. In many models, the optimization process is stopped at approximately after 140 epochs by an early stopping criteria. In summary, our compressed networks was trained for approximately 16 min for 140 epochs, while FCN-8s networks took up to 138 min.

In addition, FCN-8s based models are usually trained using (*i*) a traditional cross-entropy loss and (*ii*) cross-entropy loss with class weight balancing: 0.1 for non-polyp class and 100 for polyp class. From the experiment, both loss functions are unable to be converged, so the results evaluated on the testing set are "absolutely zero" for every metrics except the dice score because the networks predict all pixels as background class.

To further discuss the proposed strategy, the transfer learning has played an important role in improving an accuracy. Table 4 shows that initializing the networks with pre-trained weights can greatly increase the performance across multiple evaluation metrics. For example, transfer learning boosted the IoU score from 30.14 to 69.67.

Table 4. Results of detection performance in terms of IoU, Dice, F1, precision, and recall comparing between baseline (FCN-8s) with pre-trained and FCN-8s without pre-trained

Method	IoU	Dice	F1	Precision	Recall
FCN-8s w/o pre-trained	30.14	90.46	40.62	44.85	51.54
FCN-8s w/ pre-trained	69.67	95.99	79.27	88.09	78.91
% of improvement	131.15%	6.11%	95.15%	99.98%	53.1%

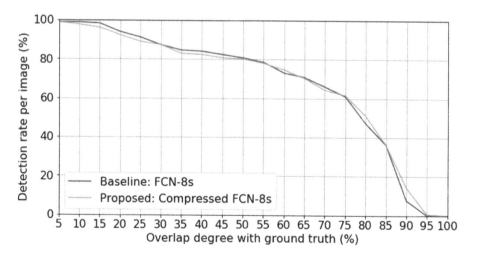

Fig. 3. Detection rate of polyps as a function of IoU. The x-axis represents the degree of overlap between ground truth and model prediction. The y-axis represents the percentage of correctly detection polyps.

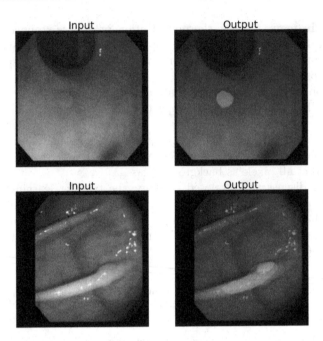

Fig. 4. Examples: green areas represent true positive areas, red areas are false positive, and blue areas are region that our model failed to detect (Color figure online)

6 Discussion

The segmentation results on the testing set are stated in Sect. 5. Our proposed system yielded results comparable to the state-of-the-art methods while running 7 times faster at the inferring stage and requiring fewer weight parameters by almost 9 times. No significant differences were found between our compressed and the FCN-8s models. This illustrates that our system can be used in a real-time polyp image segmentation in video sequences with the frame rate of 25 frames per second (or 40 milliseconds per frame; our required time constraint), while the baseline system is not able to perform at this speed [9]. Furthermore, our method can be used for video sequences with frame rate up to 125 frames per second.

Polyp miss rate is also investigated in this study, the result shows that our proposed system fails to detect only 20% of polyps which is lower than the polyp miss rate by clinicians' reported in the literature which is 22% [2].

One of the most important limitations of deep learning in medical image analysis is the limited amount of medical image data. Transfer learning is the most effective way to address this issue. Transfer learning using pre-trained weights has been proven to be successful in many medical imaging modalities [6].

7   Conclusion

In this research, a network called "a compressed fully convolutional network (C-FCN-8s)" is proposed to segment polyps within the video testing time constraint (under 40 milliseconds per frame) while still maintaining a promising detection performance. There are three improvements in our networks: (*i*) the FCN-8s network compression, (*ii*) pre-trained weight initialization, and (*iii*) the loss function customization.

The experiments were conducted on the CVC-EndoScenceStill dataset comparing between our network (C-FCN-8s) and baseline (FCN-8s). Rather than using a random weight initialization, the transferred weights can double the accuracy in terms IoU in any networks; from 30.14 to 69.67 in the baseline (FCN-8s). Furthermore, our compressed network reduces the number of parameters by removing the convolutionalized layers. The results demonstrate that our method can predict each video frame in 8 ms, which is under the 40 ms time constraint. This is 7 times faster than the baseline and can reduce the number of required parameters by more than 9 times. Furthermore, the results illustrate that the network cannot be converged without our custom loss function using a dice score only on the polyp class.

The experimental results conclude that our system has the potential to support clinicians during the analysis of colonoscopy video by automatically indicating the suspicious polyps locations. The link to our demonstration video is provided in this paper[1].

References

1. Bernal, J., Tajkbaksh, N., Sánchez, F.J., Matuszewski, B.J., Chen, H., Yu, L., Angermann, Q., Romain, O., Rustad, B., Balasingham, I., Pogorelov, K., Choi, S., Debard, Q., Maier-Hein, L., Speidel, S., Stoyanov, D., Brandao, P., Córdova, H., Sánchez-Montes, C., Gurudu, S.R., Fernández-Esparrach, G., Dray, X., Liang, J., Histace, A.: Comparative validation of polyp detection methods in video colonoscopy: results from the MICCAI 2015 endoscopic vision challenge. IEEE Trans. Med. Imaging **36**(6), 1231–1249 (2017)
2. van Rijn, J.C., Reitsma, J.B., Stoker, J., Bossuyt, P.M., van Deventer, S.J., Dekker, E.: Polyp miss rate determined by tandem colonoscopy: a systematic review. Am. J. Gastroenterol. **101**(2), 343–350 (2006)
3. Krizhevsky, A., Sutskever, I., Hinton, G.E.: Imagenet classification with deep convolutional neural networks. In: Pereira, F., Burges, C.J.C., Bottou, L., Weinberger, K.Q. (eds.) Advances in Neural Information Processing Systems 25, pp. 1097–1105. Curran Associates, Inc., Red Hook (2012)
4. Simonyan, K., Zisserman, A.: Very deep convolutional networks for large-scale image recognition. CoRR abs/1409.1556 (2014)
5. He, K., Zhang, X., Ren, S., Sun, J.: Deep residual learning for image recognition. In: The IEEE Conference on Computer Vision and Pattern Recognition (CVPR), June 2016

---

[1] https://www.cp.eng.chula.ac.th/~peerapon/MMM2018.html.

6. Litjens, G., Kooi, T., Bejnordi, B.E., Setio, A.A.A., Ciompi, F., Ghafoorian, M., van der Laak, J.A., van Ginneken, B., Sánchez, C.I.: A survey on deep learning in medical image analysis. Med. Image Anal. **42**(Suppl. C), 60–88 (2017)

7. Petscharnig, S., Schöffmann, K., Lux, M.: An inception-like CNN architecture for GI disease and anatomical landmark classification (2017)

8. Long, J., Shelhamer, E., Darrell, T.: Fully convolutional networks for semantic segmentation. In: 2015 IEEE Conference on Computer Vision and Pattern Recognition (CVPR), pp. 3431–3440, June 2015

9. Vázquez, D., Bernal, J., Sánchez, F.J., et al.: A benchmark for endoluminal scene segmentation of colonoscopy images. J. Healthc. Eng. **2017**, Article ID 4037190, 9 p. (2017). https://doi.org/10.1155/2017/4037190

10. Russakovsky, O., Deng, J., Su, H., Krause, J., Satheesh, S., Ma, S., Huang, Z., Karpathy, A., Khosla, A., Bernstein, M., Berg, A.C., Fei-Fei, L.: ImageNet large scale visual recognition challenge. Int. J. Comput. Vis. (IJCV) **115**(3), 211–252 (2015)

11. Li, H., Kadav, A., Durdanovic, I., Samet, H., Graf, H.P.: Pruning filters for efficient convnets. CoRR abs/1608.08710 (2016)

12. Gulshan, V., Peng, L., Coram, M., Stumpe, M.C., Wu, D., Narayanaswamy, A., Venugopalan, S., Widner, K., Madams, T., Cuadros, J., Kim, R., Raman, R., Nelson, P.C., Mega, J.L., Webster, D.R.: Development and validation of a deep learning algorithm for detection of diabetic retinopathy in retinal fundus photographs. JAMA **316**(22), 2402–2410 (2016)

13. Esteva, A., Kuprel, B., Novoa, R.A., Ko, J., Swetter, S.M., Blau, H.M., Thrun, S.: Dermatologist-level classification of skin cancer with deep neural networks. Nature **542**(7639), 115–118 (2017)

14. Everingham, M., Eslami, S.M.A., Van Gool, L., Williams, C.K.I., Winn, J., Zisserman, A.: The pascal visual object classes challenge: a retrospective. Int. J. Comput. Vis. **111**(1), 98–136 (2015)

Recursive Pyramid Network with Joint Attention for Cross-Media Retrieval

Yuxin Yuan and Yuxin Peng[✉]

Institute of Computer Science and Technology, Peking University, Beijing, China
{yuanyuxin,pengyuxin}@pku.edu.cn

Abstract. Cross-media retrieval has raised wide attention in recent years, for its flexibility in retrieving results across different media types by a query of any media type. Besides studying on the global information of the samples, some recent works focus on the regions of the samples to mine local information for better correlation learning of different media types. However, these works focus on the correlations of regions and sample, while ignoring the correlations between regions, including the significance of each region among all of them, and the supplementary information between the region and its sub-regions, similar to the sample and its regions. For addressing this problem, this paper proposes a new recursive pyramid network with joint attention (RPJA) for cross-media retrieval, which has two main contributions: (1) We repeatedly partition the sample into increasingly fine regions in a pyramid structure, and the representation of sample is generated by modeling the supplementary information, which is provided by the regions and their sub-regions recursively from the bottom to top of pyramid. (2) We propose a joint attention model connecting different media types in each pyramid level, which mines the intra-media information and inter-media correlations to guide the learning of significance of each region, further improving the performance of correlation learning. Experiments on two widely-used datasets compared with state-of-the-art methods verify the effectiveness of our proposed approach.

Keywords: Cross-media retrieval · Recursive pyramid network Joint attention

1 Introduction

Nowadays, multimedia data, including image, text and so on, has played an important role in people's daily life with huge amount and rapid emerging rate. For retrieving the useful information from such massive data, many researches have focused on multimedia retrieval for decades. The traditional retrieval methods, such as image retrieval [1] and video retrieval [2], mostly provide the results that share the same media type with the query. However, on one hand, results of single media type cannot offer comprehensive information as multiple media types do. On the other hand, the restriction of query type limits the flexibility

© Springer International Publishing AG 2018
K. Schoeffmann et al. (Eds.): MMM 2018, Part I, LNCS 10704, pp. 405–416, 2018.
https://doi.org/10.1007/978-3-319-73603-7_33

of retrieval and affects the user experience. Faced with these problems, a more flexible and effective retrieval paradigm has raised wide attention in recent years, namely cross-media retrieval.

Cross-media retrieval is to retrieve across the multimedia data by a query of any media type [3]. For example, users can get the relevant results of various media types like text, image or audio by submitting an image query. Unlike the direct similarity measurement between the samples with same media type, the representations of data with different media types lie in respective feature spaces, thus it is hard to measure cross-media similarity. This phenomenon is called as "heterogeneity gap", which is the main challenge for cross-media retrieval. For addressing this problem, the mainstream methods like [4–8] are to project the representations of different media types into a common space, where the correlation of them can be learned.

Most existing works focus on the correlations between the samples of different media types. Besides the global information offered by the whole sample, the regions like patches of an image or sentences of a text paragraph can provide the local information for better correlation learning of different media types. Some recent works [10,11] take regions of sample into consideration to promote cross-media retrieval. However, these works directly model the information of all regions and the whole sample, but ignore the correlations between regions. On one hand, the correlations between the region and its sub-regions are not considered. Like the complementary information provided by the regions to the whole sample, the sub-regions of the region can also offer the supplementary information for a more comprehensive understanding of the region, further resulting in more precise correlation learning and should not be ignored. On the other hand, these works treat all regions equally, while the significance of each region among all of them should be different. As the key information usually lies in some specific regions, exploiting the significance of each region can extract these key information for a better representation of sample.

To address the limitations of existing works, we propose a new recursive pyramid network with joint attention (RPJA) to deal with cross-media retrieval. The contributions of our approach are listed as follows: (1) We repeatedly partition the sample into increasingly fine regions in a pyramid structure, and the representation of each region is learned by modeling its own information and the supplementary information provided by its sub-regions, while the information of sub-regions is generated with the help of the sub-sub-regions, which forms a recursively network for all regions in the pyramid. In this way, the detailed information can be fully exploited and the final representation of the sample will be more comprehensive. (2) We propose a joint attention model connecting the different media types in each pyramid level to learn the attention weights, which refer to the significance of regions. The intra-media information within each single media sample and inter-media correlations between samples of different media types are jointly considered to guide the attention weights learning. As a result, the attention weights contain both the significance of the region in the single-media sample and the relationship between the samples of different media types, leading to more precise representation learning and better correlation learning. Experiments on two widely-used datasets named Wikipedia dataset and Pascal Sentence dataset compared with the state-of-the-art methods verify the effectiveness of our proposed approach.

2 Related Works

2.1 Cross-Media Retrieval

Cross-media retrieval aims to perform the retrieval across different media types by a query of any media type. The mainstream methods are to project the representations of multimedia data lying in different feature spaces into a common space for getting common representations, whose similarities can be measured. Based on the basic models, cross-media retrieval methods can be mainly divided into two categories, namely traditional methods and deep neural network (DNN) based methods [3].

Traditional methods. Traditional methods usually learn a linear projection matrix for each media. As one of the most representative methods, canonical correlation analysis (CCA) [4] learns the projection matrices by maximize the pairwise correlation between the common representations. By considering the category information, CCA extends to many variations [13,14]. Another classic method is cross-modal factor analysis (CFA) [15], which minimizes the Frobenus norm of pairwise common representations. Joint representation learning (JRL) [5] uses semi-supervised regularization and semantic information to learn the common representation and can be conducted on up to five media types. The previous works focus on the whole samples, ignoring the local information of the regions.

DNN-based methods. As the great power of deep learning has shown in many multimedia tasks, a lot of cross-media retrieval methods have been proposed based on the DNN model. For example, Correspondence Autoencoder (Corr-AE) [6] uses two linked autoencoders to model the multimedia data, jointly learning the correlation and reconstruction information at the code layer. Besides, CMDN [7] models the intra-modality and inter-modality correlations simultaneously by a hierarchical multi-network architecture. Wei et al. [8] use the image CNN features extracted from a pre-trained model as the inputs instead of the hand-crafted features. The above works prove the effectiveness of CNN features on cross-media retrieval.

Most existing methods directly process the whole sample, but ignore the local information provided by the regions of samples. Some recent works [10,11] take regions into consideration and improve the accuracy of cross-media retrieval. However, these works mainly focus on the correlations between sample and regions, while ignoring the correlations of the regions, including the significance of each region in all of them and the supplementary information between the region and its sub-regions.

2.2 Attention Mechanism

Attention mechanism has been widely applied for visual and language processing to find the significance of the parts of visual or text inputs. For example, Mnih et al. [9] propose a recurrent neural network model to adaptively select a sequence of regions or locations of an image or video for attention-based task-driven visual processing like image classification. Besides, the textual attention is used for natural language processing (NLP) problems like question answering [23] and text translation [24].

Except for the single media tasks, attention mechanism is also adopted to the multimedia tasks. For example, Yang et al. [12] propose stacked attention networks to deal with the visual question answering (VQA), which aims to search the regions of an image that related to the answer. Xu et al. [25] propose an attention based model that automatically learns to describe the content of images for image caption.

3 Our Proposed Approach

The architecture of our RPJA approach is shown in Fig. 1. The sample of each media type is repeatedly partitioned into increasingly fine regions, resulting in a pyramid-shaped structure. Each region in a higher pyramid level is made up of several sub-regions in the adjacent lower level. The feature of each region is generated by recursively learning the features of sub-regions, which are weighted fused into its original feature to fully make use of the supplement information provided by the sub-regions. In each pyramid level, a joint attention model is constructed to learn a more precise attention weight of each region with the help of intra-media information and inter-media correlation. At last, the final representation generated from the top level is projected into the common space for cross-media similarity measurement.

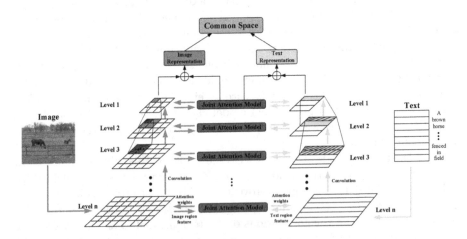

Fig. 1. An overview of our RPJA approach

We first introduce the formal definition. As two media types we used in this paper, image is denoted as I and text is T. The multimedia data is divided into training data and testing data. The training data is denoted as $D_{tr} = \{I_{tr}, T_{tr}\}$, where $I_{tr} = \{i_p, c_p\}_{p=1}^{n_{tr}}$ and $T_{tr} = \{t_p, c_p\}_{p=1}^{n_{tr}}$ refer to the image and text respectively. i_p and t_p are the p-th image/text pair with their correspond label c_p while n_{tr} is the number of training data. The testing data is denoted as $D_{te} = \{I_{te}, T_{te}\}$, where $I_{te} = \{i_q, c_q\}_{q=1}^{n_{te}}$ and $T_{te} = \{t_q, c_q\}_{q=1}^{n_{te}}$ are for image and text with n_{te} pairs.

Next we will introduce the four main parts of our proposed approach in the following subsections.

3.1   Pyramid-Shaped Partition and Feature Extraction

In this paper, we realize the partition by using convolutional network in a buttom-up way for both image and text. Actually, the convolution operation can be seen as the reverse of partitioning, which can merge several finer regions into a large region. Through the repeated convolutional operation on the sample, the increasingly fine regions can be generated in a pyramid structure, where the regions in the level 1 of pyramid contain the most areas of original sample while those in the level n may refer to the pixels of images or words in texts.

Specifically, for image, we take the resized images as inputs, and the spatial (2D) convolution layer is adopted between each two adjacent levels, for example, the level l and level $l+1$, to merge the sub-regions in level $l+1$ into the corresponding region in level l. The features of the regions in layer l can be generated by concatenating the response of each filter contained in the convolution layer, denoted as $V_l^i = \{v_{l1}^i, ..., v_{ln_l}^i\}$, where n_l means the number of image regions in level l. For the text, we first convert each word into a vector as the input though Word2Vec [22] model. We adopt the temporal (1D) convolution layer between adjacent levels instead of the spatial (2D) convolution layer used for image. The features are generated in the same way as image and denoted as $V_l^t = \{v_{l1}^t, ..., v_{lm_l}^t\}$, where m_l is the number of text regions in level l.

3.2   Joint Attention Model

In each pyramid level, we design a joint attention model to learn a more precise attention weight of each region by taking intra-media information and inter-media correlation into consideration simultaneously. For level l, given the image representation $V_l^i \in R^{n_l \times d_i}$ and text representation $V_l^t \in R^{m_l \times d_t}$, the intra-media attention weights $A_{l\_intra}^t$ for text and $A_{l\_intra}^i$ for image are calculated as follows:

$$M_l^t = tanh(V_l^t), \quad M_l^i = tanh(V_l^i), \tag{1}$$

$$A_{l\_intra}^t = softmax(M_l^t w_{l\_ta}), \quad A_{l\_intra}^i = softmax(M_l^i w_{l\_ia}), \tag{2}$$

where $w_{l\_ia} \in R^{d_i \times 1}$ and $w_{l\_ta} \in R^{d_t \times 1}$ are weight parameters of the linear layers. As to the inter-media attention weights, we use a shared-weights attention model to learn the correlation between different media types. The calculation is as follows:

$$M_l^{t'} = tanh(W_t V_l^t), \quad M_l^{i'} = tanh(W_i V_l^i), \tag{3}$$

$$A_{l\_inter}^t = softmax(M_l^{t'} w_l), \quad A_{l\_inter}^i = softmax(M_l^{i'} w_l), \tag{4}$$

where W_t and W_i are the matrices to project the features of image and text to a common space, and w_l is the shared weights. Finally, we treat intra-media and inter-media information equally and calculate the attention weights for each media type as the sum of intra-media and inter-media attention weights, which are

$$A_l^t = A_{l\_intra}^t + A_{l\_inter}^t, \quad A_l^i = A_{l\_intra}^i + A_{l\_inter}^i \tag{5}$$

With the significance of regions within a single-media sample provided by the intra-media attention weights, and the relationship between the samples of different media types provided by the inter-media attention weights, the attention weights of regions are more precise and further helpful for the correlation learning.

3.3   Recursive Feature Learning

The feature of each region is generated by recursively learning the features of its sub-regions and weighted fusing them with its original feature. The algorithm for image is shown in Algorithm 1. It is noted that the v_{lk}^i represents the feature vector of the k-th image region in the level l, while the $a_{(l+1)k_{sub}}^i$ refers to the corresponding sub-regions in the level $l+1$. Through the recursive feature learning processing, the final representation of the whole sample can be generated on the top level of the pyramid denoted as v_{ins}^i, which contains more comprehensive information than that generated only by the regions. The algorithm for text is the same as the image.

3.4   Common Representation Learning

After generating the attention vectors of image and text, we project them into the common space though a fully-connected layer to get the common representations R_i and R_t, and use a triplet loss function to constraint the correlation between them in the training stage. Specifically, the form of the loss function is

$$L = \frac{1}{N} \sum_{n=1}^{N} l_1(t_n^+, i^+, i^-) + l_2(i_n^+, t^+, t^-), \tag{6}$$

where

$$l_1(t_n, i^+, i^-) = max(0, score(t_n^+, i^-) - score(t_n^+, i^+) + \alpha) \tag{7}$$

$$l_2(i_n, t^+, t^-) = max(0, score(i_n^+, t^-) - score(i_n^+, t^+) + \alpha) \tag{8}$$

N refers to number of triplet tuples. (t_n^+, i^+) is a random image/text pair of the same category, and (t_n^+, i^-) is the pair of different category labels. The definition

---

Algorithm 1. Recursive Feature Learning for Image

Input: Original features of regions V^i, the number of levels n
Output: The final representation of the overall sample of image v_{ins}^i.
1: **function** RECURSIVELEARNING(level l)
2:     **if** $l == n$ **then**
3:         Learn the attention weights A_l^i of the regions on level l
4:     **else**
5:         v_{l+1}^i, A_{l+1}^i = RECURSIVELEARNING($l+1$)
6:         **for** $k = 1 : n_l$ **do**
7:             $v_{lk}^i = Max(a_{(l+1)k_{sub}}^i \cdot v_{(l+1)k_{sub}}^i) + v_{lk}^i$
8:         **end for**
9:         Learn the attention weights A_l^i of the regions on level l by V_l^i
10:     **end if**
11:     **return** V_l^i A_l^i
12: **end function**
13:
14: V_1^i, A_1^i = ATTENTIONLEARNING(1)
15: $v_{ins}^i = \sum_{n=1}^{n_1} a_{1n}^i v_{1n}^i$

---

of (i_n^+, t^+) and (i_n^+, t^-) is similar. α is the margin parameter. The score of each pair is calculated as the dot-product between the common representations. For example,

$$score(t_n^+, i^-) = r_{t_n^+} \cdot r_{i^-} \tag{9}$$

The common representations are normalized into unit vectors to restrict the score in $[-1, 1]$.

4   Experiments

In this section we will represent the experimental results and analysis. We verify the effectiveness of our approach on two widely-used datasets, comparing to 7 state-of-the-art methods with 2 retrieval tasks.

4.1   DataSets

Here we briefly introduce the datasets we used for the experiments, which are Wikipedia dataset and Pascal Sentence dataset.

Wikipedia dataset [13] is the most widely-used dataset for cross-media retrieval. It consists of 2,866 image and text pairs with 10 categories, selected from the "featured articles" in Wikipedia. For fair comparison, we follow [6] to split this dataset into three subsets, which are training set, testing set and validation set, including 2,173, 462 and 231 pairs respectively.

Pascal sentence dataset [16] is generated from 2008 PASCAL development kit. It has 1,000 images with 20 categories and the number of images per category is equal. Each image has 5 text descriptions generated by Amazon Mechanical Turk. Similar with Wikipedia dataset, this dataset is randomly split into three subsets, 800 image/text pairs for training, 100 pairs for testing and validation respectively.

4.2 Details of Network

The details of the implementation are presented here, including data preprocessing and parameters of the network.

Data preprocessing. The images are resized to 224×224 as the inputs of VGG net. The words of texts are converted into 300-dimensional vectors by the Word2Vec [22] model trained on GoogleNews dataset, and make up a $k \times 300$ matrix as the input of the network. k is lengths of input words, which is set as the maximum length of all the text data, and those beneath this limit are padded by zeros. Specifically, the lengths of Wikipedia dataset and Pascal Sentence dataset are 2,904 and 110 separately. The word vectors are fed into a fully-connected layer, whose weight parameters are trained in the network, and the outputs are 512-dimensional vectors.

Parameters of network. In this paper, we construct a network with two levels to verify the effectiveness of the supplementary information provided by the sub-regions for the region. For the image, we directly use the VGG net with batch normalization [20] to partition the images. The VGG model is fine-tuned on the target dataset in advance, and keeps all parameters fixed in the training phase of our approach. We set the fifth pooling layer (pool5) and fourth pooling layer (pool4) as the level 1 and level 2 in the pyramid network because the features in earlier layers are less robust [21]. The preprocessed text data is fed into a convolution module, which is inspired by the convolutional operation of WCNN [19]. The output of the convolution module refers to the top level in pyramid network and the preprocessed text data refers to the level 2. The convolution module consists of a temporal (1D) convolution layer with 512 filters, a batch normalization layer, a ReLU activation function layer and a temporal max-pooling layer. The kernel width and stride of convolution layer and max-pooling layer are customized for the specific dataset because of the variance of the input lengths. Specifically, for Wikipedia dataset, the kernel width of convolution layer is 3 and the stride is 3, and the kernel width and stride for max-pooling layer are both 8. As a result, each 24 words without overlapping make up a phrase. For the Pascal Sentence dataset, the parameter combinations for the two layers are $(2, 2)$ and $(5, 5)$, first one of each means the kernel width and the second one refers to stride, leading to that each phrase consists of 10 words. At last, the common representations are 4,096 dimensional vectors, and α in the loss function is set to 0.5.

4.3 Compared Methods

We conduct the experiments comparing with 8 state-of-the-art methods to verify the effectiveness of our approach, including CCA [4], CFA [15], JRL [5], LGCFL [18], Corr-AE [6], DCCA [17] and Deep-SM [8]. The previous four methods are traditional methods while the last four are based on DNN.

Our architecture is an end-to-end network, which takes original image and text word embedding as inputs, while the compared methods mostly conduct their experiments on the features of multimedia data. For fair comparison, for image we use the same fine-tuned VGG model and extract outputs of the final fully-connected layer (fc7) as the inputs of the compared methods. Corresponding to the image, we use the WCNN [19] method to train a classification network on the text of each dataset and extract the features transported into the classification layer. It is noted that we replace the CNN model of original WCNN architecture with the one adopted in our approach for fair comparison.

4.4 Evaluation Metrics

In this paper, we carry out two cross-media retrieval tasks, which are text retrieve image (text→image) and image retrieve text (image→text). For text→image, after generating the common representations of image and text, we measure the cosine distances between text query and all images in the testing set as similarity scores. Then the scores are sorted in descending order, and the images with higher scores are more similar with the text query. It is the same for image→text.

The Mean Average Precision (MAP) is used to evaluate the effectiveness of all methods. MAP is the mean of average precision (AP) of all queries. AP can be computed as follows:

$$AP = \frac{1}{R} \sum_{k=1}^{n} \frac{R_k}{k} \times rel_k, \tag{10}$$

where R is the number of relevant items in the testing set, while R_k is that in the top k results. n means the size of testing set, and rel_k tells the k-th result is right or not. If the result is right, rel_k is set as 1, otherwise as 0.

4.5 Experiment Results and Analysis

Table 1 shows the results of our approach as well as the compared methods on Wikipedia and Pascal Sentence datasets. As we have seen, our approach achieves the best performance on both datasets. Numerically, our RPJA approach improves the highest average MAP score of compared methods from 0.441 to 0.459 in Wikipedia dataset, while in Pascal Sentence dataset, our result surpass the compared methods by 0.025. This is because our RPJA approach not only take use of the local information lies in the regions of sample, but also mine the correlations between regions, which addresses the limitation of existing methods and results in a better correlation learning for cross-media retrieval.

Table 1. The MAP scores **Wikipedia** and **Pascal Sentence** dataset.

Method	Wikipedia dataset			Pascal Sentence dataset		
	Image→Text	Text→Image	Average	Image→Text	Text→Image	Average
Our RPJA	**0.469**	**0.449**	**0.459**	**0.560**	**0.562**	**0.561**
Deep-SM [8]	0.457	0.398	0.428	0.552	0.519	0.536
LGCFL [18]	0.455	0.403	0.429	0.556	0.464	0.510
JRL [5]	0.465	0.416	0.441	0.546	0.517	0.532
DCCA [17]	0.449	0.400	0.425	0.541	0.523	0.532
Corr-AE [6]	0.428	0.388	0.408	0.504	0.480	0.492
CFA [15]	0.376	0.254	0.315	0.516	0.408	0.462
CCA [4]	0.292	0.268	0.280	0.165	0.137	0.151

Table 2 shows the comparison of the complete RPJA approach and the baselines. RPJA-(top level) set the number of pyramid level into 1, meaning that there is no sub-regions of the region in the top level, which aims to verify the effectiveness of the supplementary information learning from the sub-regions. RPJA-intra and RPJA-inter denotes the RPJA with only intra-media attention weight and with only inter-media attention weight. We keep all other settings the same with the complete RPJA approach for fair comparison.

Table 2. The MAP scores of our RPJA and baselines.

Method	Wikipedia dataset			Pascal Sentence dataset		
	Image→Text	Text→Image	Average	Image→Text	Text→Image	Average
Our RPJA	**0.469**	**0.449**	**0.459**	**0.560**	**0.562**	**0.561**
RPJA-(top level)	0.456	0.436	0.446	0.546	0.548	0.547
RPJA-intra	0.458	0.429	0.444	0.554	0.526	0.540
RPJA-inter	0.443	0.422	0.433	0.539	0.537	0.538

As we have seen in the Table 2, the trends on both datasets are the same. The results of our RPJA are better than RPJA-(top level), which show that the supplementary information provided by the sub-regions help to improve the cross-media retrieval accuracy and should not be ignored. What's more, intra-media attention and inter-media attention promote the correlation learning together, resulting a higher MAP score than that achieved by each of them.

5   Conclusion

This paper has proposed a recursive pyramid network with joint attention (RPJA) for cross-media retrieval, which aims to not only take use of the local information lies in the regions of sample, but also mine the correlations between the regions, including the supplementary information between the region and its sub-regions, and the significance of each region among all of them. It first partitions the sample into increasingly fine regions in a pyramid structure, and models the supplementary information of each region and its sub-regions recursively. What's more, we design a joint attention model between different media types in each level to use intra-media information and inter-media correlations to learn the attention weight of each region for a better correlation learning. Experiments on two widely-used datasets verify the effectiveness of our approach. For future work, we plan to conduct our approach on more than two media types to accomplish a more flexible cross-media retrieval.

Acknowledgment. This work was supported by National Natural Science Foundation of China under Grant 61771025 and Grant 61532005.

References

1. Hu, Y., Cheng, X., Chia, L.T., et al.: Coherent phrase model for efficient image near-duplicate retrieval. IEEE Trans. Multimedia (TMM) **11**(8), 1434–1445 (2009)
2. Peng, Y., Ngo, C.W.: Clip-based similarity measure for query-dependent clip retrieval and video summarization. IEEE Trans. Circ. Syst. Video Technol. (TCSVT) **16**(5), 612–627 (2006)
3. Peng, Y., Huang, X., Zhao, Y.: An overview of cross-media retrieval: concepts, methodologies, benchmarks and challenges. IEEE Trans. Circ. Syst. Video Technol. (TCSVT) (2017)
4. Hotelling, H.: Relations between two sets of variates. Biometrika **28**(3/4), 321–377 (1936)
5. Zhai, X., Peng, Y., Xiao, J.: Learning cross-media joint representation with sparse and semi-supervised regularization. IEEE Trans. Circ. Syst. Video Technol. (TCSVT) **24**(6), 965–978 (2014)
6. Feng, F., Wang, X., Li, R.: Cross-modal retrieval with correspondence autoencoder. In: 22nd ACM International Conference on Multimedia (ACM MM), pp. 7–16 (2014)
7. Peng, Y., Huang, X., Qi, J.: Cross-media shared representation by hierarchical learning with multiple deep networks. In: International Joint Conference on Artificial Intelligence (IJCAI), pp. 3846–3853 (2016)
8. Wei, Y., Zhao, Y., Lu, C., et al.: Cross-modal retrieval with CNN visual features: a new baseline. IEEE Trans. Cybern. (TCYB) **47**(2), 449–460 (2017)
9. Mnih, V., Heess, N., Graves, A.: Recurrent models of visual attention. In: Advances in Neural Information Processing Systems (NIPS), pp. 2204–2212 (2014)
10. Peng, Y., Zhai, X., Zhao, Y., et al.: Semi-supervised cross-media feature learning with unified patch graph regularization. IEEE Trans. Circ. Syst. Video Technol. **26**(3), 583–596 (2016)
11. Peng, Y., Qi, J., Huang, X., et al.: CCL: cross-modal correlation learning with multi-grained fusion by hierarchical network. arXiv preprint arXiv:1704.02116 (2017)
12. Yang, Z., He, X., Gao, J., et al.: Stacked attention networks for image question answering. In: IEEE Conference on Computer Vision and Pattern Recognition (CVPR), pp. 21–29 (2016)

13. Rasiwasia, N., Costa Pereira, J., Coviello, E., et al.: A new approach to cross-modal multimedia retrieval. In: 18th ACM International Conference on Multimedia (ACM MM), pp. 251–260 (2010)

14. Gong, Y., Ke, Q., Isard, M., et al.: A multi-view embedding space for modeling internet images, tags, and their semantics. Int. J. Comput. Vis. (IJCV) **106**(2), 210–233 (2014)

15. Li, D., Dimitrova, N., Li, M., et al.: Multimedia content processing through cross-modal association. In: 11th ACM International Conference on Multimedia (ACM MM), pp. 604–611 (2003)

16. Rashtchian, C., Young, P., Hodosh, M., et al.: Collecting image annotations using Amazon's mechanical turk. In: NAACL HLT 2010 Workshop on Creating Speech and Language Data with Amazon's Mechanical Turk, pp. 139–147 (2010)

17. Yan, F., Mikolajczyk, K.: Deep correlation for matching images and text. In: IEEE Conference on Computer Vision and Pattern Recognition (CVPR), pp. 3441–3450 (2015)

18. Kang, C., Xiang, S., Liao, S., et al.: Learning consistent feature representation for cross-modal multimedia retrieval. IEEE Trans. Multimedia (TMM) **17**(3), 370–381 (2015)

19. Kim, Y.: Convolutional neural networks for sentence classification. In: Conference on Empirical Methods in Natural Language Processing (EMNLP), pp. 1746–1751 (2014)

20. Simon, M., Rodner, E., Denzler, J.: Imagenet pre-trained models with batch normalization. arXiv preprint arXiv:1612.01452 (2016)

21. Krause, J., Jin, H., Yang, J., et al.: Fine-grained recognition without part annotations. In: IEEE Conference on Computer Vision and Pattern Recognition (CVPR), pp. 5546–5555 (2015)

22. Mikolov, T., Sutskever, I., Chen, K., Corrado, G.S., Dean, J.: Distributed representations of words and phrases and their compositionality. In: Conference on Neural Information Processing Systems (NIPS), pp. 3111–3119 (2013)

23. Kumar, A., Irsoy, O., Ondruska, P., et al.: Ask me anything: dynamic memory networks for natural language processing. In: International Conference on Machine Learning (ICML), pp. 1378–1387 (2016)

24. Bahdanau, D., Cho, K., Bengio, Y.: Neural machine translation by jointly learning to align and translate. In: International Conference on Learning Representations (ICLR) (2015)

25. Xu, K., Ba, J., Kiros, R., et al.: Show, attend and tell: neural image caption generation with visual attention. In: International Conference on Machine Learning (ICML), pp. 2048–2057 (2015)

Reinforcing Pedestrian Parsing
on Small Scale Dataset

Qi Zheng[1,2,3(✉)], Jun Chen[1,2,3], Junjun Jiang[4], and Ruimin Hu[1,2,3]

[1] National Engineering Research Center for Multimedia Software,
School of Computer Science, Wuhan University, Wuhan, China
{zhengq,chenj}@whu.edu.cn, hurm1964@gmail.com
[2] Hubei Key Laboratory of Multimedia and Network Communication Engineering,
Wuhan University, Wuhan, China
[3] Research Institute of Wuhan University in Shenzhen, Wuhan, China
[4] School of Computer Science, China University of Geosciences, Beijing, China
junjun0595@163.com

Abstract. In this paper we address the problem of automatic pedestrian parsing in surveillance video with only a small number of training samples. Although human parsing has achieved great success with high-capacity models, it is still quite challenging to parse pedestrians in practical surveillance conditions because complicated environmental interferences need more pixel-level training samples to fit. But creating large datasets with pixel-level labels has been extremely costly due to the vast amount of human effort required. Our method is developed to capture the pedestrian information from the non-labeled datasets to update the trained model by reinforcement learning, which achieves elegant performance with only much fewer pixel-level labeled samples. Both quantitative and qualitative experiments conducted on practical surveillance datasets have shown the effectiveness of the proposed method.

Keywords: Pedestrian parsing · Reinforcement learning
Small scale dataset

1 Introduction

Human parsing is a specific image parsing task for labeling human part items, such as hair, head, body, arms, and legs, on the level of pixels. It has attracted growing attentions in wide fields, ranging from person identification [1–3], body shape estimation [4,5] and content-based image retrieval [6] to fashion images parsing [7–9]. This paper mainly focuses on parsing work about the human in surveillance environment, also called pedestrian. This work can be used as implicit cue of persons positions, identities and even their occlusions, which paly significant roles in security system.

The flourish of deep learning in recent years has paved a new way to deal with segmentation problem by high-capacity models and achieved significant successes in the area of human parsing [5,10–14]. Compared with other human

© Springer International Publishing AG 2018
K. Schoeffmann et al. (Eds.): MMM 2018, Part I, LNCS 10704, pp. 417–427, 2018.
https://doi.org/10.1007/978-3-319-73603-7_34

related applications, pedestrian parsing is a much more difficult problem under surveillance environment due to low resolution, illumination change, viewpoint variation, motion blur and etc. To deal with those diverse interferences, much more pixel-level training samples are usually used to fit high-capacity models. But creating large training dataset with pixel-wise semantic labels is also quite strenuous because of the vast amount of human effort required to trace accurate body parts boundaries.

Data augmentation is firstly introduced for enlarging the training dataset by applying image manipulations such as shifting, scaling, and other affine transformations [15]. But it performs limited improvement because of the limited increase of image details. Synthetic data has also been used for feeding deep architecture models [16–18]. To generate the synthetic data, some other resources (like depth sensors, rendering engines) are required, which are not widely available on practical surveillance environment.

Compared with those reprocessed data, pedestrian images with non-labeled are much easier to achieve. Some partially supervised learning approaches gave feasible results on extra unlabeled data for classification [19–21]. The work, though from different domain, inspires us to utilize larger pedestrian images even without pixel-wise labels to improve the pedestrian parsing model. On the other side, it means that we can use fewer pixel-level labeled images as training samples. However, those above classification work often assumes that similar feature correspond the same label. This assumption is unhelpful to segmentation problem because similar feature will not result in the same edge. To handle this problem, we proposed a reinforcement learning method with edge-sensitive model to parse pedestrian images on a very small training dataset. Unlike the classical parsing methods trying to design a complicated deep model, we explore the reinforcement framework to refine deep model which is compatible with any segmentation models.

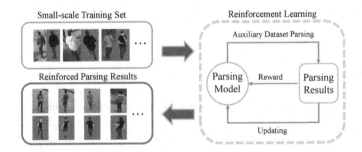

Fig. 1. Firstly, given a small scale dataset (the upper left box), an initial parsing model is trained. Then the model is reinforced in the next step with auxiliary non-labeled dataset by reinforcement learning, as the dashed box shown. Finally the reinforced model is evaluated in the test set.

In our work, an iterative method is raised to parse pedestrian images. Firstly, an initialized model is trained by only a small dataset. Then the model is used to parse non-labeled images. Finally, model update is realized via reinforcement learning with searching the best parsing results as illustrated in Fig. 1. Both quantitative and qualitative experiments show the effectiveness of the proposed method.

The major contributions of this work can be summarized as follows: (1) We propose a novel pedestrian parsing method to achieve considerable performance only based on few training samples, which means we suffer less pixel-level painstaking labeling work. (2) We carefully design an edge-sensitive value model for reinforcement learning. (3) Our experiments demonstrate the effectiveness of our approach.

2   Pedestrian Parsing Reinforcement

In this section, a pedestrian parsing method based on reinforcement learning is described in detail, including the main framework, parsing model, value model, and model update.

2.1   Overview of the Pedestrian Parsing Reinforcement Framework

We observe that pedestrian images are much easier to achieve than their pixel-level labels. But most of existing methods omit the abundant information behind those non-label images. In order to take advantage of the plentiful knowledge, we design a reinforcement learning for the surveillance parsing problem as shown in Fig. 1.

There are three key components in reinforcement learning, including model, policy and value function. Here we consider the classical deep model FCN (Fully Convolutional Network) as the model in reinforcement learning. In the first step, the FCN model is initialized on the small training dataset. Then the last layer of the initialized model is taken as the policy to parse the the larger scale pedestrian dataset. Finally a reward signal from value function is proposed for updating the model. Note that we extract the high-level and low-level information to feed the value function.

2.2   Parsing Model

Pedestrian parsing can be considered as a labeling problem, where each pixel in an image is assigned a semantic label which can be selected from background, hat, or from a large set of body items (e.g. hair, legs, upper-body). Surveillance images often suffer low-resolution, motion blur and etc., which make them more challenging to parse. To deal with those problems, the deep architecture model is an ideal solution because of its high-capacity. However the small scale training set results in overfitting, which means it needs more training samples to achieve a satisfied performance. Thus our target is exploring a feasible framework to maintain the advantages of deep architecture model but avoid the disadvantages of the insufficient training samples with pixel-accurate pedestrian part labels.

Here we take a classical deep model FCN, which has achieved remarkable results in many areas of computer vision, as our parsing model (Fig. 2). In the experiments report of [22], it showed impressive performance in human-related parsing dataset. As an extension of CNN, FCN transforming fully connected layers of CNN into convolution layers enables a classification net to output a heatmap and adds a spatial loss to produce an efficient machine for end-to-end dense learning. But the spatial information will be fuzzy after a couple of convolution layers. To resolve this problem, FCN defines 'skip' architecture to combine coarse, high layer information with fine, low layer information. As an end-to-end model, the last layer is used to predict the class per-pixel and the left layers capture features from the image, which are corresponding to the key components (policy and model respectively) in the reinforcement learning. Here we change the classes in the last output layer from 21 to 24 (including background class) to adapt to our surveillance environment.

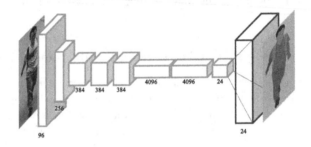

Fig. 2. Overview of the deep architecture based pedestrian parsing model. We train the end-to-end fully convolutional network with 24 classes.

2.3   Value Model

Value model predicts reward which is helpful to reinforce the model. Thus we design a simple but efficient value model to predict each image confidence in the non-labeled pedestrian dataset. The value model obtained by combining high-level feature and low-level feature is defined as

$$V = v_h \cdot v_l. \tag{1}$$

The first part v_h denotes the high-level value from classical deep model (CNN-m) [23], which evaluate the image segmentation results globally. In this phase, we mainly focus on pedestrian profile. We collect the pedestrian segmentation images from **CCP** [8] dataset as the positive samples while some failed parsing results segmentation from initial model as negative samples. Thus it could be considered as a binary classification problem here. The parsing results with high value mean relatively good results of pedestrian profile, which is beneficial to global information evaluation of those images. The **CCP** is a clothing parsing dataset whose semantic labels are different from the pedestrian set. We only leverage the human outline ground truth in the **CCP** due to the similar global segmentation information between the **CCP** and our dataset. Moreover, it makes the model independent of our dataset.

The second part v_l denotes the low-level value which considers the similarity between original image and parsing result in low-level. The segmentation result conveys relatively simple structure because pixels in a specific region share the same value. The distinct character in those results is the region shape. It is easy to know that if the original image showing the same shape with parsing result, it indicates the well-parsing performance in shape, see Fig. 3. And the gradient feature has been demonstrated to capture shape information well [24]. Therefore, we adopt the HOG representation as our low-level feature. Then the similarity value is computed by the HOG correlation coefficient between original image and parsing result as

$$v_l = \frac{Cov(H_o, H_r)}{\sigma_{H_o} \sigma_{H_r}}, \tag{2}$$

where H_o, H_r represent the HOG feature from original image and result respectively.

Finally, the reward is calculated between each two sequential update steps t and $t - 1$ from all parsing results by

$$R = \Sigma(V_t - V_{t-1}). \tag{3}$$

v_l=1.000 v_l=0.8190 v_l=0.6300 v_l=0.3295

a)   b)   c)   d)

Fig. 3. Compare between different results with original image visually. (a) The original image. (b) Combination with groud truth. (c) Combination with coarse result. (d) Combination with wrong result.

2.4   Model Update

The model update is followed by the reinforcement learning as an iterative process. And the evaluated confidence from value model plays a significant role in our framework. After parsing the non-labeled pedestrian images, we evaluate the parsing performance on each result image by value model. In the first iteration, the image will be put into the retraining set if its value V is more than threshold C. Then the retraining set is considered as pixel-level labeled set and send into next iterations. Note that in the following iteration, only the result with the highest value, $V_t = \{V\}_{\text{MAX}}$, will be used to update the retraining set, as shown in Fig. 4. The iteration process will repeat until reward signal R converged. For threshold C, we test it from 0.1 to 0.9 by step 0.1 separately, and 0.4 achieves the best performance.

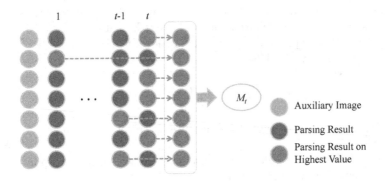

Fig. 4. For tth iteration, each highest value parsing result is used to update the parsing model.

3   Experiments

In the following part, we conduct experiments on pedestrian dataset to investigate the performance of our reinforcement approach.

3.1   Datasets

To demonstrate the performance of our method, we build a pedestrian segmentation dataset consisting of 3180 images. Our pedestrian images are captured from several surveillance cameras in the wild. Each person in the image has been cropped into its bounding box, as illustrated in Fig. 5. It includes 2180 images whose pixel-level annotation is provided with 23 items and 1 background label, see Table 1. And the left 1000 pedestrian images are captured without any pixel-level labels.

In our experiments, we extract three scales of training sets from the labeled set. Here the scales are set to 100, 500, 1980 images respectively to evaluate the trained model. Besides, there are 100 labeled images for validating, and the left 100 labeled images for testing.

3.2   Pseudocode

Our reinforcement learning mainly experiments on two small-scale training sets. To describe the main process in our experiments, we summary the pseudocode in Algorithm 1.

Fig. 5. Our dataset contains 3180 images, some of which are provided with 24 kinds of pedestrian part labels in pixel-level.

Table 1. Attributes with 23 items and background label.

face	hair	hat	sunglasses
l-shoe	r-shoe	upper-clothing	dress
pants	skirt	haversack	knapsack
handbag	Luggage	umbrella	l-arm
r-arm	l-leg	r-leg	scarf
belt	others	other persons	background

Algorithm 1. Updating Algorithm

1: Initialize model M from small scale dataset D_s
2: Initialize each results value V_0 as 0
3: **repeat**
4:      Initialize retraining dataset D as D_s
5:      **for** each image I in surveillance dataset **do**
6:          Compute parsing output $L = M(I)$
7:          Compute output value $V = v_h \cdot v_l$
8:          **if** $V > 0.4$ and $(V_t - V_{t-1}) > 0$ **then**
9:              Put I, L into D
10:          **end if**
11:      **end for**
12:      Update M from dataset D
13:      Compute total rewards $R = \Sigma(V_t - V_{t-1})$
14: **until** R converge.

3.3   Clothing Parsing Accuracy

We measure performance of pedestrian parts parsing results in average pixel accuracy and average Jaccard Index, JI (the intersection over union of the parsing results and the ground truth segmentation), on our test dataset. Table 2 shows the performance on 3 different scales of training sets, two of which are additionally trained with reinforcement strategy. In the reinforcement experiments, we set 1980 images and 1480 images as non-labeled images for 'S100+RL' and 'S500+RL' respectively. Obviously the most frequent label presented in our images is background. Predicting all regions including background (more than 80.0%) results in a reasonably better accuracies than including foreground only.

We firstly train a very small scale set over 100 image, which only achieves a poor performance (47.2% on foreground pixel accuracy, 84.1% on background pixel accuracy and 19.8% on JI). After reinforcement learning, it obtains an improved 58.9%, 86.9% accuracy and 22.1% on JI. The average JI of results presents much lower value than other measurements due to long tail problem which is more serious in small scale dataset. From the quantitative experiments, the reinforced

Table 2. Pedestrian parsing average pixel accuracy and average JI performance. S100 means training on 100 pixel-level labeled images. S100+RL means training on 100 pixel-level labeled images and being reinforced by our approach. PA-f, PA-b represent foreground pixel accuracy and images pixel accuracy respectively.

Evaluation metric	S100	S100+RL	S500	S500+RL	S1980
PA-f	0.472	**0.589**	0.579	**0.679**	0.688
PA-b	0.841	**0.869**	0.866	**0.876**	0.885
JI	0.198	**0.220**	0.223	**0.313**	0.334

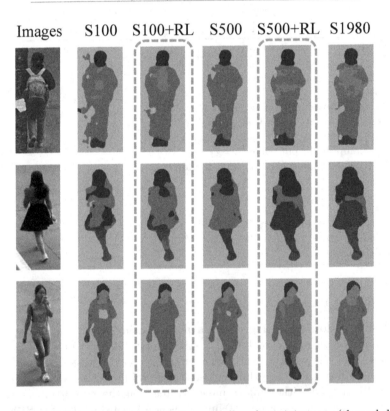

Fig. 6. Some reinforced parsing results from small scale training sets (the red dashed box) compare with original results (the second and fourth columns) and the results parsed by larger scale training set (the last column). (Color figure online)

predictions present an efficient improvement than the original ones, even better than results trained on 500 pixel-level labeled images, but only one fifth of the set scale. The following reinforcement experiment on 500 training images also shows its comparable ability with larger scale training images set. The improvement in 'S500+RL' is inferior than 'S100+RL' because the less non-labeled images supply less information for reinforcement. In conclusion, given a small scale training dataset, our reinforcement method achieves the approximated performance comparing with the much larger training dataset.

3.4   Qualitative Evaluation

In this section, we illustrate the parsing results from original models ('S100', 'S500') and reinforced models ('S100+RL', 'S500+RL') to demonstrate our improvement performance through very small scale dataset. The model trained on 100 images is confused on much semantic segmentation. Then our approach reinforces the model on those segmentation to achieve an even better performance over the model trained on 500 images, and the similar comparison are presented between 'S500' and 'S500+RL' (Fig. 6 shows the results).

4   Conclusion

This paper presents an iterative parsing optimization method for pedestrian in surveillance environment. The core idea is: utilizing the reinforcement learning to update the initial model trained on a small scale pixel-level labeled dataset. The method is proved to be effective to parse the pedestrian with the only help of pedestrian images without pixel-accurate object labels. The algorithm is simple and the effect is significantly promoted while the time and manual work cost cheaper. These make the proposed pedestrian parsing model to be suitable for the surveillance application.

In future work, we would like to explore the influence from those non-labeled images, including images scale and quality. And some label results deteriorated by the 'long tail' phenomenon, further impacting the JI performance, also will be our next work.

Acknowledgments. The research was supported by the National Nature Science Foundation of China under Grant U1611461, 61231015, 61303114, 61671332 and 61671336, by the EU FP7 QUICK project under Grant Agreement No. PIRSES-GA-2013-612652, by the National High Technology Research and Development Program of China under Grant 2015AA016306, by the Technology Research Program of Ministry of Public Security under Grant 2016JSYJA12, by the Hubei Province Technological Innovation Major Project under Grant 2016AAA015 and 2017AAA123, and by the Nature Science Foundation of Jiangsu Province under Grant BK20160386.

References

1. Li, A., Liu, L., Wang, K., Liu, S., Yan, S.: Clothing attributes assisted person reidentification. IEEE Trans. Circ. Syst. Video Technol. **25**(5), 869–878 (2015)
2. Wang, Z., Ruimin, H., Liang, C., Yi, Y., Jiang, J., Ye, M., Chen, J., Leng, Q.: Zero-shot person re-identification via cross-view consistency. IEEE Trans. Multimedia **18**(2), 260–272 (2016)
3. Ye, M., Liang, C., Yi, Y., Wang, Z., Leng, Q., Xiao, C., Chen, J., Ruimin, H.: Person reidentification via ranking aggregation of similarity pulling and dissimilarity pushing. IEEE Trans. Multimedia **18**(12), 2553–2566 (2016)
4. Zeng, M., Cao, L., Dong, H., Lin, K., Wang, M., Tong, J.: Estimation of human body shape and cloth field in front of a kinect. Neurocomputing **151**, 626–631 (2015)
5. Yang, J., Franco, J.-S., Hétroy-Wheeler, F., Wuhrer, S.: Estimation of human body shape in motion with wide clothing. In: Leibe, B., Matas, J., Sebe, N., Welling, M. (eds.) ECCV 2016. LNCS, vol. 9908, pp. 439–454. Springer, Cham (2016). https://doi.org/10.1007/978-3-319-46493-0_27
6. Weber, M., Bauml, M., Stiefelhagen, R.: Part-based clothing segmentation for person retrieval. In: 2011 8th IEEE International Conference on Advanced Video and Signal-Based Surveillance (AVSS), pp. 361–366. IEEE (2011)
7. Yamaguchi, K., Hadi Kiapour, M., Berg, T.L.: Paper doll parsing: retrieving similar styles to parse clothing items. In: IEEE International Conference on Computer Vision, pp. 3519–3526 (2013)
8. Yang, W., Luo, P., Lin, L.: Clothing co-parsing by joint image segmentation and labeling. In: Computer Vision and Pattern Recognition, pp. 3182–3189 (2014)
9. Simo-Serra, E., Fidler, S., Moreno-Noguer, F., Urtasun, R.: A high performance CRF model for clothes parsing. In: Cremers, D., Reid, I., Saito, H., Yang, M.-H. (eds.) ACCV 2014. LNCS, vol. 9005, pp. 64–81. Springer, Cham (2015). https://doi.org/10.1007/978-3-319-16811-1_5
10. Liu, S., Liang, X., Liu, L., Shen, X., Yang, J., Xu, C., Lin, L., Cao, X., Yan, S.: Matching-CNN meets KNN: quasi-parametric human parsing. In: Computer Vision and Pattern Recognition, pp. 1419–1427 (2015)
11. Liang, X., Liu, S., Shen, X., Yang, J., Liu, L., Dong, J., Lin, L., Yan, S.: Deep human parsing with active template regression. IEEE Trans. Pattern Anal. Mach. Intell. **37**(12), 2402 (2015)
12. Liu, S., Liang, X., Liu, L., Lin, L.: Transferred human parsing with video context. IEEE Trans. Multimedia **17**, 1 (2015)
13. Xia, F., Zhu, J., Wang, P., Yuille, A.L.: Pose-guided human parsing by an and/or graph using pose-context features. In: Thirtieth AAAI Conference on Artificial Intelligence, pp. 3632–3640 (2016)
14. Liang, X., Xu, C., Shen, X., Yang, J., Tang, J., Lin, L., Yan, S.: Human parsing with contextualized convolutional neural network. IEEE Trans. Pattern Anal. Mach. Intell. **39**(1), 115–127 (2016)
15. Krizhevsky, A., Sutskever, I., Hinton, G.E.: Imagenet classification with deep convolutional neural networks. In: International Conference on Neural Information Processing Systems, pp. 1097–1105 (2012)
16. Handa, A., Patraucean, V., Badrinarayanan, V., Stent, S., Cipolla, R.: Scenenet: understanding real world indoor scenes with synthetic data. Comput. Sci. 4077–4085 (2015)

17. Papon, J., Schoeler, M.: Semantic pose using deep networks trained on synthetic RGB-D. In: IEEE International Conference on Computer Vision, pp. 774–782 (2015)
18. Richter, S.R., Vineet, V., Roth, S., Koltun, V.: Playing for data: ground truth from computer games. In: Leibe, B., Matas, J., Sebe, N., Welling, M. (eds.) ECCV 2016. LNCS, vol. 9906, pp. 102–118. Springer, Cham (2016). https://doi.org/10.1007/978-3-319-46475-6_7
19. Kaboutari, A., Bagherzadeh, J., Kheradmand, F.: An evaluation of two-step techniques for positive-unlabeled learning in text classification. Int. J. Comput. Appl. Technol. Res. **3**, 592–594 (2014)
20. Day, W.Y., Chi, C.Y., Chen, R.C., Cheng, P.J.: Sampling the web as training data for text classification. Int. J. Digit. Libr. Syst. **1**(4), 24–42 (2010)
21. Benisty, H., Crammer, K.: Metric learning using labeled and unlabeled data for semi-supervised/domain adaptation classification. In: Electrical and Electronics Engineers in Israel, pp. 1–5 (2014)
22. Tangseng, P., Wu, Z., Yamaguchi, K.: Looking at Outfit to Parse Clothing (2017)
23. Chatfield, K., Simonyan, K., Vedaldi, A., Zisserman, A.: Return of the devil in the details: delving deep into convolutional nets. In: British Machine Vision Conference (2014)
24. Dalal, N., Triggs, B.: Histograms of oriented gradients for human detection. In: IEEE Computer Society Conference on Computer Vision and Pattern Recognition, pp. 886–893 (2005)

Remote Sensing Image Fusion Based on Two-Stream Fusion Network

Xiangyu Liu[1], Yunhong Wang[1], and Qingjie Liu[1,2(✉)]

[1] The State Key Laboratory of Virtual Reality Technology and Systems,
Beihang University, Beijing 100191, China
{xyliu,yhwang,qingjie.liu}@buaa.edu.cn
[2] Beijing Key Laboratory of Digital Media, School of Computer Science
and Engineering, Beihang University, Beijing 100191, China

Abstract. Remote sensing image fusion (or pan-sharpening) aims at generating high resolution multi-spectral (MS) image from inputs of a high spatial resolution single band panchromatic (PAN) image and a low spatial resolution multi-spectral image. In this paper, a deep convolutional neural network with two-stream inputs respectively for PAN and MS images is proposed for remote sensing image pan-sharpening. Firstly the network extracts features from PAN and MS images, then it fuses them to form compact feature maps that can represent both spatial and spectral information of PAN and MS images, simultaneously. Finally, the desired high spatial resolution MS image is recovered from the fused features using an encoding-decoding scheme. Experiments on Quickbird satellite images demonstrate that the proposed method can fuse the PAN and MS image effectively.

Keywords: Image fusion · Pan-sharpening
Convolutional neural networks · Deep learning · Remote sensing

1 Introduction

Most remote sensing applications require images at the highest resolution both in spatial and spectral domains which is very hard to achieve by a single sensor. To alleviate this problem, many optical Earth observation satellites, such as QuickBird, GeoEye and IKONOS, carry two kinds of optical sensors, one sensor acquires panchromatic images (PAN) at high spatial and low spectral resolution, the other sensor acquires multi-spectral images (MS) with complementary properties, i.e. low spatial and high spectral resolution. Panchromatic and multi-spectral image fusion (also known as pan-sharpening) aims to fuse information from PAN and MS image to generate images with high spatial and spectral resolutions, simultaneously.

Pan-sharpening can be helpful for a variety of remote sensing applications [26], so it has been raising much attention within remote sensing community. Many methods have been published during the last decade [28]. Most

© Springer International Publishing AG 2018
K. Schoeffmann et al. (Eds.): MMM 2018, Part I, LNCS 10704, pp. 428–439, 2018.
https://doi.org/10.1007/978-3-319-73603-7_35

of these methods can be classified into three categories: (1) component substitution (CS) methods; (2) amélioration de la résolution spatiale par injection de structures (ARSIS) concept methods (which means enhancement of the spatial resolution by structure injections) and (3) model-based methods. The CS methods assume that the geometric detail information of a MS image lies in its structural component which can be obtained by projecting it to a new space. Then, the substitution consists of the total or partial replacement of this structural component by the PAN image. The goal of pan-sharpening can be achieved after an inverse projection. The principal component analysis (PCA) [4], the intensity hue saturation (IHS) [27] and the GramSchmidt (GS) transform [11] based methods are those of the most widely known CS methods. The fundamental assumption of the ARSIS concept methods is that the missing spatial information in MS modalities can be inferred from the high frequencies [22]. To pan-sharpen a MS image, ARSIS methods apply multi-resolution algorithms, such as discrete wavelet transform (DWT) [19], à trous wavelet transform [17] on a PAN image to extract high-frequency information then inject it into a MS image. The model based methods construct a degradation models of how PAN and MS images are degraded from the desired high resolution MS image and restore it from the degradation models [3,31].

In addition to the aforementioned methods, researchers address pan-sharpening from other perspectives. For instance, Li [12] and Zhu [35] modeled remote sensing image pan-sharpening from compressed sensing theory. He et al. [8] introduced a variational model based on spatial and spectral sparsity priors for pan-sharpening. Liu et al. [13] addressed pan-sharpening from a manifold learning framework.

Recently, deep learning techniques have been applied to various research fields and achieved astonishing performance [5,9,23,33]. Inspired by SRCNN [5], Masi et al. [16] proposed a pan-sharpening method based on convolutional neural networks (CNNs). They utilized a three-layered CNN architecture modified from [5], which was original designed for image super-resolution. Zhong et al. [34] presented a CNN based hybrid pan-sharpening method. Different from Masi et al.'s method, in [34], CNN was employed to enhance the spatial resolution of the MS image, then the GramSchmidt transform was utilized to fuse the enhanced MS and PAN image to obtain the pan-sharpened image. The network used to enhance the spatial resolution of MS image is also a three-layered CNN same to SRCNN [5].

It has been reported that deeper neural networks can achieve better results than shallow ones [7,9]. And inspired by the tremendous success of deep CNN in image processing and computer vision tasks, in this paper we explore to use a much deeper two streams network to fuse PAN and MS images to generate the desired high resolution MS image (Fig. 1). The rest of this paper is organized as follows. Section 2 elaborate our two stream pan-sharpening network. Section 3 gives experiments and comparisons with other methods. Finally, this paper is concluded in Sect. 4.

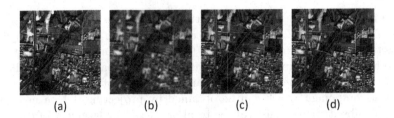

<table>
<tr><td>(a)</td><td>(b)</td><td>(c)</td><td>(d)</td></tr>
</table>

Fig. 1. An example result of the proposed method. The desired high resolution MS image (c) is generated from an input pair of PAN (a) and MS (b). (d) is referenced MS image.

2   Two-Stream Fusion Network

The architecture of the proposed Two-stream Fusion Network (TFNet) is shown in Fig. 2. The proposed TFNet consists of three parts, including feature extraction, feature fusion and image restoration.

It is generally accepted that PAN and MS images contain different information. PAN image is carrier of geometric detail (spatial) information, while MS image preserves spectral information. However, it is very hard to define what exactly spatial and spectral information are and how to represent them independently. In this paper, to make the best use of the spatial and spectral information in PAN and MS, we use two sub-networks to extract hierarchical features to capture complementary information of PAN and MS images. We believe the features extracted from PAN and MS contain spatial and spectral information. After feature extraction, the subsequent networks proceed as an auto-encoder, in which the encoder (feature fusion) fuses information extracted

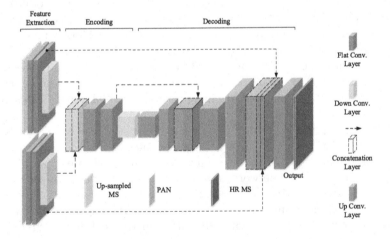

Fig. 2. The architecture of the proposed TFNet.

from PAN and MS images, then the decoder (image restoration) reconstructs the high resolution MS images from the fused features.

2.1 Feature Extraction Networks

Pan-sharpening can be considered as a special form of single image resolution [16]. However, the differences between them are obvious. Unlike image super-resolution, pan-sharpening takes two different images, PAN and MS, as input, and produces an image with both characteristics. To reuse the architecture of SRCNN [5], Masi et al. [16] did not consider different information contained in PAN and MS images. They stacked up-sampled MS bands with PAN band to form a five-band image and send it to the network. With our method, the two input images are treated separately. We use two sub-networks to extract features from PAN and MS images respectively. These two sub-networks have similar architecture but different weights. One sub-network takes a 4-band MS image as input and extracts spectral information of it. The other one takes a single band PAN image as input and extract geometric spatial information contained in it.

Each of the sub-networks consists of two successive convolutional layers followed by a leaky rectified linear unit (LeakyReLU) [15] and a down-sampling layer. Most of the CNN architectures utilize max or mean pooling to get scale- and rotational-invariance features, however the detail information is more important in pan-sharpening, so we use the convolutional kernel with a stride of 2 for down-sampling instead of simple pooling strategy.

2.2 Fusion Network

After feature extraction, we have two feature maps representing PAN and MS images respectively. The two feature maps explicitly capture complementary information of PAN and MS, i.e. spatial detail and spectral information. Considering that the desired high resolution MS image should have high resolutions both in spatial and spectral, the features of it must describe spatial and spectral information simultaneously. To this end, the two feature maps are concatenated. After that, three convolutional layers are applied to encode the concatenated feature maps into more compact representations. The end of the fusion network is a $[w/4, h/4, 256]^1$ tensor who encodes spatial and spectral information of the two input images.

2.3 Image Restoration Network

The last stage of the proposed TFNet is reconstructing the desired high resolution MS image from the features. The encoded feature maps only take up 1/16 of the input proportion. One can use traditional method such as linear interpolation to up-sample the scale of the feature maps. However, learnable way is better [14].

---

[1] w and h are the width and height of the input images.

Table 1. The network structure of TFNet.

		Layer	Filter	Stride	Output Size
Input	MS				$128 \times 128 \times 4$
	PAN				$128 \times 128 \times 1$
Feature extraction	MS	FlatConv1_M	$3 \times 3/32$	1	$128 \times 128 \times 32$
		FlatConv2_M	$3 \times 3/32$	1	$128 \times 128 \times 32$
		DownConv3_M	$2 \times 2/64$	2	$64 \times 64 \times 64$
	PAN	FlatConv1_P	$3 \times 3/32$	1	$128 \times 128 \times 32$
		FlatConv2_P	$3 \times 3/32$	1	$128 \times 128 \times 32$
		DownConv3_P	$2 \times 2/64$	2	$64 \times 64 \times 64$
Fusion		Concat1	-	-	$64 \times 64 \times 128$
		FlatConv4	$3 \times 3/128$	1	$64 \times 64 \times 128$
		FlatConv5	$3 \times 3/128$	1	$64 \times 64 \times 128$
		DownConv6	$2 \times 2/256$	2	$32 \times 32 \times 256$
Restoration		FlatConv7	$1 \times 1/256$	1	$32 \times 32 \times 256$
		FlatConv8	$3 \times 3/256$	1	$32 \times 32 \times 256$
		UpConv9	$2 \times 2/128$	2	$64 \times 64 \times 128$
		Concat2	-	-	$64 \times 64 \times 256$
		FlatConv10	$3 \times 3/128$	1	$64 \times 64 \times 128$
		UpConv11	$2 \times 2/64$	2	$128 \times 128 \times 64$
		Concat3	-	-	$128 \times 128 \times 128$
		FlatConv12	$3 \times 3/64$	1	$128 \times 128 \times 64$
		FlatConv13	$3 \times 3/4$	1	$128 \times 128 \times 4$
Output		-		-	$128 \times 128 \times 4$

We use backward strided convolutional layers (also known as transposed convolutional layers) to reconstruct the high resolution MS image. Starting with applying a convolutional layer with kernel size of 1×1 to combine the feature, we up-sample the feature map every two layers as a symmetrical structure to encoder. Inspired by the skip connection between encoder and decoder utilized in U-Net [24], we also add skip connection between the encoder and decoder of our network. Specifically, after every step of up-sampling, the feature maps in the encoder are copied to the decoder and concatenated with the corresponding feature maps to inject more details lost in down-sampling process, as shown in Fig. 2. In the next section, we will discuss how much performance improvement it will be by adding lower features in the higher level. The last layer outputs the desired high resolution 4-band MS image. Table 1 shows the parameters and details of our network.

3   Experiments

3.1   Dataset

The proposed method is tested on QuickBird images. Quickbird is a commercial satellite launched in October 18, 2001 by DigitalGlobe[2]. Quickbird carries two

---

[2] http://www.digitalglobe.com/.

sensors, one sensor acquires panchromatic images at 0.6 m spatial resolution, and the other sensor acquires 4-band (blue, green, red and near-infrared) multi-spectral images at 2.4 m resolution. Table 2 shows spectral wavelength ranges of different bands.

Table 2. Spectral bands wavelength range (in nanometer) of Quickbird.

	PAN	Blue	Green	Red	Nir
Quickbird	450–900	450–520	520–600	630–690	760–890

The dataset contains 9 pairs of MS and PAN images sized from $558 \times 2080 \times 4$ to $3162 \times 2142 \times 4$ and $2232 \times 8320 \times 1$ to $12648 \times 28568 \times 1$. For each $w \times h$ MS image, there is a corresponding $4w \times 4h$ PAN image over the same site. Our goal is to generate the MS image with the same spatial resolution as the PAN image. To assess the proposed method, the results should be compared with the referenced images, which do not exist. As a conventional method, we follow Wald's protocol [30] to assess our method and compare it with other methods. That is down-sampling both PAN and MS images by 4 of width and height, separately, then the down-sampled images are used as the inputs of the network and the original MS images are used as references. We also use bi-cubic interpolation algorithm to up-sample the input MS images to match the PANs' resolution.

3.2 Training

8 out of 9 images are used to train the network and the last one is used to test. The feature extraction net only accepts 128×128 images. We randomly sample 128×128 images from the original and the down-sampled image pairs to form training set. This will generate 64,000 training samples. The cost function is computed over the final output image and the corresponding original MS image with mean square error (MSE). Given a set of original images $\{Y_i\}$ and their corresponding PAN and MS images $\{X_i^P, X_i^M\}$, the MSE is defines as:

$$L(\Theta) = \frac{1}{n} \sum_{i=1}^{n} \| F(X_i^P, X_i^M; \Theta) - Y_i \|^2 \tag{1}$$

where n is the number of training samples. The loss is minimized using Adam optimizer [10] with a learning rate of 0.0001 and a momentum of 0.5. The mini-batch size is set to 32. The network is implemented in Tensorflow [1] and trained on a NVIDIA Titan-X GPU. It will take about 15 h to train our network.

3.3 Evaluation Indexes

We use five metrics for performance assessment.

Q_4. The Quality-index Q_4 [2] is the 4-band extension of Q index [30]. Q_4 is defined as:

$$Q_4 = \frac{4|\sigma_{z_1 z_2}| \cdot |\bar{z}_1| \cdot |\bar{z}_2|}{(\sigma_{z_1}^2 + \sigma_{z_2}^2)(|\bar{z}_1|^2 + |\bar{z}_2|^2)} \tag{2}$$

where z_1 and z_2 are two spectral vectors of MS images, $\bar{z}_1$ and $\bar{z}_2$ are the means, $\sigma_{z_1 z_2}$ denotes the covariance between z_1 and z_2, and $\sigma_{z_1}^2$ and $\sigma_{z_2}^2$ are the variances of z_1 and z_2.

SAM. Spectral angle mapper (SAM) [32] is defined as the angular between two vectors v_1 and v_2:

$$SAM(v_1, v_2) = \arccos(\frac{v_1 \cdot v_2}{\| v_1 \| \cdot \| v_2 \|}) \tag{3}$$

where v_1 and v_2 are two spectral vectors of MS images. SAM is averaged over all the images to generate a global measurement of spectral distortion. For the ideal pan-sharpened images, SAM should be zero.

sCC. To evaluate the similarity between the spatial details of pan-sharpened images and referenced images, a high pass filter is applied to the images, then the correlation coefficient (CC) between the results is calculated. This quantity index is called spatial CC (sCC). We use the high Laplacian pass filter given by,

$$F = \begin{bmatrix} -1 & -1 & -1 \\ -1 & 8 & -1 \\ -1 & -1 & -1 \end{bmatrix} \tag{4}$$

A higher sCC indicates that most of the spatial information of the PAN image is injected during the fusion process. The final sCC is averaged over all the bands of the MS images.

RASE. Relative average spectral error (RASE) is used to estimate the global spectral quality of the fused images [6]. It is defined as

$$RASE = \frac{100}{M} \sqrt{\frac{1}{N} \sum_{i=1}^{N} RMSE^2(B_i)} \tag{5}$$

where N is the number of multi-spectral images, M is the mean radiance of all multi-spectral images, B_i is the ith muliti-spectral band, $RMSE(B_i)$ is the root mean square error defines as: $RMSE^2(B_i) = bias^2(B_i) + SD^2(Bi)$, where $bias$ is the difference between the mean of the referenced image and that of the fused image and SD reflects the deviation degree of values relative to the mean of the image.

ERGAS. ERGAS is a commonly used global quality index [29], which means relative global dimensional synthesis error. It is given by,

$$\text{ERGAS} = 100\frac{h}{l}\sqrt{\frac{1}{N}\sum_{i=1}^{N}\left(\frac{\text{RMSE}(B_i)}{M(B_i)}\right)^2} \qquad (6)$$

where h and l are the spatial resolution of PAN and MS images; $\text{RMSE}(B_i)$ is the root mean square error between the ith fused band and the referenced image band; $M(B_i)$ is the mean value of the original MS band B_i.

3.4 Impacts of Detail Compensation

In order to reconstruct fine details better, as mentioned in Sect. 2.3, we concatenate the low-level feature maps with the corresponding high level feature maps in the same resolution after every up-sampling step. Since PAN images carry spatial detail information, it is reasonable to employ features of PAN to compensate spatial information. An alternative solution is compensating features from both PAN and MS images to the corresponding high level feature maps of restoration network. Surprisingly, the latter one achieves better results in terms of both spatial and spectral qualities than the first one shown in Table 3. The reason behind this may be that both PAN and MS images contain spatial and spectral information. It is impossible to separate spatial and spectral information from each other and extract only spatial details from PAN image or spectral features from MS images. To get better results, one should not focus only on how to extract spatial or spectral information separately. Both PAN and MS images should be taken into consideration.

Table 3. Performance of different concatenation strategies

	Q_4	ERGAS	RASE	sCC	SAM
None	0.9370	7.4561	29.1958	0.9596	3.9598
PAN	0.9438	6.7348	25.8415	0.9603	3.3653
MS&PAN	**0.9576**	**6.2010**	**23.9232**	**0.9625**	**2.8762**

3.5 Comparison with Other Methods

In this subsection we compare the proposed method with several widely used techniques.

- APCA: Adaptive Principal Components Analysis [25].
- AIHS: Adaptive Intensity-Hue-Saturation [21].
- AWLP: Additive Wavelet Luminance Proportional [18].
- PNN: CNN-based Pan-sharpening [16].

We re-implement the first four techniques in MATLAB, and [16] with Tensorflow with the same hyper-parameters. Table 4 shows the results in terms of five evaluation metrics. Additionally, we provide the performance using simple nearest neighbor interpolation (EMS) as the baseline [20].

Table 4. Performance comparison on the test dataset

	Q_4	ERGAS	RASE	sCC	SAM
EMS [20]	0.7687	13.6148	50.8050	0.8169	6.3484
APCA [25]	0.8590	11.8154	44.1160	0.9086	5.5634
AIHS [21]	0.8408	11.0549	41.3064	0.9156	5.0821
AWLP [18]	0.9021	11.7006	41.0487	0.9145	4.7441
PNN [16]	0.9511	6.7531	25.6368	0.9567	3.0481
TFNet	**0.9576**	**6.2010**	**23.9232**	**0.9625**	**2.8762**

From Table 4 we can see that the proposed methods guarantee performance gains on all the metrics. One can notice that our method is much better than traditional methods of APCA [25], AIHS [21] and AWLP [18]. When compared with recently proposed PCNN, which is a three-layer convolutional model, our method also has significant advantages in spectral reconstruction and detail preservation.

In Figs. 3 and 4, we show the results of different techniques on Quickbird. The pan-sharpened images generated by the proposed method look better. APCA and

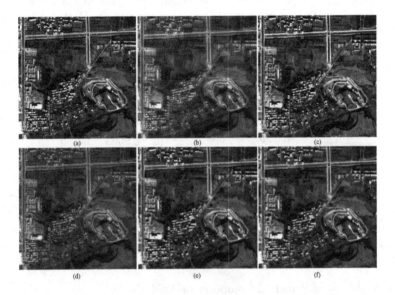

Fig. 3. Pansharpening results on the Quickbird images. (a) Referenced Image; (b) APCA [25]; (c) AWLP [18]; (d) AIHS [21]; (e) PNN [16] and (f) the proposed TFNet. Displayed in true color (RGB). (Color figure online)

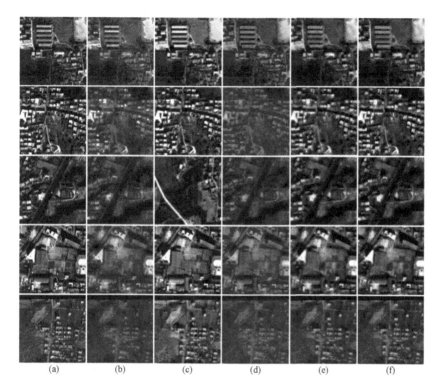

(a)   (b)   (c)   (d)   (e)   (f)

Fig. 4. Sub-regions of the results. (a) Referenced Image; (b) APCA [25]; (c) AWLP [18]; (d) AIHS [21]; (e) PNN [16] and (f) the proposed TFNet. Better viewed in color.

AIHS produce images with obvious blurring. AWLP returns images similar to the reference images with fine spatial details, but suffers from strong spectral distortions. PNN's results are similar to the proposed method. Some missing spatial details are noticable. The proposed method does better in spectral preservation and provides images with richer spatial details.

4   Conclusion

Deep learning has been drawing increasing attention from both computer vision and remote sensing communities. Significant progresses have been achieved in computer vision and image processing field, yet in remote sensing tasks there are still great advance to be achieved with the help of deep learning techniques. Based on the intuition that, the high resolution MS image should have the same features as that of PAN and MS images. In this paper, we propose a two-stream pan-sharpening network like autoencoder that extracts features from PAN and MS respectively. Encoding and decoding scheme is applied to fuse features together and reconstruct the high resolution MS images. The experiments on Quickbird images demonstrate the effectiveness of the proposed method and comparisons with other methods also shows superiority of our method.

Acknowledgments. This work is supported by the Natural Science Foundation of China (NSFC) under Grant No. 61601011.

References

1. Abadi, M., Agarwal, A., Barham, P., Brevdo, E., Chen, Z., Citro, C., Corrado, G.S., Davis, A., Dean, J., Devin, M., et al.: TensorFlow: large-scale machine learning on heterogeneous distributed systems. arXiv preprint arXiv:1603.04467 (2016)
2. Alparone, L., Baronti, S., Garzelli, A., Nencini, F.: A global quality measurement of pan-sharpened multispectral imagery. GRSL **1**(4), 313–317 (2004)
3. Aly, H.A., Sharma, G.: A regularized model-based optimization framework for pan-sharpening. TIP **23**(6), 2596–2608 (2014)
4. Chavez, P., Sides, S.C., Anderson, J.A., et al.: Comparison of three different methods to merge multiresolution and multispectral data - landsat TM and SPOT panchromatic. PE&RS **57**(3), 295–303 (1991)
5. Dong, C., Loy, C.C., He, K., Tang, X.: Image super-resolution using deep convolutional networks. TPAMI **38**(2), 295–307 (2016)
6. González-Audícana, M., Saleta, J.L., Catalán, R.G., García, R.: Fusion of multispectral and panchromatic images using improved IHS and PCA mergers based on wavelet decomposition. TGRS **42**(6), 1291–1299 (2004)
7. He, K., Zhang, X., Ren, S., Sun, J.: Deep residual learning for image recognition. In: CVPR, pp. 770–778 (2016)
8. He, X., Condat, L., Bioucas-Dias, J.M., Chanussot, J., Xia, J.: A new pansharpening method based on spatial and spectral sparsity priors. TIP **23**(9), 4160–4174 (2014)
9. Kim, J., Kwon Lee, J., Mu Lee, K.: Accurate image super-resolution using very deep convolutional networks. In: CVPR, pp. 1646–1654 (2016)
10. Kingma, D., Ba, J.: Adam: a method for stochastic optimization. arXiv preprint arXiv:1412.6980 (2014)
11. Laben, C.A., Brower, B.V.: Process for enhancing the spatial resolution of multispectral imagery using pan-sharpening. US Patent 6,011,875, 4 January 2000
12. Li, S., Yang, B.: A new pan-sharpening method using a compressed sensing technique. TGRS **49**(2), 738–746 (2011)
13. Liu, Q., Wang, Y., Zhang, Z.: Pan-sharpening based on geometric clustered neighbor embedding. OE **53**(9), 093109 (2014)
14. Long, J., Shelhamer, E., Darrell, T.: Fully convolutional networks for semantic segmentation. In: CVPR, pp. 3431–3440 (2015)
15. Maas, A.L., Hannun, A.Y., Ng, A.Y.: Rectifier nonlinearities improve neural network acoustic models. In: ICML, vol. 30 (2013)
16. Masi, G., Cozzolino, D., Verdoliva, L., Scarpa, G.: Pansharpening by convolutional neural networks. Remote Sens. **8**(7), 594 (2016)
17. Nunez, J., Otazu, X., Fors, O., Prades, A., Pala, V., Arbiol, R.: Multiresolution-based image fusion with additive wavelet decomposition. TGRS **37**(3), 1204–1211 (1999)
18. Otazu, X., González-Audícana, M., Fors, O., Núñez, J.: Introduction of sensor spectral response into image fusion methods. Application to wavelet-based methods. TGRS **43**(10), 2376–2385 (2005)

19. Pradhan, P.S., King, R.L., Younan, N.H., Holcomb, D.W.: Estimation of the number of decomposition levels for a wavelet-based multiresolution multisensor image fusion. TGRS **44**(12), 3674–3686 (2006)
20. Prashanth, H., Shashidhara, H., Balasubramanya Murthy, K.N.: Image scaling comparison using universal image quality index. In: IAC3T, pp. 859–863. IEEE (2009)
21. Rahmani, S., Strait, M., Merkurjev, D., Moeller, M., Wittman, T.: An adaptive IHS pan-sharpening method. GRSL **7**(4), 746–750 (2010)
22. Ranchin, T., Wald, L.: Fusion of high spatial and spectral resolution images: the arsis concept and its implementation. PE&RS **66**(1), 49–61 (2000)
23. Ren, S., He, K., Girshick, R., Sun, J.: Faster R-CNN: towards real-time object detection with region proposal networks. In: NIPS, pp. 91–99 (2015)
24. Ronneberger, O., Fischer, P., Brox, T.: U-Net: convolutional networks for biomedical image segmentation. In: Navab, N., Hornegger, J., Wells, W.M., Frangi, A.F. (eds.) MICCAI 2015. LNCS, vol. 9351, pp. 234–241. Springer, Cham (2015). https://doi.org/10.1007/978-3-319-24574-4_28
25. Shah, V.P., Younan, N.H., King, R.L.: An efficient pan-sharpening method via a combined adaptive PCA approach and contourlets. TGRS **46**(5), 1323–1335 (2008)
26. Thomas, C., Ranchin, T., Wald, L., Chanussot, J.: Synthesis of multispectral images to high spatial resolution: a critical review of fusion methods based on remote sensing physics. TGRS **46**(5), 1301–1312 (2008)
27. Tu, T.M., Su, S.C., Shyu, H.C., Huang, P.S.: A new look at IHS-like image fusion methods. Inf. Fusion **2**(3), 177–186 (2001)
28. Vivone, G., Alparone, L., Chanussot, J., Dalla Mura, M., Garzelli, A., Licciardi, G.A., Restaino, R., Wald, L.: A critical comparison among pansharpening algorithms. TGRS **53**(5), 2565–2586 (2015)
29. Wald, L.: Quality of high resolution synthesised images: is there a simple criterion? In: Proceedings of Fusion of Earth Data: Merging Point Measurements, Raster Maps, and Remotely Sensed image (2000)
30. Wald, L., Ranchin, T., Mangolini, M.: Fusion of satellite images of different spatial resolutions: assessing the quality of resulting images. PE&RS **63**, 691–699 (1997)
31. Wei, Q., Dobigeon, N., Tourneret, J.Y.: Bayesian fusion of multi-band images. J-STSP **9**(6), 1117–1127 (2015)
32. Yuhas, R.H., Goetz, A.F.H., Boardman, J.: Discrimination among semi-arid landscape endmembers using the spectral angle mapper (SAM) algorithm. In: Proceedings of Summaries 3rd Annual JPL Airborne Geoscience Workshop, pp. 147–149, June 1992
33. Zhang, Q., Wang, Y., Liu, Q., Liu, X., Wang, W.: CNN based suburban building detection using monocular high resolution Google earth images. In: IGARSS, pp. 661–664. IEEE (2016)
34. Zhong, J., Yang, B., Huang, G., Zhong, F., Chen, Z.: Remote sensing image fusion with convolutional neural network. Sens. Imaging **17**(1), 10 (2016)
35. Zhu, X.X., Bamler, R.: A sparse image fusion algorithm with application to pansharpening. TGRS **51**(5), 2827–2836 (2013)

REVT: Robust and Efficient Visual Tracking by Region-Convolutional Regression Network

Peng Wu, Di Huang$^{(\boxtimes)}$, and Yunhong Wang

IRIP Lab, School of Computer Science and Engineering,
Beihang University, Beijing 100191, China
dhuang@buaa.edu.cn

Abstract. This paper proposes a novel approach, namely REVT, for visual tracking based on a region convolutional regression network. REVT runs according to a coarse to fine scheme. It first builds an on-line update deep network to roughly select a candidate region in a fast way. It then refines the result by exquisitely searching the target within the candidate region by a deep regression network, which is trained off-line to account for more diverse intra-class appearance changes. REVT thus integrates the advantages of the two types of deep models, and demonstrates a good trade-off between accuracy and efficiency. We perform extensive experiments on the OTB-2013 and OTB-2015 benchmarks, and REVT reports competitive performance at a speed of 19 fps, proving its competency.

Keywords: Visual tracking · Coarse-to-fine · Deep regression network

1 Introduction

Object tracking is an important problem in computer vision and multimedia and it plays a fundamental role in a large number of applications. Given the position of an unknown specified target by a bounding box at the first frame of a video, the goal is to localize the target at each subsequence frame. Unfortunately, it is a challenging issue due to fast motion, non-uniform illumination, severe deformation, partial occlusion, low resolution, *etc.*, which result in evident variations in the target appearance. Besides, in visual tracking, the unbalance between positive and negative samples, where the positives are quite limited and much less than the negatives, making this issue even more difficult.

The past decade has witnessed the development of visual tracking from handcrafted techniques to deep learning based ones. Hand-crafted approaches include two major categories, *i.e.* generative trackers and discriminative trackers. The former depend on a reconstruction process of the appearance of the target and search for the most similar candidate at the current frame. Incremental Visual Tracking (IVT) [5] and l_1 Tracker (L1T) [11] are typical examples, and they represent the target by Principal Component Analysis (PCA) and a sparse combination of an over-complete dictionary respectively. Some later attempts based

© Springer International Publishing AG 2018
K. Schoeffmann et al. (Eds.): MMM 2018, Part I, LNCS 10704, pp. 440–452, 2018.
https://doi.org/10.1007/978-3-319-73603-7_36

on other subspace and sparse coding models [12,20] are their variants. The latter directly build a classifier to decide whether a given sampled candidate is the target, to separate it from the background. Its representatives contain Minimum Output Sum of Squared Errors (MOSSE) tracker [4], MILTrack (Multiple Instance Learning) [1], structured output tracker (Struck) [13], *etc.* Particularly, Discriminative Correlation Filters (DCF) are fully developed to construct efficient and robust trackers, taking the advantage of the models trained on a large variety of samples. In [15], kernelized correlation filter with circularly generated samples is proposed, which is further improved in [16] by adopting the HOG features. A number of popular trackers [7,18,19,22] belong to the DCF framework. In general, discriminative trackers report better performance than generative ones, since they are more tolerant to the challenges aforementioned. However, limited by hand-crafted feature based appearance representation, there still exists much space for them in improvement.

Benefiting from large scale datasets like ImageNet, deep learning approaches have shown great successes in object detection and classification. In recent years, they have also become dominant in tracking since Deep Learning Tracker (DLT) was proposed [27]. Deep learning tracking methods basically follow the discriminative framework, but enhance it by deep feature based hierarchical representation. Compared with hand-crafted features, deep convolutional features show better generalization and higher robustness. These methods can be divided into on-line update ones and off-line training ones. On-line trackers [6,21,26,27] employ relatively sophisticated deep feature based classification models to distinguish foreground from background and renew them during processing. In [27], Wang and Yeung describe the target utilizing deep features extracted by a pretrained model and fine-tune it on-line. In [21,26], the authors both analyze the characteristic of each convolutional layer and investigate combination of features at different layers to represent the target. Their models are updated on-line employing certain strategies. Wang *et al.* introduce the method to learn target-specific saliency maps and sequentially sample optimal base learners into an ensemble. In spite of competitive scores achieved, they suffer from heavy computational cost, which is probably problematic in practical scenarios. Off-line trackers [3,14,17,24] train deep models on dedicated data in advance and remain them unchanged when localizing the target. For example, Tao *et al.* [24] introduce Siamese INstance search Tracker (SINT), which makes use of image patches as input and selects the one by measuring the similarity in a Siamese network between the candidate and the target extracted at the first frame. In [3], a fully-convolutional Siamese architecture is trained off-line to generate a more general measurement. Held *et al.* [14] present Generic Object Tracking Using Regression Networks (GOTURN), which applies deep regression instead of classification with a single feed-forward pass through the network to directly find target location. Since back-propagation based model learning is not conducted on-line, the methods can operate at a very high speed. Nevertheless, they are prone to drift, since on-line variations are complex which cannot be completely modeled in off-line training.

In this paper, we propose a novel approach to visual tracking, namely REVT, which not only inherits the advantage of deep learning models for robust appearance representation, but also runs efficiently. Specifically, REVT works according to a coarse to fine scheme. It first roughly chooses a candidate region, where the target is supposed to be, based on its position information at the previous frame in a fast way, and in this period, on-line update is applied to the deep model to reduce its sensitivity to occasional changes. The tracker then exquisitely searches the target within the candidate region by a regressor, which is trained off-line to account for diverse intra-class appearance variations and keep the on-line time under control. To evaluate the proposed approach, we carry out extensive experiments on the OTB-2013 and OTB-2015 datasets, and the results are comparable to the state of the arts in literature, at the processing speed of 19 fps. It clearly demonstrates the effectiveness of REVT.

2   Overview of REVT

As mentioned in Sect. 1, although on-line update deep trackers deliver promising accuracies, their major downside lies in the test speed of a rather low fps. Several top performing trackers using deep learning models only run at 1 fps on a GPU [9,23]. Meanwhile, off-line training deep trackers show the potential in real time applications, but it is not so easy for them to guarantee a very good generalization power to unseen targets and changes. The efficient deep regression model of two streams is recently given in [14], where the tracker runs at 100 fps with a sharp decrease in performance.

To achieve a robust and fast tracker, REVT makes a balance between the two types to deep tracking methods, aiming to keep the precision at a high level while accelerating it as much as possible. The framework is depicted in Fig. 1. REVT is composed of two subnets, namely region selection subnet (SelNet) and location regression subnet (LocNet), and runs in a coarse to fine procedure.

SelNet primarily selects a coarse area as the candidate for target searching. It discriminates the candidate region from the background in terms of a similar appearance described in the deep feature space. SelNet is initialized at the first frame, and for a new frame, a Region of Interest (RoI) centered at the previous target location is cropped and propagated through this subnet. The one which has the maximum value in heat maps generated by SelNet is regarded as the candidate region. Since the model is not as complex as those in [9,23], this step operates much more efficiently for updating.

Inspired by [14], LocNet also incorporates a two-stream deep regression network for fast localization. The subset is trained off-line for a generic relationship between object appearance and motion, and the training data are expected to contribute to potential performance gain. In on-line testing, once the rough candidate region is predicted at the current frame by SelNet, the deep features of the target RoI at the previous frame are compared with the ones of the candidate for a fine search to regress the bounding box of the target.

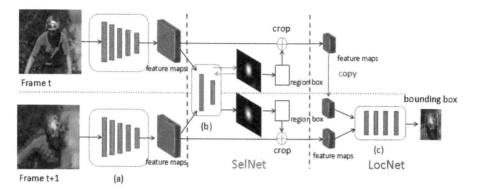

Fig. 1. Flowchart of the proposed REVT tracker: (a) The VGG network for deep feature extraction; (b) Region selection network; and (c) Location regression network, whose output is the target bounding box at frame $t + 1$.

3 REVT Tracker

In this section, we present the major components of the proposed REVT tracker, *i.e.*, SelNet and LocNet, and introduce the details of on-line tracking.

3.1 Region Selection Subnet

We formulate the region selection network (SelNet) as an adaptation module to transfer general features extracted from the pre-trained model on ImageNet to specific target objects. The SelNet architecture follows [25], which consists of a convolutional layer with 64 channels and a group convolutional layer to split the output into 32 branches as in Fig. 2. Since SelNet only has two convolutional layers, updating this network on-line is cheap in calculation. The first convolutional layer has a kernel of the size 5×5 and a mask is used for dropout. The group convolutional layer has a kernel of the size 3×3 to reduce overfitting. Both convolution layers are followed by non-linear activation. SelNet takes the feature maps of a given image region as input, and the output feature map is a 2-D Gaussian centered at the ground truth target location with the variance proportional to the target size, which highlights salient objects in the input patch.

In implementation, we concatenate the convolution features from the conv4-3 and conv5-3 layers at the VGG-16 network after individual l_2 normalization as the input feature of SelNet. The concatenated feature integrates local and global information of different resolutions, which gives more cues to on-line discriminative feature learning. For better generalization performance, ensemble learning is introduced to update SelNet. As in [25], we use the mask generated through Bernoulli distribution to select and split the convolutional feature into 32 individual branches. At the same time, we update all the 32 branches and ensemble the predict results by averaging as the final target heat map. The model is trained by minimizing the square loss between the predicted heat map $\hat{M}_i$ for the ith branch and the target heat map M:

$$L_{sel} = \sum_{i=1}^{k} ||\hat{M}_i - M||_F^2 + \beta ||W_s^i||_F^2. \tag{1}$$

where W_s^i denotes the weights of the convolutional layers; k is the branch number (in our implementation $k = 32$); and β is a trade-off parameter for weight decay.

SelNet requires being updated on-line. In tracking, we calculate the maximum value of the mean heat map as the confidence at current frame, and according to this confidence, we make two types of update strategies:

Long-term updating: we update SelNet every six frames by the history frame with the best confidence and the first frame in 2 iterations. It makes the model robust to target appearance.

Short-term updating: we update SelNet when current confidence is less than the updating threshold by the history frame with the best confidence in 2 iterations. This step helps the model to avoid introducing wrong samples.

As in Fig. 2, the architecture of SelNet is simple. Indeed, it is not necessary to predict the target location precisely, and we thus use the reliable frame and the first frame in few iterations to renew SelNet, controlling computational cost.

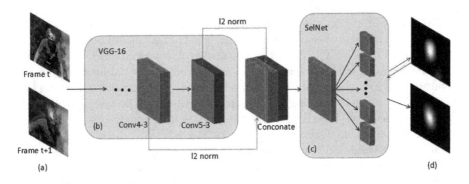

Fig. 2. Pipeline of the region selection network. The inputs are normalized and concatenated convolution feature maps, and the network output is a heat map. The network is updated on-line, where the red line indicates the training phase.

3.2   Location Regression Subnet

In [14], an off-line trained deep regression network is proposed for visual tracking. It regresses the bounding box of the target on the next frame at a high speed, and displays good robustness to fast motions and scale changes. In REVT, we follow this idea and apply a deep regression network to finely search the target location. However, the method in [14] holds a big search window, which includes much background, making the results predicted easy to drift to other objects. Fortunately, the coarse step, *i.e.* SelNet, reduces the search window and removes irrelevant background, focusing on the area whose center is close to target object.

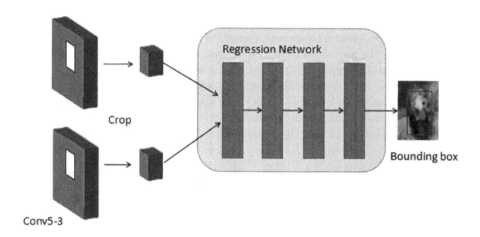

Fig. 3. Pipeline of location regression network. The features of the target region at the previous frame and those of the candidate region selected by SelNet at current frame are passed to the regression network. The output is the target bounding box at current frame.

The LocNet architecture is illustrated in Fig. 3. It is a fully convolutional network structure, consisting of four convolutional layers and an average pooling layer. All the convolution layers are followed by a batch normalization layer and non-linear activation. The network uses the cropped feature maps generated by SelNet as the input, and returns a 4×1 dimensional tensor, corresponding to the four coordinates of the object bounding box. We train the network with an Euclidean loss between the predicted bounding box and the ground-truth as:

$$L_{bbox} = ||\hat{Y} - Y|| + \gamma||W_r||^2. \tag{2}$$

where W_r denotes the weights of the convolutional layers and γ is a trade-off parameter for weight decay.

With the same strategy in [14], we train our regression network off-line by a combination of videos and images. Different from [14], we do not use ALOV300+ in training. For better performance, we train our model on some bigger datasets. ImageNet Det is adopted as the image database and ImageNet VID is employed as the video database. For each video, a subset of frames are labeled with the target bounding boxes. For each successive pair of frames, we crop the frames to feed the network and learn the motion relation of the target between successive frames. For each image, the target location is annotated. This training set helps the regression network account for a more diverse set of objects while preventing over-fitting to the objects in training videos.

3.3   On-line Tracking

At the first frame, we randomly sample 15 patches from the regions that include the target and generate corresponding ground truth heat maps to fine-tune Sel-Net. We use the Stochastic Gradient Descent (SGD) method to optimize (1) until 180 iterations or the loss is less than 0.04. In initialization, SelNet is trained using those patches, and for updating, SelNet is renewed only on single patches.

In frame t, we crop the searching region based on the target bounding box at the previous frame with two and a half times size, from which the convolutional feature is extracted as the input of SelNet. We then calculate the mean of all the 32 output heat maps and the rough target location $\hat{l}$ is determined by the maximum value on the mean heat map. Target region R_t is selected by a box whose center is $\hat{l}$ and size is 1.4 times bigger than the previous bounding box.

We fix the template region T_t by 1.4 times the size of the bounding box at the previous frame. The template region feature X_t^T as well as the target region feature X_t^R are produced by cropping the corresponding normalized features at the Conv5-3 layer of the VGG-16 network. Then X_t^T and X_t^R are feed into the location regression network to predict the bounding box at the current frame.

4   Experimental Results

To evaluate the proposed REVT method for visual tracking, we carry out extensive experiments on two frequently investigated benchmarks: OTB-2013 with 50 sequences and OTB-2015 with 100 sequences. The experimental settings and results are described in the subsequent.

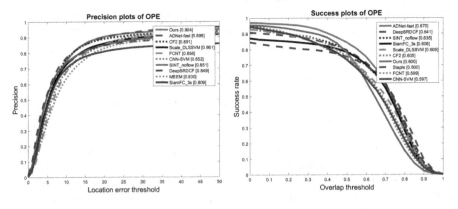

Fig. 4. Comparison in location error and overlapping accuracy plots on OTB-2013.

4.1   Settings

In our experiments, the image patch size is set at 2.5 times the width and height of the target. The target map in SelNet is generated by using a two-dimensional Gaussian function with the peak value of 1. Both the networks in this study are trained using SGD, and the learning rate is set at $1e-4$. The proposed tracker is implemented in Python at the Tensorflow platform.

We follow the standard evaluation protocols in the benchmarks. For OTB2013 and OTB2015, we exploit the One-Pass Evaluation (OPE) scheme with the precision and success plot metrics. The precision metric measures the rate of frame locations within a certain threshold distance from the ones of the ground truth. The threshold distance is set at 20 for all the trackers. The success plot metric measures the overlap ratio between predicted and ground truth bounding boxes.

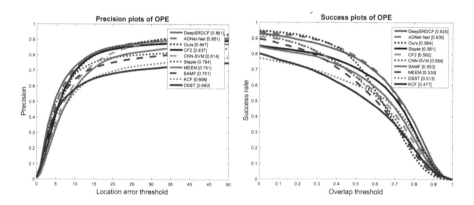

Fig. 5. Comparison in location error and overlapping accuracy plots on OTB-2015.

4.2   Quantitative Evaluation

We compare REVT with some well-performing shallow visual trackers including KCF [16], DSST [10], MEEM [29], and Staple [2], and a number of recently proposed deep trackers, namely HCFT [21], FCNT [26], DeepSRDCF [8], GOTURN [14], SINT [24], SiamFC [3], and ADNet-fast [28]. Their results on OTB-2013 and OTB-2015 are displayed in Figs. 4 and 5 respectively.

From Fig. 4 we can see that REVT outperforms all the counterparts in the location error test on OTB-2013. Figure 5 shows the evaluation results on OTB-2015, and our tracker ranks the third place in the location error, but the performance is still comparable to the best two. On the other side, one can also notice from the two figures that the scores in the overlapping test are not at the top level. The reason lies in that the regression network, *i.e.*, LocNet, is trained on ImageNet, where more semantic information is learned, leading to the fact that bounding boxes include some related parts of targets and are not so tight to the centers. For instance, when tracking the face of a person, REVT regresses the whole head as the target while only the center part of the face is labeled as ground truth in benchmark. In most cases, our regressed bounding boxes are bigger than their ground truths, thus limiting the IOU score.

Meanwhile, since our region selection network, *i.e.*, SelNet, is close to FCNT, a fully convolutional tracking method, we pay special attention to their comparison. We extract the same features by VGG-16 as FCNT does, but thanks to the

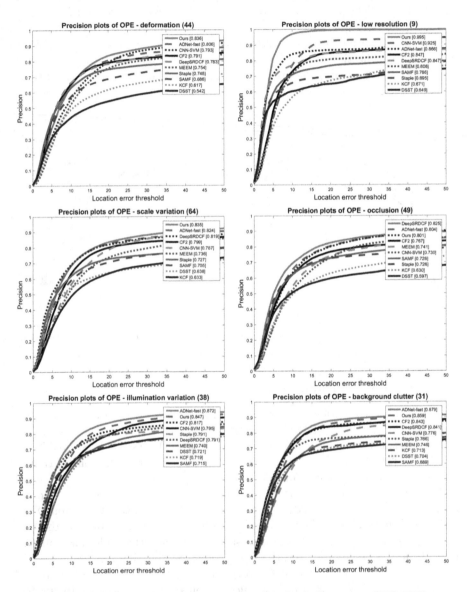

Fig. 6. Comparison of location error plots for six challenges on OTB-2015.

Table 1. Accuracy and speed comparison of different trackers on OTB-2013.

Sequence	Ours	ADNet-fast	SiamFC	HCF	FCNT	SINT	GOTURN	KCF	Struck
DP rate (%)	90.4	89.8	80.9	89.1	85.6	85.1	62.51	74.24	65.61
OS (AUC)	0.60	0.67	0.608	0.605	0.599	0.635	0.45	0.516	0.474
Speed (fps)	19	15	58	11	4	1.5	165	243	9.84

proposed coarse-to-fine working flow, REVT achieves better performance both in the location error and in the overlapping evaluation. Besides, our tracker runs about 5 times faster than FCNT does. In addition, SiamFC is a real-time deep tracker, whose speed is up to 58 fps, but its score is more than 10% below that of REVT.

In Fig. 6, we report the location error in terms of six challenges on OTB-2015, including deformation, low resolution, scale variation, occlusion, illumination variation, and background clutter. We can see that REVT performs best on deformation, scale variation, especially on low resolution, and it also achieves suboptimal performance on illumination variation and background clutter.

4.3 Qualitative Evaluation

In Fig. 7, we compare REVT with three other deep trackers including ADNet-fast, SiamFC_3s, and FCNT. The tracking results are displayed on eight chal-

Fig. 7. Results of ADNet-fast, SiamFC_3s, FCNT and our REVT on 8 challenging sequences, including carscale, freeman4, jogging, motorrolling, skating1, walking2, david, and fish (*yellow* for ADNet-fast; *green* for SiamFC_3s, *black* for FCNT; *blue* for REVT; *red* for ground truth). (Color figure online)

lenging videos. From the results of carscale, motorrolling and singer1, we can see that our tracker is not sensitive to scale variations and rotations and it predicts better bounding boxes than the counterparts do. For all the sequences, REVT always correctly tracks the targets, while in some cases, the other three lose, *e.g.*, FCNT in jogging, ADNet-fast in skating1 and walking2, and SiamFC_3s in motorrolling.

4.4   Speed Analysis

The processing speed of the tracking technique is also a crucial factor to consider especially in practice. Despite the success in terms of accuracy and robustness, the traditional CNN-based tracking methods are criticized for the low speed. We list the details of some popular deep learning trackers in Table 1 for direct comparison. The trackers proposed in [21,24,26] run slowly, which is mainly due to frequent on-line retraining and updating of the CNN model. On contrary, REVT runs at a speed of 19 fps, since no back propagation is required in the regression network while on-line updating region selection network is not expensive in computation. It indicates that REVT makes a good trade-off between performance and consumed time.

5   Conclusion

In this paper, we propose a fast and robust tracker, namely REVT. We integrate both the on-line and off-line deep modules into an unit framework. Different from traditional deep methods that need massive on-line updating, our on-line SelNet is designed to only search a coarse candidate region and thus consumes much less computational time. LocNet, a deep regression network, is then trained off-line to refine the bounding box of the target within the candidate region. Compare with existing off-line deep methods, REVT works on the smaller search windows screened out by the region selection network and is able to capture long-term context. The proposed method is finally validated on OTB-2013 and OTB-2015, reporting state of the art performance and nearly real-time processing speed.

Acknowledgement. This work was supported by the National Key Research and Development Plan (Grant No. 2016YFC0801002).

References

1. Babenko, B., Yang, M.-H., Belongie, S.: Visual tracking with online multiple instance learning. In: IEEE CVPR (2009)
2. Bertinetto, L., Valmadre, J., Golodetz, S., Miksik, O., Torr, P.H.S.: Staple: complementary learners for real-time tracking. In: IEEE CVPR (2016)
3. Bertinetto, L., Valmadre, J., Henriques, J.F., Vedaldi, A., Torr, P.H.S.: Fully-convolutional siamese networks for object tracking. In: Hua, G., Jégou, H. (eds.) ECCV 2016. LNCS, vol. 9914, pp. 850–865. Springer, Cham (2016). https://doi.org/10.1007/978-3-319-48881-3_56

4. Bolme, D.S., Beveridge, J.R., Draper, B.A., Lui, Y.M.: Visual object tracking using adaptive correlation filters. In: CVPR (2010)
5. Ross, D.A., Lim, J., Lin, R.S., Yang, M.-H.: Incremental learning for robust visual tracking. IJCV **77**, 125–141 (2008)
6. Chen, K., Tao, W.: Convolutional regression for visual tracking. arXiv preprint arXiv:1611.04215 (2016)
7. Danelljan, M., Bhat, G., Khan, F.S., Felsberg, M.: ECO: efficient convolution operators for tracking. In: IEEE CVPR (2017)
8. Danelljan, M., Hager, G., Khan, F.S., Felsberg, M.: Convolutional features for correlation filter based visual tracking. In: IEEE ICCV Workshop (2016)
9. Danelljan, M., Hager, G., Khan, F.S., Felsberg, M.: Learning spatially regularized correlation filters for visual tracking. In: IEEE ICCV (2015)
10. Danelljan, M., Hager, G., Khan, F.S., Felsberg, M.: Discriminative scale space tracking. IEEE T-PAMI **39**(8), 1561–1575 (2016)
11. Mei, X., Ling, H.: Robust visual tracking using l_1 minimization. In: ICCV (2010)
12. Bao, C., Wu, Y., Ling, H., Ji, H.: Real time robust L1 tracker using accelerated proximal gradient approach. In: IEEE CVPR (2012)
13. Hare, S., Saffari, A., Torr, P.H.S.: Struck: structured output tracking with kernels. In: IEEE ICCV (2011)
14. Held, D., Thrun, S., Savarese, S.: Learning to track at 100 FPS with deep regression networks. In: Leibe, B., Matas, J., Sebe, N., Welling, M. (eds.) ECCV 2016. LNCS, vol. 9905, pp. 749–765. Springer, Cham (2016). https://doi.org/10.1007/978-3-319-46448-0_45
15. Henriques, J.F., Caseiro, R., Martins, P., Batista, J.: Exploiting the circulant structure of tracking-by-detection with kernels. In: Fitzgibbon, A., Lazebnik, S., Perona, P., Sato, Y., Schmid, C. (eds.) ECCV 2012. LNCS, vol. 7575, pp. 702–715. Springer, Heidelberg (2012). https://doi.org/10.1007/978-3-642-33765-9_50
16. Henriques, J.F., Caseiro, R., Martins, P., Batista, J.: High-speed tracking with kernelized correlation filters. IEEE T-PAMI **37**(3), 583–596 (2015)
17. Hong, S., You, T., Kwak, S., Han, B.: Online tracking by learning discriminative saliency map with convolutional neural network. arXiv preprint arXiv:1502.06796 (2015)
18. Hong, Z., Chen, Z., Wang, C., et al.: Multi-store tracker (muster): a cognitive psychology inspired approach to object tracking. In: IEEE CVPR (2015)
19. Li, Y., Zhu, J., Hoi, S.C.H.: Reliable patch trackers: robust visual tracking by exploiting reliable patches. In: IEEE CVPR (2015)
20. Ma, B., Hu, H., Shen, J., Zhang, Y., Porikli, F.: Linearization to nonlinear learning for visual tracking. In: IEEE ICCV (2015)
21. Ma, C., Huang, J.-B., Yang, X., Yang, M.-H.: Hierarchical convolutional features for visual tracking. In: IEEE ICCV (2015)
22. Ma, C., Yang, X., Zhang, C., Yang, M.-H.: Long-term correlation tracking. In: IEEE CVPR (2015)
23. Nam, H., Han, B.: Learning multi-domain convolutional neural networks for visual tracking. In: IEEE CVPR (2016)
24. Tao, R., Gavves, E., Smeulders, A.W.M.: Siamese instance search for tracking. In: IEEE CVPR (2016)
25. Wang, L., Ouyang, W., Wang, X., Lu, H.: STCT: sequentially training convolutional networks for visual tracking. In: IEEE CVPR (2016)
26. Wang, L., Ouyang, W., Wang, X., Lu, H.: Visual tracking with fully convolutional networks. In: IEEE ICCV (2015)

27. Wang, N., Yeung, D.Y.: Learning a deep compact image representation for visual tracking. In: NIPS (2013)
28. Yun, S., Choi, J., Yoo, Y., Yun, K., Jin, Y.C.: Action-decision networks for visual tracking with deep reinforcement learning. In: IEEE CVPR (2017)
29. Zhang, J., Ma, S., Sclaroff, S.: MEEM: robust tracking via multiple experts using entropy minimization. In: Fleet, D., Pajdla, T., Schiele, B., Tuytelaars, T. (eds.) ECCV 2014. LNCS, vol. 8694, pp. 188–203. Springer, Cham (2014). https://doi.org/10.1007/978-3-319-10599-4_13

Shallow-Water Image Enhancement Using Relative Global Histogram Stretching Based on Adaptive Parameter Acquisition

Dongmei Huang[1], Yan Wang[1], Wei Song[1(✉)], Jean Sequeira[2], and Sébastien Mavromatis[2]

[1] College of Information Technology, Shanghai Ocean University,
Shanghai, China
{dmhuang,wsong}@shou.edu.cn, yanwang9310@163.com
[2] Aix-Marseille University, Marseille, France
{jean.sequeira,sebastien.mavromatis}@univ-amu.fr

Abstract. Light absorption and scattering lead to underwater image showing low contrast, fuzzy, and color cast. To solve these problems presented in various shallow-water images, we propose a simple but effective shallow-water image enhancement method - relative global histogram stretching (RGHS) based on adaptive parameter acquisition. The proposed method consists of two parts: contrast correction and color correction. The contrast correction in RGB color space firstly equalizes G and B channels and then re-distributes each R-G-B channel histogram with dynamic parameters that relate to the intensity distribution of original image and wavelength attenuation of different colors under the water. The bilateral filtering is used to eliminate the effect of noise while still preserving valuable details of the shallow-water image and even enhancing local information of the image. The color correction is performed by stretching the 'L' component and modifying 'a' and 'b' components in CIE-Lab color space. Experimental results demonstrate that the proposed method can achieve better perceptual quality, higher image information entropy, and less noise, compared to the state-of-the-art underwater image enhancement methods.

Keywords: Shallow-water image enhancement
Relative global histogram stretching (RGHS) · Adaptive parameter acquisition

1 Introduction

Restoring clear and real video of underwater image is of great importance to marine ecology, underwater archaeology, underwater biological recognition, and underwater robot vision [1]. However, in contrast with the images under natural environment, the underwater image is more complex and poorly visible. Main reason has two aspects: one is the underwater environment and the influence of water turbidity, the second is the light absorption, scattering and reflection. Assuming most clear coastal water with a high level of attenuation, the light beam absorbs and scatters, as illustrated in Fig. 1. Before reaching the camera, the light is reflected and deflected multiple times by particles present in the shallow water [2]. In the water, the longer the wavelength is, the

© Springer International Publishing AG 2018
K. Schoeffmann et al. (Eds.): MMM 2018, Part I, LNCS 10704, pp. 453–465, 2018.
https://doi.org/10.1007/978-3-319-73603-7_37

faster the light disappears. Compared with green and blue, red is the most affected, so underwater images appear blue tone. To compensate for the light absorption, underwater image acquisition is often illuminated with artificial lights.

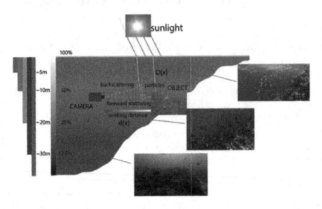

Fig. 1. The basic model of underwater optical imaging and the selective fading of underwater lighting (Color figure online)

Generally speaking, underwater images can be restored and enhanced by two categories of algorithms and techniques: physics-based methods and image-based methods [3]. The former method enhances underwater images by considering the basic physics of light propagation in the water medium. For example, Zhao et al. [4] derived inherent optical properties of water from the background color of underwater images and used for underwater image enhancement. Due to the hazing effects of underwater images caused by light scattering and color change, a phenomenon similar as the effect of heavy fog in the air, He's Dark Channel Prior (DCP) dehazing method [5] is widely used in underwater image enhancement [6, 7]. The algorithm based on wavelength compensation and image dehazing (WCID) [8] compensates the attenuation discrepancy along the propagation path and the influence of the possible presence of an artificial light source. It effectively enhances visibility and restore the color balance of underwater images, but requires high computing resources and long computing time.

Image-based methods are usually simpler and more efficient than physics-based methods. Color equalization is widely adopted approach to deal with color cast problem of underwater image, where blue or green color is dominant. Iqbal et al. proposed the integrated color model (ICM) [9] and the unsupervised color correction method (UCM) [10]. These methods used the histogram stretching in RGB color model and then saturation-intensity stretching in HSI color model to enhance the contrast of the images and correct color cast. Different from ICM, the UCM is to modify red and green channels based on the Von Kries hypothesis and stretch one side or both side according to the characteristic of each R-G-B channel. The output results of these two methods do not have significant difference and still exist blue-green illumination, and may bring serious noise to the enhanced image [11]. But, ignoring the characteristics of different channels, [11] applies the Rayleigh distribution to stretch each channel.

Considering the validity of the physical model used in the underwater image and the simplicity of the inherent nature of the underwater image, we propose a new method, namely relative global histogram stretching (RGHS). It is mainly on the basis of the equalization of G-B channels and histogram stretching in RGB color model but determines the tensile range parameters according to both the distribution features of original image and the light absorption of different wavelength under the water. The bilateral filter is a simple, non-iterative scheme for edge-preserving smoothing to be used to effectively capture the fine details after the image is stretched in RGB color model. After the contrast correction and color correction are performed, our method can preserve the image details and enhance visibility. The superiority of our method to the classic DCP, ICM and UCM methods is illustrated from having the highest value of entropy [12] and UCIQE [13], the lowest value of Q-MOS [14] and MSE [15].

The rest of the paper is organized as followed: Sect. 2 introduces related processing on the underwater image enhancement. Section 3 show the shallow-water image enhancement model in details. The results and evaluation are expressed in Sect. 4, followed by conclusion in Sect. 5.

2 Related Work

2.1 Underwater Model

A well-known haze image function model [16, 17] is often used to approximate the propagation equation of underwater scattering in the background light. The equation is as follows:

$$I_\lambda(x) = J_\lambda(x)t_\lambda(x) + (1 - t_\lambda(x))B_\lambda \tag{1}$$

where the light wavelength $\lambda \in \{red, green, blue\}$, x represents the pixel point in the underwater image $I_\lambda(x)$, $J_\lambda(x)$ is the scene radiance at point x, $t_\lambda(x)$ is the residual energy ratio of after reflecting from point x in the underwater scene and reaching the camera, B_λ is the uniform background light. $J_\lambda(x)t_\lambda(x)$ describes the direct attenuation of scene radiance in the water [20]. Note that the residual energy ratio $t_\lambda(x)$ is a function of both λ and the scene–camera distance $d(x)$, which reflects the overall effects for both light scattering and color change suffered by light with wavelength traveling the underwater distance $d(x)$. Thus, $t_\lambda(x)$ can be represented as (2):

$$t_\lambda(x) = Nrer(\lambda)^{d(x)} \tag{2}$$

$Nrer(\lambda)$ is the normalized residual energy ratio, which refers to the ratio of residual to initial energy for every unit of distance propagated. As showed in the Fig. 1, where the green and blue lights process shorter wavelength and high frequency thereby attenuates extraordinarily lower than the red counterpart. This is why the deep sea image appears the bluish tone prevalent but the performance of the shallow-water image is not obvious. The dependency of $Nrer(\lambda)$ on the light wavelength can be defined based on that of Ocean Type I as (3).

$$\text{Nrer}(\lambda) = \begin{cases} 0.8 \sim 0.85 & \text{if } \lambda = 650 \sim 750\,\mu\text{m (red)} \\ 0.93 \sim 0.97 & \text{if } \lambda = 490 \sim 550\,\mu\text{m (green)} \\ 0.95 \sim 0.99 & \text{if } \lambda = 400 \sim 490\,\mu\text{m (blue)} \end{cases} \tag{3}$$

In this paper, these equations will be considered to decide the maximum range of R-G-B channel in the RGHS.

2.2 Histogram Stretching

Due to the relative-concentrated distribution and quite low histogram range, underwater images often have low contrast and visibility. Histogram stretching is therefore adopted to provide a better pixel distribution of the image channels to the whole dynamic range and thus improve the image contrast. A linear contrast stretching function as (4) is used in [9–11, 18, 19].

$$p_o = (p_i - a)\left(\frac{c - d}{b - a}\right) + d \tag{4}$$

where p_i and p_o are the input and output pixels intensity values, respectively, a, b and c, d represent the minimum and maximum intensity of the input image and the targeted output images, respectively. In a global stretching, c and d are constant and often set to 255 and 0 respectively; a and b are selected at 0.2% and 99.8% in the whole histogram of original image.

3   Shallow-Water Image Enhancement Model

Figure 2 shows the entire processing of our proposed method, which includes three main steps: (1) contrast correction, (2) color correction and (3) quality assessment.

In the contrast correction step, we apply the color equalization and the relative global histogram stretching (RGHS) to the image after R-G-B channel decomposition. The bilateral filter is used to eliminate the noise after the above transformation when preserving the details of the desired colorful underwater image [20]. This will neutralize the low contrast and reduce color cast effect due to light scattering and absorption. In the color correction step, we apply simple global histogram stretching to the 'L' component of the image and adjust for the 'a' and 'b' components in CIE-Lab color space. The adaptive-stretching of 'L', 'a' and 'b' will improve the saturation and brightness of the image to obtain more vivid color. In the last step, we use five quality assessment models to evaluate the enhancement performance of the proposed method.

3.1   Gray-World Color Equalization

In the underwater situation, images are rarely color balanced correctly. After R-G-B channel decomposition, we firstly conduct color equalization for underwater image. Iqbal et al. adjusted the color values of the RGB components based on Von Kries hypothesis [10], which keeps the dominant color cast channel constant. Based on the

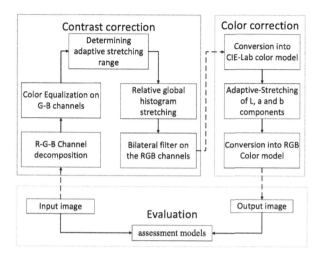

Fig. 2. The entire processing of our proposed method

UCM model, once the average of one channel is extraordinary low, the channel must multiply with a bigger multiplier, which will cause the wrong pretreatment of image color. However, Inspired by the Gray-World (GW) assumption theory [21] that the average value of color object in a perfect image is gray, we correct the G-B channel following the assumptions shown as (5) and (6).

$$\left(R_{avg} + G_{avg} + B_{avg}\right)/3 = 0.5 \tag{5}$$

where $R_{avg}, G_{avg}, B_{avg}$ are the normalized average values of the recovered red channel, green channel, blue channel, respectively.

$$G_{avg} = \frac{1}{255*MN} \sum_{i=1}^{M} \sum_{j=1}^{N} I_g(i,j), \ \theta_g = \frac{0.5}{G_{avg}}$$
$$B_{avg} = \frac{1}{255*MN} \sum_{i=1}^{M} \sum_{j=1}^{N} I_b(i,j), \ \theta_b = \frac{0.5}{B_{avg}} \tag{6}$$

We correct the G and B channels following the GW assumption theory. Here, R channel is not considered because the red light in the water is hard to compensate by simple color equalization, which may bring about red over-saturation. Equation (6) is used to calculate the G-B channel of color equalization coefficient θ_g, θ_b, where M and N are the spatial resolution of an image. Based on the coefficient θ_g, θ_b, the intensity values of G-B channel can be corrected by multiplying θ_g, θ_b, respectively. Next, we carry out dynamic histogram stretching for the image channels with the RGHS strategy.

3.2 Relative Global Histogram Stretching (RGHS)

The blind global histogram stretching usually uses the same parameters for all R-G-B channels of the images, ignoring the histogram distribution characteristics of different channels and in different images. When the fixed values (e.g., 0, 255) are applied in

Eq. (4), it may over-stretch or under-stretch certain color channel and damage the details of the original image.

According to the propagation law of underwater light, we need to apply the contrast correction method to modify the distorted images. The histogram distribution rule of RGB channels on the following observation in shallow-water images: In most of shallow-water images, the histogram of red light is focused in such values $[50, 150]$, while G channel and B channel have the most of numerical concentrated in the range $[70, 210]$. This indicates that histogram stretching should be sensitive to channels.

To differentiate from the global histogram stretching in (4), we re-write the relative global histogram stretching equation in (7).

$$p_{out} = (p_{in} - I_{min}) \left(\frac{O_{max} - O_{min}}{I_{max} - I_{min}} \right) + O_{min} \tag{7}$$

where p_{in} and p_{out} are the input and output pixels, respectively, and I_{min}, I_{max}, O_{min} and O_{max} are the adaptive parameters for the before and after stretching images, respectively. In the next step, specifically, we will introduce the calculation of the stretching range $[I_{min}, I_{max}]$ and the desired range $[O_{min}, O_{max}]$.

Adaptive parameter acquisition for the stretching range. From the histogram distribution of various shallow-water images, we can observe that the histogram distribution of R-G-B channel similar to the variation of Rayleigh distribution defined as (8), which is a continuous probability distribution for positive-valued random variables.

$$RD = \frac{x}{a^2} e^{-x^2/2a^2}, \ x \geq 0, \ a > 0 \tag{8}$$

where the scale parameter of the distribution a is mode, the peak of R-G-B channel histograms. It should be noted that when the distribution of a channel shows a normal distribution, its mode and its mid-point are almost the same. We take the mode value as a dividing line to separately decide the minimum (left) and maximum (right) intensity level values of the input image in the histogram stretching.

Because the underwater images are influenced by various factors, to reduce the impact of some extreme pixels on the relative global histogram stretching, it usually takes the stretching range between 0.1% and 99.9% of the histogram. However, if the histogram is not normally distributed, this method that removes an equal number of pixels from two tails of the histogram may not be reasonable. We split the upper and lower proportion of the intensity values to calculate the I_{min} and I_{max} for each R-G-B channel, which is showed in the Eq. (9).

$$\begin{aligned} I_{min} &= S.sort[S.sort.index(a) * 0.1\%] \\ I_{max} &= S.sort[-(S.length - S.sort.index(a)) * 0.1\%] \end{aligned} \tag{9}$$

where S is the set of image pixel values for each R-G-B channel, $S.sort$ is the sorted data set in an ascending order, $S.sort.index(a)$ is the index number of the mode in the histogram distribution, and $S.sort[x]$ represents the value in the index x of positive-sorted data set. Equation (9) means that from the peak division line, we separate the pixels which values are in the smallest 0.1% of the total number on the left side and the biggest 0.1% of the total number on the right side from the histogram distribution to perform the special method. For different images and RGB channels of the Rayleigh distributions, the I_{min} and I_{max} are both image- and channel-sensitive.

Adaptive parameter acquisition for the desired range. For the underwater images, global histogram stretching with a range of $[0, 255]$ often brings excessive blue-green illumination. In order to achieve an optimal desired range of stretching, we dynamically determine the minimum (O_{min}) and maximum (O_{max}) intensity level values for each R-G-B channel.

We first calculate the standard deviation of the Rayleigh distribution σ_λ, as (10).

$$\sigma_\lambda = \sqrt{\frac{4-\pi}{2}} a_\lambda = 0.655\, a_\lambda, \ \lambda \in \{R, G, B\} \tag{10}$$

where $\lambda \in \{R, G, B\}$ indicates the R, G, B channel, a is the mode in a channel. Then, we define the minimum value of the desired range $O_{\lambda min}$ as (11).

$$O_{\lambda min} = a_\lambda - \beta_\lambda * \sigma_\lambda, \ 0 \leq O_{\lambda min} \leq I_{\lambda min} \tag{11}$$

Here, β_λ can be derived from (11) and substitute σ_λ with (10).

$$\beta_\lambda = \frac{a_\lambda - O_{\lambda min}}{\sigma_\lambda}, \ \frac{a_\lambda - I_{min}}{\sigma_\lambda} \leq \beta_\lambda \leq \frac{a_\lambda}{\sigma_\lambda} \tag{12}$$

On the right of Eq. (12), as $a \geq I_{min}$, we can get $0 \leq \beta_\lambda$. Substitute (10) into the right of Eq. (12), we can get $\beta_\lambda \leq 1.526$. Define $\beta_\lambda \in Z$, then β_λ has a unique solution: $\beta_\lambda = 1$. Therefore, (11) can be simplified as (13).

$$O_{\lambda min} = a_\lambda - \sigma_\lambda \tag{13}$$

For the maximum parameters of the desired range, because of different degrees of attenuation of the different light bands in the water, we must take separate analysis of RGB channels to calculate. According to the simplified fuzzy imaging model (1), the haze-free image $J_\lambda(x)$ can be recovered by (14).

$$J_\lambda(x) = \frac{I_\lambda(x) - (1 - t_\lambda(x))B_\lambda}{\kappa\, t_\lambda(x)} \tag{14}$$

where $\kappa = 1.1$ and $\kappa = 0.9$ are an experiential value for red channel and green-blue channel respectively. The maximum value of the desired range O_{max} can be achieved when maximizing the recovered image $J_\lambda(x)$, as represented in (15).

$$Max((J_\lambda(x)) = Max\left(\frac{I_\lambda(x) - (1 - t_\lambda(x))B_\lambda}{\kappa\, t_\lambda(x)}\right) \tag{15}$$

When $J_\lambda(x)$ achieves the maximum value, B_λ is 0. Then, O_{max} for different color channel can be defined as (16).

$$O_{\lambda max} = \frac{I_\lambda}{\kappa t_\lambda} = \frac{a_\lambda + \mu_\lambda * \sigma_\lambda}{\kappa * t_\lambda}, \quad I_{\lambda max} \leq O_{\lambda max} \leq 255 \tag{16}$$

Here, $t_\lambda(x)$ is measured using Eq. (2) with the $Nrer(\lambda)$ values of 0.83, 0.95, 0.97 for R, G, B channels respectively (see also Eq. (3)), and $d(x)$ is set to 3 as the estimation distance between the scene and the camera. I_λ is a value on the right side of the mode in the channel histogram, and can be represented as $a_\lambda + \mu_\lambda * \sigma_\lambda$.

Based on the range value of $O_{\lambda max}$, the coefficient μ_λ meets the inequity (17).

$$\mu_\lambda = \frac{\kappa * t_\lambda * O_{\lambda max} - a_\lambda}{\sigma_\lambda}$$
$$\frac{\kappa * t_\lambda * I_\lambda}{\sigma_\lambda} \leq \mu_\lambda + 1.526 \leq \frac{\kappa * t_\lambda * 255}{\sigma_\lambda} \tag{17}$$

In (17), μ_λ will has no solution or limited solutions in integer field. When μ_λ has multiple solutions, we chose the average value of their solutions; when μ_λ has no solution, we simply set the $O_{\lambda max}$ to 255. These adaptive parameters have considered both the light transmission and the original image histogram distribution, preserving from overstretching or under-stretching.

3.3   Adaptive-Stretching in CIE-Lab Color Model

After the contrast correction in RGB color model, the image will undergo the color correction process. In this process, the underwater image is converted into CIE-Lab color model to improve color performance. In CIE-Lab color model, 'L' component, which is equivalent to the image lightness, represents the brightest value at L = 100 and the darkest value at L = 0. When a = 0 and b = 0, the color channel will present true neutral gray values. Hence, the output color gradations of 'a' and 'b' components are modified to acquire color correction accurately, meanwhile, 'L' component is used to adjust the brightness of the entire image. Firstly, the shallow-water image in CIE-Lab color model is decomposed into respective channels.

The 'L' component is applied with linear slide stretching, given by (8), which range between 0.1% and 99.9% is stretched to range [0, 100]. The 0.1% of the lower and upper values in the image are set to 0 and 100 respectively. The 'a' and 'b' components are in the range of $[-128, 127]$, of which 0 is the median value. The stretching of 'a' and 'b' is defined as an S-model curve (18).

$$p_\chi = I_\chi * \left(\varphi^{1 - \left| \frac{I_\chi}{128} \right|} \right), \quad \chi \in \{a, b\} \tag{18}$$

where I_χ and p_χ represents the input and output pixels, respectively, $\chi \in \{a, b\}$ indicates the 'a' and 'b' components, φ is optimally-experimental value, set to 1.3 in the method. Equation (18) uses an exponential function as the stretching coefficient, whereby the closer the values to 0, the further they will be stretched.

Color and brightness in an image are the important parameters of clearness and visibility. Therefore, the objects in the image can be clearly differentiated from the background. After the adaptive-stretching process of 'L', 'a' and 'b' components in CIE-Lab color model, the channels are then composed and converted back into RGB color model. A contrast-enhanced and color-corrected output image can be generated as the perceivable and visible final output image.

4   Result and Discussion

Our proposed method characterized by contrast improvement, saturation equalization and brightness enhancement is compared with three traditional image enhancement methods qualitatively and quantitatively. Single image haze removal using dark channel prior by He [5] used in comparison as it is the classic technique for dehazing and the underwater image is often considered as haze image. The other comparison methods are ICM and UCM [9, 10] because they are the effective non-physical method and are most similar to the proposed method in terms of histogram modification. In the comparison results, we only present the UCM images because the ICM has similar results to the UCM. We have tried to compare with the algorithms of Rayleigh distribution in [11, 18, 19]. Unfortunately, we failed to restore their results. In Fig. 3, our proposed method generates better visual image than the other method. The overall perception of fishes produced by He's model has slight changes which cannot improve the quality of the image and even lowers the visibility and contrast. The UCM over-saturates the image color where the blue-green color appears prominent and it leads in the noise. The result image of our method presents better contrast and color saturation as the fishers are differentiated from the background and less blue-green illumination retained. In the second row of Fig. 3, the x-axis of the histogram (original and enhanced images) ranges from 0 to 255. The gray-level histogram distributions of (a) and (b) are comparatively concentrated, used to explain the low contrast and visibility of two colorful images. The gray-level histogram of (c) and (d) are distributed in

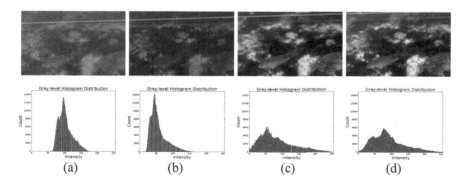

Fig. 3. (a) Original image; (b) DCP; (c) UCM; (d) our proposed model; enhanced images on the top and their corresponding gray-level histogram distributions on the bottom (Color figure online)

the whole range, but on the basis of the Gray-World (GW) assumption theory, the histogram of enhanced image (d) is more superior in the distribution.

Different methods for underwater image enhancement achieve the result images, showing in the Fig. 4. Obviously, the DCP fails to enhance the shallow-water image. In the first two rows of Fig. 4, the UCM over-saturates the image color as the blue-green color of the image becomes too bright and the enhanced images are not as natural as our results. In the last two rows of Fig. 4, the result images of the UCM exist distinct noise but our method successfully removes the noise and preserves the image details.

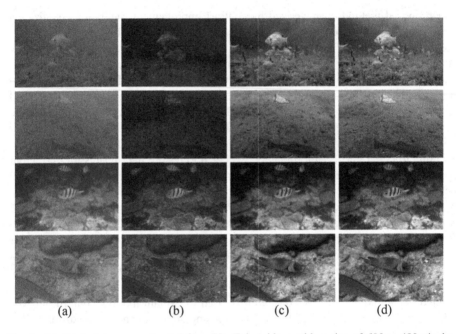

(a)   (b)   (c)   (d)

Fig. 4. (a) Original images extracted from YouTube videos with a size of 600 × 400 pixels; (b) DCP; (c) UCM; (d) our proposed model (Color figure online)

We conduct quantitative analysis, with objective metrics including entropy, underwater color image-quality evaluation (UCIQE) [13], High-Dynamic Range Visual Difference Predictor2 (HDR-VDP2) [14], mean square error (MSE) and peak signal noise ratio (PSNR) [15]. The UCIQE is very recent non-reference model for underwater color image quality assessment, which is the aggregative indicator of chroma, saturation, and contrast. Entropy represents the abundance of information, which is interpreted as the average uncertainty of information source. The higher the entropy value is, the more information contains. The HDR-VDP2 uses a fairly advanced model of human perception to predict both visibility of artifacts and overall quality in images. It produces Q-MOS value to indicate the image quality from 0 (best) to 100 (worst). MSE and PSNR are conventional metrics in image quality assessment, mainly measuring the noise degradation of image. Although the Q-MOS, MSE and PSNR are full-reference metrics, using the original underwater image as the reference image, they are useful to indicate the human perceived quality loss and the noise increase of the produced image from the original. Table 1 shows the comparison results in terms of the five assessment models.

Table 1. Quantitative analysis in terms of ENTROPY, UCIQE, Q-MOS, MSE and PSNR.

Method	ENTROPY	UCIQE	Q-MOS	MSE	PSNR
DCP	6.352	0.391	53.287	3326.736	13.537
ICM	7.221	0.476	41.369	1439.314	16.646
UCM	7.316	0.514	39.517	1375.188	16.825
RGHS	**7.552**	**0.587**	**34.636**	**963.231**	**18.643**

Our proposed method gains the best results (show in the bold) in the evaluations. It preserves the most information and details, achieves the great visibility and overall high quality and eliminates the noise. The maximum UCIQE value means that our method can effectively balance chroma, saturation, and contrast of the enhanced underwater images. The DCP produces the worst performance in four methods, which is in accordance with the visual observation of low contrast and visibility. It means that simple haze removal with the dark channel prior cannot be directly used for underwater enhancement. The ICM and UCM produce the method images with obvious noise, which causes high value of MSE and low value of PSNR. To sum up, the results show that our method can produce the high-quality shallow-water images and is superior to widely-accepted underwater image enhancement models.

5   Conclusion

In this paper, we have explored the issues related to shallow-water images and existing underwater image enhancement methods, and successfully proposed a new image enhancement method RGHS for different shallow-water images. Our proposed method firstly performs contrast correction based on simple histogram stretching with dynamic parameters acquisition in RGB color model, which takes into account both the histogram distribution feature of the raw image and underwater transmission properties of different light channels. Then, adaptive-stretching in CIE-Lab color model is conducted for color correction. Our proposed method was compared with the typical haze removal model DCP, and the underwater image enhancement model ICM and UCM which are based on histogram stretching in the RGB and HSV/HSI color models. Qualitative and quantitative results proof that our method is more effective to enhance the visibility, improve details and not to increase artifacts and noise of shallow-water image. The integration of histogram redistribution in the RGB and CIE-Lab color model can be used in other underwater image research. However, our proposed method is limited in the shallow-water image enhancement, which ignores the energy attenuation along propagation path between the surface and the scene and failing to compensate the serious-distorted channel in deeper-water image. In fact, many underwater image enhancement methods are not tested with the images from deep ocean below 1000 m. With the reasonable combination of the properties and the degraded physical model of image, we will improve the algorithm to be suitable for different kinds of underwater images.

Acknowledgment. This work was supported by the Program for Professor of Special Appointment (Eastern Scholar at Shanghai Institutions of Higher Learning No. TP2016038, the National Natural Science Foundation of China (NSFC) Grant 61702323, and the Doctoral Research Startup Fund of Shanghai Ocean University A2-0203-17-100322.

References

1. Sahu, P., Gupta, N., Sharma, N.: A survey on underwater image enhancement techniques. Int. J. Comput. Appl. **87**(13), 19–23 (2014)
2. Zaneveld, J.R.V., Pegau, W.S.: Robust underwater visibility parameter. Opt. Express **11**(23), 2997–3009 (2003)
3. Schettini, R., Corchs, S.: Underwater image processing: state of the art of restoration and image enhancement methods. EURASIP J. Adv. Sig. Process. **2010**(1), 746052 (2010)
4. Zhao, X., Jin, T., Qu, S.: Deriving inherent optical properties from background color and underwater image enhancement. Ocean Eng. **94**, 163–172 (2015)
5. He, K., Sun, J., Tang, X.: Single image haze removal using dark channel prior. IEEE Trans. Pattern Anal. Mach. Intell. **33**(12), 2341–2353 (2011)
6. Galdran, A., Pardo, D., Picón, A., Alvarez-Gila, A.: Automatic red-channel underwater image restoration. J. Vis. Commun. Image Represent. **26**, 132–145 (2015)
7. Drews, P., Nascimento, E., Moraes, F., Botelho, S., Campos, M.: Transmission estimation in underwater single images. In: Proceedings of IEEE ICCVW 2013, pp. 825–830 (2013)
8. Chiang, J.Y., Chen, Y.C.: Underwater image enhancement by wavelength compensation and dehazing. IEEE Trans. Image Process. **21**(4), 1756–1769 (2012)
9. Iqbal, K., Abdul Salam, R., Osman, M.A., Talib, A.Z.: Underwater image enhancement using an integrated colour model. IAENG Int. J. Comput. Sci. **32**(2), 239–244 (2007)
10. Iqbal, K., Odetayo, M., James, A., Salam, R.A., Talib, A.Z.H.: Enhancing the low quality images using unsupervised colour correction method. In: 2010 IEEE International Conference on Systems, Man and Cybernetics, pp. 1703–1709 (2010)
11. Ghani, A.S.A., Isa, N.A.M.: Underwater image quality enhancement through integrated color model with Rayleigh distribution. Appl. Soft Comput. **27**, 219–230 (2015)
12. Schechner, Y.Y., Karpel, N.: Recovery of underwater visibility and structure by polarization analysis. IEEE J. Ocean. Eng. **30**(3), 570–587 (2005)
13. Yang, M., Sowmya, A.: An underwater color image quality evaluation metric. IEEE Trans. Image Process. **24**(12), 6062–6071 (2015)
14. Mantiuk, R., Kim, K.J., Rempel, A.G., Heidrich, W.: HDR-VDP-2: a calibrated visual metric for visibility and quality predictions in all luminance conditions. In: ACM SIGGRAPH 2011 Papers, New York, NY, USA, vol. 40, pp. 1–14 (2011)
15. Hitam, M.S., Awalludin, E.A., Yussof, W.N.J.H.W., Bachok, Z.: Mixture contrast limited adaptive histogram equalization for underwater image enhancement. In: 2013 International Conference on Computer Applications Technology (ICCAT), pp. 1–5 (2013)
16. Schechner, Y.Y., Narasimhan, S.G., Nayar, S.K.: Instant dehazing of images using polarization. In: Proceedings of 2001 IEEE Computer Society Conference on Computer Vision and Pattern Recognition (CVPR), pp. 325–332 (2001)

17. Narasimhan, S.G., Nayar, S.K.: Vision and the atmosphere. Int. J. Comput. Vis. **48**(3), 233–254 (2002)
18. Ghani, A.S.A., Isa, N.A.M.: Underwater image quality enhancement through Rayleigh-stretching and averaging image planes. Int. J. Nav. Archit. Ocean Eng. **6**(4), 840–866 (2014)
19. Ghani, A.S.A., Isa, N.A.M.: Enhancement of low quality underwater image through integrated global and local contrast correction. Appl. Soft Comput. **37**, 332–344 (2015)
20. Paris, S., Durand, F.: A fast approximation of the bilateral filter using a signal processing approach. In: Leonardis, A., Bischof, H., Pinz, A. (eds.) ECCV 2006. LNCS, vol. 3954, pp. 568–580. Springer, Heidelberg (2006). https://doi.org/10.1007/11744085_44
21. Chambah, M., Semani, D., Renouf, A., Courtellemont, P., Rizzi, A.: Underwater color constancy: enhancement of automatic live fish recognition. In: Color Imaging IX: Processing, Hardcopy, and Applications, vol. 5293, pp. 157–168 (2003)

Spatiotemporal 3D Models of Aging Fruit from Multi-view Time-Lapse Videos

Lintao Guo, Hunter Quant, Nikolas Lamb, Benjamin Lowit, Sean Banerjee, and Natasha Kholgade Banerjee[(✉)]

Clarkson University, Potsdam, NY 13699, USA
{linguo,quanthd,lambne,lowitbp,sbanerje,nbanerje}@clarkson.edu

Abstract. We provide an approach to reconstruct spatiotemporal 3D models of aging objects such as fruit containing time-varying shape and appearance using multi-view time-lapse videos captured by a microenvironment of Raspberry Pi cameras. Our approach represents the 3D structure of the object prior to aging using a static 3D mesh reconstructed from multiple photographs of the object captured using a rotating camera track. We manually align the 3D mesh to the images at the first time instant. Our approach automatically deforms the aligned 3D mesh to match the object across the multi-viewpoint time-lapse videos. We texture map the deformed 3D meshes with intensities from the frames at each time instant to create the spatiotemporal 3D model of the object. Our results reveal the time dependence of volume loss due to transpiration and color transformation due to enzymatic browning on banana peels and in exposed parts of bitten fruit.

Keywords: Spatiotemporal · 3D model · Multi view · Time-varying
Time lapse

1 Introduction

Public repositories of 3D models of objects are expanding rapidly, with ready-to-use 3D models available for a wide variety of applications such as animation [5], physics simulations [3,4], robotic manipulation [8] and photo-editing [16]. However, the information contained in publicly available 3D models is still limited. Most 3D models only contain the geometry and textures for rigid objects. While rigged models exist for faces and bodies, current 3D model repositories lack the range of dynamic behaviors exhibited by real-world objects such as plush toys deforming under impact, metal corroding, chocolate melting, and bitten fruit such as the apple in Fig. 1 shrinking and browning when kept outside.

In this paper, we provide a data-driven approach to reconstruct spatiotemporal 3D models of objects such as fruit that undergo changes in shape and appearance due to aging when exposed to the environment. Unlike prior approaches on time-varying aging that focus on appearance transformations [11,13,19,23], our approach models both appearance change due to enzymatic browning [25] and shape deformations due to water loss.

ⓒ Springer International Publishing AG 2018
K. Schoeffmann et al. (Eds.): MMM 2018, Part I, LNCS 10704, pp. 466–478, 2018.
https://doi.org/10.1007/978-3-319-73603-7_38

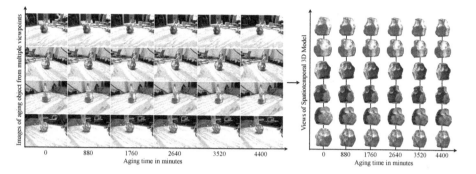

Fig. 1. Given time-lapse videos of an aging object from multiple viewpoints as shown on the left, our approach reconstructs a spatiotemporal 3D model as shown by the views on the right.

Our approach deforms a static 3D mesh of the object reconstructed prior to aging to fit synchronized time-lapse videos of the object captured from multiple viewpoints. As discussed in Sect. 3, we contribute a 3D printed camera track to automatically capture and stitch multiple photographs of the object into the static mesh. We contribute a microenvironment of multiple Raspberry Pi v2 cameras that automatically capture the synchronized time-lapse videos from various viewpoints as described in Sect. 4. We provide a manual interface to rigidly align and deform the static mesh to images at the first time instant as discussed in Sect. 5. Our approach automatically deforms the 3D mesh to match the object in the time-lapse videos and maps the deformed meshes with seam-free textures from the time-lapse images as discussed in Sects. 6 and 7.

Section 8 shows the spatiotemporal 3D models resulting from our approach. Our spatiotemporal 3D models enable data-driven analysis of the physical properties of objects aging under environmental effects as shown by our results on volume loss and appearance transformation in Sect. 8. The spatiotemporal 3D models provided by our work have the potential to enhance consumer quality of life by providing applications such as data-driven prediction of shelf-life of perishable food products from grocery store cameras, automated monitoring of the structural health of erosive materials used in building constructions, and intelligent updates to end users on the status of fruit, cooked items, and baked goods in their home environments.

2 Related Work

Many approaches simulate time-varying phenomena such as metal erosion, paint cracking, and plant aging using physics-based and biological models [10,17,26, 30]. These models often lack comprehensive representation of fine-scale appearance changes in real-world objects. Several data-driven approaches model real-world appearance by capturing material samples using a single camera [11], multiple cameras [13,19], or scanner-camera setups [23]. None of these approaches capture time-varying shape. In conjunction with appearance, our approach captures the shape deformation exhibited by fruit undergoing volume changes due to water loss. The approach of Li et al. [21] analyzes plant growth using 3D point clouds captured by rotating the plant and imaging it using a single structured light scanner. Unlike their approach, we use multiple cameras to capture the 3D structure of the object by keeping it still to avoid rotational forces from deforming the object shape. Their approach yields uncorresponded 3D point clouds, while our approach yields spatiotemporal models with mesh vertices corresponded in time.

Our work is more closely related to approaches that reconstruct spatiotemporal 3D shape and appearance models of facial and body motion from multiple viewpoint videos. These approaches need to address the challenge of estimating frame-to-frame correspondences where brightness constancy may not hold between adjacent frames due to aggressive face and body motions or due to occlusion from moving body parts. The approach of de Aguiar et al. [2] matches 3D body model points to interest point correspondences between multiple images at the same time instant, and uses silhouette rims to refine the alignment. Beeler et al. [6] cluster video frames as anchored and unanchored to a reference frame, propagate a 3D mesh to fit reference-to-anchored and anchored-to-unanchored correspondences obtained using normalized cross-correlation, and perform a global optimization to refine the propagated 3D meshes under constraints of image fidelity, mesh consistency, and geometric smoothness. Unlike such approaches, we use small time-lapses to capture slow aging transformations occurring over the span of hours to days, where brightness is nearly constant between adjacent frames, enabling the use of optic flow techniques such as [24].

3   Camera Track to Capture Static 3D Mesh

We provide a rotating camera track of diameter 620 mm shown in Fig. 2(a) to automatically capture photographs of the object from multiple viewpoints. The

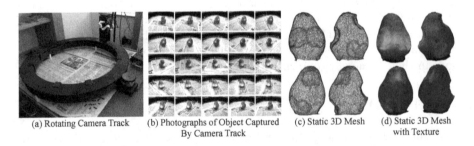

(a) Rotating Camera Track   (b) Photographs of Object Captured   (c) Static 3D Mesh   (d) Static 3D Mesh
                                        By Camera Track   with Texture

Fig. 2. (a) Rotating track with a Raspberry Pi camera attached to a tower to image an object from multiple viewpoints. (b) Photographs of a pear captured by the rotating camera. (c) Static 3D mesh reconstructed by stitching the photographs. (d) Static 3D mesh mapped with the texture from the photographs.

track is constructed by joining 12 programmatically modeled 3D printed arcs as discussed in [18], and is controlled using a Nema 23 stepper motor with a 1.8° step angle. The track rotates over ball bearings on a base assembled from slottable 3D printed segments. We use a Raspberry Pi v3 computer to program the movement of the stepper and the imaging of the object using a Raspberry Pi v2 camera. Figure 2(b) shows the images of a pear captured using the track. We stitch the photographs into a static 3D mesh using Autodesk ReMake [1] shown in Figs. 2(c) and (d).

4   Microenvironment of Multiple Raspberry Pi Cameras to Capture Time-Lapse Videos

As shown in Fig. 3(a), we use a microenvironment of four Raspberry Pi v2 cameras to capture multiple viewpoint time-lapse videos of the object aging. Details of the microenvironment construction can be found in [14]. We provide a Java graphical user interface (GUI) that allows a user to set a time-lapse duration and capture length, and run the time-lapse capture of an aging object. When a capture process is started, the server sends a parallelized capture signal to each Raspberry Pi computer at every time-lapse instant. On receiving the signal, each Raspberry Pi invokes an image capture. We manually set the exposure value and white balance to be constant. Each Raspberry Pi computer sends the captured image to the master computer to augment corresponding video sequences. Figure 3(b) shows multi-view images of a banana blackening captured using the Raspberry Pi microenvironment. We refer to each set of multi-view images at a single time instant in the videos as a frame F.

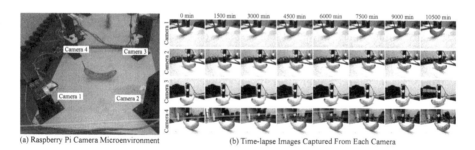

(a) Raspberry Pi Camera Microenvironment   (b) Time-lapse Images Captured From Each Camera

Fig. 3. (a) Microenvironment of four Raspberry Pi v2 cameras to capture time-varying phenomena such as aging. (b) Sample images shown from a time-lapse video of a blackening banana. While images are shown every 1000 min to show the range of the video, the time-lapse interval is finer at 5 min.

5   3D Mesh Alignment to Initial Frame

While the 3D mesh reconstructed using ReMake provides an accurate representation of the object, small-scale deviations due to ground contact, imperfect correspondences between photographs, or ambiguities in resolving illumination from reflectance often render the 3D model imprecise. We provide a manual approach that adapts the geometry correction method of Kholgade et al. [16] to match the 3D mesh to the object in multiple viewpoint images at the initial frame of the time-lapse videos, i.e., at $F = 0$, using user-provided correspondences. While automated approaches to perform 3D model alignment exist [15,22], they fail to provide unsupervised pixel-precise alignment for unstructured object collections such as the fruit in this work.

We first perform a rigid alignment of the 3D mesh to the 2D images from 2D-3D correspondences. As shown in Fig. 4(a), for the jth image in the initial frame, we mark m_j 2D points $\mathbf{x}_{k_j}$ in the image and corresponding 3D points $\mathbf{X}_{k_j}$ in the 3D mesh, where $k_j \in \{1, 2, \cdots, m_j\}$. We use the efficient Perspective n-Point algorithm (ePnP) [20] to estimate the rigid pose of each camera consisting of its rotation $\mathbf{R}_j$ and translation $\mathbf{t}_j$ with respect to the 3D mesh using $m_j \geq 4$. For each image, the ePnP algorithm requires $m_j \geq 4$ correspondences, necessitating $\sum_{j=1}^{m} m_j \geq 4m$ correspondences, where m is the number of cameras.

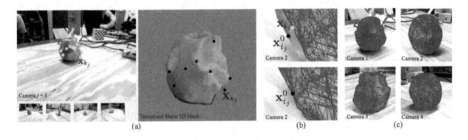

(a)   (b)   (c)

Fig. 4. Alignment of the 3D mesh to the frame at time instant 0 min, i.e., the initial frame. (a) Interface to manually perform rigid alignment of the 3D mesh on the right to the initial frame images from all four cameras on the left. The 3D mesh is texture-mapped with the stitched texture from the static mesh reconstruction for ease of point marking. (b) The user marks a single point correspondence in the second image (top) to deform the 3D mesh (bottom). (c) 3D mesh aligned to the object in all four images after several user-marked correspondences.

We use the pose $\{\mathbf{R}_j, \mathbf{t}_j\}$ of each camera to project the 3D mesh $\mathbf{X} \in \mathbb{R}^{3 \times N}$ into each camera image, where N is the number of vertices on the mesh. We manually deform $\mathbf{X}$ to mesh $\mathbf{X}^0$ with pixel-precise alignment to the object contours at the initial frame $F = 0$ by marking n_j 2D correspondences $\mathbf{x}_{i_j} \in \mathbb{R}^2$ on the 3D mesh projection and $\mathbf{x}_{i_j}^0 \in \mathbb{R}^2$ on object contours, where $i_j \in \{1, 2, \cdots, n_j\}$. The top image in Fig. 4(b) shows a single user-provided 2D-2D correspondence. We backproject rays from the camera center through $\mathbf{x}_{i_j}$ to obtain 3D points $\mathbf{X}_{i_j} \in \mathbb{R}^3$ at the intersection of the rays and the faces of $\mathbf{X}$. Similar to Kholgade et al. [16], we estimate the deformed 3D mesh $\mathbf{X}^0 \in \mathbb{R}^{3 \times N}$ from $\mathbf{X}_{i_j}$ and $\mathbf{x}_{i_j}^0$ by optimizing the objective function $E(\mathbf{X}^0)$ in $\mathbf{X}^0$, where

$$E(\mathbf{X}^0) = \lambda_{\text{ray}} E_{\text{ray}}(\mathbf{X}^0) + \lambda_{\text{lap}} E_{\text{lap}}(\mathbf{X}^0) + \lambda_{\text{small}} E_{\text{small}}(\mathbf{X}^0). \tag{1}$$

As in Kholgade et al., the term E_{ray} in Eq. (1) constrains each 3D point $\mathbf{X}_{i_j}^0$ to lie as close as possible to the projection of $\mathbf{X}_{i_j}^0$ on the ray $\mathbf{v}_{i_j}^0 = \mathbf{K}_j^{-1}\left[\mathbf{x}_{i_j}^0;1\right]$ [1] through the 2D point $\mathbf{x}_{i_j}^0$. E_{ray} is described as

$$E_{\mathrm{ray}}(\mathbf{X}^0) = \sum_{i_j=1}^{n_j}\left\|\left(\mathbf{I}_3 - \mathbf{v}_{i_j}^0(\mathbf{v}_{i_j}^0)^T / \left\|\mathbf{v}_{i_j}^0\right\|^2\right)\mathbf{R}_j\mathbf{X}_{i_j}^0\right\|^2, \qquad (2)$$

where $\mathbf{I}_3$ represents the 3×3 identity matrix. The term E_{lap} represents a simplified version of the Laplacian surface energy from the approach of Sorkine and Alexa [29]. Since our deformations are small, we eliminate co-tangent weights and local rotation estimation from their approach to yield E_{lap} as

$$E_{\mathrm{lap}}(\mathbf{X}^0) = \sum_{i=1}^{N}\left\|(\mathbf{X}_i^0 - \mathbf{X}_i) - \sum_{l\in\mathcal{N}(i)}(\mathbf{X}_l^0 - \mathbf{X}_l)/\|\mathcal{N}(i)\|\right\|^2, \qquad (3)$$

where $\mathcal{N}(i)$ is the 1-ring neighborhood of $\mathbf{X}_i^0$. We drop the symmetry term from approach of Kholgade et al., as our objects show asymmetry due to slicing or bite marks. We introduce the term E_{small} in our approach, where

$$E_{\mathrm{small}}(\mathbf{X}^0) = \sum_{i=1}^{N}\left\|(\mathbf{X}_i^0 - \mathbf{X}_i)\right\|^2 \qquad (4)$$

to restrict the deformations to be as small as possible. The term prevents an arbitrary resizing and translation of the 3D mesh due to the scale ambiguity inherent to the relationship between the 3D mesh and the cameras. The bottom image of Fig. 4(b) shows the 3D mesh deformed to match the 2D-2D correspondence marked at the top. Figure 4(c) shows the deformed 3D mesh aligned to all four images of the first time-lapse frame for an apple. We use weights $\lambda_{\mathrm{ray}} = 1$, $\lambda_{\mathrm{lap}} = 5$, and $\lambda_{\mathrm{small}} = .001$ in this work.

6   Automatic 3D Mesh Deformation to Time-Lapse Videos

Given the 3D mesh aligned to the initial frame, our approach automatically estimates a deformation of the 3D mesh to match point correspondences on the object over successive frames in the sequence of multi-view time-lapse videos. Our approach leverages the assumption that adjacent time-lapse images from a particular viewpoint show minimal change in shape and appearance, enabling the use of optic flow to estimate point correspondences between successive frames. We use the Kanade-Lucas-Tomasi (KLT) tracking approach [24] to estimate n_j^F 2D point correspondences $\mathbf{x}_{i_j}^F$ and $\mathbf{x}_{i_j}^{F+1}$ between the jth images in the current frame F and the next frame $F+1$, where $i_j \in \{1, 2, \cdots, n_j^F\}$. Figure 5(a) shows the 2D point correspondences estimated between two adjacent frames for the bitten apple. We use the projection of the 3D mesh in each image of the frame F to retain point correspondences within the object contour.

---

[1] In $\left[\mathbf{x}_{i_j}^0;1\right]$, the semi-colon appends 1 at the end of column vector $\mathbf{x}_{i_j}^0$.

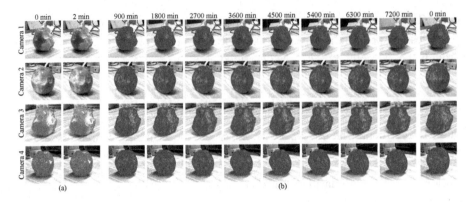

Fig. 5. Automatic deformation to multi-view time-lapse sequence of the bitten apple. (a) Point correspondences in red obtained using Kanade-Lucas-Tomasi (KLT) tracking between successive images from the first two frames. (b) Deformed 3D mesh for each camera image at various instances in the time-lapse sequence. The 3D mesh at time instant 0 min from Fig. 4(c) is shown at the right for size comparison to the 3D mesh at the last time instant of 7200 min. (Color figure online)

Given a deformed 3D mesh $\mathbf{X}^F \in \mathbb{R}^{3 \times N}$ at frame F, we determine each 3D point $\mathbf{X}_{i_j}^F$ on $\mathbf{X}^F$ by back-projecting a ray from the camera center through $\mathbf{x}_{i_j}^F$ and determining barycentric coordinates $\alpha_{l i_j}$ for vertices $\mathbf{X}_l$ on the face $\mathcal{F}_k \in \mathcal{F}$ that intersects the ray, where $l \in \mathcal{F}_k$ and $\mathcal{F}$ is the set of mesh faces. To reduce drift over the 3D model deformations, we deform the initial mesh $\mathbf{X}^0$ instead of $\mathbf{X}^F$ to fit the corresponding points $\mathbf{x}_{i_j}^{F+1}$ in frame $F + 1$. We compute 3D points on $\mathbf{X}^0$ corresponding to $\mathbf{X}_{i_j}^F$ as $\mathbf{X}_{i_j}^0 = \sum_{l \in \mathcal{F}_k} \alpha_{l i_j} \mathbf{X}_l^0$. We estimate the deformed 3D mesh $\mathbf{X}^{F+1}$ in the frame $F + 1$ by optimizing the objective function $E(\mathbf{X}^{F+1})$ in $\mathbf{X}^{F+1}$. We set up $E(\mathbf{X}^{F+1})$ by performing the substitutions $\mathbf{X} \leftarrow \mathbf{X}^0$, $\mathbf{X}^0 \leftarrow \mathbf{X}^{F+1}$, $n_j \leftarrow n_j^F$, and $\mathbf{v}_{i_j}^0 \leftarrow \mathbf{v}_{i_j}^{F+1}$ in Eqs. (1)–(4). The quantity $\mathbf{v}_{i_j}^{F+1} = \mathbf{K}_j^{-1} \left[\mathbf{x}_{i_j}^{F+1}; 1 \right]$ represents the ray through the 2D point $\mathbf{x}_{i_j}^{F+1}$ in the frame $F + 1$. Figure 5(b) shows the deformed mesh aligned to several frames in the time-lapse sequence of the bitten apple.

7   Texture Mapping the Deformed 3D Meshes

Given the 3D meshes deformed to match each time-lapse frame, we texture map each mesh with the intensities from the individual images. For the frame F of the time-lapse sequence, we use ray intersections to obtain the subset $\mathcal{F}_j^F \in \mathcal{F}$ of faces visible from the viewpoint of the jth camera. We sample the intensities at the vertices indexed by $\mathcal{F}_j^F$ in the jth image. We use the sampled intensities to create a texture mapped sub-mesh consisting of the vertices indexed by $\mathcal{F}_j^F$. Figure 6(a) shows the sub-meshes for the bitten apple from the four cameras.

We blend the sub-meshes using TextureStitcher [7] to create a seamless texture-mapped 3D mesh at frame F, as shown in Fig. 6(b). The texture-mapped meshes for all time instants form a spatiotemporal 3D model for the object.

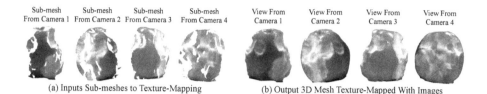

| Sub-mesh From Camera 1 | Sub-mesh From Camera 2 | Sub-mesh From Camera 3 | Sub-mesh From Camera 4 | View From Camera 1 | View From Camera 2 | View From Camera 3 | View From Camera 4 |

(a) Inputs Sub-meshes to Texture-Mapping   (b) Output 3D Mesh Texture-Mapped With Images

Fig. 6. Texture-mapping the 3D model. (a) As input to TextureStitcher [7], we provide four sub-meshes obtained by sampling the intensities from each image at the vertices of the faces visible in the corresponding camera. (b) TextureStitcher provides the complete 3D mesh as output containing seamlessly blended texture from the input sub-meshes.

8   Results

The top rows of Figs. 7 and 9(a)–(c) show spatiotemporal 3D models reconstructed for a pear, the bitten apple, a cut mango, and a unpeeled banana. Time-lapse intervals used in our captures were 10 min for the apple and banana, and 5 min for the mango and pear. We aged the apple and banana for 7200 min or 5 days, the mango for 3600 min or 2.5 days, and the pear for 2165 min or 1.503 days. The 3D models of the bitten objects reveal enzymatic browning over time when the exposed regions undergo oxidation catalyzed by polyphenol oxidase [25]. The spatiotemporal 3D model of the banana shows appearance change from yellow with black spots to nearly full black. The 3D model of the mango shows its leaning over under the influence of gravity. The mango model also shows slight browning due to decay at exposed edges.

Volume Loss Analysis. The middle rows of Figs. 7 and 9(a)–(c) show time-plots of $\log(V/V_0)$, the logarithmic rate of change of volume V expressed as a ratio of the initial volume V_0. We compute the volume of each 3D mesh using the approach of [31]. We estimate linear fits shown in red dashed lines to analyze the match between the data plot and models that describe fruit senescence in terms of exponential decay [17]. We use random sample consensus (RANSAC) [12] to eliminate outliers in the linear fit. While our estimation shows a close match between the exponential decay model and the data for the banana and the pear, it under-estimates the rate of volume change for the mango and the apple. As part of future work, we are interested in understanding the occurrence of super-exponential volume decay in fruit by extending the time duration of capture for the banana to include the underripe green phase and rotten black phase, and by creating spatiotemporal 3D models for a greater diversity of fruit.

Appearance Change Analysis. The bottom rows of Figs. 7 and 9(a)–(c) show plots of the mean color in each textured 3D mesh across the time-lapse sequence.

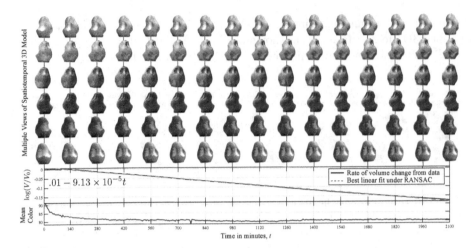

Fig. 7. Multiple views of the spatiotemporal 3D model and time plots of the log percentage of the initial volume and average color for bitten pear. (Color figure online)

For objects undergoing browning of exposed regions such as the apple and the pear, the rate of color change is high in the beginning and tapers toward the end, showing that browning occurs rapidly in the initial phases of exposure. For the banana where enzymatic browning occurs on the peel, we notice a gradual change in color in the beginning during the phase when the banana develops black spots, followed by an acceleration in color change as the spots saturate and the object becomes overripe. The mango shows a slower rate of color change over the time-lapse sequence, indicating lower levels of polyphenol oxidase compared to the apple, pear, and banana.

Brightness constancy analysis. Our 3D model deformation is based on the assumption that brightness is nearly constant over successive frames. Figure 8(a) shows a plot of root-mean-square (r.m.s.) difference in frame-to-frame appearance estimated using the textures obtained in Sect. 7. The mean value of the r.m.s. difference on a 0 to 255 intensity scale is $7.59 \pm .48$ for the apple, $7.05 \pm .60$ for the banana, $6.91 \pm .65$ for the pear, and $5.91 \pm .35$ for the mango, showing that per-frame differences in appearance are small. High values in the plot indicate

Fig. 8. (a) Plot of root-mean-square (r.m.s.) frame-to-frame appearance difference against time. (b) Frames showing interactions with a VR environment containing spatiotemporal 3D models. The user plays forward aging in the banana and pear.

lighting fluctuations, however, the slow rate of volume change introduces small point translations in the image, enabling the KLT tracker to accurately track points under slight fluctuations in illumination.

Interactions with Spatiotemporal 3D Models. The spatiotemporal 3D models created by our approach can be imported into standard 3D modeling and rendering software to create animations, games, and virtual reality (VR) environments. For instance as shown in Fig. 8(b), we use our spatiotemporal manipulation interface in VR discussed in [27] to perform spatial manipulations such as rotations, scaling, and translation and temporal manipulations such as playing, rewinding, and forwarding of changes in shape and appearance due to aging of objects.

9 Discussion

We provide an approach to reconstruct spatiotemporal 3D models of objects such as fruit that undergo aging on exposure to the environment. Our approach deforms a static 3D mesh reconstructed from photographs captured by a rotating camera track to time-lapse image sequences of the aging object captured from multiple viewpoints. The spatiotemporal 3D models provided by our approach reveal changes to shape changes due to water volume loss and appearance changes due to enzymatic browning characteristic of natural objects such as fruit.

The main limitation of our approach is that it requires manual interaction to perform precise alignment the 3D model to the initial frame. In future work, we will use matching of multi-viewpoint renders with interest point correspondences to perform automatic pixel-precise deformation of the mesh to the initial frame. Our approach retains the contribution of illumination in the texture as seen by the shadow on the surface of the pear and apple. As part of future work, we will evaluate BRDFs obtained using light probes [9] and using illumination estimation [16,28]. Since our approach relies on approximate frame-to-frame brightness constancy to identify point correspondences using KLT tracking, it may not handle rapidly occurring changes such as popping corn kernels. We will investigate supervised learning approaches to predict point correspondences between frames with dissimilar brightness.

Our work is the first step in the creation of spatiotemporal 3D model repositories enriched with information on dynamic real-world object behaviors. As part of our future work in creating these repositories, we will expand the range of behaviors captured to include melting, weathering, and corrosion, perform data-driven estimation of physical properties, and perform controlled experiments to include the effect of variation in temperature and humidity on object aging. Our long term goal is to use spatiotemporal 3D models in performing data-driven understanding of the aging status of objects such as fruit ripeness and edibility and structural health of erosive objects from images taken by ubiquitous devices.

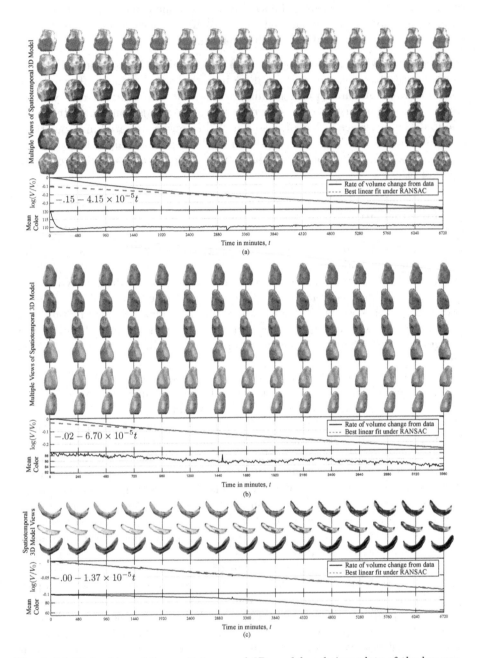

Fig. 9. Multiple views of the spatiotemporal 3D model and time plots of the log percentage of the initial volume and average color for (a) Apple (b) Mango, and (c) Banana. (Color figure online)

Acknowledgements. This work was partially supported by the National Science Foundation (NSF) grant #1730183.

References

1. Adobe: ReMake. https://remake.autodesk.com/about/
2. de Aguiar, E., Stoll, C., Theobalt, C., Ahmed, N., Seidel, H.P., Thrun, S.: Performance capture from sparse multi-view video. ACM Trans. Graph. **25**(3) (2008)
3. Baraff, D., Witkin, A.: Dynamic simulation of non-penetrating flexible bodies. In: SIGGRAPH (1992)
4. Baraff, D., Witkin, A.: Large steps in cloth simulation. In: SIGGRAPH (1998)
5. Baran, I., Popović, J.: Automatic rigging and animation of 3D characters. ACM Trans. Graph. **26**(3) (2007)
6. Beeler, T., Hahn, F., Bradley, D., Bickel, B., Beardsley, P., Gotsman, C., Sumner, R.W., Gross, M.: High-quality passive facial performance capture using anchor frames. In: SIGGRAPH (2011)
7. Chuang, M., Luo, L., Brown, B.J., Rusinkiewicz, S., Kazhdan, M.: Estimating the Laplace-Beltrami operator by restricting 3D functions. In: CGF (2009)
8. Collet, A., Berenson, D., Srinivasa, S.S., Ferguson, D.: Object recognition and full pose registration from a single image for robotic manipulation. In: ICRA (2009)
9. Debevec, P.: Rendering synthetic objects into real scenes: bridging traditional and image-based graphics with global illumination and high dynamic range photography. In: SIGGRAPH Classes (2008)
10. Dorsey, J., Pedersen, H.K., Hanrahan, P.: Flow and changes in appearance. In: SIGGRAPH Courses, p. 3 (2005)
11. Enrique, S., Koudelka, M., Belhumeur, P., Dorsey, J., Nayar, S., Ramamoorthi, R.: Time-varying textures: definition, acquisition, and synthesis. In: SIGGRAPH Sketches (2005)
12. Fischler, M.A., Bolles, R.C.: Random sample consensus: a paradigm for model fitting with applications to image analysis and automated cartoraphy. CACM **24**(6), 381–395 (1981)
13. Gu, J., Tu, C.I., Ramamoorthi, R., Belhumeur, P., Matusik, W., Nayar, S.: Time-varying surface appearance: acquisition, modeling and rendering. ACM Trans. Graph. **25**(3) (2006)
14. Guo, L., Quant, H., Lamb, N., Lowit, B., Banerjee, N.K., Banerjee, S.: Multi-camera microenvironment to capture multi-view time-lapse videos for 3D analysis of aging objects. In: International Conference on Multimedia Modeling (2018)
15. Jackson, A.S., Bulat, A., Argyriou, V., Tzimiropoulos, G.: Large pose 3D face reconstruction from a single image via direct volumetric CNN regression. arXiv preprint arXiv:1703.07834 (2017)
16. Kholgade, N., Simon, T., Efros, A., Sheikh, Y.: 3D object manipulation in a single photograph using stock 3D models. In: SIGGRAPH (2014)
17. Kider, J.T., Raja, S., Badler, N.I.: Fruit senescence and decay simulation. In: CG Forum (2011)
18. Lamb, N., Banerjee, N.K., Banerjee, S.: Programmatic 3D printing of a revolving camera track to automatically capture dense images for 3D scanning of objects. In: International Conference on Multimedia Modeling (2018)
19. Langenbucher, T., Merzbach, S., Möller, D., Ochmann, S., Vock, R., Warnecke, W., Zschippig, M.: Time-varying BTFs. In: CESCG (2010)

20. Lepetit, V., Moreno-Noguer, F., Fua, P.: EPnP: an accurate O(n) solution to the PnP problem. IJCV **81**(2), 155–166 (2009)
21. Li, Y., Fan, X., Mitra, N.J., Chamovitz, D., Cohen-Or, D., Chen, B.: Analyzing growing plants from 4D point cloud data. ACM Trans. Graph. **32**(6) (2013)
22. Lim, J.J., Khosla, A., Torralba, A.: FPM: fine pose parts-based model with 3D CAD models. In: Fleet, D., Pajdla, T., Schiele, B., Tuytelaars, T. (eds.) ECCV 2014. LNCS, vol. 8694, pp. 478–493. Springer, Cham (2014). https://doi.org/10. 1007/978-3-319-10599-4_31
23. Lu, J., Georghiades, A.S., Glaser, A., Wu, H., Wei, L.Y., Guo, B., Dorsey, J., Rushmeier, H.: Context-aware textures. ACM Trans. Graph. **26**(1) (2007)
24. Lucas, B.D., Kanade, T.: An iterative image registration technique with an application to stereo vision. In: IJCAI (1981)
25. Nicolas, J.J., Richard-Forget, F.C., Goupy, P.M., Amiot, M.J., Aubert, S.Y.: Enzymatic browning reactions in apple and apple products. Critical Rev. Food Sci. Nutr. **34**(2), 109–157 (1994)
26. Paquette, E., Poulin, P., Drettakis, G.: The simulation of paint cracking and peeling. In: GI (2002)
27. Quant, H., Banerjee, S., Banerjee, N.K.: A virtual reality interface for interactions with spatiotemporal 3D data. In: International Conference on Multimedia Modeling (2018)
28. Ramamoorthi, R., Hanrahan, P.: An efficient representation for irradiance environment maps. In: SIGGRAPH (2001)
29. Sorkine, O., Alexa, M.: As-rigid-as-possible surface modeling. In: EUROGRAPHICS (2007)
30. Yin, X., Fujimoto, T., Chiba, N., Tanaka, H.T.: Modeling of wood aging caused by biological deterioration. JACIII **22**(2), 125–131 (2008)
31. Zhang, C., Chen, T.: Efficient feature extraction for 2D/3D objects in mesh representation. In: ICIP (2001)

Stitch-Based Image Stylization for Thread Art Using Sparse Modeling

Kewei Yang, Zhengxing Sun$^{(\boxtimes)}$, Shuang Wang, and Bo Li

State Key Laboratory for Novel Software Technology, Nanjing University,
Nanjing, China
szx@nju.edu.cn

Abstract. Random-needle Embroidery (RNE) is a graceful Chinese Embroidery art enrolled in the World Intangible Heritage. In this paper, we propose a rendering method to translate a reference image into an art image with the style of random-needles. Since RNE artists create artwork by stitching thousands of intersecting threads with complex patterns into an embroidery cloth, the key of RNE rendering is to define its threads distributions in vector space (actual physical space) and generate its artistic styles in pixel space (coordinate system of the image). To this end, we first define "stitch" which is a collection of threads arranged in a certain pattern as the basic rendering primitive. A vector space stitch model is presented, which can automatically generate various thread distributions in stitches. Then, the rendering primitives are generated by rasterizing the stitches on 2D pixel arrays. During runtime, new stitches can be synthesized to portray the image content via sparse modeling based on the pre-defined stitches. In order to avoid mosaic effects, this result is further refined by incorporating local stitch vector constraints, in which we enforce the thread distribution of the local stitch to be similar to its adjacent stitches. Finally, rendering image is generated by placing stitches with different attributes on the canvas. Experiments show that our method can perform fine images with the style of random-needle.

Keywords: Image-based artistic rendering · Random-needle rendering
Stitch definition · Sparse modeling

1 Introduction

Image-based artistic rendering (IB-AR) received significant attention in the past decades which covers a broad range of techniques to render different artistic styles [11]. However, there is little previous work on embroidery simulation especially for Random-needle rendering [14–16] which attempts to emulate a new form of Chinese Embroidery art: Random-needle Embroidery. Thus, in this paper we aim to utilize thousands of intersecting threads to translate the source image into the art image with the style of random-needles based on the preservation of original main contents. According to [14, 15], the corresponding stylization process contains two procedures: style definition and style rendering.

© Springer International Publishing AG 2018
K. Schoeffmann et al. (Eds.): MMM 2018, Part I, LNCS 10704, pp. 479–492, 2018.
https://doi.org/10.1007/978-3-319-73603-7_39

For the first problem, the differences among various artistic styles are mainly reflected in the rendering primitives. Since no single thread is of critical importance and threads must work together to express certain artistic style in RNE, Yang and Sun [14] introduced the notion of "stitch" as the basic rendering primitive, which is defined inseparably both in vector and pixel space. However, they rely on skilled artists to design the thread distribution in each stitch, which involves a huge amount of tedious manual work. Thus, a stitch model that can automatically generate various threads distributions is desired. For the second problem, started with image parsing, the style transfer process aims to select appropriate primitives to portray the image content, and arrange them on the canvas for the result image. Since RNE rendering requires a relatively high degree of image content reproduction and it is hard to pre-define a complete stitch library to fit continuous image contents, selecting appropriate stitch by seriatim matching each primitive with the image [9–11] is inaccurate and may affect the rendering quality when no suitable stitch is found. To solve this problem, Yang and Sun [14] proposed a stitch selection strategy by using a linear combination of stitches to synthesize new stitches representing the image content. However, because each stitch is independently selected and they did not consider the smoothness of the selected stitch's thread distributions with its adjacent stitches, local distortion or mosaic effects can be found in the rendering result.

Accordingly, we present a stitch-based image stylization method for thread art using space modeling, which includes two contributions: (1) we define stitch inseparably both in vector space and pixel space. In vector space, we carry out a parametric stitch model which can automatically generate threads with different thread directions, lengths and widths in stitches. In pixel space, we present an efficient way to generate stitch on 2D pixel arrays by rasterizing each thread in the stitch. At last, we construct a stitch dictionary to organize the stitches and describe each stitch from vector and pixel aspects. (2) We improve the stitch selection method of paper [14] by incorporating local vector constraints. After synthesizing a new stitch to portray the image contents via sparse modeling, we refine the selection result by enforcing the thread distribution of the local stitch to be similar to its adjacent stitches to improve the local smoothness.

2   The Proposed Method

Figure 1 shows the workflow of our method which incorporates three main modules. *Stitch definition and representation* defines our rendering primitive, namely, stitch. Since the style of RNE is based on free-form threads, we first present a stitch model which can automatically generate threads with various directions, lengths and widths in stitches. Then, we rasterize stitches on pixel arrays to support image stylization on 2D pixel space. Finally, we organize the stitches into groups and describe each stitch from its thread distribution and image style, together, these stitch groups form our stitch dictionary. For *image parsing*, the input image is first segmented into object regions and corresponding features are calculated to describe the contents of the image. Then, these features are integrated by partitioning the interior of each region into sub-regions and using them to describe each sub-region. During *stitch selection and rendering*, for each sub-region, we synthesize a new stitch to express the sub-region's contents by optimizing a linear combination of the stitch dictionary atoms via sparse modeling. After that, the selection result is refined by incorporating local vector constraints. To be specific, we enforce the local stitch's directionality or average-length to be similar to its adjacent stitches, which can alleviate mosaic effects of the selection result. After stitch selection, the synthesized stitches are sequentially placed on the canvas and connected to the adjacent stitches along a minimum error boundary (called stitch quilting). This process is repeated until all the sub-regions are processed.

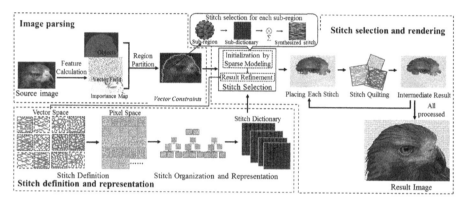

Fig. 1. The flowchart of our method.

2.1   Stitch Definition and Representation

Comparing with the traditional embroidery, the stitching style of RNE has three main characteristics: (1) traditional embroidery artwork is a kind of woven material or fabric which only use coarse and long interlacing knits of weft and warp. However, the RNE artwork utilizes short intersecting threads with numerous directions: sometimes these threads may have fixed orientation, which is called "regular stitch" in RNE. Sometimes all the threads are in a mess, which is called "stochastic stitch". The creation of RNE shows the characteristic of *region dependency*, meaning that the stitches in one region tend to belong to the same stitch category. (2) Different from the traditional embroidery which uses constant stitch pattern within one region, RNE uses various stitch patterns even for the same stitch category (directions, lengths and widths of threads can all be different), namely, *pattern flexibility*. This enables a relatively high degree of image content reproduction. (3) Another characteristic is *scale variability*, the RNE artists create artwork by using thick and long threads for smooth parts of the image, and then adding thin and short threads for the fine-scale details.

Apparently, taking one thread as individual primitive is inappropriate to design such complex thread patterns in RNE [9, 14, 15]. In this paper, our main idea is to capture the thread patterns in the form of stitch. Threads are pre-rendered into stitches, and at runtime rendering image is obtained by appropriately selecting and arranging these stitches on canvas. The stitches are defined in two spaces: vector and pixel space. In vector space, we automatically design the thread distributions in stitches. In pixel space, the rendering primitives are generated by rasterizing the stitches on 2D pixel arrays.

Stitch Design in Vector Space. Based on the characteristics of RNE, the orientations, intersection angles, lengths and widths of intersecting-threads can vary with stitches. Thus, we first design the single-layer stitch, meaning all intersection-threads in them have the same thread width. Then, the multi-layer stitch can be constructed by several stitch layers with each layer using a different thread width.

Single-Layer Stitch. Similar to Yang and Sun [14, 15], we choose to use two intersecting threads as the basic element (called intersecting-thread) to construct stitches (Fig. 2(a) shows its attributes) in a unit square, and the definition of stitch involves three parameters $\{B, \Xi, d\} : B, \Xi$ and d control global intersecting-threads' intersection angles β, lengths ξ and width respectively. Because regular and stochastic stitches have the biggest style difference and are the two most distinct stitch categories in RNE, we carry out two definition methods for regular and stochastic stitch respectively.

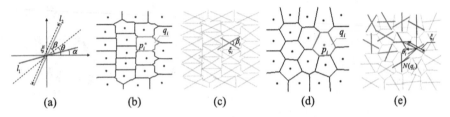

(a)   (b)   (c)   (d)   (e)

Fig. 2. Stitch design in vector space. (a) l_1 and l_2 represent two threads. Each thread has a specific length ξ and direction α. θ and β represent the intersection orientation and angle, respectively. (b) Intersecting-thread distribution for regular stitch. (c) Intersecting-thread generation for regular stitch. (d) Intersecting-thread distribution for stochastic stitch. (e) Intersecting-thread generation for stochastic stitch.

Since the threads in regular stitch have a unified orientation, we define regular stitch as a groups of horizontally orientated intersecting-threads. Given a unit square, regular stitch can be generated via three steps: (1) calculating the size of intersecting-thread through $s = \Xi^2 \sin\left(\frac{B}{2}\right)\cos\left(\frac{B}{2}\right)$, then determining their numbers through $N = S/s$ where S denotes the size of the unit square; (2) in order to make the intersecting-threads uniformly distributed, we adopt Centroidal Voronoi Tessellation by Lloyd's method to calculate their positions $\{p_1, p_2, \ldots, p_N\}$, as shown in Fig. 2(b). Since the bounding box of intersecting-thread is near rectangle, we modify the distance metric in Lloyd's method from Euclidean distance to manhattan distance: $\sin\left(\frac{B}{2}\right)|x_1 - x_2| + \cos\left(\frac{B}{2}\right)$ $|y_1 - y_2|$, where (x, y) denote coordinate of the point; (3) we put an intersecting-thread on p_i for each cell q_i in the tessellation (Fig. 2(c)), and the intersection angle and length are calculated by $\xi_i = \Xi + \Delta\xi$ and $\beta_i = B + \Delta\beta$. Here, $\Delta\xi$ and $\Delta\beta$ are a small stochastic value to express more natural randomness in reality. Generally, the pattern flexibility of regular stitch is mainly reflected in the intersection angle. Regular stitch generated by a small B can create image style with a high texture directionality in pixel space which can be measured by orientation dominance [13] (also verified in Sect. 3).

We use a similar method as before with some modifications to generate stochastic stitch. First, we use Euclidean distance in Centroidal Voronoi Tessellation to tile the square with hexagons (Fig. 2(d)), so that intersecting-threads with different orientations can be placed in each cell q_i. Second, after placing an intersecting-thread, we tune its orientation θ_i until it has enough difference between its adjacent intersecting-threads N (q_i) in order to express the chaotic patterns of stochastic stitch (Fig. 2(e)). Different from regular stitch, we use thread length to distinguish stochastic stitches. Stochastic stitch generated by a small Ξ can create image style with high image contrast (also verified in Sect. 3).

Multi-layer Stitch. In RNE, stitches constructed by multiple thread widths have stronger detail expression ability than those constructed by single thread width. Thus, besides single-layer stitch, we also design two-layer stitch and three-layer stitch, and the intersecting-threads of each layer can be generated by the above method.

Stitch Generation in Pixel Space. Yang and Sun [14] presented a stitch rendering method which includes a large number of steps and requires subtle parameter setting. In this paper, we present a more effective way to generate stitch in pixel space by rasterizing each thread in the stitch, which has comparable quality to [14]. In order to achieve more realistic appearance, we consider the characteristics of thread from three aspects: (1) lightness of the thread; (2) the tone mixing effect in the intersection area of two threads; (3) shading caused by thread occlusion.

Given a pixel array of size $e \times e$, we first map the current thread into the array by the ratio of its coordinate and e, interpolate all pixels of a thread using the Bresenham algorithm and extend this one pixel width line to d pixels (d represents the thread width). Then, we simulate the lightness of the thread by adjusting the luminance of the threads pixels. As shown in Fig. 3(a), in the radial direction of the thread, we weakening the luminance of pixels around endpoints of threads to simulate a thread exit and enter the basic fabric: $Y(P_A)' = Y(P_A)\left(0.95 - \frac{d_2}{d_1}\sigma_r\right)$ ($\sigma_r = 0.2, d_1 = \xi/2$), where $Y(P_A)$ denotes the luminance of the pixel P_A, d_2 is the distance of pixel P_A to the center of the thread. We also adjust the luminance of pixels along the normal direction of the thread to simulate cylinder appearance of a thread: $Y(P_A)' = Y(P_A)\left(1 - \frac{n_2}{n_1}\sigma_n\right)$ ($\sigma_n = 0.2$, $n_1 = d/2$), where n_2 represents the distance of pixel P_A to the center axis of the thread. Next, we mix the pixel tones in the intersection area by Gaussian blur filter, as shown in Fig. 3(b). Finally, we weaken the luminance of the boundary pixels to simulate the shading effect (Fig. 3(c)).

Stitch Organization and Representation. During rendering process, appropriate stitch should be selected from the generated stitches. Since the stitch styles and the image contents which the stitches are suitable for are very different, stitch selection by seriatim matching each stitch with the image content can be very time-consuming and inaccurate. In this paper, we first organize the stitches into groups according to their artistic styles; then proper descriptions are presented to describe each stitch in the group. During stitch selection, stitch can be selected from a specific stitch group which reduce the search space and in turn increase the efficiency.

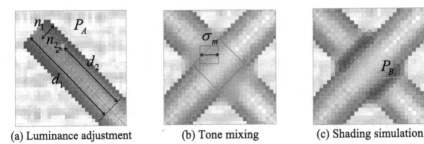

(a) Luminance adjustment   (b) Tone mixing   (c) Shading simulation

Fig. 3. Stitch generation in pixel space

Stitch Organization. We use a four-level tree structure to organize the generated stitch images. Level 1 distinguishes the regular stitch and stochastic stitch for different objects rendering. At level 2, regular stitch and stochastic stitch are further classified into single-layer stitch, two-layer stitch and three-layer stitch. Level 3 organizes stitches according to their sizes, we use stitches of seven sizes (from $e \times e = 200 \times 200-50 \times 50$, interval 25) to express image contents with different saliences. Level 4 contains stitches with different intersection angles (B)/thread lengths (Ξ). Together, we have $K(K = 2 \times 3 \times 7)$ groups of stitches. In this paper, each stitch group is viewed as a sub-dictionary, and these sub-dictionaries form our stitch dictionary denoted as $\{D^1, D^2, \ldots, D^K\}$. Additionally, for each D^i, we generate 200 stitches (namely atoms of D^i) $\zeta_j, j = 1 - 200$ by tuning the parameter B or Ξ from 0 to 1 (interval 0.005).

Stitch Representation. In this paper, we describe each stitch ζ_j in each $D^{(i)}$ in both vector and pixel space which denoted as a two-tuple $\langle V(\zeta_j), P(\zeta_j) \rangle$. According to the previous stitch definition process, for regular stitch, we use *directionality* calculated by the standard deviation of the thread directions (small intersection angles lead to a low standard deviation of the thread directions, and the directionality of this stitch is considered high) as its vector description $V(\zeta_j)$ and use *orientation dominance* [13] as its pixel description $P(\zeta_j)$ to describe its artistic styles. For stochastic stitch, we use the *average length* of the threads as its vector description $V(\zeta_j)$ and use *image contract* as its pixel description. In the stitch selection in Sect. 2.3, we use $P(\zeta_j)$ to get the initial stitch selection result and use $V(\zeta_j)$ to refine the selection result.

2.2   Image Parsing

According to the region dependency of RNE, we first adopt the image segmentation method to paint the objects using different stitch categories. The mapping relations between stitch categories and objects are hard-coded. Regular stitch is assigned for objects such as petal, hair, water surface etc., and stochastic stitch is assigned for objects such as grass, rock, background, etc. In order to simulate the pattern flexibility and scale variability of RNE, we use stitches with different styles, sizes and orientations for different parts of the image. Accordingly, we also generate an importance map E using Sobel operator [1] and a vector field Θ by ETF [5] to guide the stitch sizes and orientations assignment for different parts of the image. Then, we integrate these image features and further partition each region into sub-regions. This is done by first generating stitch positions p_i through wang tiles [6] by taking the importance map as a density map. Based on the positions, we partition each region into non-uniform connected convex polygons using voronoi diagram. By distributing stitches according to the size of each sub-region, we are able to use smaller stitches in areas containing fine details.

Finally, for each sub-region Q_i in each region partition, following attributes are calculated to guide the rendering process which including: orientation $\Theta(p_i)$, adjacent sub-regions $N(Q_i)$, average importance E_i, orientation dominance R_i, image contrast T_i and color C_i. R_i is calculated by orientation dominance [13] which measures the texture directionality of Q_i. T_i is calculated by the standard deviation of the pixel lightness in Q_i. R_i and T_i are used to select stitches with different styles in Sect. 2.3.

2.3 Stitch Selection and Rendering

Based on the image parsing result, the style transfer process refer to the task of selecting stitches from the stitch dictionary for each sub-region Q_i and then arranging them on the canvas. Since it is hard to pre-define a complete stitch library to fit continuous image contents, Yang and Sun [14] presented a stitch selection strategy by sparsely coding the image content via a linear combination of stitch dictionary atoms. However, the stitch selection result usually has local distortion or mosaic effects (Fig. 4 (a)) due to the fact that stitch for each Q_i is independently selected, which makes the result vulnerable to local image noises. Thus, in this paper, we add vector constraints according to the stitch vector description defined in Sect. 2.1 to refine the initial stitch selection result by [14]. The main idea is to enforce the local stitch's directionality or average-length to be similar to its adjacent stitches so that local distortion can be alleviated (Fig. 4(b)).

Initialization of Stitch Selection. Recall that our stitch dictionary is composed of a set of sub-dictionaries, thus, we first select an appropriate sub-dictionary for the given sub-region Q_i. According to the mapping relations defined in Sect. 2.2, regular or stochastic stitch is assigned to each Q_i depending on its object category (level 1). Then, we use E_i of each sub-region to choose the number of stitch layers at level 2. Three-layer stitch is used for sub-region containing high frequency information, two-layer stitch is used for medium E_i and single-layer stitches are used for flat parts of

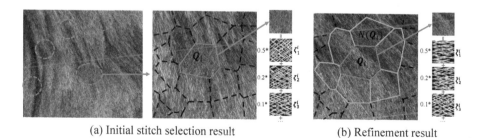

(a) Initial stitch selection result   (b) Refinement result

Fig. 4. Illustration of stitch selection refinement

the image. Finally, stitch size which has the minimum difference with the sub-region size S_i is selected (level 3). After determining the sub-dictionary $D^i \in \mathbb{R}^{e \times M}$ (e and M denote the size and number of the atoms) for each Q_i, new stitch can be synthesized via optimizing the combinations of the atoms, which is denoted as function E:

$$E = \frac{1}{2} \left\| I_i - D^i \gamma^i \right\|_2^2 + \lambda \left\| diag(\omega) \gamma^i \right\|_1 \tag{1}$$

For each sub-region Q_i, I_i is an image patch sampled at location p_i with length of side $\sqrt{e}$ and orientation $\Theta(p_i)$. $\gamma^i \in \mathbb{R}^M$ represents the combination coefficient of I_i under D^i. $\|\cdot\|_2^2$ calculates the squared differences of pixels between I_i and the synthesized stitch $D^i \gamma^i$. The second term is a l_1-norm regularization term to enforce the sparse representation. $diag(\omega) \in \mathbb{R}^{M \times M}$ is a diagonal matrix in which each diagonal element $\omega_j, j \in 1 - M$ is the combination weight of the corresponding atom ζ_j^i. By setting ω_j equals to the feature difference between sub-region Q_i (denoted as R_i and T_i) and pixel description of ζ_j^i (denoted as $P\left(\zeta_j^i\right)$), priority can be given to the atoms whose features are close to the input image, which enables to adopt strong texture directional stitches for areas with strong orientation dominances and high contrast stitches for areas with high image contrasts. $\|\cdot\|_1$ is the l_1-norm calculated by the sum of the absolute value of coefficients in $diag(\omega)\gamma^i$. We set weight factor $\lambda = 0.15$ in this paper. The Eq. (1) is also called weighted Lasso in statistics and can be efficiently solved [8].

Selection Result Refinement. Stitch selection only by sparse modeling will result in local chaotic or mosaic effect as shown in Fig. 4(a). This is because that the atoms which synthesize the stitch for sub-region Q_i have large thread distribution difference between its neighbors $N(Q_i)$ (see right of Fig. 4(a)). To alleviate this phenomenon, we re-assign the atoms by enforcing them to be similar with their neighbors (Fig. 4(b)), which can be formulated as a graph cuts problem [3] in Eq. (2). In our current implement, we find that only re-assigning the atoms which have the top three highest combination coefficients (denoted as $\zeta_1^i, \zeta_2^i, \zeta_3^i$) is enough to alleviate local distortions.

$$\varepsilon\left(\tilde{\zeta}_1\right) = \sum_i \varepsilon_D\left(i, \tilde{\zeta}_1^i\right) + \sum_{j \in N(Q_i)} \varepsilon_S\left(i, j, \tilde{\zeta}_1^i, \tilde{\zeta}_1^j\right) \tag{2}$$

where $\varepsilon_D = \left| V\left(\zeta_1^i\right) - V\left(\tilde{\zeta}_1^i\right) \right|$ is the data term which measures the penalty of changing atoms from ζ_1^i to $\tilde{\zeta}_1^i$, $V\left(\zeta_1^i\right)$ and $V\left(\tilde{\zeta}_1^i\right)$ are vector descriptions of ζ_1^i and $\tilde{\zeta}_1^i$ respectively (defined in Sect. 2.1). $\varepsilon_S\left(i, j, \tilde{\zeta}_1^i, \tilde{\zeta}_1^j\right) = B(i,j) \cdot \delta\left(\tilde{\zeta}_1^i \neq \tilde{\zeta}_1^j\right)$ is the smooth term which measures the penalty for assigning different atoms to adjacent stitches. δ is a 0–1 indicator function which returns 1 if $\tilde{\zeta}_1^i \neq \tilde{\zeta}_1^j$ else returns 0. We set $B(i,j) = \left| V\left(\zeta_1^i\right) - V\left(\zeta_1^j\right) \right|$ so that same atom will be assigned for i and j if their original differences are high. The re-assignment of ζ_2^i and ζ_3^i can be done in a similar way.

Stitch Layout and Rendering. After synthesizing the stitch for sub-region Q_i, we place the synthesized stitch on the canvas by rotating it towards orientation $\Theta(p_i)$, resizing it to size $|Q_i|$ (area of Q_i), and set its color to the average color of Q_i. In order to achieve a smooth transition between stitches, alpha blending is easy to implement but can result in artifacts such as ghosting and blurring. Graph cuts can eliminate both by finding an optimal seam between patches [7]. Thus, once a new stitch is placed, we connect it to its adjacent stitches along a minimum error boundary calculated by [7].

3   Results and Experiments

We test our method on a Core(TM) i7 CPU with 8 GB memory using *OpenCV* tools.

Evaluation of Stitch Definition. We first evaluate the effectiveness of our stitch design method in vector space. Figure 5(a) plots the relations between the intersection angles (B) and directionalities of the regular stitches. From the plots, we can see that directionality is proportional to the intersection angle, which means our algorithm can generate regular stitches with different directionalities. Comparing to regular stitch, the most distinguish characteristic of stochastic stitch is that its intersecting-threads do not have a unified orientation. We use orientation uniformity calculated by the standard deviation of the intersecting-threads' orientations to measure this characteristic. As shown in Fig. 5(b), all the plots are higher than 2.7, which means our algorithm can guarantee the randomness of intersecting-threads' orientations under different thread lengths. Finally, in order to verify that our algorithm can distribute intersecting-threads uniformly, we first partition the stitch into squares, calculate the distance m_i between each square's center $Center_i$ and its centroid $Center_i'$ (as shown in the right) and then use the m_i distribution histogram to measure the uniformity of the intersecting-thread distribution. As shown in Fig. 5(c), comparing to distribute intersecting-threads randomly, the intersecting-threads distributed by Centroidal Voronoi Tessellation are more uniform (having more m_i near 0).

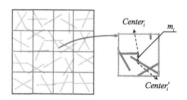

In order to verify that different thread distributions in vector space can generate various stitch styles in pixel space, Fig. 6 plots the relations between thread distributions and stitch styles. From Fig. 6(a) and (b), we can see that the orientation dominance of the regular stitch is inversely proportional to its directionality, and the image contrast of the stochastic stitch is also inversely proportional to its average-length. This also conforms to the convention of RNE. We also analyze the styles of multi-layer stitches by using the texture coarseness (Tamura [12]) to measure the fine level of stitches under different numbers of stitch layers. As shown in Fig. 6(c), three-layer stitches have the lowest coarseness, indicating they have stronger detail expression ability than the two-layer and single-layer stitches.

Evaluation of Stitch Selection and Rendering. In order to evaluate the effectiveness of our stitch selection method, we use same stitches as input, and compare our default

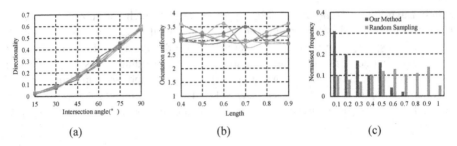

(a)   (b)   (c)

Fig. 5. (a) Relations between intersection angles and directionalities of regular stitches. (b) Relations between thread lengths and orientation uniformities of stochastic stitches. (c) distribution histograms of m_i. For (a) and (b), we test our algorithm under stitches with different numbers of intersecting-threads (distinguished by different line colors). (Color figure online)

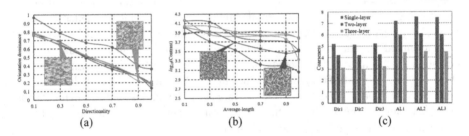

(a)   (b)   (c)

Fig. 6. Relations of thread distributions and stitch styles. (a) Orientation dominance of regular stitches with different directionalities, (b) Image contrast of stochastic stitches with different average-lengths, (c) Is the texture coarseness of single-layer, two-layer and three-layer stitch.

method (*M0*) with two downgraded versions (see Fig. 7): *M1*, not adding weight ω in Eq. (1); *M2*, not using the refinement step by Eq. (2). By comparing *M1* with *M2*, we can see that although considering the stitch pixel description in Eq. (1) can synthesize stitches with proper texture directionalities to portray the objects, it may generate results which have mosaic effects. Correspondingly, the results in Fig. 7(a) are improved greatly thanks to using stitch vector description in the refinement step.

Comparison with the State-of-the-Art Methods and the Real Artwork. In this section, we compare our method with three other RNE rendering methods (Fig. 8), two state-of-the-art style transfer methods (Fig. 9) and the real artwork (Fig. 10). Comparing to Fig. 8(a) and (b), by using sparse modeling to synthesize new and more content-adaptive stitch, the result generated by our method can better portray the image content especially for the detail part of the image. Furthermore, by means of stitch selection refinement, we can also alleviate the mosaic effects of the rendering result in Fig. 8(c).

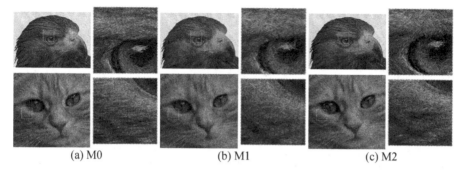

| (a) M0 | (b) M1 | (c) M2 |

Fig. 7. Comparison among rendering images generated by method M0, M1 and M2 respectively. Zoom 400% to view details.

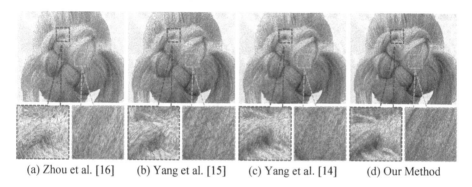

(a) Zhou et al. [16]   (b) Yang et al. [15]   (c) Yang et al. [14]   (d) Our Method

Fig. 8. Comparison with the images generated by other RNE rendering methods. Zoom 400% to view details.

Comparing to the result generated by style transfer method for traditional embroidery [2] in Fig. 9(a), our result is more visual-rich to the readers because of designing complex thread distributions in Sect. 2.1. Comparing to the style transfer method via deep learning [4] in Fig. 9(b), our method has two main advantages: (1) although the method [4] can achieve good style transfer result of oil painting or watercolor whose single stroke contains rich texture and color information, it fails to capture the texture feeling of threads in RNE rendering. On the other hand, by taking stitch as the basic rendering primitive, the aesthetic feeling of our results are superior to those generated by deep learning. (2) By using our stitch selection method, we can adaptively select the most relevant atoms which give best representation to the image, thus avoiding the subtle parameter setting in deep learning method. Figure 10 shows the comparison results with real artworks. From the figure, we can see that our method can generate rendering results which have comparable quality to those artworks produced by professional artists. Figure 11 gives more rendering images of our method.

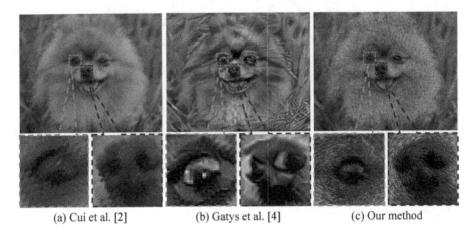

(a) Cui et al. [2]   (b) Gatys et al. [4]   (c) Our method

Fig. 9. Comparison with the images generated by other style transfer methods. Zoom 400% to view details.

(a) Our result   (b) Real artwork

Fig. 10. Comparison with the real artworks. Zoom 400% to view details.

Fig. 11. More rendering results. Zoom 400% to view details.

4   Conclusion

In this paper, we presented a stitch-based image stylization method which can translate an input image into the style of random-needle. We use intersecting-thread as the basic element to construct the basic rendering primitive called stitch, and stitches are defined by automatically generating thread distributions in vector space and generating the corresponding stitch images in pixel space. During runtime, we use sparse modeling to sparsely code the image contents. Vector constraints are also incorporated into this process to alleviate local mosaic effects of the rendering result. Experiments shows that random-needle rendering can be effectively achieved via our process.

Acknowledgement. This work was supported by National High Technology Research and Development Program of China (No. 2007AA01Z334), National Natural Science Foundation of China (Nos. 61321491 and 61272219), Innovation Fund of State Key Laboratory for Novel Software Technology (Nos. ZZKT2013A12 and ZZKT2016A11), and Program for New Century Excellent Talents in University of China (NCET-04-04605).

References

1. Collomosse, J.P., Hall, P.M.: Painterly rendering using image salience. In: Proceedings of EGUK 2002, pp. 122–128 (2002)
2. Cui, D., Sheng, Y., Zhang, G.: Image-based embroidery modeling and rendering. J. Vis. Comput. Anim. **28**(2) (2017)
3. Delong, A., Osokin, A., Isack, H.N., Boykov, Y.: Fast approximate energy minimization with label costs. In: Proceeding of CVPR, pp. 2173–2180 (2010)
4. Gatys, L.A., Ecker, A.S., Bethge, M.: A neural algorithm of artistic style. ArXiv e-prints (2015)
5. Kang, H., Lee, S., Chui, C.K.: Coherent line drawing. In: Proceedings of the 5th International Symposium on Non-photorealistic Animation and Rendering, pp. 43–50 (2007)
6. Kopf, J., Cohen-Or, D., Deussen, O., Lischinski, D.: Recursive Wang tiles for real-time blue noise. ACM Trans. Graph. (TOG) **25**(3), 509–518 (2006)
7. Kwatra, V., Schödl, A., Essa, I., Turk, G., Bobick, A.: Graphcut textures: image and video synthesis using graph cuts. ACM Trans. Graph. (ToG) **22**(3), 277–286 (2003)
8. Mairal, J., Bach, F., Ponce, J., Sapiro, G.: Online learning for matrix factorization and sparse coding. J. Mach. Learn. Res. **11**, 19–60 (2010)
9. Praun, E., Hoppe, H., Webb, M., Finkelstein, A.: Real-time hatching. In: Proceedings of SIGGRAPH 2001, pp. 581–586 (2001)
10. Qu, Y., Pang, W.M., Wong, T.T., Heng, P.A.: Richness-preserving manga screening. ACM Trans. Graph. **27**(5), 155:1–155:8 (2008)
11. Rosin, P., Collomosse, J.: Image and Video-Based Artistic Stylisation, vol. 42. Springer-Verlag, London (2013). https://doi.org/10.1007/978-1-4471-4519-6
12. Tamura, H., Mori, S., Yamawaki, T.: Textural features corresponding to visual perception. IEEE Trans. Syst. Man Cybern. **8**(6), 460–473 (1978)
13. Yang, S., Wang, M., Chen, Y., Sun, Y.: Single-image super-resolution reconstruction via learned geometric dictionaries and clustered sparse coding. IEEE Trans. Image Process. **21**(9), 4016–4028 (2012)

14. Yang, K., Sun, Z.: Paint with stitches: a style definition and image-based rendering method for random-needle embroidery. Multimedia Tools Appl. **76**(14), 1–34 (2017)
15. Yang, K., Sun, Z., Ma, C., Yang, W.: Paint with stitches: a random-needle embroidery rendering method. In: Proceedings of the 33rd Computer Graphics International, pp. 9–12 (2016)
16. Zhou, J., Sun, Z., Yang, K.: A controllable stitch layout strategy for random needle embroidery. J. Zhejiang Univ. Sci. C **15**(9), 729–743 (2014)

Teacher and Student Joint Learning for Compact Facial Landmark Detection Network

Hong Joo Lee, Wissam J. Baddar, Hak Gu Kim, Seong Tae Kim,
and Yong Man Ro[⊠]

Image and Video Systems Laboratory, School of Electrical Engineering, KAIST,
Daejeon, South Korea
{dlghdwn008, wisam.baddar, hgkim0331,
stkim4978, ymro}@kaist.ac.kr

Abstract. Compact neural networks with limited memory and computation are
demanding in recently popularized mobile applications. The reduction of network parameters is an important priority. In this paper, we address a compact
neural network for facial landmark detection. The facial landmark detection is a
frontal module that is mandatorily required for face analysis applications. We
propose a new teacher and student joint learning method applicable to a compact
facial landmark detection network. In the proposed learning scheme, the compact architecture of student regression network is learned jointly with the fully
connected layer of the teacher regression network so that they are mimicked
each other. To demonstrate the effectiveness of the proposed learning method,
experiments were performed on a public database. The experimental results
showed that the proposed method could reduce network parameters while
maintaining comparable performance to state-of-the-art methods.

Keywords: Compact neural network · Facial landmark detection
Teacher and student joint learning

1 Introduction

Facial landmark detection (FLD) is the task of localizing facial key points around facial
parts, such as eyes, nose, nose-bridge, mouth, eyebrows, and facial contour. FLD has
received much attention in the facial analysis due to its important role in a variety of face
related applications [1–4]. For instances, facial landmarks are used for face verification
[5] and pose-adjustment [6] in face recognition and head-pose estimations [7, 8]. In
addition, the GAN model, which has been studied recently, generate face image through
facial landmarks [9].

Most of the previous studies were based on hand crafted FLD [2, 10]. In Liang et al.
[11], facial landmark points were refined via an iterative optimization. Burgos-Artizzu
et al. [12] proposed a regression based approach (called as RCPR). Recently, FLD
studies focused on convolutional neural networks (CNNs) [13–16]. Sun et al. [13]
proposed three-level cascaded CNNs for FLD. Zhang et al. [16] proposed a multi-task
learning method (TCDCN). Most of the CNNs based FLD methods required a large

© Springer International Publishing AG 2018
K. Schoeffmann et al. (Eds.): MMM 2018, Part I, LNCS 10704, pp. 493–504, 2018.
https://doi.org/10.1007/978-3-319-73603-7_40

number of network parameters and associated computational cost. Therefore, these methods are inappropriate for mobile applications. In the constrained environments, compact neural network with small parameters is demanding.

Some recent research focus on handling CNN memory and computational cost issues [17–22]. Howard et al. [23] proposed MobileNets which employed depth-wise separable convolutions. By using depth-wise separable convolutions and 1×1 point-wise convolution, the number of convolution filter parameters and the computation complexity were reduced. Lee et al. [24] proposed a compact convolution layer with logarithmic group filters. Lin et al. [25] proposed global average pooling to replace fully connected layers, which reduced the parameters. In addition to these convolutional techniques and replacing fully connected layers with global average pooling, knowledge distillation method is also useful in the network parameter reduction [26, 27]. In this learning scheme, the acquired knowledge of an original 'teacher' network is utilized to train a 'student' network. The student network is trained to mimic the pre-trained teacher network. It has a limitation since it needs pre-trained teacher network. If there is no pre-trained teacher network, it takes too much time to train both the teacher network and student network.

In this paper, we propose a new compact FLD neural network to aim for a mobile application. We devise a new teacher and student joint learning scheme applicable to a compact FLD neural network. In the proposed learning scheme, the teacher regression network and the student regression network are learned jointly. This is different from the conventional teacher student learning in which student network is learned separately from the pre-trained teacher network. In the proposed learning scheme, the teacher and the student regression networks are connected to each other with a shared convolution network and they branch after it. The student regression network is compact architectures while the teacher regression network includes a fully-connected layer which has a large size of parameters. Three new loss functions are devised to concurrently train the student regression network and the teacher regression network. Two of them minimize the landmark errors of the two regression networks. Another loss function minimizes the feature difference between two regression networks. During a training stage, the compact architecture of student regression network is learned together with the fully connected layer of the teacher regression network so that they are mimicked each other. In a testing stage, the teacher regression network is removed. Therefore, in the testing stage, the network is composed of the shared convolution network and the compact regression network. Since all frameworks are end-to-end learnable, we do not need pre-trained teacher network. And the student regression network can be achieved comparable performance to the teacher regression network.

The rest of the paper is organized as follows. In Sect. 2, we describe the proposed Teacher and student joint learning method and compact network for face landmark detection in detail. In Sect. 3, experiment setup and experimental results are described. Finally, conclusions are drawn in Sect. 4.

2 Compact Network for Facial Landmark Detection

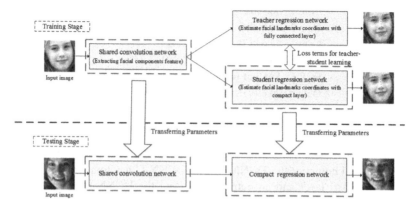

The training and testing stage for the proposed compact facial landmarks detection network

Fig. 1. Overview of the proposed compact FLD network. During the training stage, the shared convolution network, teacher regression network and student regression network are learning jointly. In the testing stage, the shared CNN and the student regression network are transferred to compact FLD network.

2.1 Overview of Proposed Compact FLD Network

Figure 1 shows an overview of the proposed learning method for compact FLD network. As shown in Fig. 1, the network in the training stage is composed of three sub-networks. The first network is a shared convolution network in which image domain features related to facial components are supposed to be extracted. The second one is a teacher regression network and the third one is a student regression network. In these teacher and student regression networks, facial landmark points are estimated by using the features encoded by the shared convolution network. Teacher and student regression networks are jointly learned with three loss functions. Two loss functions are used for minimizing the estimated landmarks error. Another loss function is used to minimize differences of the features between the teacher and student regression networks. By the last loss function, the student regression network can mimic teacher regression network. In the testing stage, the FLD network consists of the shared convolution network and a compact regression network to achieve compactness. The compact regression network uses parameters transferred from the student regression network.

2.2 Parameters Occupation in Conventional FLD Networks

Table 1 shows the number of parameters in recently reported FLD networks. One is TCDCN [16] and the other is DCNN-I/C [15]. The TCDCN [16] is a simple structure that has four convolution layers, one fully connected layer and an output layer. The DCNN-I/C [15] is the FLD network which consists of two sub networks. One sub

Table 1. The number of parameters in previous existing FLD networks

Layer	TCDCN [16]	DCNN-I/C [15]
Conv1	500 (0.2%)	1,000 (0.03%)
Conv2	24,000 (7.7%)	17,280 (0.52%)
Conv3	27,648 (8.8%)	55,296 (1.67%)
Conv4	46,080 (14.7%)	122,880 (3.73%)
FC1	**184,320 (60%)**	**3,072,000 (93.14%)**
Output	29,696 (8.6%)	29,696 (0.91%)
Total	312,244	3,298,152

network is used to detect facial contour landmarks (DCNN-C) and the other is used to detect inner-facial components (DCNN-I). The DCNN-C has four convolution layers, one fully connected layer and an output layer. And the DCNN-I has three common convolution layers and five inner-facial components convolution layers. Each inner-facial components convolution layers have their own fully connected layers and output layers. As can be seen in Table 1, more than half of all the parameters belong to the fully connected layer. This is our motivation to devise a compact FLD networks by minimizing the number of parameters in the fully connected layers.

2.3 Proposed Teacher and Student Joint Learning Scheme for Compact FLD Network

In this section, we describe the proposed learning scheme with the teacher and student regression networks in Fig. 1. In the training stage, both teacher and student networks are jointly learned at the same time along with the shared convolution network. The main idea of our learning scheme is that both teacher and student regression networks use the same features from the shared convolution network so that the student regression network can easily mimic the teacher network. This learning scheme allows the student network (a compact landmark regression network) maintains good performance while it has a small number of parameters.

Figure 2 shows details of learning scheme. As seen in Fig. 2, two networks branch at the end of the shared convolution layers as teacher and student regression networks. The fully connected layer of the teacher regression network is named as T-FC. The corresponding layer in the student regression network is named as STD-FC which consists of 1 by 1 convolution and global average pooling. The dimension of STD-FC and T-FC are the same. The features encoded by the shared convolution layer are fed into teacher regression network and student regression network at the same time. The features are converted to facial landmarks coordinates through teacher regression network and student regression network. Note that inputs of both teacher and student regression network are the same features encoded by the shared convolution layers.

The fully connected layers play an essential role in FLD network since it converts CNN feature map to landmark coordinates. Therefore, designated loss functions for the joint learning are needed so that the STD-FC layer mimics T-FC layer. To that end, in the proposed method, three loss functions are devised. The first loss function, L^1, is

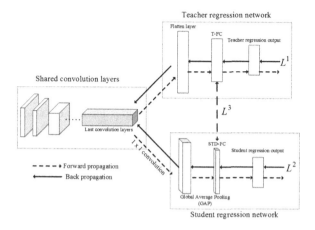

Fig. 2. Proposed learning scheme consisting of shared convolution network and two branched networks. The first branch is teacher regression network and the second one is student regression network. All networks are learned end-to-end with three loss functions (L^1, L^2, L^3).

responsible for minimizing the estimated error of the teacher regression network output (i.e., facial landmark detection by teacher regression network). The second loss function, L^3, is responsible for minimizing the estimated error of the student regression network output (i.e., facial landmark detection by student regression network). The third loss function, L^3, is differences between the output vectors of T-FC and STD-FC. In training, the loss L^3 affects all three sub-networks which are the shared convolution network, the teacher regression network and the student regression network. The three loss terms (L^1, L^2, L^3) can be written as follows:

$$L^1(y, W_{CNN}, W_T) = \frac{1}{N} \sum_{i=1}^{N} \|y_i - f(h(x_i; W_{CNN}), W_T)\|_1, \tag{1}$$

$$L^2(y, W_{CNN}, W_{STD}) = \frac{1}{N} \sum_{i=1}^{N} \|y_i - g(h(x_i; W_{CNN}), W_{STD})\|_1, \tag{2}$$

$$L^3(p, q) = \frac{1}{N} \sum_{i=1}^{N} \|p_i - q_i\|_1, \tag{3}$$

where N is the number of training images, i is the index of an input image, y_i is ground truth facial landmark coordinates and x_i is the input image. $h(.)$ is the function of shared convolution network parameterized by W_{CNN}. $f(.)$ is the function of the teacher regression network parameterized by W_T. $g(.)$ is the function of the student regression network parameterized by W_{STD}. And p_i is output vector of T-FC and q_i is that of STD-FC.

Algorithm 1.	
Input	x_i , $\alpha = 1, \beta = 0, \gamma = 0$
Output	W_{CNN}, W_T, W_{STD}
1.	**for** t = 1 to T do
2.	Feed x_i to shared convolution network : $h(x_i; W_{CNN})$
3.	Feed $h(x_i; W_{CNN})$ to the teacher regression and the student regression network : $f(h(x_i; W_{CNN}); W_T), g(h(x_i; W_{CNN}); W_{STD})$
4.	Calculate L^1, L^2, L^3
5.	$\{W_{CNN}^*, W_T^*, W_{STD}^*\} \leftarrow \underset{W_{CNN}, W_T, W_{STD}}{\arg\min} \{\alpha L^1(y, W_{CNN}, W_T) + \beta L^2(y, W_{CNN}, W_{STD}) + \gamma L^3(p, q)\}$
6.	$W_{CNN} \leftarrow W_{CNN}^*, W_T \leftarrow W_T^*, W_{STD} \leftarrow W_{STD}^*$
7.	Increase β, γ
8.	**End**

The total loss from the branched points is defined as $L_{Branch} = \alpha L^1 + \beta L^2 + \gamma L^3$. The α, β, γ represent the importance of each loss. Since all losses affect jointly to all networks, we set these parameters properly. During the training stage, the teacher regression network is supposed to be trained steadily since it has to achieve the best performance. If the teacher regression network does not achieve the best performance, the student regression network couldn't also achieve the best performance. Therefore, we fixed $\alpha = 1$ from beginning to end to achieve the best performance. Then, we increase β, γ from 0 to 1 gradually (i.e. $\beta = \gamma = 1 - e^{-t}$ or $\beta = \gamma = \tanh(t)$, where t is t-th epoch), which they affect to the teacher and student regression network and shared convolution network jointly. If we initially set $\beta = \gamma = 1$, the teacher regression network performance is saturated before it achieves the best performance. Thus, at the beginning of training, the shared convolution network and the teacher regression network are trained dominantly. After that, the student regression network is trained gradually. Algorithm 1 describes the proposed learning scheme.

2.4 Facial Landmark Detection with the Compact FLD Network Using Learned Student Regression Network

In the testing stage, the proposed compact FLD network consists of the shared convolution network and the compact regression network. The network parameters of the shared convolution network and the student regression network are transferred to the compact FLD network (refer to Fig. 1). Since the student regression network utilizes 1 by 1 convolution and global average pooling instead of the flatten layer and fully connected layer, the network parameters are significantly reduced. In addition, since the student regression network is trained to mimic the teacher regression network, it can provide a comparable performance to the teacher regression network.

3   Experiments

3.1   FLD Networks Used in Experiments to Verify the Proposed Method

To verify the effectiveness of the proposed teacher and student joint learning scheme, we applied the proposed joint learning scheme to the conventional FLD networks. We used two FLD networks which are TCDCN [16] and a modified-DCNN-I/C (M-DCNN-I/C). In TCDCN, we considered its four convolution layers as the shared convolution network. Then, the feature of the last convolution layer was fed to the proposed teacher regression network and student regression network. The proposed teacher regression network consists of the flatten layer, the fully connected layer and teacher regression output layer. On the other hand, the student regression network consists of 1 by 1 convolution layer, global average pooling layer and student regression output layer, as mentioned in Sect. 2.3.

The M-DCNN-I/C integrates facial inner part and facial contour part. It divides eyes and eyebrows convolution layers to left/right eye and left/right eyebrow convolution layers from DCNN-I/C [15] architecture. The M-DCNN-I/C consists of three convolution layers and eight facial components convolution layers (left eyebrow, right eyebrow, left eye, right eye, nose-bridge, nose, mouth and facial contour). In M-DCNN-I/C, the shared convolution network is the three convolution layers and facial component convolution layer. Each facial component convolution layer was divided into its own teacher regression network and student regression network.

3.2   Experiments Setting

In our experiment, we conducted experiments on benchmark dataset, 300-W [28] which is widely used in recent research. It provides 68 facial landmark points and face bounding boxes. This dataset for training was collected from AFW [4], HELEN [29], LFPW [30] and a subset of IBUG [28]. Specifically, 337 training images are from AFW [4], 2,000 training images are from HELEN [29] and 811 training images are from LFPW [30]. Therefore, the total number of training images is 3,148. The total number of testing images is 689. The test data set is composed of two types of test set. One is a common test set from LFPW [30] (224 test images) and HELEN [29] (330 test images). Another is a challenge set from IBUG [28] (135 test images). The challenge set contains challenging conditions such as occlusions, variation of illuminations, head poses, and expressions. To avoid overfitting and increase training data variation, we conducted data augmentation by ±3 pixels translation, in-plane rotation in the range of ±50° with 2° step size, and magnification by 1.1 to 1.2 factors with a step size of 0.002. We increased the number of training images by executing image translation, rotating, and zooming.

3.3   Experiment Results

Performance Comparison with the State-of-the-art Methods

We evaluated the network performance to verify the effectiveness of the proposed method for compact FLD network. The mean error was calculated as the distance measure between the estimated landmarks and the ground truths.

Table 2. Mean Errors (%) on 300-W [28] Dataset (68 facial landmarks)

Methods		Mean error (%)
Hand craft methods	ESR [1]	7.58
	SDM [31]	7.5
	LBF [32]	6.32
Deep learning based methods	JFA [33]	6.06
	TCDCN [16]	5.54
	TCDCN-C	**5.40**
	DCNN-I/C [15]	6.12
	M-DCNN-I/C	4.92
	M-DCNN-I/C-C (Ours)	**4.95**

$$Mean\ error = \frac{1}{N}\sum_{i=1}^{N} \frac{\frac{1}{M}\sum_{j=1}^{M} \left\| o_{i,j} - g_{i,j} \right\|_2}{\left\| l_i - r_i \right\|_2}, \tag{4}$$

where N denotes the number of images, M is the number of landmarks, j is the index of landmark points, o is the output, and g is the ground truth. l, r are the coordinates of the left eye and right eye, respectively.

To evaluate the FLD performance of the proposed method, we compared with various existing FLD methods including hand craft based methods [1, 31, 32] and deep learning based methods [15, 16, 33]. Table 2 shows the mean error comparison between previous methods and our compact FLD network on 300-W [28] dataset with 68 facial landmark points. As shown in Table 2, in the case of hand craft methods, the mean errors were over 6.3%. On the other hand, deep learning based methods achieved lower mean errors than that of the hand craft methods on 300-W [28] dataset. In Table 2, TCDCN-C is a compact version of TCDCN [16] network that was trained by our proposed joint learning method. TCDCN-C performance (5.40%) showed comparable performance to TCDCN (5.54%) [16]. The M-DCNN-I/C-C is a compact version of the M-DCNN-I/C trained by the proposed method. M-DCNN-I/C-C (4.95%) achieved comparable performance to M-DCNN-I/C (4.92%) while the number of parameters was significantly reduced (see Table 3). Therefore, the result indicates that our proposed method was well adapted to various networks.

We evaluated the total number of network parameters. As shown in Table 3, in case of the TCDCN [16], the total number of network parameters was reduced from 312,244 to 148,404 (about 52% parameters were reduced). In particular, in Table 3, the M-DCNNs-I/C had a large number of network parameters (4,331,444). On the other hand, after applying the proposed method to the M-DCNN-I/C, the total number of network parameters was significantly reduced from 4,331,444 to 399,284 (about 90% of parameters were reduced). Not only the number of parameters of M-DCNN-I/C-C is less than that of DCNN-I/C (3,298,152 in Table 1) [15] but also the error rate is lower than DCNN-I/C (6.12% in Table 2).

Table 3. Comparison of total number of network parameters

Methods	Parameters
TCDCN [16]	312,244
TCDCN-C	148,404
M-DCNN-I/C	4,331,444
M-DCNN-I/C-C	399,284

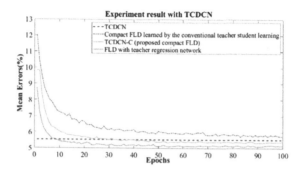

(a) Mean errors of TCDCN

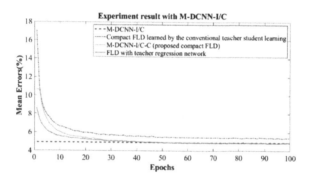

(b) Mean errors of M-DCNN-I/C

Fig. 3. Effect of the proposed method compared to previous teacher/student learning. (a) A performance using our proposed methods with TCDCN model. (b) A performance using our proposed methods with M-DCNN-I/C.

Evaluation on Teacher and Student Joint Learning. Our main contribution is that the student regression network can mimic the teacher regression network by the teacher and student joint learning without a pre-train model of teacher network. To verify this, we measured every mean error of test images at each epoch during the training stage. In the training stage, the loss balance weights were set to $\alpha = 1$, $\beta = \gamma = 1 - e^{-0.05*epochs}$. β and γ were increased exponentially from 0 to 1. At the beginning of training stage, the teacher regression network loss (L^1) was back propagated dominantly. After several epochs, the student regression network was trained gradually with L^2 and L^3. In the latter half of the training stage, all losses were played to train entire network.

Figure 3 shows the mean error comparison of two network structures which are TCDCN [16] and M-DCNN-I/C. The Fig. 3(a) is the experiment result with TCDCN [16] and the Fig. 3(b) is the experiment result with M-DCNN-I/C. Four FLD networks are compared in Fig. 3(a) and (b). 'Compact FLD with the conventional teacher student learning' is the compact network (student model) trained with the conventional teacher and student learning methods [27]. The teacher model (TCDCN, M-DCNN-I/C) and student model (consisting of the shared convolution network and the student regression network) were separately learned not jointly, i.e., the student model mimic to the pre-trained teacher model. 'FLD with teacher regression network' is the FLD network which consists of the shared convolution network and the teacher regression network, then training with the student regression network jointly.

As shown in Fig. 3, student regression networks worked well to make compact FLD both in TCDCN and M-DCNN-I/C. 'FLD with teacher regression network' achieves good performance both in the case of TCDCN and M-DCNN-I/C. The performance of TCDCN-C follows the performance of 'FLD with teacher regression network' well. In the case of M-DCNN-I/C, the performance of M-DCNN-I/C-C is almost same as the performance of 'FLD with teacher regression network' and M-DCNN-I/C. Experimental results showed that our proposed teacher and student joint learning scheme worked well to build compact FLD networks.

4   Conclusions

This paper presented a novel teacher student joint learning scheme for compact FLD networks. The network in training stage was composed of three networks: the shared convolution network and two branched networks, which are teacher and student regression networks. The shared convolution network extracted feature maps of facial components. With the feature maps from shared convolution network, the two-branch networks estimated facial landmark coordinates. By jointly learning the teacher and student regression networks end-to-end, the student regression network could mimic the teacher regression network well and it doesn't need pre-trained teacher network. In the testing stage, the shared convolution network and the student regression network were used to establish the compact FLD. Experimental results showed that the proposed compact FLD significantly reduced the number of network parameters. In particular, the proposed method achieved much lower error rate than the previous teacher/student network in FLD. These results indicated that the proposed compact network could provide a high FLD performance with a small number of network parameters in the mobile application.

Acknowledgements. This work was supported by Institute for Information and communications Technology Promotion (IITP) grant funded by the Korea government (MSIT) (No. 2017-0-00111, Practical technology development of high performing emotion recognition and facial expression based authentication using deep network).

References

1. Cao, X., Wei, Y., Wen, F., Sun, J.: Face alignment by explicit shape regression. Int. J. Comput. Vis. **107**, 177–190 (2014)
2. Cootes, T.F., Taylor, C.J., Cooper, D.H., Graham, J.: Active shape models-their training and application. Comput. Vis. Image Underst. **61**, 38–59 (1995)
3. Cristinacce, D., Cootes, T.F.: Feature detection and tracking with constrained local models. In: BMVC, p. 3 (2006)
4. Zhu, X., Ramanan, D.: Face detection, pose estimation, and landmark localization in the wild. In: 2012 IEEE Conference on Computer Vision and Pattern Recognition (CVPR), pp. 2879–2886. IEEE (2012)
5. Taigman, Y., Yang, M., Ranzato, M.A., Wolf, L.: Deepface: closing the gap to human-level performance in face verification. In: Proceedings of the IEEE Conference on Computer Vision and Pattern Recognition, pp. 1701–1708 (2014)
6. Asthana, A., Marks, T.K., Jones, M.J., Tieu, K.H., Rohith, M.: Fully automatic pose-invariant face recognition via 3D pose normalization. In: 2011 IEEE International Conference on Computer Vision (ICCV), pp. 937–944. IEEE (2011)
7. Tong, Y., Wang, Y., Zhu, Z., Ji, Q.: Robust facial feature tracking under varying face pose and facial expression. Pattern Recogn. **40**, 3195–3208 (2007)
8. Asthana, A., Zafeiriou, S., Cheng, S., Pantic, M.: Robust discriminative response map fitting with constrained local models. In: Proceedings of the IEEE Conference on Computer Vision and Pattern Recognition, pp. 3444–3451 (2013)
9. Huang, R., Zhang, S., Li, T., He, R.: Beyond face rotation: global and local perception GAN for photorealistic and identity preserving frontal view synthesis. arXiv preprint arXiv:1704.04086 (2017)
10. Matthews, I., Baker, S.: Active appearance models revisited. Int. J. Comput. Vis. **60**, 135–164 (2004)
11. Liang, L., Xiao, R., Wen, F., Sun, J.: Face alignment via component-based discriminative search. In: Forsyth, D., Torr, P., Zisserman, A. (eds.) ECCV 2008. LNCS, vol. 5303, pp. 72–85. Springer, Heidelberg (2008). https://doi.org/10.1007/978-3-540-88688-4_6
12. Burgos-Artizzu, X.P., Perona, P., Dollár, P.: Robust face landmark estimation under occlusion. In: Proceedings of the IEEE International Conference on Computer Vision, pp. 1513–1520 (2013)
13. Sun, Y., Wang, X., Tang, X.: Deep convolutional network cascade for facial point detection. In: Proceedings of the IEEE Conference on Computer Vision and Pattern Recognition, pp. 3476–3483 (2013)
14. Zhang, J., Shan, S., Kan, M., Chen, X.: Coarse-to-fine auto-encoder networks (CFAN) for real-time face alignment. In: Fleet, D., Pajdla, T., Schiele, B., Tuytelaars, T. (eds.) ECCV 2014. LNCS, vol. 8690, pp. 1–16. Springer, Cham (2014). https://doi.org/10.1007/978-3-319-10605-2_1
15. Baddar, W.J., Son, J., Kim, D.H., Kim, S.T., Ro, Y.M.: A deep facial landmarks detection with facial contour and facial components constraint. In: 2016 IEEE International Conference on Image Processing (ICIP), pp. 3209–3213. IEEE (2016)
16. Zhang, Z., Luo, P., Loy, C.C., Tang, X.: Learning deep representation for face alignment with auxiliary attributes. IEEE Trans. Pattern Anal. Mach. Intell. **38**, 918–930 (2016)
17. Rastegari, M., Ordonez, V., Redmon, J., Farhadi, A.: XNOR-Net: imagenet classification using binary convolutional neural networks. In: Leibe, B., Matas, J., Sebe, N., Welling, M. (eds.) ECCV 2016. LNCS, vol. 9908, pp. 525–542. Springer, Cham (2016). https://doi.org/10.1007/978-3-319-46493-0_32

18. Teerapittayanon, S., McDanel, B., Kung, H.: Branchynet: fast inference via early exiting from deep neural networks. In: 2016 23rd International Conference on Pattern Recognition (ICPR), pp. 2464–2469. IEEE (2016)

19. Jin, J., Dundar, A., Culurciello, E.: Flattened convolutional neural networks for feedforward acceleration. arXiv preprint arXiv:1412.5474 (2014)

20. Iandola, F.N., Han, S., Moskewicz, M.W., Ashraf, K., Dally, W.J., Keutzer, K.: SqueezeNet: AlexNet-level accuracy with 50x fewer parameters and <0.5 MB model size. arXiv preprint arXiv:1602.07360 (2016)

21. Wang, M., Liu, B., Foroosh, H.: Factorized convolutional neural networks. arXiv preprint arXiv:1608.04337 (2016)

22. Wu, J., Leng, C., Wang, Y., Hu, Q., Cheng, J.: Quantized convolutional neural networks for mobile devices. In: Proceedings of the IEEE Conference on Computer Vision and Pattern Recognition, pp. 4820–4828 (2016)

23. Howard, A.G., Zhu, M., Chen, B., Kalenichenko, D., Wang, W., Weyand, T., Andreetto, M., Adam, H.: Mobilenets: efficient convolutional neural networks for mobile vision applications. arXiv preprint arXiv:1704.04861 (2017)

24. Lee, T.K., Baddar, W.J., Kim, S.T., Ro, Y.M.: Convolution with logarithmic filter groups for efficient shallow CNN. arXiv preprint arXiv:1707.09855 (2017)

25. Lin, M., Chen, Q., Yan, S.: Network in network. arXiv preprint arXiv:1312.4400 (2013)

26. Hinton, G., Vinyals, O., Dean, J.: Distilling the knowledge in a neural network. arXiv preprint arXiv:1503.02531 (2015)

27. Romero, A., Ballas, N., Kahou, S.E., Chassang, A., Gatta, C., Bengio, Y.: Fitnets: hints for thin deep nets. arXiv preprint arXiv:1412.6550 (2014)

28. Sagonas, C., Antonakos, E., Tzimiropoulos, G., Zafeiriou, S., Pantic, M.: 300 faces in-the-wild challenge: database and results. Image Vis. Comput. **47**, 3–18 (2016)

29. Le, V., Brandt, J., Lin, Z., Bourdev, L., Huang, T.S.: Interactive facial feature localization. In: Fitzgibbon, A., Lazebnik, S., Perona, P., Sato, Y., Schmid, C. (eds.) ECCV 2012. LNCS, vol. 7574, pp. 679–692. Springer, Heidelberg (2012). https://doi.org/10.1007/978-3-642-33712-3_49

30. Belhumeur, P.N., Jacobs, D.W., Kriegman, D.J., Kumar, N.: Localizing parts of faces using a consensus of exemplars. IEEE Trans. Pattern Anal. Mach. Intell. **35**, 2930–2940 (2013)

31. Xiong, X., De la Torre, F.: Supervised descent method and its applications to face alignment. In: Proceedings of the IEEE Conference on Computer Vision and Pattern Recognition, pp. 532–539 (2013)

32. Ren, S., Cao, X., Wei, Y., Sun, J.: Face alignment at 3000 fps via regressing local binary features. In: Proceedings of the IEEE Conference on Computer Vision and Pattern Recognition, pp. 1685–1692 (2014)

33. Xu, X., Kakadiaris, I.A.: Joint head pose estimation and face alignment framework using global and local CNN features. In: Proceedings of 12th IEEE Conference on Automatic Face and Gesture Recognition, Washington, DC (2017)

Text Image Deblurring via Intensity Extremums Prior

Zhengcai Qin[1,2,3], Bin Wu[1,2,3(✉)], and Meng Li[1,2,3]

[1] State Key Laboratory of Information Security, Institute of Information Engineering, Chinese Academy of Sciences, Beijing 100093, China
{qinzhengcai,wubin,limeng2}@iie.ac.cn
[2] Shenzhen Key Laboratory of Media Security, Shenzhen University, Shenzhen 518060, China
[3] School of Cyber Security, University of Chinese Academy of Sciences, Beijing 100049, China

Abstract. A novel and effective blind text image deblurring approach which takes advantage of the intensity extremums prior is proposed in the work. Our method is inspired by the phenomenon that the black and white pixels in blurred images are less than the corresponding clear images, especially for text images. And the intensity extremums prior is proved mathematically in this paper. To deblur text images by the intensity extremums prior, an effective optimization algorithm which utilizes a half-quadratic splitting strategy is exploited. Besides the experiments on the document images, the introduced algorithm is also examined on complex text images which contain cluttered background regions, and the results manifest that our approach has outstanding performance against some state-of-the-art image deblurring methods.

Keywords: Intensity extremums prior · Blind deblurring
Text image · Half-quadratic splitting

1 Introduction

Single image blind deblurring intends to recover a clear image from a blurred input image when we know nothing about blur kernel. It's a classical problem in the field of the image processing, and it attracts considerable research attention in computer vision and graphics community. Because of the popularity of taking photos by smartphones, image deblurring becomes more and more important. It's inevitable that camera shake happens in many cases, and the generated blur image is undesirable. Mathematically, the blur process is defined as,

$$b = l \otimes k + n, \tag{1}$$

This work was supported by the Joint Funds of the National Natural Science Foundation of China (Grant No. U1536202), Fundamental theory and cutting edge technology Research Program of Institute of Information Engineering, CAS (Grant No. Y7Z0391102), SKLOIS Key Deployment Project (Grant No. Y7D0061102) and CAS Key Technology Talent Program.

K. Schoeffmann et al. (Eds.): MMM 2018, Part I, LNCS 10704, pp. 505–517, 2018.
https://doi.org/10.1007/978-3-319-73603-7_41

where the blurred image, clear image, blur kernel, and noise are denoted by b, l, k, n, respectively. Besides, the convolution operator is denoted by $\otimes$. The input only has blur image b, but clear image and corresponding blur kernel are required to be recovered. Because there are an ocean of different pairs of (l, k) that can lead to same b, the problem is severely ill-posed.

To make blind deblurring well-posed, the prior knowledge of natural images or blur kernels are utilized in most existing methods. To name only a few, heavy-tailed gradient distrbutions [1,2], normalized sparsity prior [3], L0-regularized gradient [4], patch recurrence prior [5], the dark channel prior [6] and others [16,18,21]. A lot of methods have been proposed to restore blurred image, but the priors of natural image statistics which are utilized in these methods are so weak that can not constrain text images. What's more, previous text restoration approaches [8,10,11] take advantage of the priors of text images, such as the two-tone property, intensity and gradient prior. They have achieved good performance, but there is still a lot of room for improvement.

MMM is a leading international conf
practitioners for sharing new ideas,
development experiences from all M
research papers reporting original ir

(a) Ground Truth

(b) Blur Image

MMM is a leading international conf
practitioners for sharing new ideas,
development experiences from all M
rch papers reporting original ir

(c) Pan *et al.* [11]

MMM is a leading international con
practitioners for sharing new ideas,
opment experiences from all M
rch papers reporting original ir

(d) Ours

Fig. 1. Deblurring results of a complex blurred text image.

In our work, a novel and effective blind deblurring algorithm which utilizes the intensity extremums prior is proposed for text images. Figure 1 shows one experiment result by the proposed algorithm. It illustrates that the proposed algorithm achieves favorable result even if the input image is severely blurred. The core contributions of the work are summarized as follows.

(1) It's theoretically proved that the blur operation gives rise to the intensity extremums prior, which has remarkable effect on text images deblurring.
(2) A deblurring algorithm which contains the intensity extremums prior is proposed, and we also develop a simple and effective optimization approach by a half-quadratic splitting strategy.
(3) The proposed algorithm is examined on the text images dataset, and the results manifest that our method performs favorably against the state-of-the-art deblurring approaches.

2   Related Work

In recent years, significant advances [19, 20, 22] has been witnessed in blind image deblurring. Many outstanding deblurring algorithms [3, 4, 6, 12, 13] utilize the extracted prior from sharp natural images and blur kernels. The methods mentioned above can generate favorable results for natural scene images, but their performances in text images is not well as expected. The main reason is that they utilize the prior of natural images as the regular term, not the prior of text images.

A great attention is aroused by text image deblurring in recent years. A joint estimation approach which estimates latent images from two-tone images is introduced by Li and Lii [7]. Nevertheless, the approach is suitable for two-tone images, it is not work well for complex text images. In [8], a text image deblurring method based on a content aware prior is proposed by Chen et al., but its performance is not well for images cluttered with text. A resultful deblurring method which utilizes three text-specific properties is proposed by Cho et al. [10]. The method depends largely on the text regions which are explored by the stroke width transform (SWT) [9]. But the SWT is applied in sharp images, and when it's used in blurry images, the accuracy may fall down or even the method does not work. Pan et al. [11] develop a text image deblurring algorithm which takes advantage of the L0-regularized intensity and gradient prior. The method achieves the state-of-the-art results for text images. But it depends too much on black pixels whose intensity values are zeroes. When latent image has little dark pixels, the method is unlikely to work well, and even force gray pixels to be black falsely.

A novel intensity extremums prior which utilizes the change of the amount of white and black pixels after blur process for text image deblurring is proposed in this paper. The prior is proved mathematically, and we introduce a new L_0-regularization term to encourage the amount of white and black pixels to be greater. The introduced term has more prior imformation than that in [11], and the proposed method achieves more stable and clear results.

3   Intensity Extremums Prior of Text Images

In this section, we first introduce the intensity extremums prior of text images, and then prove it mathematically. The observation that the black and white pixels in blurred images become less after blurring process inspires us to propose the prior. In order to reflect the contrast between text characters and background in text image, the normalized intensity of pixels are always close to 0 or 1. The phenomenon is more obvious for text images. So the intensity extremums prior is that the pixels whose normalized intensity value equal to 0 or 1 in blurred text images are less than that in corresponding clear text images.

To explain why the black pixels and white pixels in blurred images become less, a few of characters of the blur (convolution) operation is derived mathematically. The convolution of two discrete signals (images) can be regarded as one signal is reversed before the product of them are summed up.

$$b\left(x\right) = \sum_{z \in \Omega_k} l\left(x + \left[\frac{p}{2}\right] - z\right) k\left(z\right) \tag{2}$$

where p is the size of blur kernel and Ω_k is the domain of k, $k\left(z\right) \geq 0$ and $\sum_{z \in \Omega_k} k\left(z\right) = 1$. In addition, the rounding process is denoted as $[\cdot]$. It's found that Eq. (2) can denote the sum of a locally weighted linear combination of l.

Proposition 1. *Let b and l denote the blurred image and corresponding clear image, and $\|x\|_0$ denotes the number of nonzero elements in image x. We have*

$$\|b\|_0 \geq \|l\|_0 \tag{3}$$

Proof. From $\sum_{z \in \Omega_k} k\left(z\right) = 1$ and $k\left(z\right) \geq 0$, we can know $\|k\|_0 \geq 1$. Let the matrix k_z has the same size as k, and it satisfies $k_z(z) = k(z)$ and $k_z(r) = 0$ when $r \in \Omega_k$ and $r \neq z$. It's obvious that $k = \sum_{z \in \Omega_k} k_z$. Then let $b_z = l \otimes k_z$, we can get

$$\|b_z\|_0 = \begin{cases} \|l\|_0, & k_z \neq 0 \\ 0, & otherwise \end{cases} \tag{4}$$

Let $t \in \Omega_k$ and $k(t) \neq 0$, then the proposition can be proved.

$$\begin{aligned} \|b\|_0 &= \|l \otimes k\|_0 \\ &= \left\| \sum_{z \in \Omega_k} l \otimes k_z \right\|_0 \\ &= \left\| \sum_{z \in \Omega_k} b_z \right\|_0 \\ &= \left\| b_t + \sum_{z \neq t} b_z \right\|_0 \\ &\geq \|b_t\|_0 \\ &= \|l\|_0 \end{aligned} \tag{5}$$

Proposition 2. *Let b and l denote the blurred image and corresponding clear image, and $\|x\|_0$ denotes the number of nonzero elements in image x. We have*

$$\|b - 1\|_0 \geq \|l - 1\|_0 \tag{6}$$

Proof. Let $l' = l - 1$ and $b' = l' \otimes k$. From Eq. (2), we can get

$$
\begin{aligned}
b'(x) &= \sum_{z \in \Omega_k} l'(x + [\tfrac{p}{2}] - z)k(z) \\
&= \sum_{z \in \Omega_k} \left[l(x + [\tfrac{p}{2}] - z) - 1 \right] k(z) \\
&= \left[\sum_{z \in \Omega_k} l(x + [\tfrac{p}{2}] - z)k(z) \right] - 1 \\
&= b(x) - 1
\end{aligned}
\tag{7}
$$

So the follow equation can be derived.

$$
b - 1 = (l - 1) \otimes k \tag{8}
$$

According to Proposition 1, $\|b - 1\|_0 \geq \|l - 1\|_0$ is proved.

4   Model and Optimization

A blind text image deblurring model is presented in this section, and we develop an efficient optimization algorithm for kernel estimation. Based on the maximum a posteriori (MAP) framework [14], the deblurring problem is formulated as,

$$
\left\{ \hat{l}, \hat{k} \right\} = \arg\min_{l,k} \ell(l \otimes k, b) + \gamma p(k) + \lambda p(l) \tag{9}
$$

where $\ell(l \otimes k, b)$ denotes data fidelity term, the regular terms on the priors of blur kernel and clear image are denoted by $p(k)$ and $p(l)$, respectively.

4.1   Objective Function

From above analysis and observations, we proposed $\|l\|_0$ and $\|l - 1\|_0$ to measure sparsity of black and white pixels. These constraints and image gradients prior [4,11] are added to the standard image deblurring formulation as

$$
\left\{ \hat{l}, \hat{k} \right\} = \arg\min_{l,k} \|l \otimes k - b\|_2^2 + \gamma \|k\|_2^2 + \mu \|\nabla l\|_0 + \lambda \|l\|_0 + \eta \|l - 1\|_0 \tag{10}
$$

Every normalized element in image l is either close to 1 or 0, so we can combine $\|l\|_0$ and $\|l - 1\|_0$ into $\|l - c\|_0$, and c can be derived by the follow pixel-wise formula.

$$
c(x) = \begin{cases} 0, & l(x) < c_0 \\ 1, & l(x) > c_1 \\ l(x), & \text{otherwise} \end{cases} \tag{11}
$$

where $x \in \Omega_l$ (Ω_l denotes the domain of the image l), c_0 and c_1 are adaptive, they will be changed with the update of l in experiments. The pixels in l whose values are less than c_0 are more likely close to 0. The values of pixels are more likely to close 1 when they are greater than c_1. It's hard to determine the remaining pixels correctly, so they are not enforced to change in the introduced regularization term, and the other terms will guide them to be correct. Then the objective function which is proposed for image deblurring becomes

$$\left\{\hat{l}, \hat{k}\right\} = \arg\min_{l,k} \|l \otimes k - b\|_2^2 + \gamma\|k\|_2^2 + \mu\|\nabla l\|_0 + \lambda\|l - c\|_0 \quad (12)$$

where μ, γ, λ are three different weight parameters. The data fidelity term which is used to restrict that the convolution of deblurred result should be consistent with the blurred image b is the first term in the above formula. And the blur kernel is regularized by the second term. The L_2-norm is adopted, and we can solve it by the Fast Fourier Transform (FFT) [12,15]. The third term on image gradients can help the model to preserve obvious gradients [4,11]. The last regularization term is introduced to enforce sparsity of pixels whose normalized values are greater than 0 and less than 1 in latent image.

4.2   Optimization

Since it's hard to obtain the answer of Eq. (12) directly, an alternating minimization algorithm which takes advantage of the half-quadratic splitting algorithm [17] is adopted. Coordinate descent is used to alternatively calculate clear image l:

$$\hat{l} = \arg\min_{l} \|l \otimes k - b\|_2^2 + \mu\|\nabla l\|_0 + \lambda\|l - c\|_0 \quad (13)$$

and blur kernel k:

$$\hat{k} = \arg\min_{k} \|l \otimes k - b\|_2^2 + \gamma\|k\|_2^2 \quad (14)$$

Estimating the Latent Image l. Considering that the L_0 regulariztion term is computationally intractable, we proposed an efficient method which relys on the half-quadratic splitting approach to solve Eq. (13). New auxiliary variables u and $g(g = (g_h, g_v)^T)$ are introduced, and they correspond to $l - c$ and ∇l, respectively. So the objective function Eq. (13) can be rewrited as

$$\{\hat{l}, \hat{u}, \hat{g}\} = \arg\min_{l,u,g} \|l \otimes k - b\|_2^2 + \alpha\|\nabla l - g\|_2^2 + \beta\|l - c - u\|_2^2 + \mu\|g\|_0 + \lambda\|u\|_0. \quad (15)$$

In the case of α and β approaching infinity, the answer of Eq. (15) approches that of Eq. (13). And we can solve Eq. (15) efficiently by alternatively minimizing l, u, g respectively and fixing remaining variables. To achieve clear image l, the objective function transforms into,

$$\hat{l} = \arg\min_{l} \|l \otimes k - b\|_2^2 + \alpha\|\nabla l - g\|_2^2 + \beta\|l - c - u\|_2^2 \quad (16)$$

and the least squares minimization problem has the closed-form solution,

$$l = \mathcal{F}^{-1}\left(\frac{\overline{\mathcal{F}(k)}\mathcal{F}(b) + \beta\mathcal{F}(c + u) + \alpha F_g}{\overline{\mathcal{F}(k)}\mathcal{F}(k) + \beta + \alpha\overline{\mathcal{F}(\nabla)}\mathcal{F}(\nabla)} \right) \tag{17}$$

where $\mathcal{F}(\cdot)$ is the Fast fourier Transform (FFT), and $\mathcal{F}^{-1}(\cdot)$ is the inverse FFT. The complex conjugate operator is denoted by $\overline{(\cdot)}$. $F_g = \overline{\mathcal{F}(\nabla_h)}\mathcal{F}(g_h) + \overline{\mathcal{F}(\nabla_v)}\mathcal{F}(g_v)$, ∇_v and ∇_h are the vertical and horizontal differential operators, respectively. Fixed l, we can solve u and g separately as follows:

$$\hat{u} = \arg\min_u \beta\|l - c - u\|_2^2 + \lambda\|u\|_0 \tag{18}$$

and

$$\hat{g} = \arg\min_g \alpha\|\nabla l - g\|_2^2 + \mu\|g\|_0 \tag{19}$$

Because Eqs. (18) and (19) are pixel-wise minimization problem, u and g can be solved by [17],

$$u = \begin{cases} l - c, & |l - c|^2 \geq \frac{\lambda}{\beta} \\ 0, & \text{otherwise} \end{cases} \tag{20}$$

and

$$g = \begin{cases} \nabla l, & |\nabla l|^2 \geq \frac{\mu}{\alpha} \\ 0, & \text{otherwise} \end{cases} \tag{21}$$

Estimating Blur Kernel k. As the latent image l is fixed, the blur kernel k can be calculated by utilizing the fast deblurring method [12] on the gradient image as:

$$\hat{k} = \arg\min_k \|\nabla l \otimes k - \nabla b\|_2^2 + \gamma\|k\|_2^2, \tag{22}$$

and FFTs can help us to get the solution efficiently,

$$k = \mathcal{F}^{-1}\left(\frac{\overline{\mathcal{F}(\nabla l)}\mathcal{F}(\nabla b)}{\overline{\mathcal{F}(\nabla l)}\mathcal{F}(\nabla l) + \gamma} \right). \tag{23}$$

We adopt a coarse-to-fine strategy that utilize an image pyramid [12] to estimate blur kernel. The introduced strategy is widely used in state-of-the-art methods. What's more, the negative elements in k are set to zero and k is normalized in the end. Algorithm 1 shows the main processes of our deblurring method.

Algorithm 1. Our Proposed Algorithm

Input: Initial blur kernel k, blurred image b
  for $i = 1 \rightarrow 5$ **do**
    $l \leftarrow b, \beta \leftarrow \beta_0$
    repeat
      c is derived from (11).
      u is derived from (20).
      $\alpha \leftarrow \alpha_0$
      repeat
        g is derived from (21).
        l is derived from (16).
        $\alpha \leftarrow 2\alpha$
      until $\alpha > \alpha_{max}$
      $\beta \leftarrow 2\beta$
    until $\beta > \beta_{max}$
    blur kernel k is derived from (22).
    $\beta_0 \leftarrow 0.9\beta_0, \alpha_0 \leftarrow 0.9\alpha_0$
  end for
Output: Blur kernel k, clear image l

---

5   Experimental Results

The performances of our proposed algorithm on the document images and complex text images contain cluttered background regions is presented in this section, and we also compare it with the state-of-the-art images deblurring approaches. The parameters in all experiments are fixed as follows, $\lambda = 0.004$, $\mu = 0.004$ and $\gamma = 2$. While c_0 and c_1 in Eq. (11) will be updated with the change of l in deblurring process, we set $c_0 = (max(l) + min(l)) * 0.4$ and $c_1 = min(1, (min(l) + max(l)) * 0.6)$. The PSNR (Peak Signal to Noise Ratios) and SSIM (Structural Similarity) are used as the performance evaluation standards on deblurred results.

To better vertify the effectiveness of our proposed algorithm, the text image dataset [11] which has 8 blur kernels [2] and 15 clear text images are used here. The average PSNR and SSIM on the deblurred images generated by proposed method are computed, and they are compared with those of Krishnan *et al.* [3], Xu and Jia [4], Pan and Sun [6], Pan and Hu [11], Cho and Lee [12], Zhong *et al.* [13]. The average PSNR and SSIM values of the recovered images with these methods are shown in Table 1. It indicates that our algorithm based on intensity

Table 1. The PSNR and SSIM comparisons of the deblurring results on dataset [11]

	Blurred	[3]	[4]	[6]	[11]	[12]	[13]	Ours
PSNR	17.81	21.83	26.34	28.99	29.31	27.23	19.19	30.17
SSIM	0.57	0.58	0.69	0.70	0.70	0.60	0.49	0.72

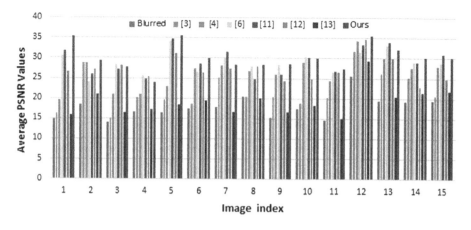

Fig. 2. Quantitative comparison of different methods on text image dataset.

extremums prior performs favorably against other approaches. What's more, we can see more details about PSNR comparison in Fig. 2. The figure manifests that the introduced algorithm achieves the highest PSNR value in these methods for over half of images. The Fig. 3 illustrates that our method performs favorably against [3, 4, 6, 11–13] for document images. The methods [3, 12, 13] fail in the challenging document image, and the results generated by [4, 6, 11] contain too much noise or ringing artifacts. We also note that the approach [11] enforces some pixels to be dark falsely as shown in Fig. 3(g). In contrast, a much better deblurred image, in terms of the sharpness of the text as well as noise level, is achieved by the our method. Overall, the proposed method has favorable performance and get the highest average metrics (PSNR, SSIM) for text images dataset.

Two examples are also presented in Figs. 4 and 5 where the input images contain complex background regions and rich text. Some outstanding image deblurring approaches perform unfavorably on these images. In contrast, the deblurred images which contain clear text and natural colors, sharp edges is generated by our method. As shown in the Fig. 4, the blurred image contain several colors and complex cluttered backgrounds. Most deblurring approaches [3, 4, 11] fail to recover a clear text image with sharp edges. The proposed method performs well against other approaches, and the generated image has little noise compare with the results by [12, 13]. The blurred image in Fig. 5 is more intricate and challenging than that in Fig. 4. Although the estimation result produced by Pan *et al.* [11] is better than other results by approaches [3, 4, 12, 13, 23], some recovered texts in the deblurred image are still not clear. While our method generates a sharp image with clear texture and legible text as shown in Fig. 5(h). The two deblur experiments on the complex text images prove that the proposed method achieve more stable and clear results than other outstanding methods even if the blur images contain rich text and cluttered background.

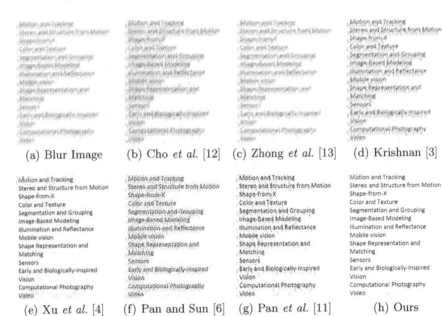

(a) Blur Image (b) Cho *et al.* [12] (c) Zhong *et al.* [13] (d) Krishnan [3]

(e) Xu *et al.* [4] (f) Pan and Sun [6] (g) Pan *et al.* [11] (h) Ours

Fig. 3. Deburring results of state-of-the-art methods on one challenging document image.

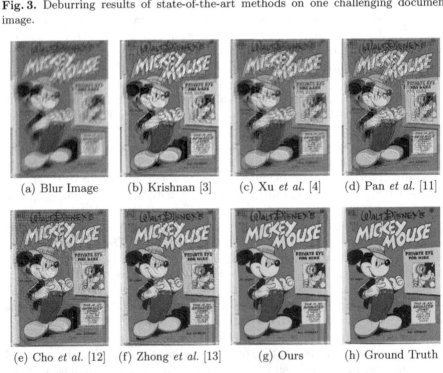

(a) Blur Image (b) Krishnan [3] (c) Xu *et al.* [4] (d) Pan *et al.* [11]

(e) Cho *et al.* [12] (f) Zhong *et al.* [13] (g) Ours (h) Ground Truth

Fig. 4. Deburring results of state-of-the-art methods on one complex text image cluttered background regions.

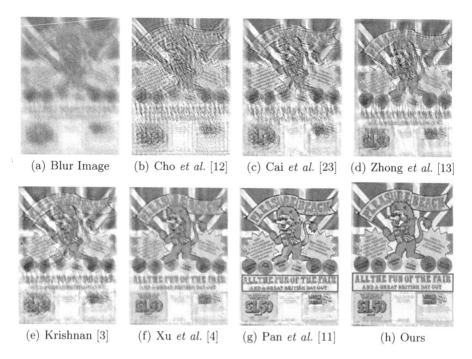

(a) Blur Image   (b) Cho *et al.* [12]   (c) Cai *et al.* [23]   (d) Zhong *et al.* [13]

(e) Krishnan [3]   (f) Xu *et al.* [4]   (g) Pan *et al.* [11]   (h) Ours

Fig. 5. Deburring results of some state-of-the-art methods on another complex image.

From these experiments, it can be found that the extremums prior based approach generates sharper deblurred results on text images than other outstanding approaches. It's theoretically proved that the blur operation produces the proposed prior. The intensity extremums prior whose energy is lower for sharp images than for blurred images can help algorithm to generate more clear results in iterations.

6   Conclusion

Based on the mathematical proof of the intensity extremums prior for text images, a novel and effective blind text image deblurring approach is introduced. To deblur text images by the intensity extremums prior, an effective optimization algorithm which utilizes a half-quadratic splitting strategy is exploited. The proposed method don't require any complex processing techniques or edge selection steps. In addition, the algorithm is examined on the document images and complex text images which contain cluttered background regions. The results manifest that the proposed method has outstanding performance against the state-of-the-art image deblurring approaches.

References

1. Fergus, R., Singh, B., Hertzmann, A., Roweis, S.T., Freeman, W.T.: Removing camera shake from a single photograph. ACM Trans. Graph. **25**, 787–794 (2006)
2. Levin, A., Weiss, Y., Durand, F., Freeman, W.: Understanding and evaluating blind deconvolution algorithms. In: Proceedings of CVPR 2009, pp. 1964–1971 (2009)
3. Krishnan, D., Tay, T., Fergus, R.: Blind deconvolution using a normalized sparsity measure. In: Proceedings of CVPR 2011, pp. 233–240 (2011)
4. Xu, L., Zheng, S., Jia, J.: Unnatural L0 sparse representation for natural image deblurring. In: Proceedings of CVPR 2013, pp. 1107–1114 (2013)
5. Michaeli, T., Irani, M.: Blind deblurring using internal patch recurrence. In: Fleet, D., Pajdla, T., Schiele, B., Tuytelaars, T. (eds.) ECCV 2014. LNCS, vol. 8691, pp. 783–798. Springer, Cham (2014). https://doi.org/10.1007/978-3-319-10578-9_51
6. Pan, J., Sun, D., Pfister, H., Yang, M.H.: Blind image deblurring using dark channel prior. In: Proceedings of CVPR 2016, pp. 1628–1636 (2016)
7. Li, T.H., Lii, K.S.: A joint estimation approach for two-tone image deblurring by blind deconvolution. IEEE Trans. Image Process. **11**, 847–858 (2002)
8. Chen, X., He, X., Yang, J., Wu, Q.: An effective document image deblurring algorithm. In: Proceedings of CVPR 2011, pp. 369–376 (2011)
9. Epshtein, B., Ofek, E., Wexler, Y.: Detecting text in natural scenes with stroke width transform. In: Proceedings of CVPR 2010, pp. 2963–2970 (2010)
10. Cho, H., Wang, J., Lee, S.: Text image deblurring using text-specific properties. In: Fitzgibbon, A., Lazebnik, S., Perona, P., Sato, Y., Schmid, C. (eds.) ECCV 2012. LNCS, vol. 7576, pp. 524–537. Springer, Heidelberg (2012). https://doi.org/10.1007/978-3-642-33715-4_38
11. Pan, J., Hu, Z., Su, Z., Yang, M.H.: Deblurring text images via L0-regularized intensity and gradient prior. In: Proceedings of CVPR 2014, pp. 2901–2908 (2014)
12. Cho, S., Lee, S.: Fast motion deblurring. In: ACM Transactions on Graphics (2009)
13. Zhong, L., Cho, S., Metaxas, D., Paris, S., Wang, J.: Handling noise in single image deblurring using directional filters. In: Proceedings of CVPR 2013, pp. 612–619 (2013)
14. Zhou, Y., Komodakis, N.: A map-estimation framework for blind deblurring using high-level edge priors. In: Fleet, D., Pajdla, T., Schiele, B., Tuytelaars, T. (eds.) ECCV 2014. LNCS, vol. 8690, pp. 142–157. Springer, Cham (2014). https://doi.org/10.1007/978-3-319-10605-2_10
15. Xu, L., Jia, J.: Two-phase kernel estimation for robust motion deblurring. In: Daniilidis, K., Maragos, P., Paragios, N. (eds.) ECCV 2010. LNCS, vol. 6311, pp. 157–170. Springer, Heidelberg (2010). https://doi.org/10.1007/978-3-642-15549-9_12
16. Ren, W., Cao, X., Pan, J., Guo, X., Zuo, W., Yang, M.H.: Image deblurring via enhanced low-rank prior. IEEE Trans. Image Process. **25**(7), 3426–3437 (2016)
17. Xu, L., Lu, C., Xu, Y., Jia, J.: Image smoothing via L0 gradient minimization. ACM Trans. Graph. **30**, 1–12 (2011)
18. Sun, L., Cho, S., Wang, J., Hays, J.: Edge-based blur kernel estimation using patch priors. In: Proceedings of ICCP 2013, pp. 1–8 (2013)
19. Joshi, N., Szeliski, R., Kriegman, D.J.: PSF estimation using sharp edge prediction. In: Proceedings of CVPR 2008, pp. 1–8 (2008)
20. Levin, A., Weiss, Y., Durand, F., Freeman, W.T.: Efficient marginal likelihood optimization in blind deconvolution. In: Proceedings of CVPR 2011, pp. 2657–2664 (2011)

21. Krishnan, D., Fergus, R.: Fast image deconvolution using hyper-Laplacian priors. In: Proceedings of NIPS 2009, pp. 1033–1041 (2009)
22. Shan, Q., Jia, J., Agarwala, A.: High-quality motion deblurring from a single image. ACM Trans. Graph. **27**(3), 1–10 (2008)
23. Cai, J.F., Ji, H., Liu, C., et al.: Framelet-based blind motion deblurring from a single image. IEEE Trans. Image Process. **21**(2), 562–572 (2012)

The CAMETRON Lecture Recording System: High Quality Video Recording and Editing with Minimal Human Supervision

Dries Hulens[✉], Bram Aerts, Punarjay Chakravarty, Ali Diba,
Toon Goedemé, Tom Roussel, Jeroen Zegers, Tinne Tuytelaars,
Luc Van Eycken, Luc Van Gool, Hugo Van Hamme, and Joost Vennekens

University of Leuven, Kasteelpark Arenberg 10, 3001 Leuven, Belgium
{dries.hulens,bram.aerts,punarjay.chakravarty,ali.diba,toon.goedem,
tom.roussel,jeroen.zegers,tinne.tuytelaars,luc.vaneycken,luc.vangool,
hugo.vanhamme,joost.vennekens}@kuleuven.be

Abstract. In this paper, we demonstrate a system that automates the process of recording video lectures in classrooms. Through special hardware (lecturer and audience facing cameras and microphone arrays), we record multiple points of view of the lecture. Person detection and tracking, along with recognition of different human actions are used to digitally zoom in on the lecturer, and alternate focus between the lecturer and the slides or the blackboard. Audio sound source localization, along with face detection and tracking, is used to detect questions from the audience, to digitally zoom in on the member of the audience asking the question and to improve the quality of the sound recording. Finally, an automatic video editing system is used to naturally switch between the different video streams and to compose a compelling end product. We demonstrate the working system in two classrooms, over two 2-h lectures, given by two lecturers.

Keywords: Lecture recording · Smart camera systems
Virtual cameraman · Virtual editor · Sound source localization
Active speaker detection

1 Introduction

Wouldn't it be nice if we could make video-lectures of all classes taught at our universities, at minimal cost yet high quality? Well, now we can ! This paper describes a system to record lectures and process multiple video-streams yielding a professional looking montage with minimal human intervention.

This work is supported by the Cametron Project grant.
Excluding the corresponding author, authors are listed in alphabetical order.

K. Schoeffmann et al. (Eds.): MMM 2018, Part I, LNCS 10704, pp. 518–530, 2018.
https://doi.org/10.1007/978-3-319-73603-7_42

The benefits for students of recording lectures and broadcasting them on-line have already been widely discussed and proven in the literature [7,12,21] and several (semi-)automatic lecture recording systems have been developed, focusing on capturing regions of interest [11,13,24] (e.g. projected slides), automated capture of lecturer notes taken in class [3] or (live) viewing over the Internet [17,18,24]. A common disadvantage of most of those systems, however, is the typically low quality of the viewing experience, which is very different from the one obtained when a human camera crew records the lecture. Indeed, a human cameraman does more than just tracking the speaker positions: he positions the speaker cinematographically correct in the frame, he zooms in on the blackboard when the lecturer is writing, he zooms in on a person in the audience asking a question, etc. This requires a high level of semantic understanding of what is going on in the scene. Lecture recording systems on the market today lack such a semantic layer, resulting in lecture captures that are rather static and not very engaging for learners, which in turn leads to ineffective learning.

The goal of this work is to improve the viewing experience with an automatic lecture recording system, while keeping the cost down. To this end, we built custom hardware that synchronously records multiple video and audio streams of both the lecturer and the audience. We use computer vision and audio processing techniques to detect any relevant information in these data streams, such as action recognition, sound source localization and face detection. This information is fed to a virtual editor that is designed to switch between video-streams depending on any actions that were detected and following standard cinematographic rules. Further, to make the video more visually appealing, a virtual cameraman zooms in on the most relevant image region, mimicking the camera motions a human cameraman would make, by tracking the lecturer while he is moving.

The resulting CAMETRON system is highly flexible thanks to its modular design. It makes minimal assumptions about the class room layout, the number of cameras used, etc. The hardware can be set up in any class room in a couple of minutes, and needs no interaction from the lecturer other than starting and stopping the recordings.

The main contributions of this paper are: (i) custom hardware for synchronized video and audio recording, (ii) a virtual cameraman making the video more visually attractive, (iii) action recognition helping the virtual editor choosing the best shot, (iv) sound source localization used to zoom-in into the audience, and (v) a virtual editor choosing the best shot and making the final video.

The remainder of this paper is organized as follows. In Sect. 2 we describe the audiovisual analysis of the recordings of the lecturer and of the audience in Sect. 3. Next, we discuss the virtual editor (Sect. 4) and the hardware setup (Sect. 5). Section 6 discusses the experimental validation of our system and Sect. 7 concludes the paper.

2   Analysis of the Lecturer Recordings

The actual video-stream chosen by the editor depends on different factors. One of the most important ones is if the lecturer is visible in that stream or not. A shot of the lecturers desk without a lecturer is not visually attractive to watch. Therefore we first run a person detector and tracker. In addition, a new video-stream is created out of the original video-stream. This new stream is a close-up shot of the lecturer where the lecturer is placed at the correct cinematographic position. Furthermore, several actions (like pointing to the blackboard) of the lecturer are detected to give the virtual editor cues whether to switch to a different video-stream or not.

2.1   Virtual Zoom of the Lecturer

The lecturer is captured by two or more HD overview cameras. To make the recordings visually more attractive, a virtual zoom is applied generating a close-up shot of the lecturer. This close-up shot is actually a cut-out (640×480 pixels) of the original image (overview shot of 1280×960 pixels). We chose not to use a Pan-Tilt-Zoom camera because there is always a transition between e.g. an overview shot and a close-up shot (zooming), which takes time and is not visually attractive to watch. The size of the cut-out shot and overview shot are both easily adjustable.

To make the close-up shot visually pleasing, some basic cinematographic rules are applied, namely the *rule of thirds* and the *head room*. The *rule of thirds* states that the lecturer should be positioned on the left of the screen (on 1/3rd of the width) when his face is looking to the right and vice versa, to leave some empty space (the other 2/3rd of the width) for the action to take place. The *head room* rule imposes that there should be some empty space between the head and the top of the frame. An example cut-out is shown in Fig. 1 in red, together with some actions that trigger the virtual editor to switch to a close-up shot.

Fig. 1. Left: The original frame (1280×960) and the cut-out (640×480) in red with the lecturer positioned on the left due to the rule of thirds and with a bit of headroom. Right: actions like writing, pointing and gesturing that trigger a close-up shot (Color figure online).

To apply these rules, first the position and gaze direction of the lecturer needs to be determined. The position is found by running a DPM (Deformable Part Model) upper-body detector [5] over the entire image. Next, the algorithm searches for the head in the upper part of the detection window. For the gaze direction estimation, we use the method described in [8], which is optimized for speed. It is based on three Viola and Jones face models [22] (frontal, left- and right-looking) and a linear interpolation of the viewing angles of the two training images with the most similar detector scores. Based on the estimated gaze direction, the desired position of the lecturer in the zoomed-in frame can be determined. Because the face angle is estimated in every frame and the zoomed-in region is adapted to that, the zoomed-in region will follow the lecturer. A PID control loop is used to move the zoomed-in region in a smooth way.

Since a log file is generated with the position and angle of the face for every frame, the virtual editor knows in which frames a face is visible or not and can switch to a different shot when the lecturer is not visible. The algorithm runs at 15 fps while the video is captured at 25 fps. This does not induce a problem in our setup since processing happens off-board and after the recordings are finished.

2.2 Action Recognition

While at times zooming in on the lecturer may be a good strategy, it is sometimes also better to show a wider view, e.g. including the projected slides when the lecturer is pointing to them, or the blackboard when the lecturer is writing on it. To enable the virtual editor to choose the right setup, we analyze the behavior of the lecturer and recognize a number of different actions.

The number of actions performed by lecturers is limited. We focus on writing on the blackboard, pointing, and talking gestures. Since there is no publicly available dataset including these categories of actions in a class environment, we created our own. It uses free on-line courses and lectures content and contains samples of the mentioned actions by different lecturers. Our method for action classification in these videos is inspired by recent progress in the field of deep convolutional neural networks [6,10] and especially two stream networks for human action recognition [4,19]. The two stream approaches utilize two modalities of data: RGB frames and motion Optical-Flow [23] frames. Each of the stream networks are trained separately on their corresponding data to recognize the actions [19].

To achieve the goal in this task accurately, we need to find the person beforehand. For this, we use the Fast-RCNN [6] object detector which is just trained to detect human bodies in video frames. After localizing the person in the video, we feed the cropped image of the person in the video frames to the action recognition neural network. Based on the score of lecturer actions, the CAMETRON system is able to decide for further steps and video editing action points.

3   Analysis of the Audience Recordings

In most lectures, a couple of questions are asked from members of the audience (questioners) and sometimes even a small discussion occurs. Most traditional lecture recording systems, however, fail to capture both the audio and the video from the questioner, which can be very frustrating for someone watching the recording. To tackle this problem we first localize the sound source, then zoom in on the active speaker. We also use this info to improve the quality of the audio.

3.1   Sound Source Localization

We propose a far distance beamforming solution together with a single wide-view camera. A microphone array (see Sect. 5) is used to locate the direction of the sound by detecting spatial correlations, using the far-field approximation. The spatial setup of the microphone array (see Fig. 2 left) allows for an estimate of both the azimuth (θ) and elevation (ϕ) angle. An angular spectrum is created over (θ, ϕ) using a Generalized Cross-Correlation with PHAse Transform (GCC-PHAT) [9], since it was shown to perform best in source localization tasks [2]. A nonlinear transform of the GCC-PHAT is taken, to emphasize larger values in the angular spectrum. Source localization is done by detecting the peak in the angular spectrum. A questioner is assumed stationary while he talks.

For sound source localization, the audio stream is divided into segments of one minute (with one second overlap) for computational reasons. For each frame in each segment a Voice Activity Detector (VAD) is used to detect voice activity from the audience [20]. Consecutive audience active frames are grouped into a fragment, and for each fragment a spatial location is estimated. Fragments shorter than 1 s are regarded as noise or false positives and thrown away.

3.2   Active Speaker Detection

Whenever the sound source localization detects a speaker in the audience, it is necessary to localize them in the video as well. To find the active speaker, we use a fast and state-of-the-art face detector: the Multi-Task Cascaded Convolutional Neural Network of [25]. This has been trained for both face detection and alignment. The resulting detections are candidates for being the active speaker. We translate the azimuth and elevation angles into a position in the image frame using a third order polynomial: $x_i(\theta) = p_1 \cdot \theta^3 + p_2 \cdot \theta^2 + p_3 \cdot \theta + p_4$, and similarly for $y_i(\phi)$. Whichever candidate is closest to this result is assumed to be the active speaker. From there we can crop the frame around the speaker. The polynomial coefficients are determined through a calibration process that needs to be repeated once in each new environment. It consists of having a single person walk around the environment and clap his hands from several positions. As there is only one face in the frame when doing this, the face detector only has a single correspondence with the clapping sound. This allows us to fit the polynomial to translate the sound source localization angles to image coordinates. Clapping is detected by a simple energy threshold on the signal of one of the microphones from the microphone array.

3.3   Speech Enhancement

Aside from positioning, the sound source localization technique can also be used to enhance the speech signal of the questioner. Since the distance of the questioner to the recording device can be up to the size of the class room, reverberation and a noisy sound source can reduce audio intelligibility for the listener. The speech signal is estimated by minimum variance distortionless response (MVDR) beamforming with diagonal loading [14]. The multichannel covariance matrix of noise is estimated over 2 s of non-speech segments in the near context. The steering vector is determined on the Time Difference Of Arrival (TDOA), which was estimated for the sound source localization. Notice that this technique is only used for speech from the audience, since the lecturer uses a wireless close-talk microphone. Moreover, the speech of a questioner close to the microphone is less influenced by reverberation and the need for beamforming is reduced.

4   Virtual Editor

Once the autonomous cameras have captured high quality footage of the event, it's time for the virtual editor system to combine the footage of the different cameras into a single, coherent and qualitative montage. Creating a video that is both interesting and easy-to-follow is not a straightforward task. Human editors typically follow a number of different cinematographic rules to accomplish this task. To develop our virtual editor, we follow a declarative approach, in which we explicitly represent these rules. This approach has the benefit that it offers a great deal of flexibility in deciding which rules should be taken into account and how they should take priority over each other. Rules can be added and removed with relative ease. For example, using this framework we can easily add rules that take new actions into account. To represent the rules, we need a suitable knowledge representation language. A particular challenge in this application is that cinematographic rules are not strict: they are guidelines that are typically followed, but not always. Indeed, the rules may sometimes contradict each other, and even if they do not, a human editor may still choose to ignore a rule, simply because the result "feels" better. A virtual editor should therefore not rigidly follow the rules, but it should sometimes deviate from them in order to give the montage a more interesting and natural flavor, thereby mimicking the creativity of a human editor. For this reason, we have chosen to make use of a Probabilistic Logic Programming (PLP) language, which allows us to represent these rules in a non-deterministic way. This has the additional benefit that – just like a human editor – the system is able to produce different montages from the same input streams.

A detailed overview of the full virtual editor system can be found in [1]. A number of adaptations have been made to the described system in order to make it more applicable in the current lecture recording setting. Below, we briefly discuss these adaptations, which at the same time serves as illustration of how rules are used in our system.

In particular, we focus on a new aspect of the lecture not present in the system of [1]: questions from the audience. When a member of the audience asks a question, the viewer should see that person speaking. For this purpose we introduce an additional shot type, the interaction shot. Switching to this shot is possible from any other shot. A question from a member of the audience triggers the switch to the interaction shot. After an interaction shot, the reaction of the lecturer is shown in a long shot, medium shot or close up. This approach also allows fluent switching between questioner and lecturer in a conversation.

5   Hardware

To record a lecture three devices have been developed, as shown in Fig. 2. The first device is the *Audience Recorder*. It records video and sound of the audience and has everything integrated in a portable flight case. Six T-Bone EM700 microphones are used in the microphone array, while the lecturer is equipped with a Shure MX53 headworn earset connected to a Shure GLXD wireless receiver. The sound of all microphones is captured by an 8 channel Focusrite Scarlett 18i20 USB audio interface and stored on a Windows laptop computer. The camera used in the Audience recorder is a Ueye XC 13 MP color camera from IDS which provides images at a framerate of 25 fps. The video is recorded on a Brix minicomputer which is connected to a WIFI hotspot for easy video transfer. To start and stop the recordings simultaneously on all devices, an Arduino is used which sends a signal to all devices (recorders) via a ZigBee wireless connection. In addition a sound signal is sent to the sound recorder to synchronize video and sound. Furthermore two smaller recorders are developed to record the lecturer. These recorders are a copy of the video recorder in the Audience Recorder box. When a start signal is sent by the Arduino, all recorders start recording simultaneously at a frame-rate of 25 fps. When a stop signal is sent, the recorders stop recording and the video of all recorders is automatically transfered to the Windows laptop where they can be processed.

6   Experiments

Before we evaluate our complete system, we zoom in on the performance of some of the components: virtual zoom of the lecturer, action recognition, active speaker detection/sound source localization and speech enhancement.

6.1   Setup

To demonstrate the CAMETRON system, two lectures were recorded, in different class rooms and with different lecturers. The first lecture is called the *seminar*

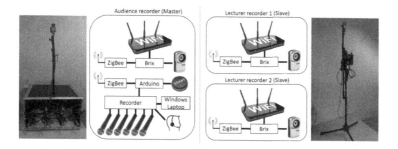

Fig. 2. Left: The main recording box aimed at the audience. Right: The individual recording devices aimed at the speaker.

recordings and the second lecture is called *Matthews lecture.* They're respectively 95 and 117 min long. For both recordings the *Audience recorder* was placed in front of the classroom facing the audience, a second recorder was placed in the audience facing the lecturer and the third recorder was placed in the back of the room also facing the lecturer in a wider shot.

6.2   Virtual Zoom of the Lecturer

The virtual zoom of the lecturer was explained in Sect. 2.1. To evaluate the correctness of the virtual zoom procedure we perform two experiments on the *seminar recordings*. In the first experiment we evaluate the detection of the lecturer. We find that the lecturer is not detected in 311 of the 142.900 frames. This yields an excellent detection accuracy of 99.8%. In the second experiment 100 frames are randomly extracted out of the *seminar recordings* and the consistency of the position of the lecturer w.r.t. the frame and the gaze direction is examined. Only in 2 frames the position of the lecturer is chosen wrongly, due to a wrong gaze direction estimation (caused by light of the beamer shining on the lecturers face). In some occasions we find the lecturer positioned in the center of the frame when looking to the left, but this is because the zoomed in frame can not move any further to the left due to the boundaries (size) of the original frame. These frames are also classified as correctly positioned frames. The Virtual zoom algorithm took respectively 158 min and 195 min to process both videos.

6.3   Action Recognition

For the action recognition, we first run an evaluation on part of the data we collected from the Internet. Half of the dataset (400 short clips) is used for training and the other half for evaluation. This setup results in a mean average precision of 87% on the three action classes (88% talking gestures, 91% writing, 82% pointing). Next, we evaluate the module on the recorded lectures. To this end, we randomly select 100 frames (out of both recordings) in which an action is recognized and visually check the correctness. In this case the performance of the module is 84%, i.e. the action class label is correct in 84 out of 100 sample points.

6.4   Active Speaker Detection and Sound Source Localization

Evaluating sound source localization in our use case is more difficult, as we do not have any ground truth values for the azimuth and elevation angles. For this reason we evaluate it jointly with the active speaker detection with a simple experiment. We go through all of the video fragments where an active speaker is detected in the audience and manually check if the correct speaker is cropped in the frame or not. We do this for both lecture recordings, giving a total of 79 detections. Using this evaluation method we get a true positive rate of 79.75%.

6.5   Speech Enhancement

The speech enhancement procedure was explained in Sect. 3.3. Its goal was to enhance the audibility of the question for the listener. Speech enhancement quality will be measured in terms of Word Error Rate (WER) of an Automatic Speech Recognizer (ASR). While optimizing speech enhancement as a preprocessing step to ASR is not identical to optimizing towards improved audibility, it does provide an indication without the need of a close-talk reference microphone for each questioner to measure, for example, signal-to-distortion ratio. For the ASR, a standard Kaldi [16] recipe is used to train an acoustic model on the AURORA-4 [15] database. This database contains utterances of read speech, while the system will be evaluated on spontaneous speech and thus poor results can be expected. Furthermore, no specific guidelines were given to the questioners and sometimes intelligibility is very low. In addition, all test speakers are non-native. The audio signal of a single microphone was used as baseline to compare with the MVDR of the microphone array. The WER for questions of multiple lectures were determined. Experiments were performed on four different lectures. In three lectures average WER was above 90% illustrating the low intelligibility. We found more acceptable results for one lecture (containing five questions). The WER of the baseline was 69.6% and was reduced to 66.1% (a relative reduction of 5.0%) using beamforming, indicating that the speech enhancement does improve audibility.

6.6   Overall System

Some snapshots of the *seminar recording* are shown in Fig. 3. The first row shows the raw video input, while the second row shows processed footage. In the first image there is a question from the audience and the system reacts by zooming-in on the person that is asking the question. In the second image nothing is happening and the virtual editor selects the overview camera as output. In the third image the teacher is pointing and a close-up shot of the teacher is shown.

Figure 4 shows a number of shot sequences (one sequence per row). We briefly discuss the underlying reasons for those shot transitions. Sequence 1 and 2 show

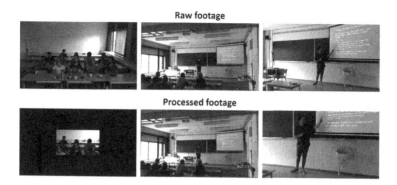

Fig. 3. Result of the overall system. First row: raw input footage of the audience (1), overview (2) and mid-shot (3) camera. Second row: Processed output: Zoom in on audience (1), overview shot (2) and crop of lecturer (3)

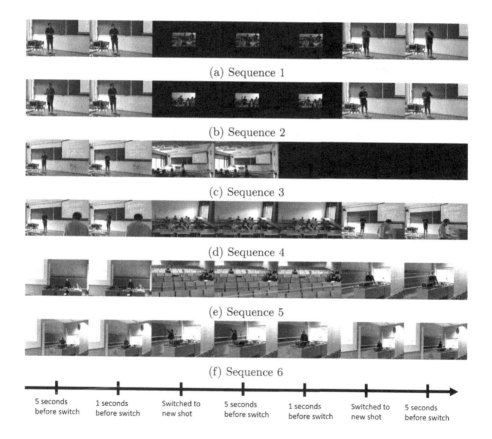

(a) Sequence 1

(b) Sequence 2

(c) Sequence 3

(d) Sequence 4

(e) Sequence 5

(f) Sequence 6

| 5 seconds before switch | 1 seconds before switch | Switched to new shot | 5 seconds before switch | 1 seconds before switch | Switched to new shot | 5 seconds before switch |

Fig. 4. Result of the overall system. Each row represents a sequence of shots, generated by the system. Sequences 1 to 4 are taken from the *seminar recording*, sequences 5 and 6 are from *Matthews lecture*.

how the system reacts to a question from the audience. When a question is asked, the system generates a close-up stream of that person. The sudden appearance of this video stream triggers the first switch in sequence 1. The first switch in sequence 2 is triggered directly by a person speaking in the audience. When the person in the audience stops talking, the close-up stream is aborted, which causes a switch back to the lecturer. Sequences 3, 4 and 5 show the behavior when a shot becomes too long. When this is about to happen, a switch to a different shot is triggered. In sequence 3, the selected shot is an overview shot, where the lecturer is still visible. In sequences 4 and 5, the system selects the overview of the audience. Here the lecturer is no longer visible, but is still talking. This is only suitable for a short period of time, so as soon as the minimal shot length has passed, the system decides to switch back to the lecturer. In sequence 6, an action (writing) is detected and a switch to a close-up shot is triggered.

Because the validation of the overall system is person-dependent we published both processed videos on Youtube[1]. In addition we added a movie of the first 5 min of the *seminar recordings* with the reasons of switching shot (determined by the virtual editor) plotted on the video[2].

7   Conclusion

In this paper we described a system to record multiple audio- and video-streams of a lecture and process these into a single video montage with as little human intervention as possible. The best video-stream is chosen by a virtual editor, taking into account the action that is taking place and cinematographic rules. To make the video more attractive, a virtual cameraman is created that zooms in on the lecturer and tracks his movement while considering the *rule of thirds* and *head-room*. When there is a question from the audience, sound source localization is used to zoom in on the person that is speaking. All processes are successfully validated individually as well as in an overall system.

References

1. Aerts, B., Goedemé, T., Vennekens, J.: A probabilistic logic programming approach to automatic video montage. In: ECAI, pp. 234–242 (2016)
2. Blandin, C., Ozerov, A., Vincent, E.: Multi-source TDOA estimation in reverberant audio using angular spectra and clustering. Signal Process. **92**(8), 1950–1960 (2012)
3. Brotherton, J.A., Abowd, G.D.: Lessons learned from eclass: assessing automated capture and access in the classroom. ACM Trans. Comput.-Hum. Interact. (TOCHI) **11**(2), 121–155 (2004)
4. Feichtenhofer, C., Pinz, A., Zisserman, A.: Convolutional two-stream network fusion for video action recognition. In: CVPR (2016)

---

[1] Seminar recordings: https://youtu.be/DalAafs38TU Matthew recordings: https://youtu.be/p3ZeFfj238g.

[2] https://youtu.be/4Ruzv9jAZ6E.

5. Felzenszwalb, P., McAllester, D., Ramanan, D.: A discriminatively trained, multiscale, deformable part model. In: IEEE Conference on Computer Vision and Pattern Recognition, CVPR 2008, pp. 1–8. IEEE (2008)
6. Girshick, R.: Fast R-CNN. In: IEEE International Conference on Computer Vision (ICCV) (2015)
7. Hahn, E.: Video lectures help enhance online information literacy course. Ref. Serv. Rev. **40**(1), 49–60 (2012)
8. Hulens, D., Van Beeck, K., Goedemé, T.: Fast and accurate face orientation measurement in low-resolution images on embedded hardware. In: Proceedings of the 11th Joint Conference on Computer Vision, Imaging and Computer Graphics Theory and Applications (VISIGRAPP 2016), vol. 4, pp. 538–544. Scitepress (2016)
9. Knapp, C., Carter, G.: The generalized correlation method for estimation of time delay. IEEE Trans. Acoust. Speech Signal Process. **24**(4), 320–327 (1976)
10. Krizhevsky, A., Sutskever, I., Hinton, G.E.: Imagenet classification with deep convolutional neural networks. In: NIPS (2012)
11. Lampi, F., Kopf, S., Benz, M., Effelsberg, W.: An automatic cameraman in a lecture recording system. In: Proceedings of the International Workshop on Educational Multimedia and Multimedia Education, pp. 11–18. ACM (2007)
12. Marchand, J.P., Pearson, M.L., Albon, S.P.: Student and faculty member perspectives on lecture capture in pharmacy education. Am. J. Pharm. Educ. **78**(4), 74 (2014)
13. Mavlankar, A., Agrawal, P., Pang, D., Halawa, S., Cheung, N.M., Girod, B.: An interactive region-of-interest video streaming system for online lecture viewing. In: 18th International Packet Video Workshop (PV), pp. 64–71. IEEE (2010)
14. Mestre, X., Lagunas, M.A.: On diagonal loading for minimum variance beamformers. In: Proceedings of the 3rd IEEE International Symposium on Signal Processing and Information Technology (ISSPIT), pp. 459–462. IEEE (2003)
15. Pearce, D.: Aurora working group: DSR front end LVCSR evaluation AU/384/02. Ph.D. thesis, Mississippi State University (2002)
16. Povey, D., Ghoshal, A., Boulianne, G., Burget, L., Glembek, O., Goel, N., Hannemann, M., Motlicek, P., Qian, Y., Schwarz, P., et al.: The kaldi speech recognition toolkit. In: Workshop on Automatic Speech Recognition and Understanding (ASRU), No. EPFL-CONF-192584. IEEE (2011)
17. Rui, Y., Gupta, A., Grudin, J., He, L.: Automating lecture capture and broadcast: technology and videography. Multimed. Syst. **10**(1), 3–15 (2004)
18. Schulte, O.A., Wunden, T., Brunner, A.: Replay: an integrated and open solution to produce, handle, and distributeaudio-visual (lecture) recordings. In: Proceedings of the 36th Annual ACM SIGUCCS Fall Conference: Moving Mountains, Blazing Trails, pp. 195–198. ACM (2008)
19. Simonyan, K., Zisserman, A.: Two-stream convolutional networks for action recognition in videos. In: NIPS (2014)
20. Tan, Z.H., Lindberg, B.: Low-complexity variable frame rate analysis for speech recognition and voice activity detection. IEEE J. Sel. Top. Signal Process. **4**(5), 798–807 (2010)
21. Tugrul, T.O.: Student perceptions of an educational technology tool: video recordings of project presentations. Procedia-Soc. Behav. Sci. **64**, 133–140 (2012)
22. Viola, P., Jones, M.: Rapid object detection using a boosted cascade of simple features. In: CVPR (2001)

23. Zach, C., Pock, T., Bischof, H.: A duality based approach for realtime TV-L^1 optical flow. In: Hamprecht, F.A., Schnörr, C., Jähne, B. (eds.) DAGM 2007. LNCS, vol. 4713, pp. 214–223. Springer, Heidelberg (2007). https://doi.org/10.1007/978-3-540-74936-3_22
24. Zhang, C., Rui, Y., Crawford, J., He, L.W.: An automated end-to-end lecture capture and broadcasting system. ACM Trans. Multimed. Comput. Commun. App. (TOMM) 4(1), 6 (2008)
25. Zhang, K., Zhang, Z., Li, Z., Qiao, Y.: Joint face detection and alignment using multitask cascaded convolutional networks. IEEE Signal Process. Lett. 23(10), 1499–1503 (2016)

Towards Demographic-Based Photographic Aesthetics Prediction for Portraitures

Magzhan Kairanbay$^{(\boxtimes)}$, John See, and Lai-Kuan Wong

Faculty of Computing and Informatics, Center for Visual Computing,
Multimedia University, 63100 Cyberjaya, Malaysia
magzhan.kairanbay@gmail.com, {johnsee,lkwong}@mmu.edu.my

Abstract. Do women look at aesthetics differently from men? Does cultural background have an influence over the perception of beauty? Has age have any role in this? Psychological and art studies reveal striking differences in perception among various demographical aspects. This warrants attention particularly with the rapid growth in automatic evaluation of photo aesthetics. In this research, we investigate the influences of demographic factors of photographer towards the aesthetic quality of portrait photos from the computational perspective. An extended version of the large-scale AVA dataset was created with the inclusion of the photographers' demographic data such as location, age and gender. We trained several demographic-centric CNN models, which are then fused together as a single multi-demographic CNN model to learn aesthetic tendencies in a holistic manner. We demonstrate the efficacy of our model in achieving state-of-the-art performance in predicting portraiture aesthetics.

1 Introduction

In a recent study on beauty and the brain, Jacobsen [1] revealed that influences of demographic attributes such as history, culture, and individual differences are important determinants of aesthetics appreciation. In a particular eye-opening work, Masuda et al. [2] studied the aesthetics preferences of East Asians and Americans for portrait photographs and concluded that the Western societies prefer object-oriented attention whereas Ease Asians desire context-oriented attention in portraiture. Apart from cultural differences, Jacobsen [1] has highlighted that within cultures, individual differences such as age, gender, expertise (training in art), and education also influence aesthetics perception. Taunton [3] investigated the influence of age on preferences for subject matter, realism, and spatial depth in painting reproductions and found significant difference in preferences across different age group. In another interesting study, Cela-Conde et al. [4] infer that men and women use different strategies in assessing aesthetic preferences, where men focus on big picture and women pay more attention to local details. All these studies support Jacobsen's [1] findings that visual aesthetics perception is highly complex and is supported by highly-configured dynamic neural networks.

© Springer International Publishing AG 2018
K. Schoeffmann et al. (Eds.): MMM 2018, Part I, LNCS 10704, pp. 531–543, 2018.
https://doi.org/10.1007/978-3-319-73603-7_43

With the explosive growth of digital mobile cameras and social media that leads to vast amount of photographs being captured and shared everyday, computational aesthetics is receiving increasing research attention. Many state-of-the-arts aesthetics prediction models focus on classifying photographs as either aesthetically high or aesthetically low. Earlier traditional approaches utilize hand-crafted features [5–8] or generic descriptors [9] to predict aesthetic quality. More recently, with the availability of the large-scale Aesthetics Visual Analysis (AVA) dataset [10], researchers explored deep learning approaches [11,12] which were successfully in outperforming traditional methods by a good measure. Notably, most of these works focus on predicting aesthetics of generic photos; very few research works investigated the aesthetics of a specific category of photos such as portraits [13–15]. In addition, despite the significant influence of demographic attributes on aesthetics, little research [14] has considered capitalizing on these attributes to improve aesthetics prediction.

In this paper, we aim to investigate the influence of photographers' demographic profiles on aesthetics prediction of portrait images, from the computational perspective. As photographers with different demographic profiles have the tendency to perceive aesthetics differently, they may likely use different photographic techniques to capture and enhance their photographs. By identifying three demographic aspects of photographers: location, age, and gender, we first categorized the photos from AVA-Portraits dataset [14] based on newly extracted demographic information. Location is a notion closely related to culture and it can thus be an indicator of the influence of culture on aesthetics. We build a pair of convolutional neural network (CNN) models for each demographic aspect to capture intrinsic tendencies. We then combine these individual demographic-based CNNs (dgCNN) into a multi-demographic-based CNN (MdgCNN) as illustrated in Fig. 1. Experimental results demonstrate that our

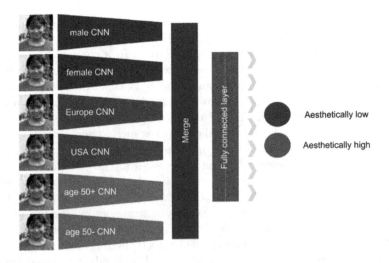

Fig. 1. Combining multiple demographic-centric CNNs for aesthetic prediction of portraitures.

proposed idea of learning demographic-centric models is one that is worth considering for subjective tasks such as the perception of aesthetics.

2   Related Work

Majority research in computational aesthetic focuses on investigation of generic photos. Little research has been performed on portrait photos. One of the earlier works that focus on portrait aesthetics [13] uses a feature set that combines template-based spatial composition features and highlight/shadow composition. According to the authors, the spatial composition features are more discriminative than highlight/shadow composition features.

Redi et al. [14] extracted a set of hand-crafted visual features based on compositional rules, semantics and scene content, basic quality metrics, portrait specific features and fuzzy properties. They highlighted that the main features that correlates with photo aesthetics are sharpness of facial landmark, contrast, exposure, uniqueness and originality. Their proposed model outperformed the method of Khan and Vogel [13] by 14.66% on the same dataset. Interestingly, their results show that demographic factors like race, gender and age of the person who are in the photo are uncorrelated with photo aesthetics. We believe that likely the correlation of culture, gender and age with photographic aesthetics lies on the photographers, and not in the person captured in the photo.

More recently, Kairanbay et al. [16] proposed a new model that employed the GoogleNet CNN model [17] with data augmentation. In their approach, the crops from the four corners and the face are feed forwarded to the GoogleNet and the layer before each softmax layer is used as the feature vector. These five feature vectors from the five crops is then concatenated to form the final feature vector and passed to a linear classifier for learning. The usage of the five crops helped to mimic the foreground-background compositional rules, which possibly contributed to the improvement in classification accuracy. However, the accuracy of their deep learning solution is only marginally better than Redi et al.'s [14] hand-crafted solution.

3   Dataset

The AVA dataset [10] is the benchmark dataset which is widely used in the photo aesthetic task. The dataset consists of 250K photos, where 230K photos are used for training and the remaining 20K photos are used for testing. Each photo is evaluated by an average of 210 users with an aesthetic score that ranges from 1 to 10. AVA dataset also provides other meta-data such as semantic tags, challenge ID and style information for each photo.

Redi et al. [14] extracted a subset of portrait images from the AVA dataset by filtering out photos that contain "Portrait" semantic tag and challenges that contain either one of these words: "Portraiture", "Portrait" and "Portraits" As some of the extracted photos do not contain real portraits, Face++ API [18] is used to filter out the non-portrait images. The final dataset (also coined as "AVA-Portraits" in [16]) consists of a total of 10,141 portrait photos.

3.1   AVA-Portraits+

The original AVA dataset does not have any information of the photographers'
demographic profile that is crucial in this research. Therefore, we set out to
extend the AVA-Portraits data by including additional data of three demographic
aspects: location, age and gender. We name this extended dataset, the "AVA-
Portraits+". The demographic profile for each photographer is extracted from
the DPChallenge web site, the original source of the AVA.

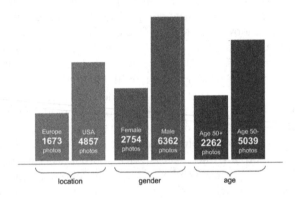

Fig. 2. The number of photos for the image subset of each demographic attribute in
AVA-Portraits+.

Figures 3, 4a and b illustrate the distribution of photographer locations, age,
and gender respectively on the full AVA dataset. From Fig. 3, we can observe
that USA (North America) and Europe are the two continents with significantly
larger number of photographers in DPChallenge. Due to lack of data from other
continents, our study on location is limited only to USA and Europe. We create
a bounding box for each continent and selected only photos from inside these
bounding boxes (See Fig. 3, hence omitting photos from other continents.

For the age data, Fig. 4a shows that there are some photographers whose age
are more than 100 or less than 5. In our experiments we ignore these outliers
and consider 15 and 85 as the minimum and maximum ages respectively. The
threshold is computed as the average of the minimum and maximum values, i.e.
50. We divide the dataset into two subsets: the first consists of images taken by
the photographers whose age is more or equal than 50, and the second subset
contains images captured by photographers whose age is less than 50.

Meanwhile, Fig. 4b shows that the number of male photographers are 2.3
times more than female photographers. Whilst the overall average aesthetic score
for males (5.45) is slightly higher than that for females (5.36), they are very
close to the mean aesthetic score (5.5) of the AVA-Portraits dataset. Figure 2
summarizes the amount of photos for each demographical subset of the AVA
Portraits+ dataset. Similar to that of the location and age data, the dataset is
also divided into two subsets for the male and female photographers.

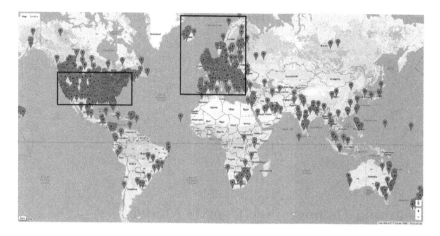

Fig. 3. The distribution of photographers' location in AVA dataset. Bounding boxes indicate the two regions where photos were selected.

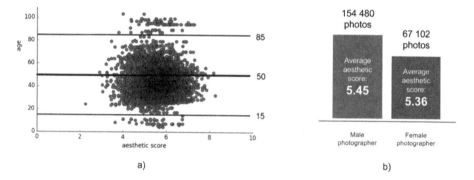

a)

b)

Fig. 4. (a) The distribution of photographers' age in AVA dataset. 85 and 15 are the upper and lower bounds, (b) The distribution of photographers' gender in AVA dataset.

Photographer-subject correlations. For further investigation into the AVA portraits+ dataset, we explore the correlation between the photographer and the subject in the photo (whose portrait was taken). Using the Face++ API [18] service, we detected the face region and demographic parameters (e.g. gender, race and age) of the subject in the photo. Table 1 depicts the demographic matches between the photographer and the subject in the photo; the numbers denote the percentage of portraits with the column attribute captured by a photographer with the row attribute. The rows indicate the photographer's demographic profile while the columns represent the subject's demographic profile. Analysis of Table 1 reveals that females often take photos of females than males, while European photographers tend to shoot portraits that are not necessarily smiling.

Table 1. Demographic attribute matching between photographer and subject in the AVA-Portraits+ photos.

	Male (%)	Female (%)	White (%)	Asian (%)	Black (%)	Smiling (%)	Avg. age
Europe	44.76	55.23	76.53	18.3	5.15	32.07	38.66
USA	43.2	56.79	76.25	17.86	5.87	39.07	36.51
Male	46.04	53.95	73.75	19.38	6.86	35.55	37.67
Female	37.02	62.97	77.11	17.69	5.18	39.42	35.53
age 50+	43.67	56.32	74.65	18.97	6.37	39.6	39.01
age 50−	42.45	57.54	75.86	18.86	5.27	35.97	35.42

4   Learning Demographic-Centric Models

AlexNet [19] is a well known deep Convolutional Neural Network (CNN) model that is effective at solving many complex computer vision tasks. Unlike its 'deeper' successors such as GoogleNet [17], the AlexNet consists of five convolutional layers and two fully connected layers followed by a final softmax layer. In this work, we opted for AlexNet as our base model as the data in this problem is only around 10K images and could very easily overfit a much deeper model. We hypothesize that finer grained features can be learned from specific subsets of a dataset, which can lead to better representation for subjective tasks such as photo aesthetics. We intend to uncover further understanding into whether better models can be learned if the photographers' intrinsic background properties can be untangled. As such, we propose to train demographic-centric CNN models on the subsets of the AVA-Portraits+ dataset to capture the natural inclinations of photographers based on their demographics profile.

4.1   Baseline Methods

The two handcrafted methods [13, 14] which were reported in [14] are used as the vanilla baselines for AVA-Portraits. We also establish a couple of deep learning baselines, which are based on transfer learning.

Firstly, we fine-tuned the ImageNet trained AlexNet CNN model [19], by replacing the final softmax layer with one that is of output dimension 2×1, corresponding to the two aesthetic classes (high and low). We use $\delta = 1.5$ setting[1], which results in around 16K photos selected for training. A classification accuracy of 75.15% was obtained on the test partition (20K photos) of the original AVA test set [10]. On the AVA-Portraits dataset, this fine-tuned CNN model attained a classification accuracy of 63.8% on a threshold value of 5.5 based on its mean rating [14], instead of 5.0 used in AVA. For fair comparison, we followed

---

[1] The authors of the AVA dataset [10] introduced the parameter δ to filter ambiguous photos during the training step; photos with average rating $[5 - \delta, 5 + \delta]$ are omitted. $\delta = 0$ in the testing step.

the same evaluation protocol and train-test partitions provided by the authors of the AVA-Portraits dataset [14].

In our second baseline, we took the first model and further fine-tuned it with only portrait photos (from AVA-Portraits) and yielded a 68.61% accuracy, which outperformed the baseline solutions [13,14] by around 4%, and also a recent work by [16] which employed deeply learned features but without transfer learning. Table 2 shows the classification accuracy of the baseline approaches and their corresponding dispersion errors. At this juncture, results showed that transfer learning is an appropriate technique to learn the aesthetics of portraits better.

Table 2. Aesthetic classification accuracy and dispersion error of the proposed methods compared against baseline methods.

Type	Methods	Accuracy (%)	Error ± (%)
HC	Khan et al. [13]	54.58	1.25
HC	Redi et al. [14]	64.24	1.76
DL	Kairanbay et al. [16]	65.33	1.01
DL	Fine-tuned CNN (AlexNet)	63.80	1.33
DL	Doubly-Fine-tuned CNN (AlexNet)	68.46	1.95

*HC: Handcrafted methods; DL: Deep learning methods

4.2 Demographic CNNs

The new AVA-Portraits+ dataset enables us to learn *demographic-based CNN* models, or **dgCNN** (in short from now on). For the six demographic attributes identified (see Fig. 2), we train a single dgCNN for each attribute individually, using samples from their respective subsets. In similar fashion to the transfer learning procedure reported earlier, we fine-tune our best model ("Doubly-Fine-tuned CNN") from Table 2 with samples from each attribute subset. A 5-fold cross validation approach is used for the evaluation of performance of the dgC-NNs. Figure 6 reports the classification accuracy of each dgCNN and its corresponding dispersion error.

To ascertain the benefits of our demographic-based sampling strategy, we randomly extracted the same number of photos from AVA, captured by photographers of the particular demographic for training purpose. We made sure there were no overlaps with the test portrait photos selected for each fold. This time round, the individual dgCNN models are trained with the randomly selected photos on the same network parameters and test set (per fold).

4.3 Multi-demographic CNNs

The demographic attributes learned from the dgCNNs can be fused together into a multi-demographic CNN model, or **MdgCNN** (in short from now on). As a photographer's profile can be of multiple demographic attributes (gender, age, location), we intend to capture the complex individual inclinations towards the aesthetic quality of portraits, all through one integrated two-level network.

Motivated by brain-inspired deep networks from [20], we attempt to learn the demographic attributes along a selected feature dimension independently by treating these dgCNNs as "parallel pathways", a concept derived from visual neuroscience. Using the individually pre-trained dgCNN models, we freeze the weights from all convolutional layers (1st to 5th) and only the fully connected (FC) layers are backpropagated during training. The activations at the respective FC layers (6th or 7th) of each dgCNN are taken as the learned demographic attributes. We merge (by concatenating) these activations together, before connecting to another FC layer which provides high-level association between features picked up at the dgCNN level and aesthetic quality. Figure 5 illustrates the architecture of the proposed model. We further experimented with an additional drop-out layer after the FC layer that is selected for merging, in order to introduce some regularization during training. All images have been feed forwadred in testing stage without taking into account its demographic attributes.

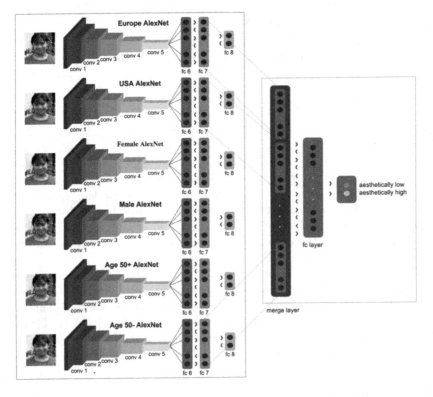

Fig. 5. The architecture of the proposed MdgCNN model

5   Results and Discussion

Figure 6 shows the aesthetic classification accuracy of the individual dgCNN models (Europe, USA, Female, Male, 50+, 50−) on their respective subsets of the AVA-Portraits+ dataset. The red markers indicate the average accuracy (across 5 folds) while the blue lines indicate the dispersion range (minimum to maximum). For comparison, we also furnish the results of the same models trained with randomly sampled photos of the same attribute. For all demographic attributes, the the classification performance of models trained with demographic specific data performed slightly better than models trained with random photos. The "USA" and "Female" attributes appear to have strong characteristics that relied on demographic-oriented samples to improve against random training samples. Attributes with larger dispersion error such as "Europe", "Female" and "Age 50+" could indicate more ambiguity in terms of what constitutes a good portrait.

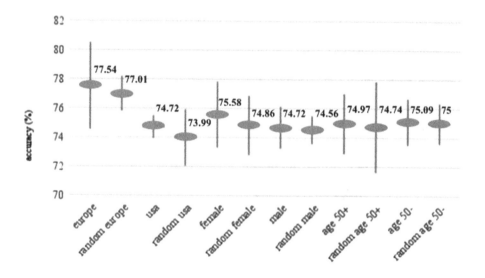

Fig. 6. Classification accuracy and dispersion errors of various dgCNN models and their respective models trained with random photos. (Color figure online)

Table 3 reports the state-of-the-art performance of our proposed MdgCNN architecture in comparison with other deep learning approaches in predicting aesthetics of portraitures. We achieve the best performance of 73.70% using the FC7 activations from the learned dgCNNs, outperforming our deep learning baseline by almost 5% albeit a marginally higher dispersion error. In both cases, adding a drop-out layer actually resulted in slightly poorer accuracy. It is crucial to mention that the results in Table 3 are for the evaluation of the entire AVA-Portraits+ dataset while results in Fig. 6 are only for each demographic subset, as outlined in Fig. 2.

Table 3. Aesthetic classification accuracy of the proposed MdgCNN method in comparison with other deep learning approaches.

Methods	Accuracy (%)	Error ± (%)
Kairanbay et al. [16]	65.33	1.02
Fine-tuned AlexNet (baseline)	68.46	1.95
MdgCNN (Merged FC6 w. drop-out)	73.10	2.92
MdgCNN (Merged FC6)	73.32	2.95
MdgCNN (Merged FC7 w. drop-out)	73.48	3.30
MdgCNN (Merged FC7)	**73.70**	3.08

Interestingly, the neurons from a specific dgCNN models are strongly activated if they contribute towards a portrait of high aesthetic score; this is akin to the MdgCNN responding towards a particular demographic attribute, and vice versa. Figure 7 depicts two sample photos of high and low aesthetic scores and their corresponding merged FC7 activations. The following figure (Fig. 8) shows some sample misclassified portrait photos. We observe that most of the false negatives (aesthetically high but misclassified as low) have unique composition or partial faces, while the false positives (aesthetically low but misclassified as high) used special effect filters such as sepia and grayscale.

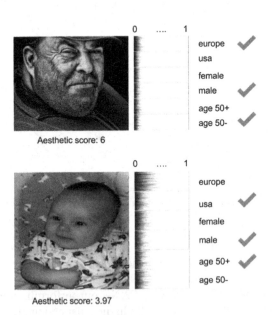

Fig. 7. Merged FC7 activations of dgCNNs for two sample photos. Ticks denote the photographer's profile.

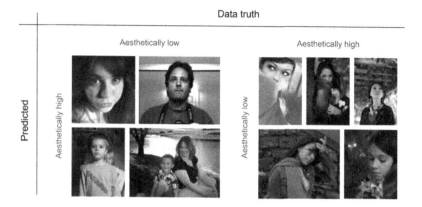

Fig. 8. Sample misclassified portraits.

Future Directions. This work presents an exploratory attempt at understanding the essence of individuality in the aesthetic quality of images, particularly portraitures, from the computational perspective. Current techniques have disregarded the aspect of the photographer which plays an important role, as we have shown in our experiments. We find Jacobsen's [1] observation of "differences in age and gender, within cultures" as a potential direction towards a more effective computational model. Our model lacks this hierarchical processing, as the simplistic merging of the dgCNNs can be improved. Also, unsupervised methods [20,21] that can capture latent information from these natural demographical tendencies, could be useful for learning disentangled factors.

Therefore, we would like to invite the research community to work on this aspect by making publicly available the AVA-Portraits+ demographic meta-data that we have extracted[2]. We also intend to release the similar meta-data for the full AVA dataset in the near future.

6 Conclusion

This paper investigates the influence of the photographer's demographic attributes such as location, age and gender on portrait photos. In order to do that, we extended the AVA-Portraits subset of the AVA dataset to include new demographical meta-data. We proposed to train demographic-based CNN models from sampled subsets of the data. By fusing together these individual models into a higher level network, we achieve state-of-the-art performance for aesthetic prediction of portraits, outperforming the vanilla baseline solution by around 5%. We envision great potential in the practical use of demographic-centric models to capture the natural inclinations of photographers of different profiles. In future, we intend to explore such multi-tiered architectures for other information such as image style, semantics and textual comments.

---

[2] AVA-Portraits+ demographic meta-data is available at https://goo.gl/jo13f3.

References

1. Jacobsen, T.: Beauty and the brain: culture, history and individual differences in aesthetic appreciation. J. Anat. **216**, 184–191 (2010)
2. Masuda, T., Gonzalez, R., Kwan, L., Nisbett, R.E.: Culture and aesthetic preference: comparing the attention to context of East Asians and Americans. Pers. Soc. Psychol. Bull. **34**, 1260–1275 (2008)
3. Taunton, M.: The influence of age on preferences for subject matter, realism, and spatial depth in painting reproductions. Stud. Art Educ. **21**, 40–53 (1980)
4. Cela-Conde, C.J., Ayala, F.J., Munar, E., Maestú, F., Nadal, M., Capó, M.A., del Río, D., López-Ibor, J.J., Ortiz, T., Mirasso, C., et al.: Sex-related similarities and differences in the neural correlates of beauty. PNAS **106**, 3847–3852 (2009)
5. Datta, R., Joshi, D., Li, J., Wang, J.Z.: Studying aesthetics in photographic images using a computational approach. In: Leonardis, A., Bischof, H., Pinz, A. (eds.) ECCV 2006. LNCS, vol. 3953, pp. 288–301. Springer, Heidelberg (2006). https://doi.org/10.1007/11744078_23
6. Ke, Y., Tang, X., Jing, F.: The design of high-level features for photo quality assessment. In: 2006 IEEE Computer Society Conference on Computer Vision and Pattern Recognition, vol. 1, pp. 419–426. IEEE (2006)
7. Luo, Y., Tang, X.: Photo and video quality evaluation: focusing on the subject. In: Forsyth, D., Torr, P., Zisserman, A. (eds.) ECCV 2008. LNCS, vol. 5304, pp. 386–399. Springer, Heidelberg (2008). https://doi.org/10.1007/978-3-540-88690-7_29
8. Lo, K.Y., Liu, K.H., Chen, C.S.: Assessment of photo aesthetics with efficiency. In: ICPR, pp. 2186–2189 (2012)
9. Marchesotti, L., Perronnin, F., Larlus, D., Csurka, G.: Assessing the aesthetic quality of photographs using generic image descriptors. In: 2011 IEEE International Conference on Computer Vision (ICCV), pp. 1784–1791. IEEE (2011)
10. Murray, N., Marchesotti, L., Perronnin, F.: AVA: a large-scale database for aesthetic visual analysis. In: 2012 IEEE Conference on Computer Vision and Pattern Recognition (CVPR), pp. 2408–2415. IEEE (2012)
11. Jin, X., Chi, J., Peng, S., Tian, Y., Ye, C., Li, X.: Deep image aesthetics classification using inception modules and fine-tuning connected layer. In: 2016 8th International Conference on Wireless Communication and Signal Processing (WCSP), pp. 1–6 (2016)
12. Deng, Y., Loy, C.C., Tang, X.: Image aesthetic assessment: an experimental survey. IEEE Sig. Process. Mag. **34**, 80–106 (2017)
13. Khan, S.S., Vogel, D.: Evaluating visual aesthetics in photographic portraiture. In: Proceedings of the Eighth Annual Symposium on Computational Aesthetics in Graphics, Visualization, and Imaging, Eurographics Association, pp. 55–62 (2012)
14. Redi, M., Rasiwasia, N., Aggarwal, G., Jaimes, A.: The beauty of capturing faces: rating the quality of digital portraits. In: Proceedings of 11th IEEE FG, pp. 1–8 (2015)
15. Lienhard, A., Ladret, P., Caplier, A.: Low level features for quality assessment of facial images. In: VISAPP, pp. 545–552 (2015)
16. Kairanbay, M., See, J., Wong, L.-K.: Aesthetic evaluation of facial portraits using compositional augmentation for deep CNNs. In: Chen, C.-S., Lu, J., Ma, K.-K. (eds.) ACCV 2016. LNCS, vol. 10117, pp. 462–474. Springer, Cham (2017). https://doi.org/10.1007/978-3-319-54427-4_34

17. Szegedy, C., Liu, W., Jia, Y., Sermanet, P., Reed, S., Anguelov, D., Erhan, D., Vanhoucke, V., Rabinovich, A.: Going deeper with convolutions. In: Proceedings of IEEE CVPR, pp. 1–9 (2015)
18. Megvii: Face++ - Leading face recognition on cloud. (http://www.faceplusplus. com/). Accessed 26 August 2016
19. Krizhevsky, A., Sutskever, I., Hinton, G.E.: Imagenet classification with deep convolutional neural networks. In: Advances in NIPS, pp. 1097–1105 (2012)
20. Wang, Z., Chang, S., Dolcos, F., Beck, D., Liu, D., Huang, T.S.: Brain-inspired deep networks for image aesthetics assessment. arXiv preprint arXiv:1601.04155 (2016)
21. Higgins, I., Matthey, L., Glorot, X., Pal, A., Uria, B., Blundell, C., Mohamed, S., Lerchner, A.: Early visual concept learning with unsupervised deep learning. arXiv preprint arXiv:1606.05579 (2016)

Triplet Convolutional Network for Music Version Identification

Xiaoyu Qi$^{(\boxtimes)}$, Deshun Yang, and Xiaoou Chen

Institute of Computer Science and Technology, Peking University,
Beijing, People's Republic of China
{xyqi,yangdeshun,chenxiaoou}@pku.edu.cn

Abstract. Music version identification has long been a difficult task in the music information retrieval field, due to the variations in tempo, key and structure. Most existing methods use hand-crafted features, which require extensive human efforts and expert participants to design the feature structures and further breakthrough is hardly achievable. Therefore, we propose a triplet convolutional embedding network for version identification, learning feature representations for music automatically in a supervised way. Triplet convolutional networks can learn segment-level features from training data, focusing on the most similar parts between music versions, rather than on the song-level. Furthermore, we compare triplet-based learning with pair-based learning. Our approach has two main advantages over existing ones: (1) Music features are embedded in an automatic and supervised way and the architecture is more promising as the music data keeps expanding; (2) Feature embedding on segment-level is more precise since the query audio can be any identifiable segment of a music work and the audio can have different lengths. Extensive experiments demonstrate the effectiveness of our method.

Keywords: Music version · Identification · Triplet network
Segmentation

1 Introduction

A version of a music piece is a new performance of a previous work. Given a query song, version identification aims to retrieve all the versions in a database. Music version identification (also called cover identification in the MIR literature) has wide application, especially in music copyright monitoring, while it remains challenging due to the variances in tempo, key, instruments, etc. For this reason, audio fingerprinting [18] can hardly be applied to this task. Previous work mainly focuses on extracting features from pitch class profiles or chroma [15], which well capture the tonal content, and have been proved to be more effective than original audio spectrum descriptors such as mel-frequency cepstral coefficients.

During the past decades, music version identification has been widely studied. Pitch histogram was a common and early-used feature in music information retrieval, proposed in 2003 by Tzanetakis et al. [19]. Bertin-Mahieux et

K. Schoeffmann et al. (Eds.): MMM 2018, Part I, LNCS 10704, pp. 544–555, 2018.
https://doi.org/10.1007/978-3-319-73603-7_44

al. [3] extracted hash code called 'jump code' from beat-aligned chroma, focusing on local features. Jensen et al. [10] used 2D autocorrelation and Bertin-Mahieux and Ellis [4] further applied 2D Fourier transformation magnitude coefficients as audio features, in order to capture the periodicity of music pitch and tempo changes. Adding general features of music pieces improves the results and Khadkevich and Omologo [12] took chord profiles as features. From then on, more methods, including information-theoretic measures of similarity [7], cognition-inspired descriptors [2] have been proposed with little performance improvement. Osmalsky et al. [14] combined nine different features with hierarchical rank aggregation, although further improved the performance but still not much. Dynamic time warping (DTW) [16] has state-of-the-art performance while it could not be applied to large scale due to large time complexity. Having seen the performance glass-ceiling for hand-crafted features, we turn to deep learning algorithms for their excellent learning capability to bridge the semantic gap in the long term.

Deep learning has recently been widely used for audio analysis, following its success in speech recognition [8], learning image descriptors [13], etc. Existing models using convolutional neural networks (CNN) for speech recognition and music segmentation have shown state-of-the-art performances. CNN is able to learn hierarchical features and is robust to distortions of input objects, which satisfies the need of version identification. But to our knowledge, the only existing work that employs deep learning to this problem is the one of Stamenovic [17], in which a stacked auto-encoder was applied to learn music features. The auto-encoder was trained in an unsupervised way, without any knowledge of music versions, so the learned features are not necessarily good for identification. In addition, the dataset used in the work is not a large scale one.

Version identification is basically a problem of melodic similarity metric learning. Our goal is to embed the music data to a feature space where the versions of a music track lie close to each other but far from music pieces which are not versions. To this end, we propose a triplet convolutional network to learn music representations from triplet inputs [9]. Each triplet consists of three music objects: a piece of music, a version, and another music piece which is not a version. Triplet network alternates convolution and pooling operations to extract features, and comprises two fully connected layers to transform extracted features into a lower dimensional space.

In most studies of music version identification, music tracks are represented as whole entities, regardless of its internal structure. Although a music track and its version do share some melody segments, they often have different parts too. With this representation, the alignment of shared melody between pieces cannot be assured, leading to mismatching between pieces. To avoid this risk, we conduct the learning process on segment-level instead of song-level, by ensuring that the first two objects of a triplet be comprised of nothing but the same melody segment. In order to prove the effectiveness of our approach, we conduct extensive experiments on a public data set [5]. The experimental results demonstrate our advantages over the hand-crafted features. Our contribution can be summarized into two points. (1) To our knowledge, this is the first time that a triplet deep learning method has been applied to music version identification. (2) We propose an end-to-end framework, a triplet convolutional neural network, which shall be applicable in large-scale commercial use.

2 Approach

2.1 Motivation and Problem Formalism

It is infeasible to consider a song as a class and deal with version identification as a classification problem, because there are millions of melodically unique songs and most songs have few versions. So we propose a novel approach to version identification in which a similarity metric is learned from the version pairs and non-version pairs specified in triplets. The objects in a triplet are song segments, mostly not whole songs. It is stipulated that the first two objects of a triplet are two versions of a recognizable melody segment of a song, and the third object a segment from another song.

We use chroma [15] as our input, which is the frame-level feature similar in spirit to a constant-Q except that pitch content is folded into a single octave of 12 discrete bins, each corresponding to a particular semitone.

Given a training set $\mathcal{D} = \{(a_i, v_i)\}_{i=1}^N$, where $a_i = \{e_{j,k}\}_{l \times d}$ is a music track chroma matrix, and v_i denotes the version it belongs to. $e_{j,k} \in [0,1]$ indicates different semitones. l is the audio duration and d is the number of semitones. Our goal is to learn a similarity metric $S(\cdot, \cdot)$ with $\mathcal{D}$ in order to make a prediction of the similarity degree given a new music pair (a_j, a_k).

Our framework includes two parts. First, we construct triplets set $\tilde{\mathcal{D}}$ from $\mathcal{D}$ on segment-level. $\tilde{\mathcal{D}} = \{(x_i, x_i^+, x_i^-)\}_{i=1}^N$, where x_i is a music segment, x_i^+ denotes a same version of x_i, while x_i^- represents a non-version one. Then, we embed music with a triplet-based network and form the similarity metric on the embedded feature.

2.2 Triplets Generation

It is a common case that one version of a song has a segment which has no counterpart in another version of the same song. Considering this, we adopt a similarity measurement which is based on segment level comparison, in order

Fig. 1. Triplets generation

to get a more detailed and precise measurement of melody similarity between music versions. Moreover, music tracks are initially represented by beat-aligned chroma sequences in our study, and therefore, music segments from different versions will have the same length of chroma sequences if the segments share the same melody.

Encoding

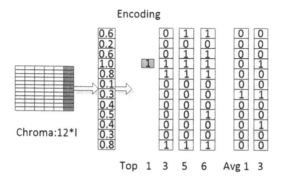

Chroma:12*l

Top 1 3 5 6   Avg 1 3

Fig. 2. Encoding

In our scheme, a training triplet consists of three distinct music segments, and it is assumed that the first two segments come from two versions of the same song and share the same melody, but the third segment has a different melody. Although we have datasets of music tracks in which version relations among tracks have already been labeled, building the training triplets of matching segments is not straightforward. Manually listening and labeling the pairs of matching segments in two versions of a song is time consuming and boring, so we design an algorithm to automatically find out in two versions the pairs of segments having the same melody and use those pairs as the first two segments of the training triplets.

The actual process is as follows. Firstly, the track of one version is divided into overlapping segments, and then for each of those segments, the most similar segment in the track of the other version is figured out. Finally, the pairs of matching segments with a similarity degree no less than a predefined threshold are selected to be used in triplets. We encode music tracks and build an index for efficient segment retrieval to construct triplets.

A song is originally represented as a sequence of beat-aligned chroma vectors. The sequence of beat-aligned chroma vectors is guaranteed robust to tempo variation in music tracks. For easy indexing and computational simplicity, chroma vectors are encoded into binary codes, in a way that the dissimilarity between two original vectors is well approximated by the Hamming distance between the two codes.

A binary code consists of two parts. One part of a code concerns the chroma vector itself, consisting of four 12-bit sub-codes. In each sub-code, the bits corresponding to the top m largest dimensions of the vector are set to 1 and others

0, with m being 6, 5, 3 and 1 respectively. In this way, the tonic is preserved, the triad and five chords are smoothed and the less significant half semitones are ignored for better noise immunity. The other part of a code represents the average of the neighbors of the vector, to be used later for key transposition prediction. The average vector is encoded in a similar way but with a lower resolution. As a result, a chroma vector is represented by a 64-bit binary code.

Create a music version dataset $\mathcal{D}$, in which song $a_i(i = 1, 2...N)$ is represented by a sequence of 64-bit codes. Based on the first parts of codes, we build a code index which indicates the occurrences of each unique code in all the songs.

Then, we divide a_i into segments $x_i, i = 1, 2...n$ of length l, with step size d (we further tested different l and d in the experiment). For each code in a segment x_i, find out through the index all occurrences of the code in a_j, and then, for each occurrence, calculate the Hamming distance between the x_i segment and the occurrence-aligned x_i^+ segment.

Generate pairs of similar music segments between x_i and x_i^+. Only segment pairs with a similarity larger than the threshold will be selected. For each similar segment pair, randomly select a chroma segment from a different song, to make a chroma segment triplet (x_i, x_i^+, x_i^-).

2.3   Triplet Embedding Network

Regarding to version identification, there exist thousands of kinds of music tracks which have different number of versions. It is hard to construct a model for each music track due to the small number of sample versions for a particular song. Thus, we learn by similarity metric and propose a triplet convolutional network.

Triplet-based network applies the CNN structure with 2 convolutional layers (the first including 20 filters and the second consisting 50, kernel size set to 3 and stride set to 1) and two max-pooling layers (kernel size and stride both set to 2). Rectified Linear Unit (ReLU) is used as an activation function following each convolutional layer. Batch Normalization is added after convolutional and

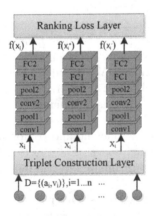

Fig. 3. Triplet network

before activation. Dropout of 0.5 is added after each pooling layer to prevent the network from overfitting.

We take the second fullly-connected layer feature as music embedding $f(x_i)$, with which we further learn the distance metric with cosine similarity proposed in [21], aiming to minimize the distance between similar audio segments. The similarity function is denoted as follows:

$$S(x_i, x_j) = f(x_i)^T f(x_j) / (||f(x_i)|| \times ||f(x_j||) \tag{1}$$

where parameters $x_i, x_j \in R^{d \times d}$, d stands for the dimension of features. The hinge loss [20] for a triplet and the whole dataset are defined in the form:

$$L_t(D; \theta) = \sum_{i=1}^{N} max(1 - S(x_i, x_i^+) + S(x_i, x_i^-), 0) \tag{2}$$

where θ represents all of the parameters in our model, and N denotes the number of training instances. θ is updated by back-propagation and each base network in the triplet network share the same architecture.

2.4   Siamese Embedding Network

For comparison of our research, we also turn to Siamese network [6], in which original images are mapped into another feature space where similar pairs lay relatively close. We conduct experiment with same network architecture to prove that learning with a triplet network outperforms siamese ones, since neural network learns better feature by comparisons of same versions and different versions. To be mentioned, triplet networks have better application prospect since labeled data with comparisons are easier to acquire. In this section, we detail the design of our contrastive siamese network.

We change the input data from triplets (x_i, x_i^+, x_i^-) to pairs (x_i, x_j), where (x_i, x_j) can be (x_i, x_i^+) or (x_i, x_i^-). We select music pairs of same and different versions as the input data for the siamese network, define the lable l as 1 for same versions and 0 for different ones. Then, we follow the same convolution and pooling strategies to process the music data. We calculate object distance with cosine distance in pairs. Without distance comparisons from triplets, we use the contrastive loss:

$$L_s(D; \theta) = \sum_{i=1}^{N} (1 - l)S(x_i, x_j) + (l)max(M - S(x_i, x_j), 0)^2 \tag{3}$$

where M is a parameter we set.

Contrastive loss becomes small when input pairs belong to the same ($l = 1$) category and lay relatively close in the embedded feature space. It punishes pairs of label 1 which lay far away and those "close" ones of label 0. In this way, we embed the music data into a new feature space which better demonstrate their semantic information.

2.5 Embedded Feature Identification

As to the testing part, given two audio chroma file (a_i, a_j), we clip them with a sliding window with different overlaps (including 0 overlap). The window size equals the segment length. For each clip x_i, we find its most similar version clip x_j and get a similarity value. We use the accumulated similarity score to represent the similarity degree for the two audio pieces. Also, we test with the max and average similarity scores of the two songs. Detailed experimental results are in the next section.

3 Experiments and Discussions

3.1 Dataset and Evaluation

We use the SecondHandSongs dataset (SHSD[1]) which is an official list of cover songs within the Million Song Dataset (MSD) [5] released in 2011. SHSD is the largest public cover song dataset up to now, including 18196 tracks in 5854 cliques.

We conduct the experiments with three parts of SHSD, which are common division for version identification task:

– **Train12960** Training set of SHSD, including 12960 tracks in 4128 cliques.
– **Query1500** A subset of Train12960 including 1500 songs, given in the form of 500 triplets (x_i, x_i^+, x_i^-).
– **Test5236** Testing set of SHSD, including 5236 music tracks in 1726 cliques.

For each song in MSD, we use the Echo Nest analyze API[2] to get beat-aligned chroma series. An intuitive vision for cover song chroma is shown in Fig. 4, with music patterns visually more similar between same versions.

We use three kinds of evaluation metrics:

– **Acc.** Acc stands for the ranking accuracy on Query1500. Given (x_i, x_i^+, x_i^-), we aim to get a smaller distance between (x_i, x_i^+) than (x_i, x_i^-). We calculate querying accuracy by comparing the similarity function results $S(x_i, x_i^+)$ and $S(x_i, x_i^-)$.

$$Acc = \frac{1}{N} \sum_{i=1}^{N} \gamma(S(x_i, x_i^+) - S(x_i, x_i^-)) \tag{4}$$

where $\gamma(c) = 1$ if $c > 0$ and $\gamma(c) = 0$ otherwise. N denotes the testing instance numbers.
– **AR.** AR stands for Average Ranking. Given a query song, we rank all songs in the dataset according to its distance from the query and calculate the average ranking. Lower AR denotes better results.
– **Top-k.** We calculate the number of correct versions that rank among top k in the database. In this experiment, k is set to 5, 10 and 100.

---

[1] http://labrosa.ee.columbia.edu/millionsong/secondhand.
[2] http://www.spotify.com.

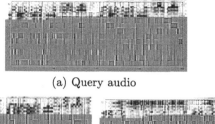

(a) Query audio

(b) Same version audio   (c) Different version audio

Fig. 4. Beat-aligned chroma

3.2 Ranking Task (Experiment on Query1500)

We clip the training audio. Then, we randomly sampled 10^6 triplets for training and 10^5 for testing, 10 to 100 times of our network parameter number complexity which is $O(10^4)$. The triplet network is implemented with caffe [11]. Empirically, we found improved results from raising the highest values relative to the lowest ones by a power-law expansion. We believe this accentuates the main patterns in the signal. In this experiment, we raise feature values to the power of 2.

The triplet network structure is described in Sect. 2.3. We test the model on the Query1500, which is a subset of Train12960. To avoid overfitting, we remove all the 1500 songs from the training set. We compare our approach with the existing methods using hand-crafted features. The experimental results are listed in Table 1.

Table 1. Performances on Query1500

Method	Acc
Random	50.0%
Pitch hist [19]	73.6%
Jump codes [3]	77.4%
DTW [16]	80.0%
Correlation [10]	76.6%
Cognitive [2]	73.2%
Triplet	**82.6%**

As is shown, triplet network features show better performance than other hand-crafted features.

3.3 Large Scale Retrieval Task (Experiment on Test5236)

Triplet-based network is also applicable for large-scale version identification. We further conduct experiment on Test5236 dataset.

Parameter Tuning. We conduct parameter tuning on three aspects: network structure, segment length and feature construction.

We custom the kernel size for audio features, filtering horizontally without doing convolution over different chroma bins. We set Triplet-1 (kernel size 3×3), Triplet-2 (kernel size 1×3) and Triplet-3 (kernel size 1×6), other network settings as described in Sect. 2.3. Then we test the proposed siamese network, in which the architecture keeps the same as that in the triplet one. The result in Table 2 shows that triplet network outperforms siamese one, with bettering learning capability via triplet comparison learning. We find that filtering horizontally without doing convolution over different semitone (Triplet-3) has better performance.

Table 2. Performances with different triplet network kernels

Method	Top-5	Top-10	Top-100	AR
Siamese-1	49	101	708	2100
Siamese-2	48	81	736	2087
Siamese-3	57	110	780	2010
Triplet-1	107	207	1415	1496
Triplet-2	97	184	1228	**1460**
Triplet-3	**149**	**270**	**1643**	1469

Due to the limitation of training data, our network is not relatively deep. We vary the layer structures and show the results in Fig. 5(a). Triplet-d1 has 1 convolution and 1 pooling layer, other settings the same as Triplet-d2, which is the current network. Triplet-d3 has 3 convolution and 3 pooling layers and Triplet-d4 has 4 for both. We find that deeper network performs slightly better, with Triplet-d3 being the best.

We then compare the effect of segment length on the feature learning results. The results are shown in Fig. 5(c). The performance of triplet network improves at first as segment length increases and then becomes worse. We get best results with segment of length 300.

To alleviate the influence of key transposition, we reconstruct the chroma vector in two ways. First, we double it in the vertical direction and change the size from $(n, 12)$ to $(n, 24)$, where n stands for chroma numbers in a music segment. Then, we transpose keys by one semitone at a time and repeat for 11 times. By stitching the original chroma matrix and 11 new ones vertically, we construct a new matrix with size $(n, 144)$.

As is shown in Fig. 5(d), increasing the chroma vector size improves the network performance, with the identical parts of music versions enhanced.

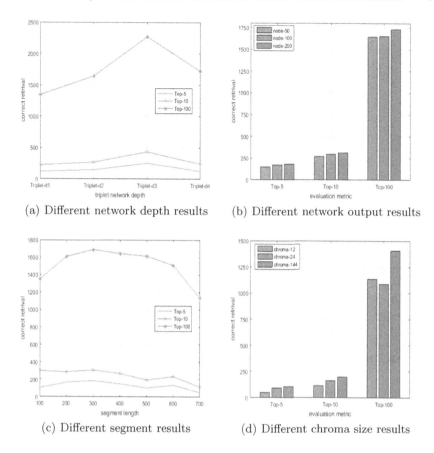

(a) Different network depth results   (b) Different network output results

(c) Different segment results   (d) Different chroma size results

Fig. 5. Performances with different segments and features

Comparison with Existing Methods. We turn to different kinds of basic machine learning algorithm, including nearest neighbors, clustered NN, multi layer perception (MLP), etc. [1] for comparison to our proposed triplet network.

The results in Table 3 demonstrate that our approach significantly increases the retrieval precision. Parts of the algorithms in the table are conducted in an unsupervised way, which may lead to relatively unsatisfactory results, such as Nearest Neighbors. With a non-precise given cluster number k, Nearest Neighbors and Clustered NN make use of spatial information of music pieces, comparing the distances between music features as triplet network and siamese network do, while they merely care for nearest neighbors or form rough clusters.

Triplet network and siamese network employ triplet or pairwise supervision information, which are more informative than traditional neural network, where information are given within a single sample, and the model is trained based on single data and label pair. Furthermore, the network structures of triplet network and siamese one is more complicated and well designed that multi layer perception, thus they demonstrate the best performance among all machine learning methods.

Table 3. Comparison on Test5236 with different existing algorithms

Method	Top-5	Top-10	Top-100
Random baseline	3.5	7	72
Nearest neighbors [1]	56	98	502
Clustered NN [1]	61	87	334
Neural network [1]	61	92	466
MLP [1]	74	111	542
Siamese	57	110	780
Triplet (Triplet-d3)	**255**	**436**	**2269**

It is obvious that given the same number of training samples, triplets tend to contain more information than pairs. With supervision information better utilized, it is reasonable that triplet network outperforms siamese one.

To summarize, among the machine learning methods, triplet network takes advantage of most supervision information with similarity comparison, given training music data and version pairs, and performs best in the experiment.

4   Conclusions

In this paper, we propose a triplet network for music version identification based on music segmentation. Our supervised network refines itself automatically, in contrast with methods based on hand-crafted features. Experiments on the current largest dataset have shown promising results.

We have conducted extensive experiments on the design of triplet convolutional neural network and compared it with siamese convolutional neural network, while there is still room for improvement. As the music data grows larger, triplet network shall be better designed (for example, with deeper network structure). It shall present better performance and may be applicable for industrial usage in the future.

Acknowledgments. This work was supported by the Natural Science Foundation of China (No. 61370116).

References

1. Aroma, M., Arijit, R., Bijaya, A., Granstedt, J.: Learning to listen matching song covers to original songs via supervised learning methods (2015). http://courses.cs. vt.edu/cs5824/Fall15/project_reports/mahendru_ray_adhikari_granstedt.pdf
2. Van Balen, J., Bountouridis, D., Wiering, F., Veltkamp, R.C., et al.: Cognition-inspired descriptors for scalable cover song retrieval. In: Proceedings of the 15th International Conference on Music Information Retrieval (2014)

3. Bertin-Mahieux, T., Ellis, D.P.: Large-scale cover song recognition using hashed chroma landmarks. In: 2011 IEEE Workshop on Applications of Signal Processing to Audio and Acoustics (WASPAA), pp. 117–120. IEEE (2011)
4. Bertin-Mahieux, T., Ellis, D.P.: Large-scale cover song recognition using the 2D Fourier transform magnitude. In: ISMIR, pp. 241–246 (2012)
5. Bertin-Mahieux, T., Ellis, D.P., Whitman, B., Lamere, P.: The million song dataset. In: ISMIR, vol. 2, p. 10 (2011)
6. Chopra, S., Hadsell, R., LeCun, Y.: Learning a similarity metric discriminatively, with application to face verification. In: 2005 IEEE Computer Society Conference on Computer Vision and Pattern Recognition (CVPR 2005), vol. 1, pp. 539–546. IEEE (2005)
7. Foster, P., Dixon, S., Klapuri, A.: Identification of cover songs using information theoretic measures of similarity. In: 2013 IEEE International Conference on Acoustics, Speech and Signal Processing, pp. 739–743. IEEE (2013)
8. Graves, A., Mohamed, A., Hinton, G.: Speech recognition with deep recurrent neural networks. In: 2013 IEEE International Conference on Acoustics, Speech And Signal Processing (ICASSP), pp. 6645–6649. IEEE (2013)
9. Hoffer, E., Ailon, N.: Deep metric learning using triplet network. In: Feragen, A., Pelillo, M., Loog, M. (eds.) SIMBAD 2015. LNCS, vol. 9370, pp. 84–92. Springer, Cham (2015). https://doi.org/10.1007/978-3-319-24261-3_7
10. Jensen, J.H., Christensen, M.G., Jensen, S.H.: A chroma-based tempo-insensitive distance measure for cover song identification using the 2D autocorrelation function. In: Fourth Music Information Retrieval Evaluation eXchange (2008)
11. Jia, Y., Shelhamer, E., Donahue, J., Karayev, S., Long, J., Girshick, R., Guadarrama, S., Darrell, T.: Caffe: Convolutional architecture for fast feature embedding. arXiv preprint arXiv:1408.5093 (2014)
12. Khadkevich, M., Omologo, M.: Large-scale cover song identification using chord profiles. In: ISMIR, pp. 233–238 (2013)
13. Lee, H., Grosse, R., Ranganath, R., Ng, A.Y.: Convolutional deep belief networks for scalable unsupervised learning of hierarchical representations. In: Proceedings of the 26th Annual International Conference on Machine Learning, pp. 609–616. ACM (2009)
14. Osmalsky, J., Van Droogenbroeck, M., Embrechts, J.J.: Enhancing cover song identification with hierarchical rank aggregation. In: Proceedings of the 17th International for Music Information Retrieval Conference (2016)
15. Serra, J., Gómez, E., Herrera, P., Serra, X.: Chroma binary similarity and local alignment applied to cover song identification. IEEE Trans. Audio Speech Lang. Process. **16**(6), 1138–1151 (2008)
16. Serra, X., Andrzejak, R.G., et al.: Cross recurrence quantification for cover song identification. New J. Phys. **11**(9), 093017 (2009)
17. Stamenovic, M.: Identifying cover songs using deep neural networks (2015)
18. Typke, R., Wiering, F., Veltkamp, R.C., et al.: A survey of music information retrieval systems. In: ISMIR, pp. 153–160 (2005)
19. Tzanetakis, G., Ermolinskyi, A., Cook, P.: Pitch histograms in audio and symbolic music information retrieval. J. New Music Res. **32**(2), 143–152 (2003)
20. Wan, J., Wang, D., Hoi, S.C.H., Wu, P., Zhu, J., Zhang, Y., Li, J.: Deep learning for content-based image retrieval: a comprehensive study. In: Proceedings of the 22nd ACM International Conference on Multimedia, pp. 157–166. ACM (2014)
21. Wu, P., Hoi, S.C., Xia, H., Zhao, P., Wang, D., Miao, C.: Online multimodal deep similarity learning with application to image retrieval. In: Proceedings of the 21st ACM International Conference on Multimedia, pp. 153–162. ACM (2013)

Two-Level Segment-Based Bitrate Control for Live ABR Streaming

Yujing Chen[1,2], Jing Xiao[1,3(✉)], Gen Zhan[1], Xu Wang[1], and Zhongyuan Wang[1,4]

[1] National Engineering Research Center for Multimedia Software,
School of Computer Science, Wuhan University, Wuhan 430072, China
Jing@whu.edu.cn
[2] Shenzhen Research Institute, Wuhan University, Wuhan, China
[3] Collaborative Innovation Center of Geospatial Technology,
Wuhan 430079, China
[4] Hubei Key Laboratory of Multimedia and Network Communication
Engineering, Wuhan University, Wuhan 430072, China

Abstract. Adaptive Bitrate (ABR) streaming has been widely used on OTT live streaming services. However, most OTT still use the traditional rate control developed for delivering a continuous bitstream, which can't achieve the best performance of ABR technology. In this paper, a two-level segment-based rate control for ABR streaming is proposed. In the segment level, we properly allocate the bits to frames depend on their types and content complexity; while in the picture level, the proposed algorithm controls the encoded picture size close to the allocated size by an improved rate prediction model. Experimental results on two representations demonstrated that the fluctuation of segment size generated from proposed algorithm can reduce from 7.615% to 0.76% compared to x264, and the PSNR can increase 0.92 dB in average.

Keywords: Adaptive Bitrate (ABR) · Rate control · Rate allocation
Segment size · Quality-of-experience (QoE)

1 Introduction

Recently, various multimedia services such as mobile streaming services, video conferencing, live video streaming platforms are developing rapidly. Over-the-top (OTT) live streaming services, such as YouTube, become more and more popular. And Cisco Visual Networking Index forecasts that video traffic will account for 82% of all consumer traffic and Content Delivery Networks (CDN) will reach two-thirds of all Internet traffic by 2020 [1].

With the rapid rising bandwidth and need of high quality-of-experience (QoE), live video streaming platforms require infrastructure updates and call for stable transmission over Adaptive Bitrate (ABR) streaming. In ABR streaming, the video is decomposed into small segments of 2 to 10 s length. Every video segment is encoded at multiple resolutions and bitrates, and then saved in small media files at the web servers or Content Delivery Networks (CDN). The video player used ABR technology on client

K. Schoeffmann et al. (Eds.): MMM 2018, Part I, LNCS 10704, pp. 556–564, 2018.
https://doi.org/10.1007/978-3-319-73603-7_45

adaptive selects an appropriate resolution of segment by the network and the performance of device [2–4].

According to the experience with ABR streaming, the following are the most affected objective metrics that capture the factors that influence the users' QoE.

(1) Overall video quality: The overall video quality directly affects QoE of users.
(2) Variations of segment sizes: Segment size determines downloading time under a certain bandwidth. The variation in the segment download times is critical for rate adaptation in low bandwidth environment [5]. If the segment size is bigger than targeted, the longer downloading time may result in stalling thus causing bad QoE to end users; on the opposite if the segment size smaller than the estimated size will produce poor video quality.

The rate control in encoder side plays a critical role in determining the performance of client platform used ABR technology. However, the traditional rate control method developed for delivering continuous bitstreams, such as average bitrate algorithm in x264, can't keep the segment size stable. To help ABR algorithms approach to their best performances, the segment size of each representation is ideally equal to the segment duration times the advertised bitrate. Thus we aim to develop a rate control algorithm that can provide the stable segment sizes.

To achieve this target, we develop a segment-based rate allocation algorithm. Inspired by the λ-domain rate control for HEVC [6], the bitrate is controlled through two levels in the proposed algorithm: segment level and picture level. In the segment level, the bits are properly allocated to pictures according to their types and content complexity; and in the picture level, the encoded picture size is controlled within a certain range of the allocated size. By adopting the two level rate control algorithm, we still allow variations on the frame sizes according to the requirement on high quality, but compromise the variations within a segment.

The proposed approach extents x264 by bringing the following main innovations:

- A novel bit allocation scheme based on segment. As fixed bits are assigned to each segment, the allocation is further implemented hierarchically to every picture in the segment according to the weight of the picture.
- To get a correct bit budget among pictures in a segment, prior information such as frame type and *SATD* cost obtained from x264 look ahead module is used to define the allocation. A new type of P frame is defined with larger weight than ordinary P frames, aim at improving the performance in cases of the scene changes and fast movement.
- We improved the prediction model in three aspects. First, we use weighting factors to compromise the prediction error from the mode. Second, only the contribution from last row is considered other than all previous rows, avoid the propagation of errors through rows. Third, re-coding of I frame and several rows of P and B frames is adopted to reduce QP fluctuations between rows.

The remainder of the paper is organized as follows: Sect. 2 describes the proposed algorithm. Experimental results are provided in Sect. 3. Section 4 is the conclusion.

2   Two-Level Segment-Based Rate Control

In this section, we give a detailed description of the proposed two-level segment-based rate control algorithm. Once the bitrate of video is appointed, the target size of segment can be computed by the segment duration times the bitrate. Then, the proposed rate control is conducted within each segment. The descriptions in this section is targeted at one segment.

Within each segment, the proposed rate control algorithm can be roughly divided into two steps. The first step is bit allocation at picture level, which will be elaborated in Sect. 2.1. The second part is how to achieve the pre-allocated bits for each picture, which will be introduced in Sect. 2.2.

2.1   Picture Bit Allocation at Segment Level

Picture Level Bit Allocation. Similar to bit rate control in HEVC [7], the bits are allocated according to the weight of each picture. Denote T_{Seg} is the target bit of current segment, the picture level target bits are calculated as:

$$T_{Pic} = \frac{T_{Seg} - B_{Coded}}{W_{Seg} - W_{Coded}} \times \omega_{PicCurr} \tag{1}$$

where B_{Coded} represents the coded bits of the current segment, W_{Seg} is the total weights of all the pictures in current segment, W_{Coded} denotes the accumulated weights of coded pictures. $\omega_{PicCurr}$ is the bit allocation weight of picture in the segment. In order to optimize video quality under a fixed segment size, we consider the hierarchical prediction structure and complexity of each picture to allocate bits more reasonably.

Picture Types and Weights. Base on the hierarchical prediction structure, x264 has four types of picture: I, P, B, B-ref. From the dependency between pictures, we give each type a weight factor indicates the significance of the picture. Considering that scene changes and fast movement create a great number of INTRA-coded macroblocks, result in P-pictures of large size, we separate P frames into two types, P_L and P_N. P_L frames are assigned with larger weight in order to allocate more bits to these large P frames. A typical P_L frame normally has large $SATD$ cost, it is detected by comparing its $SATD$ cost to the $SATD$ cost of last P_N frame $SATD_{last}$ and average $SATD$ cost of all coded P_N frames $SATD_{avg}$. And the weight used in our test are shown in Table 1. Those are experienced values calculated by counting the actual coded bits of frames in some test videos.

$$SATD_i > 3 \cdot SATD_{last} \quad \&\& \quad SATD_i > 1.5 \cdot SATD_{avg} \tag{2}$$

Estimation and Update of Total Weights. *The total weights of following pictures are calculated before bit allocation.*

Table 1. Pre-defined weight of picture

Type of picture	I	P_L	P_N	B	B-ref
Weight	120	80	20	5	3

$$W_{Seg} = \sum_{AllFramesInSegment} N_j \cdot \omega_j \tag{3}$$

where N_j denotes the number of each type of pictures and ω_j is the corresponding weight. With the change of video content, numbers of B frames and P frames are adaptive using b-adapt strategy of x264, we have to make an approximate estimation about number of each type of pictures. The numbers of P frames and B frames are predicted by the percentage of P and B in future 30 pictures computed by look ahead from start of segment. And we use the number of P_L frame in last segment as the predicted number of current segment.

During the encoding procedure, the total weights is updated to improve accuracy of bit allocation. To update number of P frames, after the encoder has coded 30 pictures from beginning of segment, each time it encounters a P frame, the actual percentage of P frames in current coded pictures is used to fix the total weights. In order to update the number of P_L frame N_{PL}, $\sum N_j$ denotes total number of pictures in segment, we check the number of appeared P_L frame at intervals of $\sum N_j/(N_p + 1)$ frames during encoding. Each time if P_L frame does not appear as expect, we update total weights by subtracting weight of P_L frame ω_{PL} from total weights.

2.2 Rate Control at Picture Level

As classic buffer-based rate control schemes used in ABR cannot accurately control the size of each frame, in order to approach to the assigned bits, we predict the size of current picture using a linear prediction model inherited form x264, and we adjust the quantization parameters in row level to make predicted picture size match the allocated bits. The predicted size of current picture can be predicted by

$$Pred = B_{RowCoded} + Pred_{Uncoded} \tag{4}$$

where $B_{RowCoded}$ is the total size of coded rows, $Pred_{Uncoded}$ is the size of all uncoded rows predicted with QP of current row determined by

$$Pred_{Uncoded} = \sum_{UncodedRows} \frac{coeff \times SATD_i + offset}{q \times count} \tag{5}$$

where $coeff$, $offset$, $count$ are parameters of the prediction model, unlike x264, these parameters are updated according to the actual bits and QP of last coded row rather than all coded rows, q denotes $qscale$ value of current row converted from QP.

$$qscale = 0.85 \times 2^{(QP-12)/6} \qquad (6)$$

Therefore, to improve performance, we reserve the adaptive quantization and MB-tree method from x264. The rate control schemes of our method are presented in Fig. 1.

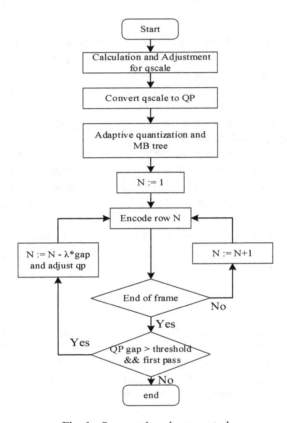

Fig. 1. Segment-based rate control

Because of the prediction error, in some pictures the upper rows are coded with small amount of bits while the majority of allocated bits are left to few rows in bottom of picture, result in bit rate waste, quality degradation and dramatic QP fluctuations between rows. We suppress these bad effects by using pre-weighting process and re-coding method.

Pre-weighting. In order to prevent uneven bit allocation between rows, weighting factors have been used in the adjustment of row QP. The upper rows are encoded with more bits and lower rows with less bits by scaling the target bits using weighting factors during the adjustment. The weighting factors can be determined by

$$\omega_y = 1 + (1 - y/n) \times \alpha \tag{7}$$

where ω_y is weighting factor of y_{th} row, n denotes the total number of rows, α is a predefined coefficient. In our experiments, α is set to 0.5.

Re-coding for I Frame and Rows. To reduce dramatic QP fluctuation between rows, we recode each I frame with recalculated QP because of its significance in prediction. For P and B frames, we recode a certain number of rows from bottom according to the magnitude of fluctuation. The number of recode rows is determined by QP gap between last two rows as the prediction error of each row are cumulated to bottom rows. The QP used in recoding process is converted from recalculated *qscale* which is calculated by

$$qscale_{Rec} = \frac{\sum\limits_{Rec} SATD_y}{\sum\limits_{Rec} (SATD_y / qscale_y)} \tag{8}$$

where $qscale_{Rec}$ is the recalculated *qscale*, $SATD_y$ and $qscale_y$ is the *SATD* cost and *qscale* value of y_{th} row.

3   Experiment

3.1   Experience Setup

In the experiment, four HEVC official tested sequences including "FourPeople", "Johnny", "KristenAndSara", "Vidyo" are connected to a bitstream with up to 2400 pictures, and the source bitstream is of 720p60 at 1 mbs. We transcode the bitstream into 240p60 and 480p60 to verify proposed method. In our experimental settings, the segments count from the first picture, namely every segment starts from I frame. Therefore, the source bitstreams can be split into 20 segments with 120 pictures per segment.

The proposed is developed based on the open source encoder x264 (libx264 (v20161024.2245) for FFmpeg (v3.1.5) on Linux). To verify proposed method, we compared our methods with the original x264. The experiments are conducted on a workstation with four-core CPU (Xeon(R) @3.10 GHz * 4) and RAM 4 GB that is also used to measure the computational complexity of our method.

3.2   Results and Analysis

In this part, we present comparisons of the results from proposed algorithm and x264 in objective aspects. The results are presented in two aspects: segment size, PSNR.

Fluctuations of Segment Sizes. The purpose of this work is to generate stable segment size under the constraint of stable PSNR, so we present the results of segment sizes first (Fig. 2). Statistics on the average size and its standard deviation (STD) is shown in Table 2. From Fig. 2 we can see that in two representations the yellow line which represent segment sizes of our method distribute around the target bits. And the yellow line is more close to the target bit than the blue line. Thus, our algorithm obtains more stable segment sizes than x264. Table 2 gives a more accuracy analysis of segment sizes. From the table we can see that the average segment sizes of our method in two different resolutions are closer to the target bits. And the STD values of our method also obtain significant reduction from x264. Ratio between STD and the target bits is used to measure fluctuations of segment sizes. Fluctuation of the proposed method on two representations range from 0.84%–2.2% whilst the fluctuations of x264 range from 6.05%–9.18%. From above analysis we can see that the proposed method obtains more stable segment size which is more suitable for living streaming.

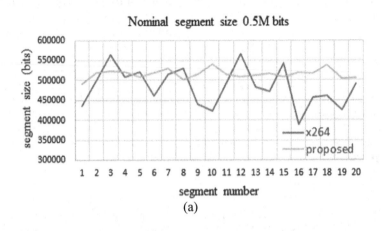

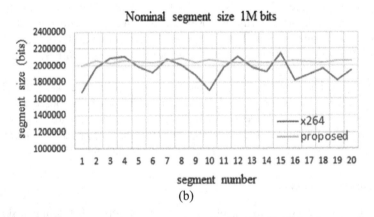

Fig. 2. The result of segment size. (a) 240p60. (b) 480p60 (Color figure online)

Overall Video Quality. As mentioned above, the generation of stable segment size should under the constraint of stable and high PSNR. Table 3 gives the comparison of PSNR from the proposed method and x264. The proposed method can generate higher PSNR compared on x264 on all representations with a bit increment in the final bitrate

Table 2. Comparison of segment size

Representation	Target (K bits)	Average size (K bits)		STD (K bits)		STD/Target (%)	
		Proposed	x264	Proposed	x264	Proposed	x264
240p60	500	503.38	472.25	11.02	45.91	2.20	9.18
480p60	2000	1997.80	1902.66	16.69	120.95	0.84	6.05

Table 3. Comparison of PSNR

Representation	PSNR (dB)		
	Proposed	x264	Improvement
240p60	42.56	41.07	1.49
480p60	43.48	43.13	0.35

and a little more time cost. The lower the resolution is, the high the improvement. On the representation of 240p60, the increment of PSNR achieves 1.49 dB.

In general, the proposed method can obtain more stable segment size than x264 and higher PSNR under the constraint computational cost. The average fluctuation of segment sizes in two resolutions reduce from 7.615% to 0.76%, and the average PSNR increased from 42.1 dB to 43.02 dB.

4   Conclusions

To meet the requirement of stable segment sizes for live ABR streaming, a two-level segment-based bitrate control algorithm is proposed. When implemented in the open source encoder x264, we can achieve very stable segment sizes with the bitrate approaching the target bitrate. The overall PSNR has an improvement of around 0.9 dB for 2 transcoded representations. However, a little more time is cost. With the proposed method, the downloading time can be more accurately estimated, thus highly reduce to stalling during playback. Our segment-based control concept can also be implemented in x265 or other encoders for their adaptations for live ABR streaming.

Acknowledgement. This work was supported by Science and Technology Program of Shenzhen (JCYJ20150029092); Hubei Province Technological Innovation Major Project (2016AAA015, 2017AAA123); EU FP7 QUICK Project under Grant Agreement No. PIRSES-GA-2013-612652; National Natural Science Foundation of China (61671332, 61671336); Applied Basic Research Program of Wuhan City (2016010101010025).

References

1. Cisco Visual Networking Index: Forecast and Methodology, 2015–2020, white paper, Cisco (2016)
2. Pires, K., Simon, G.: Dash in twitch: adaptive bitrate streaming in live game streaming platforms. In: Proceedings of the 2014 Workshop on Design, Quality and Deployment of Adaptive Video Streaming. ACM (2014)
3. Wei, S., Swaminathan, V.: Low latency live video streaming over HTTP 2.0. In: Proceedings of Network and Operating System Support on Digital Audio and Video Workshop, p. 37. ACM (2014)
4. Nam, H., Kim, K.H., Calin, D., Schulzrinne, H.: Youslow: a performance analysis tool for adaptive bitrate video streaming. ACM SIGCOMM Comput. Commun. Rev. **44**(4), 111–112 (2015)
5. Juluri, P., Tamarapalli, V., Medhi, D.: QoE management in DASH systems using the segment aware rate adaptation algorithm. In: 2016 IEEE/IFIP Network Operations and Management Symposium (NOMS), pp. 129–136. IEEE (2016)
6. Li, B., Li, H., Li, L., Zhang, J.: λ Domain rate control algorithm for high efficiency video coding. IEEE Trans. Image Process. **23**(9), 3841–3854 (2014)
7. Sullivan, G.J., Ohm, J., Han, W.J., Wiegand, T.: Overview of the high efficiency video coding (HEVC) standard. IEEE Trans. Circ. Syst. Video Technol. **22**(12), 1649–1668 (2012)
8. Wiegand, T., Sullivan, G.J., Bjontegaard, G., Luthra, A.: Overview of the H. 264/AVC video coding standard. IEEE Trans. Circ. Syst. Video Technol. **13**(7), 560–576 (2003)

Uyghur Text Localization with Fast Component Detection

Jianjun Chen[1,2], Hongtao Xie[3(✉)], Yue Hu[1,2], and Chenggang Yan[4]

[1] Institute of Information Engineering, Chinese Academy of Sciences, Beijing, China
[2] School of Cyber Security, University of Chinese Academy of Sciences,
Beijing, China
[3] School of Information Science and Technology,
University of Science and Technology of China, Hefei, China
htxie@ustc.edu.cn
[4] Institute of Information and Control, Hangzhou Dianzi University,
Hangzhou, China

Abstract. Text localization in image often is an important part of image content analysis and has broad application prospects. Even though there have been many researches focus on it, fast Uyghur text localization in complex background images is still a challenging task. The obstacles mainly come from the huge extracted candidates and the heavy computation of non-text classification. In this paper, we propose a fast framework for Uyghur text localization which handle above obstacles with two effective measures. One is that we propose a stroke-specific detector based candidate extraction scheme. Compared with the common used I-MSER detector, the presented scheme not only produces 2 times less components but also runs in twice faster. The other is a component similarity based clustering is raised, which neither need the component-level classification nor the extra computations. The experiments confirm that our method has achieved the state-of-the-art on UICBI-500 benchmark dataset and runs in near real-time. The localization results also prove that the proposed method is robust to Chinese and English.

Keywords: Uyghur · Text localization · FAST keypoint
Complex background images

1 Introduction

Uyghur text localization in complex background images has broad application prospects and there are many researches have achieved huge success [1]. But how to improve the speed and accuracy for the actual application is still a tough challenge. The first reason is that text locations in images are uncertain, the exhaustive search is time-consuming and produces a lot of candidates. The other is that the text candidates contain a lot of non-texts and the computation of text/non-text classification is heavy. Meanwhile, since the complex background

© Springer International Publishing AG 2018
K. Schoeffmann et al. (Eds.): MMM 2018, Part I, LNCS 10704, pp. 565–577, 2018.
https://doi.org/10.1007/978-3-319-73603-7_46

and variation of Uyghur text, such as font, size and color, it is difficult to find an effective method to distinguish text or non-text.

The earlier works for text localization in complex background images are roughly classified into two categories, the sliding window classification method and connected component analysis [2]. The sliding window based methods detect texts via shifting a window on multiple scales image [3–8]. The sweeping search of sliding window often achieves a high *recall*, but it needs an expensive time-cost. This is a reason of connected component analysis becomes popular. The connected component analysis usually extracts text candidates at first and the maximally stable extremal regions (MSER) is a popular extractor [9–12]. And then a text/non-text classifier is utilized to select text regions. These methods have achieved the state of the art on ICDAR 2011 dataset [11]. However, the MSERs contain a large number of repetitions and non-text candidates, which bring about the process of candidates classification is time-consuming.

In this paper, we propose a fast Uyghur text localization method which provides an efficient solution to deal with above difficulties. To quickly and accurately extract components, we put forward a FAST-like keypoint which is a stroke-feature constrained FAST. Then the component is found by a simple flood-fill algorithm with the keypoint. The detected components are constructed into lines via a component similarity clustering and the non-text lines are filtered out by a line classifier. The main contributions of this paper are:

1. We propose a FASTroke keypoint detector, which is a stroke-specific detector and can effectively discover the stroke endings, crosses and bends. The FASTroke keypoint has two advantages, as a FAST-like keypoint it can be quickly detected and as a stroke-specific detector it extracts less non-text components.
2. To construct text line candidates, a component similarity clustering algorithm is recommended. It is a two-stage clustering, in the first stage components lie on the same horizontal are organized into a group. For each group, components are clustered as line candidates in accordance with component similarity.
3. We present a novel framework for Uyghur text localization in complex background images. In this framework, the component-level classification is no longer included, which averts text components lose and extra computation.

As an additional contribution, a new benchmark dataset UICBI-500 is detailedly recommended in Sect. 3.1. The experimental component extraction results show that, compared with the common used I-MSER detector, the FAS-Troke based component extractor generates 2 times less components and runs 2 times faster. The proposed method f-measure achieves 74.4%, which improves the compared method with 11.2% on UICBI-500 dataset. The last but not least, the fast Uyghur localization framework runs almost 16 times faster than the method in [13].

The remainder of this paper is organized as follows: Sect. 2 recommends the proposed fast Uyghur text localization framework. The experimental evaluation

as well as discussion of each phase are covered in Sect. 3. Finally, we conclude
the paper in Sect. 4.

2   The Proposed Method

The flowchart of the proposed method is illustrated in Fig. 1. The proposed
method consists of five stages: the keypoint detection, the component extraction,
the component clustering, the line construction and the text line classification.
Given an image, the FASTroke keypoints are firstly detected. Then, a simple
flood-fill algorithm is employed to discover components. After that, the candidate
lines are constructed by component clustering. Finally, the non-text lines are
filtered out by a text line classifier and the survivors are texts.

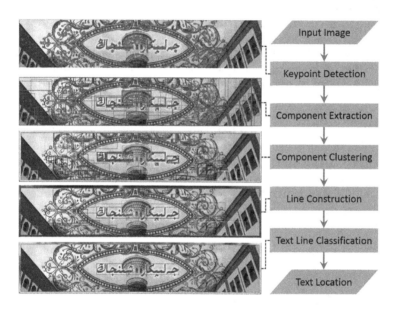

Fig. 1. Flowchart of the proposed method and corresponding results of each step.

2.1   FASTroke Keypoint Detector

We observed that there are three types of stroke feature in characters, which
are stroke endings, crosses and bends, as shown in Fig. 2(a). The classical FAST
keypoint [14] can respond to the stroke endings, such as the tail of "9". But it
loses the characters without stroke endings, such as "o, 0". Besides, the FAST
keypoint detector is not a text-specific keypoint detector and produces numerous
non-text candidates.

Hence, we propose a stroke-specific detector – the FASTroke keypoint detector, which is able to effectively catch characters and generates less candidates.

The FASTroke keypoint detector defines three types of keypoint for the three stroke features. The acute-angle keypoint correspond to the stroke ending, such as Fig. 2(b). The right-angle keypoint fires on the stroke cross as shown in Fig. 2(c). The obtuse-angle keypoint correspondingly lies on the stroke bend which is exhibited in Fig. 2(d). Following are the details of FASTroke keypoint detector.

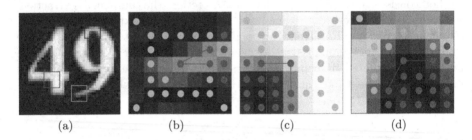

(a)   (b)   (c)   (d)

Fig. 2. (a) The three types of stroke feature. (b) The acute-angle keypoint correspond to stroke ending. (c) The right-angle keypoint correspond to stroke cross. (d) The obtuse-angle keypoint correspond tostroke bend.

For each pixel p, we defined a template to verify it belongs to which kind of keypoint. The detector template is a 7×7 rectangle, as shown in the Fig. 3(a). The center pixel of the template is the keypoint candidate p, which is marked as red. The pixels around p are grouped into 4 areas, the inner area is marked as gray, the middle area is marked as yellow, the outer area is marked as blue and the template corners are marked as green. Each pixel x in these areas is mapped into one of three values: 0, 1 and 2. The mapping function is defined as follows:

$$L(p, x) = \begin{cases} 1 & if \quad I_p - I_x \geq threshold \\ 0 & if \quad |I_x - I_p| < threshold \\ 2 & if \quad I_x - I_p \geq threshold \end{cases} \qquad (1)$$

where I_p is the image intensity value of p and *threshold* is a margin parameter. The value 1 means x is darker than p, 0 means x is similar to p and 2 means x is brighter than p.

At first, pixels in the middle area are examined. The pixel p is a keypoint candidate if there exists two contiguous sets P_0 and P_1 (or P_0 and P_2) such that $|P_0| < 8$. Then, according to $|P_0|$ the pixel p is labeled one of three kinds keypoint candidate. To further confirm p is text relevant, the corresponding pixels in the inner and outer area are checked. This text relevance examination includes two rules, the internal continuity rule and the external distinction rule. The internal continuity rule ensures the keypoint is a stroke ending rather than a isolated point. The external distinction rule is used to check the continuity of background. The details of the three types FASTroke keypoint are respectively described as follows.

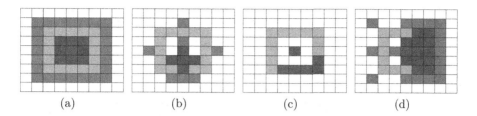

Fig. 3. (a) The detector template. (b) The acute-angle keypoint. (c) The right-angle keypoint. (d) The obtuse-angle keypoint. (Color figure online)

For the acute-angle keypoint $|P_0| \in \{1, 2, 3, 4\}$. The Fig. 3 shows three cases of the acute-angle keypoint. In the case of Fig. 3(b), $|P_0| = 1$, the pixel of P_0 is marked as red. The internal continuity verification refers to the inner (gray) and outer (blue) areas. Both in the inner and outer area, if the all of these pixels (c) are not satisfy $L(p, c) = 0$, then the current point p don't be kept. In the external distinction verification stage, the green pixels are examined, if there exist any pixels (c) which are not satisfy $L(p, c) = L(p, x)$, where x is the pixel in yellow area, then p not is a acute-angle keypoint.

The right-angle keypoints mainly fire on the stroke cross, such as "T, 4, G", as shown in Fig. 2(c). In this case $|P_0| = 5$, but $|P_0| = 5$ can't always get a regular right-angle keypoint, as can be seen from Fig. 3(c). So the regular right-angle keypoint just includes 8 cases. In the case of obtuse-angle keypoint $|P_0| \in \{6, 7\}$. The Fig. 3(d) shows three obtuse-angle keypoint verification cases. Different from the acute-angle keypoint, the internal continuity verification is more strict. In the gray area, there exist at least two contiguous pixels are similar to the center, else the current point p not is a obtuse-angle keypoint.

After the three types keypoint are detected, each type keypoints will pass a simple non-maximum suppression which is performed on a 3×3 neighborhood. Only the keypoint with the highest response is kept.

2.2 Text Component Extraction

Our text component extraction is based on the assumption that the text component has internal consistency and external distinction. According to this assumption, we can get a text component just via finding a point in it. Once we get a point of the text component, we can get the whole component via local consistency flood-fill. The seed and the similarity threshold θ are two keys which are adaptively obtained by the FASTroke keypoints. The component extraction process and results are illustrated in Fig. 4.

For the seed selection, the acute-angle keypoint can directly be viewed as a seed. Since the stroke is surrounded by P_1 or P_2, the pixel p just to be the seed point of flood-fill, as shown in Fig. 5(a). In consideration of the peculiarity of the right-angle and obtuse-angle keypoints, the seed of flood-fill is slightly different to the acute-angle keypoint. For the cases of the right-angle and obtuse-angle keypoints, the keypoint may not hit the stroke.

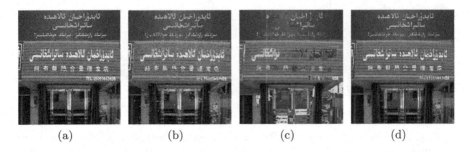

Fig. 4. (a) The source images. (b) The FASTroke keypoint detection results, the acute-angle keypoints are marked as green, right-angle keypoints as red and obtuse-angle keypoints as blue. (c) The flood fill results. (d) The bounding boxes. (Color figure online)

For example, in Fig. 5(b), the blue keypoint hit the letter "T" but the red one is not. Since we have no idea where the keypoint fires on, both these two direction should be take into consideration. Thus, both the keypoint and the middle pixel of P_1 or P_2 are regarded as a seed, as is illustrated in Fig. 5(c). If the keypoint is a dark point, then the middle pixel is a bright point, and vice versa.

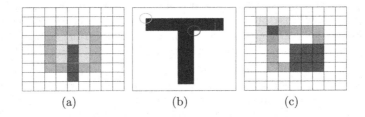

Fig. 5. The flood-fill models. The red pixel is the seed of flood-fill. (Color figure online)

For the θ decision, there are two cases: the stroke is brighter than the background and the contrary case. Given a bright keypoint, the similarity threshold θ_1 is above the extreme intensity value of pixels in P_1.

$$\theta_1 = \max(I_x) + 1 \mid x \in P_1 \tag{2}$$

Correspondingly, given a dark keypoint, the similarity threshold θ_2 is below the extreme intensity value of pixels in P_2.

$$\theta_2 = \min(I_x) - 1 \mid x \in P_2 \tag{3}$$

The proposed component extraction is an effective method for the majority of text candidate discovery. However, the loss of few text candidate is unavoidable, because of sometimes the FASTroke can't find a threshold in a low image contrast. Some of the lost candidate will be found back in the text line construction stage, whose detail is explained in Sect. 2.3.

2.3 Text Line Construction and Classification

Text Line Construction. The text line construction can be viewed as a component clustering algorithm. According to works in [15,16], text lines construction can be clustered by component local feature. The text line construction method mainly contains three part: the heuristic rule based noise-reduction, the component clustering and the line optimization. Figure 6 shows the process of line construction and classification.

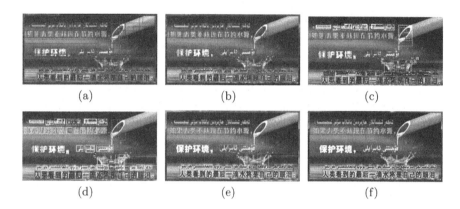

Fig. 6. The process of line construction and classification. (a) The extracted components. (b) The heuristic rules filtration result. (c) The horizontal grouping result. (d) The final clustering result. (e) The text line candidates. (f) The final text lines.

After the components are extracted, some heuristic rules are applied to remove the obvious non-text component. First, the components with too small or too big size are not text component, that is $10 \leq w_c \leq w_i/2$ and $10 \leq h_c \leq h_i/3$, where w_c is the width of component and h_c is the height, w_i is the width of image and h_i is the height. Second, the aspect ratio (r) of a text component in the range of $0.2 < r < 5$, $r = h_c/w_c$. These heuristic rules are beneficial to candidate reduction, and partly suppress the false positives.

The component similarity clustering is a two-stage algorithm, which includes a grouping stage and a clustering stage. In the grouping stage, since Uyghur text popularly is horizontal layout, our method mainly handles the horizontal texts. So the extracted components are organized into a group via horizontal position relativity. In the clustering stage, components are clustered into lines with component similarity which includes size, color and aspect-ratio. At first, the components in a group with too small or too large size are separated and the average width of the rest components is regarded as a character width (w_c). Then the components which have adjacent position and uniform color are clustered into a line candidate.

Text Line Classification. Since there are not existed a component-level text/non-text classification, the constructed line candidates contain some non-text lines which is inevitable. After the line construction, a line classifier is used to distinguish text/non-text lines. An example of text line classification is shown in the Fig. 6(e) and (f). Since Uyghur text has abundant texture feature, the HoG can effectively represent Uyghur text. The HoG-SVM system has already demonstrated valid in text/non-text line classification [13].

3   Experiments

3.1   Dataset and Evaluation Protocol

UICBI-500 Dataset. This paper recommends UICBI-500 dataset which is a expanded version of UICBI-400 [17]. The new images also consist of advertisement slogans, nature scene and born-digital images. The UICBI-500 dataset is more difficult than UICBI-400, the challenging mainly comes from two aspects. First, the diversity of the texts are much more diverse in the respect of fonts, sizes and colors. Second, the image background is more variable, and contains more patterns that are very hard to differentiate from text. In UICBI-500 dataset, the training set contains 300 images randomly selected from the superset and the rests constitute the test set.

Component Extraction Evaluation Protocol. To measure the performance of component extraction, we use the evaluation protocol in [17]. The recall, precision and repetition are defined as follows.

$$\begin{cases} recall = \dfrac{area(D \cap G)}{area(G)} \\[2mm] precision = \dfrac{N_p}{N_t} \\[2mm] repetition = \dfrac{N_r}{|D|} \end{cases}, \tag{4}$$

where D is the detection set and G is the ground-truth set, N_p is the number of positive detections which satisfy the condition $\frac{area(D \cap G)}{area(D)} \geqslant 0.8$. The condition means the most of D is fallen into the ground truth G hence we regard this D as a true detection. N_t is the total detections and N_r is the number of repetition.

Text Localization Evaluation Protocol. The most popular evaluation protocol is proposed by Wolf and Jolion [18], which considers three matching cases between the ground-truth (G) and the detection (D): one-to-one, one-to-many and many-to-one. It calculates the precision (p), recall (r) and f-measure, and is very effective to measure the text localization result. The p and r are defined as follows:

$$\begin{cases} r = \dfrac{\sum_i Match_G(G_i, D, t_r, t_p)}{|G|} \\ p = \dfrac{\sum_j Match_D(D_j, G, t_r, t_p)}{|D|} \end{cases}, \quad f = \dfrac{2pr}{p+r}, \qquad (5)$$

where t_r is the constraint on area recall and $t_r = 0.8$. t_p is the constraint on area precision and $t_p = 0.4$.

3.2   Component Candidate Extraction

At first, the compare of four typical keypoint detectors are given, as shown in Fig. 7. The text in the solid bounding box is marked by all of these detectors. But the text ("PARIS") in the dashed bounding box is lost in Fig. 7(a) and (b). In Fig. 7(c), the all texts are found, however, the number of detected keypoint is almost 1.78 times of the FASTroke keypoints. It is obvious from the above that the FASTroke keypoint detector is effective to mark text and produces less candidates.

(a)	(b)	(c)	(d)

Fig. 7. The keypoint detection results. (a) FAST detected 1098 keypoints. (b) Haaris detected 1610 keypoints. (c) FASText detected 2875 keypoints. The different mark size represents different scale of keypoints. (d) Our method detected 1615 keypoints.

In Table 1, the component extraction results of several common used detectors are compared on UICBI-500 dataset. Where "I-MSER" means that running MSER detector on single image channel of intensity and "RGB-MSER" is running on three images channel of red, green and blue (RGB). The proposed detector is faster than the rest and produces more less candidates, although it has not reached the highest *recall*. Especially, compared with I-MSER, the proposed detector obtains a higher *recall* but the detected components are less over a half.

3.3   Text Localization Results

The assessment results on UICBI-400 and UICBI-500 dataset are summarized in Tables 2 and 3. All of these methods depend on 3.2 GHz PC and OpenCV-3.0. The proposed method has achieved the highest f-measure on both UICBI-400 and UICBI-500. Moreover, the time-cost of our approach is the lowest and the process runs over 15-times as fast compared with [13]. The high *precision*

Table 1. The component extraction assessment result on UICBI-500.

Method	recall	precision	repetition	$\bar{t}$ (ms)	$|D|$
FASTroke	0.795	0.216	0.196	328.29	433
FASText	0.888	0.223	0.181	488.02	744
I-MSER	0.772	0.312	0.659	579.01	1178
RGB-MSER	0.867	0.313	0.803	1512.15	3634

Table 2. UICBI-400 evaluation result.

Method	recall	precision	f	$\bar{t}$ (s)
Our	0.846	**0.815**	**0.830**	**0.95**
[13]	**0.888**	0.776	0.828	15.43
[11]	0.522	0.749	0.616	N/A
[19]	0.313	0.479	0.300	24.59

Table 3. UICBI-500 evaluation result.

Method	recall	precision	f	$\bar{t}$ (s)
Our	**0.725**	**0.763**	**0.744**	**0.96**
[13]	0.600	0.659	0.628	14.56
[19]	0.379	0.523	0.439	25.73

benefits from three facts: the FASTroke keypoint detector is good at discovering text components, the component similarity clustering can effectively form text lines and the line classifier is accurate at text line verification. The low time-cost mainly come from the less component candidates which are produced by FASTroke keypoint detector and the framework without the extra component classification cost.

Fig. 8. Successful text localization results of several challenging images.

Several successful text localization examples are displayed in Fig. 8. These results demonstrate that the presented method is effective to localize Uyghur

Fig. 9. Several failure cases.

text in complex images and also robust to font-size, style and noise. However, there are some failures which expose a few shortcomings, as shown in Fig. 9. The FASTroke keypoint detector is sensitive to image contrast and loses the text with low contrast. The line classifier sometimes is confused on the HoG representation of Uyghur text-like non-text lines, such as fence, tree branch and so on.

4   Conclusion

Due to the complex background and text diversity, fast text localization in complex background images is still a tough problem. In this paper, we propose a novel framework for Uyghur text localization in complex background images, which contains two effective measures. One is the FASTroke keypoint detector which is a stroke-specific detector and can effectively discover the stroke endings, crosses and bends. The other is the component similarity clustering algorithm, which doesn't include component-level classification. Instead, the extracted components are directly constructed into lines according to their similarity.

A new benchmark dataset UICBI-500 is recommend, which is more challenging than the current benchmark. The experiment results on UICBI-500 show two facts. The first fact is the FASTroke keypoint detector has the fastest speed and produces the fewest candidates. The second fact is the proposed method improves the compared method with 11.2% on f-measure and achieves the state-of-the-art. These facts have demonstrated the validity of FASTroke keypoint detector and component similarity clustering algorithm. More importantly, owing to the FASTroke keypoint detector extracts less components and the similarity clustering algorithm, our method needn't the extra component classification and the speed of our approach is near real-time.

Acknowledgment. This work is supported by the National Nature Science Foundation of China (61771468 and 61327902), the Youth Innovation Promotion Association Chinese Academy of Sciences (2017209).

References

1. Liu, S., Xie, H., Zhou, C., Mao, Z.: Uyghur language text detection in complex background images using enhanced MSERs. In: Amsaleg, L., Guðmundsson, G.Þ., Gurrin, C., Jónsson, B.Þ., Satoh, S. (eds.) MMM 2017. LNCS, vol. 10132, pp. 490–500. Springer, Cham (2017). https://doi.org/10.1007/978-3-319-51811-4_40

2. Ye, Q., Doermann, D.: Text detection and recognition in imagery: a survey. IEEE Trans. Pattern Anal. Mach. Intell. **37**(7), 1480–1500 (2015)

3. Coates, A., Carpenter, B., Case, C., Satheesh, S., Suresh, B., Wang, T., Wu, D.J., Ng, A.Y.: Text detection and character recognition in scene images with unsupervised feature learning. In: 2011 International Conference on Document Analysis and Recognition (ICDAR), pp. 440–445. IEEE (2011)

4. Bissacco, A., Cummins, M., Netzer, Y., Neven, H.: Photoocr: reading text in uncontrolled conditions. In: IEEE International Conference on Computer Vision, pp. 785–792 (2013)

5. Tian, S., Pan, Y., Huang, C., Lu, S., Yu, K., Tan, C.L.: Text flow: a unified text detection system in natural scene images. In: Proceedings of the IEEE International Conference on Computer Vision, pp. 4651–4659 (2015)

6. Tian, Z., Huang, W., He, T., He, P., Qiao, Y.: Detecting text in natural image with connectionist text proposal network. In: Leibe, B., Matas, J., Sebe, N., Welling, M. (eds.) ECCV 2016. LNCS, vol. 9912, pp. 56–72. Springer, Cham (2016). https://doi.org/10.1007/978-3-319-46484-8_4

7. Fang, S., Xie, H., Chen, Z., Zhu, S., Gu, X., Gao, X.: Detecting Uyghur text in complex background images with convolutional neural network. Multimed. Tools Appl. **6**, 1–21 (2017)

8. Fang, S., Xie, H., Chen, Z., Liu, Y., Li, Y.: Uyghur text matching in graphic images for biomedical semantic analysis. Neuroinformatics (2017). https://doi.org/10.1007/s12021-017-9350-0

9. Neumann, L., Matas, J.: A method for text localization and recognition in real-world images. In: Kimmel, R., Klette, R., Sugimoto, A. (eds.) ACCV 2010. LNCS, vol. 6494, pp. 770–783. Springer, Heidelberg (2011). https://doi.org/10.1007/978-3-642-19318-7_60

10. Neumann, L., Matas, J.: Text localization in real-world images using efficiently pruned exhaustive search. In: 2011 International Conference on Document Analysis and Recognition (ICDAR), pp. 687–691. IEEE (2011)

11. Yin, X.-C., Yin, X., Huang, K., Hao, H.-W.: Robust text detection in natural scene images. IEEE Trans. Pattern Anal. Mach. Intell. **36**(5), 970–983 (2014)

12. Sung, M.-C., Jun, B., Cho, H., Kim, D.: Scene text detection with robust character candidate extraction method. In: 2015 13th International Conference on Document Analysis and Recognition (ICDAR), pp. 426–430. IEEE (2015)

13. Chen, J., Song, Y., Xie, H., Chen, X., Deng, H., Liu, Y.: Robust Uyghur text localization in complex background images. In: Chen, E., Gong, Y., Tie, Y. (eds.) PCM 2016. LNCS, vol. 9917, pp. 406–416. Springer, Cham (2016). https://doi.org/10.1007/978-3-319-48896-7_40

14. Rosten, E., Porter, R., Drummond, T.: Faster and better: a machine learning approach to corner detection. IEEE Trans. Pattern Anal. Mach. Intell. **32**(1), 105–119 (2010)

15. Xie, H., Zhang, Y., Gao, K., Tang, S., Xu, K., Guo, L., Li, J.: Robust common visual pattern discovery using graph matching. J. Vis. Commun. Image Represent. **24**(5), 635–646 (2013)

16. Xie, H., Gao, K., Zhang, Y., Li, J.: Local geometric consistency constraint for image retrieval. In: IEEE International Conference on Image Processing, pp. 101–104 (2011)
17. Song, Y., Chen, J., Xie, H., Chen, Z., Gao, X., Chen, X.: Robust and parallel Uyghur text localization in complex background images. Mach. Vis. Appl. **28**(7), 755–769 (2017). https://doi.org/10.1007/s00138-017-0837-3
18. Wolf, C., Jolion, J.-M.: Object count/area graphs for the evaluation of object detection and segmentation algorithms. Int. J. Doc. Anal. Recognit. IJDAR **8**(4), 280–296 (2006)
19. Neumann, L., Matas, J.: Real-time scene text localization and recognition. In: 2012 IEEE Conference on Computer Vision and Pattern Recognition (CVPR), pp. 3538–3545. IEEE (2012)

SS: Multimedia Analytics: Perspectives, Techniques and Applications

Approaches for Event Segmentation of Visual Lifelog Data

Rashmi Gupta and Cathal Gurrin[✉]

Insight Centre for Data Analytics, Dublin City University, Dublin, Ireland
rashmi.gupta3@mail.dcu.ie, cgurrin@computing.dcu.ie

Abstract. A personal visual lifelog can be considered to be a human memory augmentation tool and in recent years we have noticed an increased interest in the topic of lifelogging both in academic research and from industry practitioners. In this preliminary work, we explore the concept of event segmentation of visual lifelog data. Lifelog data, by its nature is continual and streams of multimodal data can easy run into thousands of wearable camera images per day, along with a significant number of other sensor sources. In this paper, we present two new approaches to event segmentation and compare them against pre-existing approaches in a user experiment with ten users. We show that our approaches based on visual concepts occurrence and image categorization perform better than the pre-existing approaches. We finalize the paper with a suggestion for next steps for the research community.

Keywords: Lifelogging · Event segmentation · Feature extraction
Memory augmentation · Information retrieval system

1 Introduction

Lifelogging is concerned with capturing and utilization of rich volumes of personal behavioural/activity data from multimodal lifelogs, gathered by individuals, who may be termed lifeloggers. These lifeloggers could be researchers or any individual who wish to capture the totality of their life [15]. Lifelog data could be collection of images, audios, videos, text documents and/or biometric data gathered using various wearable devices (e.g. wearable cameras) or software sensors. Lifelogging provides detailed information about the activities of the individual and could help to change an individual's behaviour so as to achieve positive life benefits. A variety of lifelog devices have been available with the Microsoft SenseCam [4], as used in MyLifeBits project [2], being the most well known. In addition, many other wearable sensors exist such as wearable cameras, biometric sensors, physical activity sensors, etc. can together passively contribute to a rich media digital diary which captures a representation of the individual's life activities. One aspect of such lifelog archives is that they tend to be passively captured and continuous (streamed) in nature [13], hence there exists a challenge in segmenting these continuous content streams into index-able units for

K. Schoeffmann et al. (Eds.): MMM 2018, Part I, LNCS 10704, pp. 581–593, 2018.
https://doi.org/10.1007/978-3-319-73603-7_47

analysis, retrieval and presentation. Most retrieval systems are based on the core concept of a document as an indexing unit. In lifelog search and retrieval, the document is not clearly defined, due to the continuous nature of lifelog data, and efforts have been made to impose a unit of retrieval, such as the minute [14] or the event [8], which is a document-centric unit.

In this paper, we propose two new approaches for event segmentation of visual lifelog data using a dataset of 14,132 images from 10 users over the period of 1 day each (12–14 h). These new approaches to segmentation are based on visual analysis of the visual image stream to identify objects and activities as a source for segmentation. An example of the types of data streams and their associated activities are shown in Fig. 1. The contributions of this paper are: (i) the introduction of two new approaches for event segmentation of visual lifelog data, and (ii) a dataset and evaluation approach for evaluating event segmentation approaches for visual lifelog data.

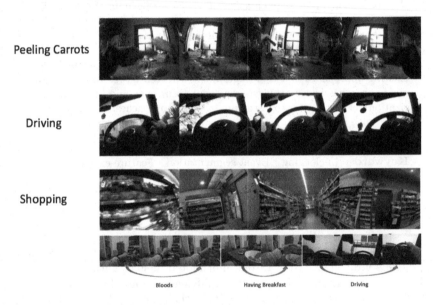

Fig. 1. Example of segmented daily life activities in lifelog dataset and signifying the transition between different activities.

2   Background

Lifelog data is typically based on passive capture of an individual's life experience. The data generated by lifelogging tends to be multimodal in nature, and streamed (as opposed to bursty in nature). Lifelogging has a long history, tracing back to Richard Buckminster Fullers Dymaxion Chronofile [7], in which he physically recorded all his personal and business data in a chronological arrangement as a very large scrapbook. Steve Mann in 1980s, introduced the idea of digitally capturing continuous everyday life data with wearable computing and streaming videos. Later in 2006, Bell and Gemmell introduced "MyLifeBits", a software database of Bell's life [12]. Following this initial work in digitally recording daily life, there has been an increase in the availability of wearable sensors such as cameras (OMG Autographer, Narrative clip, iOn SnapCam, etc.), fitness trackers (Fitbit, FuelBand, Jawbone wristband), smartphones apps (Moves, Saga), various biometric sensors, and more recently informational sensors, such as loggerman [16] which capture all computer interactions of an individual. We note that the process of capturing such rich volumes of digital multimedia data by the individual is becoming a normative activity. Recent years has seen the proliferation of visual capture devices such as cameraphones and digital video recorders, such as GoPros. What makes the content created by such devices differ from lifelog content is that they tend to produce bursty content. A cameraphone for example takes conventional photos in sequences of one (or more) at various times throughout the day. These datasets are naturally segmented into events or points in time based on the gaps between data capture. Whereas in lifelogging, the data streams are continuous and there is no clear point of segmentation. Consider an individual wearing a modern wearable camera. Such devices are usually worn attached to clothing or on a lanyard around the neck and can 'observe' the activities that the individual configured to capture images. Hence, we need to consider how to segment these data streams. In lifelogging, this segmentation process creates a contiguous set of documents that have typically been combined into a logical unit called an 'event' in a process called 'event segmentation'.

2.1 Event Segmentation of Lifelog Data

Event segmentation refers to the process whereby a continuous stream of data (typically from sensors) is segmented into discrete units. Zacks and Tversky in 2001, define the event as *"a segment of time at a given location that is conceived by an observer to have a beginning and an end"* [19]. Initial work on image-based event segmentation resulted from the ready availability of personal photo data from cameraphones. One early approach to segmentation of the bursty photo capture stream in timestamped data is discussed by Gargi in 2003 [11], which models the data stream with poisson distribution and used box-counting method.

In lifelogging, this automatic segmentation into events is similar to segmentation of video into shots and scenes and requires structuring the personal data into discrete units [15] which can be semantically enriched to form the basis of a lifelog retrieval system. Event segmentation of lifelog data has received research interest for about a decade now, yet there has not been much effort put into comparative evaluations. Doherty et al. [9] in 2007, implemented event detection for Sensecam image data by representing each image by a low-level edge histogram, a scalable colour (global), Color Histogram in HSV Color Space, accelerometer values of the Sensecam device and temperature readings as a source of evidence for the segmentation process. To determine the similarity between adjacent blocks of images, Hearst's TextTiling Algorithm was used. Following his early work,

Doherty [8] in 2008 introduced an enhanced event segmentation algorithm for wearable camera data using visual MPEG-7 features from images, which lead to an improvement over the previous approach. Various vector distance methods implemented and this work showed that the histogram intersection method and euclidean distance method based on MPEG-7 features perform best. In addition, kapur and mean thresholding approach were used as optimal thresholding techniques. Byrne et al. [5], presented an event segmentation technique based on content (using five low-level MPEG-7 feature descriptors) and contextual information (with light sensor i.e. changes in light and human motion sensor i.e. change of location/motion) of the lifelog image set using bluetooth and GPS metadata.

Chen et al. in 2011, gathered a large dataset of 450,000 images, about 2,000 h of computer activities and 18 months of context data (350,000 records) from 3 lifeloggers [6]. The fusion of this rich lifelog data is segmented based on computer activities, location and visual concepts using a TextTilling algorithm. Li et al. in 2013 [18], employed event segmentation based on multi-sensor data recorded by a wearable camera with associated gyroscope and accelerometer data. To generate the event boundaries the S-STD (sum of all standard deviations) feature is extracted from gyroscope data and to fine-tuned to enhance performance. Additionally Segment-HSV (the mean of HSV histograms) feature is utilized. Most recently, a segmentation approach based on unsupervised hierarchical agglomerate clustering was introduced by Bolanos et al. [3] and evaluated over a small dataset of 4,005 images (part of three people's days).

To conclude the previously implemented experiments to segment continuous visual data, the researchers used different volumes of image lifelog data and in some cases fused visual data with other sensors. They extracted various types of visual features from images and implemented clustering techniques such as hierarchical agglomerative clustering to segment daily life activities of the day in to specific events. In this work, we implement new approaches to event segmentation based on high-level visual concepts and categories and evaluate these against a baseline approach represented by Doherty [8]. In addition, we also define an evaluation methodology that provides a repeatable and fair comparison between the different approaches.

3   New Approaches to Event Segmentation of Lifelogs

Although there are a number of approaches to event segmentation that we could take, we have chosen to compare high-level modern visual features with the baseline low-level computer vision based features used by Doherty and Smeaton [8]. We employ two high-level sources, the open-source CAFFE framework (1000 ImageNet classes) concept detector [17] and the image categorization detector (86-categories Taxonomy) provided by the Microsoft Computer Vision API (MS) [1], which is based on [10]. The process of segmenting one day visual lifelog data into meaningful events is shown in Fig. 2 (below). The wearable camera that we used generated about two images per minute and these are organised into basic minute-long atomic units (1440 min/day) by selecting first image of each minute; visual concepts are extracted using one of two approaches (outlined below); the continuous data stream is segmented into events and then the output is evaluated.

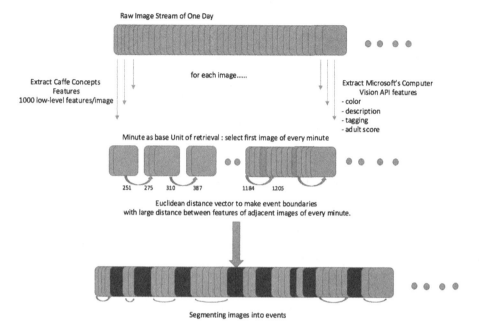

Fig. 2. Process of segmenting one day lifelog visual achieve into events.

3.1   Event Segmentation Based on Visual Concepts

In the visual concept approach to event segmentation, it is our conjecture that the change of activities of an individual would result in a change in visual objects in the field of view of the individual. Therefore, we employed the Caffe framework [17] to detect the objects visible in lifelog image content. Caffe is deep learning framework, used in conjunction with 1,000 ImageNet dataset of visual concepts [17]. Hence, the Caffe visual concepts form a 1,000 item vector for each image. The process of event segmentation of one day lifelog images based on caffe concepts in specific events by observing activity change is shown in Fig. 3.

3.2   Segmentation Based on Image Categorization

The aim of this approach is to utilize a higher-level semantic categorization of the images as a source of evidence for the segmentation process. Microsoft's

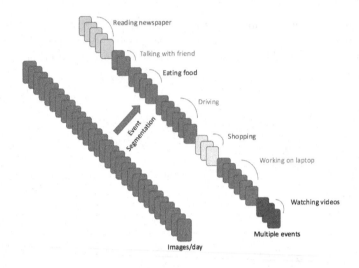

Fig. 3. Event segmentation of one day images based on visual concepts.

Computer Vision API [1] is employed for this task; it returns a taxonomy-based categorization for each image into 86 semantic categories. These categories are organised as a taxonomy into parent/child hierarchies. This taxonomy includes different categories, such as indoor category (includes indoor_churchwindow, indoor_door, indoor_room, etc.), food category (includes food_grilled, food_bread, food_pizza, etc.), outdoor category (includes outdoor_mountain, outdoor_city) and so on. This results in one vector (of size 86) representing each lifelog image with the associated confidence values. The example of identified various categories in image content and segmented images of one day based on these category taxonomy is shown in Fig. 4.

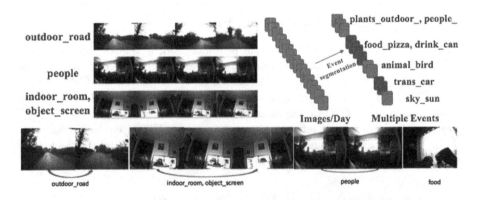

Fig. 4. Example of segmented lifelog dataset based on categories.

3.3   Baseline Approach

In order to compare against pre-existing approaches, we developed a baseline approach based on the work of Doherty and Smeaton [8]. This segmentation approach is based on, MPEG-7 low-level visual feature extraction from SenseCam images, TextTiling (block of 5 adjacent images) and Non-TextTiling approaches, various distance measures and threshold determination techniques. The approach to segment visual lifelog data implemented by Byrne [5] is similar to the Doherty and Smeaton [8] approach and performs similarly. As a consequence, for our baseline approach, we re-implemented only the Doherty approach.

3.4   Distance Measure

A key component of event boundary detection is the ability to identify the distance between subsequent lifelog images (or groups of images) and where the distance is above a certain threshold (along with other criteria), an event boundary can be declared. In order to calculate the distance, we implemented the euclidean distance measure on these vectors, which allows us to identify the event boundaries (a high distance) and fuse the images within the same event (low distance). Therefore a change in activities with high distance such as 'eating' and 'driving' would be highly distant from each other, so they would indicate an event boundary, whereas activities such as 'eating' and 'cooking' would have a lower distance and may not trigger an event boundary. This requires the selection of appropriate thresholds, and this is described in the following section.

3.5   Threshold Determination

To identify the most effective events boundaries, we need to determine the threshold values. We implemented, two automatic thresholding techniques based on pre-existing approaches; the first is a parametric technique (e.g. mean thresholding which takes mean, standard deviation and user parameters) and second is non-parametric technique (Kapur thresholding). The manual thresholding parameters we selected were 0.4, 0.5, 0.6 and 0.7, which can be subject to more fine tuning at a later date.

3.6   Avoiding Over-Segmentation

As with prior work, we needed to avoid over-segmenting the data, which could happen if there is significant visual change in a short sequence of camera images, which can commonly occur in lifelogging due to short-term variations in the activities of the individual. We propose that such small variations are not representative of changes in the overall activities of the individual, and as such, we should not segment based on these. Hence we chose five minutes as the smallest duration of a segmented event, which is chosen based on our experience of analyzing and organizing lifelog data.

4 Evaluation

The automatic event boundaries generated by the two proposed approaches and the baseline approach are compared with manual event segmentation done by the lifeloggers themselves which is considered as ground truth event segmentation. For this evaluation we developed a new purpose-built visual lifelog dataset gathered by a number of individuals.

4.1 Dataset

In this experiment, we collected total 14,132 images (average of 1,400 images over the period of 11 to 14 hours per day/each user) from 10 different participants. The OMG Autographer was used for data capture, which is a passive-capture wearable camera worn on a lanyard around the neck and therefore is oriented towards the activities of the wearer. Typically the camera will capture about 2 images per minute. All other sensors on the device, such as bluetooth and GPS were turned off to optimize battery life. All the participants are asked not to change their daily routine due to wearing the camera. Each participant manually segmented their day into a set of discrete activities, which we then take as a ground truth event segmentation. We provided the same guidance to each participant on the process to be employed when deciding what should be considered to be an event boundary. As a consequence, there is a natural variability in the number of events manually segmented due to human subjective judgments being made and the numbers of events are in line with what we would have expected. The detailed information regarding participants and the average count of images collected and segmented from each user per day is summarized in Table 1.

Table 1. The summary information of participants and their count of segmented ground truth events.

Lifelogger/User	Profession	Age group	Avg duration/day	Avg images/day	Total ground truth events/day
1	Researcher	>40	17 h	1084	46
2	Researcher	>35	12 h 35 m	1792	33
3	Researcher	>35	13 h	1895	16
4	Researcher	>35	17 h	1078	31
5	Researcher	>25	11 h	1064	31
6	Student	>30	11 h	1399	20
7	Student	>22	11 h	1494	39
8	Student	>25	14 h	1336	35
9	Businessman	>55	13 h	1708	41
10	House-maker	>45	13 h	1282	19

4.2   Evaluation Methodology

One challenge when evaluating event segmentation algorithms is how to evaluate systems that produce a segmentation that is accurate, but labels the segmentation point to be a few images before, or after, the user-defined ground truth segmentation point (close-to, but not exactly matching the subjective human segmentation). To solve this problem, we reuse the approach of Doherty (i.e. post-processing boundary gap) which defines a sliding window around the ground truth labeled segmentation-point. The size of this window could range from 0 (no sliding window allowed) up to an arbitrary figure of 16 (the upper-bound for reasonable experimentation[1]). Through experimentation, we have found that five images is a reasonable size of the sliding window around the ground truth labeled event boundary points. Every nearest boundary is considered to be true in the associated window and we used this boundary in our experimentation, explained in Fig. 5 below.

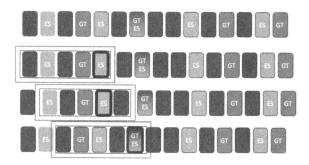

Fig. 5. Similarity between event segmentation points (ES) and user-defined ground truth event segmentation (GT) via sliding window approach (Post-processing boundary gap) [8].

In terms of evaluation measurements, we used the conventional measurements of precision, recall, F1-Measure and Matthews Correlation Coefficient (MCC). Precision and recall are the standard approaches to evaluation measurement in information retrieval. F1 score is harmonic mean of precision and recall and MCC score does not only taken into consideration for correct prediction but also measures the correlation between all values in a matrix and identifies the mis-predictions by adopting values smaller than 0.

4.3   Results

The two new approaches introduced in this paper are compared with the baseline approach discussed in Sect. 3 in a comparative study.

---

[1] Given a 16 h day, with one image per minute and 30 events identified per day (all reasonable assumptions), then an evaluation with a 16 min boundary would tend not to penalize random segmentation algorithms.

- **Baseline: Event Segmentation based on MPEG-7 Descriptors:** The two pre-existing segmentation approaches implemented by Doherty [8] is based on, TextTiling (Block of 5 adjacent images) and non-textiling are implemented. We get the highest score of precision (20.6%), recall (65.8%), F1-Measure (65.8%) and MCC (7.42%) with hearst's textiling approach and with the non-textiling approach, we get the highest score of precision (29.5%), recall (60.6%), F1-Measure (38.7%) and MCC (22%) as shown in Table 2. We found the Non-textiling approach with mean thresholding technique performs best.
- **Event Segmentation based on Visual Concepts:** The approach to segment one day lifelog data into activities by using caffe framework visual concepts, as described in (Sect. 3.1), performs better from MPEG - 7 low level features. With threshold value 0.4, we get best score of precision (70.4%), F1-Measure (69.3%) and MCC (64.3%) shown in Table 2 below.
- **Event Segmentation based on Image Categorization:** Segmentation of one day lifelog data into events based on the image categories, as described in (Sect. 3.2), we get the best evaluated scores of recall (68.3%), F1-Measure (70.1%) and MCC score (65.7%) with threshold value 0.7 shown in Table 2, which again justifies the better approach over baseline approach with MPEG-7 Descriptors.

Table 2. Overall thresholding performance based on MPEG - 7 descriptors [8], caffe visual concepts [17], image categorization via MS concepts [1] and summary of experiment results.

Experimental approaches	Threshold value	Precision	Recall	F1-score	MCC
Hearst's TexTiling based on MPEG-7 descriptors	Mean (K = 0.5)	20.6	65.4	30.7	6.98
	Kapur	20.6	65.8	31.3	7.42
Non TexTiling based on MPEG-7 descriptors	Mean (K = 0.5)	29.5	60.6	38.7	22.0
	Kapur	29.4	60	38.7	21.43
Caffe visual concepts	0.4	70.4	72	69.3	64.3
	0.5	64.6	76.5	68.5	62.9
	0.6	56.4	80.9	64.8	58.6
	0.7	40.5	88.2	54.2	46
Image categorization via MS concepts	0.4	78.3	65.5	69.2	65.2
	0.5	77.5	66.2	69.4	65.4
	0.6	77.2	67.2	69.8	61.4
	0.7	76.2	68.3	70.1	65.7
Summary results	**Threshold value**	**Precision**	**Recall**	**F1-score**	**MCC**
MS concepts	0.7	76.2	68.3	70.1	65.7
Caffe concepts	0.4	70.4	72	69.3	64.3
MPEG-7 without TexTiling	Mean (K = 0.5)	29.5	60.6	38.7	22.0
MPEG-7 with TexTiling	Kapur	20.6	65.8	31.3	7.42

4.4   Discussion

As can be seen from the previous section, we found that the segmentation based on image categorization and visual concepts provide higher-level semantic concepts that reflects the differences in the activities of the individual. For example, moving from the office desk to eat lunch, the visual concepts and objects [1,17] in the field of view would naturally change from computers to food items. Assuming this to be the case, then it is natural that a higher-level visual analysis would perform better than one that operates just on lower-level visual features such as edge histogram and colours of the MPEG-7 library [8]. Hence, we found that the event segmentation based on image categorization [1] with precision (76.2%), recall (65.5%), f1-score (70.1%) and MCC (65.7%) and event segmentation based on visual concepts [17] with precision (70.4%), recall (72%), f1-score (69.3%) and MCC (64.3%) provides the best results while re-implementation of baseline approach [8] with Non-TexTiling approach (found best approach in baseline) provides comparatively low results summarized in Table 2 above.

We note that these are preliminary approaches and are subject to optimisations and enhancements. We intend to explore more optimal thresholds as well as larger datasets [14]. The simple distance measure that we employed can also be enhanced and we intend to explore a number of alternatives, such as the wordnet-based conceptual distance, as well as the results of fusing many different approaches. This work is also limited by the fact that we only analyse the visual content. We began this paper by stating that lifelogs are multimodal data archives, so we will employ multimodal data sources for our future work, such as audio, acceleration, location, biometrics, etc.

5   Conclusion

In this preliminary work, we presented two new approaches for event segmentation of visual lifelog data based on high-level visual feature analysis. In order to place our research in the context of past state-of-the-art, we defined a baseline approach to segment visual lifelog data into retrievable events based on the work of Doherty and Smeaton [8]. We compared our two proposed approaches to the baseline approach in an experimental setting with the lifelog data of ten users. In this experiment, we showed that the higher-level approaches proposed in this paper perform significantly better than [8] across all four employed evaluation measures. This suggests that there is significant scope for enhancing the performance of event-segmentation algorithms on lifelog data and that this is far from a solved problem. In future, we plan to extend this work along the lines previously outlined. We also intend to compare our approaches with the full spectrum of alternative approaches as introduced above.

Acknowledgment. This publication has emanated from research conducted with the financial support of Science Foundation Ireland (SFI) under grant number SFI/12/RC/2289.

References

1. Microsoft's Computer Vision API. https://docs.microsoft.com/en-us/azure/cognitive-services/computer-vision/category-taxonomy
2. Bell, G., Gemmell, J.: A digital life. Sci. Am. **296**, 58–65 (2007)
3. Bolanos, M., Mestre, R., Talavera, E., Nieto, X.G., Radeva, P.: Visual summary of egocentric photostreams by representative keyframes. In: IEEE First International Workshop on Wearable and Ego-Vision Systems for Augmented Experience (WEsAX), 29 June–3 July 2015, Turin, Italy (2015)
4. Bush, V.: As we may think. Atlantic Mon. **176**(1), 101–108 (1945)
5. Byrne, D., Lavelle, B., Doherty, A.R., Jones, G.J., Smeaton, A.F.: Using bluetooth and GPS metadata to measure event similarity in SenseCam images. In: 5th International Conference on Intelligent Multimedia and Ambient Intelligence, July 2007
6. Chen, Y., Jones, G.J., Ganguly, D.: Segmenting and summarizing general events in a long-term lifelog. In: The 2nd Workshop Information Access for Personal Media Archives (IAPMA) at ECIR 2011, April 2011
7. Chu, H.Y., Trujillo, R.G.: New views on R. Buckminster Fuller, pp. 6–23 (2009)
8. Doherty, A.R., Smeaton, A.F.: Automatically segmenting lifelog data into events. In: 9th International Workshop on Image Analysis for Multimedia Interactive Services, 30 June 2008
9. Doherty, A.R., Smeaton, A.F., Lee, K., Ellis, D.P.: Multimodal segmentation of lifelog data. In: Large Scale Semantic Access to Content (Text, Image, Video, and Sound), pp. 21–38, June 2007
10. Fang, H., Gupta, S., Iandola, F., Srivastava, R., Deng, L., Dollar, P., Gao, J., He, X., Mitchell, M., Platt, J., Zitnick, L., Zweig, G.: From captions to visual concepts and back. IEEE Institute of Electrical and Electronics Engineers, June 2015
11. Gargi, U.: Modeling and clustering of photo capture streams. In: Proceedings of the 5th ACM SIGMM International Workshop on Multimedia Information Retrieval, pp. 47–54, November 2003
12. Gemmell, J., Bell, G., Lueder, R.: MyLifeBits: a personal database for everything. Commun. ACM **49**(1), 88–95 (2006)
13. Gurrin, C., Byrne, D., O'Connor, N., Jones, G.J., Smeaton, A.F.: Architecture and challenges of maintaining a large-scale, context-aware human digital memory. In: VIE 2008 - The 5th IET Visual Information Engineering 2008 Conference, July 2018
14. Gurrin, C., Joho, H., Hopfgartner, F., Zhou, L., Albatal, R.: NTCIR Lifelog: The First Test Collection for Lifelog Research (2016)
15. Gurrin, C., Smeaton, A.F., Doherty, A.R.: LifeLogging: personal big data. Found. Trends Inf. Retrieval **8**(1), 1–125 (2014)
16. Hinbarji, Z., Albatal, R., O'Connor, N., Gurrin, C.: LoggerMan, a comprehensive logging and visualization tool to capture computer usage. In: Tian, Q., Sebe, N., Qi, G.-J., Huet, B., Hong, R., Liu, X. (eds.) MMM 2016. LNCS, vol. 9517, pp. 342–347. Springer, Cham (2016). https://doi.org/10.1007/978-3-319-27674-8_31
17. Jia, Y., Shelhamer, E., Donahue, J., Karayev, S., Long, J., Girshick, R., Guadarrama, S., Darrell, T.: Caffe: convolutional architecture for fast feature embedding. arXiv preprint arXiv:1408.5093 (2014)

18. Li, Z., Wei, Z., Jia, W., Sun, M.: Daily life event segmentation for lifestyle evaluation based on multi-sensor data recorded by a wearable device. In: Conference on Proceedings of IEEE Engineering in Medicine and Biology Society, 30 October 2013

19. Zacks, M.J., Braver, S.T., Sheridan, A.M., Donaldson, I.D., Snyder, Z.A., Ollinger, M.J., Buckner, L.R., Raichle, E.M.: Human brain activity time-locked to perceptual event boundaries. Nat. Neurosci. 4(6), 651–655 (2001)

Category Specific Post Popularity Prediction

Masoud Mazloom[✉], Iliana Pappi, and Marcel Worring

Informatics Institute, University of Amsterdam, Amsterdam, Netherlands
{m.mazloom,m.worring}@uva.nl, iliana.n.pappi@gmail.com

Abstract. Social media have become dominant in everyday life during the last few years where users share their thoughts and experiences about their enjoyable events in posts. Most of these posts are related to different categories related to: *activities*, such as dancing, *landscapes*, such as beach, *people*, such as a selfie, and *animals* such as pets. While some of these posts become popular and get more attention, others are completely ignored. In order to address the desire of users to create popular posts, several researches have studied post popularity prediction. Existing works focus on predicting the popularity without considering the category type of the post. In this paper we propose category specific post popularity prediction using visual and textual content for *action, scene, people* and *animal* categories. In this way we aim to answer the question *What makes a post belonging to a specific action, scene, people or animal category popular?* To answer to this question we perform several experiments on a collection of 65K posts crawled from Instagram.

1 Introduction

A huge amount of visual and textual information is posted everyday in social media such as Twitter, Instagram, Flickr, Facebook. This is not surprising as it takes only a few seconds to share social activity in the form of an image, video, comments, and tags in any place at any time with a simple internet connection to a device such as a mobile or tablet. However the destiny of the user generated posts in social media are completely different. While some posts receive a high number of likes and gain a lot of attention, others are more or less ignored.

Predicting how popular a post will be among other users in the user's network or in public, has become interesting for marketing and business [16], political and economic sciences [12] and decision-making strategies of campaigns targeting on social media crowds [11]. Moreover, predicting post popularity is important for the self-evolution of the social media [8]. Every user would like to know the best way to interact or get noticed in a social media platform, concerning both shared posts and quotes or comments. Defining what makes a user generated post become popular has been proven to be a challenging problem to solve [9].

Many approaches have been proposed to predict the popularity of a post focusing on the effect of visual low- and high-level contents [4,6,9,13–16], textual contents such as tweets, user's tags and comments [1,7,18], and multimodal posts with visual contents along with the textual contents of a user's post [6,9,14–16].

© Springer International Publishing AG 2018
K. Schoeffmann et al. (Eds.): MMM 2018, Part I, LNCS 10704, pp. 594–607, 2018.
https://doi.org/10.1007/978-3-319-73603-7_48

Fig. 1. Each row shows five posts related to the actions climbing and running, swimming-pool scene, and selfie respectively. We aim in this paper to investigate whether there are any visual semantic features affecting the popularity of posts belonging to a specific category.

Inspired by the success of recent methods for post popularity prediction in social media [1,4,6,7,9,13–16,18] we continue the study by predicting the popularity of category-based posts. In particular, we analyze the content of posts related to the categories *actions, scenes, people,* and *animal* for the study, following the analysis of brand-related contents for brand popularity prediction in [16].

For the purpose of this paper a new dataset was created from scratch, containing posts crawled from Instagram, a broadly used social network with emphasis on visual and textual contents. Among the different social media platforms, Instagram has a strong emphasis on self-expression by images with a description through captions and hashtags and is easy to crawl. In contrast, Twitter does not always have image content in a post, Facebook is complicated to crawl and has a lot of privacy rules and Flickr is less connected with social activity and more connected to photographers' communities. Since we aim to predict the popularity of post related to what people mostly enjoy, we crawled posts in terms of enjoyable activities, places, selfie, and pets. Figure 1 show some examples of our dataset.

In this paper we propose a multimodal framework for post popularity prediction especially when action, scene, people, and animal appear in the users' posts. We investigate which semantic features affect the popularity of a post in social media most. Especially we try to study the role of low and high-level visual features, along with textual features with specific characteristics related to e.g. action and scenery, in correlation with post popularity.

We make three main contributions in this paper: (1) We study the problem of post popularity prediction inside various categories in social media, (2) We investigate the correlation of semantic features with popularity prediction of posts for different categories which allows us to propose meaningful suggestions to a user, (3) We introduce a new dataset, for category-based post popularity prediction, obtained for free from Instagram by a simple crawling procedure.

We organize the remainder of this paper as follows. We start by considering related work in Sect. 2. Section 3 describes our proposal for predicting the popularity of posts. We introduce the experimental setup on our dataset in Sect. 4. Results and conclusions are presented in Sects. 5 and 6 respectively.

2   Related Work

Several studies in the literature address the post popularity prediction based on the textual or visual features, or a combination of them.

A study for predicting popularity in Twitter by Hong et al. [7], formulates the task as a classification problem, investigating a wide spectrum of features based on the content of the messages. Bae and Lee [1] analyze Twitter posts and categorized the followers of a limited number of influential users to a positive and a negative audience. From there, they correlate the sentiment of the followers with the textual content of their posts and based on that defined a measure of influence. Szabo and Huberman in [18] investigate the popularity of videos in YouTube by analyzing the social cues, comments, and associated tags. All of these works use textual content for popularity prediction. Visual content which also holds a lot of information, is not addressed in these methods.

Visual contents of posts are investigated for their correlation with popularity prediction in [4,6,9,14–16]. Cappallo et al. in [4] developed a model for popularity prediction in social media based only on visual content. A latent ranking approach was proposed, which takes into account not only the distinctive visual cues in popular images, but also those in unpopular images. Khosla et al. in [9] report the importance of image cues such as color, gradients, low-level features and the set of objects present, as well as the importance of various social cues such as number of followers or number of photos uploaded by the user. Image popularity prediction in a "cold start" scenario, where there exists no or limited textual interaction data, by considering image context, visual appearance and user context was investigated by McParlane et al. [15]. The authors cast the problem as a classification task between highly popular and unpopular images. Mazloom et al. in [14] present an approach for identifying what aspects of posts determine their popularity. The proposed model was based on the hypothesis that brand-related posts may be popular due to several cues related to factual information, sentiment, vividness and brand engagement parameters. Gelli et al. in [6] investigate the effect of visual sentiment analysis and context features on image popularity in social media. Overgoor et al. in [16] investigate brand, as a category, popularity prediction in a spatio-temporal category representation framework. The results of this work confirm complementary of visual and textual features for predicting the popularity of a brand.

Different from [4,6,9,14,15] which perform popularity prediction of posts in a general setting, we aim to take into account the category type of a post in

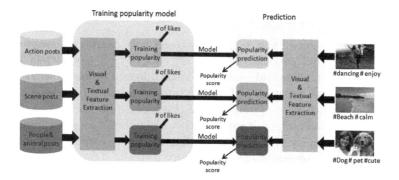

Fig. 2. Our proposal for computing popularity score for category specific posts.

predicting it's popularity. Inspired by the success of brand popularity prediction in [16], we predict the popularity of posts related to different categories such as action, scene, people and animal.

3   Our Proposal

Our category-based popularity prediction framework consists of two main components, schematically illustrated in Fig. 2. In the training phase, at first, we represent each category-based post using its visual and textual contents. We use the number of likes of each post received in social media as target value and train a popularity model. Second, in the prediction phase, we represent an unseen post and compute a popularity score. Before introducing the proposed framework for popularity prediction, the notation and key concepts will be formally introduced.

3.1   Problem Formalization

Given a specific category-based post, popularity prediction inside a category is the task of computing a score per post that shows how popular it will be in comparison to other posts in the same category. For consistency, we use P_{z_x} to indicate the given x^{th} post of category z. We aim to construct a real-valued function $f(P_{z_x})$ which produces a score for the popularity of P_x in category z. By sorting all posts of category z in the test set according to $f(:)$ in descending order, a list of most popular posts in category z will be obtained.

Suppose $C = \{C_1, C_2, ..., Cn\}$ is a dataset consist of posts related to all n categories, where each C_i is given by m_i posts, $C_i = \{(P_{i_1}, y_{i_1}), (P_{i_2}, y_{i_2})), ..., (P_{i_{m_i}}, y_{i_{m_i}})\}$ and P_{i_j} is the jth post of category C_i, carrying multimodal information, and y_{i_j} is its corresponding number of likes. We hypothesize that what makes a category-based post become popular on social media, number of likes a post will receive, depends on the content of the generated post. In other words, the output of $f(P_{z_x})$ largely depends on the representation of P_x. In Sect. 3.2 we show how to represent a post based on it's content.

3.2   Post Representation

In this section we explain how a category-based post can be represented using its visual and textual contents. Suppose $P_{i_j} = (P_{i_j}^v, P_{i_j}^t)$ consists of the two components visual and textual content. To find different representations of post P_{i_j}, we extract visual features, $F(P_{i_j}^v)$ and textual features, $F(P_{i_j}^t)$. The output of F is a representation of P_{i_j}. Similar to [14], we use both visual and textual contents in the representation of a post as they carry complementary information related to the popularity of a post. Depending on how to extract these contents, we present several representations of P_{i_j} here.

We present each P_{i_j} using it's visual channel, $P_{i_j}^v$, by three state-of-the-art features used in [14]:

- *Concept Features*: To extract Concept features we utilized a deep neural network namely the GoogleNet Inception V3 [19]. The output of $F(P_{i_j}^v)$ is the 1000-dimensional feature vector of the softmax output layer.
- *Low-level Features:* The output of $F(P_{i_j}^v)$ is the 2048-dimensional low-level feature vector for each image from the Max Pooling of the Convolutional Pool 8x8 layer of the same network.
- *Visual Sentiment Features:* The sentiment in the visual content of each post was expressed through 1200-dimensional vectors, utilizing SentiBank detectors [5] of the Visual Sentiment Ontology (VSO) [2]. This bank consist of 1,200 Adjective-Noun pairs (ANP's) detectors such as "beautiful flowers". The output of $F(P_{i_j}^v)$ in this case is a 1,200 dimensional vector with the probabilities of the ANP's being present in the image.

We also present each P_{i_j} using it's textual channel, $P_{i_j}^t$, by three state-of-the-art features used in [14]:

- *Word-to-Vec Features:* The Word-to-vec (W2V) model [17] leads to vector representations of words learned using word embeddings, where each word is represented by a 300-dimensional vector. The words for each post are represented by a W2V vector and the final representation of post, $F(P_{i_j}^t)$, is obtained by average pooling over all word vectors.
- *Bag-of-Words Features:* Bag-of-Words (BOW) is a sparse representation of the counts of each word in the post, compared to a pre-constructed vocabulary, i.e., a sorted list of all the unique words in the dataset based on their frequency. We find a representation, $F(P_{i_j}^t)$, with 1000-dimensions as the best representation by cross validation over the different dimension sizes.
- *Textual Sentiment Features:* The output of $F(P_{i_j}^t)$ is a 2-dimensional feature vector which represents the positive, ranging from 1 to 5, and negative, ranging from -1 to -5, sentiment score of the textual content in the post P_{i_j}. We use SentiStrength [20] for this task.

Next, we show how to tackle category-based post popularity prediction using different representations.

3.3   Popularity Prediction

After representing posts, we use it for the problem of post popularity prediction. Suppose C is a set of m posts, $m = \sum_{i=1}^{n} m_i$, where $C = \{(P_{i_1}, y_{i_1}), ..., (P_{i_{m_i}}, y_{i_{m_i}}), ..., (P_{n_{m_n}}, y_{n_{m_n}})\}$. We divide C into two parts, with $C = C_{tr} \cup C_{te}$ where C_{tr} is a training set consisting of k posts and C_{te} is a test set consisting of the other $m - k$ posts in C. By representing the posts in a training and test set using features explained in Sect. 3.2, we define C_{tr} and C_{te} as two matrix representations of posts, $C_{tr} = [F(P_1), ..., F(P_k)]$ and $C_{te} = [F(P_{k+1}), ..., F(P_m)]$ where each row of C_{tr} and Cte represents a post.

We consider the popularity prediction of a post as a regression problem as considered in [6,9,14,16]. Let $F(P_i)$ be a representation of post P_i from C_{te} and y_i the popularity of P_i in social media. The goal is to learn function $f(:)$ over C_{tr} to estimate the popularity of P_i, $\tilde{y}_i = f(F(P_i)) = w^T F(P_i)$, where $|y_i - \tilde{y}_i|$ as an error is small. The idea is to optimize w, parameter of function $f_w()$, on C_{tr} to minimize the error. To solve the problem and find the optimal value of w we use different regressors such as L2 regularized L2 loss Support Vector Regression as used in [9,14], Support Vector Regression using RBF kernel, Random Forest, and Multilayer Perceptron. After training the model and finding the optimum value of w on C_{tr}, we use it for prediction of post popularity on C_{te} and report the rank correlation between the predicted scores and ground truth.

4   Experimental Setup

4.1   Dataset

Since there is no existing dataset for predicting the popularity of a category-based posts, we created one by crawling Instagram. Our dataset consists of approximately 65k Instagram posts with visual and textual content as well as metadata related to *action, scene, people* and *animal* categories. All the posts in our dataset were generated between 1/1/2017 to 25/4/2017. The crawling of the posts was made according to hashtags of several enjoyable event related to the categories. The relevant hashtags used for the Instagram crawler are: for **actions**: we select those actions related to love, music, and sport such as *#playing-music, #running, #basketball, #surfing, #ski, #climbing, #cycling, #dance, #football, #horse-riding, #hug, #kiss.* For **places/scenes**: we consider those sceneries related to indoor, outdoor, nature, and hobby in particular *#art-gallery, #bar, #beach, #bedroom, #cafe, #canals, #fields, #forest, #home, #kitchen, #street, #swimming-pool, #urban.* For **people** we consider *#selfie* and *#pets* for **animal**. The statistics of our dataset are reported in Table 1[1].

In order to explore the popularity of posts in all categories or in a specific category, we define two different settings: (1) **Category-mix** where we use the whole dataset, C, to build a general model for popularity prediction.

---

[1] http://isis-data.science.uva.nl/Masoud/MMM17Data.

Table 1. Statistics of our dataset used in experiments

Category							
Action		Scene		People		Animal	
Name	Posts	Name	Posts	Name	Posts	Name	Posts
#basketball	2055	#art-gallery	1499	selfie	4500	pet	3200
#climbing	2008	#bar	2039				
#cycling	2786	#beach	2264				
#dance	2473	#bedroom	2240				
#football	2549	#cafe	2568				
#horse-riding	2258	#canals	3382				
#hug	2290	#fields	2264				
#kiss	2909	#forest	3289				
#playing-music	1850	#home	2306				
#running	2139	#kitchen	2620				
#ski	2267	#street	2408				
#surfing	1622	#swimming-pool	2915				
	27206		29794		4500		3200

(2) **Category-specific** where we used all data related to specific category C_i. We perform the training and evaluation independently for each category. In both settings we split the data randomly into training and test set. We train a model over 70% of the dataset as training set and report the popularity result over the other 30% of dataset as test set.

4.2   Implementation Details

Popularity measurement. Similar to [9,14] we consider popularity prediction of a post as a ranking problem. We use the number of likes a post received in social media as the measure of its popularity. We find the majority of posts receive little likes and the minority of them receive a high number of likes. To deal with it we follow [9,14] and consider the log number of likes.

We used different regressor methods for predicting the popularity of a post. We consider 5-fold cross-validation on training set for tuning all parameters of regressors. We find the optimal value of the regularization parameter $\lambda = 0.1$, in SVR, through $\lambda \in \{0.001, 0.1, 1, 10, 100, 1000\}$. We find Random Forrest Regressor (RFR) [3] with 100 tree estimators, as an optimal parameter giving the best results among the values $\{10, 100, 300, 1000\}$. We consider the default setting in results [10] for using Multi-layer Perceptron (MLP) as a regressor. The optimal value of $\alpha = 0.01$, the loss parameter, was tuned by considering α in the range $\{0.0001, 0.001, 0.01, 1, 10\}$.

Evaluation metric. In this paper we evaluate the post popularity prediction model using Spearman's rank correlation coefficient, a statistical metric showing the monotonic relation between two vectors as used in [9,14]. We compute the rank correlation between the prediction vector resulting from the model and ground truth vector which returns a value between $[-1, 1]$.

4.3   Experiments

Experiment 1: Post popularity prediction in Category-mix dataset. In this experiment we evaluate the effect of different visual and textual features explained in Sect. 3.2 on predicting the popularity of a post in Category-mix datasets. To find an efficient popularity model we report the result of different regressors explained in Sect. 3.3, Linear-SVR (LSVR), RBF-SVR (RSVR), Random Forest Regressor (RFR), and MLP Regressor (MLPR). We use the best regressor for the other experiments. We also report the effect of combining the best visual and textual feature, based on their rank correlation results, by average pooling in a late fusion scenario.

Experiment 2: Post popularity prediction in Category-specific. We report the result of post popularity prediction on the Category-specific dataset in this experiment. Furthermore, we evaluate the effect of various visual and textual features on the popularity of category-based posts. From there, we compare the result of applying a model which is trained on Category-specific data with the model trained on train set of Category-mix and report the result on the test set of each category. We report the result of fusing best visual and best textual features.

We also report the result of popularity prediction on each specific instance inside categories, such as popularity of dancing in the action category. We evaluate the correlation of semantic visual features, Concepts and Visual sentiments, with the popularity of posts in different instances in categories. To do that we compute the weights of regressor models separately for each category and each semantic feature. We sort them for selecting the top semantic features which have high impact on popularity of post per category.

Experiment 3: Popularity prediction using specific visual concepts. In this experiment we evaluate the effect of specific visual Concepts on the popularity of a specific category. We use the *Concepts features* explained in Sect. 3.2 in this experiment. We manually labelled the 1000-Imagenet Concepts for *action, scene, people, animals*, and *general objects*. The outcome was a set of 50-dimensional feature vectors for action, 151-dimensional vectors for scene, 10-dimensional vectors for people, 404-dimensional vectors for animals, and 525-dimensional vectors for general objects within the Imagenet 1000 concepts. Many of the concepts had to be double-labelled, and as a result participating in two categories, as a strict division of concepts was not always possible in terms of semantic meaning. We report the popularity of posts using specific concept category for each specific category.

5   Results

5.1   Post Popularity Prediction in Category-Mix Dataset

The result of post popularity prediction in the category-mix dataset is presented in Table 2. Starting with the visual features and LSVR as a regressor method, the results show the 0.229, 0.211 and 0.196 rank correlation as a popularity of a post using Concepts, Low-level, and Visual sentiment features respectively. Using an average pooling for fusing these visual features, the result reaches 0.253. The results in Table 2 also show the importance of using RFR as a regressor, instead of using the other regressors, for predicting the popularity of a post using visual features where the result reach 0.232, 0.221, 0.202 and 0.260 rank correlation using Concepts, Low-level, Visual sentiment and fusion of them respectively. The results show the advantage of using LSVR and RFR for training a popularity model over visual features in comparison with the other two regressors, RSVR and MLPR.

Table 2. Experiment 1: popularity prediction on category-mix dataset

Model	Visual features			
	Concepts	Low-level	Visual sentiment	AvgPool
RSVR	0.221	0.201	0.152	0.234
LSVR	0.229	0.211	0.196	**0.253**
RFR	0.232	0.221	0.202	**0.260**
MLPR	0.183	0.237	0.192	0.230
	Textual features			
	Word2Vec	BoW	Textual sentiment	AvgPool
RSVR	0.328	0.415	0.102	0.374
LSVR	0.339	0.402	0.104	**0.390**
RFR	0.350	0.428	0.085	**0.395**
MLPR	0.409	0.320	0.099	0.355

The result of popularity prediction using textual features in Table 2 also depict the superiority of using LSVR and RFR for training a popularity model. However the result of using RFR, over both visual and textual features, is slightly better than using LSVR, but it suffers from the time efficiency for training a model against LSVR. We keep LSVR regressor method and use it for the other experiments. By fusing the results of the best visual and textual features using the LSVR model, which are Concepts and BoW respectively, with an average operator the rank correlation reaches 0.434 which shows the complementary of visual and textual features for popularity prediction.

Table 3. Experiment 2: popularity on category-specific dataset using visual features.

Training data	Action			
	Concepts	Low-level	Visual sentiment	AvgPool
Category-mix	0.186	0.241	0.144	0.285
Category-specific	0.286	0.317	0.211	0.345
	Scene			
	Concepts	Low-level	Visual sentiment	AvgPool
Category-mix	0.151	0.201	0.112	0.221
Category-specific	0.221	0.227	0.153	0.250
	People			
	Concepts	Low-level	Visual sentiment	AvgPool
Category-mix	0.168	0.191	0.152	0.224
Category-specific	0.187	0.223	0.198	0.244
	Animal			
	Concepts	Low-level	Visual sentiment	AvgPool
Category-mix	0.221	0.201	0.162	0.234
Category-specific	0.165	0.216	0.224	0.247

5.2   Post Popularity Prediction in Category-Specific Dataset

We report the result of post popularity prediction using visual features in the category-specific dataset in Table 3. The result of predicting the popularity of post related to action category reaches 0.286, 0.317, 0.211, and 0.345 using Concepts, Low-level, Visual sentiment and fusion of them respectively where the model is trained on action specific data. However using a model trained on category-mix the result reaches to 0.186, 0.241, 0.144, and 0.285 by Concepts, Low-level, Visual sentiment and fusion of them. Thus the result of fusing features shows 38% relative improvement in popularity of action posts where we use a model trained on specific action data against a model using all data. The result in Table 3 also show 13%, 9%, and 6% relative improvement in popularity of scene, people, and animal category respectively using specific data for training a popularity model against using all data.

We report the effect of training a popularity model over specific data, using different textual features, versus training a model using all data. It shows 17%, 29%, 8%, and 5% relative improvement in predicting the popularity of post related to action, scene, people, and animal category. The result of rank correlation by combining the best visual and textual features per category reaches to 0.488, 0.481, 0.245, and 0.248 for action, scene, people, and animal category respectively.

We show the result of popularity prediction per instance inside each category using visual features in Table 4. As we can see among all actions the best results are for the action *Dancing*, where the result reaches 0.400, 0.321, and 0.255

Table 4. Experiment 2: popularity prediction for each instance of categories.

Visual features				
Category	Instance	Concepts	Low-level	Visual sentiment
Action	Basketball	0.171	0.226	0.157
	Climbing	0.088	0.158	0.201
	Cycling	0.182	0.175	0.095
	Dancing	**0.400**	**0.321**	**0.255**
	Playing-football	0.120	0.074	0.095
	Horse-riding	0.100	0.106	0.083
	Hugging	0.135	0.200	0.076
	kissing	0.086	0.157	0.065
	Playing-music	0.087	0.100	0.108
	Running	0.057	0.124	0.045
	Skiing	0.119	0.114	0.107
	Surfing	0.070	0.067	0.035
Scene	Art-gallery	0.100	0.170	0.287
	Bar	0.102	0.112	0.114
	Beach	0.064	0.107	0.158
	Bedroom	0.100	0.137	0.149
	Cafe	0.093	0.087	0.035
	Canals	0.088	0.068	0.094
	Fields	0.081	0.103	0.087
	Forest	0.100	0.125	0.154
	Home	0.046	0.068	0.099
	Kitchen	0.069	0.032	0.055
	Street	0.035	0.1092	0.112
	Swimming-pool	**0.495**	**0.598**	**0.309**
People	Selfie	0.187	0.223	0.198
Animal	Pet	0.165	0.216	0.224

rank correlation using Concepts, Low-level and visual sentiment respectively. In the scene category, *Swimming-pool* has the highest rank correlation scores using all visual features among the others. The results are pretty good for these two instances showing the effect on popularity of pleasant actions and places for everyday life hidden in visual content.

We observe from Tables 3, and 4 that the presence of visual sentiment for most of the categories and instances has a positive effect on the predicted popularity. We highlight the importance of sentiments with different impact on popularity for *Dancing, Swimming-pool, Selfie,* and *Pet* in Fig. 3.

Fig. 3. Experiment 2: visual sentiments with high impact on post popularity for (a) Dancing, (b) Swimming-pool, (c) Selfie and (d) Pet. Font size correlates with the impact of visual sentiments with the popularity of instances.

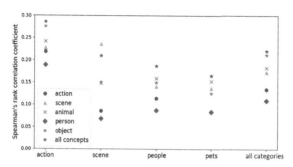

Fig. 4. Experiment 3: correlation between specific concepts and categories

The results of experiment 2 confirm the effect of visual and textual features, also the combination of them, for predicting the popularity of a post related to different categories. Moreover, in general, it emphasizes the accuracy of popularity prediction models trained on category-specific data. At the end it shows that there are some specific visual semantic features which make sense for popularity of posts in different categories.

5.3 Popularity Prediction Using Specific Visual Concepts

We report the result of experiment 3 in Fig. 4. It shows that for all categories, except for scene, all 1000 Concepts have the best descriptive power for popularity. In this case, the scene category is observed to have the highest rank correlation with the specific concepts related to scene concepts, forming 151-dimensional concept feature vectors of 1000 concepts. The reported correlation is 0.255 versus all concepts with 0.221. The rank correlation result reaches 0.286, 0.271, 0.241, 0.232, 0.215, and 0.186 using all concepts, objects, animal, scene, action, and person concepts for the action category. There are just 50 concepts out of 1000 concepts related to action. The results indicate that the low dimensional visual concepts are less effective for predicting the popularity of actions. Another reason is that the most of specific action concepts are not relevant for the actions in our dataset.

The result of experiment 3 confirm that higher-dimensional concept vector are contributing most to popularity prediction, since there are as many descriptors as possible for a subset category of posts.

6 Conclusion

We study the problem of popularity prediction of user generated post based on visual and textual content of post. Different from existing work, which investigate the effect of different visual and textual features on popularity of a post, we consider to predict the popularity of a post inside different specific categories such as action, scene, people, and animal. We study if there is any visual semantic concepts in the category which has positive effect on the popularity of category. By performing three experiments on a dataset of 65K posts related to different categories crawled from Instagram we find that: (1) Visual and textual contents have different impact on the popularity prediction of posts. Combining these contents improves the result. (2) In general, training a popularity model on specific-category data increases the accuracy of popularity per category. and (3) Concepts related to scene and different objects, have a descriptive power with the highest correlation with popularity prediction in all categories. Human faces and animals are also important for popularity prediction, as the adjective-noun pairs results show.

Acknowledgments. This research is supported by the Amsterdam Academic Alliance Data Science (AAA-DS) Program Award to the UvA and VU Universities. Thanks to Dr Efstratios Gavves for his collaboration in this project.

References

1. Bae, Y., Lee, H.: Sentiment analysis of twitter audiences: measuring the positive or negative influence of popular twitterers. J. Am. Soc. Inf. Sci. Technol. **63**(12), 2521–2535 (2012)
2. Borth, D., Ji, R., Chen, T., Breuel, T., Chang, S.-F.: Large-scale visual sentiment ontology and detectors using adjective noun pairs. In: MM (2013)
3. Breiman, L.: Random forests. Mach. Learn. **45**(1), 5–32 (2001)
4. Cappallo, S., Mensink, T., Snoek, C.G.M.: Latent factors of visual popularity prediction. In: ICMR (2015)
5. Chen, T., Borth, D., Darrell, T., Chang, S.F.: Deepsentibank: visual sentiment concept classification with deep convolutional neural networks. CoRR (2014)
6. Gelli, F., Uricchio, T., Bertini, M., Del Bimbo, A., Chang, S.F.: Image popularity prediction in social media using sentiment and context features. In: MM (2015)
7. Hong, L., Dan, O., Davison, B.D.: Predicting popular messages in Twitter. In: WWW (2011)
8. Iordache, O.: Self-Evolvable Systems: Machine Learning in Social Media. Understanding Complex Systems. Springer, Heidelberg (2012). https://doi.org/10.1007/978-3-642-28882-1
9. Khosla, A., Das Sarma, A., Hamid, R.: What makes an image popular? In: WWW (2014)
10. Kingma, D.P., Ba, J.: Adam: a method for stochastic optimization. CoRR (2014)
11. Li, C., Lu, Y., Mei, Q., Wang, D., Pandey, S.: Click-through prediction for advertising in Twitter timeline. In: KDD (2015)
12. MacKuen, M.B.: Political drama, economic conditions, and the dynamics of presidential popularity. Am. J. Polit. Sci. **27**(2), 165–192 (1983)

13. Mazloom, M., Hendriks, B., Worring, M.: Multimodal context-aware recommender for post popularity prediction in social media. In: MM (2017)
14. Mazloom, M., Rietveld, R., Rudinac, S., Worring, M., van Dolen, W.: Multimodal popularity prediction of brand-related social media posts. In: MM (2016)
15. McParlane, P.J., Moshfeghi, Y., Jose, J.M.: Nobody comes here anymore, it's too crowded; predicting image popularity on flickr. In: ICMR (2014)
16. Overgoor, G., Mazloom, M., Worring, M., Rietveld, R., van Dolen, W.: A spatio-temporal category representation for brand popularity prediction. In: ICMR (2017)
17. Rong, X.: word2vec parameter learning explained. CoRR (2014)
18. Szabo, G., Huberman, B.A.: Predicting the popularity of online content. Commun. ACM **53**(8), 80–88 (2010)
19. Szegedy, C., Vanhoucke, V., Ioffe, S., Shlens, J., Wojna, Z.: Rethinking the inception architecture for computer vision. CoRR (2015)
20. Thelwall, M., Buckley, K., Paltoglou, G., Cai, D., Kappas, A.: Sentiment strength detection in short informal text. J. Am. Soc. Inf. Sci. Technol. **61**(12), 2544–2558 (2010)

Image Aesthetics and Content in Selecting Memorable Keyframes from Lifelogs

Feiyan Hu and Alan F. Smeaton[✉]

Insight Centre for Data Analytics, Dublin City University, Dublin 9, Ireland
alan.smeaton@dcu.ie

Abstract. Visual lifelogging using wearable cameras accumulates large amounts of image data. To make them useful they are typically structured into events corresponding to episodes which occur during the wearer's day. These events can be represented as a visual storyboard, a collection of chronologically ordered images which summarise the day's happenings. In previous work, little attention has been paid to how to select the representative keyframes for a lifelogged event, apart from the fact that the image should be of good quality in terms of absence of blurring, motion artifacts, etc. In this paper we look at image aesthetics as a characteristic of wearable camera images. We show how this can be used in combination with content analysis and temporal offsets, to offer new ways for automatically selecting wearable camera keyframes. In this paper we implement several variations of the keyframe selection method and illustrate how it works using a publicly-available lifelog dataset.

Keywords: Lifelogging · Keyframes · Image aesthetics · Image quality

1 Introduction to Lifelogging

Lifelogging is a phenomenon of automatically and ambiently recording different aspects of ordinary, everyday life, in digital format [7]. This has become a topic of research interest and practical use because of the development of wearable sensors and their reduction in size and most importantly the way battery technology has improved to the point of enabling all-day continuous recording.

Lifelogs can be generated using a range of wearable sensors including physiology sensors (heart rate, respiration, etc.), activity sensors (wrist-worn accelerometers), location sensors (GPS and indoor location tracking), environmental sensors (passive infra-red for detecting presence, temperature, humidity, etc.) and wearable cameras which record what the user is doing and experiencing, from the wearers' viewpoint. The most popular wearable cameras are worn on the chest, are front-facing and have a wide-angle lens to record a broad perspective of the viewers point of view [6]. Many devices like the GoPro and similar can record continuous HD video, as well as audio. For niche applications like wearable cameras for law enforcement, this is acceptable but leads to storage requirements which are excessive for scalable lifelogging and for less specialist uses.

K. Schoeffmann et al. (Eds.): MMM 2018, Part I, LNCS 10704, pp. 608–619, 2018.
https://doi.org/10.1007/978-3-319-73603-7_49

The most popular wearable camera devices used for lifelogging is the Autographer and prior to that it was the Narrative and before that the SenseCam. Functionally these are all quite similar in that they each take several thousands of images per day, usually triggered by on-board sensors such as an accelerometer to detect movement. In general these take about 2 or 3 images per minute and store these on-board for later downloading and processing. The processing usually involves structuring a lifelog into discrete and non-overlapping events and selecting single image keyframes from each event as representative of the activity in the event [4].

The selection of the keyframe to use as the event summary has not been a subject of much investigation and simple techniques such as choosing the keyframe in the middle of the event, or the first or last, or the one with best image quality, have generally been used. In this paper we re-examine the question of "which lifelog image to use to summarise an event" by exploring different aspects of lifelog images including image quality, image content and image aesthetics, as well as combinations of them. We present results computed from a publicly available lifelog dataset which compares different approaches.

2   Keyframes from Visual Lifelogs

There are many use cases for lifelogging including self-monitoring of sleep or activity levels for health and wellness, long term monitoring for supporting behaviour change like smoking cessation, activity recording by personnel in security settings, activity and event recording in certain employment areas like health professionals [7]. The application that we are interested in is memory augmentation and memory support helping them to remember and to learn better and to remember more and to remember things that are more important. While we currently focus on people without memory impairment, ultimately this can have possibilities for people with various forms of dementia as shown in the preliminary work by Piasek et al. [16].

Harvey et al. [8] have argued that the increasing interest in and development of lifelogging does present clear possibilities for using technology, specifically technology which generates lifelogs, to augment human memory beyond what is currently done, which is mostly just about reminders and prompts. Their work does note the ethical concerns and dangers with doing this and that we should be aware of moving beyond prompts and reminders and into augmentation. Lets not forget that there are reasons why sometimes we do want to forget. Silva et al. go further in [18] and point to a lack of theory behind memory augmentation which can guide us on how to use visual lifelogging in memory augmentation or rehabilitation. Most of the studies to date have been small in scale and in sample size and evaluation of the efficacy of any form of memory augmentation has always been difficult.

The basic premise on which almost all (visual) lifelog applications are based, especially those which address memory rehabilitation or support, is to present a visual summary of each day as a storyboard of images, a selection of images taken from the wearable camera. These are usually filtered to eliminate poor quality images, including those with blurring or occlusion caused by hands similar to those shown in Fig. 1. However once the poor quality images are removed there is then little guidance on which images to select. Keyframe selection from lifelogs is different to keyframe selection from video shots when the genre is movies, TV programs, news, or any kind of post-produced material where the shot is structured. In image lifelogs, as in many videos on social media, the shots/events are not as structured and the important things can happen serendipitously.

Fig. 1. Examples of poor quality wearable camera images due to wearer movement and occlusion from the wearer's hands, respectively

Doherty *et al.* in [3] did work on automatic selection of keyframe images based on their visual uniqueness, so effectively presenting the day as an illustration of the wearers' most unusual activities, as shown in Fig. 2 below. In this rendering of a summary of the day's activities the size of the image is proportional to the visual uniqueness of the image, where uniqueness corresponds to unusual activities for the wearer. This addresses a use case for lifelogging where we want the summary to present unusual events but that's not the same as memory augmentation which is what we are interested in here.

In an early study into the management and use of digital photographs, [17] found that people are more attracted to highly aesthetically attractive pictures. In an even earlier study in [1] it was found that users tend to pick the most aesthetically appealing pictures for their portfolios when asked to choose images of themselves for authentication purposes. More recent work [11] studied the impact that aesthetic images have on people's recollection of news items associated with those images and determined that aesthetics of those associated images does have a big impact on people's views on those stories.

There are many examples in society where people are presented with the task of creating an image that a viewer will remember. That is the basis behind advertising, for example. While it may seem that image memorability is a subjective aspect, not all images are equal in their memorability as shown in [10]. Some will stick in our minds, while others are easily forgotten. It has been shown that image memorability is a characteristic of images that is constant and is shared

Fig. 2. Doherty's SenseCam Browser, a visual summary of a day taken from [3]

across viewers, in other words different people associate with the same memorability aspects of many images [9,12]. Given that this is the case, and that our ultimate use case here is triggering memory recall, especially for people with memory impairment, this gives us the rationale for looking at whether we should select the most aesthetically pleasing images from a visual lifelog as summaries of a day. This forms the main criterion for our lifelog event summarisation, computable aesthetics as a proxy for memorability of an image.

3   Computing Image Aesthetics and Uniqueness of Image Semantics

In order to test our ideas on lifelog keyframes we need a lifelog collection which is freely available to allow reproducibility of our work. Creating and releasing a lifelog collection for public use is one of the most difficult datasets to assemble because of concerns about privacy, ownership of the data. Fortunately such a collection has recently become available.

The NTCIR-13 Lifelog data consists of 5 days of data from two active lifeloggers. The dataset contains biometric data including heart rate, GSR, caloric expenditure, blood pressure, and more, activity data including locations visited, accelerometer data and mood, computer usage data, and the part of interest to us, images taken from a Narrative Clip 2 wearable camera [5]. This is set to take an image at 45 s intervals, corresponding to about 1,500 images per day. With these images there is the accompanying output from an automatic concept detector.

Aesthetics is a fairly ephemeral concept and has to do with the beauty and human appreciation of an object, or whatever is in the image. It is difficult to pin down precisely as it has a subjective element where one person can view a picture or an object as beautiful and another person can have the opposite view. So even though there is no universal agreement or even a ranking of aesthetic quality, and there would be debate about things in the "middle" there's fair enough agreement of things that are, and are not, aesthetically pleasing.

Many computer vision papers have tried to quantify and measure the aesthetic quality of images [2,13,14]. Yet this aspect of an image is subjectively derived and aesthetic values of an image will vary from subject to subject. There are some features like sky illumination or certain concepts that have been reported in [2] to have influence on aesthetic scores. With increasing computational power and especially neural networks with pre-trained models, it is now possible to predict or compute aesthetic values for an image. Mai et al. [14] used pre-trained models to extract the probability of certain semantic concepts occurring in highly-aesthetic images. Along with probability of concepts, neural networks have also been trained from scratch to compute aesthetics with adaptive pooling layers where combined high level and low level features are used to predict aesthetic scores.

To describe the problem formally we assume that each day a camera captures T images, and each image is I_t where $t = 0 \ldots T$. In order to quantify aesthetic scores, we trained a deep neural network. The network we used is ResNet, pre-trained on ImageNet images to extract image representations and on top of the image representation we add a fully connected layer to predict aesthetic scores.

The dataset used to train aesthetic net is from the DPChallenge[1]. The aesthetic score is defined as S_A:

$$S_t^A = f_{NN}(I_t(x, y, c)) \tag{1}$$

where f_{NN} is the trained neural net, and $I(x, y, c)$ is the input image with color channels. Some example lifelog images with their aesthetic scores are shown in Fig. 3.

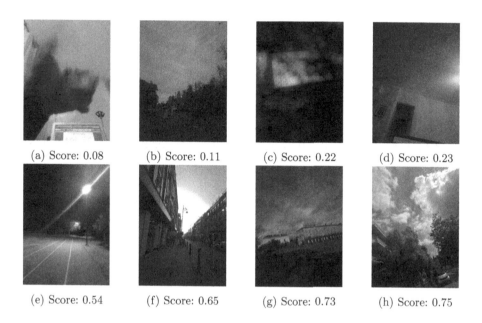

(a) Score: 0.08   (b) Score: 0.11   (c) Score: 0.22   (d) Score: 0.23

(e) Score: 0.54   (f) Score: 0.65   (g) Score: 0.73   (h) Score: 0.75

Fig. 3. Examples lifelog images with their aesthetic scores

In order to determine the uniqueness of each lifelog images in terms of its content, which is a contributing factor to memorability, we use object annotation associated with each image. In the NTCIR Lifelog task, which was described earlier, each image has a number of semantic concepts or objects labeled automatically, and we use $\{O_t\}$ to represent the set of semantics for image t. The number of semantic concepts in each image is defined as:

$$S_t^L = |O_t| \tag{2}$$

In order to define the uniqueness of a image we define a matrix A_{ij}:

$$A_{ij} = \begin{cases} \frac{S_i^L - |O_i \cap O_j|}{S_i^L} & i \neq j \text{ and } S_i^L \neq 0 \\ 0 & i = j \text{ or } S_i^L = 0 \end{cases} \tag{3}$$

---

[1] http://www.dpchallenge.com/.

The uniqueness score is then computed as:

$$S_t^U = \sum_{j=0}^{T} A_{tj} \tag{4}$$

The scores are normalized by the maximum score within a day to eliminate inter-daily bias:

$$\hat{S}_t^A = \frac{S_t^A}{\max\limits_{t} S_t^A}$$

$$\hat{S}_t^L = \frac{S_t^L}{\max\limits_{t} S_t^L} \tag{5}$$

$$\hat{S}_t^U = \frac{S_t^U}{\max\limits_{t} S_t^U}$$

The process to select key frames of each day of lifelog images is described as:

1. Find the highest n images ranked by aesthetic score S_t^A. This set is marked as $\{\mathcal{A}\}$. In our experiment $n = 100$.
2. Find the highest m images ranked by uniqueness of image semantics S_t^U. This set is marked as $\{\mathcal{U}\}$. In our experiment $m = 100$.
3. The intersection of $\{\mathcal{A}\}$ and $\{\mathcal{U}\}$ is our candidate set of keyframes $\{\mathcal{K}\} = \mathcal{A} \cap \mathcal{U}$.
4. Images in $\{\mathcal{K}\}$ are ranked in chronological order. Among those ordered images, the time interval between neighboring images less than time s is classified into one group or segment. In our experiment time s is set to 15 min.
5. We then select one keyframe from each segment according to different scores or combinations of scores S_t. Different hypothesis to compute S_t are used and these are described in the next section, along with illustrating examples.

4   Creating Storyboards from Lifelog Images

We combined uniqueness of content as represented by concept annotations, image aesthetics and image richness to select keyframes to make storyboards for single days in the NTCIR Lifelog collection. We choose one day from the collection, September 25th, and illustrate the different selection methods for that day, though we would like to have completed a fuller evaluation, which we will return to later.

1. The first method is called **Aesthetics:** and is formally defined as $S_t = \hat{S}_t^A$. The examples of it is shown in Fig. 4(a) which shows the timeline as a bar in the middle with the chosen keyframes appearing above and below, and pointing to the time of day when they were taken. There is no supplementary information in this storyboard, just the images and time taken.

2. The second method is called **Uniqueness of semantics:** formally defined as $S_t = \hat{S}_t^U$ and shown in Fig. 4(b). Once again we have a timeline and associated with each image we have the set of annotations assigned to each image. Some of these images, for example the first one of the night sky, may be semantically meaningful but they are not pleasing to look at.

3. The third method is a **Combination of semantic uniqueness and richness:** defined as $S_t = \frac{1}{2}\hat{S}_t^U + \frac{1}{2}\hat{S}_t^L$ and shown in Fig. 4(c) which once again associates semantic concepts or tags with images and also yields a set of images which are at least more pleasing to the eye.

4. In the fourth example we use a **Combination of aesthetic and semantic uniqueness:** which is defined as $S_t = \frac{1}{2}\hat{S}_t^A + \frac{1}{2}\hat{S}_t^U$ and the example is shown in Fig. 5(a). There are no concepts to illustrate in this example.

5. The final algorithm to generate storyboard keyframes is called **Combination of aesthetic, semantic uniqueness and richness:** and is defined as $S_t = \frac{1}{2}\hat{S}_t^A + \frac{1}{2}(\frac{1}{2}\hat{S}_t^U + \frac{1}{2}\hat{S}_t^L)$. A worked example can be seen in Fig. 5(b).

If we look at Fig. 4(a), in which keyframes are selected only by aesthetic scores, we notice that even though the third image above the timeline from the left above is considered aesthetically pleasing by the classifier, it doesn't provide much information except that it is an indoor wall. Interestingly when we choose keyframes by combining aesthetic and semantic uniqueness as shown in Fig. 5(a), the images chosen at the very same time seem to have much more information. We can tell this event is on a street and can even see the names of some shops. Figure 4(b) shows the storyboard result when using only semantic uniqueness, and it can be observed that most of the selected keyframes are different from those selected by aesthetic value though there are still 3 images that are overlapping, including two images with a laptop screen.

Selection by semantic uniqueness in Fig. 4(b) is sensitive to the successful performance of concept detection. A good example to illustrate this is the first image above the timeline on the left. The concepts are mis-classified as *night* and *sky*, which happen to be unique among all the semantics because the wearer did not spend much time outdoors at night. By using the number of concepts appearing in each image it seems it can have leverage on this dilemma. Figure 4(c) seems to return more reasonable results than just using semantic uniqueness alone. The result of aesthetic, semantic uniqueness and richness combined are shown in Fig. 5(b). Among the results when using different methods, there are some images that seem to appear repeatedly and have some invariant property. In future work we could extract and further analyse those images.

While the above might seem like a cursory examination of the outputs of different keyframe strategies, a full and thorough evaluation of the *memorability* of the camera images generated by different, and combined, approaches is out of scope. This would require multiple wearers to generate lifelog content and for each wearer, generate storyboards of their days via all the algorithmic variations mentioned above. We would then present memory recollection tasks to each wearer, for each method, in order to test the efficacy of the different

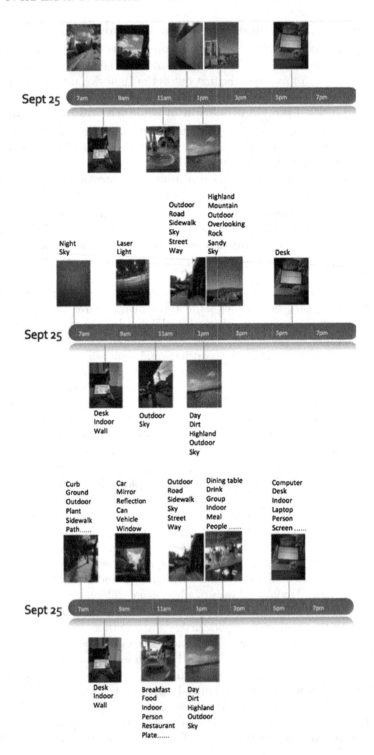

Fig. 4. (a) Aesthetics only. (b) Semantics. (c) Semantics plus some concepts.

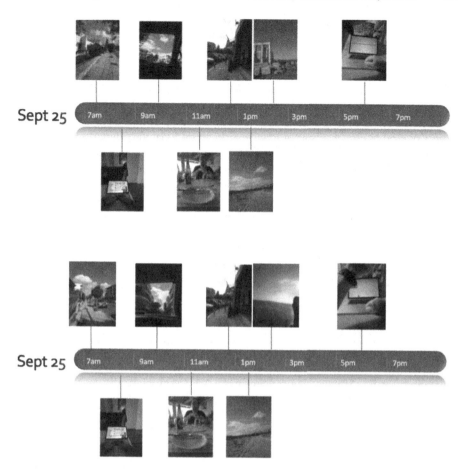

Fig. 5. (a) Aesthetics with semantics. (b) Aesthetics, semantics and some concepts.

keyframe selection approaches used to generate the storyboards. Such an experiment would need to insulate against the very many confounding variables like wearer variation, time variation, and would make this a huge user experiment. We don't have resources for that so we are limited to observational analysis of generated storyboards presented above.

5   Conclusions

Computing lifelog keyframe selections as described in this paper is not computationally expensive since the aesthetics classifier is already trained and built and all that is required is processing to extract low level features and then run it through the classifier. The early layers of the deep learning network used to compute aesthetics can be re-used as the layers used to extract features for semantic concept recognition and in fact that is what we do when we re-use the layers trained on ResNet and the ImageNet image dataset. So in total, once the training is done this is very fast to run.

There are two main directions we would like to pursue as future work. The first, and most obvious, is a thorough evaluation but we need to develop an evaluation which is not full-on with lots of users involved as sketched out in the previous section since that is neither scalable nor affordable. The second direction is to examine each image for use as a keyframe but not the whole image. Wearable camera images have a wide angle view and they do not capture what the wearer was actually looking at, just what the range of things they may have looked at. Using prior work in saliency detection such as that described in [15], we can identify "parts" or regions within a keyframe which can be a crop from the whole image and then go into the storyboard, rather than the whole image. This is interesting for the memorability application because it can be objects or features within our perspective which trigger memories and this is what that saliency-based cropping yields.

References

1. Dhamija, R., Perrig, A.: Deja-Vu a user study: using images for authentication. In: USENIX Security Symposium, vol. 9, p. 4 (2000)
2. Dhar, S., Ordonez, V., Berg, T.L.: High level describable attributes for predicting aesthetics and interestingness. In: 2011 IEEE Conference on Computer Vision and Pattern Recognition (CVPR), pp. 1657–1664. IEEE (2011)
3. Doherty, A.R., Moulin, C.J.A., Smeaton, A.F.: Automatically assisting human memory: a SenseCam browser. Memory **19**(7), 785–795 (2011)
4. Doherty, A.R., Smeaton, A.F.: Automatically segmenting lifelog data into events. In: 2008 9th International Workshop on Image Analysis for Multimedia Interactive Services, pp. 20–23, May 2008
5. Gurrin, C., Joho, H., Hopfgartner, F., Zhou, L., Albatal, R.: NTCIR lifelog: the first test collection for lifelog research. In: Proceedings of 39th International ACM SIGIR Conference on Research and Development in Information Retrieval, SIGIR 2016, pp. 705–708. ACM, New York (2016)
6. Gurrin, C., Smeaton, A.F., Byrne, D., O'Hare, N., Jones, G.J.F., O'Connor, N.: An examination of a large visual lifelog. In: Li, H., Liu, T., Ma, W.-Y., Sakai, T., Wong, K.-F., Zhou, G. (eds.) AIRS 2008. LNCS, vol. 4993, pp. 537–542. Springer, Heidelberg (2008). https://doi.org/10.1007/978-3-540-68636-1_60
7. Gurrin, C., Smeaton, A.F., Doherty, A.R.: Lifelogging: personal big data. Found. Trends Inf. Retr. **8**(1), 1–125 (2014)
8. Harvey, M., Langheinrich, M., Ward, G.: Remembering through lifelogging: a survey of human memory augmentation. Pervasive Mob. Comput. **27**, 14–26 (2016)
9. Isola, P., Parikh, D., Torralba, A., Oliva, A., Understanding the intrinsic memorability of images. In: Shawe-Taylor, J., Zemel, R.S., Bartlett, P.L., Pereira, F., Weinberger, K.Q. (eds.) Advances in Neural Information Processing Systems, vol. 24, pp. 2429–2437. Curran Associates Inc. (2011)
10. Isola, P., Xiao, J., Parikh, D., Torralba, A., Oliva, A.: What makes a photograph memorable? IEEE Trans. Pattern Anal. Mach. Intell. **36**(7), 1469–1482 (2014)
11. Kätsyri, J., Ravaja, N., Salminen, M.: Aesthetic images modulate emotional responses to reading news messages on a small screen: a psychophysiological investigation. Int. J. Hum. Comput. Stud. **70**(1), 72–87 (2012)

12. Khosla, A., Xiao, J., Isola, P., Torralba, A., Oliva, A.: Image memorability and visual inception. In: SIGGRAPH Asia 2012 Technical Briefs, SA 2012, pp. 35:1–35:4. ACM, New York (2012)
13. Lu, X., Lin, Z., Jin, H., Yang, J., Wang, J.Z.: Rating image aesthetics using deep learning. IEEE Trans. Multimedia **17**(11), 2021–2034 (2015)
14. Mai, L., Jin, H., Liu, F.: Composition-preserving deep photo aesthetics assessment. In: Proceedings of IEEE Conference on Computer Vision and Pattern Recognition, pp. 497–506 (2016)
15. Pan, J., Sayrol, E., Giro-i Nieto, X., McGuinness, K., O'Connor, N.E.: Shallow and deep convolutional networks for saliency prediction. In: Proceedings of IEEE Conference on Computer Vision and Pattern Recognition, pp. 598–606 (2016)
16. Piasek, P., Irving, K., Smeaton, A.F.: SenseCam intervention based on cognitive stimulation therapy framework for early-stage dementia. In: 2011 5th International Conference on Pervasive Computing Technologies for Healthcare (PervasiveHealth) and Workshops, pp. 522–525, May 2011
17. Rodden, K., Wood, K.R.: How do people manage their digital photographs? In: Proceedings of SIGCHI Conference on Human Factors in Computing Systems, CHI 2003, pp. 409–416. ACM, New York (2003)
18. Silva, A.R., Pinho, M.S., Macedo, L., Moulin, C.J.A.: A critical review of the effects of wearable cameras on memory. Neuropsychol. Rehabil. **26**(1), 1–25 (2016). PMID: 26732623

On the Traceability of Results from Deep Learning-Based Cloud Services

Werner Bailer[✉]

DIGITAL – Institute for Information and Communication Technologies,
JOANNEUM RESEARCH Forschungsgesellschaft mbH,
Steyrergasse 17, 8010 Graz, Austria
werner.bailer@joanneum.at

Abstract. Deep learning-based approaches have become an important method for media content analysis, and are useful tools for multimedia analytics, as they enable organising and visualising multimedia content items. However, the use of deep neural networks also raises issues of traceability, reproducability and understanding analysis results. The issues are caused by the dependency on training data sets and their possible bias, the change of training data sets over time and the lack of transparent and interoperable representations of models. In this paper we analyse these problems in detail and provide examples. We propose six recommendations to address these issues, which include having interoperable representations of trained models, the identification of training data and models (including versions) and the description of provenance of data sets, models and results.

1 Introduction

Deep learning-based approaches have become an important method for multimedia analysis, most notably classification. But also features extracted from deep neural networks (often named *deep features*) have been shown to be applicable for a wide range of tasks [14], and are useful for determining similarity between multimedia items or for instance search. All these approaches are useful for multimedia analytics, as they enable organising and visualising multimedia content items.

However, the use of deep neural networks also raises issues of traceability, reproducability and understanding analysis results. The results of these methods depend heavily on training data sets, and on choices of network structure and hyper-parameters for training. Due to the requirements of very large data sets and high computational resources for training, they are often not deployed locally, but provided as cloud services. With continuous integration and deployment, the classifiers used in the cloud services are updated, changing the results for media items. And all this happens in a black box, and is intransparent to the user.

While this may cause issues in various application scenarios, it is especially problematic in multimedia analytics, where humans in the loop gather experience

© Springer International Publishing AG 2018
K. Schoeffmann et al. (Eds.): MMM 2018, Part I, LNCS 10704, pp. 620–631, 2018.
https://doi.org/10.1007/978-3-319-73603-7_50

on the automatic tools used and their strengths and weaknesses. Especially in applications like forensics, biotechnology or medicine, where the user may make far-reaching judgements using multimedia analytics tools, a complete and traceable documentation of how decisions were made is required. This becomes hard to impossible once the tools involved become black boxes constantly changing their behaviour.

In this paper, we analyse different aspects of the problem of traceability and reproducability of deep neural network (DNN)-based multimedia analysis tools, in particular, cloud-based ones. Section 2 provides a real-world example that serves as motivation, and Sect. 3 discusses related work. In Sect. 4 we review the aspects of the problem in more detail, and outline recommendations to address them in Sect. 5. Section 6 concludes the paper.

2   A Motivating Example

As an example, we use the AWS Rekognition[1] service to perform concept detection for a photos (The service was chosen as an example, but the observations hold for most comparable services). The image used as input and the results are shown in Fig. 1. The detected concepts look appropriate for the image. If we look more closely, we see that *Guitar*, *Guitarist*, *Musical Instrument*, *Musician*, *Performer* and *Person* have exactly the same score (down to the 14th digit after the comma), and it is highly unlikely that six independent classifiers would produce this result. So it seems some concepts have been inferred from others, and the scores have been transferred between concepts – but which were those actually classified? We also cannot check the reliability of the result based on the fact that overlapping concepts were labelled (e.g., person and musician), because they were obviously not classified independently. So we lack details about the *provenance of information.*

The labels *Club* and *Night Club* (again with the same confidence) are not exactly correct in this example, but they are plausible. However, they hint at the problem of bias from training data. Many images used in the training data of cloud-based classification services seem to originate from social media, and thus have a bias towards tags used there. For example, we found that many photos showing one to a few persons from close distance are labelled with *Selfie*. In a multimedia analytics application one can handle such a bias, if one knows it is there or changes. But we do not know anything about the *training data* or when it changes.

A week later, we uploaded the same image again. The result contained the same set of concepts, but all the confidence scores had changed. The amount of change within a week was not dramatic, but over longer periods values are likely to drift further. The service only reports labels for which the confidence exceeds a certain threshold, thus labels could appear or disappear even due to small confidence changes if the scores are near the threshold. If clustering has been applied before, and the parameters have been stored, even small changes

---

[1] aws.amazon.com/de/rekognition/.

may cause images to move to another cluster. This means that both automatic tools and users working with the results cannot rely on *consistent behaviour* of the service *over time*.

3 Related Work

In the literature on multimedia analytics, some requirements closely related to the problems discussed in this paper are mentioned. In their discussion of research questions related to multimedia analytics [4], Jónsson et al. mention the topics of longitudinal analysis and the persistence of machine learning models. Zahálka et al. [16] go into more detail in their work on performance evaluation of multimedia collection analysis. The define the notion of an arbiter as "a black box producing content annotations for each item in the analyzed collection". This is exactly the role a cloud-based analysis service takes. Among others, they require an arbiter to be *consistent* ("inputting the same item twice yields identical annotations") and *semantic* ("a human can interpret the annotations and judge their presence in the item"). As we have seen in the example, these two requirements are not met.

Like all supervised machine learning approaches, deep neural networks depend heavily on training data, on *big* training data to be precise. The identification and description of data sets being used is thus an important issue. The linked open data community has identified this issue earlier and has started efforts to describe published data sets in order to improve their interoperability. One result is the Data Catalogue Vocabulary (DCAT) [8] which enables the identification and description of published data sets, together with distribution information and allows organising them in catalogues (which may be distributed over the web).

In addition to identifying data, it is also important to describe how data has been used, transformed or modified, e.g., which trained model is based on which data or that a data set has been formed by extending an existing one with new samples. This is the domain of data provenance. A recent work [6] discusses among other open challenges for machine learning with big data the issue of big data sets used in training. The challenge is not only integrating provenance management but also handling the size of the provenance data. Again, the linked data community has already addressed these issues. Typical use cases involve news distribution on the web[2], e-Science applications such as tracing disease outbreaks and tracking business processes [9]. The W3C developed the PROV family of specifications [3], with an ontology for modelling data provenance at its core. Its main classes are Agents, Entities and Activities, that allow the description of activities generating, modifying or using the data entities. To the best of our knowledge, [2] is the only work that makes use of the PROV ontology in a machine learning context for describing the relation between experiments and

---

[2] It is worth noting that this topic was addressed long before the term "fake news" came into everyday use.

```
{  "Labels": [
        {    "Confidence": 96.46748352050781,
             "Name": "Guitar" },
        {    "Confidence": 96.46748352050781,
             "Name": "Guitarist" },
        {    "Confidence": 96.46748352050781,
             "Name": "Musical Instrument" },
        {    "Confidence": 96.46748352050781,
             "Name": "Musician" },
        {    "Confidence": 96.46748352050781,
             "Name": "Performer" },
        {    "Confidence": 96.46748352050781,
             "Name": "Person" },
        {    "Confidence": 87.81559753417969,
             "Name": "Stage"  },
        {    "Confidence": 76.38549041748047,
             "Name": "Lighting" },
        {    "Confidence": 65.7210464477539,
             "Name": "Music Band" },
        {    "Confidence": 61.37468719482422,
             "Name": "Glitter" },
        {    "Confidence": 61.37468719482422,
             "Name": "Light" },
        {    "Confidence": 58.881168365478516,
             "Name": "Club" },
        {    "Confidence": 58.881168365478516,
             "Name": "Night Club" },
        {    "Confidence": 58.881168365478516,
             "Name": "Night Life" }
    ],
    "OrientationCorrection": "ROTATE_0" }
```

Fig. 1. Input image and concept detection results (photo by VRT for the ICoSOLE project, www.icosole.eu).

the data sets used. In addition it provides an ontology for describing properties of the experiments and algorithm used.

4   Problems

We discuss now the issues raised in Sect. 2 in more detail. They all apply when analysis components of multimedia analytics systems are treated as black boxes, and some are particularly relevant when cloud services are used, which may be updated at any time.

4.1   Provenance of Information

Knowing about the provenance of information answers the questions who produced it, using which inputs and which tools. Among others, it is crucial to assess the quality of data resulting from a process and establish an audit trail, that enables tracking back errors and biases introduced in the process [15]. In a multimedia analytics system, it is important to know how data has been created, i.e., whether it comes from human annotations of multimedia assets, from external sources or has been created using automatic tools. Both data created by humans and machines comes with different levels of confidence or trust, e.g., annotations created by a professional curator vs. crowd-sourced, algorithms for which benchmarking results on relevant data are known vs. experimental algorithms. In both cases there may be bias introduced through external or contextual information that is used, although this factor is hard to isolate for humans. However, if automatic tools are used, they may use external data (e.g., training data, dictionaries) that may have significant influence on the results. Many modern multimedia analysis tools are also quite complex, and make use of other components, such as feature extractors, or build on pre-trained models that are adapted. Each of these steps may impact the confidence of the results or introduce some kind of bias.

In data warehousing the term *data lineage* has been introduced to describe the series of transformation applied to data [1]. The transformations have been classified into dispatchers (one input, many output), aggregators (many inputs, one output) and black boxes (many inputs and outputs, without being able to trace their exact connections). Most multimedia analysis algorithms probably fall into the latter category. Nonetheless, the data lineage could be captured on a coarser level. For example, it can be described that a pre-trained model has been used, and referring to the data set and parameters that have been used during transfer learning when adapting it to a new problem. Coming back to our example, one could use data provenance models to identify which labels and scores are the result of a visual classifier, and which are the result of semantic reasoning on the raw set of classifier outputs.

4.2 Training Data

The availability of large training data has been a main success factor for DNN-based methods in multimedia analysis. Due the easy availability, many training data sets are harvested from social media platforms. Thus the content captured and the annotations being used may be biased, towards topics and demographics of social media in general (which may differ in some aspects from the "outside world") and towards the specifics of the platform(s) being used to collect the data.

The problem of bias has for example been reported for face recognition algorithms, which show lower performance for groups like Blacks or females [5], which is explained by the fact that the demographics of researchers are reflected in the training data sets[3]. It has been also shown that the performance of face recognition algorithms developed in certain regions of the world is better with for individuals from the local majority population [12]. As expected, balancing the training data sets across demographics can improve the performance for minority groups [5].

4.3 Variation Over Time

Consistency of analysis over time is a prerequisite to ensure that (i) identical or very similar (e.g., near duplicate) multimedia items receive very similar annotations when analysed at different points in time, (ii) a large collection that takes a long time to annotate receives the same level and quality of annotations, (iii) the parameterisation of tools that use the analysis results remains valid, and (iv) the experienced strengths and weaknesses of analysis tools that users have made are still valid for future results.

The variation of results from analysis tools may have different reasons, such as improvement of algorithms, change of parameterisation or modified/extended training data. In the case of DNN-based methods it is typically the latter. It is desired that services learn from new data, thus the training data set is extended and the model is improved. Adding new training data may not only be "more of the same", but the statistical distribution of properties in the data may shift. This problem in machine learning is known as *concept drift* [11]. While the drift helps keeping models up to date (e.g., a classifier for "mobile phone" would probably strongly rely on the existence of buttons if trained on data from the 1990s), it may also loose information because it becomes under-represented in the training data.

Figure 2 shows results of the experiment we did with AWS Rekognition. It shows that nearly 70% of the labels' confidence score changed at least once, and that 5–10% of the labels changed up to three times in the experiment duration of four weeks.

Clearly, the possibility to update the system continuously is also a strength of cloud-based services, and should not be sacrificed. However, a client using the

---

[3] https://www.recode.net/2017/1/18/14304964/data-facial-recognition-trouble-recognizing-black-white-faces-diversity.

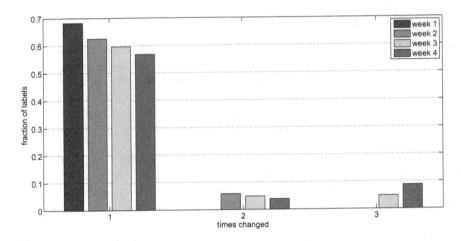

Fig. 2. Fraction of labels with changed confidence score in AWS Rekognition results (out of a set of 104 labels) over four weeks.

service should be able to obtain information whether there have been changes of the service, and in many cases it may also be relevant to get some detail of what these changes are. In cases where consistency over time is particularly crucial, it could be useful to request a specific version of a service (maybe not every version, but one could define long term maintained versions like it is done for operating systems).

4.4 Interoperable Network Representations

As DNNs get widely used in many areas, the issue of describing a (trained) neural network becomes more important, in order to ensure that results can be reproduced when models are exchanged. The issue of interoperable network representations does not only arise when DNNs are used as classifiers for multimedia analysis, but also when deep features are used as representations of content, or in optimization of video coding using DNNs (e.g., [7]). In these cases, the trained model serves as a reference, and must be available in a representation that can be used independent of a specific software framework. Such interoperability issues also arise when a trained network shall be used for inference locally, e.g., on a mobile device or in a vehicle, that requires the use of another software framework than employed for training. In this section, we first review different representations used in current deep learning frameworks, and their properties. We then look at exchange formats that have been proposed for neural networks, and are candidates to address the interoperability issue.

Representations Used in Deep Learning Frameworks. A number of deep learning frameworks define their own representations, and (trained) models of many networks proposed in literature are published using these representations. The

TensorFlow framework[4] uses protocol buffers[5] (version 3) as representation of models. Protocol buffers are a data serialisation designed for efficient transmission over networks, and can be serialised as text or binary files. The model of the network is defined using one GraphDef and a set of NodeDef objects. The operations of a node are defined in C++ code. Node attributes are stored as key value pairs. One protocol buffer file stores these serialised objects. Trained weights of the model are stored separately, represented as TensorProto objects for each NodeDef object. Like TensorFlow, Caffe[6] uses protocol buffers as representation, but relies on another model format (and the format has evolved over different versions of the framework). The representation of the model contains of three files: *train_val.prototxt* contains the structure of the network, *solver.prototxt* contains the hyper parameters for training and **.caffemodel* contains the trained model weights represented as a binary protocol buffer file. The Torch[7] framework is written in Lua, and represents models by describing the construction of the model structure with Lua objects. Weights of a trained model are stored in a separate binary file. PyTorch[8] is a Torch implementation in Python, using their own serialisation model. Either only weights are serialised, or the entire model. The latter is a serialisation of the class structure, so that full interoperability of the serialised model is only granted if nothing in the class structure changes. Keras[9] stores all information related to a model in a single HDF5[10] file: (i) the architecture of the model, (ii) the weights of the model, (iii) the training configuration (loss, optimizer), and (iv) the state of the optimizer. Theano[11] is a framework written in Python, and uses the Python pickle mechanism to serialise and deserialise the Python objects holding the network structure and data. MxNet[12] uses a JSON file with the model definition, and a binary file with the trained parameters. Darknet[13] is a DNN framework written in C. It represents trained networks as two files: a config file with the network structure (INI file style text file) and a binary weights file. Converters between many pairs of model representations are available, and are in most cases implemented using available parsers/serialisers for the involved models, and code translating the data structures.

Exchange Formats. There are some exchange formats for neural networks, but some predate the recent wave of deep neural networks. In addition, some formats are only able to represent the network structure, but not the parameters of trained models. NNML [13] is an XML format that has been designed for the

---

[4] https://www.tensorflow.org.
[5] https://developers.google.com/protocol-buffers.
[6] http://caffe.berkeleyvision.org.
[7] http://torch.ch.
[8] http://pytorch.org.
[9] https://keras.io.
[10] https://support.hdfgroup.org/HDF5/.
[11] http://deeplearning.net/software/theano/.
[12] http://mxnet.io/model_zoo.
[13] https://pjreddie.com/darknet/.

interchange of trained neural network models. Due to the nature of XML, files probably get unpractically large to handle in the case of today's deep networks. ANNeML[14] is an XML representation for representing only the network structure, but not trained models. Predictive Model Markup Language (PMML)[15] is an XML-based language which provides a way for applications to define statistical and data mining models and to share models between PMML compliant applications. It also supports feed forward NNs.

The authors of [10] proposes a data model for representing and storing information related to deep learning experiments. The model, termed POL (Parameter Optimisation for Learning), allows representing the model structure, hyperparameters and trained weights. The model is implemented in JSON and stores data in MongoDB[16].

NNEF[17] is an effort by the Khronos group to define an exchange format to execute networks trained with different frameworks on different inference engines. It seems to be the only effort of this kind up to now. The format is intended to describe the network structure and the trained parameters of the model. However, it does not describe how a network has been trained (e.g., hyperparameters for training, training data). A draft version of the specification is expected by late 2017, and a final version by mid 2018.

ONNX[18] is a recent initiative started by Facebook and Microsoft, with Intel joining a bit later. The aim is to provide an exchangeable format for trained models for AI applications. The code is available[19], and currently supports conversion between Caffe2, Cognitive Toolkit and PyTorch.

5   Recommendations

Based on the analysis of the problems encountered, we formulate a set of recommendations for representing and describing DNN-based multimedia analysis tools in order to obtain traceable results in a multimedia analytics system. Some of the recommendations are more general, and are also applicable to other machine-learning or content analysis tools.

Rec. 1: Identify Data. Any data set used for training should receive an identifier, ideally, a URL that resolves to a description of the data set and (if applicable) a link to access the data. The description should contain basic information about the version, publication details and rights of the data set, and should be available in human and machine readable form, using a standard vocabulary such as DCAT. Machine readability also applies to rights and licensing information, so that an agent accessing the data can ensure correct use of the data. This includes any constraints such as the possibility of revoking (part of) the data in future.

---

[14] github.com/adam-nnl/ANNeML.

[15] dmg.org/pmml/pmml-v4-3.html.

[16] www.mongodb.com.

[17] www.khronos.org/nnef/.

[18] http://onnx.ai/.

[19] https://github.com/onnx.

Rec. 2: Describe Data Provenance. Provide a machine-readable description of the processing and transformations that have been applied, using a vocabulary such as PROV. The description should also include references to tools applied (where relevant). The provenance description should be used together with the identification mechanism to provide a complete record of the changes (e.g., extensions) of the data set over time. For example, a new version of the data set would refer to the previous version, and the set of records (or another data set) being added.

Rec. 3: Identify Models. Like data, models and their versions should receive identifiers, that resolve to a description of the model and access information. A vocabulary such as MEX [2] could be used for this purpose.

Rec. 4: Interoperable Representation of Trained Models. Use a representation for a trained model that includes the network topology, the trained parameters and the hyper-parameters used during training. As the analysis has shown, there are a few suitable candidates. POL does propose a model, but uses a database backend and does not specify a serialisation into files. NNEF seems to be a good starting point, but for being able to reproduce the entire pipeline, also information about the training setup would be required, so it will need to be complemented with a model providing support for these hyper-parameters (e.g., MEX or POL).

Rec. 5: Describe Model Provenance and Relation to Data. Trained models rely on a data set, which is a usage relation in terms of provenance. These dependencies should be explicitly described with the model, using a vocabulary such as PROV. In addition, models may be derived from other models, e.g., by transfer learning on other data. In this case, there exist provenance relations to other models, as well as to the data set(s) used to obtain the modified model.

Rec. 6: Describe Result Provenance. If not all results of an analysis tool are generated in the same way, provide a description which subset of tools/algorithms has been used to generated the results, e.g., which are the result of a classifier or which have been inferred (possibly using external data). This description can also be formulated using a data provenance vocabulary. This is not only valuable information for the user, but also enables subsequent automated services to decide which information has been created independently and can thus be used complementarily or for validation. Result provenance may be more fine-grained and dynamic than the data and model provenance discussed above, so further work on an appropriate representation may be needed.

6   Conclusion

In this paper, we discussed issues that arise from using DNN-based media analysis tools as black boxes. The traceability of the results, which is crucial in many multimedia analytics applications is no longer granted because of these issues.

We propose six recommendations to solve these issues, which address having interoperable representations of trained models, the identification of training data and models (including versions) and the description of provenance of data sets, models and results. The availability of this information in machine-readable form enables a multimedia analytics system to control the use of the tools, to handle the results appropriately and to pass relevant about the sources and confidence of the results to the user.

Acknowledgments. The research leading to these results has received funding from the European Union's Horizon 2020 research and innovation programme under grant agreement No. 732461, ReCAP ("Real-time Content Analysis and Processing", http://recap-project.com). The author thanks Sophia Hebenstreit for collecting the data from AWS Rekognition.

References

1. Cui, Y., Widom, J.: Lineage tracing for general data warehouse transformations. VLDB J.—Int. J. Very Large Data Bases **12**(1), 41–58 (2003)
2. Esteves, D., Moussallem, D., Neto, C.B., Soru, T., Usbeck, R., Ackermann, M., Lehmann, J.: Mex vocabulary: a lightweight interchange format for machine learning experiments. In: Proceedings of the 11th International Conference on Semantic Systems, pp. 169–176. ACM (2015)
3. Groth, P., Moreau, L. (eds.) PROV-overview: an overview of the PROV family of documents. Technical report, W3C Working Group Note (2013)
4. Jónsson, B.Þ., Worring, M., Zahálka, J., Rudinac, S., Amsaleg, L.: Ten research questions for scalable multimedia analytics. In: Tian, Q., Sebe, N., Qi, G.-J., Huet, B., Hong, R., Liu, X. (eds.) MMM 2016. LNCS, vol. 9517, pp. 290–302. Springer, Cham (2016). https://doi.org/10.1007/978-3-319-27674-8_26
5. Klare, B.F., Burge, M.J., Klontz, J.C., Bruegge, R.W.V., Jain, A.K.: Face recognition performance: role of demographic information. IEEE Trans. Inf. Forensics Secur. **7**(6), 1789–1801 (2012)
6. L'Heureux, A., Grolinger, K., Elyamany, H.F., Capretz, M.A.M.: Machine learning with big data: challenges and approaches. IEEE Access **5**, 7776–7797 (2017)
7. Li, H., Trocan, M.: Deep neural network based single pixel prediction for unified video coding. Neurocomputing **272**, 558–570 (2018)
8. Maali, F., Erickson, J., Archer, P. (eds.) Data Catalog Vocabulary (DCAT). Technical report, W3C Recommendation (2014)
9. Moreau, L., Groth, P., Cheney, J., Lebo, T., Miles, S.: The rationale of prov. Web Semant.: Sci. Serv. Agents World Wide Web **35**, 235–257 (2015)
10. O'Donoghue, J., Roantree, M.: A toolkit for analysis of deep learning experiments. In: Boström, H., Knobbe, A., Soares, C., Papapetrou, P. (eds.) IDA 2016. LNCS, vol. 9897, pp. 134–145. Springer, Cham (2016). https://doi.org/10.1007/978-3-319-46349-0_12
11. Parker, C.: Unexpected challenges in large scale machine learning. In: Proceedings of the 1st International Workshop on Big Data, Streams and Heterogeneous Source Mining: Algorithms, Systems, Programming Models and Applications, BigMine 2012, pp. 1–6. ACM, New York (2012)

12. Phillips, P.J., Jiang, F., Narvekar, A., Ayyad, J., O'Toole, A.J.: An other-race effect for face recognition algorithms. ACM Trans. Appl. Percept. **8**(2), 14:1–14:11 (2011)

13. Rubtsov, D., Butakov, S.: A unified format for trained neural network description. In: Proceedings of International Joint Conference on Neural Networks, IJCNN 2001, vol. 4, pp. 2367–2372 (2001)

14. Razavian, A.S., Azizpour, H., Sullivan, J., Carlsson, S.: CNN features off-the-shelf: an astounding baseline for recognition. In: Proceedings of the IEEE Conference on Computer Vision and Pattern Recognition Workshops, pp. 806–813 (2014)

15. Simmhan, Y.L., Plale, B., Gannon, D.: A survey of data provenance techniques. Technical report, Computer Science Department, Indiana University, Bloomington, IN (2005)

16. Zahálka, J., Rudinac, S., Worring, M.: Analytic quality: evaluation of performance and insight in multimedia collection analysis. In: Proceedings of the 23rd ACM International Conference on Multimedia, pp. 231–240. ACM (2015)

Rethinking Summarization and Storytelling for Modern Social Multimedia

Stevan Rudinac[1(✉)], Tat-Seng Chua[2], Nicolas Diaz-Ferreyra[3],
Gerald Friedland[4], Tatjana Gornostaja[5], Benoit Huet[6], Rianne Kaptein[7],
Krister Lindén[8], Marie-Francine Moens[9], Jaakko Peltonen[10], Miriam Redi[11],
Markus Schedl[12], David A. Shamma[13], Alan Smeaton[14], and Lexing Xie[15]

[1] University of Amsterdam, Amsterdam, The Netherlands
s.rudinac@uva.nl
[2] National University of Singapore, Singapore, Singapore
chuats@comp.nus.edu.sg
[3] Universität Duisburg-Essen, Duisburg, Germany
nicolas.diaz-ferreyra@uni-duisburg-essen.de
[4] University of California, Berkeley, USA
fractor@icsi.berkeley.edu
[5] Tilde, Riga, Latvia
gornostay@gmail.com
[6] EURECOM, Sophia Antipolis, France
Benoit.Huet@eurecom.fr
[7] Crunchr, Amsterdam, The Netherlands
amkaptein@hotmail.com
[8] University of Helsinki, Helsinki, Finland
krister.linden@helsinki.fi
[9] KU Leuven, Leuven, Belgium
sien.moens@cs.kuleuven.be
[10] Aalto University, Espoo, Finland
jaakko.peltonen@aalto.fi
[11] Nokia Bell Labs, Cambridge, UK
miriam.redi@gmail.org
[12] Johannes Kepler Universität Linz, Linz, Austria
markus.schedl@jku.at
[13] FX Palo Alto Laboratory, Inc., Palo Alto, USA
aymans@acm.org
[14] Dublin City University, Dublin, Ireland
alan.smeaton@dcu.ie
[15] Australian National University, Canberra, Australia
lexing.xie@anu.edu.au

Abstract. Traditional summarization initiatives have been focused on specific types of documents such as articles, reviews, videos, image feeds, or tweets, a practice which may result in pigeonholing the summarization

---

This position paper resulted from a working group discussion at the Schloss Dagstuhl seminar "User-Generated Content in Social Media", July 23–28, 2017, http://www.dagstuhl.de/17301.

task in the context of modern, content-rich multimedia collections. Consequently, much of the research to date has revolved around mostly toy problems in narrow domains and working on single-source media types. We argue that summarization and story generation systems need to refocus the problem space in order to meet the information needs in the age of user-generated content in different formats and languages. Here we create a framework for flexible multimedia storytelling. Narratives, stories, and summaries carry a set of challenges in big data and dynamic multi-source media that give rise to new research in spatial-temporal representation, viewpoint generation, and explanation.

Keywords: Social multimedia · Summarization · Storytelling

1   Introduction

Social Multimedia [1] has been described as having three main components: content interaction between multimedia, social interaction around multimedia and social interaction captured in multimedia. Roughly speaking, this describes the interaction between traditional multimedia (photos and videos), mostly textual annotations on that media, and people interacting with that media. For almost a decade, fueled by the popularity of User-Generated Content (UGC), the bulk of research [2–8] has focused on meaningful extraction from any combination of these three points. With modern advancements in AI and computational resources [9,10], we now realize that multimedia summarization and story telling has worked in isolated silos, depending on the application and media (object detection, video summarization, Twitter sentiment, etc.); a broader viewpoint on the whole summarisation and reduction process is needed. Consequently, this realization gives rise to a second set of research challenges moving forward. In this paper, we revisit and propose to reshape the future challenges in multimedia summarization to identify a set of goals, prerequisites, and guidelines to address future UGC. Specifically, we address the problems associated with increasingly heterogeneous collections both in terms of multiple media and mixed content in different formats and languages, the necessity and complexities of dense knowledge extraction, and the requirements needed for sense making and storytelling.

2   Related Work

Summarization problems. Content summarisation problems arise in different application domains and are a long-standing interest of the natural language processing, computer vision, and multimedia research communities. Summarising long segments of text from a single or multiple documents is often done with extractive techniques, on which extensive surveys exist [11]. The problem of summarising image collections arises when there are e.g. large amounts of images from many users in a geographic area [12,13], or about a particular social event [14], or when it is necessary to generate a summarizing description (caption) [8]. Similarly, it is often needed to shorten or visualize long video sequences. Early solutions for video-to-image summarisation include automatic story-boards [15] and video summaries in forms of manga comic-book layout [16]. Audiovisual video summaries involve the processing of both audio and visual channels through e.g. joint optimisation of cross-modal coherence [17], or matching of audio segments [18]. In recent years, researchers have explored the summarization of ego-centric or surveillance videos by detecting important objects and actions [19] or constructing a map of key people in a known environment [20]. In the last decade, research on video summaries for real-world events increasingly focused on large-scale social events reported online [18,21]. This position paper examines the summarization problem more broadly, taking a step back from one particular media format to be summarized, and targeting a large range of applications.

Relevance criteria for summarization. Early approaches to information retrieval (IR) and summarization focused on relevance of the content presented to the user. However, by the end of 90s the community realized that users prefer diversified search results and summaries instead of results lists produced based on relevance criterion only [15]. While the application domains varied, since then most summarization approaches focused on finding a balance between relevance, representativeness and diversity. The Informedia project is one of the best known early examples following such paradigm in addressing, amongst others, the problem of video summarization [22]. However, as users may be more sensitive to irrelevant than (near) duplicate items, enforcing diversity without hurting relevance is very challenging. This is witnessed by a large body of research on e.g. image search diversification [23–27]. Social multimedia summarization has further found its way in diverse applications ranging from personalized tweet summarization [28] to visual summarization of geographic areas and tourist routes [12,13,23,29] for POI recommendation and exploration. With the increased availability of affordable wearables, in recent years lifelogging has started gaining popularity, where the goal is to generate a diary or a record of the day's activities and happenings by creating a summary or a story from the video/image data gathered [30,31]. Progress has been made in summarizing heterogeneous user-generated content with regards to relevance, representativeness, and diversity [15]. However, relevance criteria and their interplay may be much more complex than commonly assumed [12] and, in case of visual content, include additional factors such as content popularity, aesthetic appeal and sentiment. Thus we call for rethinking the foundations of summarization and storytelling.

Benchmarks and formalization efforts. For almost two decades, common datasets, tasks, and international benchmarks fueld research on summarization and storytelling [32–34]. A typical task involved automatically generating a shorter (e.g. 100-word) summary of a set of news articles. TRECVID BBC Rushes summarization was probably the first systematic effort in the multimedia and computer vision communities focusing on video summarization [35]. The task involved reducing a raw and unstructured video captured during the recording of a TV series to a short segment of just a couple of minutes. Another well-known example is the ImageCLEF 2009 Photo Task, which revolved around image diversification [25]. The participants were expected to produce image search results covering multiple aspects of a news story, such as the images of "Hillary Clinton", "Obama Clinton" and "Bill Clinton" for a query "Clinton". Image search diversification has also been a topic of an ongoing MediaEval Diverse Social Images Task, run annually since 2013 [27].

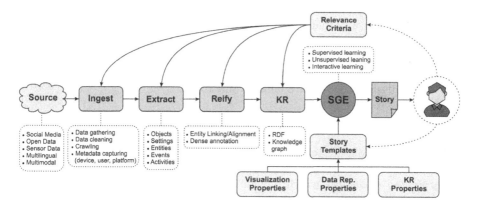

Fig. 1. Pipeline of our proposed framework for generating narratives, stories and summaries from heterogeneous collections of user generated content and beyond.

Although many people intuitively understand the concept of summarization, the complexity of the problem is best illustrated by the difficulties in even unequivocally defining a summary [36]. So, instead of focusing on strict definitions, most benchmarks took a pragmatic approach by conducting either intrinsic or extrinsic evaluation [32]. In intrinsic evaluation an automatically generated summary is compared directly against a "standard", such as summaries created by the humans. On the other hand, extrinsic evaluation measures the effectiveness of a summary in fulfilling a particular task as compared with the original set of documents (e.g. text, images or videos). Over the years many interesting metrics for evaluating (text) summaries were proposed, such as recall-oriented understudy for gisting evaluation (ROUGE) [37], bilingual evaluation understudy (BLEU) [38] and Pyramid Score [39]. Some of these were later on successfully adapted to the visual domain [12,40]. These initiatives had an impact on the progress in the field of summarization. However, their almost exclusive focus on a single modality (e.g. text or visual) or language and the traditional tasks (e.g. text document and video summarization or search diversification) does not reflect the richness of social multimedia and the complex use cases it brings.

3   Proposed Framework

First, we take a step back and look at a media-agnostic birds-eye view of the problem. We therefore imagine a generic framework that follows the requirements as driven by the user, instead of the technology. Figure 1 shows an overview of the concept, which follows the standard pattern of a media pipeline along the "ingest," "extract," "reify" paradigm. The goal of the framework is to create a story for the user, who is querying for information using a set of relevance criteria. Before doing that, we assume the user has configured the framework somehow, e.g. to choose some visualization template and define basic properties of the story. We then assume a tool that would query a set of sources from the Internet or elsewhere, download ("ingest") the data, "extract" relevant information and then "reify" it in a way that it can be added into some standardized Knowledge Representation (KR). The knowledge representation would then, in connection with the initial configuration, be used to create the final story. We will next discuss technical and other challenges to be addressed by the community in order to put flesh onto our bare bones framework.

3.1   Challenges and Example Application Domains

A framework for holistic storytelling brings a new set of research challenges and also reshapes some of the more traditional challenges in UGC. We identify these as *storytelling challenges* which include handling of time/temporality/history, dynamic labeling of noise, focused story generation, tailoring to impartiality or a viewpoint, quality assessment and explainability as well as *UGC challenges* which include ethical use, multi source fusion, multilinguality and multimodality, information extraction, knowledge update and addition of new knowledge, staying agnostic to specific application, supporting various types of open data, portability and finding a balance between depth and breadth. We now describe a set of application domains that illustrate some of the aforementioned challenges.

Smart urban spaces. Increased availability of open data and social multimedia has resulted in the birth of urban computing [41] and created new possibilities for better understanding cities. Although spontaneously captured, social multimedia may provide valuable insights about geographic city regions and their inhabitants. For example, user-generated content has been used to create summaries of geographic areas and tourist routes in location recommendation systems [12,13]. Sentiment extracted from social multimedia, in combination with neighborhood statistics was also proven invaluable for a more timely estimation of city livability and its causes [42]. Similarly, when looking for signs of issues such as neighborhood decay or suboptimal infrastructure, city administrators are increasingly monitoring diverse UGC streams, ranging from social media and designated neighborhood apps to data collected by mobile towers and wearables. Efficient approaches to summarization and storytelling are needed to facilitate exploration in such large and heterogeneous collections.

Business intelligence. User generated content is a valuable source of information for companies and institutions. Business information can be obtained by analyzing what the public is saying about a company, its products, marketing campaigns and competitors. Traditionally business intelligence relied on facts and figures collected from within the organisation, or provided by third-party reports and surveys. Instead of surveys, direct feedback can be obtained by listening to what people are saying on social media, either directed at their own social circle, or directly at the company in the case of web care conversations. Content can consist of textual messages or videos, for example product reviews. Besides the volume of messages, the sentiment of messages is important to analyze into positive and negative aspects. The amount of user generated content can easily add up to thousands of messages on a single topic, so summarization techniques are needed to efficiently process the wealth of information available [43].

Health and Wellness. There is a wealth of data about our health and wellness which is generated digitally on an individual basis. This includes genomic information from companies like 23andme[1] which uses tissue samples from individuals to generate information about our ancestry as well as about our possible susceptibility to a range of inherited diseases. We also have information about our lifestyles which can be gathered from our social media profiles and information about our physical activity levels and sports participation from any fitness trackers that we might wear or use. When we have health tests or screening we can have indications of biomarkers from our clinical tests for such things as cholesterol levels, glucose levels, etc. We have occasional once-off readings of our physiological status via heart and respiration rates and increasingly we can use wearable sensors to continuously monitor glucose, heart rate etc. to see how these change over time. From all of this personal sensor data there is a need to generate the *"story of me"*, telling my health professional and me how well or healthy I am now, whether my health and wellness is improving or is on the slide, and if there's anything derived from those trends that I should know.

Lifelogs. In this use case a large amount of first-person ethnographic video or images taken from a wearable camera over an extended period of days, weeks, months or even years, has been generated. Such a collection may be augmented and aligned with sensor data such as GPS location or biometric data like heart rate, activity levels from wearable accelerometers or stress levels from galvanic skin response sensors. There is a need to summarize each day's or week's activities to allow reviewing or perhaps to support search or browsing through the lifelog. Summaries should be visual, basically selecting a subset of images of videos, and applications could be in memory support where a summary of a day can be used to trigger memory recall [44]. In this case the visual summary should incorporate events, objects or activities which are unusual or rare throughout the lifelog in preference to those which are mundane or routine like mealtimes, watching TV or reading a newspaper which might be done every day [45].

Field study/survey. The relevance of consumer-produced multimedia often transcends the reason for creating and sharing it. As a side effect this information could be used for field studies of other kinds, if it can be retrieved in a timely fashion. The framework we propose could enable empirical scientists of many disciplines to leverage this data for field studies based on extracting required information from huge datasets. This currently constitutes a gap between the elements

---

[1] http://www.23andme.com.

of what multimedia researchers have shown is possible to do with consumer-produced big data and the follow-through of creating a comprehensive field study framework supporting scientists across other disciplines. To bravely bridge this gap, we must meet several challenges. For example, the framework must handle unlabeled and noisily labeled data to produce an altered dataset for a scientist who naturally wants it to be both as large and as clean as possible. We must also design an interface that will be intuitive and yet enable complex search queries that rely on feature and statistics generation at a large scale.

Entertainment. Multimedia summarization and storytelling can also serve to fulfill a pure entertainment need. Respective approaches could, for instance, support event-based creation of videos from pictures and video clips recorded on smart phones. To this end, they would automatically organize and structure such user-generated multimedia content, possibly in low quality, and subsequently determine the most interesting and suited parts in order to tell the story of a particular event, e.g., a wedding. The multimedia material considered by such an event-based storytelling approach is not necessarily restricted to a single user, but could automatically determine and select the best images/scenes from the whole audience at the event, or at least those choosing to share material.

3.2   Use Cases

When rethinking the requirements, we primarily analyzed two types of use cases: summarization and storyboarding.

Summarization has traditionally involved document summarization, i.e. reducing pieces of text into a shorter version, and video summarization, where multiple or long videos are reduced to a shorter version. As data is increasingly available in many modalities and languages, it is possible to generate a multilingual and multimodal summary according to the user's information request. Large events such as elections or important sports competitions are covered by many channels, including traditional media and different social media. New directions for summarization include interactive summaries of UGC opinions or sentiment-based data visualization, and forecasting including prediction of electoral results, product sales, stock market movements and influenza incidence [46]. Getting an overview of a certain music genre or style requires algorithms capable of identifying the most representative and important music [47–49], which should ideally also take cultural aspects into account when analysing meaning of a genre [50].

A **storyboard** is a summary that conveys a change over time. This may include a recount of the given input in order to tell an unbiased story of an event, e.g. the Fall of the Berlin wall or the Kennedy murder. It may also aim to present or select facts to persuade a user to perform a particular action or change opinion, e.g. pointing out the likely murderer in the Kennedy case. If the input is open-ended, the summary may be structured by background information, e.g. a composite clip giving a visual summarization of an event (such as a concert, a sports match, etc.) where the summarized input is provided by those attending the event but the story is structured according to a timeline given by background information.

4   Prerequisites

Once user generated content has been gathered, extracted, and reified, it should be expressed in a KR. This is a step prior to the generation of stories and summaries which aims to describe the information of interest following a representation formalism. Some of the knowledge representation formalisms widely adopted in the multimedia community are Resource Description Framework (RDF) and Knowledge Graph. The selection of one approach over the others is tightly connected with the purpose of the summary/story and the technique used for its construction. This means that knowledge must be represented using a language with which the Story Generation Engine can reason in order to satisfy complex relevance criteria and visualization requirements (templates) specified by the users. These relevance criteria and visualization requirements imply a set of desired properties on the data and KR, as well as the end result presented to the user, which are fundamental for summarization and storytelling.

4.1   Data Representation Properties

Complex user information needs and the relevance criteria stemming from them require novel (multimodal and multilingual) data representations. In Table 1 we list some critical prerequisites they should fulfill.

Table 1. Properties data representation should have for facilitating effective summarization and storytelling.

Data representation properties		
Location	Time	Observed
Single ⇌ Distributed	Scheduled ⇌ Unplanned	Entity-driven ⇌ Latent
Physical ⇌ Virtual	Short ⇌ Long	
Personal ⇌ Public/Shared	Recurrent ⇌ One-off	
Independent ⇌ Cascaded		

Time: The "events" described by a story could have very different properties. For example, an event could be *scheduled* (e.g. Olympic Games) or *unplanned* (e.g. a terrorist attack). In the former case relevance criteria and the visualization templates could be easier to foresee, but an effective data representation should accommodate the latter use case as well. Similarly, the events could have a *longer* (e.g., studies abroad) or *shorter* (e.g., birthday) duration. Finally, data representation should ideally accommodate both *recurrent* and *once off* events.

Location: Although multimedia analysis has found its way in modeling different aspects of geographic locations [13, 27, 51], most related work addressed specific use cases and little effort has been made in identifying general "spatial" criteria underlying data representations should satisfy. In this regard, the representation should account for the events occurring at a *single* (e.g. rock concert) or *distributed* location (e.g. Olympic Games). In both cases those locations can be further *physical* or *virtual*. On the other hand, the events of interest can be *personal* or *public/shared*. While in the former case the content interpretation and relevance criteria may have a meaning for a particular individual only, the later is usually easier to analyze due to a higher "inter-user agreement". Finally, data representation should be designed with the awareness that the aforementioned types of events could additionally be *independent* or *cascaded*.

Observed: In many analytic scenarios the summaries and stories presented to the user contain well-defined named *entities*, i.e. topics, people, places and organizations. An example would be a well-structured news article covering a political event. Yet the topics of interest may be *latent*, which is particularly common in social media discussions. For example, a public servant sifting through millions of social media posts in an attempt to verify an outbreak of a new virus may be interested in various unforeseen and seemingly unrelated conversations, which together provide conclusive evidence. Therefore, a good data representation should ideally provide support for both.

4.2   Knowledge Representation Properties

Building on best practices from the semantic web community, the results of ingestion, extraction and reification (cf. Fig. 1) should be further organized in a knowledge representation. Example candidates include RDFs and knowledge graph. The KR should be flexible enough to allow for *temporal*, *spatial* and *observed* properties of the events discussed in Sect. 4.1. It should further support both *implicit* and *explicit* relations between the items, as well as their modification "on the fly" (cf. Table 2). The events and their building blocks could further be *independent* and *correlated/causal*. To facilitate a wide range of possible relevance criteria as well as their complex interplay, the KR should also include notions of importance, representativeness and frequency. Finally, the content interpretation and user information needs can be specified at different semantic levels, which in case of multimedia range from e.g. term or pixel statistics, semantic concepts, events and actions to the level of semantic theme and complex human interpretations involving aesthetic appeal and sentiment. Supporting a wide range of relevance is therefore a necessary condition for facilitating creation of effective and engaging summaries and stories.

Table 2. Properties a knowledge representation should have.

Knowledge representation properties	
Implicit $\rightleftharpoons$ Explicit	Independent $\rightleftharpoons$ Correlated/Causal
Uniqueness/Representativeness	Support for different semantic levels

4.3 Story Properties

Given the content, data and KRs and the user information needs, the output of the pipeline depicted in Fig. 1 is the story (or summary) presented to the user. Below we enumerate a number of criteria an ideal set of "story templates" should satisfy (see Table 3). A story should satisfy both *functional* (e.g. fulfilling a purpose) and *quality* (e.g. metrical) requirements [32]. The importance of a particular requirement should ideally be learned from user interactions. The system should further support *self-contained/interpretable* and *stepping-stone/connector* type of summaries. While the former by itself provides an insight into a larger multimedia item or a collection, the later serves a goal further on the horizon, such as faster collection exploration. Additionally, the design should accommodate both *succinct* and *narrative*, as well as *abstractive* and *generative* stories. With regard to the input and output modalities and languages, support should be provided for *modality-preserving* and *cross-modal* and/or *cross-lingual* use-cases. In many scenarios, user information needs can be satisfied with a *static* story. However, the size and heterogeneity of a UGC collection as well as the complexity of user information needs make *interactive* summarization and storytelling increasingly popular. Depending on the information needs, a *factual* or *stylistic* summary may be desirable, which is why the system should support both flavors and perhaps allow for interactive learning of their balance. Finally, while a *generic* story may be sufficient for some, *personalization* should also be supported.

Table 3. Story properties that should be facilitated by the story generator engine.

Story properties	
Functional ⇌ Quality	Modality-preserving ⇌ Cross-modal
Self-contained ⇌ Stepping-stone	Static ⇌ Dynamic/Interactive
Succinct ⇌ Narrative	Factual ⇌ Stylistic
Abstractive ⇌ Generative	Generic ⇌ Personalized

5 Conclusion

Motivated by an observation about discrepancies between state of the art research on the one hand and the increasing richness of user generated content and the accompanying complex user information needs on the other, we revisit the requirements for multimedia summarization and storytelling. We reiterate the importance of summarization and storytelling for facilitating efficient and appealing access to large collections of social multimedia and interaction with them. Our proposed framework identifies a set of challenges and prerequisites related to data and KR as well as the process of their creation, i.e. ingestion, extraction and reification. We further make an inventory of the desirable properties a story should have for addressing a wide range of user information needs. Finally, we showcase a number of application domains and use cases that could serve as the catalyst for future research on the topic.

References

1. Tian, Y., Srivastava, J., Huang, T., Contractor, N.: Social multimedia computing. Computer **43**(8), 27–36 (2010)
2. Kouloumpis, E., Wilson, T., Moore, J.: Twitter sentiment analysis: the good the bad and the OMG!, pp. 538–541. AAAI Press (2011)
3. Cha, M., Kwak, H., Rodriguez, P., Ahn, Y.Y., Moon, S.: I tube, you tube, everybody tubes: analyzing the world's largest user generated content video system. In: ACM IMC 2007, pp. 1–14 (2007)
4. Shamma, D.A., Kennedy, L., Churchill, E.F.: Tweet the debates: understanding community annotation of uncollected sources. In: ACM WSM 2009, pp. 3–10 (2009)
5. Kwak, H., Lee, C., Park, H., Moon, S.: What is Twitter, a social network or a news media? In: ACM WWW 2010, pp. 591–600 (2010)
6. Bian, J., Yang, Y., Zhang, H., Chua, T.S.: Multimedia summarization for social events in microblog stream. IEEE Trans. Multimed. **17**(2), 216–228 (2015)
7. Hong, R., Tang, J., Tan, H.K., Ngo, C.W., Yan, S., Chua, T.S.: Beyond search: event-driven summarization for web videos. ACM Trans. Multimed. Comput. Commun. Appl. **7**(4), 35:1–35:18 (2011)
8. Gornostay (Gornostaja), T., Aker, A.: Development and implementation of multilingual object type toponym-referenced text corpora for optimizing automatic image description generation. In: Dialogue 2009 (2009)
9. Mikolov, T., Sutskever, I., Chen, K., Corrado, G.S., Dean, J.: Distributed representations of words and phrases and their compositionality. In: NIPS 2013, pp. 3111–3119. CAI (2013)
10. Krizhevsky, A., Sutskever, I., Hinton, G.E.: ImageNet classification with deep convolutional neural networks. In: NIPS 2012, pp. 1097–1105. CAI (2012)
11. Nenkova, A., McKeown, K.: A survey of text summarization techniques. In: Aggarwal, C., Zhai, C. (eds.) Mining Text Data, pp. 43–76. Springer, Boston (2012). https://doi.org/10.1007/978-1-4614-3223-4_3
12. Rudinac, S., Larson, M., Hanjalic, A.: Learning crowdsourced user preferences for visual summarization of image collections. IEEE Trans. Multimed. **15**(6), 1231–1243 (2013)
13. Rudinac, S., Hanjalic, A., Larson, M.: Generating visual summaries of geographic areas using community-contributed images. IEEE Trans. Multimed. **15**(4), 921–932 (2013)
14. Xie, L., Sundaram, H., Campbell, M.: Event mining in multimedia streams. Proc. IEEE **96**(4), 623–647 (2008)
15. Carbonell, J., Goldstein, J.: The use of MMR, diversity-based reranking for reordering documents and producing summaries. In: ACM SIGIR 1998, pp. 335–336. ACM, New York (1998)
16. Uchihashi, S., Foote, J., Girgensohn, A., Boreczky, J.: Video manga: generating semantically meaningful video summaries. In: ACM MM 1999, pp. 383–392. ACM (1999)

17. Sundaram, H., Xie, L., Chang, S.F.: A utility framework for the automatic generation of audio-visual skims. In: ACM MM 2002, pp. 189–198. ACM (2002)
18. Kennedy, L., Naaman, M.: Less talk, more rock: automated organization of community-contributed collections of concert videos. In: WWW 2009, pp. 311–320. ACM (2009)
19. Lu, Z., Grauman, K.: Story-driven summarization for egocentric video. In: IEEE CVPR 2013, pp. 2714–2721 (2013)
20. Yu, S.I., Yang, Y., Hauptmann, A.: Harry potter's marauder's map: localizing and tracking multiple persons-of-interest by nonnegative discretization. In: IEEE CVPR 2013, pp. 3714–3720 (2013)
21. Xie, L., Natsev, A., Kender, J.R., Hill, M., Smith, J.R.: Visual memes in social media: tracking real-world news in YouTube videos. In: ACM MM 2011, pp. 53–62. ACM (2011)
22. Wactlar, H.D., Kanade, T., Smith, M.A., Stevens, S.M.: Intelligent access to digital video: informedia project. Computer **29**(5), 46–52 (1996)
23. Kennedy, L.S., Naaman, M.: Generating diverse and representative image search results for landmarks. In: ACM WWW 2008, pp. 297–306 (2008)
24. van Leuken, R.H., Garcia, L., Olivares, X., van Zwol, R.: Visual diversification of image search results. In: ACM WWW 2009, pp. 341–350 (2009)
25. Lestari Paramita, M., Sanderson, M., Clough, P.: Diversity in photo retrieval: overview of the ImageCLEFPhoto task 2009. In: Peters, C., Caputo, B., Gonzalo, J., Jones, G.J.F., Kalpathy-Cramer, J., Müller, H., Tsikrika, T. (eds.) CLEF 2009. LNCS, vol. 6242, pp. 45–59. Springer, Heidelberg (2010). https://doi.org/10.1007/978-3-642-15751-6_6
26. Sanderson, M., Tang, J., Arni, T., Clough, P.: What else is there? Search diversity examined. In: Boughanem, M., Berrut, C., Mothe, J., Soule-Dupuy, C. (eds.) ECIR 2009. LNCS, vol. 5478, pp. 562–569. Springer, Heidelberg (2009). https://doi.org/10.1007/978-3-642-00958-7_51
27. Ionescu, B., Popescu, A., Radu, A.L., Müller, H.: Result diversification in social image retrieval: a benchmarking framework. Multimed. Tools Appl. **75**(2), 1301–1331 (2016)
28. Ren, Z., Liang, S., Meij, E., de Rijke, M.: Personalized time-aware tweets summarization. In: ACM SIGIR 2013, pp. 513–522 (2013)
29. Hao, Q., Cai, R., Wang, X.J., Yang, J.M., Pang, Y., Zhang, L.: Generating location overviews with images and tags by mining user-generated travelogues. In: ACM MM 2009, pp. 801–804. ACM, New York (2009)
30. Gurrin, C., Smeaton, A.F., Doherty, A.R.: Lifelogging: personal big data. Found. Trends Inf. Retr. **8**(1), 1–125 (2014)
31. Lee, Y.J., Ghosh, J., Grauman, K.: Discovering important people and objects for egocentric video summarization. In: IEEE CVPR 2012, pp. 1346–1353, June 2012
32. Harman, D., Over, P.: The DUC summarization evaluations. In: HLT 2002, San Francisco, CA, USA, pp. 44–51. Morgan Kaufmann Publishers Inc. (2002)
33. Dang, H.T.: Overview of DUC 2006. In: DUC 2006 (2006)
34. Owczarzak, K., Dang, H.T.: Overview of the TAC 2011 summarization track: guided task and AESOP task. In: TAC 2011 (2011)
35. Over, P., Smeaton, A.F., Awad, G.: The TRECVid 2008 BBC rushes summarization evaluation. In: ACM TVS 2008, pp. 1–20 (2008)
36. Radev, D.R., Hovy, E., McKeown, K.: Introduction to the special issue on summarization. Comput. Linguist. **28**(4), 399–408 (2002)
37. Lin, C.Y.: ROUGE: a package for automatic evaluation of summaries. In: ACL 2004 Workshop, pp. 74–81 (2004)

38. Papineni, K., Roukos, S., Ward, T., Zhu, W.J.: BLEU: a method for automatic evaluation of machine translation. In: ACL 2002, pp. 311–318 (2002)
39. Nenkova, A., Passonneau, R.J.: Evaluating content selection in summarization: the pyramid method. In: HLT-NAACL, pp. 145–152 (2004)
40. Li, Y., Merialdo, B.: VERT: automatic evaluation of video summaries. In: ACM MM 2010, pp. 851–854 (2010)
41. Zheng, Y., Capra, L., Wolfson, O., Yang, H.: Urban computing: concepts, methodologies, and applications. ACM Trans. Intell. Syst. Technol. 5(3), 38:1–38:55 (2014)
42. Boonzajer Flaes, J., Rudinac, S., Worring, M.: What multimedia sentiment analysis says about city liveability. In: Ferro, N., Crestani, F., Moens, M.-F., Mothe, J., Silvestri, F., Di Nunzio, G.M., Hauff, C., Silvello, G. (eds.) ECIR 2016. LNCS, vol. 9626, pp. 824–829. Springer, Cham (2016). https://doi.org/10.1007/978-3-319-30671-1_74
43. Dey, L., Haque, S.M., Khurdiya, A., Shroff, G.: Acquiring competitive intelligence from social media. In: MOCR AND 2011, p. 3. ACM (2011)
44. Doherty, A.R., Hodges, S.E., King, A.C., Smeaton, A.F., Berry, E., Moulin, C.J., Lindley, S., Kelly, P., Foster, C.: Wearable cameras in health. Am. J. Prev. Med. 44, 320–323 (2013)
45. Lee, H., Smeaton, A.F., O'Connor, N.E., Jones, G., Blighe, M., Byrne, D., Doherty, A., Gurrin, C.: Constructing a SenseCam visual diary as a media process. Multimed. Syst. 14(6), 341–349 (2008)
46. Schoen, H., Gayo-Avello, D., Takis Metaxas, P., Mustafaraj, E., Strohmaier, M., Gloor, P.: The power of prediction with social media. Internet Res. 23(5), 528–543 (2013)
47. Tian, M., Sandler, M.B.: Towards music structural segmentation across genres: features, structural hypotheses, and annotation principles. ACM Trans. Intell. Syst. Technol. 8(2), 23:1–23:19 (2016)
48. Goto, M.: A chorus section detection method for musical audio signals and its application to a music listening station. IEEE Trans. Audio Speech Lang. Process. 14(5), 1783–1794 (2006)
49. Chai, W.: Semantic segmentation and summarization of music. IEEE Sig. Process. Mag. 23(2), 124–132 (2006)
50. Schedl, M., Flexer, A., Urbano, J.: The neglected user in music information retrieval research. J. Intell. Inf. Syst. 41, 523–539 (2013)
51. Thomee, B., Shamma, D.A., Friedland, G., Elizalde, B., Ni, K., Poland, D., Borth, D., Li, L.J.: YFCC100M: the new data in multimedia research. Commun. ACM 59(2), 64–73 (2016)

Author Index

Printed in the United States
By Bookmasters